FI

MON ... EMENT

Real Estate Loans

Second Edition

Stephen S. Solomon
M.S., Applied Mathematics

Clifford W. Marshall
Ph.D., Applied Mathematics
Professor of Mathematics
Polytechnic University

Martin Pepper
Principal, Coopers & Lybrand
Fellow, Society of Actuaries

BARRON'S

Great effort has been made to develop accurate tables; however, no warranty of absolute accuracy is given.

All inquiries should be addressed to:
Barron's Educational Series, Inc.
250 Wireless Boulevard
Hauppauge, New York 11788

Library of Congress Catalog Card No. 92-35743

International Standard Book No. 0-8120-1618-1

Library of Congress Cataloging in Publication Data

Solomon, Stephen S.
Real estate loans / Stephen S. Solomon, Clifford W. Marshall, Martin Pepper. — 2nd ed.
p. cm. — (Barron's financial guides)
Includes index.
ISBN 0-8120-1618-1
1. Interest—Tables. I. Marshall, Clifford W., 1928– II. Pepper, Martin. III. Title. IV. Series.
HG1634.S655 1993
332.8'2'0212—dc20 92-35743
CIP

PRINTED IN THE UNITED STATES OF AMERICA

3456 9770 9876543

Contents

Introduction

The idea behind *Barron's Financial Tables for Better Money Management* is to provide assistance to anyone who invests, makes purchases, or borrows money. Since these guides require no financial or mathematical expertise, they can be used easily by the average investor or mortgage seeker. The tables are easy to read and are preceded by sample situations that show the nature and scope of the tables. Following each sample situation a short explanation tells how to use a particular table to find the desired answer and how to locate data on the table. After reading the situation and explanation you should be able to apply the same procedure to answer questions regarding your particular situation. If you spend time "walking through" all the situations given, you will better understand how to use the tables.

Because these tables are designed for the non-professional, no formulas or mathematical derivations are shown. Such derivations are not required for proper use of the tables.

Monthly Real Estate Payments

Real estate investments—whether in your primary place of residence, a second home, or rental property—are rarely made without some type of financing. Therefore, understanding mortgage financing is a very important factor in undertaking such investments.

A mortgage is an agreement between a buyer and a lender, usually a bank. Under the terms of the typical mortgage, in return for a loan the buyer agrees to make monthly payments to the lender for a specific number of years. Part of the monthly payment goes for repayment of a portion of the original loan principal and part goes for payment of an interest charge at a specified rate.

Several types of mortgages are available today. The tables in this book are for the type used most often by real estate investors, under which monthly payments are constant over a fixed repayment period.

The table that follows covers real estate loans with interest rates between 5% and 21% and shows the required monthly payment for loan amounts ranging from $100 to $250,000 with repayment periods from 1 to 40 years. Here are some illustrative situations to help you understand and use the tables:

Situation 1

Mr. Wilson wants to buy a piece of property that costs $70,000.00, and has a down payment of $20,000.00. He seeks a 30-year conventional mortgage of $50,000.00 (after paying separately all required fees, service charges, etc.). If the stipulated interest rate is 11%, he can determine the required monthly loan payment by (1) locating the 11% pages of the monthly real estate payments table, (2) finding the vertical column for 30 years, (3) looking down the left column on the same page until he finds $50,000.00, and (4) looking across to the 30-year column, which shows a monthly payment of $476.16.

Situation 2

Mrs. Bell wishes to purchase a second home for $120,000.00 and has a down payment of $40,000.00. A bank will give her an $80,000.00 mortgage for 25 years at 13¼%. Mrs. Bell can determine the monthly real estate payment by locating the 13¼% pages and the 25-year column on the top of the appropriate page. After looking down the left side of the page for the loan amount of $80,000.00, she then must look across the line to the 25-year column, where she will find a monthly payment of $917.36.

5% Monthly Payments

necessary to amortize a loan

AMOUNT	1 YEAR	2 YEARS	3 YEARS	4 YEARS	5 YEARS	6 YEARS	7 YEARS
100	8.56	4.39	3.00	2.30	1.89	1.61	1.41
200	17.12	8.77	5.99	4.61	3.77	3.22	2.83
500	42.80	21.94	14.99	11.51	9.44	8.05	7.07
1000	85.61	43.87	29.97	23.03	18.87	16.10	14.13
2000	171.21	87.74	59.94	46.06	37.74	32.21	28.27
5000	428.04	219.36	149.85	115.15	94.36	80.52	70.67
6000	513.64	263.23	179.83	138.18	113.23	96.63	84.80
7000	599.25	307.10	209.80	161.21	132.10	112.73	98.94
8000	684.86	350.97	239.77	184.23	150.97	128.84	113.07
9000	770.47	394.84	269.74	207.26	169.84	144.94	127.21
10000	856.07	438.71	299.71	230.29	188.71	161.05	141.34
15000	1284.11	658.07	449.56	345.44	283.07	241.57	212.01
20000	1712.15	877.43	599.42	460.59	377.42	322.10	282.68
25000	2140.19	1096.78	749.27	575.73	471.78	402.62	353.35
30000	2568.22	1316.14	899.13	690.88	566.14	483.15	424.02
35000	2996.26	1535.50	1048.98	806.03	660.49	563.67	494.69
36000	3081.87	1579.37	1078.95	829.05	679.36	579.78	508.82
37000	3167.48	1623.24	1108.92	852.08	698.24	595.88	522.95
38000	3253.08	1667.11	1138.89	875.11	717.11	611.99	537.09
39000	3338.69	1710.98	1168.86	898.14	735.98	628.09	551.22
40000	3424.30	1754.86	1198.84	921.17	754.85	644.20	565.36
41000	3509.91	1798.73	1228.81	944.20	773.72	660.30	579.49
42000	3595.51	1842.60	1258.78	967.23	792.59	676.41	593.62
43000	3681.12	1886.47	1288.75	990.26	811.46	692.51	607.76
44000	3766.73	1930.34	1318.72	1013.29	830.33	708.62	621.89
45000	3852.34	1974.21	1348.69	1036.32	849.21	724.72	636.03
46000	3937.94	2018.08	1378.66	1059.35	868.08	740.83	650.16
47000	4023.55	2061.96	1408.63	1082.38	886.95	756.93	664.29
48000	4109.16	2105.83	1438.60	1105.41	905.82	773.04	678.43
49000	4194.77	2149.70	1468.57	1128.44	924.69	789.14	692.56
50000	4280.37	2193.57	1498.54	1151.46	943.56	805.25	706.70
51000	4365.98	2237.44	1528.52	1174.49	962.43	821.35	720.83
52000	4451.59	2281.31	1558.49	1197.52	981.30	837.46	734.96
53000	4537.20	2325.18	1588.46	1220.55	1000.18	853.56	749.10
54000	4622.80	2369.06	1618.43	1243.58	1019.05	869.67	763.23
55000	4708.41	2412.93	1648.40	1266.61	1037.92	885.77	777.36
56000	4794.02	2456.80	1678.37	1289.64	1056.79	901.88	791.50
57000	4879.63	2500.67	1708.34	1312.67	1075.66	917.98	805.63
58000	4965.23	2544.54	1738.31	1335.70	1094.53	934.09	819.77
59000	5050.84	2588.41	1768.28	1358.73	1113.40	950.19	833.90
60000	5136.45	2632.28	1798.25	1381.76	1132.27	966.30	848.03
65000	5564.49	2851.64	1948.11	1496.90	1226.63	1046.82	918.70
70000	5992.52	3071.00	2097.96	1612.05	1320.99	1127.35	989.37
75000	6420.56	3290.35	2247.82	1727.20	1415.34	1207.87	1060.04
80000	6848.60	3509.71	2397.67	1842.34	1509.70	1288.39	1130.71
85000	7276.64	3729.07	2547.53	1957.49	1604.05	1368.92	1201.38
90000	7704.67	3948.43	2697.38	2072.64	1698.41	1449.44	1272.05
95000	8132.71	4167.78	2847.24	2187.78	1792.77	1529.97	1342.72
100000	8560.75	4387.14	2997.09	2302.93	1887.12	1610.49	1413.39
105000	8988.79	4606.50	3146.94	2418.08	1981.48	1691.02	1484.06
110000	9416.82	4825.85	3296.80	2533.22	2075.84	1771.54	1554.73
120000	10272.90	5264.57	3596.51	2763.52	2264.55	1932.59	1696.07
130000	11128.97	5703.28	3896.22	2993.81	2453.26	2093.64	1837.41
140000	11985.05	6141.99	4195.93	3224.10	2641.97	2254.69	1978.75
150000	12841.12	6580.71	4495.63	3454.39	2830.69	2415.74	2120.09
175000	14981.31	7677.49	5244.91	4030.13	3302.47	2818.36	2473.43
200000	17121.50	8774.28	5994.18	4605.86	3774.25	3220.99	2826.78
225000	19261.68	9871.06	6743.45	5181.59	4246.03	3623.61	3180.13
250000	21401.87	10967.85	7492.72	5757.32	4717.81	4026.23	3533.48

Monthly Payments **5%**

necessary to amortize a loan

AMOUNT	8 YEARS	9 YEARS	10 YEARS	11 YEARS	12 YEARS	13 YEARS	14 YEARS
100	1.27	1.15	1.06	0.99	0.92	0.87	0.83
200	2.53	2.30	2.12	1.97	1.85	1.75	1.66
500	6.33	5.76	5.30	4.93	4.62	4.37	4.14
1000	12.66	11.52	10.61	9.86	9.25	8.73	8.29
2000	25.32	23.03	21.21	19.73	18.50	17.46	16.58
5000	63.30	57.59	53.03	49.32	46.24	43.65	41.44
6000	75.96	69.10	63.64	59.19	55.49	52.38	49.73
7000	88.62	80.62	74.25	69.05	64.74	61.11	58.02
8000	101.28	92.14	84.85	78.92	73.99	69.84	66.31
9000	113.94	103.66	95.46	88.78	83.24	78.58	74.60
10000	126.60	115.17	106.07	98.64	92.49	87.31	82.89
15000	189.90	172.76	159.10	147.97	138.73	130.96	124.33
20000	253.20	230.35	212.13	197.29	184.98	174.61	165.77
25000	316.50	287.93	265.16	246.61	231.22	218.26	207.22
30000	379.80	345.52	318.20	295.93	277.47	261.92	248.66
35000	443.10	403.10	371.23	345.26	323.71	305.57	290.10
36000	455.76	414.62	381.84	355.12	332.96	314.30	298.39
37000	468.42	426.14	392.44	364.99	342.21	323.03	306.68
38000	481.08	437.66	403.05	374.85	351.46	331.76	314.97
39000	493.74	449.17	413.66	384.72	360.71	340.49	323.26
40000	506.40	460.69	424.26	394.58	369.96	349.22	331.55
41000	519.06	472.21	434.87	404.44	379.21	357.95	339.84
42000	531.72	483.73	445.48	414.31	388.45	366.69	348.13
43000	544.38	495.24	456.08	424.17	397.70	375.42	356.41
44000	557.04	506.76	466.69	434.04	406.95	384.15	364.70
45000	569.70	518.28	477.29	443.90	416.20	392.88	372.99
46000	582.36	529.79	487.90	453.77	425.45	401.61	381.28
47000	595.02	541.31	498.51	463.63	434.70	410.34	389.57
48000	607.68	552.83	509.11	473.50	443.95	419.07	397.86
49000	620.34	564.35	519.72	483.36	453.20	427.80	406.15
50000	633.00	575.86	530.33	493.22	462.45	436.53	414.44
51000	645.66	587.38	540.93	503.09	471.69	445.26	422.72
52000	658.32	598.90	551.54	512.95	480.94	453.99	431.01
53000	670.98	610.42	562.15	522.82	490.19	462.72	439.30
54000	683.64	621.93	572.75	532.68	499.44	471.45	447.59
55000	696.30	633.45	583.36	542.55	508.69	480.18	455.88
56000	708.96	644.97	593.97	552.41	517.94	488.91	464.17
57000	721.62	656.48	604.57	562.28	527.19	497.64	472.46
58000	734.28	668.00	615.18	572.14	536.44	506.37	480.75
59000	746.94	679.52	625.79	582.00	545.69	515.11	489.03
60000	759.60	691.04	636.39	591.87	554.93	523.84	497.32
65000	822.89	748.62	689.43	641.19	601.18	567.49	538.77
70000	886.19	806.21	742.46	690.51	647.42	611.14	580.21
75000	949.49	863.80	795.49	739.84	693.67	654.79	621.65
80000	1012.79	921.38	848.52	709.16	730.01	608.46	663.10
85000	1076.09	978.97	901.56	838.48	786.16	742.10	704.54
90000	1139.39	1036.55	954.59	887.80	832.40	785.75	745.98
95000	1202.69	1094.14	1007.62	937.13	878.65	829.41	787.43
100000	1265.99	1151.73	1060.66	986.45	924.89	873.06	828.87
105000	1329.29	1209.31	1113.69	1035.77	971.13	916.71	870.31
110000	1392.59	1266.90	1166.72	1085.09	1017.38	960.37	911.76
120000	1519.19	1382.07	1272.79	1183.74	1109.87	1047.67	994.64
130000	1645.79	1497.25	1378.85	1282.38	1202.36	1134.98	1077.53
140000	1772.39	1612.42	1484.92	1381.03	1294.85	1222.28	1160.42
150000	1898.99	1727.59	1590.98	1479.67	1387.34	1309.59	1243.31
175000	2215.49	2015.52	1856.15	1726.29	1618.56	1527.85	1450.52
200000	2531.98	2303.45	2121.31	1972.90	1849.78	1746.12	1657.74
225000	2848.48	2591.39	2386.47	2219.51	2081.00	1964.38	1864.96
250000	3164.98	2879.32	2651.64	2466.12	2312.23	2182.65	2072.18

5% Monthly Payments

necessary to amortize a loan

AMOUNT	15 YEARS	16 YEARS	17 YEARS	18 YEARS	19 YEARS	20 YEARS	21 YEARS
100	0.79	0.76	0.73	0.70	0.68	0.66	0.64
200	1.58	1.52	1.46	1.41	1.36	1.32	1.28
500	3.95	3.79	3.64	3.52	3.40	3.30	3.21
1000	7.91	7.58	7.29	7.03	6.80	6.60	6.42
2000	15.82	15.15	14.57	14.06	13.61	13.20	12.83
5000	39.54	37.88	36.43	35.15	34.01	33.00	32.09
6000	47.45	45.46	43.72	42.18	40.82	39.60	38.50
7000	55.36	53.04	51.01	49.21	47.62	46.20	44.92
8000	63.26	60.61	58.29	56.24	54.42	52.80	51.34
9000	71.17	68.19	65.58	63.27	61.22	59.40	57.75
10000	79.08	75.77	72.87	70.30	68.03	66.00	64.17
15000	118.62	113.65	109.30	105.46	102.04	98.99	96.26
20000	158.16	151.54	145.73	140.61	136.06	131.99	128.34
25000	197.70	189.42	182.16	175.76	170.07	164.99	160.43
30000	237.24	227.30	218.60	210.91	204.08	197.99	192.52
35000	276.78	265.19	255.03	246.06	238.10	230.98	224.60
36000	284.69	272.77	262.32	253.09	244.90	237.58	231.02
37000	292.59	280.34	269.60	260.12	251.70	244.18	237.44
38000	300.50	287.92	276.89	267.15	258.51	250.78	243.85
39000	308.41	295.50	284.18	274.18	265.31	257.38	250.27
40000	316.32	303.07	291.46	281.21	272.11	263.98	256.69
41000	324.23	310.65	298.75	288.24	278.91	270.58	263.10
42000	332.13	318.23	306.04	295.27	285.72	277.18	269.52
43000	340.04	325.80	313.32	302.30	292.52	283.78	275.94
44000	347.95	333.38	320.61	309.33	299.32	290.38	282.36
45000	355.86	340.96	327.89	316.37	306.12	296.98	288.77
46000	363.77	348.53	335.18	323.40	312.93	303.58	295.19
47000	371.67	356.11	342.47	330.43	319.73	310.18	301.61
48000	379.58	363.69	349.75	337.46	326.53	316.78	308.02
49000	387.49	371.26	357.04	344.49	333.34	323.38	314.44
50000	395.40	378.84	364.33	351.52	340.14	329.98	320.86
51000	403.30	386.42	371.61	358.55	346.94	336.58	327.28
52000	411.21	393.99	378.90	365.58	353.74	343.18	333.69
53000	419.12	401.57	386.19	372.61	360.55	349.78	340.11
54000	427.03	409.15	393.47	379.64	367.35	356.38	346.53
55000	434.94	416.72	400.76	386.67	374.15	362.98	352.95
56000	442.84	424.30	408.05	393.70	380.96	369.58	359.36
57000	450.75	431.88	415.33	400.73	387.76	376.17	365.78
58000	458.66	439.45	422.62	407.76	394.56	382.77	372.20
59000	466.57	447.03	429.91	414.79	401.36	389.37	378.61
60000	474.48	454.61	437.19	421.82	408.17	395.97	385.03
65000	514.02	492.49	473.63	456.97	442.18	428.97	417.12
70000	553.56	530.38	510.06	492.12	476.19	461.97	449.20
75000	593.10	568.26	546.49	527.28	510.21	494.97	481.29
80000	632.63	606.14	582.92	562.43	544.22	527.96	513.37
85000	672.17	644.03	619.36	597.58	578.24	560.96	545.46
90000	711.71	681.91	655.79	632.73	612.25	593.96	577.55
95000	751.25	719.80	692.22	667.88	646.26	626.96	609.63
100000	790.79	757.68	728.66	703.03	680.28	659.96	641.72
105000	830.33	795.57	765.09	738.19	714.29	692.95	673.80
110000	869.87	833.45	801.52	773.34	748.31	725.95	705.89
120000	948.95	909.22	874.39	843.64	816.33	791.95	770.06
130000	1028.03	984.99	947.25	913.94	884.36	857.94	834.23
140000	1107.11	1060.75	1020.12	984.25	952.39	923.94	898.41
150000	1186.19	1136.52	1092.98	1054.55	1020.42	989.93	962.58
175000	1383.89	1325.94	1275.15	1230.31	1190.49	1154.92	1123.01
200000	1581.59	1515.36	1457.31	1406.07	1360.56	1319.91	1283.44
225000	1779.29	1704.78	1639.47	1581.83	1530.62	1484.90	1443.87
250000	1976.98	1894.20	1821.64	1757.58	1700.69	1649.89	1604.30

Monthly Payments — 5%

necessary to amortize a loan

AMOUNT	22 YEARS	23 YEARS	24 YEARS	25 YEARS	30 YEARS	35 YEARS	40 YEARS
100	0.63	0.61	0.60	0.58	0.54	0.50	0.48
200	1.25	1.22	1.19	1.17	1.07	1.01	0.96
500	3.13	3.05	2.98	2.92	2.68	2.52	2.41
1000	6.25	6.10	5.97	5.85	5.37	5.05	4.82
2000	12.51	12.21	11.94	11.69	10.74	10.09	9.64
5000	31.26	30.52	29.84	29.23	26.84	25.23	24.11
6000	37.52	36.62	35.81	35.08	32.21	30.28	28.93
7000	43.77	42.73	41.78	40.92	37.58	35.33	33.75
8000	50.02	48.83	47.75	46.77	42.95	40.38	38.58
9000	56.28	54.94	53.72	52.61	48.31	45.42	43.40
10000	62.53	61.04	59.69	58.46	53.68	50.47	48.22
15000	93.79	91.56	89.53	87.69	80.52	75.70	72.33
20000	125.06	122.08	119.38	116.92	107.36	100.94	96.44
25000	156.32	152.60	149.22	146.15	134.21	126.17	120.55
30000	187.58	183.12	179.07	175.38	161.05	151.41	144.66
35000	218.85	213.64	208.91	204.61	187.89	176.64	168.77
36000	225.10	219.75	214.88	210.45	193.26	181.69	173.59
37000	231.35	225.85	220.85	216.30	198.62	186.73	178.41
38000	237.61	231.95	226.82	222.14	203.99	191.78	183.23
39000	243.86	238.06	232.79	227.99	209.36	196.83	188.06
40000	250.11	244.16	238.76	233.84	214.73	201.88	192.88
41000	256.37	250.27	244.73	239.68	220.10	206.92	197.70
42000	262.62	256.37	250.70	245.53	225.47	211.97	202.52
43000	268.87	262.47	256.67	251.37	230.83	217.02	207.34
44000	275.12	268.58	262.63	257.22	236.20	222.06	212.17
45000	281.38	274.68	268.60	263.07	241.57	227.11	216.99
46000	287.63	280.79	274.57	268.91	246.94	232.16	221.81
47000	293.88	286.89	280.54	274.76	252.31	237.20	226.63
48000	300.13	292.99	286.51	280.60	257.67	242.25	231.45
49000	306.39	299.10	292.48	286.45	263.04	247.30	236.28
50000	312.64	305.20	298.45	292.30	268.41	252.34	241.10
51000	318.89	311.31	304.42	298.14	273.78	257.39	245.92
52000	325.15	317.41	310.39	303.99	279.15	262.44	250.74
53000	331.40	323.52	316.36	309.83	284.52	267.48	255.56
54000	337.65	329.62	322.32	315.68	289.88	272.53	260.39
55000	343.90	335.72	328.29	321.52	295.25	277.58	265.21
56000	350.16	341.83	334.26	327.37	300.62	282.63	270.03
57000	356.41	347.93	340.23	333.22	305.99	287.67	274.85
58000	362.66	354.04	346.20	339.06	311.36	292.72	279.67
59000	368.92	360.14	352.17	344.91	316.72	297.77	284.50
60000	375.17	366.24	358.14	350.75	322.09	302.81	289.32
65000	406.43	396.76	387.98	379.98	348.93	328.05	313.43
70000	437.70	427.28	417.83	409.21	375.78	353.28	337.54
75000	468.96	457.80	447.67	438.44	402.62	378.52	361.65
80000	500.22	488.32	477.52	467.67	429.46	403.75	385.76
85000	531.49	518.85	507.36	496.90	456.30	428.98	409.87
90000	562.75	549.37	537.21	526.13	483.14	454.22	433.98
95000	594.02	579.89	567.05	555.36	509.98	479.45	458.09
100000	625.28	610.41	596.90	584.59	536.82	504.69	482.20
105000	656.54	640.93	626.74	613.82	563.66	529.92	506.31
110000	687.81	671.45	656.59	643.05	590.50	555.16	530.42
120000	750.34	732.49	716.28	701.51	644.19	605.63	578.64
130000	812.86	793.53	775.97	759.97	697.87	656.09	626.86
140000	875.39	854.57	835.66	818.43	751.55	706.56	675.08
150000	937.92	915.61	895.35	876.89	805.23	757.03	723.29
175000	1094.24	1068.21	1044.57	1023.03	939.44	883.20	843.84
200000	1250.56	1220.81	1193.80	1169.18	1073.64	1009.38	964.39
225000	1406.88	1373.41	1343.02	1315.33	1207.85	1135.55	1084.94
250000	1563.20	1526.01	1492.24	1461.48	1342.05	1261.72	1205.49

5¼% Monthly Payments

necessary to amortize a loan

AMOUNT	1 YEAR	2 YEARS	3 YEARS	4 YEARS	5 YEARS	6 YEARS	7 YEARS
100	8.57	4.40	3.01	2.31	1.90	1.62	1.43
200	17.14	8.80	6.02	4.63	3.80	3.24	2.85
500	42.86	21.99	15.04	11.57	9.49	8.11	7.13
1000	85.72	43.98	30.08	23.14	18.99	16.22	14.25
2000	171.44	87.97	60.17	46.29	37.97	32.44	28.50
5000	428.61	219.92	150.42	115.71	94.93	81.11	71.26
6000	514.33	263.90	180.50	138.86	113.92	97.33	85.51
7000	600.05	307.88	210.58	162.00	132.90	113.55	99.76
8000	685.78	351.87	240.67	185.14	151.89	129.77	114.01
9000	771.50	395.85	270.75	208.28	170.87	145.99	128.27
10000	857.22	439.83	300.83	231.43	189.86	162.21	142.52
15000	1285.83	659.75	451.25	347.14	284.79	243.32	213.78
20000	1714.44	879.67	601.67	462.85	379.72	324.42	285.03
25000	2143.05	1099.59	752.08	578.57	474.65	405.53	356.29
30000	2571.66	1319.50	902.50	694.28	569.58	486.63	427.55
35000	3000.27	1539.42	1052.91	809.99	664.51	567.74	498.81
36000	3086.00	1583.40	1083.00	833.14	683.50	583.96	513.06
37000	3171.72	1627.39	1113.08	856.28	702.48	600.18	527.31
38000	3257.44	1671.37	1143.16	879.42	721.47	616.40	541.56
39000	3343.16	1715.35	1173.25	902.57	740.45	632.62	555.82
40000	3428.88	1759.34	1203.33	925.71	759.44	648.85	570.07
41000	3514.61	1803.32	1233.41	948.85	778.43	665.07	584.32
42000	3600.33	1847.30	1263.50	971.99	797.41	681.29	598.57
43000	3686.05	1891.29	1293.58	995.14	816.40	697.51	612.82
44000	3771.77	1935.27	1323.66	1018.28	835.38	713.73	627.07
45000	3857.49	1979.25	1353.75	1041.42	854.37	729.95	641.33
46000	3943.22	2023.24	1383.83	1064.56	873.36	746.17	655.58
47000	4028.94	2067.22	1413.91	1087.71	892.34	762.39	669.83
48000	4114.66	2111.20	1444.00	1110.85	911.33	778.62	684.08
49000	4200.38	2155.19	1474.08	1133.99	930.31	794.84	698.33
50000	4286.10	2199.17	1504.16	1157.14	949.30	811.06	712.58
51000	4371.83	2243.16	1534.25	1180.28	968.29	827.28	726.84
52000	4457.55	2287.14	1564.33	1203.42	987.27	843.50	741.09
53000	4543.27	2331.12	1594.41	1226.56	1006.26	859.72	755.34
54000	4628.99	2375.11	1624.50	1249.71	1025.24	875.94	769.59
55000	4714.71	2419.09	1654.58	1272.85	1044.23	892.16	783.84
56000	4800.44	2463.07	1684.66	1295.99	1063.22	908.38	798.09
57000	4886.16	2507.06	1714.75	1319.13	1082.20	924.61	812.35
58000	4971.88	2551.04	1744.83	1342.28	1101.19	940.83	826.60
59000	5057.60	2595.02	1774.91	1365.42	1120.17	957.05	840.85
60000	5143.33	2639.01	1805.00	1388.56	1139.16	973.27	855.10
65000	5571.94	2858.92	1955.41	1504.28	1234.09	1054.37	926.36
70000	6000.55	3078.84	2105.83	1619.99	1329.02	1135.48	997.62
75000	6429.16	3298.76	2256.25	1735.70	1423.95	1216.59	1068.88
80000	6857.77	3518.67	2406.66	1851.42	1518.88	1297.69	1140.13
85000	7286.38	3738.59	2557.08	1967.13	1613.81	1378.80	1211.39
90000	7714.99	3958.51	2707.49	2082.84	1708.74	1459.90	1282.65
95000	8143.60	4178.43	2857.91	2198.56	1803.67	1541.01	1353.91
100000	8572.21	4398.34	3008.33	2314.27	1898.60	1622.12	1425.17
105000	9000.82	4618.26	3158.74	2429.98	1993.53	1703.22	1496.43
110000	9429.43	4838.18	3309.16	2545.70	2088.46	1784.33	1567.68
120000	10286.65	5278.01	3609.99	2777.13	2278.32	1946.54	1710.20
130000	11143.87	5717.85	3910.83	3008.55	2468.18	2108.75	1852.72
140000	12001.09	6157.68	4211.66	3239.98	2658.04	2270.96	1995.23
150000	12858.31	6597.52	4512.49	3471.41	2847.90	2433.17	2137.75
175000	15001.37	7697.10	5264.57	4049.97	3322.55	2838.70	2494.04
200000	17144.42	8796.69	6016.65	4628.54	3797.20	3244.23	2850.34
225000	19287.47	9896.27	6768.74	5207.11	4271.85	3649.76	3206.63
250000	21430.52	10995.86	7520.82	5785.68	4746.50	4055.29	3562.92

Monthly Payments 5¼%

necessary to amortize a loan

AMOUNT	8 YEARS	9 YEARS	10 YEARS	11 YEARS	12 YEARS	13 YEARS	14 YEARS
100	1.28	1.16	1.07	1.00	0.94	0.89	0.84
200	2.56	2.33	2.15	2.00	1.87	1.77	1.68
500	6.39	5.82	5.36	4.99	4.69	4.43	4.21
1000	12.78	11.64	10.73	9.99	9.37	8.86	8.42
2000	25.56	23.28	21.46	19.98	18.75	17.72	16.84
5000	63.90	58.19	53.65	49.94	46.87	44.29	42.09
6000	76.68	69.83	64.38	59.93	56.25	53.15	50.51
7000	89.45	81.47	75.10	69.92	65.62	62.01	58.93
8000	102.23	93.11	85.83	79.91	75.00	70.87	67.34
9000	115.01	104.74	96.56	89.90	84.37	79.72	75.76
10000	127.79	116.38	107.29	99.89	93.75	88.58	84.18
15000	191.69	174.57	160.94	149.83	140.62	132.87	126.27
20000	255.59	232.77	214.58	199.78	187.50	177.16	168.36
25000	319.48	290.96	268.23	249.72	234.37	221.45	210.45
30000	383.38	349.15	321.88	299.66	281.24	265.74	252.54
35000	447.27	407.34	375.52	349.61	328.12	310.04	294.63
36000	460.05	418.98	386.25	359.60	337.49	318.89	303.04
37000	472.83	430.62	396.98	369.58	346.87	327.75	311.46
38000	485.61	442.25	407.71	379.57	356.24	336.61	319.88
39000	498.39	453.89	418.44	389.56	365.62	345.47	328.30
40000	511.17	465.53	429.17	399.55	374.99	354.33	336.72
41000	523.95	477.17	439.90	409.54	384.37	363.18	345.13
42000	536.73	488.81	450.63	419.53	393.74	372.04	353.55
43000	549.51	500.44	461.35	429.52	403.12	380.90	361.97
44000	562.29	512.08	472.08	439.51	412.49	389.76	370.39
45000	575.07	523.72	482.81	449.49	421.87	398.62	378.81
46000	587.85	535.36	493.54	459.48	431.24	407.48	387.22
47000	600.63	547.00	504.27	469.47	440.62	416.33	395.64
48000	613.41	558.64	515.00	479.46	449.99	425.19	404.06
49000	626.18	570.27	525.73	489.45	459.37	434.05	412.48
50000	638.96	581.91	536.46	499.44	468.74	442.91	420.90
51000	651.74	593.55	547.19	509.43	478.12	451.77	429.31
52000	664.52	605.19	557.92	519.42	487.49	460.62	437.73
53000	677.30	616.83	568.65	529.40	496.87	469.48	446.15
54000	690.08	628.47	579.38	539.39	506.24	478.34	454.57
55000	702.86	640.10	590.10	549.38	515.61	487.20	462.99
56000	715.64	651.74	600.83	550.37	524.99	496.06	471.40
57000	728.42	663.38	611.56	569.36	534.36	504.91	479.82
58000	741.20	675.02	622.29	579.35	543.74	513.77	488.24
59000	753.98	686.66	633.02	589.34	553.11	522.63	496.66
60000	766.76	698.30	643.75	599.33	562.49	531.49	505.07
65000	830.65	756.49	697.40	649.27	609.36	575.78	547.16
70000	894.55	814.68	751.04	699.21	656.24	620.07	589.25
75000	958.45	872.87	804.69	749.16	703.11	664.36	631.34
80000	1022.34	931.06	858.33	799.10	749.99	708.65	673.43
85000	1086.24	989.25	911.98	849.04	796.86	752.94	715.52
90000	1150.14	1047.44	965.63	898.99	843.73	797.23	757.61
95000	1214.03	1105.63	1019.27	948.93	890.61	841.52	799.70
100000	1277.93	1163.83	1072.92	998.88	937.48	885.82	841.79
105000	1341.82	1222.02	1126.56	1048.82	984.36	930.11	883.88
110000	1405.72	1280.21	1180.21	1098.76	1031.23	974.40	925.97
120000	1533.51	1396.59	1287.50	1198.65	1124.98	1062.98	1010.15
130000	1661.31	1512.97	1394.79	1298.54	1218.73	1151.56	1094.33
140000	1789.10	1629.36	1502.08	1398.43	1312.47	1240.14	1178.51
150000	1916.89	1745.74	1609.38	1498.31	1406.22	1328.72	1262.69
175000	2236.37	2036.69	1877.60	1748.03	1640.59	1550.18	1473.13
200000	2555.86	2327.65	2145.83	1997.75	1874.96	1771.63	1683.58
225000	2875.34	2618.61	2414.06	2247.47	2109.33	1993.09	1894.03
250000	3194.82	2909.56	2682.29	2497.19	2343.70	2214.54	2104.48

5¼%

Monthly Payments

necessary to amortize a loan

AMOUNT	15 YEARS	16 YEARS	17 YEARS	18 YEARS	19 YEARS	20 YEARS	21 YEARS
100	0.80	0.77	0.74	0.72	0.69	0.67	0.66
200	1.61	1.54	1.48	1.43	1.39	1.35	1.31
500	4.02	3.85	3.71	3.58	3.47	3.37	3.28
1000	8.04	7.71	7.42	7.17	6.94	6.74	6.56
2000	16.08	15.42	14.84	14.33	13.88	13.48	13.12
5000	40.19	38.55	37.10	35.83	34.70	33.69	32.79
6000	48.23	46.26	44.52	43.00	41.64	40.43	39.35
7000	56.27	53.96	51.94	50.16	48.58	47.17	45.90
8000	64.31	61.67	59.37	57.33	55.52	53.91	52.46
9000	72.35	69.38	66.79	64.49	62.46	60.65	59.02
10000	80.39	77.09	74.21	71.66	69.40	67.38	65.58
15000	120.58	115.64	111.31	107.49	104.10	101.08	98.36
20000	160.78	154.19	148.41	143.32	138.80	134.77	131.15
25000	200.97	192.73	185.52	179.15	173.50	168.46	163.94
30000	241.16	231.28	222.62	214.98	208.20	202.15	196.73
35000	281.36	269.82	259.72	250.81	242.90	235.85	229.52
36000	289.40	277.53	267.14	257.98	249.84	242.58	236.08
37000	297.43	285.24	274.56	265.14	256.78	249.32	242.63
38000	305.47	292.95	281.98	272.31	263.72	256.06	249.19
39000	313.51	300.66	289.41	279.48	270.66	262.80	255.75
40000	321.55	308.37	296.83	286.64	277.60	269.54	262.31
41000	329.59	316.08	304.25	293.81	284.54	276.28	268.86
42000	337.63	323.79	311.67	300.97	291.48	283.01	275.42
43000	345.67	331.50	319.09	308.14	298.42	289.75	281.98
44000	353.71	339.21	326.51	315.31	305.36	296.49	288.54
45000	361.74	346.92	333.93	322.47	312.30	303.23	295.09
46000	369.78	354.63	341.35	329.64	319.24	309.97	301.65
47000	377.82	362.34	348.77	336.80	326.18	316.71	308.21
48000	385.86	370.05	356.19	343.97	333.12	323.45	314.77
49000	393.90	377.75	363.61	351.14	340.06	330.18	321.32
50000	401.94	385.46	371.03	358.30	347.00	336.92	327.88
51000	409.98	393.17	378.45	365.47	353.94	343.66	334.44
52000	418.02	400.88	385.87	372.63	360.88	350.40	341.00
53000	426.06	408.59	393.29	379.80	367.82	357.14	347.55
54000	434.09	416.30	400.71	386.97	374.76	363.88	354.11
55000	442.13	424.01	408.14	394.13	381.70	370.61	360.67
56000	450.17	431.72	415.56	401.30	388.64	377.35	367.23
57000	458.21	439.43	422.98	408.46	395.58	384.09	373.79
58000	466.25	447.14	430.40	415.63	402.52	390.83	380.34
59000	474.29	454.85	437.82	422.80	409.46	397.57	386.90
60000	482.33	462.55	445.24	429.96	416.40	404.31	393.46
65000	522.52	501.10	482.34	465.79	451.11	438.00	426.25
70000	562.71	539.65	519.45	501.62	485.81	471.69	459.03
75000	602.91	578.20	556.55	537.45	520.51	505.38	491.82
80000	643.10	616.74	593.65	573.28	555.21	539.08	524.61
85000	683.30	655.29	630.75	609.11	589.91	572.77	557.40
90000	723.49	693.84	667.86	644.94	624.61	606.46	590.19
95000	763.68	732.38	704.96	680.77	659.31	640.15	622.98
100000	803.88	770.93	742.06	716.60	694.01	673.84	655.76
105000	844.07	809.47	779.17	752.43	728.71	707.54	688.55
110000	884.27	848.02	816.27	788.26	763.41	741.23	721.34
120000	964.65	925.11	890.48	859.92	832.81	808.61	786.92
130000	1045.04	1002.21	964.68	931.59	902.21	876.00	852.49
140000	1125.43	1079.30	1038.89	1003.25	971.61	943.38	918.07
150000	1205.82	1156.39	1113.10	1074.91	1041.01	1010.77	983.65
175000	1406.79	1349.12	1298.61	1254.06	1214.51	1179.23	1147.59
200000	1607.76	1541.86	1484.13	1433.21	1388.02	1347.69	1311.53
225000	1808.72	1734.59	1669.65	1612.36	1561.52	1516.15	1475.47
250000	2009.69	1927.32	1855.16	1791.51	1735.02	1684.61	1639.41

Monthly Payments
necessary to amortize a loan

5¼%

AMOUNT	22 YEARS	23 YEARS	24 YEARS	25 YEARS	30 YEARS	35 YEARS	40 YEARS
100	0.64	0.62	0.61	0.60	0.55	0.52	0.50
200	1.28	1.25	1.22	1.20	1.10	1.04	1.00
500	3.20	3.12	3.06	3.00	2.76	2.60	2.49
1000	6.39	6.25	6.11	5.99	5.52	5.21	4.99
2000	12.79	12.50	12.23	11.98	11.04	10.41	9.98
5000	31.97	31.24	30.57	29.96	27.61	26.04	24.94
6000	38.37	37.49	36.68	35.95	33.13	31.24	29.93
7000	44.76	43.73	42.80	41.95	38.65	36.45	34.92
8000	51.16	49.98	48.91	47.94	44.18	41.66	39.91
9000	57.55	56.23	55.03	53.93	49.70	46.87	44.90
10000	63.95	62.48	61.14	59.92	55.22	52.07	49.89
15000	95.92	93.71	91.71	89.89	82.83	78.11	74.83
20000	127.90	124.95	122.28	119.85	110.44	104.16	99.77
25000	159.87	156.19	152.85	149.81	138.05	130.19	124.72
30000	191.84	187.43	183.42	179.77	165.66	156.22	149.66
35000	223.82	218.67	213.99	209.74	193.27	182.26	174.60
36000	230.21	224.91	220.11	215.73	198.79	187.47	179.59
37000	236.61	231.16	226.22	221.72	204.32	192.67	184.58
38000	243.00	237.41	232.33	227.71	209.84	197.88	189.57
39000	249.40	243.66	238.45	233.71	215.36	203.09	194.56
40000	255.79	249.90	244.56	239.70	220.88	208.30	199.55
41000	262.19	256.15	250.68	245.69	226.40	213.50	204.54
42000	268.58	262.40	256.79	251.68	231.93	218.71	209.53
43000	274.98	268.65	262.90	257.68	237.45	223.92	214.51
44000	281.37	274.89	269.02	263.67	242.97	229.13	219.50
45000	287.77	281.14	275.13	269.66	248.49	234.33	224.49
46000	294.16	287.39	281.25	275.65	254.01	239.54	229.48
47000	300.56	293.64	287.36	281.65	259.54	244.75	234.47
48000	306.95	299.89	293.47	287.64	265.06	249.96	239.46
49000	313.35	306.13	299.59	293.63	270.58	255.16	244.45
50000	319.74	312.38	305.70	299.62	276.10	260.37	249.44
51000	326.14	318.63	311.82	305.62	281.62	265.58	254.42
52000	332.53	324.88	317.93	311.61	287.15	270.79	259.41
53000	338.93	331.12	324.04	317.60	292.67	275.99	264.40
54000	345.32	337.37	330.16	323.59	298.19	281.20	269.39
55000	351.71	343.62	336.27	329.59	303.71	286.41	274.38
56000	358.11	349.87	342.39	335.58	309.23	291.62	279.37
57000	364.50	356.11	348.50	341.57	314.76	296.82	284.36
58000	370.90	362.36	354.61	347.56	320.28	302.03	289.34
59000	377.29	368.61	360.73	353.56	325.80	307.24	294.33
60000	383.69	374.86	366.84	359.55	331.32	312.45	299.32
65000	415.66	406.09	397.41	389.51	358.93	338.48	324.27
70000	447.64	437.33	427.98	419.47	386.54	364.52	349.21
75000	479.61	468.57	458.55	449.44	414.15	390.56	374.15
80000	511.59	499.81	489.12	479.40	441.76	416.59	399.10
85000	543.56	531.05	519.69	509.36	469.37	442.63	424.04
90000	575.53	562.28	550.26	539.32	496.98	468.67	448.98
95000	607.51	593.52	580.83	569.29	524.59	494.71	473.93
100000	639.48	624.76	611.40	599.25	552.20	520.74	498.87
105000	671.46	656.00	641.97	629.21	579.81	546.78	523.81
110000	703.43	687.24	672.55	659.17	607.42	572.82	548.76
120000	767.38	749.71	733.69	719.10	662.64	624.89	598.64
130000	831.33	812.19	794.83	779.02	717.86	676.97	648.53
140000	895.27	874.67	855.97	838.95	773.09	729.04	698.42
150000	959.22	937.14	917.11	898.87	828.31	781.11	748.31
175000	1119.09	1093.33	1069.96	1048.68	966.36	911.30	873.02
200000	1278.96	1249.52	1222.81	1198.50	1104.41	1041.49	997.74
225000	1438.83	1405.71	1375.66	1348.31	1242.46	1171.67	1122.46
250000	1598.70	1561.90	1528.51	1498.12	1380.51	1301.86	1247.18

5½% Monthly Payments

necessary to amortize a loan

AMOUNT	1 YEAR	2 YEARS	3 YEARS	4 YEARS	5 YEARS	6 YEARS	7 YEARS
100	8.58	4.41	3.02	2.33	1.91	1.63	1.44
200	17.17	8.82	6.04	4.65	3.82	3.27	2.87
500	42.92	22.05	15.10	11.63	9.55	8.17	7.19
1000	85.84	44.10	30.20	23.26	19.10	16.34	14.37
2000	171.67	88.19	60.39	46.51	38.20	32.68	28.74
5000	429.18	220.48	150.98	116.28	95.51	81.69	71.85
6000	515.02	264.57	181.18	139.54	114.61	98.03	86.22
7000	600.86	308.67	211.37	162.80	133.71	114.37	100.59
8000	686.69	352.77	241.57	186.05	152.81	130.70	114.96
9000	772.53	396.86	271.76	209.31	171.91	147.04	129.33
10000	858.37	440.96	301.96	232.56	191.01	163.38	143.70
15000	1287.55	661.43	452.94	348.85	286.52	245.07	215.55
20000	1716.74	881.91	603.92	465.13	382.02	326.76	287.40
25000	2145.92	1102.39	754.90	581.41	477.53	408.45	359.25
30000	2575.10	1322.87	905.88	697.69	573.03	490.14	431.10
35000	3004.29	1543.35	1056.86	813.98	668.54	571.83	502.95
36000	3090.12	1587.44	1087.05	837.23	687.64	588.16	517.32
37000	3175.96	1631.54	1117.25	860.49	706.74	604.50	531.69
38000	3261.80	1675.63	1147.44	883.75	725.84	620.84	546.06
39000	3347.63	1719.73	1177.64	907.00	744.95	637.18	560.43
40000	3433.47	1763.83	1207.84	930.26	764.05	653.52	574.80
41000	3519.31	1807.92	1238.03	953.52	783.15	669.85	589.17
42000	3605.14	1852.02	1268.23	976.77	802.25	686.19	603.54
43000	3690.98	1896.11	1298.42	1000.03	821.35	702.53	617.91
44000	3776.82	1940.21	1328.62	1023.28	840.45	718.87	632.28
45000	3862.66	1984.30	1358.82	1046.54	859.55	735.20	646.65
46000	3948.49	2028.40	1389.01	1069.80	878.65	751.54	661.02
47000	4034.33	2072.50	1419.21	1093.05	897.75	767.88	675.39
48000	4120.17	2116.59	1449.40	1116.31	916.86	784.22	689.76
49000	4206.00	2160.69	1479.60	1139.57	935.96	800.56	704.13
50000	4291.84	2204.78	1509.80	1162.82	955.06	816.89	718.50
51000	4377.68	2248.88	1539.99	1186.08	974.16	833.23	732.87
52000	4463.51	2292.97	1570.19	1209.34	993.26	849.57	747.24
53000	4549.35	2337.07	1600.38	1232.59	1012.36	865.91	761.61
54000	4635.19	2381.17	1630.58	1255.85	1031.46	882.25	775.98
55000	4721.02	2425.26	1660.77	1279.11	1050.56	898.58	790.35
56000	4806.86	2469.36	1690.97	1302.36	1069.67	914.92	804.72
57000	4892.70	2513.45	1721.17	1325.62	1088.77	931.26	819.09
58000	4978.53	2557.55	1751.36	1348.88	1107.87	947.60	833.46
59000	5064.37	2601.64	1781.56	1372.13	1126.97	963.94	847.83
60000	5150.21	2645.74	1811.75	1395.39	1146.07	980.27	862.20
65000	5579.39	2866.22	1962.73	1511.67	1241.58	1001.56	934.05
70000	6008.57	3086.70	2113.71	[illegible]	1337.08	1143.65	1005.90
75000	6437.76	3307.17	2264.69	1744.24	1432.59	1225.34	1077.75
80000	[illegible]	3527.65	2415.67	1860.52	1528.09	1307.03	1149.60
85000	7296.13	3748.13	2566.65	1976.80	1623.60	1388.72	1221.46
90000	7725.31	3968.61	2717.63	2093.08	1719.10	1470.41	1293.30
95000	8154.49	4189.09	2868.61	2209.37	1814.61	1552.10	1365.15
100000	8583.68	4409.57	3019.59	2325.65	1910.12	1633.79	1437.00
105000	9012.86	4630.04	3170.57	2441.93	2005.62	1715.48	1508.85
110000	9442.05	4850.52	3321.55	2558.21	2101.13	1797.17	1580.70
120000	10300.41	5291.48	3623.51	2790.78	2292.14	1960.55	1724.41
130000	11158.78	5732.44	3925.47	3023.34	2483.15	2123.93	1868.11
140000	12017.15	6173.39	4227.43	3255.91	2674.16	2287.30	2011.81
150000	12875.52	6614.35	4529.39	3488.47	2865.17	2450.68	2155.51
175000	15021.44	7716.74	5284.28	4069.88	3342.70	2859.13	2514.76
200000	17167.36	8819.13	6039.18	4651.30	3820.23	3267.58	2874.01
225000	19313.28	9921.52	6794.08	5232.71	4297.76	3676.02	3233.26
250000	21459.20	11023.91	7548.98	5814.12	4775.29	4084.47	3592.51

Monthly Payments 5½%

necessary to amortize a loan

AMOUNT	8 YEARS	9 YEARS	10 YEARS	11 YEARS	12 YEARS	13 YEARS	14 YEARS
100	1.29	1.18	1.09	1.01	0.95	0.90	0.85
200	2.58	2.36	2.17	2.02	1.90	1.80	1.71
500	6.45	5.88	5.43	5.06	4.75	4.49	4.27
1000	12.90	11.76	10.85	10.11	9.50	8.99	8.55
2000	25.80	23.52	21.71	20.23	19.00	17.97	17.10
5000	64.50	58.80	54.26	50.57	47.51	44.93	42.74
6000	77.40	70.56	65.12	60.68	57.01	53.92	51.29
7000	90.30	82.32	75.97	70.80	66.51	62.91	59.84
8000	103.19	94.08	86.82	80.91	76.01	71.89	68.39
9000	116.09	105.84	97.67	91.03	85.52	80.88	76.93
10000	128.99	117.60	108.53	101.14	95.02	89.87	85.48
15000	193.49	176.40	162.79	151.71	142.53	134.80	128.22
20000	257.99	235.20	217.05	202.28	190.03	179.74	170.97
25000	322.48	294.00	271.32	252.85	237.54	224.67	213.71
30000	386.98	352.80	325.58	303.42	285.05	269.60	256.45
35000	451.48	411.60	379.84	353.99	332.56	314.54	299.19
36000	464.38	423.36	390.69	364.10	342.06	323.52	307.74
37000	477.27	435.12	401.55	374.22	351.56	332.51	316.29
38000	490.17	446.88	412.40	384.33	361.07	341.50	324.83
39000	503.07	458.64	423.25	394.44	370.57	350.48	333.38
40000	515.97	470.40	434.11	404.56	380.07	359.47	341.93
41000	528.87	482.16	444.96	414.67	389.57	368.46	350.48
42000	541.77	493.92	455.81	424.79	399.07	377.44	359.03
43000	554.67	505.68	466.66	434.90	408.57	386.43	367.58
44000	567.57	517.44	477.52	445.01	418.08	395.42	376.12
45000	580.47	529.20	488.37	455.13	427.58	404.41	384.67
46000	593.37	540.96	499.22	465.24	437.08	413.39	393.22
47000	606.27	552.72	510.07	475.35	446.58	422.38	401.77
48000	619.17	564.48	520.93	485.47	456.08	431.37	410.32
49000	632.07	576.24	531.78	495.58	465.58	440.35	418.86
50000	644.97	588.00	542.63	505.70	475.09	449.34	427.41
51000	657.87	599.76	553.48	515.81	484.59	458.33	435.96
52000	670.76	611.52	564.34	525.92	494.09	467.31	444.51
53000	683.66	623.28	575.19	536.04	503.59	476.30	453.06
54000	696.56	635.04	586.04	546.15	513.09	485.29	461.61
55000	709.46	646.80	596.89	556.27	522.50	494.27	470.15
56000	722.36	658.56	607.75	566.38	532.10	503.26	478.70
57000	735.26	670.32	618.60	576.49	541.60	512.25	487.25
58000	748.16	682.08	629.45	586.61	551.10	521.23	495.80
59000	761.06	693.84	640.31	596.72	560.60	530.22	504.35
60000	773.96	705.60	651.16	606.84	570.10	539.21	512.90
65000	838.46	764.40	705.42	657.41	617.61	584.14	555.64
70000	902.95	823.20	759.68	707.98	665.12	629.07	598.38
75000	967.45	882.00	813.95	758.54	712.63	674.01	641.12
80000	1031.95	940.80	868.21	809.11	760.14	718.94	683.86
85000	1096.44	999.60	922.47	859.68	807.65	763.88	726.60
90000	1160.94	1058.40	976.74	910.25	855.15	808.81	769.34
95000	1225.44	1117.20	1031.00	960.82	902.66	853.74	812.08
100000	1289.93	1176.00	1085.26	1011.39	950.17	898.68	854.83
105000	1354.43	1234.80	1139.53	1061.96	997.68	943.61	897.57
110000	1418.93	1293.60	1193.79	1112.53	1045.19	988.55	940.31
120000	1547.92	1411.20	1302.32	1213.67	1140.21	1078.41	1025.79
130000	1676.91	1528.80	1410.84	1314.81	1235.22	1168.28	1111.27
140000	1805.91	1646.40	1519.37	1415.95	1330.24	1258.15	1196.76
150000	1934.90	1764.00	1627.89	1517.09	1425.26	1348.02	1282.24
175000	2257.38	2058.00	1899.21	1769.94	1662.80	1572.69	1495.94
200000	2579.86	2352.00	2170.53	2022.79	1900.34	1797.36	1709.65
225000	2902.35	2646.00	2441.84	2275.63	2137.89	2022.03	1923.36
250000	3224.83	2940.00	2713.16	2528.48	2375.43	2246.70	2137.06

5½% Monthly Payments

necessary to amortize a loan

AMOUNT	15 YEARS	16 YEARS	17 YEARS	18 YEARS	19 YEARS	20 YEARS	21 YEARS
100	0.82	0.78	0.76	0.73	0.71	0.69	0.67
200	1.63	1.57	1.51	1.46	1.42	1.38	1.34
500	4.09	3.92	3.78	3.65	3.54	3.44	3.35
1000	8.17	7.84	7.56	7.30	7.08	6.88	6.70
2000	16.34	15.69	15.11	14.61	14.16	13.76	13.40
5000	40.85	39.22	37.78	36.52	35.39	34.39	33.50
6000	49.03	47.06	45.34	43.82	42.47	41.27	40.20
7000	57.20	54.90	52.89	51.12	49.55	48.15	46.90
8000	65.37	62.74	60.45	58.43	56.63	55.03	53.60
9000	73.54	70.59	68.00	65.73	63.71	61.91	60.30
10000	81.71	78.43	75.56	73.03	70.79	68.79	67.00
15000	122.56	117.65	113.34	109.55	106.18	103.18	100.50
20000	163.42	156.86	151.12	146.06	141.58	137.58	133.99
25000	204.27	196.08	188.90	182.58	176.97	171.97	167.49
30000	245.13	235.29	226.68	219.09	212.37	206.37	200.99
35000	285.98	274.51	264.46	255.61	247.76	240.76	234.49
36000	294.15	282.35	272.02	262.91	254.84	247.64	241.19
37000	302.32	290.19	279.58	270.22	261.92	254.52	247.89
38000	310.49	298.04	287.13	277.52	269.00	261.40	254.59
39000	318.66	305.88	294.69	284.82	276.08	268.28	261.29
40000	326.83	313.72	302.24	292.13	283.15	275.15	267.99
41000	335.00	321.56	309.80	299.43	290.23	282.03	274.69
42000	343.18	329.41	317.36	306.73	297.31	288.91	281.39
43000	351.35	337.25	324.91	314.04	304.39	295.79	288.09
44000	359.52	345.09	332.47	321.34	311.47	302.67	294.79
45000	367.69	352.94	340.02	328.64	318.55	309.55	301.49
46000	375.86	360.78	347.58	335.95	325.63	316.43	308.19
47000	384.03	368.62	355.14	343.25	332.71	323.31	314.89
48000	392.20	376.47	362.69	350.55	339.79	330.19	321.59
49000	400.37	384.31	370.25	357.86	346.86	337.06	328.29
50000	408.54	392.15	377.80	365.16	353.94	343.94	334.99
51000	416.71	399.99	385.36	372.46	361.02	350.82	341.68
52000	424.88	407.84	392.92	379.76	368.10	357.70	348.38
53000	433.05	415.68	400.47	387.07	375.18	364.58	355.08
54000	441.23	423.52	408.03	394.37	382.26	371.46	361.78
55000	449.40	431.37	415.59	401.67	389.34	378.34	368.48
56000	457.57	439.21	423.14	408.98	396.42	385.22	375.18
57000	465.74	447.05	430.70	416.28	403.50	392.10	381.88
58000	473.91	454.90	438.25	423.58	410.57	398.97	388.58
59000	482.08	462.74	445.81	430.89	417.65	405.85	395.28
60000	490.25	470.58	453.37	438.19	424.73	412.73	401.98
65000	531.10	509.80	491.15	474.71	460.13	447.13	435.48
70000	571.96	549.01	528.93	511.22	495.52	481.52	468.98
75000	612.81	588.23	566.71	547.74	530.91	515.92	502.48
80000	653.67	627.44	604.49	584.25	566.31	550.31	535.98
85000	694.52	666.66	642.27	620.77	601.70	584.70	569.47
90000	735.38	705.87	680.05	657.28	637.10	619.10	602.97
95000	776.23	745.09	717.83	693.80	672.49	653.49	636.47
100000	817.08	784.30	755.61	730.32	707.89	687.89	669.97
105000	857.94	823.52	793.39	766.83	743.28	722.28	703.47
110000	898.79	862.73	831.17	803.35	778.67	756.68	736.97
120000	980.50	941.16	906.73	876.38	849.46	825.46	803.96
130000	1062.21	1019.60	982.29	949.41	920.25	894.25	870.96
140000	1143.92	1098.03	1057.85	1022.44	991.04	963.04	937.96
150000	1225.63	1176.46	1133.41	1095.47	1061.83	1031.83	1004.96
175000	1429.90	1372.53	1322.32	1278.05	1238.80	1203.80	1172.45
200000	1634.17	1568.61	1511.22	1460.63	1415.77	1375.77	1339.94
225000	1838.44	1764.68	1700.12	1643.21	1592.74	1547.75	1507.43
250000	2042.71	1960.76	1889.02	1825.79	1769.72	1719.72	1674.93

Monthly Payments 5½%

necessary to amortize a loan

AMOUNT	22 YEARS	23 YEARS	24 YEARS	25 YEARS	30 YEARS	35 YEARS	40 YEARS
100	0.65	0.64	0.63	0.61	0.57	0.54	0.52
200	1.31	1.28	1.25	1.23	1.14	1.07	1.03
500	3.27	3.20	3.13	3.07	2.84	2.69	2.58
1000	6.54	6.39	6.26	6.14	5.68	5.37	5.16
2000	13.08	12.79	12.52	12.28	11.36	10.74	10.32
5000	32.69	31.96	31.30	30.70	28.39	26.85	25.79
6000	39.23	38.36	37.57	36.85	34.07	32.22	30.95
7000	45.77	44.75	43.83	42.99	39.75	37.59	36.10
8000	52.31	51.14	50.09	49.13	45.42	42.96	41.26
9000	58.85	57.54	56.35	55.27	51.10	48.33	46.42
10000	65.38	63.93	62.61	61.41	56.78	53.70	51.58
15000	98.08	95.89	93.91	92.11	85.17	80.55	77.37
20000	130.77	127.86	125.22	122.82	113.56	107.40	103.15
25000	163.46	159.82	156.52	153.52	141.95	134.25	128.94
30000	196.15	191.79	187.83	184.23	170.34	161.10	154.73
35000	228.85	223.75	219.13	214.93	198.73	187.96	180.52
36000	235.39	230.14	225.39	221.07	204.40	193.33	185.68
37000	241.92	236.54	231.65	227.21	210.08	198.70	190.84
38000	248.46	242.93	237.91	233.35	215.76	204.07	195.99
39000	255.00	249.32	244.17	239.49	221.44	209.44	201.15
40000	261.54	255.72	250.44	245.63	227.12	214.81	206.31
41000	268.08	262.11	256.70	251.78	232.79	220.18	211.47
42000	274.62	268.50	262.96	257.92	238.47	225.55	216.62
43000	281.16	274.89	269.22	264.06	244.15	230.92	221.78
44000	287.69	281.29	275.48	270.20	249.83	236.29	226.94
45000	294.23	287.68	281.74	276.34	255.51	241.66	232.10
46000	300.77	294.07	288.00	282.48	261.18	247.03	237.25
47000	307.31	300.47	294.26	288.62	266.86	252.40	242.41
48000	313.85	306.86	300.52	294.76	272.54	257.77	247.57
49000	320.39	313.25	306.78	300.90	278.22	263.14	252.73
50000	326.92	319.64	313.04	307.04	283.89	268.51	257.89
51000	333.46	326.04	319.31	313.18	289.57	273.88	263.04
52000	340.00	332.43	325.57	319.33	295.25	279.25	268.20
53000	346.54	338.82	331.83	325.47	300.93	284.62	273.36
54000	353.08	345.22	338.09	331.61	306.61	289.99	278.52
55000	359.62	351.61	344.35	337.75	312.28	295.36	283.67
56000	366.16	358.00	350.61	343.89	317.96	300.73	288.83
57000	372.69	364.39	356.87	350.03	323.64	306.10	293.99
58000	379.23	370.79	363.13	356.17	329.32	311.47	299.15
59000	385.77	377.18	369.39	362.31	335.00	316.84	304.30
60000	392.31	383.57	375.65	368.45	340.67	322.21	309.46
65000	425.00	415.54	406.96	399.16	369.06	349.06	335.25
70000	457.69	447.50	438.26	429.86	397.45	375.91	361.04
75000	490.39	479.47	469.57	460.57	425.84	402.76	386.83
80000	523.08	511.43	500.87	491.27	454.23	429.61	412.62
85000	555.77	543.39	532.18	521.97	482.62	456.46	438.40
90000	588.46	575.36	563.48	552.68	511.01	483.31	464.19
95000	621.16	607.32	594.78	583.38	539.40	510.17	489.98
100000	653.85	639.29	626.09	614.09	567.79	537.02	515.77
105000	686.54	671.25	657.39	644.79	596.18	563.87	541.56
110000	719.23	703.22	688.70	675.50	624.57	590.72	567.35
120000	784.62	767.15	751.31	736.90	681.35	644.42	618.92
130000	850.00	831.07	813.92	798.31	738.13	698.12	670.50
140000	915.39	895.00	876.52	859.72	794.90	751.82	722.08
150000	980.77	958.93	939.13	921.13	851.68	805.52	773.66
175000	1144.24	1118.75	1095.66	1074.65	993.63	939.78	902.60
200000	1307.70	1278.58	1252.18	1228.17	1135.58	1074.03	1031.54
225000	1471.16	1438.40	1408.70	1381.70	1277.53	1208.29	1160.48
250000	1634.62	1598.22	1565.22	1535.22	1419.47	1342.54	1289.43

5¾%

Monthly Payments

necessary to amortize a loan

AMOUNT	1 YEAR	2 YEARS	3 YEARS	4 YEARS	5 YEARS	6 YEARS	7 YEARS
100	8.60	4.42	3.03	2.34	1.92	1.65	1.45
200	17.19	8.84	6.06	4.67	3.84	3.29	2.90
500	42.98	22.10	15.15	11.69	9.61	8.23	7.24
1000	85.95	44.21	30.31	23.37	19.22	16.46	14.49
2000	171.90	88.42	60.62	46.74	38.43	32.91	28.98
5000	429.76	221.04	151.54	116.85	96.08	82.28	72.45
6000	515.71	265.25	181.85	140.22	115.30	98.73	86.93
7000	601.66	309.46	212.16	163.59	134.52	115.19	101.42
8000	687.61	353.66	242.47	186.96	153.73	131.64	115.91
9000	773.56	397.87	272.78	210.34	172.95	148.10	130.40
10000	859.52	442.08	303.09	233.71	192.17	164.55	144.89
15000	1289.27	663.12	454.63	350.56	288.25	246.83	217.34
20000	1719.03	884.16	606.18	467.41	384.34	329.10	289.78
25000	2148.79	1105.20	757.72	584.26	480.42	411.38	362.23
30000	2578.55	1326.24	909.26	701.12	576.50	493.65	434.67
35000	3008.30	1547.28	1060.81	817.97	672.59	575.93	507.12
36000	3094.26	1591.49	1091.12	841.34	691.80	592.38	521.60
37000	3180.21	1635.70	1121.43	864.71	711.02	608.84	536.09
38000	3266.16	1679.91	1151.73	888.08	730.24	625.30	550.58
39000	3352.11	1724.11	1182.04	911.45	749.45	641.75	565.07
40000	3438.06	1768.32	1212.35	934.82	768.67	658.21	579.56
41000	3524.01	1812.53	1242.66	958.19	787.89	674.66	594.05
42000	3609.97	1856.74	1272.97	981.56	807.10	691.12	608.54
43000	3695.92	1900.95	1303.28	1004.93	826.32	707.57	623.03
44000	3781.87	1945.15	1333.59	1028.31	845.54	724.03	637.52
45000	3867.82	1989.36	1363.90	1051.68	864.75	740.48	652.01
46000	3953.77	2033.57	1394.20	1075.05	883.97	756.94	666.49
47000	4039.72	2077.78	1424.51	1098.42	903.19	773.39	680.98
48000	4125.68	2121.99	1454.82	1121.79	922.40	789.85	695.47
49000	4211.63	2166.19	1485.13	1145.16	941.62	806.30	709.96
50000	4297.58	2210.40	1515.44	1168.53	960.84	822.76	724.45
51000	4383.53	2254.61	1545.75	1191.90	980.06	839.21	738.94
52000	4469.48	2298.82	1576.06	1215.27	999.27	855.67	753.43
53000	4555.43	2343.03	1606.37	1238.64	1018.49	872.12	767.92
54000	4641.38	2387.23	1636.67	1262.01	1037.71	888.58	782.41
55000	4727.34	2431.44	1666.98	1285.38	1056.92	905.03	796.90
56000	4813.29	2475.65	1697.29	1308.75	1076.14	921.49	811.38
57000	4899.24	2519.86	1727.60	1332.12	1095.36	937.94	825.87
58000	4985.19	2564.07	1757.91	1355.49	1114.57	954.40	840.36
59000	5071.14	2608.27	1788.22	1378.86	1133.79	970.85	854.85
60000	5157.09	2652.48	1818.53	1402.23	1153.01	987.31	869.34
65000	5586.85	2873.52	1970.07	1519.09	1249.09	1069.58	941.79
70000	6016.61	3094.56	2121.62	1635.94	1345.17	1151.86	1014.23
75000	6446.37	3315.60	2273.16	1752.79	1441.26	1234.13	1086.68
80000	6876.13	3536.64	2424.70	1869.65	1537.34	1316.41	1159.12
85000	7305.88	3757.68	2576.25	1986.50	1633.43	1398.69	1231.57
90000	7735.64	3978.72	2727.79	2103.35	1729.51	1480.96	1304.01
95000	8165.40	4199.76	2879.34	2220.21	1825.59	1563.24	1376.46
100000	8595.16	4420.80	3030.88	2337.06	1921.68	1645.51	1448.90
105000	9024.91	4641.84	3182.42	2453.91	2017.76	1727.79	1521.35
110000	9454.67	4862.89	3333.97	2570.76	2113.84	1810.06	1593.79
120000	10314.19	5304.97	3637.05	2804.47	2306.01	1974.62	1738.68
130000	11173.70	5747.05	3940.14	3038.18	2498.18	2139.17	1883.57
140000	12033.22	6189.13	4243.23	3271.88	2690.35	2303.72	2028.46
150000	12892.73	6631.21	4546.32	3505.59	2882.52	2468.27	2173.35
175000	15041.52	7736.41	5304.04	4089.85	3362.93	2879.65	2535.58
200000	17190.31	8841.61	6061.76	4674.12	3843.35	3291.03	2897.80
225000	19339.10	9946.81	6819.48	5258.38	4323.77	3702.40	3260.03
250000	21487.89	11052.01	7577.20	5842.65	4804.19	4113.78	3622.25

Monthly Payments 5¾%

necessary to amortize a loan

AMOUNT	8 YEARS	9 YEARS	10 YEARS	11 YEARS	12 YEARS	13 YEARS	14 YEARS
100	1.30	1.19	1.10	1.02	0.96	0.91	0.87
200	2.60	2.38	2.20	2.05	1.93	1.82	1.74
500	6.51	5.94	5.49	5.12	4.81	4.56	4.34
1000	13.02	11.88	10.98	10.24	9.63	9.12	8.68
2000	26.04	23.76	21.95	20.48	19.26	18.23	17.36
5000	65.10	59.41	54.88	51.20	48.15	45.58	43.40
6000	78.12	71.29	65.86	61.44	57.78	54.70	52.08
7000	91.14	83.18	76.84	71.68	67.41	63.82	60.76
8000	104.16	95.06	87.82	81.92	77.04	72.93	69.44
9000	117.18	106.94	98.79	92.16	86.67	82.05	78.12
10000	130.20	118.82	109.77	102.40	96.30	91.16	86.80
15000	195.30	178.24	164.65	153.60	144.44	136.75	130.20
20000	260.40	237.65	219.54	204.80	192.59	182.33	173.59
25000	325.50	297.06	274.42	256.00	240.74	227.91	216.99
30000	390.60	356.47	329.31	307.20	288.89	273.49	260.39
35000	455.70	415.89	384.19	358.40	337.04	319.08	303.79
36000	468.72	427.77	395.17	368.64	346.67	328.19	312.47
37000	481.74	439.65	406.15	378.88	356.30	337.31	321.15
38000	494.76	451.53	417.12	389.12	365.93	346.43	329.83
39000	507.78	463.42	428.10	399.36	375.56	355.54	338.51
40000	520.80	475.30	439.08	409.60	385.18	364.66	347.19
41000	533.82	487.18	450.05	419.84	394.81	373.78	355.87
42000	546.84	499.06	461.03	430.08	404.44	382.89	364.55
43000	559.86	510.95	472.01	440.32	414.07	392.01	373.23
44000	572.88	522.83	482.98	450.56	423.70	401.13	381.91
45000	585.90	534.71	493.96	460.80	433.33	410.24	390.59
46000	598.92	546.59	504.94	471.04	442.96	419.36	399.27
47000	611.94	558.48	515.92	481.28	452.59	428.47	407.95
48000	624.96	570.36	526.89	491.52	462.22	437.59	416.63
49000	637.98	582.24	537.87	501.76	471.85	446.71	425.31
50000	651.00	594.12	548.85	512.00	481.48	455.82	433.99
51000	664.02	606.01	559.82	522.24	491.11	464.94	442.67
52000	677.04	617.89	570.80	532.48	500.74	474.06	451.35
53000	690.06	629.77	581.78	542.72	510.37	483.17	460.03
54000	703.08	641.65	592.75	552.96	520.00	492.29	468.71
55000	716.10	653.54	603.73	563.20	529.63	501.41	477.39
56000	729.12	665.42	614.71	573.44	539.26	510.52	486.07
57000	742.14	677.30	625.68	583.68	548.89	519.64	494.75
58000	755.16	689.18	636.66	593.92	558.52	528.76	503.43
59000	768.18	701.07	647.64	604.16	568.15	537.87	512.10
60000	781.20	712.95	658.62	614.40	577.78	546.99	520.78
65000	846.30	772.36	713.50	665.60	625.93	592.57	564.18
70000	911.40	831.77	768.38	716.80	674.07	638.15	607.58
75000	976.50	891.19	823.27	768.00	722.22	683.74	650.98
80000	1041.60	950.60	878.15	819.20	770.37	729.32	694.38
85000	1106.70	1010.01	933.04	870.40	818.52	774.90	737.78
90000	1171.80	1069.42	987.92	921.60	866.67	820.48	781.18
95000	1236.90	1128.84	1042.81	972.80	914.81	866.07	824.58
100000	1302.00	1188.25	1097.69	1024.00	962.96	911.65	867.97
105000	1367.10	1247.66	1152.58	1075.20	1011.11	957.23	911.37
110000	1432.20	1307.07	1207.46	1126.40	1059.26	1002.81	954.77
120000	1562.40	1425.90	1317.23	1228.80	1155.55	1093.98	1041.57
130000	1692.61	1544.72	1427.00	1331.20	1251.85	1185.14	1128.37
140000	1822.81	1663.55	1536.77	1433.60	1348.15	1276.31	1215.16
150000	1953.01	1782.37	1646.54	1536.00	1444.44	1367.47	1301.96
175000	2278.51	2079.44	1920.96	1792.00	1685.18	1595.38	1518.95
200000	2604.01	2376.50	2195.38	2048.01	1925.92	1823.30	1735.95
225000	2929.51	2673.56	2469.81	2304.01	2166.66	2051.21	1952.94
250000	3255.01	2970.62	2744.23	2560.01	2407.40	2279.12	2169.94

5¾% Monthly Payments

necessary to amortize a loan

AMOUNT	15 YEARS	16 YEARS	17 YEARS	18 YEARS	19 YEARS	20 YEARS	21 YEARS
100	0.83	0.80	0.77	0.74	0.72	0.70	0.68
200	1.66	1.60	1.54	1.49	1.44	1.40	1.37
500	4.15	3.99	3.85	3.72	3.61	3.51	3.42
1000	8.30	7.98	7.69	7.44	7.22	7.02	6.84
2000	16.61	15.96	15.39	14.88	14.44	14.04	13.69
5000	41.52	39.89	38.46	37.21	36.10	35.10	34.22
6000	49.82	47.87	46.16	44.65	43.31	42.13	41.06
7000	58.13	55.85	53.85	52.09	50.53	49.15	47.90
8000	66.43	63.82	61.54	59.53	57.75	56.17	54.75
9000	74.74	71.80	69.24	66.98	64.97	63.19	61.59
10000	83.04	79.78	76.93	74.42	72.19	70.21	68.43
15000	124.56	119.67	115.39	111.63	108.29	105.31	102.65
20000	166.08	159.56	153.86	148.83	144.38	140.42	136.87
25000	207.60	199.45	192.32	186.04	180.48	175.52	171.08
30000	249.12	239.34	230.79	223.25	216.57	210.63	205.30
35000	290.64	279.23	269.25	260.46	252.67	245.73	239.52
36000	298.95	287.21	276.94	267.90	259.89	252.75	246.36
37000	307.25	295.19	284.64	275.34	267.11	259.77	253.20
38000	315.56	303.17	292.33	282.78	274.33	266.79	260.05
39000	323.86	311.14	300.02	290.23	281.55	273.81	266.89
40000	332.16	319.12	307.72	297.67	288.76	280.83	273.73
41000	340.47	327.10	315.41	305.11	295.98	287.85	280.58
42000	348.77	335.08	323.10	312.55	303.20	294.88	287.42
43000	357.08	343.06	330.79	319.99	310.42	301.90	294.26
44000	365.38	351.04	338.49	327.43	317.64	308.92	301.11
45000	373.68	359.01	346.18	334.88	324.86	315.94	307.95
46000	381.99	366.99	353.87	342.32	332.08	322.96	314.79
47000	390.29	374.97	361.57	349.76	339.30	329.98	321.64
48000	398.60	382.95	369.26	357.20	346.52	337.00	328.48
49000	406.90	390.93	376.95	364.64	353.74	344.02	335.32
50000	415.21	398.90	384.64	372.08	360.96	351.04	342.17
51000	423.51	406.88	392.34	379.53	368.18	358.06	349.01
52000	431.81	414.86	400.03	386.97	375.39	365.08	355.85
53000	440.12	422.84	407.72	394.41	382.61	372.10	362.70
54000	448.42	430.82	415.42	401.85	389.83	379.13	369.54
55000	456.73	438.79	423.11	409.29	397.05	386.15	376.38
56000	465.03	446.77	430.80	416.73	404.27	393.17	383.23
57000	473.33	454.75	438.49	424.18	411.49	400.19	390.07
58000	481.64	462.73	446.19	431.62	418.71	407.21	396.91
59000	489.94	470.71	453.88	439.06	425.93	414.23	403.76
60000	498.25	478.68	461.57	446.50	433.15	421.25	410.60
65000	539.77	518.57	500.04	483.71	469.24	456.35	444.82
70000	581.29	558.47	538.50	520.92	505.34	491.46	479.03
75000	622.81	598.36	576.97	558.13	541.43	526.56	513.25
80000	664.33	638.25	615.43	595.34	577.53	561.67	547.47
85000	705.85	678.14	653.90	632.54	613.63	596.77	581.68
90000	747.37	718.03	692.36	669.75	649.72	631.88	615.90
95000	788.89	757.92	730.82	706.96	685.82	666.98	650.12
100000	830.41	797.81	769.29	744.17	721.91	702.08	684.34
105000	871.93	837.70	807.75	781.38	758.01	737.19	718.55
110000	913.45	877.59	846.22	818.59	794.10	772.29	752.77
120000	996.49	957.37	923.15	893.00	866.29	842.50	821.20
130000	1079.53	1037.15	1000.07	967.42	938.49	912.71	889.64
140000	1162.57	1116.93	1077.00	1041.84	1010.68	982.92	958.07
150000	1245.62	1196.71	1153.93	1116.25	1082.87	1053.13	1026.50
175000	1453.22	1396.16	1346.25	1302.30	1263.35	1228.65	1197.59
200000	1660.82	1595.61	1538.58	1488.34	1443.82	1404.17	1368.67
225000	1868.42	1795.07	1730.90	1674.38	1624.30	1579.69	1539.75
250000	2076.03	1994.52	1923.22	1860.42	1804.78	1755.21	1710.84

Monthly Payments 5¾%

necessary to amortize a loan

AMOUNT	22 YEARS	23 YEARS	24 YEARS	25 YEARS	30 YEARS	35 YEARS	40 YEARS
100	0.67	0.65	0.64	0.63	0.58	0.55	0.53
200	1.34	1.31	1.28	1.26	1.17	1.11	1.07
500	3.34	3.27	3.20	3.15	2.92	2.77	2.66
1000	6.68	6.54	6.41	6.29	5.84	5.54	5.33
2000	13.37	13.08	12.82	12.58	11.67	11.07	10.66
5000	33.42	32.70	32.05	31.46	29.18	27.68	26.64
6000	40.10	39.24	38.46	37.75	35.01	33.21	31.97
7000	46.79	45.78	44.87	44.04	40.85	38.75	37.30
8000	53.47	52.32	51.28	50.33	46.69	44.28	42.63
9000	60.15	58.86	57.69	56.62	52.52	49.82	47.96
10000	66.84	65.40	64.09	62.91	58.36	55.35	53.29
15000	100.26	98.10	96.14	94.37	87.54	83.03	79.93
20000	133.68	130.80	128.19	125.82	116.71	110.70	106.58
25000	167.10	163.50	160.24	157.28	145.89	138.38	133.22
30000	200.51	196.20	192.28	188.73	175.07	166.05	159.87
35000	233.93	228.89	224.33	220.19	204.25	193.73	186.51
36000	240.62	235.43	230.74	226.48	210.09	199.26	191.84
37000	247.30	241.97	237.15	232.77	215.92	204.80	197.17
38000	253.98	248.51	243.56	239.06	221.76	210.33	202.50
39000	260.67	255.05	249.97	245.35	227.59	215.87	207.83
40000	267.35	261.59	256.38	251.64	233.43	221.40	213.16
41000	274.04	268.13	262.79	257.93	239.26	226.94	218.48
42000	280.72	274.67	269.20	264.22	245.10	232.47	223.81
43000	287.40	281.21	275.61	270.52	250.94	238.01	229.14
44000	294.09	287.75	282.02	276.81	256.77	243.54	234.47
45000	300.77	294.29	288.43	283.10	262.61	249.08	239.80
46000	307.46	300.83	294.84	289.39	268.44	254.61	245.13
47000	314.14	307.37	301.25	295.68	274.28	260.15	250.46
48000	320.82	313.91	307.65	301.97	280.11	265.68	255.79
49000	327.51	320.45	314.06	308.26	285.95	271.22	261.11
50000	334.19	326.99	320.47	314.55	291.79	276.75	266.44
51000	340.87	333.53	326.88	320.84	297.62	282.29	271.77
52000	347.56	340.07	333.29	327.14	303.46	287.82	277.10
53000	354.24	346.61	339.70	333.43	309.29	293.36	282.43
54000	360.93	353.15	346.11	339.72	315.13	298.89	287.76
55000	367.61	359.69	352.52	346.01	320.97	304.43	293.09
56000	374.29	366.23	358.93	352.30	326.80	309.96	298.42
57000	380.98	372.77	365.34	358.59	332.64	315.50	303.75
58000	387.66	379.31	371.75	364.88	338.47	321.03	309.07
59000	394.34	385.85	378.16	371.17	344.31	326.57	314.40
60000	401.03	392.39	384.57	377.46	350.14	332.10	319.73
65000	434.45	425.09	416.62	408.92	379.32	359.78	346.38
70000	467.87	457.79	448.66	440.37	408.50	387.45	373.02
75000	501.29	490.49	480.71	471.83	437.68	415.13	399.67
80000	534.70	523.19	512.76	503.29	466.86	442.80	426.31
85000	568.12	555.89	544.81	534.74	496.04	470.48	452.95
90000	601.54	588.59	576.85	566.20	525.22	498.15	479.60
95000	634.96	621.28	608.90	597.65	554.39	525.83	506.24
100000	668.38	653.98	640.95	629.11	583.57	553.50	532.89
105000	701.80	686.68	673.00	660.56	612.75	581.18	559.53
110000	735.22	719.38	705.04	692.02	641.93	608.85	586.18
120000	802.06	784.78	769.14	754.93	700.29	664.20	639.47
130000	868.89	850.18	833.23	817.84	758.64	719.55	692.75
140000	935.73	915.58	897.33	880.75	817.00	774.90	746.04
150000	1002.57	980.98	961.42	943.66	875.36	830.25	799.33
175000	1169.67	1144.47	1121.66	1100.94	1021.25	968.63	932.55
200000	1336.76	1307.97	1281.90	1258.21	1167.15	1107.00	1065.78
225000	1503.86	1471.46	1442.13	1415.49	1313.04	1245.38	1199.00
250000	1670.95	1634.96	1602.37	1572.77	1458.93	1383.75	1332.22

6% Monthly Payments
necessary to amortize a loan

AMOUNT	1 YEAR	2 YEARS	3 YEARS	4 YEARS	5 YEARS	6 YEARS	7 YEARS
100	8.61	4.43	3.04	2.35	1.93	1.66	1.46
200	17.21	8.86	6.08	4.70	3.87	3.31	2.92
500	43.03	22.16	15.21	11.74	9.67	8.29	7.30
1000	86.07	44.32	30.42	23.49	19.33	16.57	14.61
2000	172.13	88.64	60.84	46.97	38.67	33.15	29.22
5000	430.33	221.60	152.11	117.43	96.66	82.86	73.04
6000	516.40	265.92	182.53	140.91	116.00	99.44	87.65
7000	602.47	310.24	212.95	164.40	135.33	116.01	102.26
8000	688.53	354.56	243.38	187.88	154.66	132.58	116.87
9000	774.60	398.89	273.80	211.37	174.00	149.16	131.48
10000	860.66	443.21	304.22	234.85	193.33	165.73	146.09
15000	1291.00	664.81	456.33	352.28	289.99	248.59	219.13
20000	1721.33	886.41	608.44	469.70	386.66	331.46	292.17
25000	2151.66	1108.02	760.55	587.13	483.32	414.32	365.21
30000	2581.99	1329.62	912.66	704.55	579.98	497.19	438.26
35000	3012.33	1551.22	1064.77	821.98	676.65	580.05	511.30
36000	3098.39	1595.54	1095.19	845.46	695.98	596.62	525.91
37000	3184.46	1639.86	1125.61	868.95	715.31	613.20	540.52
38000	3270.52	1684.18	1156.03	892.43	734.65	629.77	555.13
39000	3356.59	1728.50	1186.46	915.92	753.98	646.34	569.73
40000	3442.66	1772.82	1216.88	939.40	773.31	662.92	584.34
41000	3528.72	1817.15	1247.30	962.89	792.64	679.49	598.95
42000	3614.79	1861.47	1277.72	986.37	811.98	696.06	613.56
43000	3700.86	1905.79	1308.14	1009.86	831.31	712.63	628.17
44000	3786.92	1950.11	1338.57	1033.34	850.64	729.21	642.78
45000	3872.99	1994.43	1368.99	1056.83	869.98	745.78	657.38
46000	3959.06	2038.75	1399.41	1080.31	889.31	762.35	671.99
47000	4045.12	2083.07	1429.83	1103.80	908.64	778.93	686.60
48000	4131.19	2127.39	1460.25	1127.28	927.97	795.50	701.21
49000	4217.26	2171.71	1490.67	1150.77	947.31	812.07	715.82
50000	4303.32	2216.03	1521.10	1174.25	966.64	828.64	730.43
51000	4389.39	2260.35	1551.52	1197.74	985.97	845.22	745.04
52000	4475.45	2304.67	1581.94	1221.22	1005.31	861.79	759.64
53000	4561.52	2348.99	1612.36	1244.71	1024.64	878.36	774.25
54000	4647.59	2393.31	1642.78	1268.19	1043.97	894.94	788.86
55000	4733.65	2437.63	1673.21	1291.68	1063.30	911.51	803.47
56000	4819.72	2481.95	1703.63	1315.16	1082.64	928.08	818.08
57000	4905.79	2526.27	1734.05	1338.65	1101.97	944.65	832.69
58000	4991.85	2570.60	1764.47	1362.13	1121.30	961.23	847.30
59000	5077.92	2614.92	1794.89	1385.62	1140.64	977.80	861.90
60000	5163.99	2659.24	1825.32	1409.10	1159.97	994.37	876.51
65000	5594.32	2880.84	1977.43	1526.53	1256.63	1077.24	949.56
70000	6024.65	3102.44	2129.54	1643.95	1353.30	1160.10	1022.60
75000	6454.98	3324.05	2281.65	1761.38	1449.96	1242.97	1095.64
80000	6885.31	3545.65	2433.75	1878.80	1546.62	1325.83	1168.68
85000	7315.65	3767.25	2585.86	1996.23	1643.29	1408.70	1241.73
90000	7745.98	3988.85	2737.97	2113.65	1739.95	1491.56	1314.77
95000	8176.31	4210.46	2890.08	2231.08	1836.62	1574.42	1387.81
100000	8606.64	4432.06	3042.19	2348.50	1933.28	1657.29	1460.86
105000	9036.98	4653.66	3194.30	2465.93	2029.94	1740.15	1533.90
110000	9467.31	4875.27	3346.41	2583.35	2126.61	1823.02	1606.94
120000	10327.97	5318.47	3650.63	2818.20	2319.94	1988.75	1753.03
130000	11188.64	5761.68	3954.85	3053.05	2513.26	2154.48	1899.11
140000	12049.30	6204.89	4259.07	3287.90	2706.59	2320.20	2045.20
150000	12909.96	6648.09	4563.29	3522.75	2899.92	2485.93	2191.28
175000	15061.63	7756.11	5323.84	4109.88	3383.24	2900.26	2556.50
200000	17213.29	8864.12	6084.39	4697.01	3866.56	3314.58	2921.71
225000	19364.95	9972.14	6844.94	5284.13	4349.88	3728.90	3286.92
250000	21516.61	11080.15	7605.48	5871.26	4833.20	4143.22	3652.14

Monthly Payments 6%

necessary to amortize a loan

AMOUNT	8 YEARS	9 YEARS	10 YEARS	11 YEARS	12 YEARS	13 YEARS	14 YEARS
100	1.31	1.20	1.11	1.04	0.98	0.92	0.88
200	2.63	2.40	2.22	2.07	1.95	1.85	1.76
500	6.57	6.00	5.55	5.18	4.88	4.62	4.41
1000	13.14	12.01	11.10	10.37	9.76	9.25	8.81
2000	26.28	24.01	22.20	20.73	19.52	18.49	17.62
5000	65.71	60.03	55.51	51.84	48.79	46.24	44.06
6000	78.85	72.03	66.61	62.20	58.55	55.48	52.87
7000	91.99	84.04	77.71	72.57	68.31	64.73	61.69
8000	105.13	96.05	88.82	82.94	78.07	73.98	70.50
9000	118.27	108.05	99.92	93.30	87.83	83.23	79.31
10000	131.41	120.06	111.02	103.67	97.59	92.47	88.12
15000	197.12	180.09	166.53	155.51	146.38	138.71	132.19
20000	262.83	240.11	222.04	207.34	195.17	184.94	176.25
25000	328.54	300.14	277.55	259.18	243.96	231.18	220.31
30000	394.24	360.17	333.06	311.01	292.76	277.42	264.37
35000	459.95	420.20	388.57	362.85	341.55	323.65	308.43
36000	473.09	432.21	399.67	373.21	351.31	332.90	317.24
37000	486.23	444.21	410.78	383.58	361.06	342.15	326.06
38000	499.37	456.22	421.88	393.95	370.82	351.39	334.87
39000	512.52	468.22	432.98	404.31	380.58	360.64	343.68
40000	525.66	480.23	444.08	414.68	390.34	369.89	352.49
41000	538.80	492.24	455.18	425.05	400.10	379.14	361.31
42000	551.94	504.24	466.29	435.42	409.86	388.38	370.12
43000	565.08	516.25	477.39	445.78	419.62	397.63	378.93
44000	578.22	528.25	488.49	456.15	429.37	406.88	387.74
45000	591.36	540.26	499.59	466.52	439.13	416.13	396.56
46000	604.51	552.26	510.69	476.88	448.89	425.37	405.37
47000	617.65	564.27	521.80	487.25	458.65	434.62	414.18
48000	630.79	576.28	532.90	497.62	468.41	443.87	422.99
49000	643.93	588.28	544.00	507.98	478.17	453.11	431.81
50000	657.07	600.29	555.10	518.35	487.93	462.36	440.62
51000	670.21	612.29	566.20	528.72	497.68	471.61	449.43
52000	683.35	624.30	577.31	539.09	507.44	480.86	458.24
53000	696.50	636.30	588.41	549.45	517.20	490.10	467.06
54000	709.64	648.31	599.51	559.82	526.96	499.35	475.87
55000	722.78	660.32	610.61	570.19	536.72	508.60	484.68
56000	735.92	672.32	621.71	580.55	546.48	517.85	493.49
57000	749.06	684.33	632.82	590.92	556.23	527.09	502.30
58000	762.20	696.33	643.92	601.29	565.99	536.34	511.12
59000	775.34	708.34	655.02	611.66	575.75	545.59	519.93
60000	788.49	720.34	666.12	622.02	585.51	554.83	528.74
65000	854.19	780.37	721.63	673.86	634.30	601.07	572.80
70000	919.90	840.40	777.14	725.69	683.10	647.31	616.87
75000	985.61	900.43	832.65	777.53	731.89	693.54	660.93
80000	1051.31	960.46	888.16	829.36	780.68	739.78	704.99
85000	1117.02	1020.49	943.67	881.20	829.47	786.01	749.05
90000	1182.73	1080.52	999.18	933.03	878.27	832.25	793.11
95000	1248.44	1140.55	1054.69	984.87	927.06	878.49	837.17
100000	1314.14	1200.57	1110.21	1036.70	975.85	924.72	881.24
105000	1379.85	1260.60	1165.72	1088.54	1024.64	970.96	925.30
110000	1445.56	1320.63	1221.23	1140.37	1073.44	1017.20	969.36
120000	1576.97	1440.69	1332.25	1244.04	1171.02	1109.67	1057.48
130000	1708.39	1560.75	1443.27	1347.71	1268.61	1202.14	1145.61
140000	1839.80	1680.80	1554.29	1451.38	1366.19	1294.61	1233.73
150000	1971.21	1800.86	1665.31	1555.06	1463.78	1387.09	1321.85
175000	2299.75	2101.01	1942.86	1814.23	1707.74	1618.27	1542.16
200000	2628.29	2401.15	2220.41	2073.41	1951.70	1849.45	1762.47
225000	2956.82	2701.29	2497.96	2332.58	2195.66	2080.63	1982.78
250000	3285.36	3001.44	2775.51	2591.76	2439.63	2311.81	2203.09

6% Monthly Payments

necessary to amortize a loan

AMOUNT	15 YEARS	16 YEARS	17 YEARS	18 YEARS	19 YEARS	20 YEARS	21 YEARS
100	0.84	0.81	0.78	0.76	0.74	0.72	0.70
200	1.69	1.62	1.57	1.52	1.47	1.43	1.40
500	4.22	4.06	3.92	3.79	3.68	3.58	3.49
1000	8.44	8.11	7.83	7.58	7.36	7.16	6.99
2000	16.88	16.23	15.66	15.16	14.72	14.33	13.98
5000	42.19	40.57	39.16	37.91	36.80	35.82	34.94
6000	50.63	48.69	46.99	45.49	44.16	42.99	41.93
7000	59.07	56.80	54.82	53.07	51.53	50.15	48.92
8000	67.51	64.92	62.65	60.65	58.89	57.31	55.91
9000	75.95	73.03	70.48	68.23	66.25	64.48	62.90
10000	84.39	81.14	78.31	75.82	73.61	71.64	69.89
15000	126.58	121.72	117.47	113.72	110.41	107.46	104.83
20000	168.77	162.29	156.62	151.63	147.22	143.29	139.77
25000	210.96	202.86	195.78	189.54	184.02	179.11	174.71
30000	253.16	243.43	234.93	227.45	220.82	214.93	209.66
35000	295.35	284.00	274.09	265.36	257.63	250.75	244.60
36000	303.79	292.12	281.92	272.94	264.99	257.92	251.59
37000	312.23	300.23	289.75	280.52	272.35	265.08	258.58
38000	320.67	308.35	297.58	288.10	279.71	272.24	265.57
39000	329.10	316.46	305.41	295.68	287.07	279.41	272.55
40000	337.54	324.58	313.24	303.26	294.43	286.57	279.54
41000	345.98	332.69	321.07	310.85	301.79	293.74	286.53
42000	354.42	340.80	328.90	318.43	309.15	300.90	293.52
43000	362.86	348.92	336.73	326.01	316.52	308.07	300.51
44000	371.30	357.03	344.56	333.59	323.88	315.23	307.50
45000	379.74	365.15	352.40	341.17	331.24	322.39	314.49
46000	388.17	373.26	360.23	348.75	338.60	329.56	321.47
47000	396.61	381.38	368.06	356.34	345.96	336.72	328.46
48000	405.05	389.49	375.89	363.92	353.32	343.89	335.45
49000	413.49	397.60	383.72	371.50	360.68	351.05	342.44
50000	421.93	405.72	391.55	379.08	368.04	358.22	349.43
51000	430.37	413.83	399.38	386.66	375.40	365.38	356.42
52000	438.81	421.95	407.21	394.24	382.76	372.54	363.41
53000	447.24	430.06	415.04	401.83	390.12	379.71	370.39
54000	455.68	438.18	422.87	409.41	397.48	386.87	377.38
55000	464.12	446.29	430.71	416.99	404.85	394.04	384.37
56000	472.56	454.41	438.54	424.57	412.21	401.20	391.36
57000	481.00	462.52	446.37	432.15	419.57	408.37	398.35
58000	489.44	470.63	454.20	439.73	426.93	415.53	405.34
59000	497.88	478.75	462.03	447.32	434.29	422.69	412.33
60000	506.31	486.86	469.86	454.90	441.65	429.86	419.31
65000	548.51	527.43	509.02	492.81	478.45	465.68	454.26
70000	590.70	568.01	548.17	530.71	515.26	501.50	489.20
75000	632.89	608.58	587.33	568.62	552.06	537.32	524.14
80000	675.09	649.15	626.48	606.53	588.87	573.14	559.09
85000	717.28	689.72	665.64	644.44	625.67	608.97	594.03
90000	759.47	730.29	704.79	682.35	662.47	644.79	628.97
95000	801.66	770.87	743.95	720.25	699.28	680.61	663.91
100000	843.86	811.44	783.10	758.16	736.08	716.43	698.86
105000	886.05	852.01	822.26	796.07	772.89	752.25	733.80
110000	928.24	892.58	861.41	833.98	809.69	788.07	768.74
120000	1012.63	973.73	939.72	909.79	883.30	859.72	838.63
130000	1097.01	1054.87	1018.03	985.61	956.91	931.36	908.51
140000	1181.40	1136.01	1096.34	1061.43	1030.52	1003.00	978.40
150000	1265.79	1217.16	1174.65	1137.24	1104.12	1074.65	1048.29
175000	1476.75	1420.02	1370.43	1326.78	1288.15	1253.75	1223.00
200000	1687.71	1622.88	1566.20	1516.32	1472.17	1432.86	1397.71
225000	1898.68	1825.74	1761.98	1705.87	1656.19	1611.97	1572.43
250000	2109.64	2028.59	1957.75	1895.41	1840.21	1791.08	1747.14

Monthly Payments 6%

necessary to amortize a loan

AMOUNT	22 YEARS	23 YEARS	24 YEARS	25 YEARS	30 YEARS	35 YEARS	40 YEARS
100	0.68	0.67	0.66	0.64	0.60	0.57	0.55
200	1.37	1.34	1.31	1.29	1.20	1.14	1.10
500	3.42	3.34	3.28	3.22	3.00	2.85	2.75
1000	6.83	6.69	6.56	6.44	6.00	5.70	5.50
2000	13.66	13.38	13.12	12.89	11.99	11.40	11.00
5000	34.15	33.44	32.80	32.22	29.98	28.51	27.51
6000	40.98	40.13	39.36	38.66	35.97	34.21	33.01
7000	47.82	46.82	45.92	45.10	41.97	39.91	38.51
8000	54.65	53.51	52.48	51.54	47.96	45.62	44.02
9000	61.48	60.20	59.04	57.99	53.96	51.32	49.52
10000	68.31	66.88	65.60	64.43	59.96	57.02	55.02
15000	102.46	100.33	98.40	96.65	89.93	85.53	82.53
20000	136.61	133.77	131.20	128.86	119.91	114.04	110.04
25000	170.77	167.21	163.99	161.08	149.89	142.55	137.55
30000	204.92	200.65	196.79	193.29	179.87	171.06	165.06
35000	239.08	234.10	229.59	225.51	209.84	199.57	192.57
36000	245.91	240.78	236.15	231.95	215.84	205.27	198.08
37000	252.74	247.47	242.71	238.39	221.83	210.97	203.58
38000	259.57	254.16	249.27	244.83	227.83	216.67	209.08
39000	266.40	260.85	255.83	251.28	233.82	222.37	214.58
40000	273.23	267.54	262.39	257.72	239.82	228.08	220.09
41000	280.06	274.23	268.95	264.16	245.82	233.78	225.59
42000	286.89	280.92	275.51	270.61	251.81	239.48	231.09
43000	293.72	287.60	282.07	277.05	257.81	245.18	236.59
44000	300.55	294.29	288.63	283.49	263.80	250.88	242.09
45000	307.38	300.98	295.19	289.94	269.80	256.59	247.60
46000	314.21	307.67	301.75	296.38	275.79	262.29	253.10
47000	321.04	314.36	308.31	302.82	281.79	267.99	258.60
48000	327.88	321.05	314.87	309.26	287.78	273.69	264.10
49000	334.71	327.74	321.43	315.71	293.78	279.39	269.60
50000	341.54	334.42	327.99	322.15	299.78	285.09	275.11
51000	348.37	341.11	334.55	328.59	305.77	290.80	280.61
52000	355.20	347.80	341.11	335.04	311.77	296.50	286.11
53000	362.03	354.49	347.67	341.48	317.76	302.20	291.61
54000	368.86	361.18	354.23	347.92	323.76	307.90	297.12
55000	375.69	367.87	360.79	354.37	329.75	313.60	302.62
56000	382.52	374.55	367.35	360.81	335.75	319.31	308.12
57000	389.35	381.24	373.01	367.25	341.74	325.01	313.62
58000	396.18	387.93	380.47	373.69	347.74	330.71	319.12
59000	403.01	394.62	387.03	380.14	353.73	336.41	324.63
60000	409.84	401.31	393.59	386.58	359.73	342.11	330.13
65000	444.00	434.75	426.39	418.80	389.71	370.62	357.64
70000	478.15	468.19	459.18	451.01	419.69	399.13	385.15
75000	512.31	501.64	491.98	483.23	449.66	427.64	412.66
80000	546.46	535.08	524.78	515.44	479.64	456.15	440.17
85000	580.61	568.52	557.58	547.66	509.62	484.66	467.68
90000	614.77	601.96	590.38	579.87	539.60	513.17	495.19
95000	648.92	635.40	623.18	612.09	569.57	541.68	522.70
100000	683.07	668.85	655.98	644.30	599.55	570.19	550.21
105000	717.23	702.29	688.78	676.52	629.53	598.70	577.72
110000	751.38	735.73	721.58	708.73	659.51	627.21	605.24
120000	819.69	802.62	787.17	773.16	719.46	684.23	660.26
130000	888.00	869.50	852.77	837.59	779.42	741.25	715.28
140000	956.30	936.39	918.37	902.02	839.37	798.27	770.30
150000	1024.61	1003.27	983.97	966.45	899.33	855.28	825.32
175000	1195.38	1170.48	1147.96	1127.53	1049.21	997.83	962.87
200000	1366.15	1337.69	1311.96	1288.60	1199.10	1140.38	1100.43
225000	1536.92	1504.91	1475.95	1449.68	1348.99	1282.93	1237.98
250000	1707.69	1672.12	1639.95	1610.75	1498.88	1425.47	1375.53

6¼%

Monthly Payments

necessary to amortize a loan

AMOUNT	1 YEAR	2 YEARS	3 YEARS	4 YEARS	5 YEARS	6 YEARS	7 YEARS
100	8.62	4.44	3.05	2.36	1.94	1.67	1.47
200	17.24	8.89	6.11	4.72	3.89	3.34	2.95
500	43.09	22.22	15.27	11.80	9.72	8.35	7.36
1000	86.18	44.43	30.54	23.60	19.45	16.69	14.73
2000	172.36	88.87	61.07	47.20	38.90	33.38	29.46
5000	430.91	222.17	152.68	118.00	97.25	83.46	73.64
6000	517.09	266.60	183.21	141.60	116.70	100.15	88.37
7000	603.27	311.03	213.75	165.20	136.14	116.84	103.10
8000	689.45	355.47	244.28	188.80	155.59	133.53	117.83
9000	775.63	399.90	274.82	212.40	175.04	150.22	132.56
10000	861.81	444.33	305.35	236.00	194.49	166.91	147.29
15000	1292.72	666.50	458.03	354.00	291.74	250.37	220.93
20000	1723.63	888.67	610.71	472.00	388.99	333.82	294.57
25000	2154.53	1110.83	763.38	590.00	486.23	417.28	368.22
30000	2585.44	1333.00	916.06	707.99	583.48	500.73	441.86
35000	3016.35	1555.17	1068.74	825.99	680.72	584.19	515.50
36000	3102.53	1599.60	1099.27	849.59	700.17	600.88	530.23
37000	3188.71	1644.03	1129.81	873.19	719.62	617.57	544.96
38000	3274.89	1688.47	1160.34	896.79	739.07	634.26	559.69
39000	3361.07	1732.90	1190.88	920.39	758.52	650.96	574.42
40000	3447.26	1777.33	1221.41	943.99	777.97	667.65	589.15
41000	3533.44	1821.77	1251.95	967.59	797.42	684.34	603.88
42000	3619.62	1866.20	1282.48	991.19	816.87	701.03	618.61
43000	3705.80	1910.63	1313.02	1014.79	836.32	717.72	633.33
44000	3791.98	1955.07	1343.56	1038.39	855.77	734.41	648.06
45000	3878.16	1999.50	1374.09	1061.99	875.22	751.10	662.79
46000	3964.34	2043.93	1404.63	1085.59	894.67	767.79	677.52
47000	4050.52	2088.37	1435.16	1109.19	914.12	784.48	692.25
48000	4136.71	2132.80	1465.70	1132.79	933.56	801.18	706.98
49000	4222.89	2177.23	1496.23	1156.39	953.01	817.87	721.71
50000	4309.07	2221.67	1526.77	1179.99	972.46	834.56	736.43
51000	4395.25	2266.10	1557.30	1203.59	991.91	851.25	751.16
52000	4481.43	2310.53	1587.84	1227.19	1011.36	867.94	765.89
53000	4567.61	2354.97	1618.37	1250.79	1030.81	884.63	780.62
54000	4653.79	2399.40	1648.91	1274.39	1050.26	901.32	795.35
55000	4739.98	2443.83	1679.44	1297.99	1069.71	918.01	810.08
56000	4826.16	2488.27	1709.98	1321.59	1089.16	934.70	824.81
57000	4912.34	2532.70	1740.51	1345.19	1108.61	951.40	839.54
58000	4998.52	2577.13	1771.05	1368.79	1128.06	968.09	854.26
59000	5084.70	2621.57	1801.59	1392.39	1147.51	984.78	868.99
60000	5170.88	2666.00	1832.12	1415.99	1166.96	1001.47	883.72
65000	5601.79	2888.17	1984.80	1533.99	1264.20	1084.93	957.37
70000	6032.70	3110.33	2137.47	1651.99	1361.45	1168.38	1031.01
75000	6463.60	3332.50	2290.15	1769.99	1458.69	1251.84	1104.65
80000	6894.51	3554.67	2442.83	1887.99	1555.94	1335.29	1178.30
85000	7325.42	3776.83	2595.50	2005.98	1653.19	1418.75	1251.94
90000	7756.32	3999.00	2748.18	2123.98	1750.43	1502.20	1325.58
95000	8187.23	4221.17	2900.86	2241.98	1847.68	1585.66	1399.23
100000	8618.14	4443.33	3053.53	2359.98	1944.93	1669.12	1472.87
105000	9049.04	4665.50	3206.21	2477.98	2042.17	1752.57	1546.51
110000	9479.95	4887.67	3358.89	2595.98	2139.42	1836.03	1620.16
120000	10341.77	5332.00	3664.24	2831.98	2333.91	2002.94	1767.44
130000	11203.58	5776.33	3969.59	3067.98	2528.40	2169.85	1914.73
140000	12065.39	6220.67	4274.95	3303.97	2722.90	2336.76	2062.02
150000	12927.21	6665.00	4580.30	3539.97	2917.39	2503.67	2209.30
175000	15081.74	7775.84	5343.68	4129.97	3403.62	2920.95	2577.52
200000	17236.28	8886.67	6107.07	4719.96	3889.85	3338.23	2945.74
225000	19390.81	9997.50	6870.45	5309.96	4376.08	3755.51	3313.96
250000	21545.35	11108.34	7633.84	5899.95	4862.32	4172.79	3682.17

Monthly Payments 6¼%

necessary to amortize a loan

AMOUNT	8 YEARS	9 YEARS	10 YEARS	11 YEARS	12 YEARS	13 YEARS	14 YEARS
100	1.33	1.21	1.12	1.05	0.99	0.94	0.89
200	2.65	2.43	2.25	2.10	1.98	1.88	1.79
500	6.63	6.06	5.61	5.25	4.94	4.69	4.47
1000	13.26	12.13	11.23	10.49	9.89	9.38	8.95
2000	26.53	24.26	22.46	20.99	19.78	18.76	17.89
5000	66.32	60.65	56.14	52.47	49.44	46.90	44.73
6000	79.58	72.78	67.37	62.97	59.33	56.27	53.68
7000	92.84	84.91	78.60	73.46	69.22	65.65	62.62
8000	106.11	97.04	89.82	83.96	79.11	75.03	71.57
9000	119.37	109.17	101.05	94.45	89.00	84.41	80.51
10000	132.63	121.30	112.28	104.95	98.88	93.79	89.46
15000	198.95	181.95	168.42	157.42	148.33	140.69	134.19
20000	265.27	242.60	224.56	209.90	197.77	187.58	178.92
25000	331.59	303.24	280.70	262.37	247.21	234.48	223.65
30000	397.90	363.89	336.84	314.85	296.65	281.37	268.38
35000	464.22	424.54	392.98	367.32	346.09	328.27	313.11
36000	477.49	436.67	404.21	377.82	355.98	337.65	322.06
37000	490.75	448.80	415.44	388.31	365.87	347.02	331.01
38000	504.01	460.93	426.66	398.81	375.76	356.40	339.95
39000	517.28	473.06	437.89	409.30	385.65	365.78	348.90
40000	530.54	485.19	449.12	419.80	395.53	375.16	357.84
41000	543.80	497.32	460.35	430.29	405.42	384.54	366.79
42000	557.07	509.45	471.58	440.79	415.31	393.92	375.74
43000	570.33	521.58	482.80	451.28	425.20	403.30	384.68
44000	583.59	533.71	494.03	461.78	435.09	412.68	393.63
45000	596.86	545.84	505.26	472.27	444.98	422.06	402.57
46000	610.12	557.97	516.49	482.77	454.86	431.44	411.52
47000	623.38	570.10	527.72	493.26	464.75	440.82	420.47
48000	636.65	582.23	538.94	503.76	474.64	450.19	429.41
49000	649.91	594.36	550.17	514.25	484.53	459.57	438.36
50000	663.17	606.49	561.40	524.75	494.42	468.95	447.31
51000	676.44	618.62	572.63	535.24	504.31	478.33	456.25
52000	689.70	630.75	583.86	545.74	514.20	487.71	465.20
53000	702.97	642.88	595.08	556.23	524.08	497.09	474.14
54000	716.23	655.01	606.31	566.73	533.97	506.47	483.09
55000	729.49	667.14	617.54	577.22	543.86	515.85	492.04
56000	742.76	679.27	628.77	587.72	553.75	525.23	500.98
57000	756.02	691.40	640.00	598.21	563.64	534.61	509.93
58000	769.28	703.53	651.22	608.71	573.53	543.98	518.87
59000	782.55	715.66	662.45	619.20	583.41	553.36	527.82
60000	795.81	727.79	673.68	629.70	593.30	562.74	536.77
65000	862.13	788.43	729.82	682.17	642.74	609.64	581.50
70000	928.44	849.08	785.96	734.65	692.19	656.53	626.23
75000	994.76	909.73	842.10	787.12	741.63	703.43	670.96
80000	1061.08	970.38	898.24	839.60	791.07	750.32	715.69
85000	1127.40	1031.03	954.38	892.07	840.51	797.22	760.42
90000	1193.71	1091.68	1010.52	944.55	889.95	844.11	805.15
95000	1260.03	1152.33	1066.66	997.02	939.39	891.01	849.88
100000	1326.35	1212.98	1122.80	1049.49	988.84	937.90	894.61
105000	1392.67	1273.62	1178.94	1101.97	1038.28	984.80	939.34
110000	1458.98	1334.27	1235.08	1154.44	1087.72	1031.69	984.07
120000	1591.62	1455.57	1347.36	1259.39	1186.60	1125.49	1073.53
130000	1724.25	1576.87	1459.64	1364.34	1285.49	1219.28	1162.99
140000	1856.89	1698.17	1571.92	1469.29	1384.37	1313.07	1252.45
150000	1989.52	1819.46	1684.20	1574.24	1483.26	1406.86	1341.92
175000	2321.11	2122.71	1964.90	1836.62	1730.46	1641.33	1565.57
200000	2652.70	2425.95	2245.60	2098.99	1977.67	1875.81	1789.22
225000	2984.29	2729.20	2526.30	2361.36	2224.88	2110.28	2012.87
250000	3315.87	3032.44	2807.00	2623.74	2472.09	2344.76	2236.53

6¼%

Monthly Payments

necessary to amortize a loan

AMOUNT	15 YEARS	16 YEARS	17 YEARS	18 YEARS	19 YEARS	20 YEARS	21 YEARS
100	0.86	0.83	0.80	0.77	0.75	0.73	0.71
200	1.71	1.65	1.59	1.54	1.50	1.46	1.43
500	4.29	4.13	3.99	3.86	3.75	3.65	3.57
1000	8.57	8.25	7.97	7.72	7.50	7.31	7.14
2000	17.15	16.50	15.94	15.45	15.01	14.62	14.27
5000	42.87	41.26	39.85	38.61	37.52	36.55	35.68
6000	51.45	49.51	47.82	46.34	45.02	43.86	42.81
7000	60.02	57.76	55.79	54.06	52.53	51.16	49.95
8000	68.59	66.02	63.76	61.78	60.03	58.47	57.08
9000	77.17	74.27	71.73	69.51	67.54	65.78	64.22
10000	85.74	82.52	79.70	77.23	75.04	73.09	71.35
15000	128.61	123.78	119.56	115.84	112.56	109.64	107.03
20000	171.48	165.04	159.41	154.46	150.08	146.19	142.71
25000	214.36	206.30	199.26	193.07	187.60	182.73	178.38
30000	257.23	247.56	239.11	231.69	225.12	219.28	214.06
35000	300.10	288.82	278.97	270.30	262.64	255.82	249.74
36000	308.67	297.07	286.94	278.03	270.14	263.13	256.87
37000	317.25	305.32	294.91	285.75	277.65	270.44	264.01
38000	325.82	313.57	302.88	293.47	285.15	277.75	271.14
39000	334.39	321.83	310.85	301.19	292.66	285.06	278.28
40000	342.97	330.08	318.82	308.92	300.16	292.37	285.41
41000	351.54	338.33	326.79	316.64	307.66	299.68	292.55
42000	360.12	346.58	334.76	324.36	315.17	306.99	299.68
43000	368.69	354.83	342.73	332.09	322.67	314.30	306.82
44000	377.27	363.09	350.70	339.81	330.18	321.61	313.95
45000	385.84	371.34	358.67	347.53	337.68	328.92	321.09
46000	394.41	379.59	366.64	355.25	345.18	336.23	328.23
47000	402.99	387.84	374.61	362.98	352.69	343.54	335.36
48000	411.56	396.09	382.58	370.70	360.19	350.85	342.50
49000	420.14	404.35	390.55	378.42	367.70	358.15	349.63
50000	428.71	412.60	398.52	386.15	375.20	365.46	356.77
51000	437.29	420.85	406.49	393.87	382.70	372.77	363.90
52000	445.86	429.10	414.46	401.59	390.21	380.08	371.04
53000	454.43	437.35	422.43	409.32	397.71	387.39	378.17
54000	463.01	445.60	430.40	417.04	405.22	394.70	385.31
55000	471.58	453.86	438.37	424.76	412.72	402.01	392.44
56000	480.16	462.11	446.35	432.48	420.22	409.32	399.58
57000	488.73	470.36	454.32	440.21	427.73	416.63	406.71
58000	497.31	478.61	462.29	447.93	435.23	423.94	413.85
59000	505.88	486.86	470.26	455.65	442.73	431.25	420.98
60000	514.45	495.12	478.23	463.38	450.24	438.56	428.12
65000	557.32	536.38	518.08	501.99	487.76	475.10	463.80
70000	600.20	577.64	557.93	540.61	525.28	511.65	499.47
75000	643.07	618.90	597.78	579.22	562.80	548.20	535.15
80000	685.94	660.16	637.64	617.83	600.32	584.74	570.83
85000	728.81	701.42	677.49	656.45	637.84	621.29	606.50
90000	771.68	742.67	717.34	695.06	675.36	657.84	642.18
95000	814.55	783.93	757.19	733.68	712.88	694.38	677.86
100000	857.42	825.19	797.05	772.29	750.40	730.93	713.53
105000	900.29	866.45	836.90	810.91	787.92	767.47	749.21
110000	943.17	907.71	876.75	849.52	825.44	804.02	784.89
120000	1028.91	990.23	956.45	926.75	900.48	877.11	856.24
130000	1114.65	1072.75	1036.16	1003.98	975.52	950.21	927.59
140000	1200.39	1155.27	1115.86	1081.21	1050.56	1023.30	998.95
150000	1286.13	1237.79	1195.57	1158.44	1125.60	1096.39	1070.30
175000	1500.49	1444.09	1394.83	1351.51	1313.20	1279.12	1248.68
200000	1714.85	1650.39	1594.09	1544.59	1500.80	1461.86	1427.07
225000	1929.20	1856.69	1793.35	1737.66	1688.40	1644.59	1605.45
250000	2143.56	2062.99	1992.61	1930.73	1876.00	1827.32	1783.83

Monthly Payments 6¼%

necessary to amortize a loan

AMOUNT	22 YEARS	23 YEARS	24 YEARS	25 YEARS	30 YEARS	35 YEARS	40 YEARS
100	0.70	0.68	0.67	0.66	0.62	0.59	0.57
200	1.40	1.37	1.34	1.32	1.23	1.17	1.14
500	3.49	3.42	3.36	3.30	3.08	2.94	2.84
1000	6.98	6.84	6.71	6.60	6.16	5.87	5.68
2000	13.96	13.68	13.42	13.19	12.31	11.74	11.35
5000	34.90	34.19	33.56	32.98	30.79	29.35	28.39
6000	41.88	41.03	40.27	39.58	36.94	35.22	34.06
7000	48.85	47.87	46.98	46.18	43.10	41.10	39.74
8000	55.83	54.71	53.69	52.77	49.26	46.97	45.42
9000	62.81	61.55	60.41	59.37	55.41	52.84	51.10
10000	69.79	68.39	67.12	65.97	61.57	58.71	56.77
15000	104.69	102.58	100.68	98.95	92.36	88.06	85.16
20000	139.59	136.77	134.24	131.93	123.14	117.42	113.55
25000	174.48	170.97	167.79	164.92	153.93	146.77	141.93
30000	209.38	205.16	201.35	197.90	184.72	176.12	170.32
35000	244.27	239.36	234.91	230.88	215.50	205.48	198.71
36000	251.25	246.19	241.62	237.48	221.66	211.35	204.39
37000	258.23	253.03	248.34	244.08	227.82	217.22	210.06
38000	265.21	259.87	255.05	250.67	233.97	223.09	215.74
39000	272.19	266.71	261.76	257.27	240.13	228.96	221.42
40000	279.17	273.55	268.47	263.87	246.29	234.83	227.10
41000	286.15	280.39	275.18	270.46	252.44	240.70	232.77
42000	293.13	287.23	281.89	277.06	258.60	246.57	238.45
43000	300.11	294.07	288.61	283.66	264.76	252.44	244.13
44000	307.09	300.90	295.32	290.25	270.92	258.31	249.81
45000	314.07	307.74	302.03	296.85	277.07	264.18	255.48
46000	321.05	314.58	308.74	303.45	283.23	270.06	261.16
47000	328.03	321.42	315.45	310.04	289.39	275.93	266.84
48000	335.01	328.26	322.17	316.64	295.54	281.80	272.51
49000	341.98	335.10	328.88	323.24	301.70	287.67	278.19
50000	348.96	341.94	335.59	329.83	307.86	293.54	283.87
51000	355.94	348.78	342.30	336.43	314.02	299.41	289.55
52000	362.92	355.61	349.01	343.03	320.17	305.28	295.22
53000	369.90	362.45	355.72	349.62	326.33	311.15	300.90
54000	376.88	369.29	362.44	356.22	332.49	317.02	306.58
55000	383.86	376.13	369.15	362.82	338.64	322.89	312.26
56000	390.84	382.97	375.86	369.41	344.80	328.76	317.93
57000	397.82	389.81	382.57	376.01	350.96	334.63	323.61
58000	404.80	396.65	389.28	382.61	357.12	340.50	329.29
59000	411.78	403.49	395.99	389.20	363.27	346.38	334.97
60000	418.76	410.32	402.71	395.80	369.43	352.25	340.64
65000	453.65	444.52	436.27	428.79	400.22	381.60	369.03
70000	488.55	478.71	469.82	461.77	431.00	410.95	397.42
75000	523.45	512.91	503.38	494.75	461.79	440.31	425.80
80000	558.34	547.10	536.94	527.74	492.57	469.66	454.19
85000	593.24	581.29	570.50	560.72	523.36	499.02	482.58
90000	628.14	615.49	604.06	593.70	554.15	528.37	510.97
95000	663.03	649.68	637.62	626.69	584.93	557.72	539.35
100000	697.93	683.87	671.18	659.67	615.72	587.08	567.74
105000	732.82	718.07	704.74	692.65	646.50	616.43	596.13
110000	767.72	752.26	738.30	725.64	677.29	645.78	624.51
120000	837.51	820.65	805.41	791.60	738.86	704.49	681.29
130000	907.31	889.04	872.53	857.57	800.43	763.20	738.06
140000	977.10	957.42	939.65	923.54	862.00	821.91	794.84
150000	1046.89	1025.81	1006.77	989.50	923.58	880.61	851.61
175000	1221.37	1196.78	1174.56	1154.42	1077.51	1027.38	993.54
200000	1395.86	1367.75	1342.35	1319.34	1231.43	1174.15	1135.48
225000	1570.34	1538.72	1510.15	1484.26	1385.36	1320.92	1277.41
250000	1744.82	1709.69	1677.94	1649.17	1539.29	1467.69	1419.35

6½% Monthly Payments

necessary to amortize a loan

AMOUNT	1 YEAR	2 YEARS	3 YEARS	4 YEARS	5 YEARS	6 YEARS	7 YEARS
100	8.63	4.45	3.06	2.37	1.96	1.68	1.48
200	17.26	8.91	6.13	4.74	3.91	3.36	2.97
500	43.15	22.27	15.32	11.86	9.78	8.40	7.42
1000	86.30	44.55	30.65	23.71	19.57	16.81	14.85
2000	172.59	89.09	61.30	47.43	39.13	33.62	29.70
5000	431.48	222.73	153.25	118.57	97.83	84.05	74.25
6000	517.78	267.28	183.89	142.29	117.40	100.86	89.10
7000	604.07	311.82	214.54	166.00	136.96	117.67	103.95
8000	690.37	356.37	245.19	189.72	156.53	134.48	118.80
9000	776.67	400.92	275.84	213.43	176.10	151.29	133.64
10000	862.96	445.46	306.49	237.15	195.66	168.10	148.49
15000	1294.45	668.19	459.74	355.72	293.49	252.15	222.74
20000	1725.93	890.93	612.98	474.30	391.32	336.20	296.99
25000	2157.41	1113.66	766.23	592.87	489.15	420.25	371.24
30000	2588.89	1336.39	919.47	711.45	586.98	504.30	445.48
35000	3020.37	1559.12	1072.72	830.02	684.82	588.35	519.73
36000	3106.67	1603.67	1103.36	853.74	704.38	605.16	534.58
37000	3192.97	1648.21	1134.01	877.45	723.95	621.97	549.43
38000	3279.26	1692.76	1164.66	901.17	743.51	638.78	564.28
39000	3365.56	1737.30	1195.31	924.88	763.08	655.59	579.13
40000	3451.86	1781.85	1225.96	948.60	782.65	672.40	593.98
41000	3538.15	1826.40	1256.61	972.31	802.21	689.21	608.83
42000	3624.45	1870.94	1287.26	996.03	821.78	706.02	623.68
43000	3710.75	1915.49	1317.91	1019.74	841.34	722.83	638.53
44000	3797.04	1960.04	1348.56	1043.46	860.91	739.64	653.38
45000	3883.34	2004.58	1379.21	1067.17	880.48	756.45	668.22
46000	3969.64	2049.13	1409.85	1090.89	900.04	773.26	683.07
47000	4055.93	2093.67	1440.50	1114.60	919.61	790.07	697.92
48000	4142.23	2138.22	1471.15	1138.32	939.18	806.88	712.77
49000	4228.52	2182.77	1501.80	1162.03	958.74	823.69	727.62
50000	4314.82	2227.31	1532.45	1185.75	978.31	840.50	742.47
51000	4401.12	2271.86	1563.10	1209.46	997.87	857.31	757.32
52000	4487.41	2316.41	1593.75	1233.18	1017.44	874.12	772.17
53000	4573.71	2360.95	1624.40	1256.89	1037.01	890.93	787.02
54000	4660.01	2405.50	1655.05	1280.61	1056.57	907.74	801.87
55000	4746.30	2450.04	1685.70	1304.32	1076.14	924.55	816.72
56000	4832.60	2494.59	1716.34	1328.04	1095.70	941.36	831.57
57000	4918.90	2539.14	1746.99	1351.75	1115.27	958.17	846.42
58000	5005.19	2583.68	1777.64	1375.47	1134.84	974.98	861.27
59000	5091.49	2628.23	1808.29	1399.18	1154.40	991.79	876.12
60000	5177.79	2672.78	1838.94	1422.90	1173.97	1008.60	890.97
65000	5609.27	2895.51	1992.19	1541.47	1271.80	1092.65	965.21
70000	6040.75	3118.24	2145.43	1660.05	1369.63	1176.70	1039.46
75000	6472.23	3340.97	2298.68	1778.62	1467.46	1260.74	1113.71
80000	6903.71	3563.70	2451.92	1897.20	1565.29	1344.79	1187.95
85000	7335.20	3786.43	2605.17	2015.77	1663.12	1428.84	1262.20
90000	7766.68	4009.16	2758.41	2134.35	1760.95	1512.89	1336.45
95000	8198.16	4231.89	2911.66	2252.92	1858.78	1596.94	1410.70
100000	8629.64	4454.63	3064.90	2371.50	1956.61	1680.99	1484.94
105000	9061.12	4677.36	3218.15	2490.07	2054.45	1765.04	1559.19
110000	9492.61	4900.09	3371.39	2608.64	2152.28	1849.09	1633.44
120000	10355.57	5345.55	3677.88	2845.79	2347.94	2017.19	1781.93
130000	11218.53	5791.01	3984.37	3082.94	2543.60	2185.29	1930.43
140000	12081.50	6236.48	4290.86	3320.09	2739.26	2353.39	2078.92
150000	12944.46	6681.94	4597.35	3557.24	2934.92	2521.49	2227.42
175000	15101.87	7795.59	5363.58	4150.12	3424.08	2941.74	2598.65
200000	17259.28	8909.25	6129.80	4742.99	3913.23	3361.99	2969.89
225000	19416.69	10022.91	6896.03	5335.86	4402.38	3782.23	3341.12
250000	21574.10	11136.56	7662.25	5928.74	4891.54	4202.48	3712.36

Monthly Payments 6½%

necessary to amortize a loan

AMOUNT	8 YEARS	9 YEARS	10 YEARS	11 YEARS	12 YEARS	13 YEARS	14 YEARS
100	1.34	1.23	1.14	1.06	1.00	0.95	0.91
200	2.68	2.45	2.27	2.12	2.00	1.90	1.82
500	6.69	6.13	5.68	5.31	5.01	4.76	4.54
1000	13.39	12.25	11.35	10.62	10.02	9.51	9.08
2000	26.77	24.51	22.71	21.25	20.04	19.02	18.16
5000	66.93	61.27	56.77	53.12	50.10	47.56	45.40
6000	80.32	73.53	68.13	63.74	60.12	57.07	54.49
7000	93.70	85.78	79.48	74.37	70.13	66.58	63.57
8000	107.09	98.04	90.84	84.99	80.15	76.10	72.65
9000	120.48	110.29	102.19	95.61	90.17	85.61	81.73
10000	133.86	122.55	113.55	106.24	100.19	95.12	90.81
15000	200.79	183.82	170.32	159.36	150.29	142.68	136.21
20000	267.72	245.09	227.10	212.48	200.38	190.24	181.62
25000	334.66	306.36	283.87	265.59	250.48	237.80	227.02
30000	401.59	367.64	340.64	318.71	300.58	285.36	272.43
35000	468.52	428.91	397.42	371.83	350.67	332.92	317.83
36000	481.90	441.16	408.77	382.46	360.69	342.43	326.91
37000	495.29	453.42	420.13	393.08	370.71	351.94	336.00
38000	508.68	465.67	431.48	403.70	380.73	361.45	345.08
39000	522.06	477.93	442.84	414.33	390.75	370.96	354.16
40000	535.45	490.18	454.19	424.95	400.77	380.48	363.24
41000	548.84	502.44	465.55	435.57	410.79	389.99	372.32
42000	562.22	514.69	476.90	446.20	420.81	399.50	381.40
43000	575.61	526.94	488.26	456.82	430.83	409.01	390.48
44000	588.99	539.20	499.61	467.45	440.85	418.52	399.56
45000	602.38	551.45	510.97	478.07	450.86	428.04	408.64
46000	615.77	563.71	522.32	488.69	460.88	437.55	417.72
47000	629.15	575.96	533.68	499.32	470.90	447.06	426.81
48000	642.54	588.22	545.03	509.94	480.92	456.57	435.89
49000	655.93	600.47	556.39	520.56	490.94	466.08	444.97
50000	669.31	612.73	567.74	531.19	500.96	475.60	454.05
51000	682.70	624.98	579.09	541.81	510.98	485.11	463.13
52000	696.08	637.23	590.45	552.44	521.00	494.62	472.21
53000	709.47	649.49	601.80	563.06	531.02	504.13	481.29
54000	722.86	661.74	613.16	573.68	541.04	513.64	490.37
55000	736.24	674.00	624.51	584.31	551.06	523.15	499.45
56000	749.63	686.25	635.87	594.93	561.08	532.67	508.53
57000	763.02	698.51	647.22	605.55	571.10	542.18	517.61
58000	776.40	710.76	658.58	616.18	581.11	551.69	526.70
59000	789.79	723.02	669.93	626.80	591.13	561.20	535.78
60000	803.17	735.27	681.29	637.43	601.15	570.71	544.86
65000	870.11	796.54	738.06	690.54	651.25	618.27	590.26
70000	937.04	857.82	794.84	743.66	701.34	665.83	635.67
75000	1003.97	919.09	851.61	796.78	751.44	713.39	681.07
80000	1070.90	980.36	908.38	849.90	801.54	760.95	726.48
85000	1137.83	1041.63	965.16	903.02	851.63	808.51	771.88
90000	1204.76	1102.91	1021.93	956.14	901.73	856.07	817.29
95000	1271.69	1164.18	1078.71	1009.26	951.83	903.63	862.69
100000	1338.62	1225.45	1135.48	1062.38	1001.92	951.19	908.10
105000	1405.55	1286.72	1192.25	1115.50	1052.02	998.75	953.50
110000	1472.49	1348.00	1249.03	1168.61	1102.11	1046.31	998.91
120000	1606.35	1470.54	1362.58	1274.85	1202.31	1141.43	1089.72
130000	1740.21	1593.09	1476.12	1381.09	1302.50	1236.55	1180.52
140000	1874.07	1715.63	1589.67	1487.33	1402.69	1331.67	1271.33
150000	2007.93	1838.18	1703.22	1593.57	1502.88	1426.79	1362.14
175000	2342.59	2144.54	1987.09	1859.16	1753.36	1664.58	1589.17
200000	2677.25	2450.90	2270.96	2124.75	2003.84	1902.38	1816.19
225000	3011.90	2757.27	2554.83	2390.35	2254.32	2140.18	2043.22
250000	3346.56	3063.63	2838.70	2655.94	2504.80	2377.98	2270.24

6½% Monthly Payments

necessary to amortize a loan

AMOUNT	15 YEARS	16 YEARS	17 YEARS	18 YEARS	19 YEARS	20 YEARS	21 YEARS
100	0.87	0.84	0.81	0.79	0.76	0.75	0.73
200	1.74	1.68	1.62	1.57	1.53	1.49	1.46
500	4.36	4.20	4.06	3.93	3.82	3.73	3.64
1000	8.71	8.39	8.11	7.87	7.65	7.46	7.28
2000	17.42	16.78	16.22	15.73	15.30	14.91	14.57
5000	43.56	41.95	40.56	39.33	38.24	37.28	36.42
6000	52.27	50.34	48.67	47.19	45.89	44.73	43.70
7000	60.98	58.74	56.78	55.06	53.54	52.19	50.99
8000	69.69	67.13	64.89	62.92	61.19	59.65	58.27
9000	78.40	75.52	73.00	70.79	68.84	67.10	65.55
10000	87.11	83.91	81.11	78.66	76.49	74.56	72.84
15000	130.67	125.86	121.67	117.98	114.73	111.84	109.25
20000	174.22	167.82	162.22	157.31	152.97	149.11	145.67
25000	217.78	209.77	202.78	196.64	191.21	186.39	182.09
30000	261.33	251.72	243.34	235.97	229.46	223.67	218.51
35000	304.89	293.68	283.89	275.30	267.70	260.95	254.93
36000	313.60	302.07	292.00	283.16	275.35	268.41	262.21
37000	322.31	310.46	300.11	291.03	283.00	275.86	269.49
38000	331.02	318.85	308.23	298.89	290.65	283.32	276.78
39000	339.73	327.24	316.34	306.76	298.29	290.77	284.06
40000	348.44	335.63	324.45	314.62	305.94	298.23	291.35
41000	357.15	344.02	332.56	322.49	313.59	305.68	298.63
42000	365.87	352.41	340.67	330.36	321.24	313.14	305.91
43000	374.58	360.80	348.78	338.22	328.89	320.60	313.20
44000	383.29	369.19	356.89	346.09	336.54	328.05	320.48
45000	392.00	377.58	365.00	353.95	344.19	335.51	327.76
46000	400.71	385.97	373.12	361.82	351.83	342.96	335.05
47000	409.42	394.37	381.23	369.68	359.48	350.42	342.33
48000	418.13	402.76	389.34	377.55	367.13	357.88	349.61
49000	426.84	411.15	397.45	385.42	374.78	365.33	356.90
50000	435.55	419.54	405.56	393.28	382.43	372.79	364.18
51000	444.26	427.93	413.67	401.15	390.08	380.24	371.47
52000	452.98	436.32	421.78	409.01	397.73	387.70	378.75
53000	461.69	444.71	429.89	416.88	405.37	395.15	386.03
54000	470.40	453.10	438.01	424.74	413.02	402.61	393.32
55000	479.11	461.49	446.12	432.61	420.67	410.07	400.60
56000	487.82	469.88	454.23	440.47	428.32	417.52	407.88
57000	496.53	478.27	462.34	448.34	435.97	424.98	415.17
58000	505.24	486.66	470.45	456.21	443.62	432.43	422.45
59000	513.95	495.05	478.56	464.07	451.27	439.89	429.73
60000	522.66	503.45	486.67	471.94	458.91	447.34	437.02
65000	566.22	545.40	527.23	511.26	497.16	484.62	473.44
70000	609.78	587.35	567.78	550.59	535.40	521.90	509.85
75000	653.33	629.31	608.34	589.92	573.64	559.18	546.27
80000	696.89	671.26	648.90	629.25	611.88	596.46	582.69
85000	740.44	713.21	689.45	668.58	650.13	633.74	619.11
90000	784.00	755.17	730.01	707.91	688.37	671.02	655.53
95000	827.55	797.12	770.57	747.23	726.61	708.29	691.94
100000	871.11	839.08	811.12	786.56	764.86	745.57	728.36
105000	914.66	881.03	851.68	825.89	803.10	782.85	764.78
110000	958.22	922.98	892.23	865.22	841.34	820.13	801.20
120000	1045.33	1006.89	973.35	943.87	917.83	894.69	874.04
130000	1132.44	1090.80	1054.46	1022.53	994.31	969.25	946.87
140000	1219.55	1174.71	1135.57	1101.19	1070.80	1043.80	1019.71
150000	1306.66	1258.61	1216.68	1179.84	1147.28	1118.36	1092.54
175000	1524.44	1468.38	1419.46	1376.48	1338.50	1304.75	1274.64
200000	1742.21	1678.15	1622.24	1573.12	1529.71	1491.15	1456.73
225000	1959.99	1887.92	1825.02	1769.76	1720.93	1677.54	1638.82
250000	2177.77	2097.69	2027.80	1966.40	1912.14	1863.93	1820.91

Monthly Payments 6½%

necessary to amortize a loan

AMOUNT	22 YEARS	23 YEARS	24 YEARS	25 YEARS	30 YEARS	35 YEARS	40 YEARS
100	0.71	0.70	0.69	0.68	0.63	0.60	0.59
200	1.43	1.40	1.37	1.35	1.26	1.21	1.17
500	3.56	3.50	3.43	3.38	3.16	3.02	2.93
1000	7.13	6.99	6.87	6.75	6.32	6.04	5.85
2000	14.26	13.98	13.73	13.50	12.64	12.08	11.71
5000	35.65	34.95	34.33	33.76	31.60	30.21	29.27
6000	42.78	41.94	41.19	40.51	37.92	36.25	35.13
7000	49.91	48.93	48.06	47.26	44.24	42.29	40.98
8000	57.04	55.93	54.92	54.02	50.57	48.33	46.84
9000	64.16	62.92	61.79	60.77	56.89	54.37	52.69
10000	71.29	69.91	68.65	67.52	63.21	60.42	58.55
15000	106.94	104.86	102.98	101.28	94.81	90.62	87.82
20000	142.59	139.81	137.31	135.04	126.41	120.83	117.09
25000	178.23	174.77	171.64	168.80	158.02	151.04	146.36
30000	213.88	209.72	205.96	202.56	189.62	181.25	175.64
35000	249.53	244.67	240.29	236.32	221.22	211.45	204.91
36000	256.66	251.66	247.16	243.07	227.54	217.50	210.76
37000	263.79	258.65	254.02	249.83	233.87	223.54	216.62
38000	270.92	265.64	260.89	256.58	240.19	229.58	222.47
39000	278.05	272.64	267.75	263.33	246.51	235.62	228.33
40000	285.18	279.63	274.62	270.08	252.83	241.66	234.18
41000	292.30	286.62	281.48	276.83	259.15	247.70	240.04
42000	299.43	293.61	288.35	283.59	265.47	253.74	245.89
43000	306.56	300.60	295.21	290.34	271.79	259.79	251.75
44000	313.69	307.59	302.08	297.09	278.11	265.83	257.60
45000	320.82	314.58	308.94	303.84	284.43	271.87	263.46
46000	327.95	321.57	315.81	310.60	290.75	277.91	269.31
47000	335.08	328.56	322.68	317.35	297.07	283.95	275.16
48000	342.21	335.55	329.54	324.10	303.39	289.99	281.02
49000	349.34	342.54	336.41	330.85	309.71	296.04	286.87
50000	356.47	349.53	343.27	337.60	316.03	302.08	292.73
51000	363.60	356.52	350.14	344.36	322.35	308.12	298.58
52000	370.73	363.51	357.00	351.11	328.68	314.16	304.44
53000	377.86	370.50	363.87	357.86	335.00	320.20	310.29
54000	384.99	377.49	370.73	364.61	341.32	326.24	316.15
55000	392.12	384.49	377.60	371.36	347.64	332.28	322.00
56000	399.25	391.48	384.46	378.12	353.96	338.33	327.86
57000	406.38	398.47	391.33	384.87	360.28	344.37	333.71
58000	413.50	405.46	398.19	391.62	366.60	350.41	339.56
59000	420.63	412.45	405.06	398.37	372.92	356.45	345.42
60000	427.76	419.44	411.93	405.12	379.24	362.49	351.27
65000	463.41	454.39	446.25	438.88	410.84	392.70	380.55
70000	499.06	489.35	480.58	472.65	442.45	422.91	409.82
75000	534.70	524.30	514.91	506.41	474.05	453.12	439.09
80000	570.35	559.25	549.23	540.17	505.65	483.32	468.37
85000	606.00	594.20	583.56	573.93	537.26	513.53	497.64
90000	641.65	629.16	617.89	607.69	568.86	543.74	526.91
95000	677.29	664.11	652.22	641.45	600.46	573.95	556.18
100000	712.94	699.06	686.54	675.21	632.07	604.15	585.46
105000	748.59	734.02	720.87	708.97	663.67	634.36	614.73
110000	784.23	768.97	755.20	742.73	695.27	664.57	644.00
120000	855.53	838.88	823.85	810.25	758.48	724.99	702.55
130000	926.82	908.78	892.51	877.77	821.69	785.40	761.09
140000	998.11	978.69	961.16	945.29	884.90	845.82	819.64
150000	1069.41	1048.60	1029.81	1012.81	948.10	906.23	878.19
175000	1247.64	1223.38	1201.45	1181.61	1106.12	1057.27	1024.55
200000	1425.88	1398.13	1373.09	1350.41	1264.14	1208.31	1170.91
225000	1604.11	1572.90	1544.72	1519.22	1422.15	1359.35	1317.28
250000	1782.35	1747.66	1716.36	1688.02	1580.17	1510.39	1463.64

6¾%

Monthly Payments

necessary to amortize a loan

AMOUNT	1 YEAR	2 YEARS	3 YEARS	4 YEARS	5 YEARS	6 YEARS	7 YEARS
100	8.64	4.47	3.08	2.38	1.97	1.69	1.50
200	17.28	8.93	6.15	4.77	3.94	3.39	2.99
500	43.21	22.33	15.38	11.92	9.84	8.46	7.49
1000	86.41	44.66	30.76	23.83	19.68	16.93	14.97
2000	172.82	89.32	61.53	47.66	39.37	33.86	29.94
5000	432.06	223.30	153.81	119.15	98.42	84.65	74.85
6000	518.47	267.96	184.58	142.98	118.10	101.58	89.82
7000	604.88	312.62	215.34	166.81	137.78	118.50	104.80
8000	691.29	357.27	246.10	190.64	157.47	135.43	119.77
9000	777.70	401.93	276.87	214.47	177.15	152.36	134.74
10000	864.12	446.59	307.63	238.30	196.83	169.29	149.71
15000	1296.17	669.89	461.44	357.46	295.25	253.94	224.56
20000	1728.23	893.19	615.26	476.61	393.67	338.58	299.42
25000	2160.29	1116.48	769.07	595.76	492.09	423.23	374.27
30000	2592.35	1339.78	922.89	714.91	590.50	507.88	449.12
35000	3024.40	1563.08	1076.70	834.06	688.92	592.52	523.98
36000	3110.82	1607.74	1107.47	857.90	708.60	609.45	538.95
37000	3197.23	1652.40	1138.23	881.73	728.29	626.38	553.92
38000	3283.64	1697.05	1168.99	905.56	747.97	643.31	568.89
39000	3370.05	1741.71	1199.75	929.39	767.65	660.24	583.86
40000	3456.46	1786.37	1230.52	953.22	787.34	677.17	598.83
41000	3542.87	1831.03	1261.28	977.05	807.02	694.10	613.80
42000	3629.28	1875.69	1292.04	1000.88	826.71	711.03	628.77
43000	3715.70	1920.35	1322.81	1024.71	846.39	727.96	643.74
44000	3802.11	1965.01	1353.57	1048.54	866.07	744.89	658.71
45000	3888.52	2009.67	1384.33	1072.37	885.76	761.81	673.68
46000	3974.93	2054.33	1415.09	1096.20	905.44	778.74	688.66
47000	4061.34	2098.99	1445.86	1120.03	925.12	795.67	703.63
48000	4147.75	2143.65	1476.62	1143.86	944.81	812.60	718.60
49000	4234.17	2188.31	1507.38	1167.69	964.49	829.53	733.57
50000	4320.58	2232.97	1538.15	1191.52	984.17	846.46	748.54
51000	4406.99	2277.63	1568.91	1215.35	1003.86	863.39	763.51
52000	4493.40	2322.29	1599.67	1239.18	1023.54	880.32	778.48
53000	4579.81	2366.94	1630.43	1263.01	1043.22	897.25	793.45
54000	4666.22	2411.60	1661.20	1286.84	1062.91	914.18	808.42
55000	4752.63	2456.26	1691.96	1310.67	1082.59	931.11	823.39
56000	4839.05	2500.92	1722.72	1334.50	1102.27	948.04	838.36
57000	4925.46	2545.58	1753.49	1358.33	1121.96	964.97	853.33
58000	5011.87	2590.24	1784.25	1382.16	1141.64	981.89	868.30
59000	5098.28	2634.90	1815.01	1406.00	1161.32	998.82	883.28
60000	5184.69	2679.56	1845.78	1429.83	1181.01	1015.75	898.25
65000	5616.75	2902.86	1999.59	1548.98	1279.42	1100.40	973.10
70000	6048.81	3126.15	2153.40	1668.13	1377.84	1185.04	1047.95
75000	6480.87	3349.45	2307.22	1787.28	1476.26	1269.69	1122.81
80000	6912.92	3572.75	2461.03	1906.43	1574.68	1354.34	1197.66
85000	7344.98	3796.04	2614.85	2025.59	1673.09	1438.98	1272.51
90000	7777.04	4019.34	2768.66	2144.74	1771.51	1523.63	1347.37
95000	8209.10	4242.64	2922.48	2263.89	1869.93	1608.28	1422.22
100000	8641.15	4465.93	3076.29	2383.04	1968.35	1692.92	1497.08
105000	9073.21	4689.23	3230.11	2502.19	2066.76	1777.57	1571.93
110000	9505.27	4912.53	3383.92	2621.35	2165.18	1862.21	1646.78
120000	10369.38	5359.12	3691.55	2859.65	2362.02	2031.51	1796.49
130000	11233.50	5805.71	3999.18	3097.96	2558.85	2200.80	1946.20
140000	12097.62	6252.31	4306.81	3336.26	2755.68	2370.09	2095.91
150000	12961.73	6698.90	4614.44	3574.56	2952.52	2539.38	2245.61
175000	15122.02	7815.38	5383.51	4170.32	3444.61	2962.61	2619.88
200000	17282.31	8931.87	6152.58	4766.09	3936.69	3385.84	2994.15
225000	19442.60	10048.35	6921.66	5361.85	4428.78	3809.07	3368.42
250000	21602.88	11164.83	7690.73	5957.61	4920.87	4232.30	3742.69

Monthly Payments 6¾%

necessary to amortize a loan

AMOUNT	8 YEARS	9 YEARS	10 YEARS	11 YEARS	12 YEARS	13 YEARS	14 YEARS
100	1.35	1.24	1.15	1.08	1.02	0.96	0.92
200	2.70	2.48	2.30	2.15	2.03	1.93	1.84
500	6.75	6.19	5.74	5.38	5.08	4.82	4.61
1000	13.51	12.38	11.48	10.75	10.15	9.65	9.22
2000	27.02	24.76	22.96	21.51	20.30	19.29	18.43
5000	67.55	61.90	57.41	53.77	50.76	48.23	46.08
6000	81.06	74.28	68.89	64.52	60.91	57.87	55.30
7000	94.57	86.66	80.38	75.27	71.06	67.52	64.52
8000	108.08	99.04	91.86	86.03	81.21	77.17	73.74
9000	121.59	111.42	103.34	96.78	91.36	86.81	82.95
10000	135.10	123.80	114.82	107.53	101.51	96.46	92.17
15000	202.64	185.70	172.24	161.30	152.27	144.69	138.25
20000	270.19	247.60	229.65	215.07	203.02	192.92	184.34
25000	337.74	309.50	287.06	268.84	253.78	241.15	230.42
30000	405.29	371.40	344.47	322.60	304.53	289.37	276.51
35000	472.84	433.30	401.88	376.37	355.29	337.60	322.59
36000	486.35	445.68	413.37	387.13	365.44	347.25	331.81
37000	499.86	458.06	424.85	397.88	375.59	356.89	341.03
38000	513.37	470.44	436.33	408.63	385.74	366.54	350.24
39000	526.88	482.82	447.81	419.39	395.89	376.19	359.46
40000	540.39	495.20	459.30	430.14	406.04	385.83	368.68
41000	553.90	507.58	470.78	440.89	416.19	395.48	377.89
42000	567.40	519.96	482.26	451.65	426.34	405.12	387.11
43000	580.91	532.34	493.74	462.40	436.49	414.77	396.33
44000	594.42	544.72	505.23	473.15	446.65	424.42	405.54
45000	607.93	557.10	516.71	483.91	456.80	434.06	414.76
46000	621.44	569.48	528.19	494.66	466.95	443.71	423.98
47000	634.95	581.86	539.67	505.41	477.10	453.35	433.20
48000	648.46	594.24	551.16	516.17	487.25	463.00	442.41
49000	661.97	606.62	562.64	526.92	497.40	472.64	451.63
50000	675.48	619.00	574.12	537.67	507.55	482.29	460.85
51000	688.99	631.38	585.60	548.43	517.70	491.94	470.06
52000	702.50	643.76	597.09	559.18	527.85	501.58	479.28
53000	716.01	656.14	608.57	569.93	538.00	511.23	488.50
54000	729.52	668.52	620.05	580.69	548.16	520.87	497.71
55000	743.03	680.90	631.53	591.44	558.31	530.52	506.93
56000	756.54	693.28	643.02	602.20	568.46	540.16	516.15
57000	770.05	705.66	654.50	612.95	578.61	549.81	525.37
58000	783.56	718.04	665.98	623.70	588.76	559.46	534.58
59000	797.07	730.42	677.46	634.46	598.91	569.10	543.80
60000	810.58	742.80	688.94	645.21	609.06	578.75	553.02
65000	878.13	804.70	746.36	698.98	659.82	626.98	599.10
70000	945.67	866.60	803.77	752.74	710.57	675.21	645.19
75000	1013.22	928.50	861.18	806.51	761.33	723.44	691.27
80000	1080.77	990.40	918.59	860.28	812.08	771.66	737.35
85000	1148.32	1052.30	976.00	914.05	862.84	819.89	783.44
90000	1215.87	1114.20	1033.42	967.81	913.59	868.12	829.52
95000	1283.42	1176.10	1090.83	1021.58	964.35	916.35	875.61
100000	1350.96	1238.00	1148.24	1075.35	1015.10	964.58	921.69
105000	1418.51	1299.90	1205.65	1129.12	1065.86	1012.81	967.78
110000	1486.06	1361.80	1263.07	1182.88	1116.61	1061.04	1013.86
120000	1621.16	1485.60	1377.89	1290.42	1218.12	1157.50	1106.03
130000	1756.25	1609.40	1492.71	1397.95	1319.63	1253.95	1198.20
140000	1891.35	1733.20	1607.54	1505.49	1421.14	1350.41	1290.37
150000	2026.45	1857.00	1722.36	1613.02	1522.65	1446.87	1382.54
175000	2364.19	2166.50	2009.42	1881.86	1776.43	1688.02	1612.96
200000	2701.93	2476.00	2296.48	2150.70	2030.21	1929.16	1843.39
225000	3039.67	2785.51	2583.54	2419.53	2283.98	2170.31	2073.81
250000	3377.41	3095.01	2870.60	2688.37	2537.76	2411.45	2304.23

6¾%

Monthly Payments

necessary to amortize a loan

AMOUNT	15 YEARS	16 YEARS	17 YEARS	18 YEARS	19 YEARS	20 YEARS	21 YEARS
100	0.88	0.85	0.83	0.80	0.78	0.76	0.74
200	1.77	1.71	1.65	1.60	1.56	1.52	1.49
500	4.42	4.27	4.13	4.00	3.90	3.80	3.72
1000	8.85	8.53	8.25	8.01	7.79	7.60	7.43
2000	17.70	17.06	16.51	16.02	15.59	15.21	14.87
5000	44.25	42.65	41.27	40.05	38.97	38.02	37.17
6000	53.09	51.18	49.52	48.06	46.77	45.62	44.60
7000	61.94	59.72	57.77	56.07	54.56	53.23	52.03
8000	70.79	68.25	66.03	64.08	62.36	60.83	59.47
9000	79.64	76.78	74.28	72.09	70.15	68.43	66.90
10000	88.49	85.31	82.53	80.10	77.95	76.04	74.33
15000	132.74	127.96	123.80	120.14	116.92	114.05	111.50
20000	176.98	170.62	165.07	160.19	155.89	152.07	148.67
25000	221.23	213.27	206.33	200.24	194.86	190.09	185.84
30000	265.47	255.92	247.60	240.29	233.84	228.11	223.00
35000	309.72	298.58	288.86	280.34	272.81	266.13	260.17
36000	318.57	307.11	297.12	288.35	280.60	273.73	267.60
37000	327.42	315.64	305.37	296.36	288.40	281.33	275.04
38000	336.27	324.17	313.62	304.37	296.19	288.94	282.47
39000	345.11	332.70	321.88	312.38	303.99	296.54	289.90
40000	353.96	341.23	330.13	320.39	311.78	304.15	297.34
41000	362.81	349.76	338.38	328.40	319.58	311.75	304.77
42000	371.66	358.29	346.64	336.41	327.37	319.35	312.20
43000	380.51	366.82	354.89	344.41	335.17	326.96	319.64
44000	389.36	375.36	363.14	352.42	342.96	334.56	327.07
45000	398.21	383.89	371.40	360.43	350.75	342.16	334.50
46000	407.06	392.42	379.65	368.44	358.55	349.77	341.94
47000	415.91	400.95	387.90	376.45	366.34	357.37	349.37
48000	424.76	409.48	396.16	384.46	374.14	364.97	356.80
49000	433.61	418.01	404.41	392.47	381.93	372.58	364.24
50000	442.45	426.54	412.66	400.48	389.73	380.18	371.67
51000	451.30	435.07	420.92	408.49	397.52	387.79	379.10
52000	460.15	443.60	429.17	416.50	405.32	395.39	386.54
53000	469.00	452.13	437.42	424.51	413.11	402.99	393.97
54000	477.85	460.66	445.68	432.52	420.91	410.60	401.41
55000	486.70	469.19	453.93	440.53	428.70	418.20	408.84
56000	495.55	477.72	462.18	448.54	436.49	425.80	416.27
57000	504.40	486.26	470.44	456.55	444.29	433.41	423.71
58000	513.25	494.79	478.69	464.56	452.08	441.01	431.14
59000	522.10	503.32	486.94	472.57	459.88	448.61	438.57
60000	530.95	511.85	495.20	480.58	467.67	456.22	446.01
65000	575.19	554.50	536.46	520.63	506.65	494.24	483.17
70000	619.44	597.16	577.73	560.68	545.62	532.25	520.34
75000	663.68	639.81	618.99	600.72	584.59	570.27	557.51
80000	707.93	682.46	660.26	640.77	623.56	608.29	594.67
85000	752.17	725.12	701.53	680.82	662.54	646.31	631.84
90000	796.42	767.77	742.79	720.87	701.51	684.33	669.01
95000	840.66	810.43	784.06	760.92	740.48	722.35	706.18
100000	884.91	853.08	825.33	800.96	779.45	760.36	743.34
105000	929.15	895.73	866.59	841.01	818.43	798.38	780.51
110000	973.40	938.39	907.86	881.06	857.40	836.40	817.68
120000	1061.89	1023.70	990.39	961.16	935.35	912.44	892.01
130000	1150.38	1109.00	1072.92	1041.25	1013.29	988.47	966.35
140000	1238.87	1194.31	1155.46	1121.35	1091.24	1064.51	1040.68
150000	1327.36	1279.62	1237.99	1201.45	1169.18	1140.55	1115.01
175000	1548.59	1492.89	1444.32	1401.69	1364.05	1330.64	1300.85
200000	1769.82	1706.16	1650.65	1601.93	1558.91	1520.73	1486.69
225000	1991.05	1919.43	1856.98	1802.17	1753.77	1710.82	1672.52
250000	2212.27	2132.70	2063.32	2002.41	1948.64	1900.91	1858.36

Monthly Payments 6¾%

necessary to amortize a loan

AMOUNT	22 YEARS	23 YEARS	24 YEARS	25 YEARS	30 YEARS	35 YEARS	40 YEARS
100	0.73	0.71	0.70	0.69	0.65	0.62	0.60
200	1.46	1.43	1.40	1.38	1.30	1.24	1.21
500	3.64	3.57	3.51	3.45	3.24	3.11	3.02
1000	7.28	7.14	7.02	6.91	6.49	6.21	6.03
2000	14.56	14.29	14.04	13.82	12.97	12.43	12.07
5000	36.41	35.72	35.10	34.55	32.43	31.07	30.17
6000	43.69	42.86	42.12	41.45	38.92	37.28	36.20
7000	50.97	50.01	49.14	48.36	45.40	43.50	42.23
8000	58.25	57.15	56.17	55.27	51.89	49.71	48.27
9000	65.53	64.30	63.19	62.18	58.37	55.93	54.30
10000	72.81	71.44	70.21	69.09	64.86	62.14	60.34
15000	109.22	107.16	105.31	103.64	97.29	93.21	90.50
20000	145.62	142.88	140.41	138.18	129.72	124.28	120.67
25000	182.03	178.60	175.52	172.73	162.15	155.35	150.84
30000	218.43	214.32	210.62	207.27	194.58	186.42	181.01
35000	254.84	250.04	245.72	241.82	227.01	217.50	211.17
36000	262.12	257.19	252.75	248.73	233.50	223.71	217.21
37000	269.40	264.33	259.77	255.64	239.98	229.92	223.24
38000	276.68	271.48	266.79	262.55	246.47	236.14	229.28
39000	283.96	278.62	273.81	269.46	252.95	242.35	235.31
40000	291.24	285.77	280.83	276.36	259.44	248.57	241.34
41000	298.52	292.91	287.85	283.27	265.93	254.78	247.38
42000	305.80	300.05	294.87	290.18	272.41	260.99	253.41
43000	313.09	307.20	301.89	297.09	278.90	267.21	259.44
44000	320.37	314.34	308.91	304.00	285.38	273.42	265.48
45000	327.65	321.49	315.93	310.91	291.87	279.64	271.51
46000	334.93	328.63	322.95	317.82	298.36	285.85	277.54
47000	342.21	335.77	329.97	324.73	304.84	292.07	283.58
48000	349.49	342.92	336.99	331.64	311.33	298.28	289.61
49000	356.77	350.06	344.01	338.55	317.81	304.49	295.64
50000	364.05	357.21	351.04	345.46	324.30	310.71	301.68
51000	371.33	364.35	358.06	352.36	330.79	316.92	307.71
52000	378.61	371.50	365.08	359.27	337.27	323.14	313.75
53000	385.90	378.64	372.10	366.18	343.76	329.35	319.78
54000	393.18	385.78	379.12	373.09	350.24	335.56	325.81
55000	400.46	392.93	386.14	380.00	356.73	341.78	331.85
56000	407.74	400.07	393.16	386.91	363.21	347.99	337.88
57000	415.02	407.22	400.18	393.82	369.70	354.21	343.91
58000	422.30	414.36	407.20	400.73	376.19	360.42	349.95
59000	429.58	421.50	414.22	407.64	382.67	366.64	355.98
60000	436.86	428.65	421.24	414.55	389.16	372.85	362.01
65000	473.27	464.37	456.35	449.09	421.59	403.92	392.18
70000	509.67	500.09	491.45	483.64	454.02	434.99	422.35
75000	546.08	535.81	526.55	518.18	486.45	466.06	452.52
80000	582.48	571.53	561.66	552.73	518.88	497.13	482.69
85000	618.89	607.25	596.76	587.27	551.31	528.20	512.85
90000	655.29	642.97	631.86	621.82	583.74	559.27	543.02
95000	691.70	678.69	666.97	656.37	616.17	590.35	573.19
100000	728.11	714.41	702.07	690.91	648.60	621.42	603.36
105000	764.51	750.13	737.17	725.46	681.03	652.49	633.52
110000	800.92	785.86	772.28	760.00	713.46	683.56	663.69
120000	873.73	857.30	842.49	829.09	778.32	745.70	724.03
130000	946.54	928.74	912.69	898.18	843.18	807.84	784.36
140000	1019.35	1000.18	982.90	967.28	908.04	869.98	844.70
150000	1092.16	1071.62	1053.11	1036.37	972.90	932.12	905.04
175000	1274.18	1250.22	1228.62	1209.10	1135.05	1087.48	1055.87
200000	1456.21	1428.83	1404.14	1381.82	1297.20	1242.83	1206.71
225000	1638.24	1607.43	1579.66	1554.55	1459.35	1398.19	1357.55
250000	1820.26	1786.03	1755.18	1727.28	1621.50	1553.54	1508.39

7%

Monthly Payments
necessary to amortize a loan

AMOUNT	1 YEAR	2 YEARS	3 YEARS	4 YEARS	5 YEARS	6 YEARS	7 YEARS
100	8.65	4.48	3.09	2.39	1.98	1.70	1.51
200	17.31	8.95	6.18	4.79	3.96	3.41	3.02
500	43.26	22.39	15.44	11.97	9.90	8.52	7.55
1000	86.53	44.77	30.88	23.95	19.80	17.05	15.09
2000	173.05	89.55	61.75	47.89	39.60	34.10	30.19
5000	432.63	223.86	154.39	119.73	99.01	85.25	75.46
6000	519.16	268.64	185.26	143.68	118.81	102.29	90.56
7000	605.69	313.41	216.14	167.62	138.61	119.34	105.65
8000	692.21	358.18	247.02	191.57	158.41	136.39	120.74
9000	778.74	402.95	277.89	215.52	178.21	153.44	135.83
10000	865.27	447.73	308.77	239.46	198.01	170.49	150.93
15000	1297.90	671.59	463.16	359.19	297.02	255.74	226.39
20000	1730.53	895.45	617.54	478.92	396.02	340.98	301.85
25000	2163.17	1119.31	771.93	598.66	495.03	426.23	377.32
30000	2595.80	1343.18	926.31	718.39	594.04	511.47	452.78
35000	3028.44	1567.04	1080.70	838.12	693.04	596.72	528.24
36000	3114.96	1611.81	1111.58	862.06	712.84	613.76	543.34
37000	3201.49	1656.59	1142.45	886.01	732.64	630.81	558.43
38000	3288.02	1701.36	1173.33	909.96	752.45	647.86	573.52
39000	3374.54	1746.13	1204.21	933.90	772.25	664.91	588.61
40000	3461.07	1790.90	1235.08	957.85	792.05	681.96	603.71
41000	3547.60	1835.68	1265.96	981.80	811.85	699.01	618.80
42000	3634.12	1880.45	1296.84	1005.74	831.65	716.06	633.89
43000	3720.65	1925.22	1327.72	1029.69	851.45	733.11	648.99
44000	3807.18	1969.99	1358.59	1053.63	871.25	750.16	664.08
45000	3893.70	2014.77	1389.47	1077.58	891.05	767.21	679.17
46000	3980.23	2059.54	1420.35	1101.53	910.86	784.25	694.26
47000	4066.76	2104.31	1451.22	1125.47	930.66	801.30	709.36
48000	4153.28	2149.08	1482.10	1149.42	950.46	818.35	724.45
49000	4239.81	2193.86	1512.98	1173.37	970.26	835.40	739.54
50000	4326.34	2238.63	1543.85	1197.31	990.06	852.45	754.63
51000	4412.86	2283.40	1574.73	1221.26	1009.86	869.50	769.73
52000	4499.39	2328.17	1605.61	1245.20	1029.66	886.55	784.82
53000	4585.92	2372.95	1636.49	1269.15	1049.46	903.60	799.91
54000	4672.44	2417.72	1667.36	1293.10	1069.26	920.65	815.00
55000	4758.97	2462.49	1698.24	1317.04	1089.07	937.70	830.10
56000	4845.50	2507.26	1729.12	1340.99	1108.87	954.74	845.19
57000	4932.02	2552.04	1759.99	1364.94	1128.67	971.79	860.28
58000	5018.55	2596.81	1790.87	1388.88	1148.47	988.84	875.38
59000	5105.08	2641.58	1821.75	1412.83	1168.27	1005.89	890.47
60000	5191.60	2686.35	1852.63	1436.77	1188.07	1022.94	905.56
65000	5624.24	2910.22	2007.01	1556.51	1287.08	1108.19	981.02
70000	6056.87	3134.08	2161.40	1676.24	1386.08	1193.43	1056.49
75000	6489.51	3357.94	2315.78	1795.97	1485.09	1278.68	1131.95
80000	6922.14	3581.81	2470.17	1915.70	1584.10	1363.92	1207.41
85000	7354.77	3805.67	2624.55	2035.43	1683.10	1449.17	1282.88
90000	7787.41	4029.53	2778.94	2155.16	1782.11	1534.41	1358.34
95000	8220.04	4253.40	2933.32	2274.89	1881.11	1619.66	1433.80
100000	8652.67	4477.26	3087.71	2394.62	1980.12	1704.90	1509.27
105000	9085.31	4701.12	3242.10	2514.36	2079.13	1790.15	1584.73
110000	9517.94	4924.98	3396.48	2634.09	2178.13	1875.39	1660.19
120000	10383.21	5372.71	3705.25	2873.55	2376.14	2045.88	1811.12
130000	11248.48	5820.44	4014.02	3113.01	2574.16	2216.37	1962.05
140000	12113.74	6268.16	4322.79	3352.47	2772.17	2386.86	2112.98
150000	12979.01	6715.89	4631.56	3591.94	2970.18	2557.35	2263.90
175000	15142.18	7835.20	5403.49	4190.59	3465.21	2983.58	2641.22
200000	17305.35	8954.52	6175.42	4789.25	3960.24	3409.80	3018.54
225000	19468.52	10073.83	6947.35	5387.91	4455.27	3836.03	3395.85
250000	21631.69	11193.14	7719.27	5986.56	4950.30	4262.25	3773.17

Monthly Payments 7%

necessary to amortize a loan

AMOUNT	8 YEARS	9 YEARS	10 YEARS	11 YEARS	12 YEARS	13 YEARS	14 YEARS
100	1.36	1.25	1.16	1.09	1.03	0.98	0.94
200	2.73	2.50	2.32	2.18	2.06	1.96	1.87
500	6.82	6.25	5.81	5.44	5.14	4.89	4.68
1000	13.63	12.51	11.61	10.88	10.28	9.78	9.35
2000	27.27	25.01	23.22	21.77	20.57	19.56	18.71
5000	68.17	62.53	58.05	54.42	51.42	48.90	46.77
6000	81.80	75.04	69.67	65.30	61.70	58.68	56.12
7000	95.44	87.54	81.28	76.19	71.99	68.47	65.48
8000	109.07	100.05	92.89	87.07	82.27	78.25	74.83
9000	122.70	112.56	104.50	97.96	92.55	88.03	84.19
10000	136.34	125.06	116.11	108.84	102.84	97.81	93.54
15000	204.51	187.59	174.16	163.26	154.26	146.71	140.31
20000	272.67	250.13	232.22	217.68	205.68	195.61	187.08
25000	340.84	312.66	290.27	272.10	257.10	244.52	233.85
30000	409.01	375.19	348.33	326.52	308.51	293.42	280.62
35000	477.18	437.72	406.38	380.94	359.93	342.33	327.39
36000	490.81	450.23	417.99	391.83	370.22	352.11	336.74
37000	504.45	462.73	429.60	402.71	380.50	361.89	346.10
38000	518.08	475.24	441.21	413.60	390.78	371.67	355.45
39000	531.71	487.74	452.82	424.48	401.07	381.45	364.81
40000	545.35	500.25	464.43	435.36	411.35	391.23	374.16
41000	558.98	512.76	476.04	446.25	421.64	401.01	383.51
42000	572.62	525.26	487.66	457.13	431.92	410.79	392.87
43000	586.25	537.77	499.27	468.02	442.20	420.57	402.22
44000	599.88	550.28	510.88	478.90	452.49	430.35	411.58
45000	613.52	562.78	522.49	489.78	462.77	440.13	420.93
46000	627.15	575.29	534.10	500.67	473.06	449.91	430.28
47000	640.78	587.79	545.71	511.55	483.34	459.69	439.64
48000	654.42	600.30	557.32	522.44	493.62	469.48	448.99
49000	668.05	612.81	568.93	533.32	503.91	479.26	458.35
50000	681.69	625.31	580.54	544.21	514.19	489.04	467.70
51000	695.32	637.82	592.15	555.09	524.47	498.82	477.05
52000	708.95	650.33	603.76	565.97	534.76	508.60	486.41
53000	722.59	662.83	615.37	576.86	545.04	518.38	495.76
54000	736.22	675.34	626.99	587.74	555.33	528.16	505.12
55000	749.85	687.85	638.60	598.63	565.61	537.94	514.47
56000	763.49	700.35	650.21	609.51	575.89	547.72	523.82
57000	777.12	712.86	661.82	620.39	586.18	557.50	533.18
58000	790.76	725.36	673.43	631.28	596.46	567.28	542.53
59000	804.39	737.87	685.04	642.16	606.74	577.06	551.89
60000	818.02	750.38	696.65	653.05	617.03	586.84	561.24
65000	886.19	812.91	754.71	707.47	668.45	635.75	608.01
70000	954.36	875.44	812.76	761.89	719.87	684.65	654.78
75000	1022.53	937.97	870.81	816.31	771.29	733.56	701.55
80000	1090.70	1000.50	928.87	870.73	822.70	782.46	748.32
85000	1158.87	1063.03	986.92	925.15	874.12	831.36	795.09
90000	1227.03	1125.56	1044.98	979.57	925.54	880.27	841.86
95000	1295.20	1188.10	1103.03	1033.99	976.96	929.17	888.63
100000	1363.37	1250.63	1161.08	1088.41	1028.38	978.07	935.40
105000	1431.54	1313.16	1219.14	1142.83	1079.80	1026.98	982.17
110000	1499.71	1375.69	1277.19	1197.25	1131.22	1075.88	1028.94
120000	1636.05	1500.75	1393.30	1306.09	1234.06	1173.69	1122.48
130000	1772.38	1625.82	1509.41	1414.93	1336.90	1271.50	1216.02
140000	1908.72	1750.88	1625.52	1523.77	1439.73	1369.30	1309.56
150000	2045.06	1875.94	1741.63	1632.62	1542.57	1467.11	1403.10
175000	2385.90	2188.60	2031.90	1904.72	1799.67	1711.63	1636.95
200000	2726.74	2501.26	2322.17	2176.82	2056.76	1956.15	1870.80
225000	3067.59	2813.91	2612.44	2448.92	2313.86	2200.67	2104.65
250000	3408.43	3126.57	2902.71	2721.03	2570.95	2445.19	2338.50

7% Monthly Payments

necessary to amortize a loan

AMOUNT	15 YEARS	16 YEARS	17 YEARS	18 YEARS	19 YEARS	20 YEARS	21 YEARS
100	0.90	0.87	0.84	0.82	0.79	0.78	0.76
200	1.80	1.73	1.68	1.63	1.59	1.55	1.52
500	4.49	4.34	4.20	4.08	3.97	3.88	3.79
1000	8.99	8.67	8.40	8.16	7.94	7.75	7.58
2000	17.98	17.34	16.79	16.31	15.88	15.51	15.17
5000	44.94	43.36	41.98	40.78	39.71	38.76	37.92
6000	53.93	52.03	50.38	48.93	47.65	46.52	45.51
7000	62.92	60.70	58.78	57.09	55.59	54.27	53.09
8000	71.91	69.38	67.17	65.24	63.54	62.02	60.68
9000	80.89	78.05	75.57	73.40	71.48	69.78	68.26
10000	89.88	86.72	83.97	81.55	79.42	77.53	75.85
15000	134.82	130.08	125.95	122.33	119.13	116.29	113.77
20000	179.77	173.44	167.93	163.10	158.84	155.06	151.69
25000	224.71	216.80	209.92	203.88	198.55	193.82	189.62
30000	269.65	260.16	251.90	244.65	238.26	232.59	227.54
35000	314.59	303.52	293.88	285.43	277.97	271.35	265.47
36000	323.58	312.19	302.28	293.58	285.91	279.11	273.05
37000	332.57	320.87	310.67	301.74	293.85	286.86	280.63
38000	341.55	329.54	319.07	309.89	301.79	294.61	288.22
39000	350.54	338.21	327.47	318.05	309.74	302.37	295.80
40000	359.53	346.88	335.86	326.20	317.68	310.12	303.39
41000	368.52	355.56	344.26	334.36	325.62	317.87	310.97
42000	377.51	364.23	352.66	342.51	333.56	325.63	318.56
43000	386.50	372.90	361.05	350.67	341.50	333.38	326.14
44000	395.48	381.57	369.45	358.82	349.44	341.13	333.73
45000	404.47	390.24	377.85	366.98	357.39	348.88	341.31
46000	413.46	398.92	386.24	375.13	365.33	356.64	348.90
47000	422.45	407.59	394.64	383.29	373.27	364.39	356.48
48000	431.44	416.26	403.04	391.44	381.21	372.14	364.07
49000	440.43	424.93	411.43	399.60	389.15	379.90	371.65
50000	449.41	433.60	419.83	407.75	397.10	387.65	379.24
51000	458.40	442.28	428.23	415.91	405.04	395.40	386.82
52000	467.39	450.95	436.62	424.06	412.98	403.16	394.41
53000	476.38	459.62	445.02	432.22	420.92	410.91	401.99
54000	485.37	468.29	453.42	440.37	428.86	418.66	409.57
55000	494.36	476.96	461.81	448.53	436.81	426.41	417.16
56000	503.34	485.64	470.21	456.68	444.75	434.17	424.74
57000	512.33	494.31	478.61	464.84	452.69	441.92	432.33
58000	521.32	502.98	487.00	472.99	460.63	449.67	439.91
59000	530.31	511.65	495.40	481.15	468.57	457.43	447.50
60000	539.30	520.32	503.80	489.30	476.52	465.18	455.08
65000	584.24	563.69	545.78	530.08	516.23	503.94	493.01
70000	629.18	607.05	587.76	570.85	555.93	542.71	530.93
75000	674.12	650.41	629.75	611.63	595.64	581.47	568.85
80000	719.06	693.77	671.73	652.40	635.35	620.24	606.78
85000	764.00	737.13	713.71	693.18	675.06	659.00	644.70
90000	808.95	780.49	755.69	733.95	714.77	697.77	682.62
95000	853.89	823.85	797.68	774.73	754.48	736.53	720.55
100000	898.83	867.21	839.66	815.50	794.19	775.30	758.47
105000	943.77	910.57	881.64	856.28	833.90	814.06	796.40
110000	988.71	953.93	923.63	897.05	873.61	852.83	834.32
120000	1078.59	1040.65	1007.59	978.60	953.03	930.36	910.17
130000	1168.48	1127.37	1091.56	1060.15	1032.45	1007.89	986.01
140000	1258.36	1214.09	1175.52	1141.70	1111.87	1085.42	1061.86
150000	1348.24	1300.81	1259.49	1223.25	1191.29	1162.95	1137.71
175000	1572.95	1517.61	1469.41	1427.13	1389.84	1356.77	1327.33
200000	1797.66	1734.42	1679.32	1631.00	1588.38	1550.60	1516.94
225000	2022.36	1951.22	1889.24	1834.88	1786.93	1744.42	1706.56
250000	2247.07	2168.02	2099.15	2038.76	1985.48	1938.25	1896.18

Monthly Payments 7%

necessary to amortize a loan

AMOUNT	22 YEARS	23 YEARS	24 YEARS	25 YEARS	30 YEARS	35 YEARS	40 YEARS
100	0.74	0.73	0.72	0.71	0.67	0.64	0.62
200	1.49	1.46	1.44	1.41	1.33	1.28	1.24
500	3.72	3.65	3.59	3.53	3.33	3.19	3.11
1000	7.43	7.30	7.18	7.07	6.65	6.39	6.21
2000	14.87	14.60	14.36	14.14	13.31	12.78	12.43
5000	37.17	36.50	35.89	35.34	33.27	31.94	31.07
6000	44.61	43.80	43.07	42.41	39.92	38.33	37.29
7000	52.04	51.09	50.24	49.47	46.57	44.72	43.50
8000	59.47	58.39	57.42	56.54	53.22	51.11	49.71
9000	66.91	65.69	64.60	63.61	59.88	57.50	55.93
10000	74.34	72.99	71.78	70.68	66.53	63.89	62.14
15000	111.51	109.49	107.66	106.02	99.80	95.83	93.21
20000	148.68	145.98	143.55	141.36	133.06	127.77	124.29
25000	185.86	182.48	179.44	176.69	166.33	159.71	155.36
30000	223.03	218.98	215.33	212.03	199.59	191.66	186.43
35000	260.20	255.47	251.22	247.37	232.86	223.60	217.50
36000	267.63	262.77	258.39	254.44	239.51	229.99	223.72
37000	275.07	270.07	265.57	261.51	246.16	236.38	229.93
38000	282.50	277.37	272.75	268.58	252.81	242.77	236.14
39000	289.94	284.67	279.93	275.64	259.47	249.15	242.36
40000	297.37	291.97	287.10	282.71	266.12	255.54	248.57
41000	304.80	299.27	294.28	289.78	272.77	261.93	254.79
42000	312.24	306.57	301.46	296.85	279.43	268.32	261.00
43000	319.67	313.87	308.64	303.92	286.08	274.71	267.22
44000	327.11	321.16	315.81	310.98	292.73	281.10	273.43
45000	334.54	328.46	322.99	318.05	299.39	287.49	279.64
46000	341.98	335.76	330.17	325.12	306.04	293.87	285.86
47000	349.41	343.06	337.35	332.19	312.69	300.26	292.07
48000	356.84	350.36	344.52	339.25	319.35	306.65	298.29
49000	364.28	357.66	351.70	346.32	326.00	313.04	304.50
50000	371.71	364.96	358.88	353.39	332.65	319.43	310.72
51000	379.15	372.26	366.06	360.46	339.30	325.82	316.93
52000	386.58	379.56	373.23	367.53	345.96	332.21	323.14
53000	394.01	386.86	380.41	374.59	352.61	338.59	329.36
54000	401.45	394.16	387.59	381.66	359.26	344.98	335.57
55000	408.88	401.46	394.77	388.73	365.92	351.37	341.79
56000	416.32	408.75	401.95	395.80	372.57	357.76	348.00
57000	423.75	416.05	409.12	402.86	379.22	364.15	354.22
58000	431.19	423.35	416.30	409.93	385.88	370.54	360.43
59000	438.62	430.65	423.48	417.00	392.53	376.93	366.64
60000	446.05	437.95	430.66	424.07	399.18	383.31	372.86
65000	483.23	474.45	466.54	459.41	432.45	415.26	403.93
70000	520.40	510.94	502.43	494.75	465.71	447.20	435.00
75000	557.57	547.44	538.32	530.08	498.98	479.14	466.07
80000	594.74	583.94	574.21	565.42	532.24	511.09	497.15
85000	631.91	620.43	610.10	600.76	565.51	543.03	528.22
90000	669.08	656.93	645.98	636.10	598.77	574.97	559.29
95000	706.25	693.42	681.87	671.44	632.04	606.91	590.36
100000	743.42	729.92	717.76	706.78	665.30	638.86	621.43
105000	780.60	766.42	753.65	742.12	698.57	670.80	652.50
110000	817.77	802.91	789.54	777.46	731.83	702.74	683.57
120000	892.11	875.90	861.31	848.14	798.36	766.63	745.72
130000	966.45	948.89	933.09	918.81	864.89	830.51	807.86
140000	1040.79	1021.89	1004.86	989.49	931.42	894.40	870.00
150000	1115.14	1094.88	1076.64	1060.17	997.95	958.28	932.15
175000	1300.99	1277.36	1256.08	1236.86	1164.28	1118.00	1087.50
200000	1486.85	1459.84	1435.52	1413.56	1330.60	1277.71	1242.86
225000	1672.70	1642.32	1614.96	1590.25	1496.93	1437.43	1398.22
250000	1858.56	1824.80	1794.40	1766.95	1663.26	1597.14	1553.58

7¼%

Monthly Payments

necessary to amortize a loan

AMOUNT	1 YEAR	2 YEARS	3 YEARS	4 YEARS	5 YEARS	6 YEARS	7 YEARS
100	8.66	4.49	3.10	2.41	1.99	1.72	1.52
200	17.33	8.98	6.20	4.81	3.98	3.43	3.04
500	43.32	22.44	15.50	12.03	9.96	8.58	7.61
1000	86.64	44.89	30.99	24.06	19.92	17.17	15.22
2000	173.28	89.77	61.98	48.12	39.84	34.34	30.43
5000	433.21	224.43	154.96	120.31	99.60	85.85	76.08
6000	519.85	269.32	185.95	144.37	119.52	103.02	91.29
7000	606.49	314.20	216.94	168.44	139.44	120.19	106.51
8000	693.14	359.09	247.93	192.50	159.35	137.35	121.72
9000	779.78	403.97	278.92	216.56	179.27	154.52	136.94
10000	866.42	448.86	309.92	240.62	199.19	171.69	152.15
15000	1299.63	673.29	464.87	360.94	298.79	257.54	228.23
20000	1732.84	897.72	619.83	481.25	398.39	343.39	304.30
25000	2166.05	1122.15	774.79	601.56	497.98	429.23	380.38
30000	2599.26	1346.58	929.75	721.87	597.58	515.08	456.46
35000	3032.47	1571.01	1084.70	842.18	697.18	600.93	532.53
36000	3119.11	1615.90	1115.70	866.25	717.10	618.10	547.75
37000	3205.76	1660.78	1146.69	890.31	737.02	635.26	562.96
38000	3292.40	1705.67	1177.68	914.37	756.94	652.43	578.18
39000	3379.04	1750.55	1208.67	938.43	776.86	669.60	593.39
40000	3465.68	1795.44	1239.66	962.50	796.77	686.77	608.61
41000	3552.32	1840.33	1270.65	986.56	816.69	703.94	623.82
42000	3638.97	1885.21	1301.64	1010.62	836.61	721.11	639.04
43000	3725.61	1930.10	1332.64	1034.68	856.53	738.28	654.25
44000	3812.25	1974.98	1363.63	1058.75	876.45	755.45	669.47
45000	3898.89	2019.87	1394.62	1082.81	896.37	772.62	684.68
46000	3985.53	2064.76	1425.61	1106.87	916.29	789.79	699.90
47000	4072.18	2109.64	1456.60	1130.93	936.21	806.96	715.11
48000	4158.82	2154.53	1487.59	1155.00	956.13	824.13	730.33
49000	4245.46	2199.41	1518.58	1179.06	976.05	841.30	745.54
50000	4332.10	2244.30	1549.58	1203.12	995.97	858.47	760.76
51000	4418.74	2289.19	1580.57	1227.18	1015.89	875.63	775.97
52000	4505.39	2334.07	1611.56	1251.24	1035.81	892.80	791.19
53000	4592.03	2378.96	1642.55	1275.31	1055.73	909.97	806.40
54000	4678.67	2423.84	1673.54	1299.37	1075.65	927.14	821.62
55000	4765.31	2468.73	1704.53	1323.43	1095.56	944.31	836.84
56000	4851.95	2513.62	1735.53	1347.49	1115.48	961.48	852.05
57000	4938.60	2558.50	1766.52	1371.56	1135.40	978.65	867.27
58000	5025.24	2603.39	1797.51	1395.62	1155.32	995.82	882.48
59000	5111.88	2648.27	1828.50	1419.68	1175.24	1012.99	897.70
60000	5198.52	2693.16	1859.49	1443.74	1195.16	1030.16	912.91
65000	5631.73	2917.59	2014.45	1564.06	1294.76	1116.00	988.99
70000	6064.94	3142.02	2169.41	1684.37	1394.36	1201.85	1065.06
75000	6498.15	3366.45	2324.36	1804.68	1493.95	1287.70	1141.14
80000	6931.36	3590.88	2479.32	1924.99	1593.55	1373.54	1217.21
85000	7364.57	3815.31	2634.28	2045.30	1693.15	1459.39	1293.29
90000	7797.78	4039.74	2789.24	2165.62	1792.74	1545.24	1369.37
95000	8230.99	4264.17	2944.20	2285.93	1892.34	1631.08	1445.44
100000	8664.20	4488.60	3099.15	2406.24	1991.94	1716.93	1521.52
105000	9097.41	4713.03	3254.11	2526.55	2091.53	1802.78	1597.59
110000	9530.62	4937.46	3409.07	2646.86	2191.13	1888.62	1673.67
120000	10397.04	5386.32	3718.98	2887.49	2390.32	2060.32	1825.82
130000	11263.47	5835.18	4028.90	3128.11	2589.52	2232.01	1977.97
140000	12129.89	6284.04	4338.81	3368.74	2788.71	2403.70	2130.13
150000	12996.31	6732.90	4648.73	3609.36	2987.90	2575.40	2282.28
175000	15162.36	7855.05	5423.52	4210.92	3485.89	3004.63	2662.66
200000	17328.41	8977.20	6198.31	4812.48	3983.87	3433.86	3043.04
225000	19494.46	10099.35	6973.09	5414.04	4481.86	3863.09	3423.42
250000	21660.51	11221.50	7747.88	6015.60	4979.84	4292.33	3803.80

Monthly Payments 7¼%

necessary to amortize a loan

AMOUNT	8 YEARS	9 YEARS	10 YEARS	11 YEARS	12 YEARS	13 YEARS	14 YEARS
100	1.38	1.26	1.17	1.10	1.04	0.99	0.95
200	2.75	2.53	2.35	2.20	2.08	1.98	1.90
500	6.88	6.32	5.87	5.51	5.21	4.96	4.75
1000	13.76	12.63	11.74	11.02	10.42	9.92	9.49
2000	27.52	25.27	23.48	22.03	20.84	19.83	18.98
5000	68.79	63.17	58.70	55.08	52.09	49.58	47.46
6000	82.55	75.80	70.44	66.09	62.51	59.50	56.95
7000	96.31	88.43	82.18	77.11	72.92	69.42	66.45
8000	110.07	101.07	93.92	88.12	83.34	79.33	75.94
9000	123.83	113.70	105.66	99.14	93.76	89.25	85.43
10000	137.58	126.33	117.40	110.16	104.18	99.17	94.92
15000	206.38	189.50	176.10	165.23	156.26	148.75	142.38
20000	275.17	252.67	234.80	220.31	208.35	198.33	189.84
25000	343.96	315.83	293.50	275.39	260.44	247.92	237.30
30000	412.75	379.00	352.20	330.47	312.53	297.50	284.77
35000	481.55	442.16	410.90	385.55	364.61	347.08	332.23
36000	495.30	454.80	422.64	396.56	375.03	357.00	341.72
37000	509.06	467.43	434.38	407.58	385.45	366.92	351.21
38000	522.82	480.06	446.12	418.59	395.87	376.84	360.70
39000	536.58	492.70	457.86	429.61	406.28	386.75	370.19
40000	550.34	505.33	469.60	440.62	416.70	396.67	379.69
41000	564.10	517.96	481.34	451.64	427.12	406.59	389.18
42000	577.86	530.60	493.08	462.66	437.54	416.50	398.67
43000	591.61	543.23	504.82	473.67	447.95	426.42	408.16
44000	605.37	555.86	516.56	484.69	458.37	436.34	417.66
45000	619.13	568.50	528.30	495.70	468.79	446.25	427.15
46000	632.89	581.13	540.04	506.72	479.21	456.17	436.64
47000	646.65	593.76	551.78	517.73	489.63	466.09	446.13
48000	660.41	606.40	563.52	528.75	500.04	476.00	455.62
49000	674.16	619.03	575.27	539.76	510.46	485.92	465.12
50000	687.92	631.66	587.01	550.78	520.88	495.84	474.61
51000	701.68	644.30	598.75	561.80	531.30	505.75	484.10
52000	715.44	656.93	610.49	572.81	541.71	515.67	493.59
53000	729.20	669.56	622.23	583.83	552.13	525.59	503.09
54000	742.96	682.20	633.97	594.84	562.55	535.50	512.58
55000	756.72	694.83	645.71	605.86	572.97	545.42	522.07
56000	770.47	707.46	657.45	616.87	583.38	555.34	531.56
57000	784.23	720.10	669.19	627.89	593.80	565.25	541.05
58000	797.99	732.73	680.93	638.91	604.22	575.17	550.55
59000	811.75	745.36	692.67	649.92	614.64	585.09	560.04
60000	825.51	758.00	704.41	660.94	625.05	595.00	569.53
65000	894.30	821.16	763.11	716.01	677.14	644.59	616.99
70000	963.09	884.33	821.81	771.09	729.23	694.17	664.45
75000	1031.88	947.50	880.51	826.17	781.32	743.75	711.91
80000	1100.68	1010.66	939.21	881.25	833.40	793.34	759.37
85000	1169.47	1073.83	997.91	936.33	885.49	842.92	806.83
90000	1238.26	1136.99	1056.61	991.40	937.58	892.50	854.30
95000	1307.05	1200.16	1115.31	1046.48	989.67	942.09	901.76
100000	1375.85	1263.33	1174.01	1101.56	1041.76	991.67	949.22
105000	1444.64	1326.49	1232.71	1156.64	1093.84	1041.25	996.68
110000	1513.43	1389.66	1291.41	1211.72	1145.93	1090.84	1044.14
120000	1651.02	1515.99	1408.81	1321.87	1250.11	1190.01	1139.06
130000	1788.60	1642.33	1526.21	1432.03	1354.28	1289.17	1233.98
140000	1926.18	1768.66	1643.61	1542.19	1458.46	1388.34	1328.90
150000	2063.77	1894.99	1761.02	1652.34	1562.63	1487.51	1423.83
175000	2407.73	2210.82	2054.52	1927.73	1823.07	1735.42	1661.13
200000	2751.69	2526.66	2348.02	2203.12	2083.51	1983.34	1898.44
225000	3095.65	2842.49	2641.52	2478.51	2343.95	2231.26	2135.74
250000	3439.62	3158.32	2935.03	2753.90	2604.39	2479.18	2373.04

7¼% Monthly Payments

necessary to amortize a loan

AMOUNT	15 YEARS	16 YEARS	17 YEARS	18 YEARS	19 YEARS	20 YEARS	21 YEARS
100	0.91	0.88	0.85	0.83	0.81	0.79	0.77
200	1.83	1.76	1.71	1.66	1.62	1.58	1.55
500	4.56	4.41	4.27	4.15	4.05	3.95	3.87
1000	9.13	8.81	8.54	8.30	8.09	7.90	7.74
2000	18.26	17.63	17.08	16.60	16.18	15.81	15.47
5000	45.64	44.07	42.71	41.51	40.45	39.52	38.69
6000	54.77	52.89	51.25	49.81	48.54	47.42	46.42
7000	63.90	61.70	59.79	58.11	56.63	55.33	54.16
8000	73.03	70.52	68.33	66.41	64.73	63.23	61.90
9000	82.16	79.33	76.87	74.72	72.82	71.13	69.64
10000	91.29	88.15	85.41	83.02	80.91	79.04	77.37
15000	136.93	132.22	128.12	124.53	121.36	118.56	116.06
20000	182.57	176.29	170.82	166.03	161.81	158.08	154.75
25000	228.22	220.36	213.53	207.54	202.27	197.59	193.44
30000	273.86	264.44	256.24	249.05	242.72	237.11	232.12
35000	319.50	308.51	298.94	290.56	283.17	276.63	270.81
36000	328.63	317.32	307.48	298.86	291.26	284.54	278.55
37000	337.76	326.14	316.03	307.16	299.36	292.44	286.29
38000	346.89	334.95	324.57	315.47	307.45	300.34	294.02
39000	356.02	343.77	333.11	323.77	315.54	308.25	301.76
40000	365.15	352.58	341.65	332.07	323.63	316.15	309.50
41000	374.27	361.40	350.19	340.37	331.72	324.05	317.24
42000	383.40	370.21	358.73	348.67	339.81	331.96	324.97
43000	392.53	379.03	367.27	356.97	347.90	339.86	332.71
44000	401.66	387.84	375.81	365.28	355.99	347.77	340.45
45000	410.79	396.66	384.35	373.58	364.08	355.67	348.19
46000	419.92	405.47	392.90	381.88	372.17	363.57	355.92
47000	429.05	414.29	401.44	390.18	380.26	371.48	363.66
48000	438.17	423.10	409.98	398.48	388.35	379.38	371.40
49000	447.30	431.91	418.52	406.78	396.44	387.28	379.14
50000	456.43	440.73	427.06	415.09	404.53	395.19	386.87
51000	465.56	449.54	435.60	423.39	412.62	403.09	394.61
52000	474.69	458.36	444.14	431.69	420.72	411.00	402.35
53000	483.82	467.17	452.68	439.99	428.81	418.90	410.09
54000	492.95	475.99	461.23	448.29	436.90	426.80	417.82
55000	502.07	484.80	469.77	456.59	444.99	434.71	425.56
56000	511.20	493.62	478.31	464.90	453.08	442.61	433.30
57000	520.33	502.43	486.85	473.20	461.17	450.51	441.04
58000	529.46	511.25	495.39	481.50	469.26	458.42	448.77
59000	538.59	520.06	503.93	489.80	477.35	466.32	456.51
60000	547.72	528.87	512.47	498.10	485.44	474.23	464.25
65000	593.36	572.95	555.18	539.61	525.89	513.74	502.94
70000	639.00	617.02	597.89	581.12	566.35	553.26	541.62
75000	684.65	661.09	640.59	622.63	606.80	592.78	580.31
80000	730.29	705.17	683.30	664.14	647.25	632.30	619.00
85000	775.93	749.24	726.00	705.65	687.71	671.82	657.68
90000	821.58	793.31	768.71	747.15	728.16	711.34	696.37
95000	867.22	837.38	811.42	788.66	768.61	750.86	735.06
100000	912.86	881.46	854.12	830.17	809.07	790.38	773.75
105000	958.51	925.53	896.83	871.68	849.52	829.89	812.43
110000	1004.15	969.60	939.53	913.19	889.97	869.41	851.12
120000	1095.44	1057.75	1024.95	996.21	970.88	948.45	928.50
130000	1186.72	1145.89	1110.36	1079.22	1051.79	1027.49	1005.87
140000	1278.01	1234.04	1195.77	1162.24	1132.69	1106.53	1083.25
150000	1369.29	1322.19	1281.18	1245.26	1213.60	1185.56	1160.62
175000	1597.51	1542.55	1494.71	1452.80	1415.87	1383.16	1354.06
200000	1825.73	1762.92	1708.24	1660.34	1618.14	1580.75	1547.49
225000	2053.94	1983.28	1921.77	1867.89	1820.40	1778.35	1740.93
250000	2282.16	2203.64	2135.31	2075.43	2022.67	1975.94	1934.37

Monthly Payments 7¼%

necessary to amortize a loan

AMOUNT	22 YEARS	23 YEARS	24 YEARS	25 YEARS	30 YEARS	35 YEARS	40 YEARS
100	0.76	0.75	0.73	0.72	0.68	0.66	0.64
200	1.52	1.49	1.47	1.45	1.36	1.31	1.28
500	3.79	3.73	3.67	3.61	3.41	3.28	3.20
1000	7.59	7.46	7.34	7.23	6.82	6.56	6.40
2000	15.18	14.91	14.67	14.46	13.64	13.13	12.79
5000	37.94	37.28	36.68	36.14	34.11	32.82	31.98
6000	45.53	44.73	44.02	43.37	40.93	39.39	38.38
7000	53.12	52.19	51.35	50.60	47.75	45.95	44.78
8000	60.71	59.65	58.69	57.82	54.57	52.52	51.17
9000	68.30	67.10	66.02	65.05	61.40	59.08	57.57
10000	75.89	74.56	73.36	72.28	68.22	65.65	63.97
15000	113.83	111.84	110.04	108.42	102.33	98.47	95.95
20000	151.78	149.12	146.72	144.56	136.44	131.29	127.93
25000	189.72	186.39	183.40	180.70	170.54	164.12	159.92
30000	227.67	223.67	220.08	216.84	204.65	196.94	191.90
35000	265.61	260.95	256.76	252.98	238.76	229.76	223.89
36000	273.20	268.41	264.10	260.21	245.58	236.33	230.28
37000	280.79	275.86	271.43	267.44	252.41	242.89	236.68
38000	288.38	283.32	278.77	274.67	259.23	249.46	243.08
39000	295.97	290.78	286.11	281.89	266.05	256.02	249.47
40000	303.56	298.23	293.44	289.12	272.87	262.59	255.87
41000	311.15	305.69	300.78	296.35	279.69	269.15	262.27
42000	318.74	313.14	308.11	303.58	286.51	275.72	268.66
43000	326.32	320.60	315.45	310.81	293.34	282.28	275.06
44000	333.91	328.05	322.79	318.04	300.16	288.85	281.46
45000	341.50	335.51	330.12	325.26	306.98	295.41	287.85
46000	349.09	342.97	337.46	332.49	313.80	301.97	294.25
47000	356.68	350.42	344.79	339.72	320.62	308.54	300.65
48000	364.27	357.88	352.13	346.95	327.44	315.10	307.04
49000	371.86	365.33	359.47	354.18	334.27	321.67	313.44
50000	379.45	372.79	366.80	361.40	341.09	328.23	319.84
51000	387.04	380.25	374.14	368.63	347.91	334.80	326.23
52000	394.62	387.70	381.47	375.86	354.73	341.36	332.63
53000	402.21	395.16	388.81	383.09	361.55	347.93	339.03
54000	409.80	402.61	396.15	390.32	368.38	354.49	345.42
55000	417.39	410.07	403.48	397.54	375.20	361.06	351.82
56000	424.98	417.52	410.82	404.77	382.02	367.62	358.22
57000	432.57	424.98	418.15	412.00	388.84	374.18	364.61
58000	440.16	432.44	425.49	419.23	395.66	380.75	371.01
59000	447.75	439.89	432.83	426.46	402.48	387.32	377.41
60000	455.34	447.35	440.16	433.68	409.31	393.88	383.80
65000	493.28	484.63	476.84	469.82	443.41	426.70	415.79
70000	531.23	521.91	513.52	505.96	477.52	459.53	447.77
75000	569.17	559.18	550.20	542.11	511.63	492.35	479.75
80000	607.11	596.46	586.88	578.25	545.74	525.17	511.74
85000	645.06	633.74	623.56	614.39	579.85	558.00	543.72
90000	683.00	671.02	660.24	650.53	613.96	590.82	575.70
95000	720.95	708.30	696.92	686.67	648.07	623.64	607.69
100000	758.89	745.58	733.61	722.81	682.18	656.47	639.67
105000	796.84	782.86	770.29	758.95	716.29	689.29	671.66
110000	834.78	820.14	806.97	795.09	750.39	722.11	703.64
120000	910.67	894.69	880.33	867.37	818.61	787.76	767.61
130000	986.56	969.25	953.69	939.65	886.83	853.41	831.57
140000	1062.45	1043.81	1027.05	1011.93	955.05	919.05	895.54
150000	1138.34	1118.37	1100.41	1084.21	1023.26	984.70	959.51
175000	1328.06	1304.76	1283.81	1264.91	1193.81	1148.82	1119.43
200000	1517.79	1491.16	1467.21	1445.61	1364.35	1312.93	1279.34
225000	1707.51	1677.55	1650.61	1626.32	1534.90	1477.05	1439.26
250000	1897.23	1863.95	1834.01	1807.02	1705.44	1641.17	1599.18

7½% Monthly Payments

necessary to amortize a loan

AMOUNT	1 YEAR	2 YEARS	3 YEARS	4 YEARS	5 YEARS	6 YEARS	7 YEARS
100	8.68	4.50	3.11	2.42	2.00	1.73	1.53
200	17.35	9.00	6.22	4.84	4.01	3.46	3.07
500	43.38	22.50	15.55	12.09	10.02	8.65	7.67
1000	86.76	45.00	31.11	24.18	20.04	17.29	15.34
2000	173.51	90.00	62.21	48.36	40.08	34.58	30.68
5000	433.79	225.00	155.53	120.89	100.19	86.45	76.69
6000	520.54	270.00	186.64	145.07	120.23	103.74	92.03
7000	607.30	315.00	217.74	169.25	140.27	121.03	107.37
8000	694.06	360.00	248.85	193.43	160.30	138.32	122.71
9000	780.82	405.00	279.96	217.61	180.34	155.61	138.04
10000	867.57	450.00	311.06	241.79	200.38	172.90	153.38
15000	1301.36	674.99	466.59	362.68	300.57	259.35	230.07
20000	1735.15	899.99	622.12	483.58	400.76	345.80	306.77
25000	2168.94	1124.99	777.66	604.47	500.95	432.25	383.46
30000	2602.72	1349.99	933.19	725.37	601.14	518.70	460.15
35000	3036.51	1574.99	1088.72	846.26	701.33	605.15	536.84
36000	3123.27	1619.99	1119.82	870.44	721.37	622.44	552.18
37000	3210.02	1664.98	1150.93	894.62	741.40	639.73	567.52
38000	3296.78	1709.98	1182.04	918.80	761.44	657.02	582.85
39000	3383.54	1754.98	1213.14	942.98	781.48	674.31	598.19
40000	3470.30	1799.98	1244.25	967.16	801.52	691.60	613.53
41000	3557.05	1844.98	1275.35	991.33	821.56	708.89	628.87
42000	3643.81	1889.98	1306.46	1015.51	841.59	726.18	644.21
43000	3730.57	1934.98	1337.57	1039.69	861.63	743.47	659.55
44000	3817.33	1979.98	1368.67	1063.87	881.67	760.76	674.88
45000	3904.08	2024.98	1399.78	1088.05	901.71	778.06	690.22
46000	3990.84	2069.98	1430.89	1112.23	921.75	795.35	705.56
47000	4077.60	2114.98	1461.99	1136.41	941.78	812.64	720.90
48000	4164.36	2159.98	1493.10	1160.59	961.82	829.93	736.24
49000	4251.11	2204.98	1524.20	1184.77	981.86	847.22	751.58
50000	4337.87	2249.98	1555.31	1208.95	1001.90	864.51	766.91
51000	4424.63	2294.98	1586.42	1233.12	1021.94	881.80	782.25
52000	4511.39	2339.98	1617.52	1257.30	1041.97	899.09	797.59
53000	4598.14	2384.98	1648.63	1281.48	1062.01	916.38	812.93
54000	4684.90	2429.98	1679.74	1305.66	1082.05	933.67	828.27
55000	4771.66	2474.98	1710.84	1329.84	1102.09	950.96	843.61
56000	4858.42	2519.98	1741.95	1354.02	1122.13	968.25	858.94
57000	4945.17	2564.98	1773.05	1378.20	1142.16	985.54	874.28
58000	5031.93	2609.98	1804.16	1402.38	1162.20	1002.83	889.62
59000	5118.69	2654.98	1835.27	1426.56	1182.24	1020.12	904.96
60000	5205.45	2699.98	1866.37	1450.73	1202.28	1037.41	920.30
65000	5639.23	2924.97	2021.90	1571.63	1302.47	1123.86	996.99
70000	6073.02	3149.97	2177.44	1692.52	1402.66	1210.31	1073.68
75000	6506.81	3374.97	2332.97	1813.42	1502.85	1296.76	1150.37
80000	6940.59	3599.97	2488.50	1934.31	1603.04	1383.21	1227.06
85000	7374.38	3824.97	2644.03	2055.21	1703.23	1469.66	1303.75
90000	7808.17	4049.96	2799.56	2176.10	1803.42	1556.11	1380.44
95000	8241.95	4274.96	2955.09	2297.00	1903.61	1642.56	1457.14
100000	8675.74	4499.96	3110.62	2417.89	2003.79	1729.01	1533.83
105000	9109.53	4724.96	3266.15	2538.78	2103.98	1815.46	1610.52
110000	9543.32	4949.96	3421.68	2659.68	2204.17	1901.91	1687.21
120000	10410.89	5399.95	3732.75	2901.47	2404.55	2074.81	1840.59
130000	11278.46	5849.95	4043.81	3143.26	2604.93	2247.71	1993.98
140000	12146.04	6299.94	4354.87	3385.05	2805.31	2420.62	2147.36
150000	13013.61	6749.94	4665.93	3626.84	3005.69	2593.52	2300.74
175000	15182.55	7874.93	5443.59	4231.31	3506.64	3025.77	2684.20
200000	17351.48	8999.92	6221.24	4835.78	4007.59	3458.02	3067.66
225000	19520.42	10124.91	6998.90	5440.25	4508.54	3890.28	3451.11
250000	21689.35	11249.90	7776.55	6044.73	5009.49	4322.53	3834.57

Monthly Payments

necessary to amortize a loan

7½%

AMOUNT	8 YEARS	9 YEARS	10 YEARS	11 YEARS	12 YEARS	13 YEARS	14 YEARS
100	1.39	1.28	1.19	1.11	1.06	1.01	0.96
200	2.78	2.55	2.37	2.23	2.11	2.01	1.93
500	6.94	6.38	5.94	5.57	5.28	5.03	4.82
1000	13.88	12.76	11.87	11.15	10.55	10.05	9.63
2000	27.77	25.52	23.74	22.30	21.10	20.11	19.26
5000	69.42	63.81	59.35	55.74	52.76	50.27	48.16
6000	83.30	76.57	71.22	66.89	63.31	60.32	57.79
7000	97.19	89.33	83.09	78.04	73.87	70.38	67.42
8000	111.07	102.09	94.96	89.18	84.42	80.43	77.05
9000	124.95	114.85	106.83	100.33	94.97	90.48	86.68
10000	138.84	127.61	118.70	111.48	105.52	100.54	96.31
15000	208.26	191.42	178.05	167.22	158.28	150.81	144.47
20000	277.68	255.22	237.40	222.96	211.05	201.07	192.63
25000	347.10	319.03	296.75	278.70	263.81	251.34	240.79
30000	416.52	382.83	356.11	334.44	316.57	301.61	288.94
35000	485.94	446.64	415.46	390.18	369.33	351.88	337.10
36000	499.82	459.40	427.33	401.33	379.88	361.93	346.73
37000	513.70	472.16	439.20	412.48	390.43	371.99	356.36
38000	527.59	484.92	451.07	423.62	400.99	382.04	365.99
39000	541.47	497.68	462.94	434.77	411.54	392.09	375.63
40000	555.35	510.44	474.81	445.92	422.09	402.15	385.26
41000	569.24	523.20	486.68	457.07	432.64	412.20	394.89
42000	583.12	535.96	498.55	468.22	443.20	422.26	404.52
43000	597.01	548.72	510.42	479.36	453.75	432.31	414.15
44000	610.89	561.48	522.29	490.51	464.30	442.36	423.78
45000	624.77	574.25	534.16	501.66	474.85	452.42	433.41
46000	638.66	587.01	546.03	512.81	485.40	462.47	443.05
47000	652.54	599.77	557.90	523.96	495.96	472.52	452.68
48000	666.43	612.53	569.77	535.10	506.51	482.58	462.31
49000	680.31	625.29	581.64	546.25	517.06	492.63	471.94
50000	694.19	638.05	593.51	557.40	527.61	502.69	481.57
51000	708.08	650.81	605.38	568.55	538.17	512.74	491.20
52000	721.96	663.57	617.25	579.70	548.72	522.79	500.83
53000	735.85	676.33	629.12	590.84	559.27	532.85	510.47
54000	749.73	689.09	640.99	601.99	569.82	542.90	520.10
55000	763.61	701.86	652.86	613.14	580.37	552.95	529.73
56000	777.50	714.62	664.73	624.29	590.93	563.01	539.36
57000	791.38	727.38	676.60	635.44	601.48	573.06	548.99
58000	805.26	740.14	688.47	646.58	612.03	583.11	558.62
59000	819.15	752.90	700.34	657.73	622.58	593.17	568.25
60000	833.03	765.66	712.21	668.88	633.14	603.22	577.89
65000	902.45	829.47	771.56	724.62	685.90	653.49	626.04
70000	971.87	893.27	830.91	780.36	738.66	703.76	674.20
75000	1041.29	957.08	890.26	836.10	791.42	754.03	722.36
80000	1110.71	1020.88	949.61	891.84	844.18	804.30	770.51
85000	1180.13	1084.69	1008.97	947.58	896.94	854.56	818.67
90000	1249.55	1148.49	1068.32	1003.32	949.70	904.83	866.83
95000	1318.97	1212.30	1127.67	1059.06	1002.46	955.10	914.99
100000	1388.39	1276.10	1187.02	1114.80	1055.23	1005.37	963.14
105000	1457.81	1339.91	1246.37	1170.54	1107.99	1055.64	1011.30
110000	1527.23	1403.71	1305.72	1226.28	1160.75	1105.91	1059.46
120000	1666.06	1531.32	1424.42	1337.76	1266.27	1206.44	1155.77
130000	1804.90	1658.93	1543.12	1449.24	1371.79	1306.98	1252.09
140000	1943.74	1786.54	1661.82	1560.72	1477.32	1407.52	1348.40
150000	2082.58	1914.15	1780.53	1672.20	1582.84	1508.06	1444.72
175000	2429.68	2233.18	2077.28	1950.90	1846.65	1759.40	1685.50
200000	2776.77	2552.20	2374.04	2229.60	2110.45	2010.74	1926.29
225000	3123.87	2871.23	2670.79	2508.30	2374.26	2262.08	2167.07
250000	3470.97	3190.25	2967.54	2787.00	2638.07	2513.43	2407.86

7½% Monthly Payments

necessary to amortize a loan

AMOUNT	15 YEARS	16 YEARS	17 YEARS	18 YEARS	19 YEARS	20 YEARS	21 YEARS
100	0.93	0.90	0.87	0.84	0.82	0.81	0.79
200	1.85	1.79	1.74	1.69	1.65	1.61	1.58
500	4.64	4.48	4.34	4.22	4.12	4.03	3.95
1000	9.27	8.96	8.69	8.45	8.24	8.06	7.89
2000	18.54	17.92	17.37	16.90	16.48	16.11	15.78
5000	46.35	44.79	43.44	42.25	41.20	40.28	39.46
6000	55.62	53.75	52.12	50.70	49.44	48.34	47.35
7000	64.89	62.71	60.81	59.15	57.69	56.39	55.24
8000	74.16	71.67	69.50	67.60	65.93	64.45	63.13
9000	83.43	80.62	78.18	76.05	74.17	72.50	71.02
10000	92.70	89.58	86.87	84.50	82.41	80.56	78.92
15000	139.05	134.37	130.31	126.75	123.61	120.84	118.37
20000	185.40	179.17	173.74	168.99	164.82	161.12	157.83
25000	231.75	223.96	217.18	211.24	206.02	201.40	197.29
30000	278.10	268.75	260.61	253.49	247.22	241.68	236.75
35000	324.45	313.54	304.05	295.74	288.43	281.96	276.21
36000	333.72	322.50	312.74	304.19	296.67	290.01	284.10
37000	342.99	331.46	321.42	312.64	304.91	298.07	291.99
38000	352.26	340.41	330.11	321.09	313.15	306.13	299.88
39000	361.53	349.37	338.80	329.54	321.39	314.18	307.77
40000	370.80	358.33	347.48	337.99	329.63	322.24	315.67
41000	380.08	367.29	356.17	346.44	337.87	330.29	323.56
42000	389.35	376.25	364.86	354.89	346.11	338.35	331.45
43000	398.62	385.21	373.55	363.34	354.35	346.41	339.34
44000	407.89	394.16	382.23	371.79	362.59	354.46	347.23
45000	417.16	403.12	390.92	380.24	370.84	362.52	355.12
46000	426.43	412.08	399.61	388.69	379.08	370.57	363.02
47000	435.70	421.04	408.29	397.14	387.32	378.63	370.91
48000	444.97	430.00	416.98	405.59	395.56	386.68	378.80
49000	454.24	438.96	425.67	414.04	403.80	394.74	386.69
50000	463.51	447.91	434.35	422.49	412.04	402.80	394.58
51000	472.78	456.87	443.04	430.94	420.28	410.85	402.47
52000	482.05	465.83	451.73	439.39	428.52	418.91	410.37
53000	491.32	474.79	460.42	447.84	436.76	426.96	418.26
54000	500.59	483.75	469.10	456.29	445.00	435.02	426.15
55000	509.86	492.71	477.79	464.74	453.24	443.08	434.04
56000	519.13	501.66	486.48	473.19	461.48	451.13	441.93
57000	528.40	510.62	495.16	481.63	469.72	459.19	449.82
58000	537.67	519.58	503.85	490.08	477.97	467.24	457.72
59000	546.94	528.54	512.54	498.53	486.21	475.30	465.61
60000	556.21	537.50	521.23	506.98	494.45	483.36	473.50
65000	602.56	582.29	564.66	549.23	535.65	523.64	512.96
70000	648.91	627.08	608.10	591.48	576.86	563.92	552.42
75000	695.26	671.87	651.53	633.73	618.06	604.19	591.87
80000	741.61	716.66	694.97	675.98	659.26	644.47	631.33
85000	787.96	761.45	738.40	718.23	700.47	684.75	670.79
90000	834.31	806.24	781.84	760.48	741.67	725.03	710.25
95000	880.66	851.04	825.27	802.72	782.87	765.31	749.71
100000	927.01	895.83	868.71	844.97	824.08	805.59	789.17
105000	973.36	940.62	912.14	887.22	865.28	845.87	828.62
110000	1019.71	985.41	955.58	929.47	906.49	886.15	868.08
120000	1112.41	1074.99	1042.45	1013.97	988.89	966.71	947.00
130000	1205.12	1164.58	1129.32	1098.47	1071.30	1047.27	1025.92
140000	1297.82	1254.16	1216.19	1182.96	1153.71	1127.83	1104.83
150000	1390.52	1343.74	1303.06	1267.46	1236.12	1208.39	1183.75
175000	1622.27	1567.70	1520.24	1478.70	1442.14	1409.79	1381.04
200000	1854.02	1791.66	1737.42	1689.95	1648.16	1611.19	1578.33
225000	2085.78	2015.61	1954.60	1901.19	1854.18	1812.58	1775.62
250000	2317.53	2239.57	2171.77	2112.43	2060.20	2013.98	1972.92

Monthly Payments 7½%

necessary to amortize a loan

AMOUNT	22 YEARS	23 YEARS	24 YEARS	25 YEARS	30 YEARS	35 YEARS	40 YEARS
100	0.77	0.76	0.75	0.74	0.70	0.67	0.66
200	1.55	1.52	1.50	1.48	1.40	1.35	1.32
500	3.87	3.81	3.75	3.69	3.50	3.37	3.29
1000	7.75	7.61	7.50	7.39	6.99	6.74	6.58
2000	15.49	15.23	14.99	14.78	13.98	13.48	13.16
5000	38.73	38.07	37.48	36.95	34.96	33.71	32.90
6000	46.47	45.68	44.98	44.34	41.95	40.45	39.48
7000	54.22	53.30	52.47	51.73	48.95	47.20	46.06
8000	61.96	60.91	59.97	59.12	55.94	53.94	52.65
9000	69.71	68.53	67.46	66.51	62.93	60.68	59.23
10000	77.45	76.14	74.96	73.90	69.92	67.42	65.81
15000	116.18	114.21	112.44	110.85	104.88	101.14	98.71
20000	154.90	152.28	149.92	147.80	139.84	134.85	131.61
25000	193.63	190.35	187.40	184.75	174.80	168.56	164.52
30000	232.35	228.42	224.88	221.70	209.76	202.27	197.42
35000	271.08	266.49	262.36	258.65	244.73	235.98	230.32
36000	278.82	274.10	269.86	266.04	251.72	242.73	236.91
37000	286.57	281.71	277.35	273.43	258.71	249.47	243.49
38000	294.31	289.33	284.85	280.82	265.70	.256.21	250.07
39000	302.06	296.94	292.35	288.21	272.69	262.95	256.65
40000	309.80	304.56	299.84	295.60	279.69	269.70	263.23
41000	317.55	312.17	307.34	302.99	286.68	276.44	269.81
42000	325.29	319.78	314.83	310.38	293.67	283.18	276.39
43000	333.04	327.40	322.33	317.77	300.66	289.92	282.97
44000	340.78	335.01	329.83	325.16	307.65	296.67	289.55
45000	348.53	342.63	337.32	332.55	314.65	303.41	296.13
46000	356.27	350.24	344.82	339.94	321.64	310.15	302.71
47000	364.02	357.85	352.31	347.33	328.63	316.89	309.29
48000	371.76	365.47	359.81	354.72	335.62	323.64	315.87
49000	379.51	373.08	367.31	362.11	342.62	330.38	322.45
50000	387.26	380.69	374.80	369.50	349.61	337.12	329.04
51000	395.00	388.31	382.30	376.89	356.60	343.86	335.62
52000	402.75	395.92	389.79	384.28	363.59	350.61	342.20
53000	410.49	403.54	397.29	391.67	370.58	357.35	348.78
54000	418.24	411.15	404.79	399.06	377.58	364.09	355.36
55000	425.98	418.76	412.28	406.45	384.57	370.83	361.94
56000	433.73	426.38	419.78	413.84	391.56	377.58	368.52
57000	441.47	433.99	427.27	421.22	398.56	384.32	375.10
58000	449.22	441.61	434.77	428.61	405.54	391.06	381.68
59000	456.96	449.22	442.27	436.00	412.61	397.80	388.26
60000	464.71	456.83	449.76	443.39	419.53	404.55	394.84
65000	503.43	494.90	487.24	480.34	454.49	438.26	427.75
70000	542.16	632.97	524.72	517.29	489.45	471.97	460.65
75000	580.88	571.04	562.20	554.24	524.41	505.68	493.55
80000	619.61	609.11	599.68	591.19	559.37	539.39	526.46
85000	658.33	647.18	637.16	628.14	594.33	573.11	559.36
90000	697.06	685.25	674.64	665.09	629.29	606.82	592.26
95000	735.78	723.32	712.12	702.04	664.25	640.53	625.17
100000	774.51	761.39	749.60	738.99	699.21	674.24	658.07
105000	813.24	799.46	787.09	775.94	734.18	707.95	690.97
110000	851.96	837.53	824.57	812.89	769.14	741.67	723.88
120000	929.41	913.67	899.53	886.79	839.06	809.09	789.68
130000	1006.86	989.81	974.49	960.69	908.98	876.52	855.49
140000	1084.31	1065.94	1049.45	1034.59	978.90	943.94	921.30
150000	1161.77	1142.08	1124.41	1108.49	1048.82	1011.36	987.11
175000	1355.39	1332.43	1311.81	1293.23	1223.63	1179.92	1151.62
200000	1549.02	1522.78	1499.21	1477.98	1398.43	1348.49	1316.14
225000	1742.65	1713.13	1686.61	1662.73	1573.23	1517.05	1480.66
250000	1936.28	1903.47	1874.01	1847.48	1748.04	1685.61	1645.18

7¾% Monthly Payments

necessary to amortize a loan

AMOUNT	1 YEAR	2 YEARS	3 YEARS	4 YEARS	5 YEARS	6 YEARS	7 YEARS
100	8.69	4.51	3.12	2.43	2.02	1.74	1.55
200	17.37	9.02	6.24	4.86	4.03	3.48	3.09
500	43.44	22.56	15.61	12.15	10.08	8.71	7.73
1000	86.87	45.11	31.22	24.30	20.16	17.41	15.46
2000	173.75	90.23	62.44	48.59	40.31	34.82	30.92
5000	434.36	225.57	156.11	121.48	100.78	87.06	77.31
6000	521.24	270.68	187.33	145.77	120.94	104.47	92.77
7000	608.11	315.79	218.55	170.07	141.10	121.88	108.23
8000	694.98	360.91	249.77	194.37	161.26	139.29	123.70
9000	781.86	406.02	280.99	218.66	181.41	156.70	139.16
10000	868.73	451.13	312.21	242.96	201.57	174.11	154.62
15000	1303.09	676.70	468.32	364.44	302.35	261.17	231.93
20000	1737.46	902.27	624.42	485.91	403.14	348.23	309.24
25000	2171.82	1127.83	780.53	607.39	503.92	435.29	386.55
30000	2606.19	1353.40	936.63	728.87	604.71	522.34	463.86
35000	3040.55	1578.97	1092.74	850.35	705.49	609.40	541.17
36000	3127.42	1624.08	1123.96	874.65	725.65	626.81	556.63
37000	3214.30	1669.19	1155.18	898.94	745.81	644.22	572.09
38000	3301.17	1714.31	1186.40	923.24	765.96	661.63	587.55
39000	3388.04	1759.42	1217.63	947.53	786.12	679.05	603.02
40000	3474.92	1804.53	1248.85	971.83	806.28	696.46	618.48
41000	3561.79	1849.65	1280.07	996.13	826.44	713.87	633.94
42000	3648.66	1894.76	1311.29	1020.42	846.59	731.28	649.40
43000	3735.53	1939.87	1342.51	1044.72	866.75	748.69	664.86
44000	3822.41	1984.99	1373.73	1069.01	886.91	766.10	680.33
45000	3909.28	2030.10	1404.95	1093.31	907.06	783.51	695.79
46000	3996.15	2075.21	1436.17	1117.60	927.22	800.93	711.25
47000	4083.03	2120.33	1467.39	1141.90	947.38	818.34	726.71
48000	4169.90	2165.44	1498.62	1166.20	967.53	835.75	742.17
49000	4256.77	2210.55	1529.84	1190.49	987.69	853.16	757.64
50000	4343.64	2255.67	1561.06	1214.79	1007.85	870.57	773.10
51000	4430.52	2300.78	1592.28	1239.08	1028.00	887.98	788.56
52000	4517.39	2345.89	1623.50	1263.38	1048.16	905.39	804.02
53000	4604.26	2391.01	1654.72	1287.67	1068.32	922.81	819.48
54000	4691.14	2436.12	1685.94	1311.97	1088.48	940.22	834.95
55000	4778.01	2481.23	1717.16	1336.27	1108.63	957.63	850.41
56000	4864.88	2526.35	1748.39	1360.56	1128.79	975.04	865.87
57000	4951.75	2571.46	1779.61	1384.86	1148.95	992.45	881.33
58000	5038.63	2616.57	1810.83	1409.15	1169.10	1009.86	896.79
59000	5125.50	2661.69	1842.05	1433.45	1189.26	1027.27	912.26
60000	5212.37	2706.80	1873.27	1457.74	1209.42	1044.69	927.72
65000	5646.74	2932.37	2029.38	1579.22	1310.20	1131.74	1005.03
70000	6081.10	3157.93	2185.48	1700.70	1410.99	1218.80	1082.34
75000	6515.47	3383.50	2341.59	1822.18	1511.77	1305.86	1159.65
80000	6949.83	3609.07	2497.69	1943.66	1612.56	1392.91	1236.96
85000	7384.19	3834.64	2653.80	2065.14	1713.34	1479.97	1314.27
90000	7818.56	4060.20	2809.90	2186.62	1814.13	1567.03	1391.58
95000	8252.92	4285.77	2966.01	2308.10	1914.91	1654.09	1468.89
100000	8687.29	4511.34	3122.12	2429.57	2015.70	1741.14	1546.20
105000	9121.65	4736.90	3278.22	2551.05	2116.48	1828.20	1623.51
110000	9556.02	4962.47	3434.33	2672.53	2217.27	1915.26	1700.81
120000	10424.75	5413.60	3746.54	2915.49	2418.84	2089.37	1855.43
130000	11293.47	5864.74	4058.75	3158.45	2620.40	2263.49	2010.05
140000	12162.20	6315.87	4370.96	3401.40	2821.97	2437.60	2164.67
150000	13030.93	6767.00	4683.17	3644.36	3023.54	2611.71	2319.29
175000	15202.75	7894.84	5463.70	4251.75	3527.47	3047.00	2705.84
200000	17374.58	9022.67	6244.23	4859.15	4031.39	3482.28	3092.39
225000	19546.40	10150.51	7024.76	5466.54	4535.32	3917.57	3478.94
250000	21718.22	11278.34	7805.29	6073.94	5039.24	4352.86	3865.49

Monthly Payments 7¾%

necessary to amortize a loan

AMOUNT	8 YEARS	9 YEARS	10 YEARS	11 YEARS	12 YEARS	13 YEARS	14 YEARS
100	1.40	1.29	1.20	1.13	1.07	1.02	0.98
200	2.80	2.58	2.40	2.26	2.14	2.04	1.95
500	7.00	6.44	6.00	5.64	5.34	5.10	4.89
1000	14.01	12.89	12.00	11.28	10.69	10.19	9.77
2000	28.02	25.78	24.00	22.56	21.38	20.38	19.54
5000	70.05	64.45	60.01	56.41	53.44	50.96	48.86
6000	84.06	77.34	72.01	67.69	64.13	61.15	58.63
7000	98.07	90.23	84.01	78.97	74.82	71.34	68.40
8000	112.08	103.12	96.01	90.25	85.50	81.53	78.17
9000	126.09	116.01	108.01	101.53	96.19	91.73	87.95
10000	140.10	128.89	120.01	112.81	106.88	101.92	97.72
15000	210.15	193.34	180.02	169.22	160.32	152.88	146.58
20000	280.20	257.79	240.02	225.63	213.76	203.83	195.44
25000	350.25	322.24	300.03	282.03	267.20	254.79	244.29
30000	420.30	386.68	360.03	338.44	320.64	305.75	293.15
35000	490.35	451.13	420.04	394.85	374.08	356.71	342.01
36000	504.36	464.02	432.04	406.13	384.77	366.90	351.78
37000	518.37	476.91	444.04	417.41	395.45	377.09	361.56
38000	532.38	489.80	456.04	428.69	406.14	387.29	371.33
39000	546.39	502.69	468.04	439.97	416.83	397.48	381.10
40000	560.40	515.58	480.04	451.25	427.52	407.67	390.87
41000	574.41	528.47	492.04	462.53	438.20	417.86	400.64
42000	588.42	541.36	504.04	473.81	448.89	428.05	410.41
43000	602.43	554.25	516.05	485.10	459.58	438.24	420.19
44000	616.44	567.14	528.05	496.38	470.27	448.44	429.96
45000	630.45	580.03	540.05	507.66	480.96	458.63	439.73
46000	644.46	592.92	552.05	518.94	491.64	468.82	449.50
47000	658.47	605.81	564.05	530.22	502.33	479.01	459.27
48000	672.48	618.70	576.05	541.50	513.02	489.20	469.05
49000	686.49	631.59	588.05	552.78	523.71	499.39	478.82
50000	700.50	644.47	600.05	564.06	534.40	509.59	488.59
51000	714.51	657.36	612.05	575.35	545.08	519.78	498.36
52000	728.52	670.25	624.06	586.63	555.77	529.97	508.13
53000	742.53	683.14	636.06	597.91	566.46	540.16	517.90
54000	756.54	696.03	648.06	609.19	577.15	550.35	527.68
55000	770.55	708.92	660.06	620.47	587.84	560.54	537.45
56000	784.56	721.81	672.06	631.75	598.52	570.74	547.22
57000	798.57	734.70	684.06	643.03	609.21	580.93	556.99
58000	812.58	747.59	696.06	654.31	619.90	591.12	566.76
59000	820.59	760.48	708.06	665.60	630.59	601.31	576.53
60000	840.60	773.37	720.06	676.88	641.28	611.50	586.31
65000	910.65	837.82	780.07	733.28	694.71	662.46	635.17
70000	980.70	902.26	840.07	789.69	748.15	713.42	684.02
75000	1050.75	966.71	900.08	846.10	801.50	764.00	[illegible]
80000	1120.80	1031.16	960.09	902.50	855.03	815.34	781.74
85000	1190.85	1095.61	1020.09	958.91	908.47	866.30	830.60
90000	1260.89	1160.05	1080.10	1015.32	961.91	917.25	879.46
95000	1330.94	1224.50	1140.10	1071.72	1015.35	968.21	928.32
100000	1400.99	1288.95	1200.11	1128.13	1068.79	1019.17	977.18
105000	1471.04	1353.40	1260.11	1184.54	1122.23	1070.13	1026.04
110000	1541.09	1417.84	1320.12	1240.94	1175.67	1121.09	1074.89
120000	1681.19	1546.74	1440.13	1353.75	1282.55	1223.01	1172.61
130000	1821.29	1675.63	1560.14	1466.57	1389.43	1324.92	1270.33
140000	1961.39	1804.53	1680.15	1579.38	1496.31	1426.84	1368.05
150000	2101.49	1933.42	1800.16	1692.19	1603.19	1528.76	1465.77
175000	2451.74	2255.66	2100.19	1974.23	1870.39	1783.55	1710.06
200000	2801.99	2577.90	2400.21	2256.26	2137.58	2038.34	1954.35
225000	3152.24	2900.14	2700.24	2538.29	2404.78	2293.14	2198.65
250000	3502.49	3222.37	3000.27	2820.32	2671.98	2547.93	2442.94

7¾%

Monthly Payments

necessary to amortize a loan

AMOUNT	15 YEARS	16 YEARS	17 YEARS	18 YEARS	19 YEARS	20 YEARS	21 YEARS
100	0.94	0.91	0.88	0.86	0.84	0.82	0.80
200	1.88	1.82	1.77	1.72	1.68	1.64	1.61
500	4.71	4.55	4.42	4.30	4.20	4.10	4.02
1000	9.41	9.10	8.83	8.60	8.39	8.21	8.05
2000	18.83	18.21	17.67	17.20	16.78	16.42	16.09
5000	47.06	45.52	44.17	43.00	41.96	41.05	40.24
6000	56.48	54.62	53.01	51.59	50.35	49.26	48.28
7000	65.89	63.72	61.84	60.19	58.75	57.47	56.33
8000	75.30	72.83	70.67	68.79	67.14	65.68	64.38
9000	84.71	81.93	79.51	77.39	75.53	73.89	72.43
10000	94.13	91.03	88.34	85.99	83.92	82.09	80.47
15000	141.19	136.55	132.51	128.99	125.88	123.14	120.71
20000	188.26	182.06	176.68	171.98	167.84	164.19	160.95
25000	235.32	227.58	220.86	214.98	209.81	205.24	201.18
30000	282.38	273.10	265.03	257.97	251.77	246.28	241.42
35000	329.45	318.61	309.20	300.97	293.73	287.33	281.65
36000	338.86	327.71	318.03	309.57	302.12	295.54	289.70
37000	348.27	336.82	326.87	318.16	310.51	303.75	297.75
38000	357.68	345.92	335.70	326.76	318.91	311.96	305.80
39000	367.10	355.02	344.53	335.36	327.30	320.17	313.84
40000	376.51	364.13	353.37	343.96	335.69	328.38	321.89
41000	385.92	373.23	362.20	352.56	344.08	336.59	329.94
42000	395.34	382.33	371.04	361.16	352.47	344.80	337.99
43000	404.75	391.44	379.87	369.76	360.87	353.01	346.03
44000	414.16	400.54	388.71	378.36	369.26	361.22	354.08
45000	423.57	409.64	397.54	386.96	377.65	369.43	362.13
46000	432.99	418.75	406.37	395.56	386.04	377.64	370.17
47000	442.40	427.85	415.21	404.15	394.44	385.85	378.22
48000	451.81	436.95	424.04	412.75	402.83	394.06	386.27
49000	461.23	446.06	432.88	421.35	411.22	402.26	394.32
50000	470.64	455.16	441.71	429.95	419.61	410.47	402.36
51000	480.05	464.26	450.54	438.55	428.00	418.68	410.41
52000	489.46	473.36	459.38	447.15	436.40	426.89	418.46
53000	498.88	482.47	468.21	455.75	444.79	435.10	426.51
54000	508.29	491.57	477.05	464.35	453.18	443.31	434.55
55000	517.70	500.67	485.88	472.95	461.57	451.52	442.60
56000	527.11	509.78	494.72	481.55	469.97	459.73	450.65
57000	536.53	518.88	503.55	490.15	478.36	467.94	458.69
58000	545.94	527.98	512.38	498.74	486.75	476.15	466.74
59000	555.35	537.09	521.22	507.34	495.14	484.36	474.79
60000	564.77	546.19	530.05	515.94	503.53	492.57	482.84
65000	611.83	591.71	574.22	558.94	545.50	533.62	523.07
70000	658.89	637.22	618.40	601.93	587.46	574.66	563.31
75000	705.96	682.74	662.57	644.93	629.42	615.71	603.55
80000	753.02	728.25	706.74	687.92	671.38	656.76	643.78
85000	800.08	773.77	750.91	730.92	713.34	697.81	684.02
90000	847.15	819.29	795.08	773.91	755.30	738.85	724.25
95000	894.21	864.80	839.25	816.91	797.26	779.90	764.49
100000	941.28	910.32	883.42	859.90	839.22	820.95	804.73
105000	988.34	955.83	927.59	902.90	881.19	862.00	844.96
110000	1035.40	1001.35	971.76	945.89	923.15	903.04	885.20
120000	1129.53	1092.38	1060.11	1031.88	1007.07	985.14	965.67
130000	1223.66	1183.41	1148.45	1117.88	1090.99	1067.23	1046.15
140000	1317.79	1274.44	1236.79	1203.87	1174.91	1149.33	1126.62
150000	1411.91	1365.48	1325.13	1289.86	1258.84	1231.42	1207.09
175000	1647.23	1593.06	1545.99	1504.83	1468.64	1436.66	1408.27
200000	1882.55	1820.63	1766.84	1719.81	1678.45	1641.90	1609.45
225000	2117.87	2048.21	1987.70	1934.78	1888.25	1847.13	1810.64
250000	2353.19	2275.79	2208.55	2149.76	2098.06	2052.37	2011.82

Monthly Payments 7¾%

necessary to amortize a loan

AMOUNT	22 YEARS	23 YEARS	24 YEARS	25 YEARS	30 YEARS	35 YEARS	40 YEARS
100	0.79	0.78	0.77	0.76	0.72	0.69	0.68
200	1.58	1.55	1.53	1.51	1.43	1.38	1.35
500	3.95	3.89	3.83	3.78	3.58	3.46	3.38
1000	7.90	7.77	7.66	7.55	7.16	6.92	6.77
2000	15.81	15.55	15.32	15.11	14.33	13.84	13.53
5000	39.51	38.87	38.29	37.77	35.82	34.61	33.83
6000	47.42	46.64	45.95	45.32	42.98	41.53	40.60
7000	55.32	54.41	53.60	52.87	50.15	48.45	47.36
8000	63.22	62.19	61.26	60.43	57.31	55.37	54.13
9000	71.12	69.96	68.92	67.98	64.48	62.30	60.90
10000	79.03	77.73	76.58	75.53	71.64	69.22	67.66
15000	118.54	116.60	114.86	113.30	107.46	103.83	101.49
20000	158.05	155.47	153.15	151.07	143.28	138.44	135.32
25000	197.57	194.34	191.44	188.83	179.10	173.04	169.15
30000	237.08	233.20	229.73	226.60	214.92	207.65	202.99
35000	276.60	272.07	268.01	264.37	250.74	242.26	236.82
36000	284.50	279.85	275.67	271.92	257.91	249.18	243.58
37000	292.40	287.62	283.33	279.47	265.07	256.11	250.35
38000	300.30	295.39	290.99	287.02	272.24	263.03	257.12
39000	308.21	303.17	298.64	294.58	279.40	269.95	263.88
40000	316.11	310.94	306.30	302.13	286.56	276.87	270.65
41000	324.01	318.71	313.96	309.68	293.73	283.79	277.41
42000	331.91	326.49	321.62	317.24	300.89	290.71	284.18
43000	339.82	334.26	329.27	324.79	308.06	297.64	290.95
44000	347.72	342.03	336.93	332.34	315.22	304.56	297.71
45000	355.62	349.81	344.59	339.90	322.39	311.48	304.48
46000	363.53	357.58	352.25	347.45	329.55	318.40	311.25
47000	371.43	365.35	359.91	355.00	336.71	325.32	318.01
48000	379.33	373.13	367.56	362.56	343.88	332.24	324.78
49000	387.23	380.90	375.22	370.11	351.04	339.17	331.54
50000	395.14	388.67	382.88	377.66	358.21	346.09	338.31
51000	403.04	396.45	390.54	385.22	365.37	353.01	345.08
52000	410.94	404.22	398.19	392.77	372.53	359.93	351.84
53000	418.84	411.99	405.85	400.32	379.70	366.85	358.61
54000	426.75	419.77	413.51	407.88	386.86	373.78	365.37
55000	434.65	427.54	421.17	415.43	394.03	380.70	372.14
56000	442.55	435.31	428.82	422.98	401.19	387.62	378.91
57000	450.46	443.09	436.48	430.54	408.35	394.54	385.67
58000	458.36	450.86	444.14	438.09	415.52	401.46	392.44
59000	466.26	458.64	451.80	445.64	422.68	408.30	399.21
60000	474.16	466.41	459.45	453.20	429.85	415.31	405.97
65000	513.68	505.28	497.74	490.96	465.67	449.91	439.80
70000	553.19	544.14	536.03	528.73	501.49	484.52	473.63
75000	592.70	583.01	574.32	566.50	537.31	519.13	507.46
80000	632.22	621.88	612.60	604.26	573.13	553.74	541.30
85000	671.73	660.75	650.89	642.03	608.95	588.35	575.13
90000	711.25	699.61	689.18	679.80	644.77	622.96	608.96
95000	750.76	738.48	727.47	717.56	680.59	657.57	642.79
100000	790.27	777.35	765.76	755.33	716.41	692.18	676.62
105000	829.79	816.22	804.04	793.10	752.23	726.78	710.45
110000	869.30	855.08	842.33	830.86	788.05	761.39	744.28
120000	948.33	932.82	918.91	906.39	859.69	830.61	811.94
130000	1027.35	1010.55	995.48	981.93	931.34	899.83	879.61
140000	1106.38	1088.29	1072.06	1057.46	1002.98	969.05	947.27
150000	1185.41	1166.02	1148.63	1132.99	1074.62	1038.26	1014.93
175000	1382.98	1360.36	1340.07	1321.83	1253.72	1211.31	1184.08
200000	1580.55	1554.70	1531.51	1510.66	1432.82	1384.35	1353.24
225000	1778.11	1749.03	1722.95	1699.49	1611.93	1557.40	1522.39
250000	1975.68	1943.37	1914.39	1888.32	1791.03	1730.44	1691.55

8% Monthly Payments

necessary to amortize a loan

AMOUNT	1 YEAR	2 YEARS	3 YEARS	4 YEARS	5 YEARS	6 YEARS	7 YEARS
100	8.70	4.52	3.13	2.44	2.03	1.75	1.56
200	17.40	9.05	6.27	4.88	4.06	3.51	3.12
500	43.49	22.61	15.67	12.21	10.14	8.77	7.79
1000	86.99	45.23	31.34	24.41	20.28	17.53	15.59
2000	173.98	90.45	62.67	48.83	40.55	35.07	31.17
5000	434.94	226.14	156.68	122.06	101.38	87.67	77.93
6000	521.93	271.36	188.02	146.48	121.66	105.20	93.52
7000	608.92	316.59	219.35	170.89	141.93	122.73	109.10
8000	695.91	361.82	250.69	195.30	162.21	140.27	124.69
9000	782.90	407.05	282.03	219.72	182.49	157.80	140.28
10000	869.88	452.27	313.36	244.13	202.76	175.33	155.86
15000	1304.83	678.41	470.05	366.19	304.15	263.00	233.79
20000	1739.77	904.55	626.73	488.26	405.53	350.66	311.72
25000	2174.71	1130.68	783.41	610.32	506.91	438.33	389.66
30000	2609.65	1356.82	940.09	732.39	608.29	526.00	467.59
35000	3044.60	1582.96	1096.77	854.45	709.67	613.66	545.52
36000	3131.58	1628.18	1128.11	878.87	729.95	631.20	561.10
37000	3218.57	1673.41	1159.45	903.28	750.23	648.73	576.69
38000	3305.56	1718.64	1190.78	927.69	770.50	666.26	592.28
39000	3392.55	1763.86	1222.12	952.10	790.78	683.80	607.86
40000	3479.54	1809.09	1253.45	976.52	811.06	701.33	623.45
41000	3566.53	1854.32	1284.79	1000.93	831.33	718.86	639.03
42000	3653.51	1899.55	1316.13	1025.34	851.61	736.40	654.62
43000	3740.50	1944.77	1347.46	1049.76	871.88	753.93	670.21
44000	3827.49	1990.00	1378.80	1074.17	892.16	771.46	685.79
45000	3914.48	2035.23	1410.14	1098.58	912.44	789.00	701.38
46000	4001.47	2080.46	1441.47	1122.99	932.71	806.53	716.97
47000	4088.46	2125.68	1472.81	1147.41	952.99	824.06	732.55
48000	4175.44	2170.91	1504.15	1171.82	973.27	841.60	748.14
49000	4262.43	2216.14	1535.48	1196.23	993.54	859.13	763.72
50000	4349.42	2261.36	1566.82	1220.65	1013.82	876.66	779.31
51000	4436.41	2306.59	1598.15	1245.06	1034.10	894.20	794.90
52000	4523.40	2351.82	1629.49	1269.47	1054.37	911.73	810.48
53000	4610.39	2397.05	1660.83	1293.88	1074.65	929.26	826.07
54000	4697.38	2442.27	1692.16	1318.30	1094.93	946.79	841.66
55000	4784.36	2487.50	1723.50	1342.71	1115.20	964.33	857.24
56000	4871.35	2532.73	1754.84	1367.12	1135.48	981.86	872.83
57000	4958.34	2577.96	1786.17	1391.54	1155.75	999.39	888.41
58000	5045.33	2623.18	1817.51	1415.95	1176.03	1016.93	904.00
59000	5132.32	2668.41	1848.85	1440.36	1196.31	1034.46	919.59
60000	5219.31	2713.64	1880.18	1464.78	1216.58	1051.99	935.17
65000	5654.25	2939.77	2036.86	1586.84	1317.97	1139.66	1013.10
70000	6089.19	3165.91	2193.55	1708.90	1419.35	1227.33	1091.04
75000	6524.13	3392.05	2350.23	1830.97	1520.73	1314.99	1168.97
80000	6959.07	3618.18	2506.91	1953.03	1622.11	1402.66	1246.90
85000	7394.02	3844.32	2663.59	2075.10	1723.49	1490.33	1324.83
90000	7828.96	4070.46	2820.27	2197.16	1824.88	1577.99	1402.76
95000	8263.90	4296.59	2976.95	2319.23	1926.26	1665.66	1480.69
100000	8698.84	4522.73	3133.64	2441.29	2027.64	1753.32	1558.62
105000	9133.79	4748.87	3290.32	2563.36	2129.02	1840.99	1636.55
110000	9568.73	4975.00	3447.00	2685.42	2230.40	1928.66	1714.48
120000	10438.61	5427.27	3760.36	2929.55	2433.17	2103.99	1870.35
130000	11308.50	5879.55	4073.73	3173.68	2635.93	2279.32	2026.21
140000	12178.38	6331.82	4387.09	3417.81	2838.70	2454.65	2182.07
150000	13048.26	6784.09	4700.45	3661.94	3041.46	2629.99	2337.93
175000	15222.98	7914.78	5483.86	4272.26	3548.37	3068.32	2727.59
200000	17397.69	9045.46	6267.27	4882.58	4055.28	3506.65	3117.24
225000	19572.40	10176.14	7050.68	5492.91	4562.19	3944.98	3506.90
250000	21747.11	11306.82	7834.09	6103.23	5069.10	4383.31	3896.55

Monthly Payments 8%

necessary to amortize a loan

AMOUNT	8 YEARS	9 YEARS	10 YEARS	11 YEARS	12 YEARS	13 YEARS	14 YEARS
100	1.41	1.30	1.21	1.14	1.08	1.03	0.99
200	2.83	2.60	2.43	2.28	2.16	2.07	1.98
500	7.07	6.51	6.07	5.71	5.41	5.17	4.96
1000	14.14	13.02	12.13	11.42	10.82	10.33	9.91
2000	28.27	26.04	24.27	22.83	21.65	20.66	19.83
5000	70.68	65.09	60.66	57.08	54.12	51.65	49.57
6000	84.82	78.11	72.80	68.49	64.95	61.98	59.48
7000	98.96	91.13	84.93	79.91	75.77	72.32	69.39
8000	113.09	104.15	97.06	91.32	86.60	82.65	79.31
9000	127.23	117.17	109.19	102.74	97.42	92.98	89.22
10000	141.37	130.19	121.33	114.15	108.25	103.31	99.13
15000	212.05	195.28	181.99	171.23	162.37	154.96	148.70
20000	282.73	260.37	242.66	228.31	216.49	206.61	198.26
25000	353.42	325.47	303.32	285.39	270.61	258.27	247.83
30000	424.10	390.56	363.98	342.46	324.74	309.92	297.40
35000	494.78	455.66	424.65	399.54	378.86	361.58	346.96
36000	508.92	468.67	436.78	410.96	389.68	371.91	356.87
37000	523.06	481.69	448.91	422.37	400.51	382.24	366.79
38000	537.19	494.71	461.04	433.79	411.33	392.57	376.70
39000	551.33	507.73	473.18	445.20	422.16	402.90	386.61
40000	565.47	520.75	485.31	456.62	432.98	413.23	396.53
41000	579.60	533.77	497.44	468.03	443.81	423.56	406.44
42000	593.74	546.79	509.58	479.45	454.63	433.89	416.35
43000	607.88	559.80	521.71	490.86	465.45	444.22	426.27
44000	622.01	572.82	533.84	502.28	476.28	454.55	436.18
45000	636.15	585.84	545.97	513.70	487.10	464.88	446.09
46000	650.29	598.86	558.11	525.11	497.93	475.21	456.01
47000	664.42	611.88	570.24	536.53	508.75	485.54	465.92
48000	678.56	624.90	582.37	547.94	519.58	495.88	475.83
49000	692.70	637.92	594.51	559.36	530.40	506.21	485.75
50000	706.83	650.94	606.64	570.77	541.23	516.54	495.66
51000	720.97	663.95	618.77	582.19	552.05	526.87	505.57
52000	735.11	676.97	630.90	593.60	562.88	537.20	515.49
53000	749.24	689.99	643.04	605.02	573.70	547.53	525.40
54000	763.38	703.01	655.17	616.43	584.52	557.86	535.31
55000	777.52	716.03	667.30	627.85	595.35	568.19	545.23
56000	791.65	729.05	679.43	639.27	606.17	578.52	555.14
57000	805.79	742.07	691.57	650.68	617.00	588.85	565.05
58000	819.93	755.09	703.70	662.10	627.82	599.18	574.96
59000	834.06	768.10	715.83	673.51	630.65	609.51	584.88
60000	848.20	781.12	727.97	684.93	649.47	619.84	594.79
65000	918.88	846.22	788.63	742.00	703.59	671.50	644.36
70000	989.57	911.31	849.29	799.08	757.72	723.15	693.92
75000	1060.25	976.40	909.96	856.16	811.84	774.81	743.49
80000	1130.93	1041.50	970.62	913.24	865.96	826.46	793.05
85000	1201.62	1106.59	1031.28	970.31	920.08	878.11	842.62
90000	1272.30	1171.68	1091.95	1027.39	974.21	929.77	892.10
95000	1342.98	1236.78	1152.61	1084.47	1028.33	981.42	941.75
100000	1413.67	1301.87	1213.28	1141.54	1082.45	1033.07	991.32
105000	1484.35	1366.97	1273.94	1198.62	1136.58	1084.73	1040.88
110000	1555.03	1432.06	1334.60	1255.70	1190.70	1136.38	1090.45
120000	1696.40	1562.25	1455.93	1369.85	1298.94	1239.69	1189.58
130000	1837.77	1692.43	1577.26	1484.01	1407.19	1343.00	1288.71
140000	1979.14	1822.62	1698.59	1598.16	1515.43	1446.30	1387.85
150000	2120.50	1952.81	1819.91	1712.32	1623.68	1549.61	1486.98
175000	2473.92	2278.28	2123.23	1997.70	1894.29	1807.88	1734.81
200000	2827.34	2603.74	2426.55	2283.09	2164.91	2066.15	1982.64
225000	3180.75	2929.21	2729.87	2568.48	2435.52	2324.42	2230.47
250000	3534.17	3254.68	3033.19	2853.86	2706.13	2582.68	2478.30

8%

Monthly Payments

necessary to amortize a loan

AMOUNT	15 YEARS	16 YEARS	17 YEARS	18 YEARS	19 YEARS	20 YEARS	21 YEARS
100	0.96	0.92	0.90	0.87	0.85	0.84	0.82
200	1.91	1.85	1.80	1.75	1.71	1.67	1.64
500	4.78	4.62	4.49	4.37	4.27	4.18	4.10
1000	9.56	9.25	8.98	8.75	8.55	8.36	8.20
2000	19.11	18.50	17.97	17.50	17.09	16.73	16.41
5000	47.78	46.25	44.91	43.75	42.73	41.82	41.02
6000	57.34	55.50	53.90	52.50	51.27	50.19	49.23
7000	66.90	64.74	62.88	61.25	59.82	58.55	57.43
8000	76.45	73.99	71.86	70.00	68.36	66.92	65.63
9000	86.01	83.24	80.84	78.75	76.91	75.28	73.84
10000	95.57	92.49	89.83	87.50	85.45	83.64	82.04
15000	143.35	138.74	134.74	131.24	128.18	125.47	123.06
20000	191.13	184.99	179.65	174.99	170.90	167.29	164.09
25000	238.91	231.23	224.56	218.74	213.63	209.11	205.11
30000	286.70	277.48	269.48	262.49	256.35	250.93	246.13
35000	334.48	323.72	314.39	306.24	299.08	292.75	287.15
36000	344.03	332.97	323.37	314.99	307.62	301.12	295.35
37000	353.59	342.22	332.36	323.74	316.17	309.48	303.56
38000	363.15	351.47	341.34	332.49	324.71	317.85	311.76
39000	372.70	360.72	350.32	341.24	333.26	326.21	319.97
40000	382.26	369.97	359.30	349.99	341.80	334.58	328.17
41000	391.82	379.22	368.29	358.73	350.35	342.94	336.38
42000	401.37	388.47	377.27	367.48	358.89	351.30	344.58
43000	410.93	397.72	386.25	376.23	367.44	359.67	352.78
44000	420.49	406.97	395.23	384.98	375.98	368.03	360.99
45000	430.04	416.22	404.22	393.73	384.53	376.40	369.19
46000	439.60	425.47	413.20	402.48	393.07	384.76	377.40
47000	449.16	434.71	422.18	411.23	401.62	393.13	385.60
48000	458.71	443.96	431.16	419.98	410.16	401.49	393.81
49000	468.27	453.21	440.15	428.73	418.71	409.86	402.01
50000	477.83	462.46	449.13	437.48	427.25	418.22	410.21
51000	487.38	471.71	458.11	446.23	435.80	426.58	418.42
52000	496.94	480.96	467.09	454.98	444.34	434.95	426.62
53000	506.50	490.21	476.08	463.73	452.89	443.31	434.83
54000	516.05	499.46	485.06	472.48	461.43	451.68	443.03
55000	525.61	508.71	494.04	481.23	469.98	460.04	451.24
56000	535.17	517.96	503.02	489.98	478.52	468.41	459.44
57000	544.72	527.21	512.01	498.73	487.07	476.77	467.64
58000	554.28	536.46	520.99	507.48	495.61	485.14	475.85
59000	563.83	545.71	529.97	516.23	504.16	493.50	484.05
60000	573.39	554.96	538.95	524.98	512.70	501.86	492.26
65000	621.17	601.20	583.87	568.73	555.43	543.69	533.28
70000	668.96	647.45	628.78	612.47	598.15	585.51	574.30
75000	716.74	693.69	673.69	656.22	640.88	627.33	615.32
80000	764.52	739.94	718.61	699.97	683.60	669.15	656.34
85000	812.30	786.19	763.52	743.72	726.33	710.97	697.36
90000	860.09	832.43	808.43	787.47	769.05	752.80	738.39
95000	907.87	878.68	853.34	831.21	811.78	794.62	779.41
100000	955.65	924.93	898.26	874.96	854.50	836.44	820.43
105000	1003.43	971.17	943.17	918.71	897.23	878.26	861.45
110000	1051.22	1017.42	988.08	962.46	939.95	920.08	902.47
120000	1146.78	1109.91	1077.91	1049.96	1025.40	1003.73	984.51
130000	1242.35	1202.40	1167.73	1137.45	1110.85	1087.37	1066.56
140000	1337.91	1294.90	1257.56	1224.95	1196.30	1171.02	1148.60
150000	1433.48	1387.39	1347.39	1312.44	1281.75	1254.66	1230.64
175000	1672.39	1618.62	1571.95	1531.18	1495.38	1463.77	1435.75
200000	1911.30	1849.85	1796.51	1749.93	1709.00	1672.88	1640.86
225000	2150.22	2081.08	2021.08	1968.67	1922.63	1881.99	1845.96
250000	2389.13	2312.31	2245.64	2187.41	2136.25	2091.10	2051.07

Monthly Payments **8%**

necessary to amortize a loan

AMOUNT	22 YEARS	23 YEARS	24 YEARS	25 YEARS	30 YEARS	35 YEARS	40 YEARS
100	0.81	0.79	0.78	0.77	0.73	0.71	0.70
200	1.61	1.59	1.56	1.54	1.47	1.42	1.39
500	4.03	3.97	3.91	3.86	3.67	3.55	3.48
1000	8.06	7.93	7.82	7.72	7.34	7.10	6.95
2000	16.12	15.87	15.64	15.44	14.68	14.21	13.91
5000	40.31	39.67	39.10	38.59	36.69	35.51	34.77
6000	48.37	47.61	46.92	46.31	44.03	42.62	41.72
7000	56.43	55.54	54.74	54.03	51.36	49.72	48.67
8000	64.49	63.48	62.56	61.75	58.70	56.82	55.62
9000	72.56	71.41	70.38	69.46	66.04	63.92	62.58
10000	80.62	79.35	78.21	77.18	73.38	71.03	69.53
15000	120.93	119.02	117.31	115.77	110.06	106.54	104.30
20000	161.24	158.69	156.41	154.36	146.75	142.05	139.06
25000	201.54	198.36	195.51	192.95	183.44	177.57	173.83
30000	241.85	238.04	234.62	231.54	220.13	213.08	208.59
35000	282.16	277.71	273.72	270.14	256.82	248.59	243.36
36000	290.22	285.64	281.54	277.85	264.16	255.69	250.31
37000	298.29	293.58	289.36	285.57	271.49	262.80	257.27
38000	306.35	301.51	297.18	293.29	278.83	269.90	264.22
39000	314.41	309.45	305.00	301.01	286.17	277.00	271.17
40000	322.47	317.38	312.82	308.73	293.51	284.10	278.12
41000	330.53	325.32	320.64	316.44	300.84	291.21	285.08
42000	338.59	333.25	328.46	324.16	308.18	298.31	292.03
43000	346.66	341.18	336.28	331.88	315.52	305.41	298.98
44000	354.72	349.12	344.10	339.60	322.86	312.51	305.94
45000	362.78	357.05	351.92	347.32	330.19	319.62	312.89
46000	370.84	364.99	359.74	355.04	337.53	326.72	319.84
47000	378.90	372.92	367.57	362.75	344.87	333.82	326.80
48000	386.97	380.86	375.39	370.47	352.21	340.93	333.75
49000	395.03	388.79	383.21	378.19	359.54	348.03	340.70
50000	403.09	396.73	391.03	385.91	366.88	355.13	347.66
51000	411.15	404.66	398.85	393.63	374.22	362.23	354.61
52000	419.21	412.60	406.67	401.34	381.56	369.34	361.56
53000	427.27	420.53	414.49	409.06	388.90	376.44	368.52
54000	435.34	428.46	422.31	416.78	396.23	383.54	375.47
55000	443.40	436.40	430.13	424.50	403.57	390.64	382.42
56000	451.46	444.33	437.95	432.22	410.91	397.75	389.37
57000	459.52	452.27	445.77	439.94	418.25	404.85	396.33
58000	467.58	460.20	453.59	447.65	425.58	411.95	403.28
59000	475.64	468.14	461.41	455.37	432.92	419.05	410.23
60000	483.71	476.07	469.23	463.09	440.26	426.16	417.19
65000	524.02	515.74	508.34	501.68	476.95	461.67	451.95
70000	564.32	555.42	547.44	540.27	513.64	497.18	486.72
75000	604.63	595.09	586.54	578.86	550.32	532.70	521.48
80000	644.94	634.76	625.64	617.45	587.01	568.21	556.25
85000	685.25	674.43	664.75	656.04	623.70	603.72	591.01
90000	725.56	714.11	703.85	694.63	660.39	639.23	625.78
95000	765.87	753.78	742.95	733.23	697.08	674.75	660.55
100000	806.18	793.45	782.05	771.82	733.76	710.26	695.31
105000	846.49	833.13	821.16	810.41	770.45	745.77	730.08
110000	886.80	872.80	860.26	849.00	807.14	781.29	764.84
120000	967.41	952.14	938.46	926.18	880.52	852.31	834.37
130000	1048.03	1031.49	1016.67	1003.36	953.89	923.34	903.91
140000	1128.65	1110.83	1094.88	1080.54	1027.27	994.37	973.44
150000	1209.27	1190.18	1173.08	1157.72	1100.65	1065.39	1042.97
175000	1410.81	1388.54	1368.59	1350.68	1284.09	1242.96	1216.80
200000	1612.36	1586.91	1564.11	1543.63	1467.53	1420.52	1390.62
225000	1813.90	1785.27	1759.62	1736.59	1650.97	1598.09	1564.45
250000	2015.44	1983.63	1955.14	1929.54	1834.41	1775.65	1738.28

8¼% Monthly Payments

necessary to amortize a loan

AMOUNT	1 YEAR	2 YEARS	3 YEARS	4 YEARS	5 YEARS	6 YEARS	7 YEARS
100	8.71	4.53	3.15	2.45	2.04	1.77	1.57
200	17.42	9.07	6.29	4.91	4.08	3.53	3.14
500	43.55	22.67	15.73	12.27	10.20	8.83	7.86
1000	87.10	45.34	31.45	24.53	20.40	17.66	15.71
2000	174.21	90.68	62.90	49.06	40.79	35.31	31.42
5000	435.52	226.71	157.26	122.65	101.98	88.28	78.56
6000	522.62	272.05	188.71	147.18	122.38	105.93	94.27
7000	609.73	317.39	220.16	171.71	142.77	123.59	109.98
8000	696.83	362.73	251.61	196.24	163.17	141.24	125.69
9000	783.94	408.07	283.07	220.77	183.57	158.90	141.40
10000	871.04	453.41	314.52	245.30	203.96	176.56	157.11
15000	1306.56	680.12	471.78	367.96	305.94	264.83	235.67
20000	1742.08	906.83	629.04	490.61	407.93	353.11	314.22
25000	2177.60	1133.53	786.30	613.26	509.91	441.39	392.78
30000	2613.12	1360.24	943.55	735.91	611.89	529.67	471.33
35000	3048.64	1586.95	1100.81	858.57	713.87	617.94	549.89
36000	3135.75	1632.29	1132.27	883.10	734.27	635.60	565.60
37000	3222.85	1677.63	1163.72	907.63	754.66	653.26	581.31
38000	3309.95	1722.97	1195.17	932.16	775.06	670.91	597.02
39000	3397.06	1768.31	1226.62	956.69	795.45	688.57	612.73
40000	3484.16	1813.66	1258.07	981.22	815.85	706.22	628.44
41000	3571.27	1859.00	1289.52	1005.75	836.25	723.88	644.15
42000	3658.37	1904.34	1320.98	1030.28	856.64	741.53	659.86
43000	3745.47	1949.68	1352.43	1054.81	877.04	759.19	675.58
44000	3832.58	1995.02	1383.88	1079.34	897.44	776.84	691.29
45000	3919.68	2040.36	1415.33	1103.87	917.83	794.50	707.00
46000	4006.79	2085.70	1446.78	1128.40	938.23	812.16	722.71
47000	4093.89	2131.05	1478.24	1152.93	958.62	829.81	738.42
48000	4181.00	2176.39	1509.69	1177.46	979.02	847.47	754.13
49000	4268.10	2221.73	1541.14	1201.99	999.42	865.12	769.84
50000	4355.20	2267.07	1572.59	1226.52	1019.81	882.78	785.55
51000	4442.31	2312.41	1604.04	1251.05	1040.21	900.43	801.26
52000	4529.41	2357.75	1635.49	1275.58	1060.61	918.09	816.98
53000	4616.52	2403.09	1666.95	1300.11	1081.00	935.74	832.69
54000	4703.62	2448.44	1698.40	1324.64	1101.40	953.40	848.40
55000	4790.72	2493.78	1729.85	1349.17	1121.79	971.06	864.11
56000	4877.83	2539.12	1761.30	1373.70	1142.19	988.71	879.82
57000	4964.93	2584.46	1792.75	1398.24	1162.59	1006.37	895.53
58000	5052.04	2629.80	1824.21	1422.77	1182.98	1024.02	911.24
59000	5139.14	2675.14	1855.66	1447.30	1203.38	1041.68	926.95
60000	5226.24	2720.48	1887.11	1471.83	1223.78	1059.33	942.66
65000	5661.76	2947.19	2044.37	1594.48	1325.76	1147.61	1021.22
70000	6097.28	3173.90	2201.63	1717.13	1427.74	1235.89	1099.77
75000	6532.80	3400.60	2358.89	1839.78	1529.72	1324.17	1178.33
80000	6968.33	3627.31	2516.15	1962.44	1631.70	1412.44	1256.88
85000	7403.85	3854.02	2673.40	2085.09	1733.68	1500.72	1335.44
90000	7839.37	4080.73	2830.66	2207.74	1835.66	1589.00	1414.00
95000	8274.89	4307.43	2987.92	2330.39	1937.64	1677.28	1492.55
100000	8710.41	4534.14	3145.18	2453.04	2039.63	1765.56	1571.11
105000	9145.93	4760.85	3302.44	2575.70	2141.61	1853.83	1649.66
110000	9581.45	4987.55	3459.70	2698.35	2243.59	1942.11	1728.22
120000	10452.49	5440.97	3774.22	2943.65	2447.55	2118.67	1885.33
130000	11323.53	5894.38	4088.74	3188.96	2651.51	2295.22	2042.44
140000	12194.57	6347.80	4403.26	3434.26	2855.48	2471.78	2199.55
150000	13065.61	6801.21	4717.77	3679.57	3059.44	2648.33	2356.66
175000	15243.21	7934.74	5504.07	4292.83	3569.34	3089.72	2749.44
200000	17420.81	9068.28	6290.36	4906.09	4079.25	3531.11	3142.21
225000	19598.41	10201.81	7076.66	5519.35	4589.16	3972.50	3534.99
250000	21776.02	11335.35	7862.96	6132.61	5099.06	4413.89	3927.76

Monthly Payments — 8¼%

necessary to amortize a loan

AMOUNT	8 YEARS	9 YEARS	10 YEARS	11 YEARS	12 YEARS	13 YEARS	14 YEARS
100	1.43	1.31	1.23	1.16	1.10	1.05	1.01
200	2.85	2.63	2.45	2.31	2.19	2.09	2.01
500	7.13	6.57	6.13	5.78	5.48	5.24	5.03
1000	14.26	13.15	12.27	11.55	10.96	10.47	10.06
2000	28.53	26.30	24.53	23.10	21.92	20.94	20.11
5000	71.32	65.74	61.33	57.75	54.81	52.35	50.28
6000	85.58	78.89	73.59	69.30	65.77	62.82	60.33
7000	99.85	92.04	85.86	80.85	76.73	73.30	70.39
8000	114.11	105.19	98.12	92.40	87.70	83.77	80.45
9000	128.38	118.34	110.39	103.95	98.66	94.24	90.50
10000	142.64	131.49	122.65	115.50	109.62	104.71	100.56
15000	213.96	197.23	183.98	173.26	164.43	157.06	150.83
20000	285.28	262.97	245.31	231.01	219.24	209.42	201.11
25000	356.60	328.72	306.63	288.76	274.05	261.77	251.39
30000	427.92	394.46	367.96	346.51	328.86	314.12	301.67
35000	499.24	460.20	429.28	404.27	383.67	366.48	351.95
36000	513.51	473.35	441.55	415.82	394.63	376.95	362.00
37000	527.77	486.50	453.81	427.37	405.60	387.42	372.06
38000	542.03	499.65	466.08	438.92	416.56	397.89	382.11
39000	556.30	512.80	478.35	450.47	427.52	408.36	392.17
40000	570.56	525.95	490.61	462.02	438.48	418.83	402.23
41000	584.83	539.10	502.88	473.57	449.44	429.30	412.28
42000	599.09	552.24	515.14	485.12	460.41	439.77	422.34
43000	613.36	565.39	527.41	496.67	471.37	450.24	432.39
44000	627.62	578.54	539.67	508.22	482.33	460.71	442.45
45000	641.88	591.69	551.94	519.77	493.29	471.18	452.50
46000	656.15	604.84	564.20	531.32	504.26	481.66	462.56
47000	670.41	617.99	576.47	542.87	515.22	492.13	472.62
48000	684.68	631.14	588.73	554.42	526.18	502.60	482.67
49000	698.94	644.28	601.00	565.97	537.14	513.07	492.73
50000	713.20	657.43	613.26	577.52	548.10	523.54	502.78
51000	727.47	670.58	625.53	589.07	559.07	534.01	512.84
52000	741.73	683.73	637.79	600.63	570.03	544.48	522.89
53000	756.00	696.88	650.06	612.18	580.99	554.95	532.95
54000	770.26	710.03	662.32	623.73	591.95	565.42	543.01
55000	784.52	723.18	674.59	635.28	602.91	575.89	553.06
56000	798.79	736.33	686.85	646.83	613.88	586.36	563.12
57000	813.05	749.47	699.12	658.38	624.84	596.83	573.17
58000	827.32	762.62	711.39	669.93	635.80	607.30	583.23
59000	841.58	775.77	723.65	681.48	646.76	617.78	593.28
60000	855.84	788.92	735.92	693.03	657.72	628.25	603.34
65000	927.16	854.66	797.24	750.78	712.53	680.60	653.62
70000	998.49	920.41	858.57	808.53	767.35	732.95	703.90
75000	1069.81	986.15	919.89	866.29	822.16	785.31	754.17
80000	1141.13	1051.89	981.22	924.04	876.97	837.66	804.45
85000	1212.45	1117.64	1042.55	981.79	931.78	890.02	854.73
90000	1283.77	1183.38	1103.87	1039.64	986.60	942.37	905.01
95000	1355.09	1249.12	1165.20	1097.30	1041.40	994.72	955.29
100000	1426.41	1314.87	1226.53	1155.05	1096.21	1047.08	1005.57
105000	1497.73	1380.61	1287.85	1212.80	1151.02	1099.43	1055.84
110000	1569.05	1446.35	1349.18	1270.55	1205.83	1151.78	1106.12
120000	1711.69	1577.84	1471.83	1386.06	1315.45	1256.49	1206.68
130000	1854.33	1709.33	1594.48	1501.56	1425.07	1361.20	1307.24
140000	1996.97	1840.81	1717.14	1617.07	1534.69	1465.91	1407.79
150000	2139.61	1972.30	1839.79	1732.57	1644.31	1570.61	1508.35
175000	2496.21	2301.02	2146.42	2021.33	1918.36	1832.38	1759.74
200000	2852.81	2629.73	2453.05	2310.10	2192.41	2094.15	2011.13
225000	3209.42	2958.45	2759.68	2598.86	2466.47	2355.92	2262.52
250000	3566.02	3287.17	3066.32	2887.62	2740.52	2617.69	2513.91

8¼% Monthly Payments

necessary to amortize a loan

AMOUNT	15 YEARS	16 YEARS	17 YEARS	18 YEARS	19 YEARS	20 YEARS	21 YEARS
100	0.97	0.94	0.91	0.89	0.87	0.85	0.84
200	1.94	1.88	1.83	1.78	1.74	1.70	1.67
500	4.85	4.70	4.57	4.45	4.35	4.26	4.18
1000	9.70	9.40	9.13	8.90	8.70	8.52	8.36
2000	19.40	18.79	18.26	17.80	17.40	17.04	16.73
5000	48.51	46.98	45.66	44.51	43.50	42.60	41.81
6000	58.21	56.38	54.79	53.41	52.19	51.12	50.18
7000	67.91	65.78	63.92	62.31	60.89	59.64	58.54
8000	77.61	75.17	73.06	71.21	69.59	68.17	66.90
9000	87.31	84.57	82.19	80.11	78.29	76.69	75.26
10000	97.01	93.97	91.32	89.01	86.99	85.21	83.63
15000	145.52	140.95	136.98	133.52	130.49	127.81	125.44
20000	194.03	187.93	182.64	178.03	173.98	170.41	167.25
25000	242.54	234.91	228.30	222.54	217.48	213.02	209.07
30000	291.04	281.90	273.96	267.04	260.97	255.62	250.88
35000	339.55	328.88	319.62	311.55	304.47	298.22	292.69
36000	349.25	338.27	328.76	320.45	313.17	306.74	301.06
37000	358.95	347.67	337.89	329.35	321.87	315.26	309.42
38000	368.65	357.07	347.02	338.26	330.57	323.78	317.78
39000	378.35	366.46	356.15	347.16	339.26	332.31	326.14
40000	388.06	375.86	365.29	356.06	347.96	340.83	334.51
41000	397.76	385.26	374.42	364.96	356.66	349.35	342.87
42000	407.46	394.65	383.55	373.86	365.36	357.87	351.23
43000	417.16	404.05	392.68	382.76	374.06	366.39	359.59
44000	426.86	413.45	401.81	391.66	382.76	374.91	367.96
45000	436.56	422.84	410.95	400.57	391.46	383.43	376.32
46000	446.26	432.24	420.08	409.47	400.16	391.95	384.68
47000	455.97	441.64	429.21	418.37	408.86	400.47	393.05
48000	465.67	451.03	438.34	427.27	417.56	408.99	401.41
49000	475.37	460.43	447.47	436.17	426.26	417.51	409.77
50000	485.07	469.83	456.61	445.07	434.95	426.03	418.13
51000	494.77	479.22	465.74	453.98	443.65	434.55	426.50
52000	504.47	488.62	474.87	462.88	452.35	443.07	434.86
53000	514.17	498.01	484.00	471.78	461.05	451.59	443.22
54000	523.88	507.41	493.14	480.68	469.75	460.12	451.58
55000	533.58	516.81	502.27	489.58	478.45	468.64	459.95
56000	543.28	526.20	511.40	498.48	487.15	477.16	468.31
57000	552.98	535.60	520.53	507.38	495.85	485.68	476.67
58000	562.68	545.00	529.66	516.29	504.55	494.20	485.03
59000	572.38	554.39	538.80	525.19	513.25	502.72	493.40
60000	582.08	563.79	547.93	534.09	521.95	511.24	501.76
65000	630.59	610.77	593.59	578.60	565.44	553.84	543.57
70000	679.10	657.76	639.25	623.10	608.94	596.45	585.39
75000	727.61	704.74	684.91	667.61	652.43	639.05	627.20
80000	776.11	751.72	730.57	712.12	695.93	681.65	669.01
85000	824.62	798.70	776.23	756.63	739.42	724.26	710.83
90000	873.13	845.69	821.89	801.13	782.92	766.86	752.64
95000	921.63	892.67	867.55	845.64	826.41	809.46	794.45
100000	970.14	939.65	913.21	890.15	869.91	852.07	836.27
105000	1018.65	986.63	958.87	934.66	913.40	894.67	878.08
110000	1067.15	1033.62	1004.54	979.16	956.90	937.27	919.89
120000	1164.17	1127.58	1095.86	1068.18	1043.89	1022.48	1003.52
130000	1261.18	1221.55	1187.18	1157.19	1130.88	1107.69	1087.15
140000	1358.20	1315.51	1278.50	1246.21	1217.87	1192.89	1170.77
150000	1455.21	1409.48	1369.82	1335.22	1304.86	1278.10	1254.40
175000	1697.75	1644.39	1598.12	1557.76	1522.34	1491.11	1463.47
200000	1940.28	1879.30	1826.43	1780.30	1739.82	1704.13	1672.53
225000	2182.82	2114.21	2054.73	2002.83	1957.30	1917.15	1881.60
250000	2425.35	2349.13	2283.04	2225.37	2174.77	2130.16	2090.67

Monthly Payments 8¼%

necessary to amortize a loan

AMOUNT	22 YEARS	23 YEARS	24 YEARS	25 YEARS	30 YEARS	35 YEARS	40 YEARS
100	0.82	0.81	0.80	0.79	0.75	0.73	0.71
200	1.64	1.62	1.60	1.58	1.50	1.46	1.43
500	4.11	4.05	3.99	3.94	3.76	3.64	3.57
1000	8.22	8.10	7.98	7.88	7.51	7.28	7.14
2000	16.44	16.19	15.97	15.77	15.03	14.57	14.28
5000	41.11	40.48	39.92	39.42	37.56	36.42	35.71
6000	49.33	48.58	47.91	47.31	45.08	43.71	42.85
7000	57.56	56.68	55.89	55.19	52.59	50.99	49.99
8000	65.78	64.78	63.88	63.08	60.10	58.28	57.13
9000	74.00	72.87	71.86	70.96	67.61	65.56	64.27
10000	82.22	80.97	79.85	78.85	75.13	72.85	71.41
15000	123.33	121.45	119.77	118.27	112.69	109.27	107.12
20000	164.44	161.94	159.70	157.69	150.25	145.70	142.83
25000	205.56	202.42	199.62	197.11	187.82	182.12	178.53
30000	246.67	242.91	239.55	236.54	225.38	218.55	214.24
35000	287.78	283.39	279.47	275.96	262.94	254.97	249.95
36000	296.00	291.49	287.46	283.84	270.46	262.26	257.09
37000	304.22	299.59	295.44	291.73	277.97	269.54	264.23
38000	312.44	307.69	303.43	299.61	285.48	276.83	271.37
39000	320.67	315.78	311.41	307.50	292.99	284.11	278.51
40000	328.89	323.88	319.40	315.38	300.51	291.40	285.66
41000	337.11	331.98	327.38	323.26	308.02	298.68	292.80
42000	345.33	340.07	335.37	331.15	315.53	305.97	299.94
43000	353.56	348.17	343.35	339.03	323.04	313.25	307.08
44000	361.78	356.27	351.34	346.92	330.56	320.54	314.22
45000	370.00	364.36	359.32	354.80	338.07	327.82	321.36
46000	378.22	372.46	367.31	362.69	345.58	335.11	328.50
47000	386.44	380.56	375.29	370.57	353.10	342.39	335.65
48000	394.67	388.66	383.28	378.46	360.61	349.68	342.79
49000	402.89	396.75	391.26	386.34	368.12	356.96	349.93
50000	411.11	404.85	399.25	394.23	375.63	364.25	357.07
51000	419.33	412.95	407.23	402.11	383.15	371.53	364.21
52000	427.56	421.04	415.22	409.99	390.66	378.82	371.35
53000	435.78	429.14	423.20	417.88	398.17	386.10	378.49
54000	444.00	437.24	431.19	425.76	405.68	393.39	385.63
55000	452.22	445.33	439.17	433.65	413.20	400.67	392.78
56000	460.45	453.43	447.16	441.53	420.71	407.96	399.92
57000	468.67	461.53	455.14	449.42	428.22	415.24	407.06
58000	476.89	469.63	463.13	457.30	435.73	422.52	414.20
59000	485.11	477.72	471.11	465.10	443.25	429.01	421.34
60000	493.33	485.82	479.10	473.07	450.76	437.09	428.48
65000	534.45	526.30	519.02	512.49	488.32	473.52	464.19
70000	575.56	566.79	558.95	551.92	525.89	509.94	499.90
75000	616.67	607.27	598.87	591.34	563.45	546.37	535.60
80000	657.78	647.76	638.80	630.76	601.01	582.79	571.31
85000	698.89	688.24	678.72	670.18	638.58	619.22	607.02
90000	740.00	728.73	718.65	709.61	676.14	655.64	642.72
95000	781.11	769.21	758.57	749.03	713.70	692.07	678.43
100000	822.22	809.70	798.50	788.45	751.27	728.49	714.14
105000	863.33	850.18	838.42	827.87	788.83	764.92	749.85
110000	904.45	890.67	878.35	867.30	826.39	801.34	785.55
120000	986.67	971.64	958.20	946.14	901.52	874.19	856.97
130000	1068.89	1052.61	1038.05	1024.99	976.65	947.04	928.38
140000	1151.11	1133.58	1117.90	1103.83	1051.77	1019.89	999.79
150000	1233.33	1214.55	1197.75	1182.68	1126.90	1092.74	1071.21
175000	1438.89	1416.97	1397.37	1379.79	1314.72	1274.86	1249.74
200000	1644.45	1619.40	1596.99	1576.90	1502.53	1456.98	1428.28
225000	1850.00	1821.82	1796.62	1774.01	1690.35	1639.11	1606.81
250000	2055.56	2024.25	1996.24	1971.13	1878.17	1821.23	1785.35

8½%

Monthly Payments

necessary to amortize a loan

AMOUNT	1 YEAR	2 YEARS	3 YEARS	4 YEARS	5 YEARS	6 YEARS	7 YEARS
100	8.72	4.55	3.16	2.46	2.05	1.78	1.58
200	17.44	9.09	6.31	4.93	4.10	3.56	3.17
500	43.61	22.73	15.78	12.32	10.26	8.89	7.92
1000	87.22	45.46	31.57	24.65	20.52	17.78	15.84
2000	174.44	90.91	63.14	49.30	41.03	35.56	31.67
5000	436.10	227.28	157.84	123.24	102.58	88.89	79.18
6000	523.32	272.73	189.41	147.89	123.10	106.67	95.02
7000	610.54	318.19	220.97	172.54	143.62	124.45	110.86
8000	697.76	363.65	252.54	197.19	164.13	142.23	126.69
9000	784.98	409.10	284.11	221.83	184.65	160.01	142.53
10000	872.20	454.56	315.68	246.48	205.17	177.78	158.36
15000	1308.30	681.84	473.51	369.72	307.75	266.68	237.55
20000	1744.40	909.11	631.35	492.97	410.33	355.57	316.73
25000	2180.49	1136.39	789.19	616.21	512.91	444.46	395.91
30000	2616.59	1363.67	947.03	739.45	615.50	533.35	475.09
35000	3052.69	1590.95	1104.86	862.69	718.08	622.24	554.28
36000	3139.91	1636.40	1136.43	887.34	738.60	640.02	570.11
37000	3227.13	1681.86	1168.00	911.99	759.11	657.80	585.95
38000	3314.35	1727.32	1199.57	936.64	779.63	675.58	601.79
39000	3401.57	1772.77	1231.13	961.28	800.14	693.36	617.62
40000	3488.79	1818.23	1262.70	985.93	820.66	711.14	633.46
41000	3576.01	1863.68	1294.27	1010.58	841.18	728.91	649.30
42000	3663.23	1909.14	1325.84	1035.23	861.69	746.69	665.13
43000	3750.45	1954.59	1357.40	1059.88	882.21	764.47	680.97
44000	3837.67	2000.05	1388.97	1084.53	902.73	782.25	696.81
45000	3924.89	2045.51	1420.54	1109.17	923.24	800.03	712.64
46000	4012.11	2090.96	1452.11	1133.82	943.76	817.81	728.48
47000	4099.33	2136.42	1483.67	1158.47	964.28	835.58	744.31
48000	4186.55	2181.87	1515.24	1183.12	984.79	853.36	760.15
49000	4273.77	2227.33	1546.81	1207.77	1005.31	871.14	775.99
50000	4360.99	2272.78	1578.38	1232.42	1025.83	888.92	791.82
51000	4448.21	2318.24	1609.94	1257.06	1046.34	906.70	807.66
52000	4535.43	2363.70	1641.51	1281.71	1066.86	924.48	823.50
53000	4622.65	2409.15	1673.08	1306.36	1087.38	942.25	839.33
54000	4709.87	2454.61	1704.65	1331.01	1107.89	960.03	855.17
55000	4797.09	2500.06	1736.21	1355.66	1128.41	977.81	871.01
56000	4884.31	2545.52	1767.78	1380.30	1148.93	995.59	886.84
57000	4971.53	2590.97	1799.35	1404.95	1169.44	1013.37	902.68
58000	5058.75	2636.43	1830.92	1429.60	1189.96	1031.15	918.52
59000	5145.97	2681.88	1862.48	1454.25	1210.48	1048.92	934.35
60000	5233.19	2727.34	1894.05	1478.90	1230.99	1066.70	950.19
65000	5669.29	2954.62	2051.89	1602.14	1333.57	1155.59	1029.37
70000	6105.38	3181.90	2209.73	1725.38	1436.16	1244.49	1108.55
75000	6541.48	3409.18	2367.57	1848.62	1538.74	1333.38	1187.74
80000	6977.58	3636.45	2525.40	1971.86	1641.32	1422.27	1266.92
85000	7413.68	3863.73	2683.24	2095.11	1743.91	1511.16	1346.10
90000	7849.78	4091.01	2841.08	2218.35	1846.49	1600.05	1425.28
95000	8285.88	4318.29	2998.92	2341.59	1949.07	1688.95	1504.47
100000	8721.98	4545.57	3156.75	2464.83	2051.65	1777.84	1583.65
105000	9158.08	4772.85	3314.59	2588.07	2154.24	1866.73	1662.83
110000	9594.18	5000.12	3472.43	2711.31	2256.82	1955.62	1742.01
120000	10466.37	5454.68	3788.10	2957.80	2461.98	2133.41	1900.38
130000	11338.57	5909.24	4103.78	3204.28	2667.15	2311.19	2058.74
140000	12210.77	6363.79	4419.46	3450.76	2872.31	2488.97	2217.11
150000	13082.97	6818.35	4735.13	3697.25	3077.48	2666.76	2375.47
175000	15263.46	7954.74	5524.32	4313.45	3590.39	3111.22	2771.38
200000	17443.96	9091.13	6313.51	4929.66	4103.31	3555.68	3167.30
225000	19624.45	10227.53	7102.70	5545.87	4616.22	4000.14	3563.21
250000	21804.95	11363.92	7891.88	6162.08	5129.13	4444.60	3959.12

Monthly Payments 8½%

necessary to amortize a loan

AMOUNT	8 YEARS	9 YEARS	10 YEARS	11 YEARS	12 YEARS	13 YEARS	14 YEARS
100	1.44	1.33	1.24	1.17	1.11	1.06	1.02
200	2.88	2.66	2.48	2.34	2.22	2.12	2.04
500	7.20	6.64	6.20	5.84	5.55	5.31	5.10
1000	14.39	13.28	12.40	11.69	11.10	10.61	10.20
2000	28.78	26.56	24.80	23.37	22.20	21.22	20.40
5000	71.96	66.40	61.99	58.43	55.50	53.06	51.00
6000	86.35	79.68	74.39	70.12	66.60	63.67	61.20
7000	100.74	92.96	86.79	81.80	77.70	74.28	71.39
8000	115.14	106.23	99.19	93.49	88.80	84.89	81.59
9000	129.53	119.51	111.59	105.18	99.91	95.51	91.79
10000	143.92	132.79	123.99	116.86	111.01	106.12	101.99
15000	215.88	199.19	185.98	175.30	166.51	159.18	152.99
20000	287.84	265.59	247.97	233.73	222.01	212.24	203.98
25000	359.80	331.98	309.96	292.16	277.51	265.29	254.98
30000	431.76	398.38	371.96	350.59	333.02	318.35	305.98
35000	503.72	464.78	433.95	409.02	388.52	371.41	356.97
36000	518.12	478.06	446.35	420.71	399.62	382.02	367.17
37000	532.51	491.34	458.75	432.40	410.72	392.64	377.37
38000	546.90	504.62	471.15	444.08	421.82	403.25	387.57
39000	561.29	517.89	483.54	455.77	432.92	413.86	397.77
40000	575.69	531.17	495.94	467.46	444.02	424.47	407.97
41000	590.08	544.45	508.34	479.14	455.12	435.08	418.17
42000	604.47	557.73	520.74	490.83	466.22	445.70	428.37
43000	618.86	571.01	533.14	502.51	477.32	456.31	438.56
44000	633.25	584.29	545.54	514.20	488.42	466.92	448.76
45000	647.65	597.57	557.94	525.89	499.53	477.53	458.96
46000	662.04	610.85	570.33	537.57	510.63	488.14	469.16
47000	676.43	624.13	582.73	549.26	521.73	498.75	479.36
48000	690.82	637.41	595.13	560.95	532.83	509.37	489.56
49000	705.21	650.69	607.53	572.63	543.93	519.98	499.76
50000	719.61	663.97	619.93	584.32	555.03	530.59	509.96
51000	734.00	677.25	632.33	596.01	566.13	541.20	520.16
52000	748.39	690.53	644.73	607.69	577.23	551.81	530.36
53000	762.78	703.81	657.12	619.38	588.33	562.42	540.56
54000	777.17	717.09	669.52	631.07	599.43	573.04	550.76
55000	791.57	730.36	681.92	642.75	610.53	583.65	560.96
56000	805.96	743.64	694.32	654.44	621.63	594.26	571.15
57000	820.35	756.92	706.72	666.12	632.73	604.87	581.35
58000	834.74	770.20	719.12	677.81	643.83	615.48	591.55
59000	849.14	783.48	731.52	689.50	654.93	626.10	601.75
60000	863.53	796.76	743.91	701.18	666.03	636.71	611.95
65000	935.49	863.16	805.91	759.62	721.54	689.77	662.95
70000	1007.45	929.55	867.90	818.05	777.04	742.83	713.94
75000	1079.41	995.95	929.89	876.48	832.54	795.88	764.94
80000	1151.37	1062.35	991.89	934.91	888.04	848.94	815.93
85000	1223.33	1128.74	1053.88	993.34	943.55	902.00	866.93
90000	1295.29	1195.14	1115.87	1051.78	999.05	955.06	917.93
95000	1367.25	1261.54	1177.86	1110.21	1054.55	1008.12	968.92
100000	1439.21	1327.94	1239.86	1168.64	1110.06	1061.18	1019.92
105000	1511.17	1394.33	1301.85	1227.07	1165.56	1114.24	1070.91
110000	1583.13	1460.73	1363.84	1285.50	1221.06	1167.30	1121.91
120000	1727.06	1593.52	1487.83	1402.37	1332.07	1273.41	1223.90
130000	1870.98	1726.32	1611.81	1519.23	1443.07	1379.53	1325.89
140000	2014.90	1859.11	1735.80	1636.09	1554.08	1485.65	1427.89
150000	2158.82	1991.90	1859.79	1752.96	1665.08	1591.77	1529.88
175000	2518.62	2323.89	2169.75	2045.12	1942.60	1857.06	1784.86
200000	2878.43	2655.87	2479.71	2337.28	2220.11	2122.36	2039.84
225000	3238.23	2987.85	2789.68	2629.44	2497.63	2387.65	2294.82
250000	3598.03	3319.84	3099.64	2921.60	2775.14	2652.95	2549.80

8½%

Monthly Payments

necessary to amortize a loan

AMOUNT	15 YEARS	16 YEARS	17 YEARS	18 YEARS	19 YEARS	20 YEARS	21 YEARS
100	0.98	0.95	0.93	0.91	0.89	0.87	0.85
200	1.97	1.91	1.86	1.81	1.77	1.74	1.70
500	4.92	4.77	4.64	4.53	4.43	4.34	4.26
1000	9.85	9.54	9.28	9.05	8.85	8.68	8.52
2000	19.69	19.09	18.57	18.11	17.71	17.36	17.04
5000	49.24	47.72	46.41	45.27	44.27	43.39	42.61
6000	59.08	57.27	55.70	54.33	53.13	52.07	51.13
7000	68.93	66.81	64.98	63.38	61.98	60.75	59.66
8000	78.78	76.36	74.26	72.44	70.84	69.43	68.18
9000	88.63	85.90	83.55	81.49	79.69	78.10	76.70
10000	98.47	95.45	92.83	90.55	88.54	86.78	85.22
15000	147.71	143.17	139.24	135.82	132.82	130.17	127.84
20000	196.95	190.90	185.66	181.09	177.09	173.56	170.45
25000	246.18	238.62	232.07	226.36	221.36	216.96	213.06
30000	295.42	286.35	278.49	271.64	265.63	260.35	255.67
35000	344.66	334.07	324.90	316.91	309.91	303.74	298.28
36000	354.51	343.62	334.19	325.96	318.76	312.42	306.81
37000	364.35	353.16	343.47	335.02	327.61	321.09	315.33
38000	374.20	362.71	352.75	344.07	336.47	329.77	323.85
39000	384.05	372.25	362.03	353.13	345.32	338.45	332.37
40000	393.90	381.80	371.32	362.18	354.18	347.13	340.90
41000	403.74	391.34	380.60	371.24	363.03	355.81	349.42
42000	413.59	400.89	389.88	380.29	371.89	364.49	357.94
43000	423.44	410.43	399.17	389.35	380.74	373.16	366.46
44000	433.29	419.98	408.45	398.40	389.60	381.84	374.99
45000	443.13	429.52	417.73	407.46	398.45	390.52	383.51
46000	452.98	439.07	427.01	416.51	407.30	399.20	392.03
47000	462.83	448.61	436.30	425.57	416.16	407.88	400.55
48000	472.67	458.16	445.58	434.62	425.01	416.56	409.07
49000	482.52	467.70	454.86	443.67	433.87	425.23	417.60
50000	492.37	477.25	464.15	452.73	442.72	433.91	426.12
51000	502.22	486.79	473.43	461.78	451.58	442.59	434.64
52000	512.06	496.34	482.71	470.84	460.43	451.27	443.16
53000	521.91	505.88	491.99	479.89	469.29	459.95	451.69
54000	531.76	515.43	501.28	488.95	478.14	468.62	460.21
55000	541.61	524.97	510.56	498.00	487.00	477.30	468.73
56000	551.45	534.51	519.84	507.06	495.85	485.98	477.25
57000	561.30	544.06	529.13	516.11	504.70	494.66	485.78
58000	571.15	553.60	538.41	525.17	513.56	503.34	494.30
59000	581.00	563.15	547.69	534.22	522.41	512.02	502.82
60000	590.84	572.69	556.98	543.27	531.27	520.69	511.34
65000	640.08	620.42	603.39	588.55	575.54	564.09	553.96
70000	689.32	668.14	649.80	633.82	619.81	607.48	596.57
75000	738.55	715.87	696.22	679.09	664.08	650.87	639.18
80000	787.79	763.59	742.63	724.37	708.36	694.26	681.79
85000	837.03	811.32	789.05	769.64	752.63	737.65	724.40
90000	886.27	859.04	835.46	814.91	796.90	781.04	767.02
95000	935.50	906.77	881.88	860.18	841.17	824.43	809.63
100000	984.74	954.49	928.29	905.46	885.45	867.82	852.24
105000	1033.98	1002.22	974.71	950.73	929.72	911.21	894.85
110000	1083.21	1049.94	1021.12	996.00	973.99	954.61	937.46
120000	1181.69	1145.39	1113.95	1086.55	1062.53	1041.39	1022.69
130000	1280.16	1240.84	1206.78	1177.09	1151.08	1128.17	1107.91
140000	1378.64	1336.29	1299.61	1267.64	1239.62	1214.95	1193.13
150000	1477.11	1431.74	1392.44	1358.19	1328.17	1301.73	1278.36
175000	1723.29	1670.36	1624.51	1584.55	1549.53	1518.69	1491.42
200000	1969.48	1908.98	1856.58	1810.91	1770.89	1735.65	1704.48
225000	2215.66	2147.60	2088.66	2037.28	1992.25	1952.60	1917.54
250000	2461.85	2386.23	2320.73	2263.64	2213.61	2169.56	2130.60

Monthly Payments 8½%

necessary to amortize a loan

AMOUNT	22 YEARS	23 YEARS	24 YEARS	25 YEARS	30 YEARS	35 YEARS	40 YEARS
100	0.84	0.83	0.82	0.81	0.77	0.75	0.73
200	1.68	1.65	1.63	1.61	1.54	1.49	1.47
500	4.19	4.13	4.08	4.03	3.84	3.73	3.67
1000	8.38	8.26	8.15	8.05	7.69	7.47	7.33
2000	16.77	16.52	16.30	16.10	15.38	14.94	14.66
5000	41.92	41.30	40.75	40.26	38.45	37.34	36.65
6000	50.30	49.57	48.90	48.31	46.13	44.81	43.99
7000	58.69	57.83	57.06	56.37	53.82	52.28	51.32
8000	67.07	66.09	65.21	64.42	61.51	59.75	58.65
9000	75.46	74.35	73.36	72.47	69.20	67.22	65.98
10000	83.84	82.61	81.51	80.52	76.89	74.69	73.31
15000	125.76	123.91	122.26	120.78	115.34	112.03	109.96
20000	167.68	165.22	163.02	161.05	153.78	149.37	146.62
25000	209.60	206.52	203.77	201.31	192.23	186.72	183.27
30000	251.52	247.83	244.52	241.57	230.67	224.06	219.93
35000	293.44	289.13	285.28	281.83	269.12	261.40	256.58
36000	301.83	297.39	293.43	289.88	276.81	268.87	263.91
37000	310.21	305.65	301.58	297.93	284.50	276.34	271.24
38000	318.59	313.91	309.73	305.99	292.19	283.81	278.58
39000	326.98	322.17	317.88	314.04	299.88	291.28	285.91
40000	335.36	330.43	326.03	322.09	307.57	298.74	293.24
41000	343.75	338.70	334.18	330.14	315.25	306.21	300.57
42000	352.13	346.96	342.33	338.20	322.94	313.68	307.90
43000	360.51	355.22	350.49	346.25	330.63	321.15	315.23
44000	368.90	363.48	358.64	354.30	338.32	328.62	322.56
45000	377.28	371.74	366.79	362.35	346.01	336.09	329.89
46000	385.67	380.00	374.94	370.40	353.70	343.56	337.22
47000	394.05	388.26	383.09	378.46	361.39	351.02	344.55
48000	402.43	396.52	391.24	386.51	369.08	358.49	351.89
49000	410.82	404.78	399.39	394.56	376.77	365.96	359.22
50000	419.20	413.04	407.54	402.61	384.46	373.43	366.55
51000	427.59	421.30	415.69	410.67	392.15	380.90	373.88
52000	435.97	429.57	423.84	418.72	399.84	388.37	381.21
53000	444.36	437.83	431.99	426.77	407.52	395.84	388.54
54000	452.74	446.09	440.14	434.82	415.21	403.30	395.87
55000	461.12	454.35	448.30	442.87	422.90	410.77	403.20
56000	469.51	462.61	456.45	450.93	430.59	418.24	410.53
57000	477.89	470.87	464.60	458.98	438.28	425.71	417.86
58000	486.28	479.13	472.76	467.03	445.07	433.10	425.19
59000	494.66	487.39	480.90	475.08	453.66	440.65	432.53
60000	503.04	495.65	489.05	483.14	461.35	448.12	439.86
65000	544.96	536.96	529.80	523.40	499.79	485.46	476.51
70000	586.88	578.26	570.56	563.66	538.24	522.80	513.17
75000	628.80	619.56	611.31	603.92	576.69	560.15	549.82
80000	670.72	660.87	652.07	644.18	615.13	597.49	586.48
85000	712.05	702.17	092.82	084.44	653.58	634.83	623.13
90000	754.57	743.48	733.57	724.70	692.02	672.17	659.78
95000	796.49	784.78	774.33	764.97	730.47	709.52	696.44
100000	838.41	826.09	015.08	805.23	768.91	746.86	733.09
105000	880.33	867.39	855.84	845.49	807.36	784.20	769.75
110000	922.25	908.70	896.59	885.75	845.80	821.55	806.40
120000	1006.09	991.30	978.10	966.27	922.70	896.23	879.71
130000	1089.93	1073.91	1059.61	1046.80	999.59	970.92	953.02
140000	1173.77	1156.52	1141.12	1127.32	1076.48	1045.60	1026.33
150000	1257.61	1239.13	1222.62	1207.84	1153.37	1120.29	1099.64
175000	1467.21	1445.65	1426.39	1409.15	1345.60	1307.01	1282.91
200000	1676.81	1652.17	1630.16	1610.45	1537.83	1493.72	1466.19
225000	1886.41	1858.69	1833.94	1811.76	1730.06	1680.44	1649.46
250000	2096.02	2065.22	2037.71	2013.07	1922.28	1867.15	1832.74

8¾%

Monthly Payments
necessary to amortize a loan

AMOUNT	1 YEAR	2 YEARS	3 YEARS	4 YEARS	5 YEARS	6 YEARS	7 YEARS
100	8.73	4.56	3.17	2.48	2.06	1.79	1.60
200	17.47	9.11	6.34	4.95	4.13	3.58	3.19
500	43.67	22.79	15.84	12.38	10.32	8.95	7.98
1000	87.34	45.57	31.68	24.77	20.64	17.90	15.96
2000	174.67	91.14	63.37	49.53	41.27	35.80	31.92
5000	436.68	227.85	158.42	123.83	103.19	89.51	79.81
6000	524.01	273.42	190.10	148.60	123.82	107.41	95.77
7000	611.35	318.99	221.78	173.37	144.46	125.31	111.74
8000	698.68	364.56	253.47	198.13	165.10	143.21	127.70
9000	786.02	410.13	285.15	222.90	185.74	161.12	143.66
10000	873.36	455.70	316.84	247.67	206.37	179.02	159.62
15000	1310.03	683.55	475.25	371.50	309.56	268.53	239.44
20000	1746.71	911.40	633.67	495.33	412.74	358.03	319.25
25000	2183.39	1139.25	792.09	619.16	515.93	447.54	399.06
30000	2620.07	1367.10	950.51	743.00	619.12	537.05	478.87
35000	3056.75	1594.95	1108.92	866.83	722.30	626.56	558.69
36000	3144.08	1640.52	1140.61	891.59	742.94	644.46	574.65
37000	3231.42	1686.09	1172.29	916.36	763.58	662.36	590.61
38000	3318.75	1731.66	1203.97	941.13	784.21	680.26	606.57
39000	3406.09	1777.23	1235.66	965.89	804.85	698.17	622.54
40000	3493.42	1822.80	1267.34	990.66	825.49	716.07	638.50
41000	3580.76	1868.38	1299.02	1015.43	846.13	733.97	654.46
42000	3668.09	1913.95	1330.71	1040.19	866.76	751.87	670.42
43000	3755.43	1959.52	1362.39	1064.96	887.40	769.77	686.39
44000	3842.77	2005.09	1394.07	1089.73	908.04	787.68	702.35
45000	3930.10	2050.66	1425.76	1114.49	928.68	805.58	718.31
46000	4017.44	2096.23	1457.44	1139.26	949.31	823.48	734.27
47000	4104.77	2141.80	1489.12	1164.03	969.95	841.38	750.24
48000	4192.11	2187.37	1520.81	1188.79	990.59	859.28	766.20
49000	4279.44	2232.94	1552.49	1213.56	1011.22	877.18	782.16
50000	4366.78	2278.51	1584.18	1238.33	1031.86	895.09	798.12
51000	4454.11	2324.08	1615.86	1263.09	1052.50	912.99	814.09
52000	4541.45	2369.65	1647.54	1287.86	1073.14	930.89	830.05
53000	4628.79	2415.22	1679.23	1312.62	1093.77	948.79	846.01
54000	4716.12	2460.79	1710.91	1337.39	1114.41	966.69	861.97
55000	4803.46	2506.36	1742.59	1362.16	1135.05	984.59	877.94
56000	4890.79	2551.93	1774.28	1386.92	1155.69	1002.50	893.90
57000	4978.13	2597.50	1805.96	1411.69	1176.32	1020.40	909.86
58000	5065.46	2643.07	1837.64	1436.46	1196.96	1038.30	925.82
59000	5152.80	2688.64	1869.33	1461.22	1217.60	1056.20	941.79
60000	5240.14	2734.21	1901.01	1485.99	1238.23	1074.10	957.75
65000	5676.81	2962.06	2059.43	1609.82	1341.42	1163.61	1037.56
70000	6113.49	3189.91	2217.85	1733.66	1444.61	1253.12	1117.37
75000	6550.17	3417.76	2376.26	1857.49	1547.79	1342.63	1197.19
80000	6986.85	3645.61	2534.68	1981.32	1650.98	1432.14	1277.00
85000	7423.52	3873.46	2693.10	2105.15	1754.16	1521.65	1356.81
90000	7860.20	4101.31	2851.52	2228.99	1857.35	1611.15	1436.62
95000	8296.88	4329.16	3009.93	2352.82	1960.54	1700.66	1516.44
100000	8733.56	4557.01	3168.35	2476.65	2063.72	1790.17	1596.25
105000	9170.24	4784.86	3326.77	2600.48	2166.91	1879.68	1676.06
110000	9606.91	5012.71	3485.19	2724.32	2270.10	1969.19	1755.87
120000	10480.27	5468.41	3802.02	2971.98	2476.47	2148.21	1915.50
130000	11353.63	5924.12	4118.86	3219.65	2682.84	2327.22	2075.12
140000	12226.98	6379.82	4435.69	3467.31	2889.21	2506.24	2234.75
150000	13100.34	6835.52	4752.53	3714.98	3095.58	2685.26	2394.37
175000	15283.73	7974.77	5544.61	4334.14	3611.52	3132.80	2793.44
200000	17467.12	9114.02	6336.70	4953.30	4127.45	3580.34	3192.50
225000	19650.51	10253.28	7128.79	5572.46	4643.38	4027.88	3591.56
250000	21833.90	11392.53	7920.88	6191.63	5159.31	4475.43	3990.62

Monthly Payments 8¾%

necessary to amortize a loan

AMOUNT	8 YEARS	9 YEARS	10 YEARS	11 YEARS	12 YEARS	13 YEARS	14 YEARS
100	1.45	1.34	1.25	1.18	1.12	1.08	1.03
200	2.90	2.68	2.51	2.36	2.25	2.15	2.07
500	7.26	6.71	6.27	5.91	5.62	5.38	5.17
1000	14.52	13.41	12.53	11.82	11.24	10.75	10.34
2000	29.04	26.82	25.07	23.65	22.48	21.51	20.69
5000	72.60	67.05	62.66	59.12	56.20	53.77	51.72
6000	87.13	80.46	75.20	70.94	67.44	64.52	62.06
7000	101.65	93.88	87.73	82.76	78.68	75.28	72.41
8000	116.17	107.29	100.26	94.59	89.92	86.03	82.75
9000	130.69	120.70	112.79	106.41	101.16	96.78	93.09
10000	145.21	134.11	125.33	118.23	112.40	107.54	103.44
15000	217.81	201.16	187.99	177.35	168.60	161.31	155.16
20000	290.42	268.22	250.65	236.46	224.80	215.08	206.88
25000	363.02	335.27	313.32	295.58	281.00	268.85	258.59
30000	435.63	402.32	375.98	354.70	337.20	322.61	310.31
35000	508.23	469.38	438.64	413.81	393.40	376.38	362.03
36000	522.75	482.79	451.18	425.63	404.64	387.14	372.38
37000	537.27	496.20	463.71	437.46	415.88	397.89	382.72
38000	551.79	509.61	476.24	449.28	427.12	408.64	393.06
39000	566.31	523.02	488.77	461.10	438.36	419.40	403.41
40000	580.83	536.43	501.31	472.93	449.60	430.15	413.75
41000	595.35	549.84	513.84	484.75	460.84	440.91	424.09
42000	609.88	563.25	526.37	496.57	472.08	451.66	434.44
43000	624.40	576.66	538.91	508.40	483.32	462.41	444.78
44000	638.92	590.07	551.44	520.22	494.56	473.17	455.13
45000	653.44	603.48	563.97	532.04	505.80	483.92	465.47
46000	667.96	616.90	576.50	543.87	517.04	494.68	475.81
47000	682.48	630.31	589.04	555.69	528.28	505.43	486.16
48000	697.00	643.72	601.57	567.51	539.52	516.18	496.50
49000	711.52	657.13	614.10	579.34	550.76	526.94	506.84
50000	726.04	670.54	626.63	591.16	562.00	537.69	517.19
51000	740.56	683.95	639.17	602.98	573.24	548.44	527.53
52000	755.08	697.36	651.70	614.80	584.48	559.20	537.88
53000	769.60	710.77	664.23	626.63	595.72	569.95	548.22
54000	784.13	724.18	676.76	638.45	606.96	580.71	558.56
55000	798.65	737.59	689.30	650.27	618.20	591.46	568.91
56000	813.17	751.00	701.83	662.10	629.44	602.21	579.25
57000	827.69	764.41	714.36	673.92	640.68	612.97	589.59
58000	842.21	777.82	726.90	685.74	651.92	623.72	599.94
59000	856.73	791.24	739.43	697.57	663.16	634.47	610.28
60000	871.25	804.65	751.96	709.39	674.40	645.23	620.63
65000	943.85	871.70	814.62	768.51	730.60	699.00	672.34
70000	1016.46	938.75	877.29	827.62	786.80	752.77	724.06
75000	1080.06	1006.01	000.05	000.74	843.00	806.54	775.78
80000	1161.67	1072.86	1002.61	945.85	899.20	860.30	827.50
85000	1234.27	1139.92	1065.28	1004.97	955.40	914.07	879.22
90000	1306.88	1206.97	1127.94	1064.09	1011.60	967.84	930.94
95000	1379.48	1274.02	1190.60	1123.20	1067.80	1021.61	982.66
100000	1452.08	1341.08	1253.27	1182.32	1124.00	1075.38	1034.38
105000	1524.69	1408.13	1315.93	1241.43	1180.20	1129.15	1086.09
110000	1597.29	1475.18	1378.59	1300.55	1236.40	1182.92	1137.81
120000	1742.50	1609.29	1503.92	1418.78	1348.80	1290.46	1241.25
130000	1887.71	1743.40	1629.25	1537.01	1461.20	1397.99	1344.69
140000	2032.92	1877.51	1754.57	1655.24	1573.60	1505.53	1448.13
150000	2178.13	2011.62	1879.90	1773.48	1686.00	1613.07	1551.56
175000	2541.15	2346.88	2193.22	2069.05	1966.99	1881.92	1810.16
200000	2904.17	2682.15	2506.54	2364.63	2247.99	2150.76	2068.75
225000	3267.19	3017.42	2819.85	2660.21	2528.99	2419.61	2327.35
250000	3630.21	3352.69	3133.17	2955.79	2809.99	2688.45	2585.94

8¾%

Monthly Payments

necessary to amortize a loan

AMOUNT	15 YEARS	16 YEARS	17 YEARS	18 YEARS	19 YEARS	20 YEARS	21 YEARS
100	1.00	0.97	0.94	0.92	0.90	0.88	0.87
200	2.00	1.94	1.89	1.84	1.80	1.77	1.74
500	5.00	4.85	4.72	4.60	4.51	4.42	4.34
1000	9.99	9.69	9.43	9.21	9.01	8.84	8.68
2000	19.99	19.39	18.87	18.42	18.02	17.67	17.37
5000	49.97	48.47	47.17	46.04	45.06	44.19	43.42
6000	59.97	58.17	56.61	55.25	54.07	53.02	52.10
7000	69.96	67.86	66.04	64.46	63.08	61.86	60.78
8000	79.96	77.56	75.48	73.67	72.09	70.70	69.47
9000	89.95	87.25	84.91	82.88	81.10	79.53	78.15
10000	99.94	96.94	94.35	92.09	90.11	88.37	86.83
15000	149.92	145.42	141.52	138.13	135.17	132.56	130.25
20000	199.89	193.89	188.70	184.18	180.22	176.74	173.67
25000	249.86	242.36	235.87	230.22	225.28	220.93	217.09
30000	299.83	290.83	283.05	276.27	270.33	265.11	260.50
35000	349.81	339.31	330.22	322.31	315.39	309.30	303.92
36000	359.80	349.00	339.66	331.52	324.40	318.14	312.60
37000	369.80	358.70	349.09	340.73	333.41	326.97	321.29
38000	379.79	368.39	358.53	349.94	342.42	335.81	329.97
39000	389.78	378.08	367.96	359.15	351.43	344.65	338.65
40000	399.78	387.78	377.40	368.36	360.44	353.48	347.34
41000	409.77	397.47	386.83	377.57	369.45	362.32	356.02
42000	419.77	407.17	396.27	386.77	378.47	371.16	364.70
43000	429.76	416.86	405.70	395.98	387.48	380.00	373.39
44000	439.76	426.56	415.14	405.19	396.49	388.83	382.07
45000	449.75	436.25	424.57	414.40	405.50	397.67	390.76
46000	459.75	445.95	434.01	423.61	414.51	406.51	399.44
47000	469.74	455.64	443.44	432.82	423.52	415.34	408.12
48000	479.74	465.33	452.87	442.03	432.53	424.18	416.81
49000	489.73	475.03	462.31	451.24	441.54	433.02	425.49
50000	499.72	484.72	471.74	460.45	450.55	441.86	434.17
51000	509.72	494.42	481.18	469.65	459.57	450.69	442.86
52000	519.71	504.11	490.61	478.86	468.58	459.53	451.54
53000	529.71	513.81	500.05	488.07	477.59	468.37	460.22
54000	539.70	523.50	509.48	497.28	486.60	477.20	468.91
55000	549.70	533.20	518.92	506.49	495.61	486.04	477.59
56000	559.69	542.89	528.35	515.70	504.62	494.88	486.27
57000	569.69	552.58	537.79	524.91	513.63	503.72	494.96
58000	579.68	562.28	547.22	534.12	522.64	512.55	503.64
59000	589.67	571.97	556.66	543.33	531.65	521.39	512.32
60000	599.67	581.67	566.09	552.53	540.67	530.23	521.01
65000	649.64	630.14	613.27	598.58	585.72	574.41	564.42
70000	699.61	678.61	660.44	644.62	630.78	618.60	607.84
75000	749.59	727.09	707.62	690.67	675.83	662.78	651.26
80000	799.56	775.56	754.79	736.71	720.89	706.97	694.68
85000	849.53	824.03	801.97	782.76	765.94	751.15	738.09
90000	899.50	872.50	849.14	828.80	811.00	795.34	781.51
95000	949.48	920.97	896.31	874.85	856.05	839.53	824.93
100000	999.45	969.45	943.49	920.89	901.11	883.71	868.34
105000	1049.42	1017.92	990.66	966.93	946.16	927.90	911.76
110000	1099.39	1066.39	1037.84	1012.98	991.22	972.08	955.18
120000	1199.34	1163.34	1132.19	1105.07	1081.33	1060.45	1042.01
130000	1299.28	1260.28	1226.54	1197.16	1171.44	1148.82	1128.85
140000	1399.23	1357.23	1320.88	1289.25	1261.55	1237.19	1215.68
150000	1499.17	1454.17	1415.23	1381.34	1351.66	1325.57	1302.52
175000	1749.04	1696.53	1651.11	1611.56	1576.94	1546.49	1519.60
200000	1998.90	1938.89	1886.98	1841.78	1802.22	1767.42	1736.69
225000	2248.76	2181.26	2122.85	2072.00	2027.49	1988.35	1953.78
250000	2498.62	2423.62	2358.72	2302.23	2252.77	2209.28	2170.86

Monthly Payments 8¾%

necessary to amortize a loan

AMOUNT	22 YEARS	23 YEARS	24 YEARS	25 YEARS	30 YEARS	35 YEARS	40 YEARS
100	0.85	0.84	0.83	0.82	0.79	0.77	0.75
200	1.71	1.69	1.66	1.64	1.57	1.53	1.50
500	4.27	4.21	4.16	4.11	3.93	3.83	3.76
1000	8.55	8.43	8.32	8.22	7.87	7.65	7.52
2000	17.09	16.86	16.64	16.44	15.73	15.31	15.04
5000	42.74	42.13	41.59	41.11	39.34	38.27	37.61
6000	51.28	50.56	49.91	49.33	47.20	45.92	45.13
7000	59.83	58.98	58.23	57.55	55.07	53.58	52.65
8000	68.38	67.41	66.54	65.77	62.94	61.23	60.17
9000	76.93	75.83	74.86	73.99	70.80	68.88	67.70
10000	85.47	84.26	83.18	82.21	78.67	76.54	75.22
15000	128.21	126.39	124.77	123.32	118.01	114.80	112.83
20000	170.94	168.52	166.36	164.43	157.34	153.07	150.43
25000	213.68	210.65	207.95	205.54	196.68	191.34	188.04
30000	256.42	252.78	249.54	246.64	236.01	229.61	225.65
35000	299.15	294.91	291.13	287.75	275.35	267.88	263.26
36000	307.70	303.34	299.45	295.97	283.21	275.53	270.78
37000	316.25	311.77	307.77	304.19	291.08	283.18	278.30
38000	324.80	320.19	316.09	312.41	298.95	290.84	285.82
39000	333.34	328.62	324.40	320.64	306.81	298.49	293.35
40000	341.89	337.04	332.72	328.86	314.68	306.15	300.87
41000	350.44	345.47	341.04	337.08	322.55	313.80	308.39
42000	358.98	353.90	349.36	345.30	330.41	321.45	315.91
43000	367.53	362.32	357.68	353.52	338.28	329.11	323.43
44000	376.08	370.75	365.99	361.74	346.15	336.76	330.96
45000	384.63	379.17	374.31	369.96	354.02	344.41	338.48
46000	393.17	387.60	382.63	378.19	361.88	352.07	346.00
47000	401.72	396.03	390.95	386.41	369.75	359.72	353.52
48000	410.27	404.45	399.27	394.63	377.62	367.37	361.04
49000	418.81	412.88	407.58	402.85	385.48	375.03	368.56
50000	427.36	421.31	415.90	411.07	393.35	382.68	376.09
51000	435.91	429.73	424.22	419.29	401.22	390.34	383.61
52000	444.46	438.16	432.54	427.51	409.08	397.99	391.13
53000	453.00	446.58	440.86	435.74	416.95	405.64	398.65
54000	461.55	455.01	449.18	443.96	424.82	413.30	406.17
55000	470.10	463.44	457.49	452.18	432.69	420.95	413.69
56000	478.65	471.86	465.81	460.40	440.55	428.60	421.22
57000	487.19	480.29	474.13	468.62	448.42	436.26	420.74
58000	495.74	488.71	482.45	476.84	456.29	443.91	436.26
59000	504.29	497.14	490.77	485.06	464.15	451.56	443.78
60000	512.83	505.57	499.08	493.29	472.02	459.22	451.30
65000	555.57	547.70	540.67	534.39	511.36	497.49	488.91
70000	598.31	589.83	582.26	575.50	550.69	535.75	526.52
75000	641.04	631.96	623.85	616.61	590.03	574.02	564.13
80000	683.78	674.09	665.44	657.71	629.36	612.29	601.74
85000	726.52	716.22	707.03	698.82	668.70	650.56	639.34
90000	769.25	758.35	748.63	739.93	708.03	688.83	676.95
95000	811.99	800.48	790.22	781.04	747.37	727.09	714.56
100000	854.72	842.61	831.81	822.14	786.70	765.36	752.17
105000	897.46	884.74	873.40	863.25	826.04	803.63	789.78
110000	940.20	926.87	914.99	904.36	865.37	841.90	827.39
120000	1025.67	1011.13	998.17	986.57	944.04	918.44	902.60
130000	1111.14	1095.39	1081.35	1068.79	1022.71	994.97	977.82
140000	1196.61	1179.65	1164.53	1151.00	1101.38	1071.51	1053.04
150000	1282.09	1263.92	1247.71	1233.22	1180.05	1148.04	1128.26
175000	1495.77	1474.57	1455.66	1438.75	1376.73	1339.39	1316.30
200000	1709.45	1685.22	1663.61	1644.29	1573.40	1530.73	1504.34
225000	1923.13	1895.87	1871.56	1849.82	1770.08	1722.07	1692.38
250000	2136.81	2106.53	2079.51	2055.36	1966.75	1913.41	1880.43

9%

Monthly Payments
necessary to amortize a loan

AMOUNT	1 YEAR	2 YEARS	3 YEARS	4 YEARS	5 YEARS	6 YEARS	7 YEARS
100	8.75	4.57	3.18	2.49	2.08	1.80	1.61
200	17.49	9.14	6.36	4.98	4.15	3.61	3.22
500	43.73	22.84	15.90	12.44	10.38	9.01	8.04
1000	87.45	45.68	31.80	24.89	20.76	18.03	16.09
2000	174.90	91.37	63.60	49.77	41.52	36.05	32.18
5000	437.26	228.42	159.00	124.43	103.79	90.13	80.45
6000	524.71	274.11	190.80	149.31	124.55	108.15	96.53
7000	612.16	319.79	222.60	174.20	145.31	126.18	112.62
8000	699.61	365.48	254.40	199.08	166.07	144.20	128.71
9000	787.06	411.16	286.20	223.97	186.83	162.23	144.80
10000	874.51	456.85	318.00	248.85	207.58	180.26	160.89
15000	1311.77	685.27	477.00	373.28	311.38	270.38	241.34
20000	1749.03	913.69	635.99	497.70	415.17	360.51	321.78
25000	2186.29	1142.12	794.99	622.13	518.96	450.64	402.23
30000	2623.54	1370.54	953.99	746.55	622.75	540.77	482.67
35000	3060.80	1598.97	1112.99	870.98	726.54	630.89	563.12
36000	3148.25	1644.65	1144.79	895.86	747.30	648.92	579.21
37000	3235.70	1690.34	1176.59	920.75	768.06	666.94	595.30
38000	3323.16	1736.02	1208.39	945.63	788.82	684.97	611.38
39000	3410.61	1781.70	1240.19	970.52	809.58	703.00	627.47
40000	3498.06	1827.39	1271.99	995.40	830.33	721.02	643.56
41000	3585.51	1873.07	1303.79	1020.29	851.09	739.05	659.65
42000	3672.96	1918.76	1335.59	1045.17	871.85	757.07	675.74
43000	3760.41	1964.44	1367.39	1070.06	892.61	775.10	691.83
44000	3847.86	2010.13	1399.19	1094.94	913.37	793.12	707.92
45000	3935.32	2055.81	1430.99	1119.83	934.13	811.15	724.01
46000	4022.77	2101.50	1462.79	1144.71	954.88	829.17	740.10
47000	4110.22	2147.18	1494.59	1169.60	975.64	847.20	756.19
48000	4197.67	2192.87	1526.39	1194.48	996.40	865.23	772.28
49000	4285.12	2238.55	1558.19	1219.37	1017.16	883.25	788.36
50000	4372.57	2284.24	1589.99	1244.25	1037.92	901.28	804.45
51000	4460.03	2329.92	1621.79	1269.14	1058.68	919.30	820.54
52000	4547.48	2375.61	1653.59	1294.02	1079.43	937.33	836.63
53000	4634.93	2421.29	1685.39	1318.91	1100.19	955.35	852.72
54000	4722.38	2466.98	1717.19	1343.79	1120.95	973.38	868.81
55000	4809.83	2512.66	1748.99	1368.68	1141.71	991.40	884.90
56000	4897.28	2558.35	1780.79	1393.56	1162.47	1009.43	900.99
57000	4984.73	2604.03	1812.58	1418.45	1183.23	1027.46	917.08
58000	5072.19	2649.72	1844.38	1443.33	1203.98	1045.48	933.17
59000	5159.64	2695.40	1876.18	1468.22	1224.74	1063.51	949.26
60000	5247.09	2741.08	1907.98	1493.10	1245.50	1081.53	965.34
65000	5684.35	2969.51	2066.98	1617.53	1349.29	1171.66	1045.79
70000	6121.60	3197.93	2225.98	1741.95	1453.08	1261.79	1126.24
75000	6558.86	3426.36	2384.98	1866.38	1556.88	1351.92	1206.68
80000	6996.12	3654.78	2543.98	1990.80	1660.67	1442.04	1287.13
85000	7433.38	3883.20	2702.98	2115.23	1764.46	1532.17	1367.57
90000	7870.63	4111.63	2861.98	2239.65	1868.25	1622.30	1448.02
95000	8307.89	4340.05	3020.97	2364.08	1972.04	1712.43	1528.46
100000	8745.15	4568.47	3179.97	2488.50	2075.84	1802.55	1608.91
105000	9182.41	4796.90	3338.97	2612.93	2179.63	1892.68	1689.35
110000	9619.66	5025.32	3497.97	2737.35	2283.42	1982.81	1769.80
120000	10494.18	5482.17	3815.97	2986.21	2491.00	2163.06	1930.69
130000	11368.69	5939.02	4133.97	3235.06	2698.59	2343.32	2091.58
140000	12243.21	6395.86	4451.96	3483.91	2906.17	2523.58	2252.47
150000	13117.72	6852.71	4769.96	3732.76	3113.75	2703.83	2413.36
175000	15304.01	7994.83	5564.95	4354.88	3632.71	3154.47	2815.59
200000	17490.30	9136.95	6359.95	4977.01	4151.67	3605.11	3217.82
225000	19676.58	10279.07	7154.94	5599.13	4670.63	4055.75	3620.04
250000	21862.87	11421.19	7949.93	6221.26	5189.59	4506.38	4022.27

Monthly Payments 9%

necessary to amortize a loan

AMOUNT	8 YEARS	9 YEARS	10 YEARS	11 YEARS	12 YEARS	13 YEARS	14 YEARS
100	1.47	1.35	1.27	1.20	1.14	1.09	1.05
200	2.93	2.71	2.53	2.39	2.28	2.18	2.10
500	7.33	6.77	6.33	5.98	5.69	5.45	5.24
1000	14.65	13.54	12.67	11.96	11.38	10.90	10.49
2000	29.30	27.09	25.34	23.92	22.76	21.79	20.98
5000	73.25	67.71	63.34	59.80	56.90	54.48	52.45
6000	87.90	81.26	76.01	71.76	68.28	65.38	62.94
7000	102.55	94.80	88.67	83.73	79.66	76.28	73.43
8000	117.20	108.34	101.34	95.69	91.04	87.17	83.92
9000	131.85	121.89	114.01	107.65	102.42	98.07	94.40
10000	146.50	135.43	126.68	119.61	113.80	108.97	104.89
15000	219.75	203.14	190.01	179.41	170.70	163.45	157.34
20000	293.00	270.86	253.35	239.22	227.61	217.94	209.79
25000	366.26	338.57	316.69	299.02	284.51	272.42	262.23
30000	439.51	406.29	380.03	358.82	341.41	326.90	314.68
35000	512.76	474.00	443.37	418.63	398.31	381.39	367.13
36000	527.41	487.54	456.03	430.59	409.69	392.28	377.62
37000	542.06	501.09	468.70	442.55	421.07	403.18	388.11
38000	556.71	514.63	481.37	454.51	432.45	414.08	398.60
39000	571.36	528.17	494.04	466.47	443.83	424.98	409.09
40000	586.01	541.72	506.70	478.43	455.21	435.87	419.58
41000	600.66	555.26	519.37	490.39	466.59	446.77	430.06
42000	615.31	568.80	532.04	502.35	477.97	457.67	440.55
43000	629.96	582.35	544.71	514.31	489.35	468.56	451.04
44000	644.61	595.89	557.37	526.28	500.73	479.46	461.53
45000	659.26	609.43	570.04	538.24	512.11	490.36	472.02
46000	673.91	622.97	582.71	550.20	523.49	501.25	482.51
47000	688.56	636.52	595.38	562.16	534.87	512.15	493.00
48000	703.21	650.06	608.04	574.12	546.25	523.05	503.49
49000	717.86	663.60	620.71	586.08	557.64	533.94	513.98
50000	732.51	677.15	633.38	598.04	569.02	544.84	524.47
51000	747.16	690.69	646.05	610.00	580.40	555.74	534.96
52000	761.81	704.23	658.71	621.96	591.78	566.63	545.45
53000	776.46	717.77	671.38	633.92	603.16	577.53	555.94
54000	791.11	731.32	684.05	645.88	614.54	588.43	566.43
55000	805.76	744.86	696.72	657.84	625.92	599.32	576.92
56000	820.41	758.40	709.38	669.81	637.30	610.22	587.41
57000	835.06	771.95	722.05	681.77	648.68	621.12	597.89
58000	849.71	785.49	734.72	693.73	660.06	632.01	608.38
59000	864.36	799.03	747.39	705.69	671.44	642.91	618.87
60000	879.01	812.57	760.05	717.65	682.82	653.81	629.36
65000	952.26	880.29	823.39	777.45	739.72	708.29	681.81
70000	1025.51	948.00	886.73	837.26	796.62	762.78	734.26
75000	1098.77	1015.72	950.07	897.06	853.52	817.26	786.70
80000	1172.02	1083.43	1013.41	956.86	910.42	871.74	839.15
85000	1245.27	1151.15	1076.74	1016.67	067.33	026.23	801.60
90000	1318.52	1218.86	1140.08	1076.47	1024.23	980.71	944.04
95000	1391.77	1286.58	1203.42	1136.28	1081.13	1035.20	996.49
100000	1465.02	1354.29	1266.76	1196.08	1138.03	1089.68	1048.94
105000	1538.27	1422.01	1330.10	1255.88	1194.93	1144.16	1101.38
110000	1611.52	1489.72	1393.43	1315.69	1251.83	1198.65	1153.83
120000	1758.02	1625.15	1520.11	1435.30	1365.64	1307.62	1258.73
130000	1904.53	1760.58	1646.79	1554.90	1479.44	1416.58	1363.62
140000	2051.03	1896.01	1773.46	1674.51	1593.24	1525.55	1468.51
150000	2197.53	2031.44	1900.14	1794.12	1707.05	1634.52	1573.41
175000	2563.79	2370.01	2216.83	2093.14	1991.55	1906.94	1835.64
200000	2930.04	2708.58	2533.52	2392.16	2276.06	2179.36	2097.88
225000	3296.30	3047.15	2850.20	2691.18	2560.57	2451.78	2360.11
250000	3662.55	3385.73	3166.89	2990.20	2845.08	2724.20	2622.34

9%

Monthly Payments

necessary to amortize a loan

AMOUNT	15 YEARS	16 YEARS	17 YEARS	18 YEARS	19 YEARS	20 YEARS	21 YEARS
100	1.01	0.98	0.96	0.94	0.92	0.90	0.88
200	2.03	1.97	1.92	1.87	1.83	1.80	1.77
500	5.07	4.92	4.79	4.68	4.58	4.50	4.42
1000	10.14	9.85	9.59	9.36	9.17	9.00	8.85
2000	20.29	19.69	19.18	18.73	18.34	17.99	17.69
5000	50.71	49.23	47.94	46.82	45.84	44.99	44.23
6000	60.86	59.07	57.53	56.19	55.01	53.98	53.07
7000	71.00	68.92	67.12	65.55	64.18	62.98	61.92
8000	81.14	78.76	76.70	74.92	73.35	71.98	70.77
9000	91.28	88.61	86.29	84.28	82.52	80.98	79.61
10000	101.43	98.45	95.88	93.64	91.69	89.97	88.46
15000	152.14	147.68	143.82	140.47	137.53	134.96	132.69
20000	202.85	196.90	191.76	187.29	183.38	179.95	176.92
25000	253.57	246.13	239.70	234.11	229.22	224.93	221.15
30000	304.28	295.35	287.64	280.93	275.07	269.92	265.37
35000	354.99	344.58	335.58	327.76	320.91	314.90	309.60
36000	365.14	354.43	345.17	337.12	330.08	323.90	318.45
37000	375.28	364.27	354.76	346.48	339.25	332.90	327.29
38000	385.42	374.12	364.35	355.85	348.42	341.90	336.14
39000	395.56	383.96	373.93	365.21	357.59	350.89	344.99
40000	405.71	393.81	383.52	374.58	366.76	359.89	353.83
41000	415.85	403.65	393.11	383.94	375.93	368.89	362.68
42000	425.99	413.50	402.70	393.31	385.10	377.88	371.52
43000	436.13	423.34	412.29	402.67	394.27	386.88	380.37
44000	446.28	433.19	421.87	412.04	403.43	395.88	389.22
45000	456.42	443.03	431.46	421.40	412.60	404.88	398.06
46000	466.56	452.88	441.05	430.76	421.77	413.87	406.91
47000	476.71	462.72	450.64	440.13	430.94	422.87	415.75
48000	486.85	472.57	460.23	449.49	440.11	431.87	424.60
49000	496.99	482.41	469.81	458.86	449.28	440.87	433.44
50000	507.13	492.26	479.40	468.22	458.45	449.86	442.29
51000	517.28	502.10	488.99	477.59	467.62	458.86	451.14
52000	527.42	511.95	498.58	486.95	476.79	467.86	459.98
53000	537.56	521.79	508.17	496.32	485.96	476.85	468.83
54000	547.70	531.64	517.75	505.68	495.12	485.85	477.67
55000	557.85	541.48	527.34	515.04	504.29	494.85	486.52
56000	567.99	551.33	536.93	524.41	513.46	503.85	495.37
57000	578.13	561.17	546.52	533.77	522.63	512.84	504.21
58000	588.27	571.02	556.11	543.14	531.80	521.84	513.06
59000	598.42	580.86	565.69	552.50	540.97	530.84	521.90
60000	608.56	590.71	575.28	561.87	550.14	539.84	530.75
65000	659.27	639.94	623.22	608.69	595.98	584.82	574.98
70000	709.99	689.16	671.16	655.51	641.83	629.81	619.21
75000	760.70	738.39	719.10	702.33	687.67	674.79	663.44
80000	811.41	787.61	767.04	749.16	733.52	719.78	707.66
85000	862.13	836.84	814.98	795.98	779.36	764.77	751.89
90000	912.84	886.06	862.92	842.80	825.21	809.75	796.12
95000	963.55	935.29	910.86	889.62	871.05	854.74	840.35
100000	1014.27	984.52	958.80	936.44	916.90	899.73	884.58
105000	1064.98	1033.74	1006.74	983.27	962.74	944.71	928.81
110000	1115.69	1082.97	1054.68	1030.09	1008.59	989.70	973.04
120000	1217.12	1181.42	1150.56	1123.73	1100.28	1079.67	1061.50
130000	1318.55	1279.87	1246.45	1217.38	1191.97	1169.64	1149.96
140000	1419.97	1378.32	1342.33	1311.02	1283.66	1259.62	1238.41
150000	1521.40	1476.77	1438.21	1404.67	1375.35	1349.59	1326.87
175000	1774.97	1722.90	1677.91	1638.78	1604.57	1574.52	1548.02
200000	2028.53	1969.03	1917.61	1872.89	1833.79	1799.45	1769.16
225000	2282.10	2215.16	2157.31	2107.00	2063.02	2024.38	1990.31
250000	2535.67	2461.29	2397.01	2341.11	2292.24	2249.31	2211.45

Monthly Payments 9%

necessary to amortize a loan

AMOUNT	22 YEARS	23 YEARS	24 YEARS	25 YEARS	30 YEARS	35 YEARS	40 YEARS
100	0.87	0.86	0.85	0.84	0.80	0.78	0.77
200	1.74	1.72	1.70	1.68	1.61	1.57	1.54
500	4.36	4.30	4.24	4.20	4.02	3.92	3.86
1000	8.71	8.59	8.49	8.39	8.05	7.84	7.71
2000	17.42	17.19	16.97	16.78	16.09	15.68	15.43
5000	43.56	42.96	42.43	41.96	40.23	39.20	38.57
6000	52.27	51.56	50.92	50.35	48.28	47.04	46.28
7000	60.98	60.15	59.41	58.74	56.32	54.88	54.00
8000	69.69	68.74	67.89	67.14	64.37	62.72	61.71
9000	78.41	77.33	76.38	75.53	72.42	70.56	69.42
10000	87.12	85.93	84.87	83.92	80.46	78.40	77.14
15000	130.68	128.89	127.30	125.88	120.69	117.60	115.70
20000	174.23	171.85	169.73	167.84	160.92	156.80	154.27
25000	217.79	214.82	212.17	209.80	201.16	196.00	192.84
30000	261.35	257.78	254.60	251.76	241.39	235.20	231.41
35000	304.91	300.74	297.03	293.72	281.62	274.40	269.98
36000	313.62	309.34	305.52	302.11	289.66	282.24	277.69
37000	322.33	317.93	314.01	310.50	297.71	290.08	285.40
38000	331.05	326.52	322.49	318.89	305.76	297.92	293.12
39000	339.76	335.11	330.98	327.29	313.80	305.76	300.83
40000	348.47	343.71	339.47	335.68	321.85	313.60	308.54
41000	357.18	352.30	347.95	344.07	329.90	321.44	316.26
42000	365.89	360.89	356.44	352.46	337.94	329.28	323.97
43000	374.60	369.49	364.93	360.85	345.99	337.12	331.69
44000	383.32	378.08	373.41	369.25	354.03	344.96	339.40
45000	392.03	386.67	381.90	377.64	362.08	352.80	347.11
46000	400.74	395.26	390.39	386.03	370.13	360.64	354.83
47000	409.45	403.86	398.87	394.42	378.17	368.48	362.54
48000	418.16	412.45	407.36	402.81	386.22	376.32	370.25
49000	426.88	421.04	415.85	411.21	394.27	384.16	377.97
50000	435.59	429.63	424.33	419.60	402.31	392.00	385.68
51000	444.30	438.23	432.82	427.99	410.36	399.84	393.39
52000	453.01	446.82	441.31	436.38	418.40	407.68	401.11
53000	461.72	455.41	449.79	444.77	426.45	415.52	408.82
54000	470.43	464.00	458.28	453.17	434.50	423.36	416.54
55000	479.15	472.60	466.77	461.56	442.54	431.20	424.25
56000	487.86	481.19	475.25	469.95	450.59	439.04	431.96
57000	496.57	489.78	483.74	478.34	458.63	446.88	439.68
58000	505.28	498.38	492.23	400.73	400.00	454.72	447.30
59000	513.99	506.97	500.71	495.13	474.73	462.56	455.10
60000	522.70	515.56	509.20	503.52	482.77	470.40	462.82
65000	566.26	558.52	551.63	545.48	523.00	509.60	501.38
70000	609.82	601.49	594.07	587.44	563.24	548.80	539.95
75000	653.38	644.45	636.50	629.40	603.47	587.99	578.52
80000	696.94	687.41	678.93	671.36	643.70	627.19	617.09
85000	740.50	730.38	721.36	713.32	683.93	666.39	655.66
90000	784.06	773.34	763.80	755.28	724.16	705.59	694.23
95000	827.62	816.30	806.23	797.24	764.39	744.79	732.79
100000	871.17	859.27	848.66	839.20	804.62	783.99	771.36
105000	914.73	902.23	891.10	881.16	844.85	823.19	809.93
110000	958.29	945.19	933.53	923.12	885.08	862.39	848.50
120000	1045.41	1031.12	1018.40	1007.04	965.55	940.79	925.63
130000	1132.53	1117.05	1103.26	1090.96	1046.01	1019.19	1002.77
140000	1219.64	1202.98	1188.13	1174.87	1126.47	1097.59	1079.91
150000	1306.76	1288.90	1273.00	1258.79	1206.93	1175.99	1157.04
175000	1524.56	1503.72	1485.16	1468.59	1408.09	1371.99	1349.88
200000	1742.35	1718.54	1697.33	1678.39	1609.25	1567.99	1542.72
225000	1960.14	1933.35	1909.49	1888.19	1810.40	1763.98	1735.56
250000	2177.94	2148.17	2121.66	2097.99	2011.56	1959.98	1928.40

9¼%

Monthly Payments
necessary to amortize a loan

AMOUNT	1 YEAR	2 YEARS	3 YEARS	4 YEARS	5 YEARS	6 YEARS	7 YEARS
100	8.76	4.58	3.19	2.50	2.09	1.81	1.62
200	17.51	9.16	6.38	5.00	4.18	3.63	3.24
500	43.78	22.90	15.96	12.50	10.44	9.07	8.11
1000	87.57	45.80	31.92	25.00	20.88	18.15	16.22
2000	175.13	91.60	63.83	50.01	41.76	36.30	32.43
5000	437.84	229.00	159.58	125.02	104.40	90.75	81.08
6000	525.40	274.80	191.50	150.02	125.28	108.90	97.30
7000	612.97	320.60	223.41	175.03	146.16	127.05	113.51
8000	700.54	366.40	255.33	200.03	167.04	145.20	129.73
9000	788.11	412.20	287.25	225.04	187.92	163.35	145.95
10000	875.67	458.00	319.16	250.04	208.80	181.50	162.16
15000	1313.51	686.99	478.74	375.06	313.20	272.25	243.24
20000	1751.35	915.99	638.32	500.08	417.60	363.00	324.32
25000	2189.19	1144.99	797.91	625.10	522.00	453.75	405.41
30000	2627.02	1373.99	957.49	750.12	626.40	544.50	486.49
35000	3064.86	1602.98	1117.07	875.14	730.80	635.25	567.57
36000	3152.43	1648.78	1148.98	900.14	751.68	653.40	583.78
37000	3240.00	1694.58	1180.90	925.15	772.56	671.54	600.00
38000	3327.56	1740.38	1212.82	950.15	793.44	689.69	616.22
39000	3415.13	1786.18	1244.73	975.15	814.32	707.84	632.43
40000	3502.70	1831.98	1276.65	1000.16	835.20	725.99	648.65
41000	3590.27	1877.78	1308.56	1025.16	856.08	744.14	664.87
42000	3677.83	1923.58	1340.48	1050.16	876.96	762.29	681.08
43000	3765.40	1969.38	1372.40	1075.17	897.84	780.44	697.30
44000	3852.97	2015.18	1404.31	1100.17	918.72	798.59	713.51
45000	3940.54	2060.98	1436.23	1125.18	939.60	816.74	729.73
46000	4028.10	2106.78	1468.15	1150.18	960.48	834.89	745.95
47000	4115.67	2152.58	1500.06	1175.18	981.36	853.04	762.16
48000	4203.24	2198.38	1531.98	1200.19	1002.24	871.19	778.38
49000	4290.81	2244.18	1563.89	1225.19	1023.12	889.34	794.60
50000	4378.37	2289.98	1595.81	1250.20	1043.99	907.49	810.81
51000	4465.94	2335.78	1627.73	1275.20	1064.87	925.64	827.03
52000	4553.51	2381.58	1659.64	1300.20	1085.75	943.79	843.24
53000	4641.07	2427.38	1691.56	1325.21	1106.63	961.94	859.46
54000	4728.64	2473.17	1723.48	1350.21	1127.51	980.09	875.68
55000	4816.21	2518.97	1755.39	1375.22	1148.39	998.24	891.89
56000	4903.78	2564.77	1787.31	1400.22	1169.27	1016.39	908.11
57000	4991.34	2610.57	1819.22	1425.22	1190.15	1034.54	924.33
58000	5078.91	2656.37	1851.14	1450.23	1211.03	1052.69	940.54
59000	5166.48	2702.17	1883.06	1475.23	1231.91	1070.84	956.76
60000	5254.05	2747.97	1914.97	1500.24	1252.79	1088.99	972.97
65000	5691.88	2976.97	2074.55	1625.25	1357.19	1179.74	1054.06
70000	6129.72	3205.97	2234.13	1750.27	1461.59	1270.49	1135.14
75000	6567.56	3434.96	2393.72	1875.29	1565.99	1361.24	1216.22
80000	7005.40	3663.96	2553.30	2000.31	1670.39	1451.99	1297.30
85000	7443.23	3892.96	2712.88	2125.33	1774.79	1542.74	1378.38
90000	7881.07	4121.96	2872.46	2250.35	1879.19	1633.49	1459.46
95000	8318.91	4350.96	3032.04	2375.37	1983.59	1724.24	1540.54
100000	8756.75	4579.95	3191.62	2500.39	2087.99	1814.99	1621.62
105000	9194.58	4808.95	3351.20	2625.41	2192.39	1905.74	1702.71
110000	9632.42	5037.95	3510.78	2750.43	2296.79	1996.49	1783.79
120000	10508.09	5495.94	3829.95	3000.47	2505.59	2177.98	1945.95
130000	11383.77	5953.94	4149.11	3250.51	2714.39	2359.48	2108.11
140000	12259.44	6411.93	4468.27	3500.55	2923.19	2540.98	2270.27
150000	13135.12	6869.93	4787.43	3750.59	3131.98	2722.48	2432.44
175000	15324.30	8014.92	5585.34	4375.69	3653.98	3176.23	2837.84
200000	17513.49	9159.91	6383.24	5000.78	4175.98	3629.97	3243.25
225000	19702.68	10304.89	7181.15	5625.88	4697.98	4083.72	3648.65
250000	21891.86	11449.88	7979.05	6250.98	5219.97	4537.47	4054.06

Monthly Payments 9¼%

necessary to amortize a loan

AMOUNT	8 YEARS	9 YEARS	10 YEARS	11 YEARS	12 YEARS	13 YEARS	14 YEARS
100	1.48	1.37	1.28	1.21	1.15	1.10	1.06
200	2.96	2.74	2.56	2.42	2.30	2.21	2.13
500	7.39	6.84	6.40	6.05	5.76	5.52	5.32
1000	14.78	13.68	12.80	12.10	11.52	11.04	10.64
2000	29.56	27.35	25.61	24.20	23.04	22.08	21.27
5000	73.90	68.38	64.02	60.50	57.61	55.20	53.18
6000	88.68	82.05	76.82	72.60	69.13	66.24	63.82
7000	103.46	95.73	89.62	84.70	80.65	77.29	74.45
8000	118.24	109.41	102.43	96.79	92.17	88.33	85.09
9000	133.02	123.08	115.23	108.89	103.69	99.37	95.72
10000	147.80	136.76	128.03	120.99	115.22	110.41	106.36
15000	221.70	205.14	192.05	181.49	172.82	165.61	159.54
20000	295.60	273.52	256.07	241.99	230.43	220.82	212.72
25000	369.51	341.89	320.08	302.48	288.04	276.02	265.90
30000	443.41	410.27	384.10	362.98	345.65	331.22	319.08
35000	517.31	478.65	448.11	423.48	403.25	386.43	372.26
36000	532.09	492.33	460.92	435.57	414.78	397.47	382.90
37000	546.87	506.00	473.72	447.67	426.30	408.51	393.53
38000	561.65	519.68	486.52	459.77	437.82	419.55	404.17
39000	576.43	533.36	499.33	471.87	449.34	430.59	414.80
40000	591.21	547.03	512.13	483.97	460.86	441.63	425.44
41000	605.99	560.71	524.93	496.07	472.38	452.67	436.08
42000	620.77	574.38	537.74	508.17	483.91	463.71	446.71
43000	635.55	588.06	550.54	520.27	495.43	474.75	457.35
44000	650.33	601.73	563.34	532.37	506.95	485.79	467.98
45000	665.11	615.41	576.15	544.47	518.47	496.84	478.62
46000	679.89	629.09	588.95	556.57	529.99	507.88	489.26
47000	694.67	642.76	601.75	568.67	541.51	518.92	499.89
48000	709.45	656.44	614.56	580.77	553.04	529.96	510.53
49000	724.23	670.11	627.36	592.87	564.56	541.00	521.16
50000	739.01	683.79	640.16	604.96	576.08	552.04	531.80
51000	753.79	697.46	652.97	617.06	587.60	563.08	542.44
52000	768.57	711.14	665.77	629.16	599.12	574.12	553.07
53000	783.35	724.82	678.57	641.26	610.64	585.16	563.71
54000	798.13	738.49	691.38	653.36	622.16	596.20	574.34
55000	812.91	752.17	704.18	665.46	633.69	607.24	584.98
56000	827.69	765.84	716.98	677.56	645.21	618.28	595.62
57000	842.47	779.52	729.79	689.66	656.73	629.32	606.25
58000	057.25	703.10	742.60	701.76	668.25	640.37	616.89
59000	872.03	806.87	755.39	713.86	679.77	651.41	627.53
60000	886.81	820.55	768.20	725.96	691.29	662.45	638.16
65000	960.71	888.93	832.21	786.45	748.90	717.65	691.34
70000	1034.62	957.30	896.23	846.95	806.51	772.85	744.52
75000	1108.52	1025.68	960.25	907.45	864.12	828.06	797.70
80000	1182.42	1094.06	1024.26	967.94	921.73	883.26	850.88
85000	1256.32	1162.44	1088.28	1028.44	979.33	938.47	904.06
90000	1330.22	1230.82	1152.29	1088.94	1036.94	993.67	957.24
95000	1404.12	1299.20	1216.31	1149.43	1094.55	1048.87	1010.42
100000	1478.02	1367.58	1280.33	1209.93	1152.16	1104.08	1063.60
105000	1551.92	1435.96	1344.34	1270.43	1209.76	1159.28	1116.78
110000	1625.82	1504.34	1408.36	1330.92	1267.37	1214.49	1169.96
120000	1773.63	1641.09	1536.39	1451.92	1382.59	1324.89	1276.32
130000	1921.43	1777.85	1664.43	1572.91	1497.80	1435.30	1382.68
140000	2069.23	1914.61	1792.46	1693.90	1613.02	1545.71	1489.04
150000	2217.03	2051.37	1920.49	1814.89	1728.23	1656.12	1595.40
175000	2586.54	2393.26	2240.57	2117.38	2016.27	1932.14	1861.30
200000	2956.04	2735.15	2560.65	2419.86	2304.31	2208.16	2127.20
225000	3325.55	3077.05	2880.74	2722.34	2592.35	2484.18	2393.10
250000	3695.06	3418.94	3200.82	3024.82	2880.39	2760.19	2659.00

9¼%

Monthly Payments

necessary to amortize a loan

AMOUNT	15 YEARS	16 YEARS	17 YEARS	18 YEARS	19 YEARS	20 YEARS	21 YEARS
100	1.03	1.00	0.97	0.95	0.93	0.92	0.90
200	2.06	2.00	1.95	1.90	1.87	1.83	1.80
500	5.15	5.00	4.87	4.76	4.66	4.58	4.50
1000	10.29	10.00	9.74	9.52	9.33	9.16	9.01
2000	20.58	19.99	19.48	19.04	18.66	18.32	18.02
5000	51.46	49.98	48.71	47.61	46.64	45.79	45.05
6000	61.75	59.98	58.45	57.13	55.97	54.95	54.06
7000	72.04	69.98	68.20	66.65	65.30	64.11	63.07
8000	82.34	79.98	77.94	76.17	74.62	73.27	72.08
9000	92.63	89.97	87.68	85.69	83.95	82.43	81.09
10000	102.92	99.97	97.42	95.21	93.28	91.59	90.09
15000	154.38	149.95	146.14	142.82	139.92	137.38	135.14
20000	205.84	199.94	194.85	190.42	186.56	183.17	180.19
25000	257.30	249.92	243.56	238.03	233.20	228.97	225.24
30000	308.76	299.91	292.27	285.64	279.84	274.76	270.28
35000	360.22	349.89	340.98	333.24	326.48	320.55	315.33
36000	370.51	359.89	350.72	342.76	335.81	329.71	324.34
37000	380.80	369.89	360.47	352.28	345.14	338.87	333.35
38000	391.09	379.88	370.21	361.81	354.47	348.03	342.36
39000	401.38	389.88	379.95	371.33	363.80	357.19	351.37
40000	411.68	399.88	389.69	380.85	373.12	366.35	360.38
41000	421.97	409.88	399.44	390.37	382.45	375.51	369.39
42000	432.26	419.87	409.18	399.89	391.78	384.66	378.40
43000	442.55	429.87	418.92	409.41	401.11	393.82	387.41
44000	452.84	439.87	428.66	418.93	410.44	402.98	396.42
45000	463.14	449.86	438.41	428.45	419.76	412.14	405.43
46000	473.43	459.86	448.15	437.97	429.09	421.30	414.43
47000	483.72	469.86	457.89	447.50	438.42	430.46	423.44
48000	494.01	479.85	467.63	457.02	447.75	439.62	432.45
49000	504.30	489.85	477.38	466.54	457.08	448.77	441.46
50000	514.60	499.85	487.12	476.06	466.40	457.93	450.47
51000	524.89	509.85	496.86	485.58	475.73	467.09	459.48
52000	535.18	519.84	506.60	495.10	485.06	476.25	468.49
53000	545.47	529.84	516.34	504.62	494.39	485.41	477.50
54000	555.76	539.84	526.09	514.14	503.72	494.57	486.51
55000	566.06	549.83	535.83	523.67	513.04	503.73	495.52
56000	576.35	559.83	545.57	533.19	522.37	512.89	504.53
57000	586.64	569.83	555.31	542.71	531.70	522.04	513.54
58000	596.93	579.82	565.06	552.23	541.03	531.20	522.55
59000	607.22	589.82	574.80	561.75	550.36	540.36	531.56
60000	617.52	599.82	584.54	571.27	559.68	549.52	540.57
65000	668.97	649.80	633.25	618.88	606.33	595.31	585.61
70000	720.43	699.79	681.96	666.48	652.97	641.11	630.66
75000	771.89	749.77	730.68	714.09	699.61	686.90	675.71
80000	823.35	799.76	779.39	761.70	746.25	732.69	720.76
85000	874.81	849.74	828.10	809.30	792.89	778.49	765.80
90000	926.27	899.73	876.81	856.91	839.53	824.28	810.85
95000	977.73	949.71	925.52	904.51	886.17	870.07	855.90
100000	1029.19	999.70	974.23	952.12	932.81	915.87	900.94
105000	1080.65	1049.68	1022.95	999.73	979.45	961.66	945.99
110000	1132.11	1099.67	1071.66	1047.33	1026.09	1007.45	991.04
120000	1235.03	1199.64	1169.08	1142.54	1119.37	1099.04	1081.13
130000	1337.95	1299.61	1266.51	1237.75	1212.65	1190.63	1171.23
140000	1440.87	1399.58	1363.93	1332.97	1305.93	1282.21	1261.32
150000	1543.79	1499.55	1461.35	1428.18	1399.21	1373.80	1351.42
175000	1801.09	1749.47	1704.91	1666.21	1632.41	1602.77	1576.65
200000	2058.38	1999.39	1948.47	1904.24	1865.62	1831.73	1801.89
225000	2315.68	2249.32	2192.03	2142.27	2098.82	2060.70	2027.13
250000	2572.98	2499.24	2435.59	2380.30	2332.02	2289.67	2252.36

Monthly Payments 9¼%

necessary to amortize a loan

AMOUNT	22 YEARS	23 YEARS	24 YEARS	25 YEARS	30 YEARS	35 YEARS	40 YEARS
100	0.89	0.88	0.87	0.86	0.82	0.80	0.79
200	1.78	1.75	1.73	1.71	1.65	1.61	1.58
500	4.44	4.38	4.33	4.28	4.11	4.01	3.95
1000	8.88	8.76	8.66	8.56	8.23	8.03	7.91
2000	17.76	17.52	17.31	17.13	16.45	16.05	15.81
5000	44.39	43.80	43.28	42.82	41.13	40.14	39.53
6000	53.27	52.56	51.94	51.38	49.36	48.16	47.44
7000	62.14	61.32	60.60	59.95	57.59	56.19	55.35
8000	71.02	70.08	69.25	68.51	65.81	64.22	63.25
9000	79.90	78.85	77.91	77.07	74.04	72.25	71.16
10000	88.78	87.61	86.57	85.64	82.27	80.27	79.07
15000	133.16	131.41	129.85	128.46	123.40	120.41	118.60
20000	177.55	175.21	173.13	171.28	164.54	160.55	158.13
25000	221.94	219.01	216.41	214.10	205.67	200.69	197.67
30000	266.33	262.82	259.70	256.91	246.80	240.82	237.20
35000	310.71	306.62	302.98	299.73	287.94	280.96	276.73
36000	319.59	315.38	311.64	308.30	296.16	288.99	284.64
37000	328.47	324.14	320.29	316.86	304.39	297.02	292.54
38000	337.35	332.90	328.95	325.43	312.62	305.04	300.45
39000	346.22	341.66	337.61	333.99	320.84	313.07	308.36
40000	355.10	350.42	346.26	342.55	329.07	321.10	316.26
41000	363.98	359.18	354.92	351.12	337.30	329.13	324.17
42000	372.86	367.94	363.58	359.68	345.52	337.15	332.08
43000	381.73	376.70	372.23	368.24	353.75	345.18	339.98
44000	390.61	385.47	380.89	376.81	361.98	353.21	347.89
45000	399.49	394.23	389.54	385.37	370.20	361.23	355.80
46000	408.37	402.99	398.20	393.94	378.43	369.26	363.70
47000	417.24	411.75	406.86	402.50	386.66	377.29	371.61
48000	426.12	420.51	415.51	411.06	394.88	385.32	379.52
49000	435.00	429.27	424.17	419.63	403.11	393.34	387.42
50000	443.88	438.03	432.83	428.19	411.34	401.37	395.33
51000	452.75	446.79	441.48	436.75	419.56	409.40	403.24
52000	461.63	455.55	450.14	445.32	427.79	417.43	411.14
53000	470.51	464.31	458.80	453.88	436.02	425.45	419.05
54000	479.39	473.07	467.45	462.45	444.24	433.48	426.96
55000	488.26	481.83	476.11	471.01	452.47	441.51	434.86
56000	497.14	490.59	404.77	479.57	460.70	449.54	442.77
57000	506.02	499.35	493.42	488.14	468.92	457.56	450.68
58000	514.00	500.11	502.08	406.70	477.16	465.60	458.58
59000	523.78	516.87	510.74	505.27	485.38	473.62	466.49
60000	532.65	525.63	519.39	513.83	493.61	481.65	474.40
65000	577.04	569.44	562.68	556.65	534.74	521.78	513.93
70000	621.43	613.24	605.96	599.47	575.87	561.92	553.46
75000	665.82	657.04	649.24	642.29	617.01	602.06	593.00
80000	710.20	700.85	692.52	685.11	658.14	642.20	632.53
85000	754.59	744.65	735.81	727.92	699.27	682.33	672.06
90000	798.98	788.45	779.09	770.74	740.41	722.47	711.59
95000	843.37	832.25	822.37	813.56	781.54	762.61	751.13
100000	887.75	876.06	865.66	856.38	822.68	802.74	790.66
105000	932.14	919.86	908.94	899.20	863.81	842.88	830.19
110000	976.53	963.66	952.22	942.02	904.94	883.02	869.73
120000	1065.31	1051.27	1038.79	1027.66	987.21	963.29	948.79
130000	1154.08	1138.87	1125.35	1113.30	1069.48	1043.57	1027.86
140000	1242.86	1226.48	1211.92	1198.93	1151.75	1123.84	1106.92
150000	1331.63	1314.09	1298.48	1284.57	1234.01	1204.12	1185.99
175000	1553.57	1533.10	1514.90	1498.67	1439.68	1404.80	1383.66
200000	1775.51	1752.11	1731.31	1712.76	1645.35	1605.49	1581.32
225000	1997.45	1971.13	1947.72	1926.86	1851.02	1806.17	1778.99
250000	2219.39	2190.14	2164.14	2140.95	2056.69	2006.86	1976.65

9½%

Monthly Payments

necessary to amortize a loan

AMOUNT	1 YEAR	2 YEARS	3 YEARS	4 YEARS	5 YEARS	6 YEARS	7 YEARS
100	8.77	4.59	3.20	2.51	2.10	1.83	1.63
200	17.54	9.18	6.41	5.02	4.20	3.65	3.27
500	43.84	22.96	16.02	12.56	10.50	9.14	8.17
1000	87.68	45.91	32.03	25.12	21.00	18.27	16.34
2000	175.37	91.83	64.07	50.25	42.00	36.55	32.69
5000	438.42	229.57	160.16	125.62	105.01	91.37	81.72
6000	526.10	275.49	192.20	150.74	126.01	109.65	98.06
7000	613.78	321.40	224.23	175.86	147.01	127.92	114.41
8000	701.47	367.32	256.26	200.99	168.01	146.20	130.75
9000	789.15	413.23	288.30	226.11	189.02	164.47	147.10
10000	876.84	459.14	320.33	251.23	210.02	182.75	163.44
15000	1315.25	688.72	480.49	376.85	315.03	274.12	245.16
20000	1753.67	918.29	640.66	502.46	420.04	365.49	326.88
25000	2192.09	1147.86	800.82	628.08	525.05	456.87	408.60
30000	2630.51	1377.43	960.99	753.69	630.06	548.24	490.32
35000	3068.92	1607.01	1121.15	879.31	735.07	639.61	572.04
36000	3156.61	1652.92	1153.19	904.43	756.07	657.89	588.38
37000	3244.29	1698.84	1185.22	929.56	777.07	676.16	604.73
38000	3331.97	1744.75	1217.25	954.68	798.07	694.44	621.07
39000	3419.66	1790.67	1249.29	979.80	819.07	712.71	637.42
40000	3507.34	1836.58	1281.32	1004.93	840.07	730.99	653.76
41000	3595.02	1882.49	1313.35	1030.05	861.08	749.26	670.10
42000	3682.71	1928.41	1345.38	1055.17	882.08	767.54	686.45
43000	3770.39	1974.32	1377.42	1080.29	903.08	785.81	702.79
44000	3858.07	2020.24	1409.45	1105.42	924.08	804.09	719.14
45000	3945.76	2066.15	1441.48	1130.54	945.08	822.36	735.48
46000	4033.44	2112.07	1473.52	1155.66	966.09	840.64	751.82
47000	4121.13	2157.98	1505.55	1180.79	987.09	858.91	768.17
48000	4208.81	2203.90	1537.58	1205.91	1008.09	877.19	784.51
49000	4296.49	2249.81	1569.61	1231.03	1029.09	895.46	800.86
50000	4384.18	2295.72	1601.65	1256.16	1050.09	913.73	817.20
51000	4471.86	2341.64	1633.68	1281.28	1071.09	932.01	833.54
52000	4559.54	2387.55	1665.71	1306.40	1092.10	950.28	849.89
53000	4647.23	2433.47	1697.75	1331.53	1113.10	968.56	866.23
54000	4734.91	2479.38	1729.78	1356.65	1134.10	986.83	882.58
55000	4822.59	2525.30	1761.81	1381.77	1155.10	1005.11	898.92
56000	4910.28	2571.21	1793.85	1406.90	1176.10	1023.38	915.26
57000	4997.96	2617.13	1825.88	1432.02	1197.11	1041.66	931.61
58000	5085.64	2663.04	1857.91	1457.14	1218.11	1059.93	947.95
59000	5173.33	2708.96	1889.94	1482.27	1239.11	1078.21	964.29
60000	5261.01	2754.87	1921.98	1507.39	1260.11	1096.48	980.64
65000	5699.43	2984.44	2082.14	1633.00	1365.12	1187.85	1062.36
70000	6137.85	3214.01	2242.31	1758.62	1470.13	1279.23	1144.08
75000	6576.26	3443.59	2402.47	1884.24	1575.14	1370.60	1225.80
80000	7014.68	3673.16	2562.64	2009.85	1680.15	1461.98	1307.52
85000	7453.10	3902.73	2722.80	2135.47	1785.16	1553.35	1389.24
90000	7891.52	4132.30	2882.97	2261.08	1890.17	1644.72	1470.96
95000	8329.93	4361.88	3043.13	2386.70	1995.18	1736.10	1552.68
100000	8768.35	4591.45	3203.29	2512.31	2100.19	1827.47	1634.40
105000	9206.77	4821.02	3363.46	2637.93	2205.20	1918.84	1716.12
110000	9645.19	5050.59	3523.62	2763.55	2310.20	2010.22	1797.84
120000	10522.02	5509.74	3843.95	3014.78	2520.22	2192.96	1961.28
130000	11398.86	5968.88	4164.28	3266.01	2730.24	2375.71	2124.72
140000	12275.69	6428.03	4484.61	3517.24	2940.26	2558.46	2288.16
150000	13152.53	6887.17	4804.94	3768.47	3150.28	2741.20	2451.60
175000	15344.61	8035.04	5605.77	4396.55	3675.33	3198.07	2860.20
200000	17536.70	9182.90	6406.59	5024.63	4200.37	3654.94	3268.80
225000	19728.79	10330.76	7207.41	5652.71	4725.42	4111.81	3677.40
250000	21920.88	11478.62	8008.24	6280.78	5250.47	4568.67	4086.00

Monthly Payments

necessary to amortize a loan

9½%

AMOUNT	8 YEARS	9 YEARS	10 YEARS	11 YEARS	12 YEARS	13 YEARS	14 YEARS
100	1.49	1.38	1.29	1.22	1.17	1.12	1.08
200	2.98	2.76	2.59	2.45	2.33	2.24	2.16
500	7.46	6.90	6.47	6.12	5.83	5.59	5.39
1000	14.91	13.81	12.94	12.24	11.66	11.19	10.78
2000	29.82	27.62	25.88	24.48	23.33	22.37	21.57
5000	74.55	69.05	64.70	61.19	58.32	55.93	53.92
6000	89.47	82.86	77.64	73.43	69.98	67.11	64.70
7000	104.38	96.67	90.58	85.67	81.65	78.30	75.49
8000	119.29	110.47	103.52	97.91	93.31	89.49	86.27
9000	134.20	124.28	116.46	110.15	104.97	100.67	97.05
10000	149.11	138.09	129.40	122.39	116.64	111.86	107.84
15000	223.66	207.14	194.10	183.58	174.96	167.79	161.76
20000	298.22	276.19	258.80	244.77	233.27	223.71	215.67
25000	372.77	345.23	323.49	305.97	291.59	279.64	269.59
30000	447.33	414.28	388.19	367.16	349.91	335.57	323.51
35000	521.88	483.33	452.89	428.35	408.23	391.50	377.43
36000	536.79	497.14	465.83	440.59	419.89	402.69	388.21
37000	551.70	510.95	478.77	452.83	431.56	413.87	399.00
38000	566.61	524.76	491.71	465.07	443.22	425.06	409.78
39000	581.52	538.57	504.65	477.31	454.89	436.24	420.56
40000	596.44	552.37	517.59	489.55	466.55	447.43	431.35
41000	611.35	566.18	530.53	501.78	478.21	458.61	442.13
42000	626.26	579.99	543.47	514.02	489.88	469.80	452.91
43000	641.17	593.80	556.41	526.26	501.54	480.99	463.70
44000	656.08	607.61	569.35	538.50	513.20	492.17	474.48
45000	670.99	621.42	582.29	550.74	524.87	503.36	485.27
46000	685.90	635.23	595.23	562.98	536.53	514.54	496.05
47000	700.81	649.04	608.17	575.22	548.20	525.73	506.83
48000	715.72	662.85	621.11	587.45	559.86	536.91	517.62
49000	730.63	676.66	634.05	599.69	571.52	548.10	528.40
50000	745.54	690.47	646.99	611.93	583.19	559.29	539.18
51000	760.46	704.28	659.93	624.17	594.85	570.47	549.97
52000	775.37	718.09	672.87	636.41	606.51	581.66	560.75
53000	790.28	731.90	685.81	648.65	618.18	592.84	571.54
54000	805.19	745.71	698.75	660.89	629.84	604.03	582.32
55000	820.10	759.51	711.69	673.13	641.51	615.21	593.10
56000	835.01	773.32	724.63	685.36	653.17	626.40	603.89
57000	849.92	787.13	737.57	697.60	664.83	637.59	614.67
58000	864.83	800.94	750.51	709.84	676.50	648.77	625.45
59000	879.74	814.75	763.45	722.08	688.16	659.96	636.24
60000	894.65	828.56	776.39	734.32	699.82	671.14	647.02
65000	969.21	897.61	841.08	795.51	758.14	727.07	700.94
70000	1043.76	966.66	905.78	856.71	816.46	783.00	754.86
75000	1118.32	1035.70	970.48	917.90	874.78	838.93	808.78
80000	1192.87	1104.75	1035.18	979.09	933.10	894.86	862.69
85000	1207.43	1173.80	1000.88	1040.28	991.42	950.79	916.61
90000	1341.98	1242.84	1164.58	1101.48	1049.74	1006.71	970.53
95000	1416.53	1311.89	1229.20	1162.67	1108.05	1062.64	1024.45
100000	1491.09	1380.94	1293.98	1223.86	1166.37	1118.57	1078.37
105000	1565.64	1449.98	1358.67	1285.06	1224.69	1174.50	1132.29
110000	1640.20	1519.03	1423.37	1346.25	1283.01	1230.43	1186.20
120000	1789.31	1657.12	1552.77	1468.64	1399.65	1342.29	1294.04
130000	1938.42	1795.22	1682.17	1591.02	1516.29	1454.14	1401.88
140000	2087.52	1933.31	1811.57	1713.41	1632.92	1566.00	1509.72
150000	2236.63	2071.40	1940.96	1835.80	1749.56	1677.86	1617.55
175000	2609.41	2416.64	2264.46	2141.76	2041.15	1957.50	1887.14
200000	2982.18	2761.87	2587.95	2447.73	2332.75	2237.14	2156.74
225000	3354.95	3107.11	2911.45	2753.70	2624.34	2516.79	2426.33
250000	3727.72	3452.34	3234.94	3059.66	2915.93	2796.43	2695.92

9½%

Monthly Payments
necessary to amortize a loan

AMOUNT	15 YEARS	16 YEARS	17 YEARS	18 YEARS	19 YEARS	20 YEARS	21 YEARS
100	1.04	1.01	0.99	0.97	0.95	0.93	0.92
200	2.09	2.03	1.98	1.94	1.90	1.86	1.83
500	5.22	5.07	4.95	4.84	4.74	4.66	4.59
1000	10.44	10.15	9.90	9.68	9.49	9.32	9.17
2000	20.88	20.30	19.80	19.36	18.98	18.64	18.35
5000	52.21	50.75	49.49	48.40	47.44	46.61	45.87
6000	62.65	60.90	59.39	58.07	56.93	55.93	55.05
7000	73.10	71.05	69.28	67.75	66.42	65.25	64.22
8000	83.54	81.20	79.18	77.43	75.91	74.57	73.39
9000	93.98	91.35	89.08	87.11	85.40	83.89	82.57
10000	104.42	101.50	98.98	96.79	94.88	93.21	91.74
15000	156.63	152.25	148.47	145.19	142.33	139.82	137.62
20000	208.84	203.00	197.96	193.58	189.77	186.43	183.49
25000	261.06	253.75	247.45	241.98	237.21	233.03	229.36
30000	313.27	304.50	296.93	290.37	284.65	279.64	275.23
35000	365.48	355.25	346.42	338.77	332.09	326.25	321.10
36000	375.92	365.40	356.32	348.45	341.58	335.57	330.28
37000	386.36	375.55	366.22	358.13	351.07	344.89	339.45
38000	396.81	385.70	376.12	367.81	360.56	354.21	348.63
39000	407.25	395.85	386.01	377.49	370.05	363.53	357.80
40000	417.69	406.00	395.91	387.16	379.54	372.85	366.97
41000	428.13	416.15	405.81	396.84	389.02	382.17	376.15
42000	438.57	426.30	415.71	406.52	398.51	391.50	385.32
43000	449.02	436.45	425.61	416.20	408.00	400.82	394.50
44000	459.46	446.60	435.50	425.88	417.49	410.14	403.67
45000	469.90	456.75	445.40	435.56	426.98	419.46	412.85
46000	480.34	466.90	455.30	445.24	436.47	428.78	422.02
47000	490.79	477.05	465.20	454.92	445.95	438.10	431.19
48000	501.23	487.19	475.09	464.60	455.44	447.42	440.37
49000	511.67	497.34	484.99	474.28	464.93	456.74	449.54
50000	522.11	507.49	494.89	483.96	474.42	466.07	458.72
51000	532.55	517.64	504.79	493.63	483.91	475.39	467.89
52000	543.00	527.79	514.69	503.31	493.40	484.71	477.07
53000	553.44	537.94	524.58	512.99	502.89	494.03	486.24
54000	563.88	548.09	534.48	522.67	512.37	503.35	495.41
55000	574.32	558.24	544.38	532.35	521.86	512.67	504.59
56000	584.77	568.39	554.28	542.03	531.35	521.99	513.76
57000	595.21	578.54	564.17	551.71	540.84	531.31	522.94
58000	605.65	588.69	574.07	561.39	550.33	540.64	532.11
59000	616.09	598.84	583.97	571.07	559.82	549.96	541.29
60000	626.53	608.99	593.87	580.75	569.30	559.28	550.46
65000	678.75	659.74	643.36	629.14	616.75	605.89	596.33
70000	730.96	710.49	692.85	677.54	664.19	652.49	642.20
75000	783.17	761.24	742.34	725.93	711.63	699.10	688.08
80000	835.38	811.99	791.82	774.33	759.07	745.70	733.95
85000	887.59	862.74	841.31	822.72	806.51	792.31	779.82
90000	939.80	913.49	890.80	871.12	853.96	838.92	825.69
95000	992.01	964.24	940.29	919.52	901.40	885.52	871.56
100000	1044.22	1014.99	989.78	967.91	948.84	932.13	917.43
105000	1096.44	1065.74	1039.27	1016.31	996.28	978.74	963.31
110000	1148.65	1116.49	1088.76	1064.70	1043.72	1025.34	1009.18
120000	1253.07	1217.99	1187.74	1161.49	1138.61	1118.56	1100.92
130000	1357.49	1319.49	1286.71	1258.28	1233.49	1211.77	1192.66
140000	1461.91	1420.99	1385.69	1355.08	1328.38	1304.98	1284.41
150000	1566.34	1522.48	1484.67	1451.87	1423.26	1398.20	1376.15
175000	1827.39	1776.23	1732.12	1693.85	1660.47	1631.23	1605.51
200000	2088.45	2029.98	1979.56	1935.82	1897.68	1864.26	1834.87
225000	2349.51	2283.73	2227.01	2177.80	2134.89	2097.30	2064.23
250000	2610.56	2537.47	2474.45	2419.78	2372.10	2330.33	2293.59

Monthly Payments — 9½%

necessary to amortize a loan

AMOUNT	22 YEARS	23 YEARS	24 YEARS	25 YEARS	30 YEARS	35 YEARS	40 YEARS
100	0.90	0.89	0.88	0.87	0.84	0.82	0.81
200	1.81	1.79	1.77	1.75	1.68	1.64	1.62
500	4.52	4.46	4.41	4.37	4.20	4.11	4.05
1000	9.04	8.93	8.83	8.74	8.41	8.22	8.10
2000	18.09	17.86	17.66	17.47	16.82	16.43	16.20
5000	45.22	44.65	44.14	43.68	42.04	41.08	40.50
6000	54.27	53.58	52.97	52.42	50.45	49.30	48.60
7000	63.31	62.51	61.79	61.16	58.86	57.51	56.70
8000	72.36	71.44	70.62	69.90	67.27	65.73	64.80
9000	81.40	80.37	79.45	78.63	75.68	73.95	72.91
10000	90.45	89.30	88.28	87.37	84.09	82.16	81.01
15000	135.67	133.95	132.42	131.05	126.13	123.24	121.51
20000	180.89	178.59	176.55	174.74	168.17	164.32	162.01
25000	226.12	223.24	220.69	218.42	210.21	205.40	202.52
30000	271.34	267.89	264.83	262.11	252.26	246.48	243.02
35000	316.56	312.54	308.97	305.79	294.30	287.56	283.52
36000	325.61	321.47	317.80	314.53	302.71	295.78	291.62
37000	334.65	330.40	326.63	323.27	311.12	304.00	299.72
38000	343.70	339.33	335.45	332.00	319.52	312.21	307.82
39000	352.74	348.26	344.28	340.74	327.93	320.43	315.92
40000	361.78	357.19	353.11	349.48	336.34	328.64	324.02
41000	370.83	366.12	361.94	358.22	344.75	336.86	332.13
42000	379.87	375.05	370.77	366.95	353.16	345.08	340.23
43000	388.92	383.98	379.59	375.69	361.57	353.29	348.33
44000	397.96	392.91	388.42	384.43	369.98	361.51	356.43
45000	407.01	401.84	397.25	393.16	378.38	369.73	364.53
46000	416.05	410.77	406.08	401.90	386.79	377.94	372.63
47000	425.10	419.70	414.90	410.64	395.20	386.16	380.73
48000	434.14	428.63	423.73	419.37	403.61	394.37	388.83
49000	443.19	437.56	432.56	428.11	412.02	402.59	396.93
50000	452.23	446.49	441.39	436.85	420.43	410.81	405.03
51000	461.28	455.42	450.22	445.59	428.84	419.02	413.13
52000	470.32	464.35	459.04	454.32	437.24	427.24	421.23
53000	479.36	473.28	467.87	463.06	445.65	435.45	429.33
54000	488.41	482.21	476.70	471.80	454.06	443.67	437.43
55000	497.45	491.14	485.53	480.53	462.47	451.89	445.53
56000	506.60	500.07	494.35	489.27	470.88	460.10	453.63
57000	515.54	509.00	503.18	498.01	479.29	468.32	461.74
58000	524.69	517.93	512.01	506.74	487.70	476.53	469.84
59000	533.63	526.85	520.84	515.48	496.10	484.75	477.94
60000	542.68	535.78	529.66	524.22	504.51	492.97	486.04
65000	587.90	580.43	573.80	567.90	546.56	534.05	526.54
70000	633.12	625.08	617.94	611.59	588.60	575.13	567.04
75000	678.35	669.73	662.08	655.27	630.64	616.21	607.55
80000	723.57	714.38	706.22	698.96	672.68	657.29	648.05
85000	768.79	759.03	750.36	742.64	714.73	698.37	688.56
90000	814.02	803.68	794.50	786.33	756.77	739.45	729.06
95000	859.24	848.33	838.64	830.01	798.81	780.53	769.56
100000	904.46	892.97	882.77	873.70	840.86	821.61	810.06
105000	949.68	937.62	926.91	917.38	882.90	862.69	850.56
110000	994.91	982.27	971.05	961.07	924.94	903.77	891.07
120000	1085.35	1071.57	1059.33	1048.44	1009.03	985.93	972.07
130000	1175.80	1160.87	1147.61	1135.81	1093.11	1068.10	1053.08
140000	1266.25	1250.16	1235.88	1223.18	1177.20	1150.26	1134.09
150000	1356.69	1339.46	1324.16	1310.54	1261.28	1232.42	1215.09
175000	1582.81	1562.70	1544.86	1528.97	1471.49	1437.82	1417.61
200000	1808.92	1785.95	1765.55	1747.39	1681.71	1643.22	1620.12
225000	2035.04	2009.19	1986.24	1965.82	1891.92	1848.63	1822.64
250000	2261.15	2232.44	2206.94	2184.24	2102.14	2054.03	2025.15

9¾%

Monthly Payments
necessary to amortize a loan

AMOUNT	1 YEAR	2 YEARS	3 YEARS	4 YEARS	5 YEARS	6 YEARS	7 YEARS
100	8.78	4.60	3.21	2.52	2.11	1.84	1.65
200	17.56	9.21	6.43	5.05	4.22	3.68	3.29
500	43.90	23.01	16.07	12.62	10.56	9.20	8.24
1000	87.80	46.03	32.15	25.24	21.12	18.40	16.47
2000	175.60	92.06	64.30	50.49	42.25	36.80	32.94
5000	439.00	230.15	160.75	126.21	105.62	92.00	82.36
6000	526.80	276.18	192.90	151.46	126.75	110.40	98.83
7000	614.60	322.21	225.05	176.70	147.87	128.80	115.31
8000	702.40	368.24	257.20	201.94	168.99	147.20	131.78
9000	790.20	414.27	289.35	227.18	190.12	165.60	148.25
10000	878.00	460.30	321.50	252.43	211.24	184.00	164.72
15000	1316.99	690.44	482.25	378.64	316.86	276.00	247.08
20000	1755.99	920.59	643.00	504.85	422.48	368.00	329.45
25000	2194.99	1150.74	803.75	631.07	528.11	460.00	411.81
30000	2633.99	1380.89	964.50	757.28	633.73	552.00	494.17
35000	3072.99	1611.04	1125.25	883.49	739.35	644.00	576.53
36000	3160.79	1657.07	1157.40	908.74	760.47	662.40	593.00
37000	3248.59	1703.10	1189.55	933.98	781.60	680.80	609.47
38000	3336.39	1749.13	1221.70	959.22	802.72	699.20	625.95
39000	3424.19	1795.16	1253.85	984.46	823.85	717.60	642.42
40000	3511.99	1841.18	1286.00	1009.71	844.97	736.00	658.89
41000	3599.79	1887.21	1318.15	1034.95	866.09	754.40	675.36
42000	3687.59	1933.24	1350.30	1060.19	887.22	772.80	691.84
43000	3775.39	1979.27	1382.45	1085.44	908.34	791.20	708.31
44000	3863.18	2025.30	1414.60	1110.68	929.47	809.60	724.78
45000	3950.98	2071.33	1446.75	1135.92	950.59	828.00	741.25
46000	4038.78	2117.36	1478.90	1161.16	971.72	846.40	757.73
47000	4126.58	2163.39	1511.05	1186.41	992.84	864.80	774.20
48000	4214.38	2209.42	1543.20	1211.65	1013.96	883.20	790.67
49000	4302.18	2255.45	1575.35	1236.89	1035.09	901.60	807.14
50000	4389.98	2301.48	1607.50	1262.13	1056.21	920.00	823.61
51000	4477.78	2347.51	1639.65	1287.38	1077.34	938.40	840.09
52000	4565.58	2393.54	1671.80	1312.62	1098.46	956.80	856.56
53000	4653.38	2439.57	1703.95	1337.86	1119.58	975.20	873.03
54000	4741.18	2485.60	1736.10	1363.11	1140.71	993.60	889.50
55000	4828.98	2531.63	1768.25	1388.35	1161.83	1012.00	905.98
56000	4916.78	2577.66	1800.40	1413.59	1182.96	1030.40	922.45
57000	5004.58	2623.69	1832.55	1438.83	1204.08	1048.80	938.92
58000	5092.38	2669.72	1864.70	1464.08	1225.21	1067.20	955.39
59000	5180.18	2715.75	1896.85	1489.32	1246.33	1085.60	971.87
60000	5267.98	2761.78	1929.00	1514.56	1267.45	1104.00	988.34
65000	5706.98	2991.93	2089.75	1640.77	1373.08	1196.00	1070.70
70000	6145.98	3222.07	2250.50	1766.99	1478.70	1288.00	1153.06
75000	6584.97	3452.22	2411.25	1893.20	1584.32	1380.00	1235.42
80000	7023.97	3682.37	2572.00	2019.42	1689.94	1472.00	1317.78
85000	7462.97	3912.52	2732.74	2145.63	1795.56	1564.00	1400.15
90000	7901.97	4142.67	2893.49	2271.84	1901.18	1656.00	1482.51
95000	8340.97	4372.81	3054.24	2398.06	2006.80	1748.00	1564.87
100000	8779.97	4602.96	3214.99	2524.27	2112.42	1840.00	1647.23
105000	9218.96	4833.11	3375.74	2650.48	2218.05	1932.00	1729.59
110000	9657.96	5063.26	3536.49	2776.70	2323.67	2024.00	1811.95
120000	10535.96	5523.55	3857.99	3029.12	2534.91	2208.00	1976.68
130000	11413.96	5983.85	4179.49	3281.55	2746.15	2392.00	2141.40
140000	12291.95	6444.15	4500.99	3533.98	2957.39	2576.00	2306.12
150000	13169.95	6904.44	4822.49	3786.40	3168.64	2760.00	2470.84
175000	15364.94	8055.18	5626.24	4417.47	3696.74	3220.00	2882.65
200000	17559.93	9205.92	6429.99	5048.54	4224.85	3680.00	3294.46
225000	19754.92	10356.67	7233.74	5679.61	4752.95	4140.00	3706.27
250000	21949.91	11507.41	8037.49	6310.67	5281.06	4600.00	4118.07

Monthly Payments 9¾%

necessary to amortize a loan

AMOUNT	8 YEARS	9 YEARS	10 YEARS	11 YEARS	12 YEARS	13 YEARS	14 YEARS
100	1.50	1.39	1.31	1.24	1.18	1.13	1.09
200	3.01	2.79	2.62	2.48	2.36	2.27	2.19
500	7.52	6.97	6.54	6.19	5.90	5.67	5.47
1000	15.04	13.94	13.08	12.38	11.81	11.33	10.93
2000	30.08	27.89	26.15	24.76	23.61	22.66	21.86
5000	75.21	69.72	65.39	61.89	59.03	56.66	54.66
6000	90.25	83.66	78.46	74.27	70.84	67.99	65.59
7000	105.30	97.61	91.54	86.65	82.65	79.32	76.53
8000	120.34	111.55	104.62	99.03	94.45	90.65	87.46
9000	135.38	125.49	117.69	111.41	106.26	101.98	98.39
10000	150.42	139.44	130.77	123.79	118.07	113.32	109.32
15000	225.63	209.15	196.16	185.68	177.10	169.97	163.99
20000	300.84	278.87	261.54	247.58	236.14	226.63	218.65
25000	376.06	348.59	326.93	309.47	295.17	283.29	273.31
30000	451.27	418.31	392.31	371.37	354.20	339.95	327.97
35000	526.48	488.03	457.70	433.26	413.24	396.61	382.63
36000	541.52	501.97	470.77	445.64	425.05	407.94	393.56
37000	556.56	515.92	483.85	458.02	436.85	419.27	404.50
38000	571.60	529.86	496.93	470.40	448.66	430.60	415.43
39000	586.65	543.80	510.00	482.77	460.47	441.93	426.36
40000	601.69	557.75	523.08	495.15	472.27	453.27	437.29
41000	616.73	571.69	536.16	507.53	484.08	464.60	448.23
42000	631.77	585.63	549.24	519.91	495.89	475.93	459.16
43000	646.81	599.58	562.31	532.29	507.69	487.26	470.09
44000	661.86	613.52	575.39	544.67	519.50	498.59	481.02
45000	676.90	627.46	588.47	557.05	531.31	509.92	491.96
46000	691.94	641.41	601.54	569.43	543.11	521.25	502.89
47000	706.98	655.35	614.62	581.81	554.92	532.59	513.82
48000	722.03	669.30	627.70	594.18	566.73	543.92	524.75
49000	737.07	683.24	640.77	606.56	578.53	555.25	535.69
50000	752.11	697.18	653.85	618.94	590.34	566.58	546.62
51000	767.15	711.13	666.93	631.32	602.15	577.91	557.55
52000	782.19	725.07	680.01	643.70	613.95	589.24	568.48
53000	797.24	739.01	693.08	656.08	625.76	600.58	579.41
54000	812.28	752.96	706.16	668.46	637.57	611.91	590.35
55000	827.32	766.90	719.24	680.84	649.37	623.24	601.28
56000	842.36	780.85	732.31	693.22	661.18	634.57	612.21
57000	857.41	794.79	745.39	705.59	672.99	645.90	623.14
58000	872.45	808.73	758.47	717.97	684.79	657.23	634.08
59000	887.49	822.68	771.54	730.35	696.60	668.57	645.01
60000	902.53	836.62	784.62	742.73	708.41	679.90	655.94
65000	977.74	906.34	850.01	804.62	767.44	736.56	710.60
70000	1052.95	976.06	915.39	866.52	826.48	793.21	765.26
75000	1128.17	1045.77	980.78	928.41	885.51	849.87	819.93
80000	1203.38	1115.49	1046.16	990.31	944.54	906.53	874.59
85000	1278.60	1185.21	1111.55	1052.20	1003.58	963.19	929.25
90000	1353.80	1254.93	1176.93	1114.10	1062.61	1019.85	983.91
95000	1429.01	1324.65	1242.32	1175.99	1121.65	1076.50	1038.57
100000	1504.22	1394.37	1307.70	1237.88	1180.68	1133.16	1093.24
105000	1579.43	1464.08	1373.09	1299.78	1239.71	1189.82	1147.90
110000	1654.64	1533.80	1438.47	1361.67	1298.75	1246.48	1202.56
120000	1805.06	1673.24	1569.24	1485.46	1416.82	1359.80	1311.88
130000	1955.49	1812.68	1700.01	1609.25	1534.88	1473.11	1421.21
140000	2105.91	1952.11	1830.78	1733.04	1652.95	1586.43	1530.53
150000	2256.33	2091.55	1961.55	1856.83	1771.02	1699.74	1639.85
175000	2632.39	2440.14	2288.48	2166.30	2066.19	1983.03	1913.16
200000	3008.44	2788.73	2615.40	2475.77	2361.36	2266.33	2186.47
225000	3384.50	3137.32	2942.33	2785.24	2656.53	2549.62	2459.78
250000	3760.55	3485.92	3269.26	3094.71	2951.70	2832.91	2733.09

9¾%

Monthly Payments

necessary to amortize a loan

AMOUNT	15 YEARS	16 YEARS	17 YEARS	18 YEARS	19 YEARS	20 YEARS	21 YEARS
100	1.06	1.03	1.01	0.98	0.96	0.95	0.93
200	2.12	2.06	2.01	1.97	1.93	1.90	1.87
500	5.30	5.15	5.03	4.92	4.82	4.74	4.67
1000	10.59	10.30	10.05	9.84	9.65	9.49	9.34
2000	21.19	20.61	20.11	19.68	19.30	18.97	18.68
5000	52.97	51.52	50.27	49.19	48.25	47.43	46.70
6000	63.56	61.82	60.33	59.03	57.90	56.91	56.04
7000	74.16	72.13	70.38	68.87	67.55	66.40	65.38
8000	84.75	82.43	80.44	78.71	77.20	75.88	74.72
9000	95.34	92.74	90.49	88.54	86.85	85.37	84.06
10000	105.94	103.04	100.54	98.38	96.50	94.85	93.40
15000	158.90	154.56	150.82	147.57	144.75	142.28	140.11
20000	211.87	206.08	201.09	196.76	193.00	189.70	186.81
25000	264.84	257.60	251.36	245.96	241.25	237.13	233.51
30000	317.81	309.12	301.63	295.15	289.50	284.56	280.21
35000	370.78	360.64	351.90	344.34	337.75	331.98	326.92
36000	381.37	370.94	361.96	354.18	347.40	341.47	336.26
37000	391.96	381.24	372.01	364.01	357.05	350.95	345.60
38000	402.56	391.55	382.07	373.85	366.70	360.44	354.94
39000	413.15	401.85	392.12	383.69	376.35	369.92	364.28
40000	423.75	412.16	402.18	393.53	386.00	379.41	373.62
41000	434.34	422.46	412.23	403.37	395.65	388.89	382.96
42000	444.93	432.76	422.28	413.20	405.30	398.38	392.30
43000	455.53	443.07	432.34	423.04	414.95	407.86	401.64
44000	466.12	453.37	442.39	432.88	424.60	417.35	410.98
45000	476.71	463.68	452.45	442.72	434.25	426.83	420.32
46000	487.31	473.98	462.50	452.56	443.90	436.32	429.66
47000	497.90	484.28	472.56	462.40	453.55	445.80	439.00
48000	508.49	494.59	482.61	472.23	463.20	455.29	448.34
49000	519.09	504.89	492.67	482.07	472.85	464.77	457.68
50000	529.68	515.20	502.72	491.91	482.50	474.26	467.02
51000	540.27	525.50	512.77	501.75	492.15	483.74	476.36
52000	550.87	535.80	522.83	511.59	501.80	493.23	485.70
53000	561.46	546.11	532.88	521.42	511.45	502.71	495.04
54000	572.06	556.41	542.94	531.26	521.09	512.20	504.39
55000	582.65	566.72	552.99	541.10	530.74	521.68	513.73
56000	593.24	577.02	563.05	550.94	540.39	531.17	523.07
57000	603.84	587.32	573.10	560.78	550.04	540.65	532.41
58000	614.43	597.63	583.16	570.62	559.69	550.14	541.75
59000	625.02	607.93	593.21	580.45	569.34	559.62	551.09
60000	635.62	618.23	603.26	590.29	578.99	569.11	560.43
65000	688.59	669.75	653.54	639.48	627.24	616.54	607.13
70000	741.55	721.27	703.81	688.67	675.49	663.96	653.83
75000	794.52	772.79	754.08	737.87	723.74	711.39	700.54
80000	847.49	824.31	804.35	787.06	771.99	758.81	747.24
85000	900.46	875.83	854.62	836.25	820.24	806.24	793.94
90000	953.43	927.35	904.90	885.44	868.49	853.67	840.64
95000	1006.39	978.87	955.17	934.63	916.74	901.09	887.34
100000	1059.36	1030.39	1005.44	983.82	964.99	948.52	934.05
105000	1112.33	1081.91	1055.71	1033.01	1013.24	995.94	980.75
110000	1165.30	1133.43	1105.98	1082.20	1061.49	1043.37	1027.45
120000	1271.24	1236.47	1206.53	1180.58	1157.99	1138.22	1120.86
130000	1377.17	1339.51	1307.07	1278.97	1254.49	1233.07	1214.26
140000	1483.11	1442.55	1407.62	1377.35	1350.99	1327.92	1307.67
150000	1589.04	1545.59	1508.16	1475.73	1447.49	1422.78	1401.07
175000	1853.88	1803.19	1759.52	1721.69	1688.73	1659.90	1634.58
200000	2118.73	2060.78	2010.88	1967.64	1929.98	1897.03	1868.09
225000	2383.57	2318.38	2262.24	2213.60	2171.23	2134.16	2101.61
250000	2648.41	2575.98	2513.60	2459.55	2412.48	2371.29	2335.12

Monthly Payments **9¾%**

necessary to amortize a loan

AMOUNT	22 YEARS	23 YEARS	24 YEARS	25 YEARS	30 YEARS	35 YEARS	40 YEARS
100	0.92	0.91	0.90	0.89	0.86	0.84	0.83
200	1.84	1.82	1.80	1.78	1.72	1.68	1.66
500	4.61	4.55	4.50	4.46	4.30	4.20	4.15
1000	9.21	9.10	9.00	8.91	8.59	8.41	8.30
2000	18.43	18.20	18.00	17.82	17.18	16.81	16.59
5000	46.06	45.50	45.00	44.56	42.96	42.03	41.48
6000	55.28	54.60	54.00	53.47	51.55	50.44	49.77
7000	64.49	63.70	63.00	62.38	60.14	58.84	58.07
8000	73.70	72.80	72.00	71.29	68.73	67.25	66.36
9000	82.92	81.90	81.00	80.20	77.32	75.65	74.66
10000	92.13	91.00	90.00	89.11	85.92	84.06	82.96
15000	138.19	136.50	135.00	133.67	128.87	126.09	124.43
20000	184.26	182.00	180.00	178.23	171.83	168.12	165.91
25000	230.32	227.50	225.01	222.78	214.79	210.15	207.39
30000	276.39	273.01	270.01	267.34	257.75	252.18	248.87
35000	322.45	318.51	315.01	311.90	300.70	294.21	290.35
36000	331.67	327.61	324.01	320.81	309.30	302.61	298.64
37000	340.88	336.71	333.01	329.72	317.89	311.02	306.94
38000	350.09	345.81	342.01	338.63	326.48	319.42	315.23
39000	359.30	354.91	351.01	347.54	335.07	327.83	323.53
40000	368.52	364.01	360.01	356.45	343.66	336.24	331.82
41000	377.73	373.11	369.01	365.37	352.25	344.64	340.12
42000	386.94	382.21	378.01	374.28	360.84	353.05	348.41
43000	396.16	391.31	387.01	383.19	369.44	361.45	356.71
44000	405.37	400.41	396.01	392.10	378.03	369.86	365.01
45000	414.58	409.51	405.01	401.01	386.62	378.27	373.30
46000	423.79	418.61	414.01	409.92	395.21	386.67	381.60
47000	433.01	427.71	423.01	418.83	403.80	395.08	389.89
48000	442.22	436.81	432.01	427.75	412.39	403.48	398.19
49000	451.43	445.91	441.01	436.66	420.99	411.89	406.48
50000	460.65	455.01	450.01	445.57	429.58	420.29	414.78
51000	469.86	464.11	459.01	454.48	438.17	428.70	423.07
52000	479.07	473.21	468.01	463.39	446.76	437.11	431.37
53000	488.29	482.31	477.01	472.30	455.35	445.51	439.67
54000	497.50	491.41	486.01	481.21	463.94	453.92	447.96
55000	506.71	500.51	495.01	490.13	472.53	462.32	456.26
56000	515.92	509.61	504.01	499.04	481.13	470.73	404.55
57000	525.14	518.71	513.01	507.95	489.72	479.14	472.85
58000	534.35	527.81	522.01	510.80	498.31	487.54	481.14
59000	543.56	536.91	531.01	525.77	506.90	495.95	489.44
60000	552.78	546.01	540.01	534.68	515.49	504.35	497.74
65000	598.84	591.51	585.01	579.24	558.45	546.38	539.21
70000	644.90	637.01	630.01	623.80	601.41	588.41	580.69
75000	690.97	682.51	675.02	668.35	644.37	630.44	622.17
80000	737.03	728.01	720.02	712.91	687.32	672.47	663.65
85000	783.10	773.51	765.02	757.47	730.28	714.50	705.12
90000	829.16	819.02	810.02	802.02	773.24	756.53	746.60
95000	875.23	864.52	855.02	846.58	816.20	798.56	788.08
100000	921.29	910.02	900.02	891.14	859.15	840.59	829.56
105000	967.36	955.52	945.02	935.69	902.11	882.62	871.04
110000	1013.42	1001.02	990.02	980.25	945.07	924.65	912.51
120000	1105.55	1092.02	1080.02	1069.36	1030.99	1008.71	995.47
130000	1197.68	1183.02	1170.03	1158.48	1116.90	1092.77	1078.43
140000	1289.81	1274.02	1260.03	1247.59	1202.82	1176.83	1161.38
150000	1381.94	1365.03	1350.03	1336.71	1288.73	1260.88	1244.34
175000	1612.26	1592.53	1575.04	1559.49	1503.52	1471.03	1451.73
200000	1842.59	1820.03	1800.04	1782.27	1718.31	1681.18	1659.12
225000	2072.91	2047.54	2025.05	2005.06	1933.10	1891.33	1866.51
250000	2303.23	2275.04	2250.05	2227.84	2147.89	2101.47	2073.90

10% Monthly Payments

necessary to amortize a loan

AMOUNT	1 YEAR	2 YEARS	3 YEARS	4 YEARS	5 YEARS	6 YEARS	7 YEARS
100	8.79	4.61	3.23	2.54	2.12	1.85	1.66
200	17.58	9.23	6.45	5.07	4.25	3.71	3.32
500	43.96	23.07	16.13	12.68	10.62	9.26	8.30
1000	87.92	46.14	32.27	25.36	21.25	18.53	16.60
2000	175.83	92.29	64.53	50.73	42.49	37.05	33.20
5000	439.58	230.72	161.34	126.81	106.24	92.63	83.01
6000	527.50	276.87	193.60	152.18	127.48	111.16	99.61
7000	615.41	323.01	225.87	177.54	148.73	129.68	116.21
8000	703.33	369.16	258.14	202.90	169.98	148.21	132.81
9000	791.24	415.30	290.40	228.26	191.22	166.73	149.41
10000	879.16	461.45	322.67	253.63	212.47	185.26	166.01
15000	1318.74	692.17	484.01	380.44	318.71	277.89	249.02
20000	1758.32	922.90	645.34	507.25	424.94	370.52	332.02
25000	2197.90	1153.62	806.68	634.06	531.18	463.15	415.03
30000	2637.48	1384.35	968.02	760.88	637.41	555.78	498.04
35000	3077.06	1615.07	1129.35	887.69	743.65	648.40	581.04
36000	3164.97	1661.22	1161.62	913.05	764.89	666.93	597.64
37000	3252.89	1707.36	1193.89	938.42	786.14	685.46	614.24
38000	3340.80	1753.51	1226.15	963.78	807.39	703.98	630.84
39000	3428.72	1799.65	1258.42	989.14	828.63	722.51	647.45
40000	3516.64	1845.80	1290.69	1014.50	849.88	741.03	664.05
41000	3604.55	1891.94	1322.95	1039.87	871.13	759.56	680.65
42000	3692.47	1938.09	1355.22	1065.23	892.38	778.09	697.25
43000	3780.38	1984.23	1387.49	1090.59	913.62	796.61	713.85
44000	3868.30	2030.38	1419.76	1115.95	934.87	815.14	730.45
45000	3956.21	2076.52	1452.02	1141.32	956.12	833.66	747.05
46000	4044.13	2122.67	1484.29	1166.68	977.36	852.19	763.65
47000	4132.05	2168.81	1516.56	1192.04	998.61	870.71	780.26
48000	4219.96	2214.96	1548.82	1217.40	1019.86	889.24	796.86
49000	4307.88	2261.10	1581.09	1242.77	1041.11	907.77	813.46
50000	4395.79	2307.25	1613.36	1268.13	1062.35	926.29	830.06
51000	4483.71	2353.39	1645.63	1293.49	1083.60	944.82	846.66
52000	4571.63	2399.54	1677.89	1318.85	1104.85	963.34	863.26
53000	4659.54	2445.68	1710.16	1344.22	1126.09	981.87	879.86
54000	4747.46	2491.83	1742.43	1369.58	1147.34	1000.40	896.46
55000	4835.37	2537.97	1774.70	1394.94	1168.59	1018.92	913.07
56000	4923.29	2584.12	1806.96	1420.30	1189.83	1037.45	929.67
57000	5011.21	2630.26	1839.23	1445.67	1211.08	1055.97	946.27
58000	5099.12	2676.41	1871.50	1471.03	1232.33	1074.50	962.87
59000	5187.04	2722.55	1903.76	1496.39	1253.58	1093.02	979.47
60000	5274.95	2768.70	1936.03	1521.76	1274.82	1111.55	996.07
65000	5714.53	2999.42	2097.37	1648.57	1381.06	1204.18	1079.08
70000	6154.11	3230.14	2258.70	1775.38	1487.29	1296.81	1162.08
75000	6593.69	3460.87	2420.04	1902.19	1593.53	1389.44	1245.09
80000	7033.27	3691.59	2581.37	2029.01	1699.76	1482.07	1328.09
85000	7472.85	3922.32	2742.71	2156.02	1806.00	1574.70	1411.10
90000	7912.43	4153.04	2904.05	2282.63	1912.23	1667.33	1494.11
95000	8352.01	4383.77	3065.38	2409.45	2018.47	1759.95	1577.11
100000	8791.59	4614.49	3226.72	2536.26	2124.70	1852.58	1660.12
105000	9231.17	4845.22	3388.05	2663.07	2230.94	1945.21	1743.12
110000	9670.75	5075.94	3549.39	2789.88	2337.17	2037.84	1826.13
120000	10549.91	5537.39	3872.06	3043.51	2549.65	2223.10	1992.14
130000	11429.07	5998.84	4194.73	3297.14	2762.12	2408.36	2158.15
140000	12308.22	6460.29	4517.41	3550.76	2974.59	2593.62	2324.17
150000	13187.38	6921.74	4840.08	3804.39	3187.06	2778.88	2490.18
175000	15385.28	8075.36	5646.76	4438.45	3718.23	3242.02	2905.21
200000	17583.18	9228.99	6453.44	5072.52	4249.41	3705.17	3320.24
225000	19781.07	10382.61	7260.12	5706.58	4780.59	4168.31	3735.27
250000	21978.97	11536.23	8066.80	6340.65	5311.76	4631.46	4150.30

Monthly Payments 10%

necessary to amortize a loan

AMOUNT	8 YEARS	9 YEARS	10 YEARS	11 YEARS	12 YEARS	13 YEARS	14 YEARS
100	1.52	1.41	1.32	1.25	1.20	1.15	1.11
200	3.03	2.82	2.64	2.50	2.39	2.30	2.22
500	7.59	7.04	6.61	6.26	5.98	5.74	5.54
1000	15.17	14.08	13.22	12.52	11.95	11.48	11.08
2000	30.35	28.16	26.43	25.04	23.90	22.96	22.16
5000	75.87	70.39	66.08	62.60	59.75	57.39	55.41
6000	91.04	84.47	79.29	75.12	71.70	68.87	66.49
7000	106.22	98.55	92.51	87.64	83.66	80.35	77.57
8000	121.39	112.63	105.72	100.16	95.61	91.83	88.66
9000	136.57	126.71	118.94	112.68	107.56	103.31	99.74
10000	151.74	140.79	132.15	125.20	119.51	114.78	110.82
15000	227.61	211.18	198.23	187.80	179.26	172.18	166.23
20000	303.48	281.57	264.30	250.40	239.02	229.57	221.64
25000	379.35	351.97	330.38	313.00	298.77	286.96	277.05
30000	455.22	422.36	396.45	375.60	358.52	344.35	332.46
35000	531.10	492.75	462.53	438.20	418.28	401.75	387.87
36000	546.27	506.83	475.74	450.72	430.23	413.23	398.95
37000	561.44	520.91	488.96	463.24	442.18	424.70	410.03
38000	576.62	534.99	502.17	475.76	454.13	436.18	421.12
39000	591.79	549.07	515.39	488.28	466.08	447.66	432.20
40000	606.97	563.15	528.60	500.80	478.03	459.14	443.28
41000	622.14	577.23	541.82	513.31	489.98	470.62	454.36
42000	637.31	591.30	555.03	525.83	501.93	482.10	465.45
43000	652.49	605.38	568.25	538.35	513.88	493.57	476.53
44000	667.66	619.46	581.46	550.87	525.83	505.05	487.61
45000	682.84	633.54	594.68	563.39	537.79	516.53	498.69
46000	698.01	647.62	607.89	575.91	549.74	528.01	509.77
47000	713.19	661.70	621.11	588.43	561.69	539.49	520.86
48000	728.36	675.78	634.32	600.95	573.64	550.97	531.94
49000	743.53	689.86	647.54	613.47	585.59	562.45	543.02
50000	758.71	703.93	660.75	625.99	597.54	573.92	554.10
51000	773.88	718.01	673.97	638.51	609.49	585.40	565.18
52000	789.06	732.09	687.18	651.03	621.44	596.88	576.27
53000	804.23	746.17	700.40	663.55	633.39	608.36	587.35
54000	819.40	760.25	713.61	676.07	645.34	619.84	598.43
55000	834.58	774.33	726.83	688.59	657.29	631.32	609.51
56000	849.75	788.41	740.04	701.11	669.24	642.79	620.59
57000	864.93	802.49	753.26	713.63	681.19	654.27	631.68
58000	880.10	816.56	766.47	726.15	693.15	665.75	642.76
59000	895.28	830.64	779.69	738.67	705.10	677.23	653.84
60000	910.45	844.72	792.90	751.19	717.05	688.71	664.92
65000	986.32	915.11	858.98	813.79	776.80	746.10	720.33
70000	1062.19	985.51	925.06	876.39	836.55	803.49	775.74
75000	1138.06	1055.90	991.13	938.99	896.31	860.89	831.15
80000	1213.93	1126.29	1057.21	1001.59	956.06	918.28	886.56
85000	1289.80	1196.69	1123.28	1064.19	1015.82	975.67	941.97
90000	1365.67	1267.08	1189.36	1126.79	1075.57	1033.06	997.38
95000	1441.55	1337.48	1255.43	1189.39	1135.32	1090.46	1052.79
100000	1517.42	1407.87	1321.51	1251.99	1195.08	1147.85	1108.20
105000	1593.29	1478.26	1387.58	1314.59	1254.83	1205.24	1163.61
110000	1669.16	1548.66	1453.66	1377.19	1314.59	1262.63	1219.02
120000	1820.90	1689.44	1585.81	1502.39	1434.09	1377.42	1329.84
130000	1972.64	1830.23	1717.96	1627.58	1553.60	1492.20	1440.66
140000	2124.38	1971.02	1850.11	1752.78	1673.11	1606.99	1551.48
150000	2276.12	2111.80	1982.26	1877.98	1792.62	1721.77	1662.30
175000	2655.48	2463.77	2312.64	2190.98	2091.39	2008.73	1939.35
200000	3034.83	2815.74	2643.01	2503.98	2390.16	2295.70	2216.41
225000	3414.19	3167.70	2973.39	2816.97	2688.93	2582.66	2493.46
250000	3793.54	3519.67	3303.77	3129.97	2987.70	2869.62	2770.51

10%

Monthly Payments
necessary to amortize a loan

AMOUNT	15 YEARS	16 YEARS	17 YEARS	18 YEARS	19 YEARS	20 YEARS	21 YEARS
100	1.07	1.05	1.02	1.00	0.98	0.97	0.95
200	2.15	2.09	2.04	2.00	1.96	1.93	1.90
500	5.37	5.23	5.11	5.00	4.91	4.83	4.75
1000	10.75	10.46	10.21	10.00	9.81	9.65	9.51
2000	21.49	20.92	20.42	20.00	19.63	19.30	19.02
5000	53.73	52.30	51.06	49.99	49.06	48.25	47.54
6000	64.48	62.75	61.27	59.99	58.88	57.90	57.05
7000	75.22	73.21	71.48	69.99	68.69	67.55	66.55
8000	85.97	83.67	81.70	79.99	78.50	77.20	76.06
9000	96.71	94.13	91.91	89.99	88.31	86.85	85.57
10000	107.46	104.59	102.12	99.98	98.13	96.50	95.08
15000	161.19	156.89	153.18	149.98	147.19	144.75	142.62
20000	214.92	209.18	204.24	199.97	196.25	193.00	190.16
25000	268.65	261.48	255.30	249.96	245.31	241.26	237.70
30000	322.38	313.77	306.36	299.95	294.38	289.51	285.23
35000	376.11	366.07	357.42	349.95	343.44	337.76	332.77
36000	386.86	376.52	367.64	359.94	353.25	347.41	342.28
37000	397.60	386.98	377.85	369.94	363.07	357.06	351.79
38000	408.35	397.44	388.06	379.94	372.88	366.71	361.30
39000	419.10	407.90	398.27	389.94	382.69	376.36	370.80
40000	429.84	418.36	408.48	399.94	392.50	386.01	380.31
41000	440.59	428.82	418.70	409.94	402.32	395.66	389.82
42000	451.33	439.28	428.91	419.93	412.13	405.31	399.33
43000	462.08	449.74	439.12	429.93	421.94	414.96	408.84
44000	472.83	460.20	449.33	439.93	431.75	424.61	418.34
45000	483.57	470.66	459.54	449.93	441.57	434.26	427.85
46000	494.32	481.11	469.76	459.93	451.38	443.91	437.36
47000	505.06	491.57	479.97	469.93	461.19	453.56	446.87
48000	515.81	502.03	490.18	479.92	471.00	463.21	456.37
49000	526.56	512.49	500.39	489.92	480.82	472.86	465.88
50000	537.30	522.95	510.61	499.92	490.63	482.51	475.39
51000	548.05	533.41	520.82	509.92	500.44	492.16	484.90
52000	558.79	543.87	531.03	519.92	510.25	501.81	494.41
53000	569.54	554.33	541.24	529.92	520.07	511.46	503.91
54000	580.29	564.79	551.45	539.92	529.88	521.11	513.42
55000	591.03	575.25	561.67	549.91	539.69	530.76	522.93
56000	601.78	585.71	571.88	559.91	549.50	540.41	532.44
57000	612.52	596.16	582.09	569.91	559.32	550.06	541.94
58000	623.27	606.62	592.30	579.91	569.13	559.71	551.45
59000	634.02	617.08	602.51	589.91	578.94	569.36	560.96
60000	644.76	627.54	612.73	599.91	588.76	579.01	570.47
65000	698.49	679.84	663.79	649.90	637.82	627.26	618.01
70000	752.22	732.13	714.85	699.89	686.88	675.52	665.55
75000	805.95	784.43	765.91	749.88	735.94	723.77	713.09
80000	859.68	836.72	816.97	799.87	785.01	772.02	760.62
85000	913.41	889.02	868.03	849.87	834.07	820.27	808.16
90000	967.14	941.31	919.09	899.86	883.13	868.52	855.70
95000	1020.87	993.61	970.15	949.85	932.20	916.77	903.24
100000	1074.61	1045.90	1021.21	999.84	981.26	965.02	950.78
105000	1128.34	1098.20	1072.27	1049.84	1030.32	1013.27	998.32
110000	1182.07	1150.49	1123.33	1099.83	1079.38	1061.52	1045.86
120000	1289.53	1255.08	1225.45	1199.81	1177.51	1158.03	1140.94
130000	1396.99	1359.67	1327.57	1299.80	1275.64	1254.53	1236.01
140000	1504.45	1464.26	1429.69	1399.78	1373.76	1351.03	1331.09
150000	1611.91	1568.85	1531.82	1499.77	1471.89	1447.53	1426.17
175000	1880.56	1830.33	1787.12	1749.73	1717.20	1688.79	1663.87
200000	2149.21	2091.80	2042.42	1999.69	1962.52	1930.04	1901.56
225000	2417.86	2353.28	2297.72	2249.65	2207.83	2171.30	2139.26
250000	2686.51	2614.75	2553.03	2499.61	2453.15	2412.55	2376.95

Monthly Payments **10%**

necessary to amortize a loan

AMOUNT	22 YEARS	23 YEARS	24 YEARS	25 YEARS	30 YEARS	35 YEARS	40 YEARS
100	0.94	0.93	0.92	0.91	0.88	0.86	0.85
200	1.88	1.85	1.83	1.82	1.76	1.72	1.70
500	4.69	4.64	4.59	4.54	4.39	4.30	4.25
1000	9.38	9.27	9.17	9.09	8.78	8.60	8.49
2000	18.76	18.54	18.35	18.17	17.55	17.19	16.98
5000	46.91	46.36	45.87	45.44	43.88	42.98	42.46
6000	56.29	55.63	55.04	54.52	52.65	51.58	50.95
7000	65.68	64.90	64.22	63.61	61.43	60.18	59.44
8000	75.06	74.17	73.39	72.70	70.21	68.77	67.93
9000	84.44	83.45	82.56	81.78	78.98	77.37	76.42
10000	93.82	92.72	91.74	90.87	87.76	85.97	84.91
15000	140.74	139.08	137.61	136.31	131.64	128.95	127.37
20000	187.65	185.44	183.48	181.74	175.51	171.93	169.83
25000	234.56	231.80	229.35	227.18	219.39	214.92	212.29
30000	281.47	278.15	275.22	272.61	263.27	257.90	254.74
35000	328.39	324.51	321.09	318.05	307.15	300.89	297.20
36000	337.77	333.79	330.26	327.13	315.93	309.48	305.69
37000	347.15	343.06	339.43	336.22	324.70	318.08	314.18
38000	356.53	352.33	348.61	345.31	333.48	326.68	322.68
39000	365.92	361.60	357.78	354.39	342.25	335.27	331.17
40000	375.30	370.87	366.96	363.48	351.03	343.87	339.66
41000	384.68	380.14	376.13	372.57	359.80	352.47	348.15
42000	394.06	389.42	385.30	381.65	368.58	361.06	356.64
43000	403.45	398.69	394.48	390.74	377.36	369.66	365.13
44000	412.83	407.96	403.65	399.83	386.13	378.26	373.62
45000	422.21	417.23	412.82	408.92	394.91	386.85	382.12
46000	431.59	426.50	422.00	418.00	403.68	395.45	390.61
47000	440.98	435.78	431.17	427.09	412.46	404.05	399.10
48000	450.36	445.05	440.35	436.18	421.23	412.64	407.59
49000	459.74	454.32	449.52	445.26	430.01	421.24	416.08
50000	469.12	463.59	458.69	454.35	438.79	429.84	424.57
51000	478.51	472.86	467.87	463.44	447.56	438.43	433.06
52000	487.89	482.13	477.04	472.52	456.34	447.03	441.56
53000	497.27	491.41	486.22	481.61	465.11	455.63	450.05
54000	506.65	500.68	495.39	490.70	473.89	464.22	458.54
55000	516.04	509.95	504.56	499.79	482.66	472.82	467.03
56000	525.42	519.22	513.74	508.87	491.44	481.42	475.52
57000	534.80	528.49	522.91	517.96	500.22	490.01	484.01
58000	544.18	537.77	532.09	527.05	508.99	498.61	492.50
59000	553.57	547.04	541.26	536.13	517.77	507.21	501.00
60000	562.95	556.31	550.43	545.22	526.54	515.80	509.49
65000	609.86	602.67	596.30	590.66	570.42	558.79	551.94
70000	656.77	649.03	642.17	636.09	614.30	601.77	594.40
75000	703.68	605.39	688.04	681.53	658.18	644.75	636.86
80000	750.60	741.75	733.91	726.96	702.06	687.74	679.32
85000	797.51	788.10	779.78	772.40	745.94	730.72	721.77
90000	844.42	834.46	825.65	817.83	789.81	773.71	764.23
95000	891.33	880.82	871.52	863.27	833.69	816.69	806.69
100000	938.25	927.18	917.39	908.70	877.57	859.67	849.15
105000	985.16	973.54	963.26	954.14	921.45	902.66	891.60
110000	1032.07	1019.90	1009.13	999.57	965.33	945.64	934.06
120000	1125.90	1112.62	1100.87	1090.44	1053.09	1031.61	1018.98
130000	1219.72	1205.34	1192.61	1181.31	1140.84	1117.57	1103.89
140000	1313.54	1298.05	1284.34	1272.18	1228.60	1203.54	1188.80
150000	1407.37	1390.77	1376.08	1363.05	1316.36	1289.51	1273.72
175000	1641.93	1622.57	1605.43	1590.23	1535.75	1504.43	1486.01
200000	1876.49	1854.36	1834.78	1817.40	1755.14	1719.34	1698.29
225000	2111.05	2086.16	2064.12	2044.58	1974.54	1934.26	1910.58
250000	2345.61	2317.95	2293.47	2271.75	2193.93	2149.18	2122.86

10¼%

Monthly Payments

necessary to amortize a loan

AMOUNT	1 YEAR	2 YEARS	3 YEARS	4 YEARS	5 YEARS	6 YEARS	7 YEARS
100	8.80	4.63	3.24	2.55	2.14	1.87	1.67
200	17.61	9.25	6.48	5.10	4.27	3.73	3.35
500	44.02	23.13	16.19	12.74	10.69	9.33	8.37
1000	88.03	46.26	32.38	25.48	21.37	18.65	16.73
2000	176.06	92.52	64.77	50.97	42.74	37.30	33.46
5000	440.16	231.30	161.92	127.41	106.85	93.26	83.65
6000	528.19	277.56	194.31	152.90	128.22	111.91	100.38
7000	616.23	323.82	226.69	178.38	149.59	130.57	117.11
8000	704.26	370.08	259.08	203.86	170.96	149.22	133.85
9000	792.29	416.34	291.46	229.35	192.33	167.87	150.58
10000	880.32	462.60	323.85	254.83	213.70	186.52	167.31
15000	1320.48	693.91	485.77	382.24	320.55	279.78	250.96
20000	1760.64	925.21	647.69	509.66	427.41	373.04	334.61
25000	2200.81	1156.51	809.62	637.07	534.26	466.30	418.27
30000	2640.97	1387.81	971.54	764.48	641.11	559.56	501.92
35000	3081.13	1619.11	1133.46	891.90	747.96	652.83	585.57
36000	3169.16	1665.37	1165.85	917.38	769.33	671.48	602.30
37000	3257.19	1711.63	1198.23	942.86	790.70	690.13	619.03
38000	3345.22	1757.90	1230.62	968.35	812.07	708.78	635.76
39000	3433.26	1804.16	1263.00	993.83	833.44	727.43	652.50
40000	3521.29	1850.42	1295.39	1019.31	854.81	746.09	669.23
41000	3609.32	1896.68	1327.77	1044.80	876.18	764.74	685.96
42000	3697.35	1942.94	1360.16	1070.28	897.55	783.39	702.69
43000	3785.38	1989.20	1392.54	1095.76	918.92	802.04	719.42
44000	3873.42	2035.46	1424.93	1121.24	940.29	820.69	736.15
45000	3961.45	2081.72	1457.31	1146.73	961.66	839.35	752.88
46000	4049.48	2127.98	1489.70	1172.21	983.03	858.00	769.61
47000	4137.51	2174.24	1522.08	1197.69	1004.40	876.65	786.34
48000	4225.55	2220.50	1554.47	1223.18	1025.77	895.30	803.07
49000	4313.58	2266.76	1586.85	1248.66	1047.14	913.96	819.80
50000	4401.61	2313.02	1619.23	1274.14	1068.51	932.61	836.53
51000	4489.64	2359.28	1651.62	1299.62	1089.88	951.26	853.26
52000	4577.67	2405.54	1684.00	1325.11	1111.25	969.91	869.99
53000	4665.71	2451.80	1716.39	1350.59	1132.62	988.56	886.72
54000	4753.74	2498.06	1748.77	1376.07	1153.99	1007.22	903.45
55000	4841.77	2544.32	1781.16	1401.55	1175.36	1025.87	920.19
56000	4929.80	2590.58	1813.54	1427.04	1196.73	1044.52	936.92
57000	5017.84	2636.84	1845.93	1452.52	1218.11	1063.17	953.65
58000	5105.87	2683.10	1878.31	1478.00	1239.48	1081.83	970.38
59000	5193.90	2729.36	1910.70	1503.49	1260.85	1100.48	987.11
60000	5281.93	2775.62	1943.08	1528.97	1282.22	1119.13	1003.84
65000	5722.09	3006.93	2105.00	1656.38	1389.07	1212.39	1087.49
70000	6162.25	3238.23	2266.93	1783.80	1495.92	1305.65	1171.15
75000	6602.42	3469.53	2428.85	1911.21	1602.77	1398.91	1254.80
80000	7042.58	3700.83	2590.78	2038.63	1709.62	1492.17	1338.45
85000	7482.74	3932.13	2752.70	2166.04	1816.47	1585.43	1422.10
90000	7922.90	4163.44	2914.62	2293.45	1923.32	1678.69	1505.76
95000	8363.06	4394.74	3076.55	2420.87	2030.18	1771.95	1589.41
100000	8803.22	4626.04	3238.47	2548.28	2137.03	1865.22	1673.06
105000	9243.38	4857.34	3400.39	2675.70	2243.88	1958.48	1756.72
110000	9683.54	5088.64	3562.32	2803.11	2350.73	2051.74	1840.37
120000	10563.86	5551.25	3886.16	3057.94	2564.43	2238.26	2007.68
130000	11444.19	6013.85	4210.01	3312.77	2778.13	2424.78	2174.98
140000	12324.51	6476.46	4533.86	3567.59	2991.84	2611.30	2342.29
150000	13204.83	6939.06	4857.70	3822.42	3205.54	2797.82	2509.60
175000	15405.64	8095.57	5667.32	4459.49	3739.80	3264.13	2927.86
200000	17606.44	9252.08	6476.94	5096.56	4274.05	3730.43	3346.13
225000	19807.25	10408.59	7286.55	5733.63	4808.31	4196.74	3764.39
250000	22008.05	11565.10	8096.17	6370.70	5342.57	4663.04	4182.66

Monthly Payments 10¼%

necessary to amortize a loan

AMOUNT	8 YEARS	9 YEARS	10 YEARS	11 YEARS	12 YEARS	13 YEARS	14 YEARS
100	1.53	1.42	1.34	1.27	1.21	1.16	1.12
200	3.06	2.84	2.67	2.53	2.42	2.33	2.25
500	7.65	7.11	6.68	6.33	6.05	5.81	5.62
1000	15.31	14.21	13.35	12.66	12.10	11.63	11.23
2000	30.61	28.43	26.71	25.32	24.19	23.25	22.47
5000	76.53	71.07	66.77	63.31	60.48	58.13	56.16
6000	91.84	85.29	80.12	75.97	72.57	69.76	67.40
7000	107.15	99.50	93.48	88.63	84.67	81.38	78.63
8000	122.45	113.72	106.83	101.29	96.77	93.01	89.86
9000	137.76	127.93	120.19	113.96	108.86	104.64	101.09
10000	153.07	142.14	133.54	126.62	120.96	116.26	112.33
15000	229.60	213.22	200.31	189.93	181.43	174.39	168.49
20000	306.14	284.29	267.08	253.24	241.91	232.53	224.65
25000	382.67	355.36	333.85	316.54	302.39	290.66	280.82
30000	459.20	426.43	400.62	379.85	362.87	348.79	336.98
35000	535.74	497.50	467.39	443.16	423.35	406.92	393.14
36000	551.04	511.72	480.74	455.82	435.44	418.55	404.38
37000	566.35	525.93	494.09	468.48	447.54	430.17	415.61
38000	581.66	540.15	507.45	481.15	459.63	441.80	426.84
39000	596.96	554.36	520.80	493.81	471.73	453.42	438.08
40000	612.27	568.58	534.16	506.47	483.83	465.05	449.31
41000	627.58	582.79	547.51	519.13	495.92	476.68	460.54
42000	642.88	597.01	560.86	531.79	508.02	488.30	471.77
43000	658.19	611.22	574.22	544.46	520.11	499.93	483.01
44000	673.50	625.43	587.57	557.12	532.21	511.56	494.24
45000	688.80	639.65	600.93	569.78	544.30	523.18	505.47
46000	704.11	653.86	614.28	582.44	556.40	534.81	516.70
47000	719.42	668.08	627.63	595.10	568.50	546.44	527.94
48000	734.72	682.29	640.99	607.76	580.59	558.06	539.17
49000	750.03	696.51	654.34	620.43	592.69	569.69	550.40
50000	765.34	710.72	667.70	633.09	604.78	581.31	561.63
51000	780.65	724.94	681.05	645.75	616.88	592.94	572.87
52000	795.95	739.15	694.40	658.41	628.97	604.57	584.10
53000	811.26	753.36	707.76	671.07	641.07	616.19	595.33
54000	826.57	767.58	721.11	683.73	653.17	627.82	606.57
55000	841.87	781.79	734.46	696.40	665.26	639.45	617.80
56000	857.18	796.01	747.82	709.06	677.36	651.07	629.03
57000	872.49	810.22	761.17	721.72	689.45	662.70	640.26
58000	887.79	824.44	774.53	734.38	701.55	674.32	651.50
59000	903.10	838.65	787.88	747.04	713.64	685.95	662.73
60000	918.41	852.87	801.23	759.71	725.74	697.58	673.96
65000	994.94	923.94	868.00	823.01	786.22	755.71	730.13
70000	1071.47	995.01	934.77	886.32	846.70	813.84	786.29
75000	1148.01	1066.08	1001.54	949.63	907.17	871.97	842.45
80000	1224.54	1137.15	1068.31	1012.94	967.65	930.10	898.62
85000	1301.08	1208.23	1135.08	1076.25	1028.13	988.23	954.70
90000	1377.61	1279.30	1201.85	1139.56	1088.61	1046.37	1010.94
95000	1454.14	1350.37	1268.62	1202.87	1149.09	1104.50	1067.11
100000	1530.68	1421.44	1335.39	1266.18	1209.57	1162.63	1123.27
105000	1607.21	1492.51	1402.16	1329.48	1270.04	1220.76	1179.43
110000	1683.74	1563.59	1468.93	1392.79	1330.52	1278.89	1235.60
120000	1836.81	1705.73	1602.47	1519.41	1451.48	1395.15	1347.92
130000	1989.88	1847.87	1736.01	1646.03	1572.43	1511.42	1460.25
140000	2142.95	1990.02	1869.55	1772.65	1693.39	1627.68	1572.58
150000	2296.02	2132.16	2003.09	1899.26	1814.35	1743.94	1684.90
175000	2678.68	2487.52	2336.93	2215.81	2116.74	2034.60	1965.72
200000	3061.35	2842.88	2670.78	2532.35	2419.13	2325.26	2246.54
225000	3444.02	3198.24	3004.63	2848.89	2721.52	2615.91	2527.36
250000	3826.69	3553.60	3338.48	3165.44	3023.91	2906.57	2808.17

10¼%

Monthly Payments
necessary to amortize a loan

AMOUNT	15 YEARS	16 YEARS	17 YEARS	18 YEARS	19 YEARS	20 YEARS	21 YEARS
100	1.09	1.06	1.04	1.02	1.00	0.98	0.97
200	2.18	2.12	2.07	2.03	2.00	1.96	1.94
500	5.45	5.31	5.19	5.08	4.99	4.91	4.84
1000	10.90	10.62	10.37	10.16	9.98	9.82	9.68
2000	21.80	21.23	20.74	20.32	19.95	19.63	19.35
5000	54.50	53.08	51.85	50.80	49.88	49.08	48.38
6000	65.40	63.69	62.23	60.96	59.86	58.90	58.06
7000	76.30	74.31	72.60	71.12	69.83	68.72	67.73
8000	87.20	84.92	82.97	81.28	79.81	78.53	77.41
9000	98.10	95.54	93.34	91.44	89.79	88.35	87.09
10000	109.00	106.15	103.71	101.60	99.76	98.16	96.76
15000	163.49	159.23	155.56	152.40	149.65	147.25	145.14
20000	217.99	212.30	207.42	203.20	199.53	196.33	193.53
25000	272.49	265.38	259.27	254.00	249.41	245.41	241.91
30000	326.99	318.46	311.13	304.79	299.29	294.49	290.29
35000	381.48	371.53	362.98	355.59	349.17	343.58	338.67
36000	392.38	382.15	373.35	365.75	359.15	353.39	348.35
37000	403.28	392.76	383.72	375.91	369.13	363.21	358.02
38000	414.18	403.38	394.09	386.07	379.10	373.02	367.70
39000	425.08	413.99	404.47	396.23	389.08	382.84	377.38
40000	435.98	424.61	414.84	406.39	399.06	392.66	387.05
41000	446.88	435.22	425.21	416.55	409.03	402.47	396.73
42000	457.78	445.84	435.58	426.71	419.01	412.29	406.41
43000	468.68	456.45	445.95	436.87	428.99	422.11	416.08
44000	479.58	467.07	456.32	447.03	438.96	431.92	425.76
45000	490.48	477.68	466.69	457.19	448.94	441.74	435.43
46000	501.38	488.30	477.06	467.35	458.92	451.56	445.11
47000	512.28	498.91	487.43	477.51	468.89	461.37	454.79
48000	523.18	509.53	497.80	487.67	478.87	471.19	464.46
49000	534.08	520.14	508.17	497.83	488.84	481.01	474.14
50000	544.98	530.76	518.55	507.99	498.82	490.82	483.82
51000	555.87	541.37	528.92	518.15	508.80	500.64	493.49
52000	566.77	551.99	539.29	528.31	518.77	510.45	503.17
53000	577.67	562.61	549.66	538.47	528.75	520.27	512.84
54000	588.57	573.22	560.03	548.63	538.73	530.09	522.52
55000	599.47	583.84	570.40	558.79	548.70	539.90	532.20
56000	610.37	594.45	580.77	568.95	558.68	549.72	541.87
57000	621.27	605.07	591.14	579.11	568.66	559.54	551.55
58000	632.17	615.68	601.51	589.27	578.63	569.35	561.23
59000	643.07	626.30	611.88	599.43	588.61	579.17	570.90
60000	653.97	636.91	622.25	609.59	598.59	588.99	580.58
65000	708.47	689.99	674.11	660.39	648.47	638.07	628.96
70000	762.97	743.06	725.96	711.19	698.35	687.15	677.34
75000	817.46	796.14	777.82	761.99	748.23	736.23	725.72
80000	871.96	849.22	829.67	812.78	798.11	785.31	774.11
85000	926.46	902.29	881.53	863.58	848.00	834.40	822.49
90000	980.96	955.37	933.38	914.38	897.88	883.48	870.87
95000	1035.45	1008.44	985.24	965.18	947.76	932.56	919.25
100000	1089.95	1061.52	1037.09	1015.98	997.64	981.64	967.63
105000	1144.45	1114.60	1088.95	1066.78	1047.52	1030.73	1016.01
110000	1198.95	1167.67	1140.80	1117.58	1097.41	1079.81	1064.39
120000	1307.94	1273.82	1244.51	1219.18	1197.17	1177.97	1161.16
130000	1416.94	1379.98	1348.22	1320.77	1296.93	1276.14	1257.92
140000	1525.93	1486.13	1451.93	1422.37	1396.70	1374.30	1354.68
150000	1634.93	1592.28	1555.64	1523.97	1496.46	1472.47	1451.45
175000	1907.41	1857.66	1814.91	1777.97	1745.87	1717.88	1693.35
200000	2179.90	2123.04	2074.18	2031.96	1995.28	1963.29	1935.26
225000	2452.39	2388.42	2333.46	2285.96	2244.70	2208.70	2177.17
250000	2724.88	2653.80	2592.73	2539.95	2494.11	2454.11	2419.08

Monthly Payments 10¼%

necessary to amortize a loan

AMOUNT	22 YEARS	23 YEARS	24 YEARS	25 YEARS	30 YEARS	35 YEARS	40 YEARS
100	0.96	0.94	0.93	0.93	0.90	0.88	0.87
200	1.91	1.89	1.87	1.85	1.79	1.76	1.74
500	4.78	4.72	4.67	4.63	4.48	4.39	4.34
1000	9.55	9.44	9.35	9.26	8.96	8.79	8.69
2000	19.11	18.89	18.70	18.53	17.92	17.58	17.38
5000	47.77	47.22	46.74	46.32	44.81	43.94	43.44
6000	57.32	56.67	56.09	55.58	53.77	52.73	52.13
7000	66.87	66.11	65.44	64.85	62.73	61.52	60.82
8000	76.43	75.56	74.79	74.11	71.69	70.31	69.51
9000	85.98	85.00	84.14	83.37	80.65	79.10	78.19
10000	95.53	94.45	93.49	92.64	89.61	87.89	86.88
15000	143.30	141.67	140.23	138.96	134.42	131.83	130.32
20000	191.06	188.89	186.98	185.28	179.22	175.77	173.76
25000	238.83	236.12	233.72	231.60	224.03	219.71	217.20
30000	286.60	283.34	280.46	277.91	268.83	263.66	260.65
35000	334.36	330.56	327.21	324.23	313.64	307.60	304.09
36000	343.91	340.01	336.56	333.50	322.60	316.39	312.77
37000	353.47	349.45	345.90	342.76	331.56	325.18	321.46
38000	363.02	358.90	355.25	352.03	340.52	333.97	330.15
39000	372.57	368.34	364.60	361.29	349.48	342.75	338.84
40000	382.13	377.79	373.95	370.55	358.44	351.54	347.53
41000	391.68	387.23	383.30	379.82	367.40	360.33	356.22
42000	401.23	396.68	392.65	389.08	376.36	369.12	364.90
43000	410.79	406.12	402.00	398.34	385.32	377.91	373.59
44000	420.34	415.57	411.35	407.61	394.28	386.70	382.28
45000	429.89	425.01	420.69	416.87	403.25	395.49	390.97
46000	439.45	434.45	430.04	426.14	412.21	404.27	399.66
47000	449.00	443.90	439.39	435.40	421.17	413.06	408.34
48000	458.55	453.34	448.74	444.66	430.13	421.85	417.03
49000	468.11	462.79	458.09	453.93	439.09	430.64	425.72
50000	477.66	472.23	467.44	463.19	448.05	439.43	434.41
51000	487.21	481.68	476.79	472.46	457.01	448.22	443.10
52000	496.77	491.12	486.14	481.72	465.97	457.00	451.79
53000	506.32	500.57	495.48	490.98	474.93	465.79	460.47
54000	515.87	510.01	504.83	500.25	483.89	474.58	469.16
55000	525.43	519.46	514.18	509.51	492.86	483.37	477.85
56000	534.90	528.90	523.53	518.77	501.82	492.16	486.54
57000	544.53	538.35	532.88	528.04	510.78	500.95	495.23
58000	554.00	547.79	542.23	537.30	519.74	509.74	503.91
59000	563.64	557.24	551.58	546.57	528.70	518.52	512.60
60000	573.19	566.68	560.93	555.83	537.66	527.31	521.29
65000	620.96	613.90	607.67	602.15	582.47	571.26	564.73
70000	668.72	661.13	654.41	648.47	627.27	615.20	608.17
75000	716.49	708.35	701.16	694.79	672.08	659.14	651.61
80000	764.25	755.57	747.90	741.11	716.88	703.08	695.05
85000	812.02	802.80	794.65	787.43	761.69	747.03	738.50
90000	859.79	850.02	841.39	833.74	806.49	790.97	781.94
95000	907.55	897.24	888.13	880.06	851.30	834.91	825.38
100000	955.32	944.47	934.88	926.38	896.10	878.86	868.82
105000	1003.08	991.69	981.62	972.70	940.91	922.80	912.26
110000	1050.85	1038.91	1028.36	1019.02	985.71	966.74	955.70
120000	1146.38	1133.36	1121.85	1111.66	1075.32	1054.63	1042.58
130000	1241.91	1227.81	1215.34	1204.30	1164.93	1142.51	1129.46
140000	1337.45	1322.25	1308.83	1296.94	1254.54	1230.40	1216.35
150000	1432.98	1416.70	1402.31	1389.57	1344.15	1318.28	1303.23
175000	1671.81	1652.82	1636.03	1621.17	1568.18	1538.00	1520.43
200000	1910.64	1888.93	1869.75	1852.77	1792.20	1757.71	1737.64
225000	2149.47	2125.05	2103.47	2084.36	2016.23	1977.43	1954.84
250000	2388.30	2361.17	2337.19	2315.96	2240.25	2197.14	2172.05

10½%

Monthly Payments

necessary to amortize a loan

AMOUNT	1 YEAR	2 YEARS	3 YEARS	4 YEARS	5 YEARS	6 YEARS	7 YEARS
100	8.81	4.64	3.25	2.56	2.15	1.88	1.69
200	17.63	9.28	6.50	5.12	4.30	3.76	3.37
500	44.07	23.19	16.25	12.80	10.75	9.39	8.43
1000	88.15	46.38	32.50	25.60	21.49	18.78	16.86
2000	176.30	92.75	65.00	51.21	42.99	37.56	33.72
5000	440.74	231.88	162.51	128.02	107.47	93.89	84.30
6000	528.89	278.26	195.01	153.62	128.96	112.67	101.16
7000	617.04	324.63	227.52	179.22	150.46	131.45	118.02
8000	705.19	371.01	260.02	204.83	171.95	150.23	134.89
9000	793.34	417.38	292.52	230.43	193.45	169.01	151.75
10000	881.49	463.76	325.02	256.03	214.94	187.79	168.61
15000	1322.23	695.64	487.54	384.05	322.41	281.68	252.91
20000	1762.97	927.52	650.05	512.07	429.88	375.58	337.21
25000	2203.72	1159.40	812.56	640.08	537.35	469.47	421.52
30000	2644.46	1391.28	975.07	768.10	644.82	563.37	505.82
35000	3085.20	1623.16	1137.59	896.12	752.29	657.26	590.12
36000	3173.35	1669.54	1170.09	921.72	773.78	676.04	606.98
37000	3261.50	1715.91	1202.59	947.33	795.27	694.82	623.84
38000	3349.65	1762.29	1235.09	972.93	816.77	713.60	640.71
39000	3437.80	1808.67	1267.60	998.53	838.26	732.38	657.57
40000	3525.94	1855.04	1300.10	1024.14	859.76	751.16	674.43
41000	3614.09	1901.42	1332.60	1049.74	881.25	769.94	691.29
42000	3702.24	1947.79	1365.10	1075.34	902.74	788.72	708.15
43000	3790.39	1994.17	1397.61	1100.95	924.24	807.50	725.01
44000	3878.54	2040.55	1430.11	1126.55	945.73	826.27	741.87
45000	3966.69	2086.92	1462.61	1152.15	967.23	845.05	758.73
46000	4054.84	2133.30	1495.11	1177.76	988.72	863.83	775.59
47000	4142.98	2179.67	1527.61	1203.36	1010.21	882.61	792.45
48000	4231.13	2226.05	1560.12	1228.96	1031.71	901.39	809.31
49000	4319.28	2272.43	1592.62	1254.57	1053.20	920.17	826.17
50000	4407.43	2318.80	1625.12	1280.17	1074.70	938.95	843.03
51000	4495.58	2365.18	1657.62	1305.77	1096.19	957.73	859.89
52000	4583.73	2411.55	1690.13	1331.38	1117.68	976.51	876.76
53000	4671.88	2457.93	1722.63	1356.98	1139.18	995.29	893.62
54000	4760.02	2504.31	1755.13	1382.58	1160.67	1014.06	910.48
55000	4848.17	2550.68	1787.63	1408.19	1182.16	1032.84	927.34
56000	4936.32	2597.06	1820.14	1433.79	1203.66	1051.62	944.20
57000	5024.47	2643.43	1852.64	1459.39	1225.15	1070.40	961.06
58000	5112.62	2689.81	1885.14	1485.00	1246.65	1089.18	977.92
59000	5200.77	2736.19	1917.64	1510.60	1268.14	1107.96	994.78
60000	5288.92	2782.56	1950.15	1536.20	1289.63	1126.74	1011.64
65000	5729.66	3014.44	2112.66	1664.22	1397.10	1220.63	1095.94
70000	6170.40	3246.32	2275.17	1792.24	1504.57	1314.53	1180.25
75000	6611.15	3478.20	2437.68	1920.25	1612.04	1408.42	1264.55
80000	7051.89	3710.08	2600.20	2048.27	1719.51	1502.32	1348.85
85000	7492.63	3941.96	2762.71	2176.29	1826.98	1596.21	1433.16
90000	7933.37	4173.84	2925.22	2304.30	1934.45	1690.11	1517.46
95000	8374.12	4405.72	3087.73	2432.32	2041.92	1784.00	1601.76
100000	8814.86	4637.60	3250.24	2560.34	2149.39	1877.90	1686.07
105000	9255.60	4869.48	3412.76	2688.35	2256.86	1971.79	1770.37
110000	9696.35	5101.36	3575.27	2816.37	2364.33	2065.69	1854.67
120000	10577.83	5565.12	3900.29	3072.41	2579.27	2253.48	2023.28
130000	11459.32	6028.89	4225.32	3328.44	2794.21	2441.27	2191.89
140000	12340.80	6492.65	4550.34	3584.47	3009.15	2629.06	2360.49
150000	13222.29	6956.41	4875.37	3840.51	3224.09	2816.85	2529.10
175000	15426.01	8115.81	5687.93	4480.59	3761.43	3286.32	2950.62
200000	17629.72	9275.21	6500.49	5120.68	4298.78	3755.79	3372.13
225000	19833.44	10434.61	7313.05	5760.76	4836.13	4225.27	3793.65
250000	22037.15	11594.01	8125.61	6400.84	5373.48	4694.74	4215.17

Monthly Payments 10½%

necessary to amortize a loan

AMOUNT	8 YEARS	9 YEARS	10 YEARS	11 YEARS	12 YEARS	13 YEARS	14 YEARS
100	1.54	1.44	1.35	1.28	1.22	1.18	1.14
200	3.09	2.87	2.70	2.56	2.45	2.36	2.28
500	7.72	7.18	6.75	6.40	6.12	5.89	5.69
1000	15.44	14.35	13.49	12.80	12.24	11.78	11.38
2000	30.88	28.70	26.99	25.61	24.48	23.55	22.77
5000	77.20	71.75	67.47	64.02	61.21	58.88	56.92
6000	92.64	86.11	80.96	76.83	73.45	70.65	68.31
7000	108.08	100.46	94.45	89.63	85.69	82.43	79.69
8000	123.52	114.81	107.95	102.44	97.93	94.20	91.07
9000	138.96	129.16	121.44	115.24	110.17	105.98	102.46
10000	154.40	143.51	134.93	128.04	122.41	117.75	113.84
15000	231.60	215.26	202.40	192.07	183.62	176.63	170.77
20000	308.80	287.02	269.87	256.09	244.83	235.50	227.69
25000	386.00	358.77	337.34	320.11	306.04	294.38	284.61
30000	463.20	430.53	404.80	384.13	367.24	353.25	341.53
35000	540.40	502.28	472.27	448.16	428.45	412.13	398.45
36000	555.84	516.63	485.77	460.96	440.69	423.90	409.84
37000	571.28	530.98	499.26	473.76	452.93	435.68	421.22
38000	586.72	545.33	512.75	486.57	465.17	447.45	432.60
39000	602.16	559.68	526.25	499.37	477.41	459.23	443.99
40000	617.60	574.03	539.74	512.18	489.66	471.00	455.37
41000	633.04	588.39	553.23	524.98	501.90	482.78	466.76
42000	648.48	602.74	566.73	537.79	514.14	494.55	478.14
43000	663.92	617.09	580.22	550.59	526.38	506.33	489.53
44000	679.36	631.44	593.71	563.40	538.62	518.10	500.91
45000	694.80	645.79	607.21	576.20	550.86	529.88	512.30
46000	710.24	660.14	620.70	589.01	563.10	541.65	523.68
47000	725.68	674.49	634.19	601.81	575.35	553.43	535.06
48000	741.12	688.84	647.69	614.61	587.59	565.20	546.45
49000	756.56	703.19	661.18	627.42	599.83	576.98	557.83
50000	772.00	717.54	674.67	640.22	612.07	588.75	569.22
51000	787.44	731.89	688.17	653.03	624.31	600.53	580.60
52000	802.88	746.24	701.66	665.83	636.55	612.30	591.99
53000	818.32	760.60	715.16	678.64	648.79	624.08	603.37
54000	833.76	774.95	728.65	691.44	661.04	635.85	614.75
55000	849.20	789.30	742.14	704.25	673.28	647.63	626.14
56000	864.64	803.65	755.64	717.05	685.52	659.40	637.52
57000	880.08	818.00	769.13	729.85	697.76	671.18	648.91
58000	895.52	832.35	782.62	742.66	710.00	682.95	660.29
59000	910.96	846.70	796.12	755.46	722.24	694.73	671.68
60000	926.40	861.05	809.61	768.27	734.48	706.50	683.06
65000	1003.60	932.81	877.08	832.29	795.69	765.38	739.98
70000	1080.80	1004.56	944.54	898.31	850.90	824.25	796.90
75000	1158.00	1076.31	1012.01	960.33	918.11	883.13	853.83
80000	1235.20	1148.07	1079.48	1024.36	979.31	942.00	910.75
85000	1312.40	1219.82	1146.95	1088.38	1040.52	1000.88	967.67
90000	1389.60	1291.58	1214.41	1152.40	1101.73	1059.75	1024.59
95000	1466.80	1363.33	1281.88	1216.42	1162.93	1118.63	1081.51
100000	1544.00	1435.09	1349.35	1280.45	1224.14	1177.50	1138.43
105000	1621.20	1506.84	1416.82	1344.47	1285.35	1236.38	1195.36
110000	1698.40	1578.59	1484.28	1408.49	1346.55	1295.25	1252.28
120000	1852.80	1722.10	1619.22	1536.54	1468.97	1413.00	1366.12
130000	2007.20	1865.61	1754.15	1664.58	1591.38	1530.75	1479.96
140000	2161.60	2009.12	1889.09	1792.62	1713.80	1648.50	1593.81
150000	2316.00	2152.63	2024.02	1920.67	1836.21	1766.25	1707.65
175000	2702.00	2511.40	2361.36	2240.78	2142.25	2060.63	1992.26
200000	3088.00	2870.17	2698.70	2560.89	2448.28	2355.00	2276.87
225000	3474.00	3228.94	3036.04	2881.00	2754.32	2649.38	2561.48
250000	3860.00	3587.72	3373.37	3201.11	3060.35	2943.75	2846.09

10½%

Monthly Payments
necessary to amortize a loan

AMOUNT	15 YEARS	16 YEARS	17 YEARS	18 YEARS	19 YEARS	20 YEARS	21 YEARS
100	1.11	1.08	1.05	1.03	1.01	1.00	0.98
200	2.21	2.15	2.11	2.06	2.03	2.00	1.97
500	5.53	5.39	5.27	5.16	5.07	4.99	4.92
1000	11.05	10.77	10.53	10.32	10.14	9.98	9.85
2000	22.11	21.54	21.06	20.64	20.28	19.97	19.69
5000	55.27	53.86	52.65	51.61	50.71	49.92	49.23
6000	66.32	64.63	63.18	61.93	60.85	59.90	59.08
7000	77.38	75.41	73.72	72.26	70.99	69.89	68.92
8000	88.43	86.18	84.25	82.58	81.13	79.87	78.77
9000	99.49	96.95	94.78	92.90	91.27	89.85	88.61
10000	110.54	107.72	105.31	103.22	101.41	99.84	98.46
15000	165.81	161.59	157.96	154.83	152.12	149.76	147.69
20000	221.08	215.45	210.62	206.45	202.83	199.68	196.92
25000	276.35	269.31	263.27	258.06	253.53	249.59	246.15
30000	331.62	323.17	315.92	309.67	304.24	299.51	295.38
35000	386.89	377.03	368.58	361.28	354.95	349.43	344.61
36000	397.94	387.81	379.11	371.60	365.09	359.42	354.46
37000	409.00	398.58	389.64	381.92	375.23	369.40	364.30
38000	420.05	409.35	400.17	392.25	385.37	379.38	374.15
39000	431.11	420.12	410.70	402.57	395.51	389.37	383.99
40000	442.16	430.90	421.23	412.89	405.66	399.35	393.84
41000	453.21	441.67	431.76	423.21	415.80	409.34	403.69
42000	464.27	452.44	442.29	433.54	425.94	419.32	413.53
43000	475.32	463.21	452.82	443.86	436.08	429.30	423.38
44000	486.38	473.99	463.36	454.18	446.22	439.29	433.22
45000	497.43	484.76	473.89	464.50	456.36	449.27	443.07
46000	508.48	495.53	484.42	474.82	466.50	459.25	452.92
47000	519.54	506.30	494.95	485.15	476.65	469.24	462.76
48000	530.59	517.08	505.48	495.47	486.79	479.22	472.61
49000	541.65	527.85	516.01	505.79	496.93	489.21	482.45
50000	552.70	538.62	526.54	516.11	507.07	499.19	492.30
51000	563.75	549.39	537.07	526.44	517.21	509.17	502.15
52000	574.81	560.17	547.60	536.76	527.35	519.16	511.99
53000	585.86	570.94	558.13	547.08	537.49	529.14	521.84
54000	596.92	581.71	568.66	557.40	547.64	539.13	531.68
55000	607.97	592.48	579.19	567.73	557.78	549.11	541.53
56000	619.02	603.26	589.73	578.05	567.92	559.09	551.38
57000	630.08	614.03	600.26	588.37	578.06	569.08	561.22
58000	641.13	624.80	610.79	598.69	588.20	579.06	571.07
59000	652.19	635.57	621.32	609.01	598.34	589.04	580.91
60000	663.24	646.35	631.85	619.34	608.48	599.03	590.76
65000	718.51	700.21	684.50	670.95	659.19	648.95	639.99
70000	773.78	754.07	737.16	722.56	709.90	698.87	689.22
75000	829.05	807.93	789.81	774.17	760.60	748.78	738.45
80000	884.32	861.79	842.46	825.78	811.31	798.70	787.68
85000	939.59	915.66	895.12	877.39	862.02	848.62	836.91
90000	994.86	969.52	947.77	929.00	912.73	898.54	886.14
95000	1050.13	1023.38	1000.43	980.62	963.43	948.46	935.37
100000	1105.40	1077.24	1053.08	1032.23	1014.14	998.38	984.60
105000	1160.67	1131.10	1105.74	1083.84	1064.85	1048.30	1033.83
110000	1215.94	1184.97	1158.39	1135.45	1115.55	1098.22	1083.06
120000	1326.48	1292.69	1263.70	1238.67	1216.97	1198.06	1181.52
130000	1437.02	1400.42	1369.01	1341.90	1318.38	1297.89	1279.98
140000	1547.56	1508.14	1474.31	1445.12	1419.79	1397.73	1378.44
150000	1658.10	1615.86	1579.62	1548.34	1521.21	1497.57	1476.90
175000	1934.45	1885.17	1842.89	1806.40	1774.74	1747.16	1723.05
200000	2210.80	2154.48	2106.16	2064.46	2028.28	1996.76	1969.20
225000	2487.15	2423.80	2369.43	2322.51	2281.81	2246.35	2215.35
250000	2763.50	2693.11	2632.70	2580.57	2535.35	2495.95	2461.50

Monthly Payments 10½%

necessary to amortize a loan

AMOUNT	22 YEARS	23 YEARS	24 YEARS	25 YEARS	30 YEARS	35 YEARS	40 YEARS
100	0.97	0.96	0.95	0.94	0.91	0.90	0.89
200	1.95	1.92	1.90	1.89	1.83	1.80	1.78
500	4.86	4.81	4.76	4.72	4.57	4.49	4.44
1000	9.73	9.62	9.52	9.44	9.15	8.98	8.89
2000	19.45	19.24	19.05	18.88	18.29	17.96	17.77
5000	48.63	48.09	47.62	47.21	45.74	44.91	44.43
6000	58.35	57.71	57.15	56.65	54.88	53.89	53.31
7000	68.08	67.33	66.67	66.09	64.03	62.87	62.20
8000	77.80	76.95	76.20	75.53	73.18	71.85	71.09
9000	87.53	86.57	85.72	84.98	82.33	80.83	79.97
10000	97.25	96.19	95.25	94.42	91.47	89.81	88.86
15000	145.88	144.28	142.87	141.63	137.21	134.72	133.29
20000	194.50	192.37	190.50	188.84	182.95	179.63	177.71
25000	243.13	240.47	238.12	236.05	228.68	224.53	222.14
30000	291.75	288.56	285.74	283.25	274.42	269.44	266.57
35000	340.38	336.65	333.37	330.46	320.16	314.35	311.00
36000	350.10	346.27	342.89	339.91	329.31	323.33	319.89
37000	359.83	355.89	352.42	349.35	338.45	332.31	328.77
38000	369.55	365.51	361.94	358.79	347.60	341.29	337.66
39000	379.28	375.13	371.47	368.23	356.75	350.27	346.54
40000	389.00	384.75	380.99	377.67	365.90	359.25	355.43
41000	398.73	394.37	390.52	387.11	375.04	368.23	364.31
42000	408.45	403.98	400.04	396.56	384.19	377.22	373.20
43000	418.18	413.60	409.57	406.00	393.34	386.20	382.09
44000	427.90	423.22	419.09	415.44	402.49	395.18	390.97
45000	437.63	432.84	428.62	424.88	411.63	404.16	399.86
46000	447.35	442.46	438.14	434.32	420.78	413.14	408.74
47000	457.08	452.08	447.67	443.77	429.93	422.12	417.63
48000	466.80	461.70	457.19	453.21	439.07	431.10	426.51
49000	476.53	471.31	466.72	462.65	448.22	440.09	435.40
50000	486.25	480.93	476.24	472.09	457.37	449.07	444.29
51000	495.98	490.55	485.77	481.53	466.52	458.05	453.17
52000	505.70	500.17	495.29	490.97	475.66	467.03	462.06
53000	515.43	509.79	504.81	500.42	484.81	476.01	470.94
54000	525.15	519.41	514.34	509.86	493.96	484.99	479.83
55000	534.88	529.03	523.86	519.30	503.11	493.97	488.71
56000	544.60	538.65	533.39	528.74	512.25	502.96	497.60
57000	554.33	548.26	542.91	538.18	521.40	511.94	506.49
58000	564.05	557.88	552.44	547.63	530.55	520.92	515.37
59000	573.78	567.50	561.96	557.07	539.70	529.90	524.26
60000	583.50	577.12	571.49	566.51	548.84	538.88	533.14
65000	632.13	625.21	619.11	613.72	594.58	583.79	577.57
70000	680.75	673.31	666.74	660.93	640.32	628.69	622.00
75000	729.38	721.40	714.36	708.14	686.05	673.60	666.43
80000	778.01	769.49	761.98	755.35	731.79	718.51	710.86
85000	826.63	817.59	809.61	802.55	777.53	763.41	755.28
90000	875.26	865.68	857.23	849.76	823.27	808.32	799.71
95000	923.88	913.77	904.86	896.97	869.00	853.23	844.14
100000	972.51	961.87	952.48	944.18	914.74	898.13	888.57
105000	1021.13	1009.96	1000.10	991.39	960.48	943.04	933.00
110000	1069.76	1058.05	1047.73	1038.60	1006.21	987.95	977.43
120000	1167.01	1154.24	1142.98	1133.02	1097.69	1077.76	1066.28
130000	1264.26	1250.43	1238.23	1227.44	1189.16	1167.57	1155.14
140000	1361.51	1346.61	1333.47	1321.85	1280.64	1257.39	1244.00
150000	1458.76	1442.80	1428.72	1416.27	1372.11	1347.20	1332.86
175000	1701.89	1683.27	1666.84	1652.32	1600.79	1571.73	1555.00
200000	1945.01	1923.73	1904.96	1888.36	1829.48	1796.27	1777.14
225000	2188.14	2164.20	2143.08	2124.41	2058.16	2020.80	1999.28
250000	2431.27	2404.67	2381.20	2360.45	2286.85	2245.34	2221.43

10¾%

Monthly Payments

necessary to amortize a loan

AMOUNT	1 YEAR	2 YEARS	3 YEARS	4 YEARS	5 YEARS	6 YEARS	7 YEARS
100	8.83	4.65	3.26	2.57	2.16	1.89	1.70
200	17.65	9.30	6.52	5.14	4.32	3.78	3.40
500	44.13	23.25	16.31	12.86	10.81	9.45	8.50
1000	88.27	46.49	32.62	25.72	21.62	18.91	16.99
2000	176.53	92.98	65.24	51.45	43.24	37.81	33.98
5000	441.33	232.46	163.10	128.62	108.09	94.53	84.96
6000	529.59	278.95	195.72	154.35	129.71	113.44	101.95
7000	617.86	325.44	228.34	180.07	151.33	132.34	118.94
8000	706.12	371.93	260.96	205.79	172.94	151.25	135.93
9000	794.39	418.43	293.58	231.52	194.56	170.16	152.92
10000	882.65	464.92	326.20	257.24	216.18	189.06	169.91
15000	1323.98	697.38	489.31	385.86	324.27	283.59	254.87
20000	1765.30	929.84	652.41	514.49	432.36	378.13	339.83
25000	2206.63	1162.30	815.51	643.11	540.45	472.66	424.78
30000	2647.95	1394.76	978.61	771.73	648.54	567.19	509.74
35000	3089.28	1627.21	1141.72	900.35	756.63	661.72	594.69
36000	3177.54	1673.71	1174.34	926.07	778.25	680.63	611.69
37000	3265.81	1720.20	1206.96	951.80	799.86	699.53	628.68
38000	3354.07	1766.69	1239.58	977.52	821.48	718.44	645.67
39000	3442.34	1813.18	1272.20	1003.25	843.10	737.34	662.66
40000	3530.60	1859.67	1304.82	1028.97	864.72	756.25	679.65
41000	3618.87	1906.17	1337.44	1054.70	886.34	775.16	696.64
42000	3707.13	1952.66	1370.06	1080.42	907.95	794.06	713.63
43000	3795.40	1999.15	1402.68	1106.14	929.57	812.97	730.62
44000	3883.66	2045.64	1435.30	1131.87	951.19	831.88	747.62
45000	3971.93	2092.13	1467.92	1157.59	972.81	850.78	764.61
46000	4060.19	2138.63	1500.54	1183.32	994.43	869.69	781.60
47000	4148.46	2185.12	1533.16	1209.04	1016.04	888.60	798.59
48000	4236.72	2231.61	1565.78	1234.77	1037.66	907.50	815.58
49000	4324.99	2278.10	1598.40	1260.49	1059.28	926.41	832.57
50000	4413.25	2324.59	1631.02	1286.21	1080.90	945.31	849.56
51000	4501.52	2371.08	1663.64	1311.94	1102.52	964.22	866.55
52000	4589.78	2417.58	1696.26	1337.66	1124.13	983.13	883.55
53000	4678.05	2464.07	1728.88	1363.39	1145.75	1002.03	900.54
54000	4766.31	2510.56	1761.50	1389.11	1167.37	1020.94	917.53
55000	4854.58	2557.05	1794.12	1414.84	1188.99	1039.85	934.52
56000	4942.84	2603.54	1826.75	1440.56	1210.61	1058.75	951.51
57000	5031.11	2650.04	1859.37	1466.28	1232.22	1077.66	968.50
58000	5119.38	2696.53	1891.99	1492.01	1253.84	1096.56	985.49
59000	5207.64	2743.02	1924.61	1517.73	1275.46	1115.47	1002.49
60000	5295.91	2789.51	1957.23	1543.46	1297.08	1134.38	1019.48
65000	5737.23	3021.97	2120.33	1672.08	1405.17	1228.91	1104.43
70000	6178.56	3254.43	2283.43	1800.70	1513.26	1323.44	1189.39
75000	6619.88	3486.89	2446.53	1929.32	1621.35	1417.97	1274.35
80000	7061.21	3719.35	2609.64	2057.94	1729.44	1512.50	1359.30
85000	7502.53	3951.81	2772.74	2186.56	1837.53	1607.03	1444.26
90000	7943.86	4184.27	2935.84	2315.19	1945.62	1701.57	1529.21
95000	8385.18	4416.73	3098.94	2443.81	2053.71	1796.10	1614.17
100000	8826.51	4649.19	3262.05	2572.43	2161.80	1890.63	1699.13
105000	9267.83	4881.64	3425.15	2701.05	2269.89	1985.16	1784.08
110000	9709.16	5114.10	3588.25	2829.67	2377.97	2079.69	1869.04
120000	10591.81	5579.02	3914.45	3086.91	2594.15	2268.75	2038.95
130000	11474.46	6043.94	4240.66	3344.16	2810.33	2457.82	2208.87
140000	12357.11	6508.86	4566.86	3601.40	3026.51	2646.88	2378.78
150000	13239.76	6973.78	4893.07	3858.64	3242.69	2835.94	2548.69
175000	15446.39	8136.07	5708.58	4501.75	3783.14	3308.60	2973.47
200000	17653.02	9298.37	6524.09	5144.86	4323.59	3781.26	3398.25
225000	19859.64	10460.67	7339.60	5787.96	4864.04	4253.91	3823.04
250000	22066.27	11622.96	8155.11	6431.07	5404.49	4726.57	4247.82

Monthly Payments **10¾%**

necessary to amortize a loan

AMOUNT	8 YEARS	9 YEARS	10 YEARS	11 YEARS	12 YEARS	13 YEARS	14 YEARS
100	1.56	1.45	1.36	1.29	1.24	1.19	1.15
200	3.11	2.90	2.73	2.59	2.48	2.38	2.31
500	7.79	7.24	6.82	6.47	6.19	5.96	5.77
1000	15.57	14.49	13.63	12.95	12.39	11.92	11.54
2000	31.15	28.98	27.27	25.90	24.78	23.85	23.07
5000	77.87	72.44	68.17	64.74	61.94	59.62	57.68
6000	93.44	86.93	81.80	77.69	74.33	71.55	69.22
7000	109.02	101.42	95.44	90.64	86.72	83.47	80.76
8000	124.59	115.90	109.07	103.58	99.10	95.40	92.30
9000	140.17	130.39	122.70	116.53	111.49	107.32	103.83
10000	155.74	144.88	136.34	129.48	123.88	119.25	115.37
15000	233.61	217.32	204.51	194.22	185.82	178.87	173.05
20000	311.48	289.76	272.68	258.96	247.76	238.49	230.74
25000	389.35	362.20	340.85	323.70	309.70	298.12	288.42
30000	467.22	434.64	409.02	388.44	371.64	357.74	346.11
35000	545.09	507.08	477.19	453.18	433.58	417.36	403.79
36000	560.66	521.57	490.82	466.13	445.97	429.29	415.33
37000	576.23	536.06	504.45	479.08	458.36	441.21	426.87
38000	591.81	550.54	518.09	492.02	470.75	453.14	438.40
39000	607.38	565.03	531.72	504.97	483.13	465.06	449.94
40000	622.96	579.52	545.35	517.92	495.52	476.99	461.48
41000	638.53	594.01	558.99	530.87	507.91	488.91	473.02
42000	654.10	608.50	572.62	543.82	520.30	500.84	484.55
43000	669.68	622.98	586.26	556.76	532.69	512.76	496.09
44000	685.25	637.47	599.89	569.71	545.07	524.69	507.63
45000	700.83	651.96	613.52	582.66	557.46	536.61	519.16
46000	716.40	666.45	627.16	595.61	569.85	548.54	530.70
47000	731.97	680.94	640.79	608.56	582.24	560.46	542.24
48000	747.55	695.42	654.43	621.50	594.63	572.38	553.77
49000	763.12	709.91	668.06	634.45	607.01	584.31	565.31
50000	778.70	724.40	681.69	647.40	619.40	596.23	576.85
51000	794.27	738.89	695.33	660.35	631.79	608.16	588.38
52000	809.84	753.38	708.96	673.30	644.18	620.08	599.92
53000	825.42	767.86	722.60	686.24	656.57	632.01	611.46
54000	840.99	782.35	736.23	699.19	668.95	643.93	623.00
55000	856.56	796.84	749.86	712.14	681.34	655.86	634.53
56000	872.14	811.33	763.50	725.09	693.73	667.78	646.07
57000	887.71	825.02	777.13	738.04	706.12	679.71	657.61
58000	903.29	840.30	790.76	750.98	718.51	691.63	669.14
59000	918.86	854.79	804.40	763.93	730.89	703.56	680.68
60000	934.43	869.28	818.03	776.88	743.28	715.48	692.22
65000	1012.30	941.72	886.20	841.62	805.22	775.10	749.90
70000	1090.17	1014.16	954.27	906.36	867.16	834.73	807.59
75000	1168.04	1086.60	1022.54	971.10	929.10	894.35	865.27
80000	1245.91	1159.04	1090.71	1035.84	991.04	953.97	922.96
85000	1323.78	1231.48	1158.88	1100.58	1052.98	1013.60	980.64
90000	1401.65	1303.92	1227.05	1165.32	1114.92	1073.22	1038.33
95000	1479.52	1376.36	1295.22	1230.06	1176.86	1132.85	1096.01
100000	1557.39	1448.80	1363.39	1294.80	1238.80	1192.47	1153.70
105000	1635.26	1521.24	1431.56	1359.54	1300.74	1252.09	1211.38
110000	1713.13	1593.68	1499.73	1424.28	1362.68	1311.72	1269.07
120000	1868.87	1738.56	1636.06	1553.76	1486.57	1430.96	1384.44
130000	2024.61	1883.44	1772.40	1683.24	1610.45	1550.21	1499.80
140000	2180.35	2028.32	1908.74	1812.72	1734.33	1669.46	1615.17
150000	2336.09	2173.20	2045.08	1942.20	1858.21	1788.70	1730.54
175000	2725.43	2535.40	2385.93	2265.90	2167.91	2086.82	2018.97
200000	3114.78	2897.60	2726.77	2589.60	2477.61	2384.94	2307.39
225000	3504.13	3259.80	3067.62	2913.30	2787.31	2683.05	2595.82
250000	3893.48	3622.00	3408.47	3237.00	3097.01	2981.17	2884.24

10¾%

Monthly Payments

necessary to amortize a loan

AMOUNT	15 YEARS	16 YEARS	17 YEARS	18 YEARS	19 YEARS	20 YEARS	21 YEARS
100	1.12	1.09	1.07	1.05	1.03	1.02	1.00
200	2.24	2.19	2.14	2.10	2.06	2.03	2.00
500	5.60	5.47	5.35	5.24	5.15	5.08	5.01
1000	11.21	10.93	10.69	10.49	10.31	10.15	10.02
2000	22.42	21.86	21.38	20.97	20.61	20.30	20.03
5000	56.05	54.65	53.46	52.43	51.54	50.76	50.08
6000	67.26	65.58	64.15	62.92	61.84	60.91	60.10
7000	78.47	76.51	74.84	73.40	72.15	71.07	70.12
8000	89.68	87.45	85.53	83.89	82.46	81.22	80.13
9000	100.89	98.38	96.23	94.37	92.77	91.37	90.15
10000	112.09	109.31	106.92	104.86	103.07	101.52	100.17
15000	168.14	163.96	160.38	157.29	154.61	152.28	150.25
20000	224.19	218.61	213.84	209.72	206.15	203.05	200.34
25000	280.24	273.27	267.29	262.15	257.69	253.81	250.42
30000	336.28	327.92	320.75	314.58	309.22	304.57	300.50
35000	392.33	382.57	374.21	367.00	360.76	355.33	350.59
36000	403.54	393.51	384.90	377.49	371.07	365.48	360.60
37000	414.75	404.44	395.60	387.98	381.38	375.63	370.62
38000	425.96	415.37	406.29	398.46	391.68	385.79	380.64
39000	437.17	426.30	416.98	408.95	401.99	395.94	390.65
40000	448.38	437.23	427.67	419.43	412.30	406.09	400.67
41000	459.59	448.16	438.36	429.92	422.61	416.24	410.69
42000	470.80	459.09	449.05	440.41	432.91	426.40	420.71
43000	482.01	470.02	459.75	450.89	443.22	436.55	430.72
44000	493.22	480.95	470.44	461.38	453.53	446.70	440.74
45000	504.43	491.88	481.13	471.86	463.84	456.85	450.76
46000	515.64	502.81	491.82	482.35	474.14	467.01	460.77
47000	526.85	513.74	502.51	492.83	484.45	477.16	470.79
48000	538.06	524.67	513.21	503.32	494.76	487.31	480.81
49000	549.26	535.60	523.90	513.81	505.07	497.46	490.82
50000	560.47	546.53	534.59	524.29	515.37	507.61	500.84
51000	571.68	557.47	545.28	534.78	525.68	517.77	510.86
52000	582.89	568.40	555.97	545.26	535.99	527.92	520.87
53000	594.10	579.33	566.66	555.75	546.30	538.07	530.89
54000	605.31	590.26	577.36	566.24	556.60	548.22	540.91
55000	616.52	601.19	588.05	576.72	566.91	558.38	550.92
56000	627.73	612.12	598.74	587.21	577.22	568.53	560.94
57000	638.94	623.05	609.43	597.69	587.53	578.68	570.96
58000	650.15	633.98	620.12	608.18	597.83	588.83	580.97
59000	661.36	644.91	630.82	618.67	608.14	598.99	590.99
60000	672.57	655.84	641.51	629.15	618.45	609.14	601.01
65000	728.62	710.50	694.97	681.58	669.99	659.90	651.09
70000	784.66	765.15	748.42	734.01	721.52	710.66	701.18
75000	840.71	819.80	801.88	786.44	773.06	761.42	751.26
80000	896.76	874.46	855.34	838.87	824.60	812.18	801.34
85000	952.81	929.11	908.80	891.30	876.13	862.94	851.43
90000	1008.85	983.76	962.26	943.73	927.67	913.71	901.51
95000	1064.90	1038.42	1015.72	996.16	979.21	964.47	951.60
100000	1120.95	1093.07	1069.18	1048.58	1030.75	1015.23	1001.68
105000	1177.00	1147.72	1122.64	1101.01	1082.28	1065.99	1051.76
110000	1233.04	1202.38	1176.10	1153.44	1133.82	1116.75	1101.85
120000	1345.14	1311.68	1283.01	1258.30	1236.90	1218.27	1202.02
130000	1457.23	1420.99	1389.93	1363.16	1339.97	1319.80	1302.18
140000	1569.33	1530.30	1496.85	1468.02	1443.05	1421.32	1402.35
150000	1681.42	1639.60	1603.77	1572.88	1546.12	1522.84	1502.52
175000	1961.66	1912.87	1871.06	1835.02	1803.81	1776.65	1752.94
200000	2241.90	2186.14	2138.36	2097.17	2061.49	2030.46	2003.36
225000	2522.13	2459.41	2405.65	2359.32	2319.18	2284.27	2253.78
250000	2802.37	2732.67	2672.95	2621.46	2576.87	2538.07	2504.20

Monthly Payments 10¾%

necessary to amortize a loan

AMOUNT	22 YEARS	23 YEARS	24 YEARS	25 YEARS	30 YEARS	35 YEARS	40 YEARS
100	0.99	0.98	0.97	0.96	0.93	0.92	0.91
200	1.98	1.96	1.94	1.92	1.87	1.84	1.82
500	4.95	4.90	4.85	4.81	4.67	4.59	4.54
1000	9.90	9.79	9.70	9.62	9.33	9.18	9.08
2000	19.80	19.59	19.40	19.24	18.67	18.35	18.17
5000	49.49	48.97	48.51	48.10	46.67	45.88	45.42
6000	59.39	58.76	58.21	57.73	56.01	55.05	54.50
7000	69.29	68.56	67.91	67.35	65.34	64.23	63.59
8000	79.18	78.35	77.62	76.97	74.68	73.40	72.67
9000	89.08	88.14	87.32	86.59	84.01	82.58	81.76
10000	98.98	97.94	97.02	96.21	93.35	91.75	90.84
15000	148.47	146.91	145.53	144.31	140.02	137.63	136.26
20000	197.96	195.88	194.04	192.42	186.70	183.50	181.68
25000	247.45	244.85	242.55	240.52	233.37	229.38	227.10
30000	296.94	293.81	291.06	288.63	280.04	275.25	272.52
35000	346.43	342.78	339.57	336.73	326.72	321.13	317.94
36000	356.33	352.58	349.27	346.35	336.05	330.30	327.02
37000	366.23	362.37	358.97	355.97	345.39	339.48	336.11
38000	376.13	372.17	368.68	365.60	354.72	348.65	345.19
39000	386.03	381.96	378.38	375.22	364.06	357.83	354.27
40000	395.92	391.75	388.08	384.84	373.39	367.00	363.36
41000	405.82	401.55	397.78	394.46	382.73	376.18	372.44
42000	415.72	411.34	407.48	404.08	392.06	385.35	381.53
43000	425.62	421.13	417.19	413.70	401.40	394.53	390.61
44000	435.52	430.93	426.89	423.32	410.73	403.70	399.69
45000	445.41	440.72	436.59	432.94	420.07	412.88	408.78
46000	455.31	450.52	446.29	442.56	429.40	422.05	417.86
47000	465.21	460.31	455.99	452.18	438.74	431.23	426.95
48000	475.11	470.10	465.70	461.80	448.07	440.40	436.03
49000	485.01	479.90	475.40	471.43	457.41	449.58	445.11
50000	494.90	489.69	485.10	481.05	466.74	458.75	454.20
51000	504.80	499.48	494.80	490.67	476.08	467.93	463.28
52000	514.70	509.28	504.50	500.29	485.41	477.10	472.37
53000	524.60	519.07	514.21	509.91	494.75	486.28	481.45
54000	534.50	528.87	523.91	519.53	504.08	495.45	490.53
55000	544.40	538.66	533.61	529.15	513.41	504.63	499.62
56000	554.29	548.45	543.31	538.77	522.75	513.80	508.70
57000	564.19	558.25	553.01	548.39	532.08	522.98	517.79
58000	574.09	568.04	562.72	558.01	541.42	532.15	526.87
59000	583.99	577.84	572.42	567.63	550.75	541.33	535.95
60000	593.89	587.63	582.12	577.26	560.09	550.50	545.04
65000	643.38	636.60	630.63	625.36	606.76	596.38	590.46
70000	692.87	685.57	679.14	673.46	653.44	642.25	635.88
75000	742.36	734.54	727.65	721.57	700.11	688.13	681.30
80000	791.85	783.51	776.16	769.67	746.79	734.00	726.72
85000	841.34	832.47	824.67	817.78	793.46	779.88	772.14
90000	890.83	881.44	873.18	865.88	840.13	825.75	817.56
95000	940.32	930.41	921.69	913.99	886.81	871.63	862.98
100000	989.81	979.38	970.20	962.09	933.48	917.50	908.40
105000	1039.30	1028.35	1018.71	1010.20	980.16	963.38	953.82
110000	1088.79	1077.32	1067.22	1058.30	1026.83	1009.25	999.24
120000	1187.77	1175.26	1164.24	1154.51	1120.18	1101.00	1090.08
130000	1286.75	1273.20	1261.26	1250.72	1213.53	1192.75	1180.92
140000	1385.73	1371.13	1358.28	1346.93	1306.87	1284.50	1271.76
150000	1484.71	1469.07	1455.30	1443.14	1400.22	1376.25	1362.60
175000	1732.17	1713.92	1697.85	1683.66	1633.59	1605.63	1589.70
200000	1979.62	1958.76	1940.40	1924.19	1866.96	1835.01	1816.79
225000	2227.07	2203.61	2182.95	2164.71	2100.33	2064.38	2043.89
250000	2474.52	2448.46	2425.50	2405.23	2333.70	2293.76	2270.99

11% Monthly Payments

necessary to amortize a loan

AMOUNT	1 YEAR	2 YEARS	3 YEARS	4 YEARS	5 YEARS	6 YEARS	7 YEARS
100	8.84	4.66	3.27	2.58	2.17	1.90	1.71
200	17.68	9.32	6.55	5.17	4.35	3.81	3.42
500	44.19	23.30	16.37	12.92	10.87	9.52	8.56
1000	88.38	46.61	32.74	25.85	21.74	19.03	17.12
2000	176.76	93.22	65.48	51.69	43.48	38.07	34.24
5000	441.91	233.04	163.69	129.23	108.71	95.17	85.61
6000	530.29	279.65	196.43	155.07	130.45	114.20	102.73
7000	618.67	326.25	229.17	180.92	152.20	133.24	119.86
8000	707.05	372.86	261.91	206.76	173.94	152.27	136.98
9000	795.43	419.47	294.65	232.61	195.68	171.31	154.10
10000	883.82	466.08	327.39	258.46	217.42	190.34	171.22
15000	1325.72	699.12	491.08	387.68	326.14	285.51	256.84
20000	1767.63	932.16	654.77	516.91	434.85	380.68	342.45
25000	2209.54	1165.20	818.47	646.14	543.56	475.85	428.06
30000	2651.45	1398.24	982.16	775.37	652.27	571.02	513.67
35000	3093.36	1631.27	1145.86	904.59	760.98	666.19	599.29
36000	3181.74	1677.88	1178.59	930.44	782.73	685.23	616.41
37000	3270.12	1724.49	1211.33	956.28	804.47	704.26	633.53
38000	3358.50	1771.10	1244.07	982.13	826.21	723.30	650.65
39000	3446.88	1817.71	1276.81	1007.98	847.95	742.33	667.78
40000	3535.27	1864.31	1309.55	1033.82	869.70	761.36	684.90
41000	3623.65	1910.92	1342.29	1059.67	891.44	780.40	702.02
42000	3712.03	1957.53	1375.03	1085.51	913.18	799.43	719.14
43000	3800.41	2004.14	1407.76	1111.36	934.92	818.47	736.26
44000	3888.79	2050.74	1440.50	1137.20	956.67	837.50	753.39
45000	3977.17	2097.35	1473.24	1163.05	978.41	856.53	770.51
46000	4065.56	2143.96	1505.98	1188.89	1000.15	875.57	787.63
47000	4153.94	2190.57	1538.72	1214.74	1021.89	894.60	804.75
48000	4242.32	2237.18	1571.46	1240.59	1043.64	913.64	821.88
49000	4330.70	2283.78	1604.20	1266.43	1065.38	932.67	839.00
50000	4419.08	2330.39	1636.94	1292.28	1087.12	951.70	856.12
51000	4507.46	2377.00	1669.67	1318.12	1108.86	970.74	873.24
52000	4595.85	2423.61	1702.41	1343.97	1130.61	989.77	890.37
53000	4684.23	2470.22	1735.15	1369.81	1152.35	1008.81	907.49
54000	4772.61	2516.82	1767.89	1395.66	1174.09	1027.84	924.61
55000	4860.99	2563.43	1800.63	1421.50	1195.83	1046.87	941.73
56000	4949.37	2610.04	1833.37	1447.35	1217.58	1065.91	958.86
57000	5037.75	2656.65	1866.11	1473.19	1239.32	1084.94	975.98
58000	5126.14	2703.25	1898.85	1499.04	1261.06	1103.98	993.10
59000	5214.52	2749.86	1931.58	1524.89	1282.80	1123.01	1010.22
60000	5302.90	2796.47	1964.32	1550.73	1304.55	1142.04	1027.35
65000	5744.81	3029.51	2128.02	1679.96	1413.26	1237.22	1112.96
70000	6186.72	3262.55	2291.71	1809.19	1521.97	1332.39	1198.57
75000	6628.62	3495.59	2455.40	1938.41	1630.68	1427.56	1284.18
80000	7070.53	3728.63	2619.10	2067.64	1739.39	1522.73	1369.79
85000	7512.44	3961.67	2782.79	2196.87	1848.11	1617.90	1455.41
90000	7954.35	4194.71	2946.48	2326.10	1956.82	1713.07	1541.02
95000	8396.26	4427.74	3110.18	2455.32	2065.53	1808.24	1626.63
100000	8838.17	4660.78	3273.87	2584.55	2174.24	1903.41	1712.24
105000	9280.07	4893.82	3437.57	2713.78	2282.95	1998.58	1797.86
110000	9721.98	5126.86	3601.26	2843.01	2391.67	2093.75	1883.47
120000	10605.80	5592.94	3928.65	3101.46	2609.09	2284.09	2054.69
130000	11489.62	6059.02	4256.03	3359.92	2826.51	2474.43	2225.92
140000	12373.43	6525.10	4583.42	3618.37	3043.94	2664.77	2397.14
150000	13257.25	6991.18	4910.81	3876.83	3261.36	2855.11	2568.37
175000	15466.79	8156.37	5729.28	4522.97	3804.92	3330.96	2996.43
200000	17676.33	9321.57	6547.74	5169.10	4348.48	3806.82	3424.49
225000	19885.87	10486.76	7366.21	5815.24	4892.05	4282.67	3852.55
250000	22095.41	11651.96	8184.68	6461.38	5435.61	4758.52	4280.61

Monthly Payments 11%
necessary to amortize a loan

AMOUNT	8 YEARS	9 YEARS	10 YEARS	11 YEARS	12 YEARS	13 YEARS	14 YEARS
100	1.57	1.46	1.38	1.31	1.25	1.21	1.17
200	3.14	2.93	2.76	2.62	2.51	2.42	2.34
500	7.85	7.31	6.89	6.55	6.27	6.04	5.85
1000	15.71	14.63	13.78	13.09	12.54	12.08	11.69
2000	31.42	29.25	27.55	26.18	25.07	24.15	23.38
5000	78.54	73.13	68.88	65.46	62.68	60.38	58.45
6000	94.25	87.76	82.65	78.55	75.21	72.45	70.14
7000	109.96	102.38	96.43	91.65	87.75	84.53	81.83
8000	125.67	117.01	110.20	104.74	100.28	96.60	93.52
9000	141.38	131.63	123.98	117.83	112.82	108.68	105.21
10000	157.08	146.26	137.75	130.92	125.36	120.75	116.91
15000	235.63	219.39	206.63	196.39	188.03	181.13	175.36
20000	314.17	292.52	275.50	261.85	250.71	241.51	233.81
25000	392.71	365.65	344.38	327.31	313.39	301.88	292.26
30000	471.25	438.78	413.25	392.77	376.07	362.26	350.72
35000	549.79	511.91	482.13	458.23	438.74	422.63	409.17
36000	565.50	526.53	495.90	471.32	451.28	434.71	420.86
37000	581.21	541.16	509.68	484.42	463.82	446.79	432.55
38000	596.92	555.78	523.45	497.51	476.35	458.86	444.24
39000	612.63	570.41	537.23	510.60	488.89	470.94	455.93
40000	628.34	585.03	551.00	523.69	501.42	483.01	467.62
41000	644.05	599.66	564.78	536.79	513.96	495.09	479.31
42000	659.75	614.29	578.55	549.88	526.49	507.16	491.00
43000	675.46	628.91	592.33	562.97	539.03	519.24	502.69
44000	691.17	643.54	606.10	576.06	551.56	531.31	514.38
45000	706.88	658.16	619.88	589.16	564.10	543.39	526.07
46000	722.59	672.79	633.65	602.25	576.64	555.46	537.76
47000	738.30	687.42	647.43	615.34	589.17	567.54	549.46
48000	754.00	702.04	661.20	628.43	601.71	579.61	561.15
49000	769.71	716.67	674.98	641.53	614.24	591.69	572.84
50000	785.42	731.29	688.75	654.62	626.78	603.76	584.53
51000	801.13	745.92	702.53	667.71	639.31	615.84	596.22
52000	816.84	760.54	716.30	680.80	651.85	627.91	607.91
53000	832.55	775.17	730.08	693.89	664.38	639.99	619.60
54000	848.25	789.80	743.85	706.99	676.92	652.06	631.29
55000	863.96	804.42	757.63	720.08	689.46	664.14	642.98
56000	879.67	819.05	771.40	733.17	701.99	676.22	654.67
57000	895.38	833.67	785.18	746.26	714.53	688.29	666.36
58000	911.09	848.30	798.95	759.36	727.06	700.37	678.06
59000	926.80	862.93	812.73	772.45	739.60	712.44	689.74
60000	942.51	877.55	826.50	785.54	752.13	724.52	701.43
65000	1021.05	950.68	895.38	851.00	814.81	784.89	759.89
70000	1099.59	1023.81	964.25	916.46	877.49	845.27	818.34
75000	1178.13	1096.94	1033.13	981.93	940.17	905.65	876.79
80000	1256.67	1170.07	1102.00	1047.39	1002.84	966.02	935.24
85000	1335.22	1243.20	1170.88	1112.85	1065.52	1026.40	993.70
90000	1413.76	1316.33	1239.75	1178.31	1128.20	1086.77	1052.15
95000	1492.30	1389.46	1308.63	1243.77	1190.88	1147.15	1110.60
100000	1570.84	1462.59	1377.50	1309.23	1253.56	1207.53	1169.05
105000	1649.38	1535.72	1446.38	1374.70	1316.23	1267.90	1227.51
110000	1727.93	1608.84	1515.25	1440.16	1378.91	1328.28	1285.96
120000	1885.01	1755.10	1653.00	1571.08	1504.27	1449.03	1402.87
130000	2042.10	1901.36	1790.75	1702.01	1629.62	1569.79	1519.77
140000	2199.18	2047.62	1928.50	1832.93	1754.98	1690.54	1636.68
150000	2356.26	2193.88	2066.25	1963.85	1880.33	1811.29	1753.58
175000	2748.97	2559.53	2410.63	2291.16	2193.72	2113.17	2045.84
200000	3141.69	2925.17	2755.00	2618.47	2507.11	2415.05	2338.11
225000	3534.40	3290.82	3099.38	2945.78	2820.50	2716.94	2630.37
250000	3927.11	3656.47	3443.75	3273.09	3133.89	3018.82	2922.64

11% Monthly Payments

necessary to amortize a loan

AMOUNT	15 YEARS	16 YEARS	17 YEARS	18 YEARS	19 YEARS	20 YEARS	21 YEARS
100	1.14	1.11	1.09	1.07	1.05	1.03	1.02
200	2.27	2.22	2.17	2.13	2.09	2.06	2.04
500	5.68	5.55	5.43	5.33	5.24	5.16	5.09
1000	11.37	11.09	10.85	10.65	10.47	10.32	10.19
2000	22.73	22.18	21.71	21.30	20.95	20.64	20.38
5000	56.83	55.45	54.27	53.25	52.37	51.61	50.94
6000	68.20	66.54	65.12	63.90	62.85	61.93	61.13
7000	79.56	77.63	75.98	74.55	73.32	72.25	71.32
8000	90.93	88.72	86.83	85.20	83.80	82.58	81.51
9000	102.29	99.81	97.68	95.85	94.27	92.90	91.70
10000	113.66	110.90	108.54	106.50	104.75	103.22	101.89
15000	170.49	166.35	162.81	159.76	157.12	154.83	152.83
20000	227.32	221.80	217.08	213.01	209.49	206.44	203.77
25000	284.15	277.25	271.35	266.26	261.87	258.05	254.72
30000	340.98	332.70	325.61	319.51	314.24	309.66	305.66
35000	397.81	388.15	379.88	372.77	366.61	361.27	356.60
36000	409.17	399.24	390.74	383.42	377.09	371.59	366.79
37000	420.54	410.33	401.59	394.07	387.56	381.91	376.98
38000	431.91	421.42	412.44	404.72	398.04	392.23	387.17
39000	443.27	432.51	423.30	415.37	408.51	402.55	397.36
40000	454.64	443.60	434.15	426.02	418.99	412.88	407.55
41000	466.00	454.69	445.01	436.67	429.46	423.20	417.74
42000	477.37	465.78	455.86	447.32	439.93	433.52	427.93
43000	488.74	476.87	466.71	457.97	450.41	443.84	438.11
44000	500.10	487.96	477.57	468.62	460.88	454.16	448.30
45000	511.47	499.05	488.42	479.27	471.36	464.48	458.49
46000	522.83	510.14	499.28	489.92	481.83	474.81	468.68
47000	534.20	521.23	510.13	500.57	492.31	485.13	478.87
48000	545.57	532.32	520.98	511.22	502.78	495.45	489.06
49000	556.93	543.41	531.84	521.87	513.26	505.77	499.25
50000	568.30	554.50	542.69	532.52	523.73	516.09	509.44
51000	579.66	565.59	553.54	543.18	534.21	526.42	519.62
52000	591.03	576.68	564.40	553.83	544.68	536.74	529.81
53000	602.40	587.77	575.25	564.48	555.16	547.06	540.00
54000	613.76	598.86	586.11	575.13	565.63	557.38	550.19
55000	625.13	609.95	596.96	585.78	576.11	567.70	560.38
56000	636.49	621.04	607.81	596.43	586.58	578.03	570.57
57000	647.86	632.13	618.67	607.08	597.05	588.35	580.76
58000	659.23	643.22	629.52	617.73	607.53	598.67	590.95
59000	670.59	654.31	640.37	628.38	618.00	608.99	601.13
60000	681.96	665.40	651.23	639.03	628.48	619.31	611.32
65000	738.79	720.85	705.50	692.28	680.85	670.92	662.27
70000	795.62	776.30	759.77	745.53	733.22	722.53	713.21
75000	852.45	831.75	814.04	798.79	785.60	774.14	764.15
80000	909.28	887.20	868.30	852.04	837.97	825.75	815.10
85000	966.11	942.65	922.57	905.29	890.34	877.36	866.04
90000	1022.94	998.10	976.84	958.54	942.72	928.97	916.98
95000	1079.77	1053.55	1031.11	1011.80	995.09	980.58	967.93
100000	1136.60	1109.00	1085.38	1065.05	1047.46	1032.19	1018.87
105000	1193.43	1164.45	1139.65	1118.30	1099.84	1083.80	1069.81
110000	1250.26	1219.90	1193.92	1171.55	1152.21	1135.41	1120.76
120000	1363.92	1330.80	1302.46	1278.06	1256.96	1238.63	1222.65
130000	1477.58	1441.70	1410.99	1384.56	1361.70	1341.84	1324.53
140000	1591.24	1552.60	1519.53	1491.07	1466.45	1445.06	1426.42
150000	1704.90	1663.50	1628.07	1597.57	1571.20	1548.28	1528.31
175000	1989.04	1940.75	1899.42	1863.84	1833.06	1806.33	1783.02
200000	2273.19	2218.00	2170.76	2130.10	2094.93	2064.38	2037.74
225000	2557.34	2495.25	2442.11	2396.36	2356.79	2322.42	2292.46
250000	2841.49	2772.50	2713.45	2662.62	2618.66	2580.47	2547.18

Monthly Payments

necessary to amortize a loan

11%

AMOUNT	22 YEARS	23 YEARS	24 YEARS	25 YEARS	30 YEARS	35 YEARS	40 YEARS
100	1.01	1.00	0.99	0.98	0.95	0.94	0.93
200	2.01	1.99	1.98	1.96	1.90	1.87	1.86
500	5.04	4.99	4.94	4.90	4.76	4.68	4.64
1000	10.07	9.97	9.88	9.80	9.52	9.37	9.28
2000	20.14	19.94	19.76	19.60	19.05	18.74	18.57
5000	50.36	49.85	49.40	49.01	47.62	46.85	46.41
6000	60.43	59.82	59.28	58.81	57.14	56.22	55.70
7000	70.51	69.79	69.16	68.61	66.66	65.59	64.98
8000	80.58	79.76	79.04	78.41	76.19	74.96	74.26
9000	90.65	89.73	88.92	88.21	85.71	84.33	83.55
10000	100.72	99.70	98.80	98.01	95.23	93.70	92.83
15000	151.08	149.55	148.20	147.02	142.85	140.54	139.24
20000	201.44	199.40	197.61	196.02	190.46	187.39	185.66
25000	251.81	249.25	247.01	245.03	238.08	234.24	232.07
30000	302.17	299.10	296.41	294.03	285.70	281.09	278.49
35000	352.53	348.95	345.81	343.04	333.31	327.94	324.90
36000	362.60	358.92	355.69	352.84	342.84	337.30	334.19
37000	372.67	368.89	365.57	362.64	352.36	346.67	343.47
38000	382.74	378.86	375.45	372.44	361.88	356.04	352.75
39000	392.82	388.83	385.33	382.24	371.41	365.41	362.03
40000	402.89	398.80	395.21	392.05	380.93	374.78	371.32
41000	412.96	408.77	405.09	401.85	390.45	384.15	380.60
42000	423.03	418.74	414.97	411.65	399.98	393.52	389.88
43000	433.11	428.71	424.85	421.45	409.50	402.89	399.17
44000	443.18	438.68	434.73	431.25	419.02	412.26	408.45
45000	453.25	448.65	444.61	441.05	428.55	421.63	417.73
46000	463.32	458.62	454.49	450.85	438.07	431.00	427.02
47000	473.40	468.59	464.37	460.65	447.59	440.37	436.30
48000	483.47	478.56	474.25	470.45	457.12	449.74	445.58
49000	493.54	488.53	484.13	480.26	466.64	459.11	454.86
50000	503.61	498.50	494.01	490.06	476.16	468.48	464.15
51000	513.68	508.47	503.89	499.86	485.68	477.85	473.43
52000	523.76	518.44	513.77	509.66	495.21	487.22	482.71
53000	533.83	528.41	523.65	519.46	504.73	496.59	492.00
54000	543.90	538.38	533.53	529.26	514.25	505.96	501.28
55000	553.97	548.35	543.41	539.06	523.78	515.33	510.56
56000	564.05	558.32	553.29	548.86	533.30	524.70	519.84
57000	574.12	568.29	563.18	558.66	542.82	534.07	529.13
58000	584.19	578.26	573.06	568.47	552.35	543.44	538.41
59000	594.26	588.23	582.94	578.27	561.07	552.81	547.69
60000	604.33	598.20	592.82	588.07	571.39	562.17	556.98
65000	654.70	648.06	642.22	637.07	619.01	609.02	603.39
70000	705.06	697.91	691.62	686.00	666.63	655.87	649.81
75000	755.42	747.76	741.02	735.08	714.24	702.72	696.22
80000	805.78	797.61	790.42	784.09	761.86	749.57	742.64
85000	856.14	847.46	839.82	833.10	809.47	796.41	789.05
90000	906.50	897.31	889.22	882.10	857.09	843.26	835.46
95000	956.86	947.16	938.63	931.11	904.71	890.11	881.88
100000	1007.22	997.01	988.03	980.11	952.32	936.96	928.29
105000	1057.58	1046.86	1037.43	1029.12	999.94	983.81	974.71
110000	1107.95	1096.71	1086.83	1078.12	1047.56	1030.65	1021.12
120000	1208.67	1196.41	1185.63	1176.14	1142.79	1124.35	1113.95
130000	1309.39	1296.11	1284.43	1274.15	1238.02	1218.04	1206.78
140000	1410.11	1395.81	1383.24	1372.16	1333.25	1311.74	1299.61
150000	1510.84	1495.51	1482.04	1470.17	1428.49	1405.44	1392.44
175000	1762.64	1744.76	1729.05	1715.20	1666.57	1639.68	1624.52
200000	2014.45	1994.02	1976.05	1960.23	1904.65	1873.92	1856.59
225000	2266.25	2243.27	2223.06	2205.25	2142.73	2108.15	2088.66
250000	2518.06	2492.52	2470.07	2450.28	2380.81	2342.39	2320.74

11¼%

Monthly Payments

necessary to amortize a loan

AMOUNT	1 YEAR	2 YEARS	3 YEARS	4 YEARS	5 YEARS	6 YEARS	7 YEARS
100	8.85	4.67	3.29	2.60	2.19	1.92	1.73
200	17.70	9.34	6.57	5.19	4.37	3.83	3.45
500	44.25	23.36	16.43	12.98	10.93	9.58	8.63
1000	88.50	46.72	32.86	25.97	21.87	19.16	17.25
2000	177.00	93.45	65.71	51.93	43.73	38.32	34.51
5000	442.49	233.62	164.29	129.84	109.34	95.81	86.27
6000	530.99	280.34	197.14	155.80	131.20	114.97	103.53
7000	619.49	327.07	230.00	181.77	153.07	134.14	120.78
8000	707.99	373.79	262.86	207.74	174.94	153.30	138.03
9000	796.48	420.52	295.72	233.70	196.81	172.46	155.29
10000	884.98	467.24	328.57	259.67	218.67	191.62	172.54
15000	1327.47	700.86	492.86	389.51	328.01	287.44	258.81
20000	1769.97	934.48	657.14	519.34	437.35	383.25	345.08
25000	2212.46	1168.10	821.43	649.18	546.68	479.06	431.35
30000	2654.95	1401.72	985.72	779.01	656.02	574.87	517.63
35000	3097.44	1635.34	1150.00	908.85	765.36	670.68	603.90
36000	3185.94	1682.06	1182.86	934.82	787.22	689.85	621.15
37000	3274.44	1728.79	1215.72	960.78	809.09	709.01	638.40
38000	3362.94	1775.51	1248.57	986.75	830.96	728.17	655.66
39000	3451.43	1822.24	1281.43	1012.72	852.83	747.33	672.91
40000	3539.93	1868.96	1314.29	1038.68	874.69	766.49	690.17
41000	3628.43	1915.68	1347.15	1064.65	896.56	785.66	707.42
42000	3716.93	1962.41	1380.00	1090.62	918.43	804.82	724.68
43000	3805.43	2009.13	1412.86	1116.59	940.29	823.98	741.93
44000	3893.93	2055.86	1445.72	1142.55	962.16	843.14	759.18
45000	3982.42	2102.58	1478.58	1168.52	984.03	862.31	776.44
46000	4070.92	2149.30	1511.43	1194.49	1005.90	881.47	793.69
47000	4159.42	2196.03	1544.29	1220.45	1027.76	900.63	810.95
48000	4247.92	2242.75	1577.15	1246.42	1049.63	919.79	828.20
49000	4336.42	2289.48	1610.00	1272.39	1071.50	938.96	845.45
50000	4424.92	2336.20	1642.86	1298.35	1093.37	958.12	862.71
51000	4513.41	2382.92	1675.72	1324.32	1115.23	977.28	879.96
52000	4601.91	2429.65	1708.58	1350.29	1137.10	996.44	897.22
53000	4690.41	2476.37	1741.43	1376.26	1158.97	1015.61	914.47
54000	4778.91	2523.10	1774.29	1402.22	1180.83	1034.77	931.73
55000	4867.41	2569.82	1807.15	1428.19	1202.70	1053.93	948.98
56000	4955.91	2616.54	1840.01	1454.16	1224.57	1073.09	966.23
57000	5044.40	2663.27	1872.86	1480.12	1246.44	1092.26	983.49
58000	5132.90	2709.99	1905.72	1506.09	1268.30	1111.42	1000.74
59000	5221.40	2756.72	1938.58	1532.06	1290.17	1130.58	1018.00
60000	5309.90	2803.44	1971.43	1558.03	1312.04	1149.74	1035.25
65000	5752.39	3037.06	2135.72	1687.86	1421.38	1245.55	1121.52
70000	6194.88	3270.68	2300.01	1817.70	1530.71	1341.37	1207.79
75000	6637.37	3504.30	2464.29	1947.53	1640.05	1437.18	1294.06
80000	7079.87	3737.92	2628.58	2077.37	1749.38	1532.99	1380.33
85000	7522.36	3971.54	2792.86	2207.20	1858.72	1628.80	1466.60
90000	7964.85	4205.16	2957.15	2337.04	1968.06	1724.61	1552.88
95000	8407.34	4438.78	3121.44	2466.87	2077.39	1820.43	1639.15
100000	8849.83	4672.40	3285.72	2596.71	2186.73	1916.24	1725.42
105000	9292.32	4906.02	3450.01	2726.55	2296.07	2012.05	1811.69
110000	9734.81	5139.64	3614.30	2856.38	2405.40	2107.86	1897.96
120000	10619.80	5606.88	3942.87	3116.05	2624.08	2299.48	2070.50
130000	11504.78	6074.12	4271.44	3375.72	2842.75	2491.11	2243.04
140000	12389.76	6541.36	4600.01	3635.39	3061.42	2682.73	2415.58
150000	13274.75	7008.60	4928.59	3895.06	3280.10	2874.36	2588.13
175000	15487.20	8176.70	5750.02	4544.24	3826.78	3353.42	3019.48
200000	17699.66	9344.80	6571.45	5193.42	4373.46	3832.47	3450.83
225000	19912.12	10512.90	7392.88	5842.60	4920.14	4311.53	3882.19
250000	22124.58	11681.00	8214.31	6491.77	5466.83	4790.59	4313.54

Monthly Payments 11¼%

necessary to amortize a loan

AMOUNT	8 YEARS	9 YEARS	10 YEARS	11 YEARS	12 YEARS	13 YEARS	14 YEARS
100	1.58	1.48	1.39	1.32	1.27	1.22	1.18
200	3.17	2.95	2.78	2.65	2.54	2.45	2.37
500	7.92	7.38	6.96	6.62	6.34	6.11	5.92
1000	15.84	14.76	13.92	13.24	12.68	12.23	11.85
2000	31.69	29.53	27.83	26.48	25.37	24.45	23.69
5000	79.22	73.82	69.58	66.19	63.42	61.13	59.23
6000	95.06	88.59	83.50	79.43	76.10	73.36	71.07
7000	110.91	103.35	97.42	92.66	88.79	85.59	82.92
8000	126.75	118.12	111.34	105.90	101.47	97.81	94.76
9000	142.59	132.88	125.25	119.14	114.16	110.04	106.61
10000	158.44	147.64	139.17	132.38	126.84	122.27	118.45
15000	237.65	221.47	208.75	198.56	190.26	183.40	177.68
20000	316.87	295.29	278.34	264.75	253.68	244.54	236.90
25000	396.09	369.11	347.92	330.94	317.10	305.67	296.13
30000	475.31	442.93	417.51	397.13	380.52	366.80	355.35
35000	554.53	516.75	487.09	463.31	443.94	427.94	414.58
36000	570.37	531.52	501.01	476.55	456.62	440.16	426.42
37000	586.21	546.28	514.93	489.79	469.31	452.39	438.27
38000	602.06	561.05	528.84	503.03	481.99	464.62	450.11
39000	617.90	575.81	542.76	516.26	494.67	476.84	461.96
40000	633.74	590.58	556.68	529.50	507.36	489.07	473.80
41000	649.59	605.34	570.59	542.74	520.04	501.30	485.65
42000	665.43	620.11	584.51	555.98	532.73	513.52	497.49
43000	681.27	634.87	598.43	569.21	545.41	525.75	509.34
44000	697.12	649.63	612.34	582.45	558.09	537.98	521.18
45000	712.96	664.40	626.26	595.69	570.78	550.20	533.03
46000	728.80	679.16	640.18	608.93	583.46	562.43	544.87
47000	744.65	693.93	654.09	622.16	596.14	574.66	556.72
48000	760.49	708.69	668.01	635.40	608.83	586.89	568.56
49000	776.34	723.46	681.93	648.64	621.51	599.11	580.41
50000	792.18	738.22	695.84	661.88	634.20	611.34	592.25
51000	808.02	752.99	709.76	675.11	646.88	623.57	604.10
52000	823.87	767.75	723.68	688.35	659.56	635.79	615.94
53000	839.71	782.51	737.60	701.59	672.25	648.02	627.79
54000	855.55	797.28	751.51	714.83	684.93	660.25	639.63
55000	871.40	812.04	765.43	728.06	697.62	672.47	651.48
56000	887.24	826.81	779.35	741.30	710.30	684.70	663.32
57000	903.08	841.57	793.26	754.54	722.98	696.93	675.17
58000	918.93	856.34	807.18	767.78	735.67	709.15	687.01
59000	934.77	871.10	821.10	781.01	748.35	721.38	698.86
60000	950.62	885.86	835.01	794.25	761.04	733.61	710.70
65000	1029.03	959.69	904.60	860.44	824.46	794.74	769.93
70000	1109.05	1033.51	974.18	926.63	887.88	855.87	829.16
75000	1188.27	1107.33	1043.77	992.81	951.29	917.01	888.38
80000	1267.49	1181.15	1113.35	1059.00	1014.71	978.14	947.61
85000	1346.70	1254.98	1182.94	1125.19	1078.13	1039.28	1006.83
90000	1425.92	1328.80	1252.52	1191.38	1141.55	1100.41	1066.06
95000	1505.14	1402.62	1322.10	1257.56	1204.97	1161.54	1125.28
100000	1584.36	1476.44	1391.69	1323.75	1268.39	1222.68	1184.51
105000	1663.58	1550.26	1461.27	1389.94	1331.81	1283.81	1243.73
110000	1742.79	1624.09	1530.86	1456.13	1395.23	1344.95	1302.96
120000	1901.23	1771.73	1670.03	1588.50	1522.07	1467.21	1421.41
130000	2059.67	1919.37	1809.20	1720.88	1648.91	1589.48	1539.86
140000	2218.10	2067.02	1948.37	1853.25	1775.75	1711.75	1658.31
150000	2376.54	2214.66	2087.53	1985.63	1902.59	1834.02	1776.76
175000	2772.63	2583.77	2435.46	2316.57	2219.69	2139.69	2072.89
200000	3168.72	2952.88	2783.38	2647.50	2536.79	2445.35	2369.02
225000	3564.81	3321.99	3131.30	2978.44	2853.88	2751.02	2665.14
250000	3960.90	3691.10	3479.22	3309.38	3170.98	3056.69	2961.27

11¼% Monthly Payments

necessary to amortize a loan

AMOUNT	15 YEARS	16 YEARS	17 YEARS	18 YEARS	19 YEARS	20 YEARS	21 YEARS
100	1.15	1.13	1.10	1.08	1.06	1.05	1.04
200	2.30	2.25	2.20	2.16	2.13	2.10	2.07
500	5.76	5.63	5.51	5.41	5.32	5.25	5.18
1000	11.52	11.25	11.02	10.82	10.64	10.49	10.36
2000	23.05	22.50	22.03	21.63	21.29	20.99	20.72
5000	57.62	56.25	55.08	54.08	53.21	52.46	51.81
6000	69.14	67.50	66.10	64.90	63.86	62.96	62.17
7000	80.66	78.75	77.12	75.71	74.50	73.45	72.53
8000	92.19	90.00	88.13	86.53	85.14	83.94	82.89
9000	103.71	101.25	99.15	97.35	95.79	94.43	93.26
10000	115.23	112.50	110.17	108.16	106.43	104.93	103.62
15000	172.85	168.75	165.25	162.24	159.64	157.39	155.43
20000	230.47	225.01	220.34	216.32	212.86	209.85	207.23
25000	288.09	281.26	275.42	270.41	266.07	262.31	259.04
30000	345.70	337.51	330.51	324.49	319.29	314.78	310.85
35000	403.32	393.76	385.59	378.57	372.50	367.24	362.66
36000	414.84	405.01	396.61	389.38	383.14	377.73	373.02
37000	426.37	416.26	407.62	400.20	393.79	388.22	383.38
38000	437.89	427.51	418.64	411.02	404.43	398.72	393.75
39000	449.41	438.76	429.66	421.83	415.07	409.21	404.11
40000	460.94	450.01	440.67	432.65	425.72	419.70	414.47
41000	472.46	461.26	451.69	443.46	436.36	430.19	424.83
42000	483.98	472.51	462.71	454.28	447.00	440.69	435.19
43000	495.51	483.76	473.73	465.10	457.64	451.18	445.55
44000	507.03	495.01	484.74	475.91	468.29	461.67	455.92
45000	518.56	506.26	495.76	486.73	478.93	472.17	466.28
46000	530.08	517.51	506.78	497.55	489.57	482.66	476.64
47000	541.60	528.77	517.79	508.36	500.22	493.15	487.00
48000	553.13	540.02	528.81	519.18	510.86	503.64	497.36
49000	564.65	551.27	539.83	529.99	521.50	514.14	507.72
50000	576.17	562.52	550.84	540.81	532.14	524.63	518.09
51000	587.70	573.77	561.86	551.63	542.79	535.12	528.45
52000	599.22	585.02	572.88	562.44	553.43	545.61	538.81
53000	610.74	596.27	583.89	573.26	564.07	556.11	549.17
54000	622.27	607.52	594.91	584.07	574.72	566.60	559.53
55000	633.79	618.77	605.93	594.89	585.36	577.09	569.89
56000	645.31	630.02	616.94	605.71	596.00	587.58	580.26
57000	656.84	641.27	627.96	616.52	606.64	598.08	590.62
58000	668.36	652.52	638.98	627.34	617.29	608.57	600.98
59000	679.88	663.77	650.00	638.16	627.93	619.06	611.34
60000	691.41	675.02	661.01	648.97	638.57	629.55	621.70
65000	749.02	731.27	716.10	703.05	691.79	682.02	673.51
70000	806.64	787.52	771.18	757.13	745.00	734.48	725.32
75000	864.26	843.77	826.27	811.22	798.22	786.94	777.13
80000	921.88	900.03	881.35	865.30	851.43	839.40	828.94
85000	979.49	956.28	936.43	919.38	904.65	891.87	880.75
90000	1037.11	1012.53	991.52	973.46	957.86	944.33	932.55
95000	1094.73	1068.78	1046.60	1027.54	1011.07	996.79	984.36
100000	1152.34	1125.03	1101.69	1081.62	1064.29	1049.26	1036.17
105000	1209.96	1181.28	1156.77	1135.70	1117.50	1101.72	1087.98
110000	1267.58	1237.54	1211.86	1189.78	1170.72	1154.18	1139.79
120000	1382.81	1350.04	1322.02	1297.94	1277.15	1259.11	1243.41
130000	1498.05	1462.54	1432.19	1406.11	1383.57	1364.03	1347.02
140000	1613.28	1575.05	1542.36	1514.27	1490.00	1468.96	1450.64
150000	1728.52	1687.55	1652.53	1622.43	1596.43	1573.88	1554.26
175000	2016.60	1968.81	1927.95	1892.84	1862.50	1836.20	1813.30
200000	2304.69	2250.07	2203.37	2163.24	2128.58	2098.51	2072.34
225000	2592.78	2531.32	2478.80	2433.65	2394.65	2360.83	2331.39
250000	2880.86	2812.58	2754.22	2704.05	2660.72	2623.14	2590.43

Monthly Payments 11¼%

necessary to amortize a loan

AMOUNT	22 YEARS	23 YEARS	24 YEARS	25 YEARS	30 YEARS	35 YEARS	40 YEARS
100	1.02	1.01	1.01	1.00	0.97	0.96	0.95
200	2.05	2.03	2.01	2.00	1.94	1.91	1.90
500	5.12	5.07	5.03	4.99	4.86	4.78	4.74
1000	10.25	10.15	10.06	9.98	9.71	9.56	9.48
2000	20.49	20.29	20.12	19.96	19.43	19.13	18.97
5000	51.24	50.74	50.30	49.91	48.56	47.82	47.41
6000	61.48	60.88	60.36	59.89	58.28	57.39	56.90
7000	71.73	71.03	70.42	69.88	67.99	66.95	66.38
8000	81.98	81.18	80.48	79.86	77.70	76.52	75.86
9000	92.23	91.33	90.54	89.84	87.41	86.08	85.34
10000	102.47	101.47	100.60	99.82	97.13	95.65	94.83
15000	153.71	152.21	150.89	149.74	145.69	143.47	142.24
20000	204.95	202.95	201.19	199.65	194.25	191.30	189.65
25000	256.19	253.69	251.49	249.56	242.82	239.12	237.06
30000	307.42	304.42	301.79	299.47	291.38	286.95	284.48
35000	358.66	355.16	352.09	349.38	339.94	334.77	331.89
36000	368.91	365.31	362.15	359.37	349.65	344.34	341.37
37000	379.16	375.45	372.21	369.35	359.37	353.90	350.86
38000	389.40	385.60	382.27	379.33	369.08	363.47	360.34
39000	399.65	395.75	392.33	389.31	378.79	373.03	369.82
40000	409.90	405.90	402.38	399.30	388.50	382.60	379.30
41000	420.15	416.04	412.44	409.28	398.22	392.16	388.79
42000	430.39	426.19	422.50	419.26	407.93	401.73	398.27
43000	440.64	436.34	432.56	429.24	417.64	411.29	407.75
44000	450.89	446.49	442.62	439.23	427.36	420.86	417.23
45000	461.14	456.63	452.68	449.21	437.07	430.42	426.72
46000	471.38	466.78	462.74	459.19	446.78	439.99	436.20
47000	481.63	476.93	472.80	469.17	456.49	449.55	445.68
48000	491.88	487.08	482.86	479.15	466.21	459.12	455.16
49000	502.13	497.22	492.92	489.14	475.92	468.68	464.65
50000	512.37	507.37	502.98	499.12	485.63	478.25	474.13
51000	522.62	517.52	513.04	509.10	495.34	487.81	483.61
52000	532.87	527.67	523.10	519.08	505.06	497.38	493.09
53000	543.12	537.81	533.16	529.07	514.77	506.94	502.58
54000	553.36	547.96	543.22	539.05	524.48	516.51	512.06
55000	563.61	558.11	553.28	549.03	534.19	526.07	521.54
56000	573.86	568.26	563.34	559.01	543.91	535.64	531.02
57000	584.11	578.40	573.40	569.00	553.62	545.20	540.51
58000	594.36	588.55	583.46	578.98	563.33	554.77	549.99
59000	604.60	598.70	593.52	588.96	573.04	564.33	559.47
60000	614.85	608.85	603.58	598.94	582.76	573.90	568.95
65000	666.08	659.58	653.88	648.86	631.32	621.72	616.37
70000	717.32	710.32	704.17	698.77	679.88	669.55	663.78
75000	768.56	761.06	754.47	748.68	728.45	717.37	711.19
80000	819.80	811.79	804.77	798.59	777.01	765.20	758.61
85000	871.03	862.53	855.07	848.50	825.57	813.02	806.02
90000	922.27	913.27	905.37	898.42	874.14	860.84	853.43
95000	973.51	964.00	955.66	948.33	922.70	908.67	900.84
100000	1024.75	1014.74	1005.96	998.24	971.26	956.49	948.26
105000	1075.98	1065.48	1056.26	1048.15	1019.82	1004.32	995.67
110000	1127.22	1116.22	1106.56	1098.06	1068.39	1052.14	1043.08
120000	1229.69	1217.69	1207.15	1197.89	1165.51	1147.79	1137.91
130000	1332.17	1319.16	1307.75	1297.71	1262.64	1243.44	1232.73
140000	1434.64	1420.64	1408.35	1397.54	1359.77	1339.09	1327.56
150000	1537.12	1522.11	1508.94	1497.36	1456.89	1434.74	1422.39
175000	1793.31	1775.80	1760.43	1746.92	1699.71	1673.86	1659.45
200000	2049.49	2029.48	2011.92	1996.48	1942.52	1912.99	1896.51
225000	2305.68	2283.17	2263.41	2246.04	2185.34	2152.11	2133.58
250000	2561.86	2536.85	2514.90	2495.60	2428.15	2391.23	2370.64

11½%

Monthly Payments

necessary to amortize a loan

AMOUNT	1 YEAR	2 YEARS	3 YEARS	4 YEARS	5 YEARS	6 YEARS	7 YEARS
100	8.86	4.68	3.30	2.61	2.20	1.93	1.74
200	17.72	9.37	6.60	5.22	4.40	3.86	3.48
500	44.31	23.42	16.49	13.04	11.00	9.65	8.69
1000	88.62	46.84	32.98	26.09	21.99	19.29	17.39
2000	177.23	93.68	65.95	52.18	43.99	38.58	34.77
5000	443.08	234.20	164.88	130.45	109.96	96.46	86.93
6000	531.69	281.04	197.86	156.53	131.96	115.75	104.32
7000	620.31	327.88	230.83	182.62	153.95	135.04	121.71
8000	708.92	374.72	263.81	208.71	175.94	154.33	139.09
9000	797.54	421.56	296.78	234.80	197.93	173.62	156.48
10000	886.15	468.40	329.76	260.89	219.93	192.91	173.86
15000	1329.23	702.60	494.64	391.34	329.89	289.37	260.80
20000	1772.30	936.81	659.52	521.78	439.85	385.82	347.73
25000	2215.38	1171.01	824.40	652.23	549.82	482.28	434.66
30000	2658.45	1405.21	989.28	782.67	659.78	578.73	521.59
35000	3101.53	1639.41	1154.16	913.12	769.74	675.19	608.53
36000	3190.14	1686.25	1187.14	939.20	791.73	694.48	625.91
37000	3278.76	1733.09	1220.11	965.29	813.73	713.77	643.30
38000	3367.37	1779.93	1253.09	991.38	835.72	733.06	660.69
39000	3455.99	1826.77	1286.06	1017.47	857.71	752.36	678.07
40000	3544.60	1873.61	1319.04	1043.56	879.70	771.65	695.46
41000	3633.22	1920.45	1352.02	1069.65	901.70	790.94	712.84
42000	3721.83	1967.29	1384.99	1095.74	923.69	810.23	730.23
43000	3810.45	2014.13	1417.97	1121.83	945.68	829.52	747.62
44000	3899.06	2060.97	1450.94	1147.92	967.67	848.81	765.00
45000	3987.68	2107.81	1483.92	1174.01	989.67	868.10	782.39
46000	4076.29	2154.65	1516.90	1200.09	1011.66	887.39	799.78
47000	4164.91	2201.49	1549.87	1226.18	1033.65	906.68	817.16
48000	4253.52	2248.34	1582.85	1252.27	1055.65	925.98	834.55
49000	4342.14	2295.18	1615.82	1278.36	1077.64	945.27	851.94
50000	4430.75	2342.02	1648.80	1304.45	1099.63	964.56	869.32
51000	4519.37	2388.86	1681.78	1330.54	1121.62	983.85	886.71
52000	4607.98	2435.70	1714.75	1356.63	1143.62	1003.14	904.10
53000	4696.60	2482.54	1747.73	1382.72	1165.61	1022.43	921.48
54000	4785.21	2529.38	1780.70	1408.81	1187.60	1041.72	938.87
55000	4873.83	2576.22	1813.68	1434.90	1209.59	1061.01	956.26
56000	4962.44	2623.06	1846.66	1460.98	1231.59	1080.30	973.64
57000	5051.06	2669.90	1879.63	1487.07	1253.58	1099.60	991.03
58000	5139.67	2716.74	1912.61	1513.16	1275.57	1118.89	1008.41
59000	5228.29	2763.58	1945.58	1539.25	1297.56	1138.18	1025.80
60000	5316.90	2810.42	1978.56	1565.34	1319.56	1157.47	1043.19
65000	5759.98	3044.62	2143.44	1695.79	1429.52	1253.93	1130.12
70000	6203.05	3278.82	2308.32	1826.23	1539.48	1350.38	1217.05
75000	6646.13	3513.02	2473.20	1956.68	1649.45	1446.84	1303.98
80000	7089.20	3747.23	2638.08	2087.12	1759.41	1543.29	1390.92
85000	7532.28	3981.43	2802.96	2217.57	1869.37	1639.75	1477.85
90000	7975.35	4215.63	2967.84	2348.01	1979.33	1736.20	1564.78
95000	8418.43	4449.83	3132.72	2478.46	2089.30	1832.66	1651.71
100000	8861.51	4684.03	3297.60	2608.90	2199.26	1929.12	1738.65
105000	9304.58	4918.23	3462.48	2739.35	2309.22	2025.57	1825.58
110000	9747.66	5152.43	3627.36	2869.79	2419.19	2122.03	1912.51
120000	10633.81	5620.84	3957.12	3130.68	2639.11	2314.94	2086.38
130000	11519.96	6089.24	4286.88	3391.57	2859.04	2507.85	2260.24
140000	12406.11	6557.64	4616.64	3652.46	3078.97	2700.76	2434.10
150000	13292.26	7026.05	4946.40	3913.35	3298.89	2893.67	2607.97
175000	15507.63	8197.06	5770.80	4565.58	3848.71	3375.95	3042.63
200000	17723.01	9368.06	6595.20	5217.80	4398.52	3858.23	3477.29
225000	19938.39	10539.07	7419.60	5870.03	4948.34	4340.51	3911.95
250000	22153.76	11710.08	8244.00	6522.25	5498.15	4822.79	4346.62

Monthly Payments 11½%

necessary to amortize a loan

AMOUNT	8 YEARS	9 YEARS	10 YEARS	11 YEARS	12 YEARS	13 YEARS	14 YEARS
100	1.60	1.49	1.41	1.34	1.28	1.24	1.20
200	3.20	2.98	2.81	2.68	2.57	2.48	2.40
500	7.99	7.45	7.03	6.69	6.42	6.19	6.00
1000	15.98	14.90	14.06	13.38	12.83	12.38	12.00
2000	31.96	29.81	28.12	26.77	25.67	24.76	24.00
5000	79.90	74.52	70.30	66.92	64.17	61.90	60.00
6000	95.88	89.42	84.36	80.30	77.00	74.28	72.00
7000	111.86	104.33	98.42	93.68	89.83	86.65	84.00
8000	127.83	119.23	112.48	107.07	102.67	99.03	96.00
9000	143.81	134.13	126.54	120.45	115.50	111.41	108.00
10000	159.79	149.04	140.60	133.84	128.33	123.79	120.01
15000	239.69	223.55	210.89	200.75	192.50	185.69	180.01
20000	319.59	298.07	281.19	267.67	256.66	247.58	240.01
25000	399.48	372.59	351.49	334.59	320.83	309.48	300.01
30000	479.38	447.11	421.79	401.51	384.99	371.38	360.02
35000	559.28	521.63	492.08	468.42	449.16	433.27	420.02
36000	575.26	536.53	506.14	481.81	461.99	445.65	432.02
37000	591.24	551.44	520.20	495.19	474.83	458.03	444.02
38000	607.22	566.34	534.26	508.57	487.66	470.41	456.02
39000	623.20	581.24	548.32	521.96	500.49	482.79	468.02
40000	639.17	596.15	562.38	535.34	513.33	495.17	480.02
41000	655.15	611.05	576.44	548.72	526.16	507.55	492.02
42000	671.13	625.95	590.50	562.11	538.99	519.93	504.02
43000	687.11	640.86	604.56	575.49	551.83	532.30	516.02
44000	703.09	655.76	618.62	588.87	564.66	544.68	528.02
45000	719.07	670.66	632.68	602.26	577.49	557.06	540.02
46000	735.05	685.57	646.74	615.64	590.33	569.44	552.03
47000	751.03	700.47	660.80	629.02	603.16	581.82	564.03
48000	767.01	715.38	674.86	642.41	615.99	594.20	576.03
49000	782.99	730.28	688.92	655.79	628.83	606.58	588.03
50000	798.97	745.18	702.98	669.18	641.66	618.96	600.03
51000	814.95	760.09	717.04	682.56	654.49	631.34	612.03
52000	830.93	774.99	731.10	695.94	667.32	643.72	624.03
53000	846.91	789.89	745.16	709.33	680.16	656.10	636.03
54000	862.89	804.80	759.22	722.71	692.99	668.48	648.03
55000	878.87	819.70	773.27	736.09	705.82	680.85	660.03
56000	894.84	834.60	787.33	749.48	718.66	693.23	672.03
57000	910.82	849.51	801.39	762.86	731.49	705.61	684.03
58000	820.00	864.41	815.45	776.24	744.32	717.99	696.03
59000	942.78	879.32	829.51	780.63	757.16	730.37	708.03
60000	958.76	894.22	843.57	803.01	769.99	742.75	720.03
65000	1038.66	968.74	913.87	869.93	834.16	804.65	780.04
70000	1118.56	1043.26	984.17	936.85	898.32	866.54	840.04
75000	1198.45	1117.77	1054.47	1003.76	962.49	928.44	900.04
80000	1278.35	1192.29	1124.76	1070.68	1026.65	990.33	960.04
85000	1358.25	1200.01	1195.06	1137.60	1090.82	1052.23	1020.05
90000	1438.14	1341.33	1265.36	1204.52	1154.98	1114.13	1080.05
95000	1518.04	1415.85	1335.66	1271.43	1219.15	1176.02	1140.05
100000	1597.94	1490.37	1405.95	1338.35	1283.32	1237.92	1200.06
105000	1677.83	1564.88	1476.25	1405.27	1347.48	1299.81	1260.06
110000	1757.73	1639.40	1546.55	1472.19	1411.65	1361.71	1320.06
120000	1917.52	1788.44	1687.15	1606.02	1539.98	1485.50	1440.07
130000	2077.32	1937.48	1827.74	1739.86	1668.31	1609.29	1560.07
140000	2237.11	2086.51	1968.34	1873.69	1796.64	1733.08	1680.08
150000	2396.91	2235.55	2108.93	2007.53	1924.97	1856.88	1800.08
175000	2796.39	2608.14	2460.42	2342.11	2245.80	2166.36	2100.10
200000	3195.87	2980.73	2811.01	2676.70	2566.63	2475.84	2400.11
225000	3595.36	3353.32	3163.40	3011.29	2887.46	2785.31	2700.12
250000	3994.84	3725.92	3514.89	3345.88	3208.29	3094.79	3000.14

11½%

Monthly Payments
necessary to amortize a loan

AMOUNT	15 YEARS	16 YEARS	17 YEARS	18 YEARS	19 YEARS	20 YEARS	21 YEARS
100	1.17	1.14	1.12	1.10	1.08	1.07	1.05
200	2.34	2.28	2.24	2.20	2.16	2.13	2.11
500	5.84	5.71	5.59	5.49	5.41	5.33	5.27
1000	11.68	11.41	11.18	10.98	10.81	10.66	10.54
2000	23.36	22.82	22.36	21.97	21.62	21.33	21.07
5000	58.41	57.06	55.90	54.91	54.06	53.32	52.68
6000	70.09	68.47	67.09	65.90	64.87	63.99	63.21
7000	81.77	79.88	78.27	76.88	75.69	74.65	73.75
8000	93.46	91.29	89.45	87.86	86.50	85.31	84.29
9000	105.14	102.70	100.63	98.85	97.31	95.98	94.82
10000	116.82	114.12	111.81	109.83	108.12	106.64	105.36
15000	175.23	171.17	167.71	164.74	162.18	159.96	158.04
20000	233.64	228.23	223.62	219.66	216.24	213.29	210.72
25000	292.05	285.29	279.52	274.57	270.30	266.61	263.39
30000	350.46	342.35	335.43	329.49	324.37	319.93	316.07
35000	408.87	399.41	391.33	384.40	378.43	373.25	368.75
36000	420.55	410.82	402.51	395.39	389.24	383.91	379.29
37000	432.23	422.23	413.70	406.37	400.05	394.58	389.82
38000	443.91	433.64	424.88	417.35	410.86	405.24	400.36
39000	455.59	445.05	436.06	428.34	421.68	415.91	410.90
40000	467.28	456.47	447.24	439.32	432.49	426.57	421.43
41000	478.96	467.88	458.42	450.30	443.30	437.24	431.97
42000	490.64	479.29	469.60	461.28	454.11	447.90	442.50
43000	502.32	490.70	480.78	472.27	464.92	458.56	453.04
44000	514.00	502.11	491.96	483.25	475.74	469.23	463.57
45000	525.69	513.52	503.14	494.23	486.55	479.89	474.11
46000	537.37	524.94	514.32	505.22	497.36	490.56	484.65
47000	549.05	536.35	525.51	516.20	508.17	501.22	495.18
48000	560.73	547.76	536.69	527.18	518.98	511.89	505.72
49000	572.41	559.17	547.87	538.16	529.80	522.55	516.25
50000	584.09	570.58	559.05	549.15	540.61	533.21	526.79
51000	595.78	581.99	570.23	560.13	551.42	543.88	537.32
52000	607.46	593.41	581.41	571.11	562.23	554.54	547.86
53000	619.14	604.82	592.59	582.10	573.05	565.21	558.40
54000	630.82	616.23	603.77	593.08	583.86	575.87	568.93
55000	642.50	627.64	614.95	604.06	594.67	586.54	579.47
56000	654.19	639.05	626.13	615.05	605.48	597.20	590.00
57000	665.87	650.46	637.31	626.03	616.29	607.86	600.54
58000	677.55	661.88	648.50	637.01	627.11	618.53	611.08
59000	689.23	673.29	659.68	647.99	637.92	629.19	621.61
60000	700.91	684.70	670.86	658.98	648.73	639.86	632.15
65000	759.32	741.76	726.76	713.89	702.79	693.18	684.83
70000	817.73	798.82	782.67	768.81	756.85	746.50	737.50
75000	876.14	855.87	838.57	823.72	810.91	799.82	790.18
80000	934.55	912.93	894.48	878.64	864.97	853.14	842.86
85000	992.96	969.99	950.38	933.55	919.04	906.47	895.54
90000	1051.37	1027.05	1006.29	988.47	973.10	959.79	948.22
95000	1109.78	1084.11	1062.19	1043.38	1027.16	1013.11	1000.90
100000	1168.19	1141.16	1118.10	1098.30	1081.22	1066.43	1053.58
105000	1226.60	1198.22	1174.00	1153.21	1135.28	1119.75	1106.26
110000	1285.01	1255.28	1229.91	1208.12	1189.34	1173.07	1158.94
120000	1401.83	1369.40	1341.72	1317.95	1297.46	1279.72	1264.29
130000	1518.65	1483.51	1453.53	1427.78	1405.58	1386.36	1369.65
140000	1635.47	1597.63	1565.33	1537.61	1513.71	1493.00	1475.01
150000	1752.28	1711.75	1677.14	1647.44	1621.83	1599.64	1580.37
175000	2044.33	1997.04	1956.67	1922.02	1892.13	1866.25	1843.76
200000	2336.38	2282.33	2236.19	2196.59	2162.44	2132.86	2107.16
225000	2628.43	2567.62	2515.72	2471.16	2432.74	2399.47	2370.55
250000	2920.47	2852.91	2795.24	2745.74	2703.05	2666.07	2633.94

Monthly Payments 11½%

necessary to amortize a loan

AMOUNT	22 YEARS	23 YEARS	24 YEARS	25 YEARS	30 YEARS	35 YEARS	40 YEARS
100	1.04	1.03	1.02	1.02	0.99	0.98	0.97
200	2.08	2.07	2.05	2.03	1.98	1.95	1.94
500	5.21	5.16	5.12	5.08	4.95	4.88	4.84
1000	10.42	10.33	10.24	10.16	9.90	9.76	9.68
2000	20.85	20.65	20.48	20.33	19.81	19.52	19.37
5000	52.12	51.63	51.20	50.82	49.51	48.81	48.41
6000	62.54	61.95	61.44	60.99	59.42	58.57	58.10
7000	72.97	72.28	71.68	71.15	69.32	68.33	67.78
8000	83.39	82.61	81.92	81.32	79.22	78.09	77.46
9000	93.81	92.93	92.16	91.48	89.13	87.85	87.15
10000	104.24	103.26	102.40	101.65	99.03	97.61	96.83
15000	156.36	154.89	153.60	152.47	148.54	146.42	145.24
20000	208.47	206.52	204.80	203.29	198.06	195.22	193.66
25000	260.59	258.15	256.00	254.12	247.57	244.03	242.07
30000	312.71	309.77	307.20	304.94	297.09	292.83	290.48
35000	364.83	361.40	358.40	355.76	346.60	341.64	338.90
36000	375.25	371.73	368.64	365.93	356.50	351.40	348.58
37000	385.68	382.06	378.88	376.09	366.41	361.16	358.26
38000	396.10	392.38	389.12	386.26	376.31	370.92	367.95
39000	406.53	402.71	399.36	396.42	386.21	380.68	377.63
40000	416.95	413.03	409.60	406.59	396.12	390.44	387.31
41000	427.37	423.36	419.84	416.75	406.02	400.20	397.00
42000	437.80	433.68	430.08	426.92	415.92	409.97	406.68
43000	448.22	444.01	440.32	437.08	425.83	419.73	416.36
44000	458.64	454.34	450.56	447.25	435.73	429.49	426.04
45000	469.07	464.66	460.80	457.41	445.63	439.25	435.73
46000	479.49	474.99	471.04	467.58	455.53	449.01	445.41
47000	489.92	485.31	481.28	477.74	465.44	458.77	455.09
48000	500.34	495.64	491.52	487.91	475.34	468.53	464.78
49000	510.76	505.96	501.76	498.07	485.24	478.29	474.46
50000	521.19	516.29	512.00	508.23	495.15	488.05	484.14
51000	531.61	526.62	522.24	518.40	505.05	497.81	493.82
52000	542.03	536.94	532.48	528.56	514.95	507.58	503.51
53000	552.46	547.27	542.72	538.73	524.85	517.34	513.19
54000	562.88	557.59	552.96	548.89	534.76	527.10	522.87
55000	573.31	567.92	563.20	559.06	544.66	536.86	532.56
56000	583.73	578.25	573.44	569.22	554.56	546.62	542.24
57000	594.15	588.57	583.68	579.39	564.47	556.38	551.92
58000	604.58	598.90	593.92	589.55	574.37	566.14	561.60
59000	615.00	609.22	604.16	599.72	584.27	575.90	571.29
60000	625.42	619.55	614.40	609.88	594.17	585.66	580.97
65000	677.54	671.18	665.60	660.70	643.69	634.47	629.38
70000	729.66	722.81	716.80	711.53	693.20	683.28	677.80
75000	781.78	774.44	768.00	762.35	742.72	732.08	726.21
80000	833.90	826.07	819.20	813.18	792.23	780.89	774.63
85000	886.02	877.69	870.40	864.00	841.75	829.69	823.04
90000	938.14	929.32	921.60	914.82	891.26	878.50	871.45
95000	990.26	980.95	972.80	965.65	940.78	927.30	919.87
100000	1042.37	1032.58	1024.00	1016.47	990.29	976.11	968.28
105000	1094.49	1084.21	1075.20	1067.29	1039.81	1024.91	1016.70
110000	1146.61	1135.84	1126.40	1118.12	1089.32	1073.72	1065.11
120000	1250.85	1239.10	1228.80	1219.76	1188.35	1171.33	1161.94
130000	1355.09	1342.36	1331.20	1321.41	1287.38	1268.94	1258.77
140000	1459.32	1445.61	1433.60	1423.06	1386.41	1366.55	1355.59
150000	1563.56	1548.87	1536.00	1524.70	1485.44	1464.16	1452.42
175000	1824.15	1807.02	1792.00	1778.82	1733.01	1708.19	1694.49
200000	2084.75	2065.16	2048.00	2032.94	1980.58	1952.21	1936.56
225000	2345.34	2323.31	2304.00	2287.06	2228.16	2196.24	2178.63
250000	2605.94	2581.45	2560.00	2541.17	2475.73	2440.27	2420.70

11¾% Monthly Payments

necessary to amortize a loan

AMOUNT	1 YEAR	2 YEARS	3 YEARS	4 YEARS	5 YEARS	6 YEARS	7 YEARS
100	8.87	4.70	3.31	2.62	2.21	1.94	1.75
200	17.75	9.39	6.62	5.24	4.42	3.88	3.50
500	44.37	23.48	16.55	13.11	11.06	9.71	8.76
1000	88.73	46.96	33.10	26.21	22.12	19.42	17.52
2000	177.46	93.91	66.19	52.42	44.24	38.84	35.04
5000	443.66	234.78	165.48	131.06	110.59	97.10	87.60
6000	532.39	281.74	198.57	157.27	132.71	116.52	105.12
7000	621.12	328.70	231.67	183.48	154.83	135.94	122.64
8000	709.86	375.65	264.76	209.69	176.95	155.36	140.15
9000	798.59	422.61	297.86	235.90	199.06	174.78	157.67
10000	887.32	469.57	330.95	262.11	221.18	194.20	175.19
15000	1330.98	704.35	496.43	393.17	331.77	291.31	262.79
20000	1774.64	939.14	661.90	524.23	442.37	388.41	350.39
25000	2218.30	1173.92	827.38	655.28	552.96	485.51	437.98
30000	2661.96	1408.70	992.85	786.34	663.55	582.61	525.58
35000	3105.62	1643.49	1158.33	917.39	774.14	679.72	613.18
36000	3194.35	1690.45	1191.42	943.61	796.26	699.14	630.70
37000	3283.08	1737.40	1224.52	969.82	818.38	718.56	648.21
38000	3371.81	1784.36	1257.61	996.03	840.50	737.98	665.73
39000	3460.54	1831.32	1290.71	1022.24	862.61	757.40	683.25
40000	3549.28	1878.27	1323.80	1048.45	884.73	776.82	700.77
41000	3638.01	1925.23	1356.90	1074.66	906.85	796.24	718.29
42000	3726.74	1972.19	1389.99	1100.87	928.97	815.66	735.81
43000	3815.47	2019.14	1423.09	1127.08	951.09	835.08	753.33
44000	3904.20	2066.10	1456.18	1153.30	973.21	854.50	770.85
45000	3992.93	2113.06	1489.28	1179.51	995.32	873.92	788.37
46000	4081.67	2160.01	1522.37	1205.72	1017.44	893.34	805.89
47000	4170.40	2206.97	1555.47	1231.93	1039.56	912.76	823.41
48000	4259.13	2253.93	1588.56	1258.14	1061.68	932.18	840.93
49000	4347.86	2300.88	1621.66	1284.35	1083.80	951.60	858.45
50000	4436.59	2347.84	1654.75	1310.56	1105.92	971.02	875.97
51000	4525.33	2394.80	1687.85	1336.77	1128.03	990.44	893.49
52000	4614.06	2441.75	1720.94	1362.99	1150.15	1009.86	911.00
53000	4702.79	2488.71	1754.04	1389.20	1172.27	1029.28	928.52
54000	4791.52	2535.67	1787.13	1415.41	1194.39	1048.70	946.04
55000	4880.25	2582.62	1820.23	1441.62	1216.51	1068.12	963.56
56000	4968.99	2629.58	1853.32	1467.83	1238.63	1087.54	981.08
57000	5057.72	2676.54	1886.42	1494.04	1260.74	1106.96	998.60
58000	5146.45	2723.49	1919.51	1520.25	1282.86	1126.38	1016.12
59000	5235.18	2770.45	1952.61	1546.46	1304.98	1145.81	1033.64
60000	5323.91	2817.41	1985.70	1572.68	1327.10	1165.23	1051.16
65000	5767.57	3052.19	2151.18	1703.73	1437.69	1262.33	1138.76
70000	6211.23	3286.98	2316.65	1834.79	1548.28	1359.43	1226.35
75000	6654.89	3521.76	2482.13	1965.84	1658.87	1456.53	1313.95
80000	7098.55	3756.54	2647.60	2096.90	1769.47	1553.63	1401.55
85000	7542.21	3991.33	2813.08	2227.96	1880.06	1650.74	1489.14
90000	7985.87	4226.11	2978.55	2359.01	1990.65	1747.84	1576.74
95000	8429.53	4460.90	3144.03	2490.07	2101.24	1844.94	1664.34
100000	8873.19	4695.68	3309.50	2621.13	2211.83	1942.04	1751.93
105000	9316.85	4930.46	3474.98	2752.18	2322.42	2039.15	1839.53
110000	9760.51	5165.25	3640.45	2883.24	2433.02	2136.25	1927.12
120000	10647.83	5634.82	3971.40	3145.35	2654.20	2330.45	2102.32
130000	11535.14	6104.39	4302.35	3407.46	2875.38	2524.66	2277.51
140000	12422.46	6573.95	4633.30	3669.58	3096.56	2718.86	2452.70
150000	13309.78	7043.52	4964.25	3931.69	3317.75	2913.06	2627.90
175000	15528.08	8217.44	5791.63	4586.97	3870.71	3398.58	3065.88
200000	17746.38	9391.36	6619.01	5242.25	4423.66	3884.09	3503.86
225000	19964.67	10565.28	7446.38	5897.53	4976.62	4369.60	3941.85
250000	22182.97	11739.20	8273.76	6552.81	5529.58	4855.11	4379.83

Monthly Payments 11¾%

necessary to amortize a loan

AMOUNT	8 YEARS	9 YEARS	10 YEARS	11 YEARS	12 YEARS	13 YEARS	14 YEARS
100	1.61	1.50	1.42	1.35	1.30	1.25	1.22
200	3.22	3.01	2.84	2.71	2.60	2.51	2.43
500	8.06	7.52	7.10	6.77	6.49	6.27	6.08
1000	16.12	15.04	14.20	13.53	12.98	12.53	12.16
2000	32.23	30.09	28.41	27.06	25.97	25.06	24.31
5000	80.58	75.22	71.01	67.65	64.92	62.66	60.78
6000	96.69	90.26	85.22	81.18	77.90	75.19	72.94
7000	112.81	105.31	99.42	94.71	90.88	87.73	85.10
8000	128.93	120.35	113.62	108.24	103.87	100.26	97.26
9000	145.04	135.39	127.83	121.77	116.85	112.79	109.41
10000	161.16	150.44	142.03	135.30	129.83	125.32	121.57
15000	241.74	225.65	213.04	202.95	194.75	187.99	182.35
20000	322.32	300.87	284.06	270.61	259.67	250.65	243.14
25000	402.89	376.09	355.07	338.26	324.58	313.31	303.92
30000	483.47	451.31	426.09	405.91	389.50	375.97	364.71
35000	564.05	526.53	497.10	473.56	454.41	438.64	425.49
36000	580.17	541.57	511.31	487.09	467.40	451.17	437.65
37000	596.28	556.61	525.51	500.62	480.38	463.70	449.81
38000	612.40	571.66	539.71	514.15	493.36	476.23	461.96
39000	628.52	586.70	553.91	527.68	506.35	488.77	474.12
40000	644.63	601.74	568.12	541.21	519.33	501.30	486.28
41000	660.75	616.79	582.32	554.74	532.31	513.83	498.44
42000	676.86	631.83	596.52	568.27	545.30	526.36	510.59
43000	692.98	646.87	610.73	581.80	558.28	538.90	522.75
44000	709.09	661.92	624.93	595.33	571.26	551.43	534.91
45000	725.21	676.96	639.13	608.86	584.25	563.96	547.06
46000	741.33	692.01	653.34	622.39	597.23	576.49	559.22
47000	757.44	707.05	667.54	635.92	610.21	589.03	571.38
48000	773.56	722.09	681.74	649.45	623.20	601.56	583.53
49000	789.67	737.14	695.94	662.98	636.18	614.09	595.69
50000	805.79	752.18	710.15	676.51	649.16	626.62	607.85
51000	821.91	767.22	724.35	690.04	662.15	639.16	620.01
52000	838.02	782.27	738.55	703.58	675.13	651.69	632.16
53000	854.14	797.31	752.76	717.11	688.11	664.22	644.32
54000	870.25	812.35	766.96	730.64	701.10	676.75	656.48
55000	886.37	827.40	781.16	744.17	714.08	689.29	668.63
56000	902.48	842.44	795.36	757.70	727.06	701.82	680.79
57000	918.60	857.49	809.57	771.23	740.05	714.35	692.95
58000	934.72	872.53	823.77	784.76	753.03	726.88	705.10
59000	950.83	887.57	837.97	798.29	766.01	739.42	717.26
60000	966.95	902.62	852.18	811.82	779.00	751.95	729.42
65000	1047.53	977.83	923.19	879.47	843.91	814.61	790.20
70000	1128.11	1053.05	994.21	947.12	908.83	877.27	850.99
75000	1208.68	1128.27	1065.22	1014.77	973.74	939.94	911.77
80000	1289.26	1203.49	1136.24	1082.42	1038.66	1002.60	972.56
85000	1369.84	1278.71	1207.25	1150.07	1103.58	1065.26	1033.34
90000	1450.42	1353.92	1278.27	1217.73	1168.49	1127.92	1094.13
95000	1531.00	1429.14	1349.28	1285.38	1233.41	1190.59	1154.91
100000	1611.58	1504.36	1420.29	1353.03	1298.33	1253.25	1215.70
105000	1692.16	1579.58	1491.31	1420.68	1363.24	1315.91	1276.48
110000	1772.74	1654.80	1562.32	1488.33	1428.16	1378.57	1337.27
120000	1933.90	1805.23	1704.35	1623.63	1557.99	1503.90	1458.84
130000	2095.05	1955.67	1846.38	1758.94	1687.82	1629.22	1580.41
140000	2256.21	2106.10	1988.41	1894.24	1817.66	1754.55	1701.97
150000	2417.37	2256.54	2130.44	2029.54	1947.49	1879.87	1823.54
175000	2820.26	2632.63	2485.52	2367.80	2272.07	2193.18	2127.47
200000	3223.16	3008.72	2840.59	2706.06	2596.65	2506.50	2431.39
225000	3626.05	3384.81	3195.66	3044.32	2921.23	2819.81	2735.32
250000	4028.95	3760.90	3550.74	3382.57	3245.81	3133.12	3039.24

11¾%

Monthly Payments
necessary to amortize a loan

AMOUNT	15 YEARS	16 YEARS	17 YEARS	18 YEARS	19 YEARS	20 YEARS	21 YEARS
100	1.18	1.16	1.13	1.12	1.10	1.08	1.07
200	2.37	2.31	2.27	2.23	2.20	2.17	2.14
500	5.92	5.79	5.67	5.58	5.49	5.42	5.36
1000	11.84	11.57	11.35	11.15	10.98	10.84	10.71
2000	23.68	23.15	22.69	22.30	21.97	21.67	21.42
5000	59.21	57.87	56.73	55.75	54.91	54.19	53.55
6000	71.05	69.44	68.08	66.90	65.90	65.02	64.27
7000	82.89	81.02	79.42	78.06	76.88	75.86	74.98
8000	94.73	92.59	90.77	89.21	87.86	86.70	85.69
9000	106.57	104.17	102.11	100.36	98.84	97.53	96.40
10000	118.41	115.74	113.46	111.51	109.83	108.37	107.11
15000	177.62	173.61	170.19	167.26	164.74	162.56	160.66
20000	236.83	231.48	226.92	223.01	219.65	216.74	214.22
25000	296.03	289.35	283.65	278.77	274.56	270.93	267.77
30000	355.24	347.22	340.38	334.52	329.48	325.11	321.33
35000	414.45	405.09	397.11	390.28	384.39	379.30	374.88
36000	426.29	416.66	408.46	401.43	395.37	390.13	385.59
37000	438.13	428.24	419.80	412.58	406.35	400.97	396.30
38000	449.97	439.81	431.15	423.73	417.34	411.81	407.01
39000	461.81	451.38	442.50	434.88	428.32	422.65	417.72
40000	473.65	462.96	453.84	446.03	439.30	433.48	428.44
41000	485.49	474.53	465.19	457.18	450.28	444.32	439.15
42000	497.34	486.11	476.53	468.33	461.27	455.16	449.86
43000	509.18	497.68	487.88	479.48	472.25	465.99	460.57
44000	521.02	509.25	499.23	490.63	483.23	476.83	471.28
45000	532.86	520.83	510.57	501.78	494.21	487.67	481.99
46000	544.70	532.40	521.92	512.93	505.20	498.51	492.70
47000	556.54	543.98	533.26	524.08	516.18	509.34	503.41
48000	568.38	555.55	544.61	535.23	527.16	520.18	514.12
49000	580.22	567.12	555.96	546.39	538.14	531.02	524.83
50000	592.07	578.70	567.30	557.54	549.13	541.85	535.54
51000	603.91	590.27	578.65	568.69	560.11	552.69	546.25
52000	615.75	601.85	590.00	579.84	571.09	563.53	556.97
53000	627.59	613.42	601.34	590.99	582.07	574.36	567.68
54000	639.43	624.99	612.69	602.14	593.06	585.20	578.39
55000	651.27	636.57	624.03	613.29	604.04	596.04	589.10
56000	663.11	648.14	635.38	624.44	615.02	606.88	599.81
57000	674.95	659.72	646.73	635.59	626.00	617.71	610.52
58000	686.80	671.29	658.07	646.74	636.99	628.55	621.23
59000	698.64	682.86	669.42	657.89	647.97	639.39	631.94
60000	710.48	694.44	680.76	669.04	658.95	650.22	642.65
65000	769.69	752.31	737.49	724.80	713.86	704.41	696.21
70000	828.89	810.18	794.22	780.55	768.78	758.59	749.76
75000	888.10	868.05	850.95	836.30	823.69	812.78	803.32
80000	947.31	925.92	907.68	892.06	878.60	866.97	856.87
85000	1006.51	983.79	964.42	947.81	933.51	921.15	910.42
90000	1065.72	1041.66	1021.15	1003.57	988.43	975.34	963.98
95000	1124.92	1099.53	1077.88	1059.32	1043.34	1029.52	1017.53
100000	1184.13	1157.40	1134.61	1115.07	1098.25	1083.71	1071.09
105000	1243.34	1215.27	1191.34	1170.83	1153.16	1137.89	1124.64
110000	1302.54	1273.14	1248.07	1226.58	1208.08	1192.08	1178.20
120000	1420.96	1388.88	1361.53	1338.09	1317.90	1300.45	1285.31
130000	1539.37	1504.62	1474.99	1449.59	1427.73	1408.82	1392.41
140000	1657.78	1620.35	1588.45	1561.10	1537.55	1517.19	1499.52
150000	1776.20	1736.09	1701.91	1672.61	1647.38	1625.56	1606.63
175000	2072.23	2025.44	1985.56	1951.38	1921.94	1896.49	1874.40
200000	2368.26	2314.79	2269.21	2230.15	2196.50	2167.41	2142.18
225000	2664.30	2604.14	2552.86	2508.91	2471.07	2438.34	2409.95
250000	2960.33	2893.49	2836.52	2787.68	2745.63	2709.27	2677.72

Monthly Payments 11¾%

necessary to amortize a loan

AMOUNT	22 YEARS	23 YEARS	24 YEARS	25 YEARS	30 YEARS	35 YEARS	40 YEARS
100	1.06	1.05	1.04	1.03	1.01	1.00	0.99
200	2.12	2.10	2.08	2.07	2.02	1.99	1.98
500	5.30	5.25	5.21	5.17	5.05	4.98	4.94
1000	10.60	10.51	10.42	10.35	10.09	9.96	9.88
2000	21.20	21.01	20.84	20.70	20.19	19.92	19.77
5000	53.01	52.53	52.11	51.74	50.47	49.79	49.42
6000	63.61	63.03	62.53	62.09	60.56	59.75	59.30
7000	74.21	73.54	72.95	72.44	70.66	69.71	69.19
8000	84.81	84.04	83.37	82.78	80.75	79.66	79.07
9000	95.41	94.55	93.79	93.13	90.85	89.62	88.95
10000	106.01	105.05	104.21	103.48	100.94	99.58	98.84
15000	159.02	157.58	156.32	155.22	151.41	149.37	148.25
20000	212.02	210.10	208.43	206.96	201.88	199.16	197.67
25000	265.03	262.63	260.54	258.70	252.35	248.95	247.09
30000	318.03	315.16	312.64	310.44	302.82	298.74	296.51
35000	371.04	367.68	364.75	362.18	353.29	348.53	345.93
36000	381.64	378.19	375.17	372.53	363.39	358.49	355.81
37000	392.24	388.69	385.59	382.88	373.48	368.44	365.69
38000	402.84	399.20	396.01	393.22	383.58	378.40	375.58
39000	413.44	409.70	406.44	403.57	393.67	388.36	385.46
40000	424.04	420.21	416.86	413.92	403.76	398.32	395.35
41000	434.64	430.71	427.28	424.27	413.86	408.28	405.23
42000	445.24	441.22	437.70	434.62	423.95	418.23	415.11
43000	455.85	451.72	448.12	444.96	434.05	428.19	425.00
44000	466.45	462.23	458.54	455.31	444.14	438.15	434.88
45000	477.05	472.74	468.96	465.66	454.23	448.11	444.76
46000	487.65	483.24	479.39	476.01	464.33	458.07	454.65
47000	498.25	493.75	489.81	486.36	474.42	468.02	464.53
48000	508.85	504.25	500.23	496.70	484.52	477.98	474.41
49000	519.45	514.76	510.65	507.05	494.61	487.94	484.30
50000	530.05	525.26	521.07	517.40	504.70	497.90	494.18
51000	540.65	535.77	531.49	527.75	514.80	507.85	504.07
52000	551.26	546.27	541.91	538.10	524.89	517.81	513.95
53000	561.86	556.78	552.34	548.44	534.99	527.77	523.83
54000	572.46	567.28	562.76	558.79	545.08	537.73	533.72
55000	583.06	577.79	573.18	569.14	555.18	547.69	543.60
56000	593.66	588.29	583.60	579.49	565.27	557.64	553.48
57000	604.26	598.80	594.02	588.83	575.36	567.60	563.37
58000	614.86	609.30	604.44	600.18	585.46	577.56	573.25
59000	625.46	619.81	614.00	610.53	595.55	587.52	583.13
60000	636.06	630.31	625.29	620.88	605.65	597.48	593.02
65000	689.07	682.84	677.39	672.62	656.12	647.27	642.44
70000	742.07	735.37	729.50	724.36	706.59	697.06	691.85
75000	795.08	787.89	781.61	776.10	757.06	746.85	741.27
80000	848.08	840.42	833.71	827.84	807.53	796.64	790.69
85000	901.09	892.94	885.82	879.58	858.00	846.42	840.11
90000	954.10	945.47	937.93	931.32	908.47	896.21	889.53
95000	1007.10	998.00	990.04	983.06	958.94	946.00	938.95
100000	1060.11	1050.52	1042.14	1034.80	1009.41	995.79	988.36
105000	1113.11	1103.05	1094.25	1086.54	1059.88	1045.58	1037.78
110000	1166.12	1155.58	1146.36	1138.28	1110.35	1095.37	1087.20
120000	1272.13	1260.63	1250.57	1241.76	1211.29	1194.95	1186.04
130000	1378.14	1365.68	1354.79	1345.24	1312.23	1294.53	1284.87
140000	1484.15	1470.73	1459.00	1448.72	1413.17	1394.11	1383.71
150000	1590.16	1575.78	1563.21	1552.20	1514.11	1493.69	1482.55
175000	1855.19	1838.42	1823.75	1810.90	1766.47	1742.64	1729.64
200000	2120.21	2101.05	2084.28	2069.60	2018.82	1991.59	1976.73
225000	2385.24	2363.68	2344.82	2328.30	2271.17	2240.54	2223.82
250000	2650.26	2626.31	2605.36	2587.00	2523.52	2489.48	2470.91

12% Monthly Payments

necessary to amortize a loan

AMOUNT	1 YEAR	2 YEARS	3 YEARS	4 YEARS	5 YEARS	6 YEARS	7 YEARS
100	8.88	4.71	3.32	2.63	2.22	1.96	1.77
200	17.77	9.41	6.64	5.27	4.45	3.91	3.53
500	44.42	23.54	16.61	13.17	11.12	9.78	8.83
1000	88.85	47.07	33.21	26.33	22.24	19.55	17.65
2000	177.70	94.15	66.43	52.67	44.49	39.10	35.31
5000	444.24	235.37	166.07	131.67	111.22	97.75	88.26
6000	533.09	282.44	199.29	158.00	133.47	117.30	105.92
7000	621.94	329.51	232.50	184.34	155.71	136.85	123.57
8000	710.79	376.59	265.71	210.67	177.96	156.40	141.22
9000	799.64	423.66	298.93	237.00	200.20	175.95	158.87
10000	888.49	470.73	332.14	263.34	222.44	195.50	176.53
15000	1332.73	706.10	498.21	395.01	333.67	293.25	264.79
20000	1776.98	941.47	664.29	526.68	444.89	391.00	353.05
25000	2221.22	1176.84	830.36	658.35	556.11	488.75	441.32
30000	2665.46	1412.20	996.43	790.02	667.33	586.51	529.58
35000	3109.71	1647.57	1162.50	921.68	778.56	684.26	617.85
36000	3198.56	1694.65	1195.72	948.02	800.80	703.81	635.50
37000	3287.41	1741.72	1228.93	974.35	823.04	723.36	653.15
38000	3376.25	1788.79	1262.14	1000.69	845.29	742.91	670.80
39000	3465.10	1835.87	1295.36	1027.02	867.53	762.46	688.46
40000	3553.95	1882.94	1328.57	1053.35	889.78	782.01	706.11
41000	3642.80	1930.01	1361.79	1079.69	912.02	801.56	723.76
42000	3731.65	1977.09	1395.00	1106.02	934.27	821.11	741.41
43000	3820.50	2024.16	1428.22	1132.35	956.51	840.66	759.07
44000	3909.35	2071.23	1461.43	1158.69	978.76	860.21	776.72
45000	3998.20	2118.31	1494.64	1185.02	1001.00	879.76	794.37
46000	4087.04	2165.38	1527.86	1211.36	1023.24	899.31	812.03
47000	4175.89	2212.45	1561.07	1237.69	1045.49	918.86	829.68
48000	4264.74	2259.53	1594.29	1264.02	1067.73	938.41	847.33
49000	4353.59	2306.60	1627.50	1290.36	1089.98	957.96	864.98
50000	4442.44	2353.67	1660.72	1316.69	1112.22	977.51	882.64
51000	4531.29	2400.75	1693.93	1343.03	1134.47	997.06	900.29
52000	4620.14	2447.82	1727.14	1369.36	1156.71	1016.61	917.94
53000	4708.99	2494.89	1760.36	1395.69	1178.96	1036.16	935.59
54000	4797.83	2541.97	1793.57	1422.03	1201.20	1055.71	953.25
55000	4886.68	2589.04	1826.79	1448.36	1223.44	1075.26	970.90
56000	4975.53	2636.11	1860.00	1474.69	1245.69	1094.81	988.55
57000	5064.38	2683.19	1893.22	1501.03	1267.93	1114.36	1006.21
58000	5153.23	2730.26	1926.43	1527.36	1290.18	1133.91	1023.86
59000	5242.08	2777.33	1959.64	1553.70	1312.42	1153.46	1041.51
60000	5330.93	2824.41	1992.86	1580.03	1334.67	1173.01	1059.16
65000	5775.17	3059.78	2158.93	1711.70	1445.89	1270.76	1147.43
70000	6219.42	3295.14	2325.00	1843.37	1557.11	1368.51	1235.69
75000	6663.66	3530.51	2491.07	1975.04	1668.33	1466.26	1323.95
80000	7107.90	3765.88	2657.14	2106.71	1779.56	1564.02	1412.22
85000	7552.15	4001.25	2823.22	2238.38	1890.78	1661.77	1500.48
90000	7996.39	4236.61	2989.29	2370.05	2002.00	1759.52	1588.75
95000	8440.63	4471.98	3155.36	2501.71	2113.22	1857.27	1677.01
100000	8884.88	4707.35	3321.43	2633.38	2224.44	1955.02	1765.27
105000	9329.12	4942.71	3487.50	2765.05	2335.67	2052.77	1853.54
110000	9773.37	5178.08	3653.57	2896.72	2446.89	2150.52	1941.80
120000	10661.85	5648.82	3985.72	3160.06	2669.33	2346.02	2118.33
130000	11550.34	6119.55	4317.86	3423.40	2891.78	2541.53	2294.86
140000	12438.83	6590.29	4650.00	3686.74	3114.22	2737.03	2471.38
150000	13327.32	7061.02	4982.15	3950.08	3336.67	2932.53	2647.91
175000	15548.54	8237.86	5812.50	4608.42	3892.78	3421.28	3089.23
200000	17769.76	9414.69	6642.86	5266.77	4448.89	3910.04	3530.55
225000	19990.98	10591.53	7473.22	5925.11	5005.00	4398.79	3971.86
250000	22212.20	11768.37	8303.58	6583.46	5561.11	4887.55	4413.18

Monthly Payments — 12%

necessary to amortize a loan

AMOUNT	8 YEARS	9 YEARS	10 YEARS	11 YEARS	12 YEARS	13 YEARS	14 YEARS
100	1.63	1.52	1.43	1.37	1.31	1.27	1.23
200	3.25	3.04	2.87	2.74	2.63	2.54	2.46
500	8.13	7.59	7.17	6.84	6.57	6.34	6.16
1000	16.25	15.18	14.35	13.68	13.13	12.69	12.31
2000	32.51	30.37	28.69	27.36	26.27	25.37	24.63
5000	81.26	75.92	71.74	68.39	65.67	63.43	61.57
6000	97.52	91.11	86.08	82.07	78.81	76.12	73.89
7000	113.77	106.29	100.43	95.75	91.94	88.81	86.20
8000	130.02	121.47	114.78	109.42	105.07	101.49	98.51
9000	146.28	136.66	129.12	123.10	118.21	114.18	110.83
10000	162.53	151.84	143.47	136.78	131.34	126.87	123.14
15000	243.79	227.76	215.21	205.17	197.01	190.30	184.71
20000	325.06	303.68	286.94	273.56	262.68	253.73	246.29
25000	406.32	379.61	358.68	341.95	328.35	317.17	307.86
30000	487.59	455.53	430.41	410.34	394.03	380.60	369.43
35000	568.85	531.45	502.15	478.73	459.70	444.03	431.00
36000	585.10	546.63	516.50	492.40	472.83	456.72	443.31
37000	601.36	561.82	530.84	506.08	485.97	469.41	455.63
38000	617.61	577.00	545.19	519.76	499.10	482.09	467.94
39000	633.86	592.19	559.54	533.44	512.23	494.78	480.26
40000	650.11	607.37	573.88	547.12	525.37	507.47	492.57
41000	666.37	622.55	588.23	560.79	538.50	520.15	504.89
42000	682.62	637.74	602.58	574.47	551.64	532.84	517.20
43000	698.87	652.92	616.93	588.15	564.77	545.53	529.51
44000	715.13	668.11	631.27	601.83	577.90	558.21	541.83
45000	731.38	683.29	645.62	615.50	591.04	570.90	554.14
46000	747.63	698.47	659.97	629.18	604.17	583.59	566.46
47000	763.88	713.66	674.31	642.86	617.31	596.27	578.77
48000	780.14	728.84	688.66	656.54	630.44	608.96	591.09
49000	796.39	744.03	703.01	670.22	643.58	621.65	603.40
50000	812.64	759.21	717.35	683.89	656.71	634.33	615.71
51000	828.89	774.40	731.70	697.57	669.84	647.02	628.03
52000	845.15	789.58	746.05	711.25	682.98	659.71	640.34
53000	861.40	804.76	760.40	724.93	696.11	672.39	652.66
54000	877.65	819.95	774.74	738.61	709.25	685.08	664.97
55000	893.91	835.13	789.09	752.28	722.38	697.77	677.20
56000	910.16	850.32	803.44	765.96	735.51	710.45	689.60
57000	926.41	805.50	817.78	779.64	748.65	723.14	701.91
58000	942.66	880.69	832.13	793.32	761.78	735.83	714.23
59000	958.92	895.07	846.48	806.99	774.92	748.51	726.54
60000	975.17	911.05	860.83	820.67	788.05	761.20	738.86
65000	1056.43	986.98	932.56	889.06	853.72	824.63	800.43
70000	1137.70	1062.90	1004.30	957.45	919.39	888.07	862.00
75000	1218.96	1138.82	1076.03	1025.84	985.06	951.50	923.57
80000	1300.23	1214.74	1147.77	1094.23	1050.74	1014.93	985.14
85000	1381.49	1290.66	1219.50	1162.62	1116.41	1078.37	1046.72
90000	1462.76	1366.58	1291.24	1231.01	1182.08	1141.80	1108.29
95000	1544.02	1442.50	1362.97	1299.40	1247.75	1205.23	1169.86
100000	1625.28	1518.42	1434.71	1367.79	1313.42	1268.67	1231.43
105000	1706.55	1594.34	1506.44	1436.18	1379.09	1332.10	1293.00
110000	1787.81	1670.27	1578.18	1504.57	1444.76	1395.53	1354.57
120000	1950.34	1822.11	1721.65	1641.35	1576.10	1522.40	1477.72
130000	2112.87	1973.95	1865.12	1778.12	1707.44	1649.27	1600.86
140000	2275.40	2125.79	2008.59	1914.90	1838.79	1776.13	1724.00
150000	2437.93	2277.63	2152.06	2051.68	1970.13	1903.00	1847.14
175000	2844.25	2657.24	2510.74	2393.63	2298.48	2220.17	2155.00
200000	3250.57	3036.85	2869.42	2735.58	2626.84	2537.33	2462.86
225000	3656.89	3416.45	3228.10	3077.52	2955.19	2854.50	2770.72
250000	4063.21	3796.06	3586.77	3419.47	3283.55	3171.67	3078.57

12%

Monthly Payments

necessary to amortize a loan

AMOUNT	15 YEARS	16 YEARS	17 YEARS	18 YEARS	19 YEARS	20 YEARS	21 YEARS
100	1.20	1.17	1.15	1.13	1.12	1.10	1.09
200	2.40	2.35	2.30	2.26	2.23	2.20	2.18
500	6.00	5.87	5.76	5.66	5.58	5.51	5.44
1000	12.00	11.74	11.51	11.32	11.15	11.01	10.89
2000	24.00	23.47	23.02	22.64	22.31	22.02	21.77
5000	60.01	58.69	57.56	56.60	55.77	55.05	54.43
6000	72.01	70.42	69.07	67.92	66.92	66.07	65.32
7000	84.01	82.16	80.59	79.24	78.08	77.08	76.21
8000	96.01	93.90	92.10	90.56	89.23	88.09	87.10
9000	108.02	105.64	103.61	101.88	100.38	99.10	97.98
10000	120.02	117.37	115.12	113.20	111.54	110.11	108.87
15000	180.03	176.06	172.68	169.79	167.31	165.16	163.30
20000	240.03	234.75	230.24	226.39	223.08	220.22	217.74
25000	300.04	293.43	287.80	282.99	278.85	275.27	272.17
30000	360.05	352.12	345.36	339.59	334.62	330.33	326.61
35000	420.06	410.80	402.93	396.18	390.38	385.38	381.04
36000	432.06	422.54	414.44	407.50	401.54	396.39	391.93
37000	444.06	434.28	425.95	418.82	412.69	407.40	402.82
38000	456.06	446.02	437.46	430.14	423.85	418.41	413.71
39000	468.07	457.75	448.97	441.46	435.00	429.42	424.59
40000	480.07	469.49	460.49	452.78	446.15	440.43	435.48
41000	492.07	481.23	472.00	464.10	457.31	451.45	446.37
42000	504.07	492.96	483.51	475.42	468.46	462.46	457.25
43000	516.07	504.70	495.02	486.74	479.62	473.47	468.14
44000	528.07	516.44	506.53	498.06	490.77	484.48	479.03
45000	540.08	528.18	518.05	509.38	501.92	495.49	489.91
46000	552.08	539.91	529.56	520.70	513.08	506.50	500.80
47000	564.08	551.65	541.07	532.02	524.23	517.51	511.69
48000	576.08	563.39	552.58	543.34	535.39	528.52	522.58
49000	588.08	575.13	564.10	554.66	546.54	539.53	533.46
50000	600.08	586.86	575.61	565.98	557.69	550.54	544.35
51000	612.09	598.60	587.12	577.29	568.85	561.55	555.24
52000	624.09	610.34	598.63	588.61	580.00	572.56	566.12
53000	636.09	622.07	610.14	599.93	591.15	583.58	577.01
54000	648.09	633.81	621.66	611.25	602.31	594.59	587.90
55000	660.09	645.55	633.17	622.57	613.46	605.60	598.78
56000	672.09	657.29	644.68	633.89	624.62	616.61	609.67
57000	684.10	669.02	656.19	645.21	635.77	627.62	620.56
58000	696.10	680.76	667.71	656.53	646.92	638.63	631.45
59000	708.10	692.50	679.22	667.85	658.08	649.64	642.33
60000	720.10	704.24	690.73	679.17	669.23	660.65	653.22
65000	780.11	762.92	748.29	735.77	725.00	715.71	707.65
70000	840.12	821.61	805.85	792.37	780.77	770.76	762.09
75000	900.13	880.29	863.41	848.96	836.54	825.81	816.52
80000	960.13	938.98	920.97	905.56	892.31	880.87	870.96
85000	1020.14	997.67	978.53	962.16	948.08	935.92	925.39
90000	1080.15	1056.35	1036.09	1018.76	1003.85	990.98	979.83
95000	1140.16	1115.04	1093.65	1075.35	1059.62	1046.03	1034.26
100000	1200.17	1173.73	1151.22	1131.95	1115.39	1101.09	1088.70
105000	1260.18	1232.41	1208.78	1188.55	1171.15	1156.14	1143.13
110000	1320.18	1291.10	1266.34	1245.15	1226.92	1211.19	1197.57
120000	1440.20	1408.47	1381.46	1358.34	1338.46	1321.30	1306.44
130000	1560.22	1525.84	1496.58	1471.54	1450.00	1431.41	1415.31
140000	1680.24	1643.22	1611.70	1584.73	1561.54	1541.52	1524.18
150000	1800.25	1760.59	1726.82	1697.93	1673.08	1651.63	1633.05
175000	2100.29	2054.02	2014.63	1980.91	1951.92	1926.90	1905.22
200000	2400.34	2347.45	2302.43	2263.90	2230.77	2202.17	2177.40
225000	2700.38	2640.88	2590.23	2546.89	2509.62	2477.44	2449.57
250000	3000.42	2934.31	2878.04	2829.88	2788.46	2752.72	2721.75

Monthly Payments

necessary to amortize a loan

12%

AMOUNT	22 YEARS	23 YEARS	24 YEARS	25 YEARS	30 YEARS	35 YEARS	40 YEARS
100	1.08	1.07	1.06	1.05	1.03	1.02	1.01
200	2.16	2.14	2.12	2.11	2.06	2.03	2.02
500	5.39	5.34	5.30	5.27	5.14	5.08	5.04
1000	10.78	10.69	10.60	10.53	10.29	10.16	10.08
2000	21.56	21.37	21.21	21.06	20.57	20.31	20.17
5000	53.90	53.43	53.02	52.66	51.43	50.78	50.42
6000	64.68	64.11	63.62	63.19	61.72	60.93	60.51
7000	75.46	74.80	74.23	73.73	72.00	71.09	70.59
8000	86.24	85.49	84.83	84.26	82.29	81.24	80.68
9000	97.01	96.17	95.43	94.79	92.58	91.40	90.76
10000	107.79	106.86	106.04	105.32	102.86	101.55	100.85
15000	161.69	160.28	159.06	157.98	154.29	152.33	151.27
20000	215.59	213.71	212.08	210.64	205.72	203.11	201.70
25000	269.48	267.14	265.10	263.31	257.15	253.89	252.12
30000	323.38	320.57	318.11	315.97	308.58	304.66	302.55
35000	377.28	374.00	371.13	368.63	360.01	355.44	352.97
36000	388.06	384.68	381.74	379.16	370.30	365.60	363.06
37000	398.84	395.37	392.34	389.69	380.59	375.75	373.14
38000	409.62	406.05	402.95	400.23	390.87	385.91	383.23
39000	420.40	416.74	413.55	410.76	401.16	396.06	393.31
40000	431.18	427.43	424.15	421.29	411.45	406.22	403.40
41000	441.95	438.11	434.76	431.82	421.73	416.38	413.48
42000	452.73	448.80	445.36	442.35	432.02	426.53	423.57
43000	463.51	459.48	455.96	452.89	442.30	436.69	433.65
44000	474.29	470.17	466.57	463.42	452.59	446.84	443.74
45000	485.07	480.85	477.17	473.95	462.88	457.00	453.82
46000	495.85	491.54	487.78	484.48	473.16	467.15	463.91
47000	506.63	502.23	498.38	495.02	483.45	477.31	473.99
48000	517.41	512.91	508.98	505.55	493.73	487.46	484.08
49000	528.19	523.60	519.59	516.08	504.02	497.62	494.16
50000	538.97	534.28	530.19	526.61	514.31	507.77	504.25
51000	549.75	544.97	540.79	537.14	524.59	517.93	514.33
52000	560.53	555.65	551.40	547.68	534.88	528.09	524.42
53000	571.31	566.34	562.00	558.21	545.16	538.24	534.50
54000	582.09	577.03	572.61	568.74	555.45	548.40	544.59
55000	592.87	587.71	583.21	579.27	565.74	558.55	554.67
56000	603.65	598.40	593.81	589.81	576.02	568.71	564.76
57000	614.42	609.00	604.42	600.34	586.31	578.86	574.84
58000	625.20	619.77	615.02	610.87	596.60	589.02	584.93
59000	635.98	630.45	625.63	621.40	606.88	599.17	595.01
60000	646.76	641.14	636.23	631.93	617.17	609.33	605.10
65000	700.66	694.57	689.25	684.60	668.60	660.11	655.52
70000	754.56	748.00	742.27	737.26	720.03	710.88	705.95
75000	808.45	801.42	795.29	789.92	771.46	761.66	750.37
80000	862.35	854.85	848.31	842.58	822.89	812.44	806.80
85000	916.25	908.28	901.32	895.24	874.32	863.22	857.22
90000	970.14	961.71	954.34	947.90	925.75	913.99	907.65
95000	1024.04	1015.14	1007.36	1000.56	977.18	964.77	958.07
100000	1077.94	1068.56	1060.38	1053.22	1028.61	1015.55	1008.50
105000	1131.84	1121.99	1113.40	1105.89	1080.04	1066.33	1058.92
110000	1185.73	1175.42	1166.42	1158.55	1131.47	1117.10	1109.35
120000	1293.53	1282.28	1272.46	1263.87	1234.34	1218.66	1210.20
130000	1401.32	1389.13	1378.50	1369.19	1337.20	1320.21	1311.05
140000	1509.11	1495.99	1484.53	1474.51	1440.06	1421.77	1411.90
150000	1616.91	1602.85	1590.57	1579.84	1542.92	1523.32	1512.75
175000	1886.39	1869.99	1855.67	1843.14	1800.07	1777.21	1764.87
200000	2155.88	2137.13	2120.76	2106.45	2057.23	2031.10	2017.00
225000	2425.36	2404.27	2385.86	2369.75	2314.38	2284.99	2269.12
250000	2694.85	2671.41	2650.95	2633.06	2571.53	2538.87	2521.25

12¼%

Monthly Payments
necessary to amortize a loan

AMOUNT	1 YEAR	2 YEARS	3 YEARS	4 YEARS	5 YEARS	6 YEARS	7 YEARS
100	8.90	4.72	3.33	2.65	2.24	1.97	1.78
200	17.79	9.44	6.67	5.29	4.47	3.94	3.56
500	44.48	23.60	16.67	13.23	11.19	9.84	8.89
1000	88.97	47.19	33.33	26.46	22.37	19.68	17.79
2000	177.93	94.38	66.67	52.91	44.74	39.36	35.57
5000	444.83	235.95	166.67	132.28	111.85	98.40	88.93
6000	533.79	283.14	200.00	158.74	134.23	118.08	106.72
7000	622.76	330.33	233.34	185.20	156.60	137.76	124.51
8000	711.73	377.52	266.67	211.65	178.97	157.44	142.29
9000	800.69	424.71	300.00	238.11	201.34	177.12	160.08
10000	889.66	471.90	333.34	264.57	223.71	196.80	177.87
15000	1334.49	707.85	500.01	396.85	335.56	295.21	266.80
20000	1779.32	943.81	666.68	529.14	447.42	393.61	355.73
25000	2224.14	1179.76	833.35	661.42	559.27	492.01	444.67
30000	2668.97	1415.71	1000.02	793.70	671.13	590.41	533.60
35000	3113.80	1651.66	1166.68	925.99	782.98	688.82	622.53
36000	3202.77	1698.85	1200.02	952.44	805.36	708.50	640.32
37000	3291.73	1746.04	1233.35	978.90	827.73	728.18	658.11
38000	3380.70	1793.23	1266.69	1005.36	850.10	747.86	675.89
39000	3469.67	1840.42	1300.02	1031.81	872.47	767.54	693.68
40000	3558.63	1887.61	1333.35	1058.27	894.84	787.22	711.47
41000	3647.60	1934.80	1366.69	1084.73	917.21	806.90	729.25
42000	3736.56	1981.99	1400.02	1111.18	939.58	826.58	747.04
43000	3825.53	2029.18	1433.36	1137.64	961.95	846.26	764.83
44000	3914.49	2076.37	1466.69	1164.10	984.32	865.94	782.62
45000	4003.46	2123.56	1500.02	1190.55	1006.69	885.62	800.40
46000	4092.43	2170.75	1533.36	1217.01	1029.07	905.30	818.19
47000	4181.39	2217.94	1566.69	1243.47	1051.44	924.98	835.98
48000	4270.36	2265.13	1600.02	1269.92	1073.81	944.66	853.76
49000	4359.32	2312.32	1633.36	1296.38	1096.18	964.34	871.55
50000	4448.29	2359.52	1666.69	1322.84	1118.55	984.02	889.34
51000	4537.25	2406.71	1700.03	1349.29	1140.92	1003.70	907.12
52000	4626.22	2453.90	1733.36	1375.75	1163.29	1023.38	924.91
53000	4715.19	2501.09	1766.69	1402.21	1185.66	1043.06	942.70
54000	4804.15	2548.28	1800.03	1428.66	1208.03	1062.74	960.48
55000	4893.12	2595.47	1833.36	1455.12	1230.40	1082.42	978.27
56000	4982.08	2642.66	1866.70	1481.58	1252.78	1102.10	996.06
57000	5071.05	2689.85	1900.03	1508.03	1275.15	1121.79	1013.84
58000	5160.02	2737.04	1933.36	1534.49	1297.52	1141.47	1031.63
59000	5248.98	2784.23	1966.70	1560.95	1319.89	1161.15	1049.42
60000	5337.95	2831.42	2000.03	1587.41	1342.26	1180.83	1067.20
65000	5782.78	3067.37	2166.70	1719.69	1454.11	1279.23	1156.14
70000	6227.60	3303.32	2333.37	1851.97	1565.97	1377.63	1245.07
75000	6672.43	3539.27	2500.04	1984.26	1677.82	1476.03	1334.00
80000	7117.26	3775.22	2666.71	2116.54	1789.68	1574.44	1422.94
85000	7562.09	4011.18	2833.38	2248.82	1901.53	1672.84	1511.87
90000	8006.92	4247.13	3000.05	2381.11	2013.39	1771.24	1600.80
95000	8451.75	4483.08	3166.71	2513.39	2125.24	1869.64	1689.74
100000	8896.58	4719.03	3333.38	2645.68	2237.10	1968.04	1778.67
105000	9341.41	4954.98	3500.05	2777.96	2348.95	2066.45	1867.60
110000	9786.24	5190.93	3666.72	2910.24	2460.81	2164.85	1956.54
120000	10675.89	5662.84	4000.06	3174.81	2684.52	2361.65	2134.40
130000	11565.55	6134.74	4333.40	3439.38	2908.23	2558.46	2312.27
140000	12455.21	6606.64	4666.74	3703.95	3131.94	2755.26	2490.14
150000	13344.87	7078.55	5000.08	3968.51	3355.65	2952.07	2668.01
175000	15569.01	8258.30	5833.42	4629.93	3914.92	3444.08	3112.67
200000	17793.16	9438.06	6666.77	5291.35	4474.20	3936.09	3557.34
225000	20017.30	10617.82	7500.11	5952.77	5033.47	4428.10	4002.01
250000	22241.45	11797.58	8333.46	6614.19	5592.75	4920.11	4446.68

Monthly Payments 12¼%

necessary to amortize a loan

AMOUNT	8 YEARS	9 YEARS	10 YEARS	11 YEARS	12 YEARS	13 YEARS	14 YEARS
100	1.64	1.53	1.45	1.38	1.33	1.28	1.25
200	3.28	3.07	2.90	2.77	2.66	2.57	2.49
500	8.20	7.66	7.25	6.91	6.64	6.42	6.24
1000	16.39	15.33	14.49	13.83	13.29	12.84	12.47
2000	32.78	30.65	28.98	27.65	26.57	25.68	24.95
5000	81.95	76.63	72.46	69.13	66.43	64.21	62.36
6000	98.34	91.95	86.95	82.96	79.72	77.05	74.84
7000	114.73	107.28	101.44	96.78	93.00	89.89	87.31
8000	131.12	122.60	115.94	110.61	106.29	102.73	99.78
9000	147.51	137.93	130.43	124.44	119.57	115.58	112.25
10000	163.91	153.26	144.92	138.26	132.86	128.42	124.73
15000	245.86	229.88	217.38	207.39	199.29	192.63	187.09
20000	327.81	306.51	289.84	276.53	265.72	256.83	249.45
25000	409.76	383.14	362.30	345.66	332.15	321.04	311.81
30000	491.72	459.77	434.76	414.79	398.58	385.25	374.18
35000	573.67	536.39	507.22	483.92	465.01	449.46	436.54
36000	590.06	551.72	521.71	497.75	478.29	462.30	449.01
37000	606.45	567.05	536.20	511.57	491.58	475.14	461.48
38000	622.84	582.37	550.70	525.40	504.87	487.99	473.96
39000	639.23	597.70	565.19	539.22	518.15	500.83	486.43
40000	655.62	613.02	579.68	553.05	531.44	513.67	498.90
41000	672.01	628.35	594.17	566.88	544.72	526.51	511.37
42000	688.40	643.67	608.66	580.70	558.01	539.35	523.85
43000	704.79	659.00	623.16	594.53	571.30	552.19	536.32
44000	721.18	674.32	637.65	608.36	584.58	565.04	548.79
45000	737.57	689.65	652.14	622.18	597.87	577.88	561.26
46000	753.96	704.98	666.63	636.01	611.15	590.72	573.74
47000	770.35	720.30	681.12	649.83	624.44	603.56	586.21
48000	786.74	735.63	695.62	663.66	637.73	616.40	598.68
49000	803.14	750.95	710.11	677.49	651.01	629.24	611.15
50000	819.53	766.28	724.60	691.31	664.30	642.09	623.63
51000	835.92	781.60	739.09	705.14	677.58	654.93	636.10
52000	852.31	796.93	753.58	718.97	690.87	667.77	648.57
53000	868.70	812.25	768.08	732.79	704.16	680.61	661.04
54000	885.09	827.58	782.57	746.62	717.44	693.45	673.52
55000	901.48	842.91	797.06	760.44	730.73	706.29	685.99
56000	917.87	858.23	811.55	774.27	744.01	719.14	698.46
57000	934.26	873.56	826.04	788.10	757.30	731.98	710.93
58000	950.65	888.88	840.54	801.92	770.59	744.82	723.41
59000	967.04	904.21	855.03	815.75	783.87	757.66	735.88
60000	983.43	919.53	869.52	829.58	797.16	770.50	748.35
65000	1065.38	996.16	941.98	898.71	863.59	834.71	810.72
70000	1147.34	1072.79	1014.44	967.84	930.02	898.92	873.08
75000	1229.29	1149.42	1086.90	1036.97	996.45	963.13	935.44
80000	1311.24	1226.04	1159.36	1106.10	1062.88	1027.34	997.80
85000	1393.19	1302.67	1231.82	1175.23	1129.31	1091.55	1060.17
90000	1475.15	1379.30	1304.28	1244.36	1195.74	1155.76	1122.53
95000	1557.10	1455.93	1376.74	1313.49	1262.17	1219.96	1184.89
100000	1639.05	1532.56	1449.20	1382.63	1328.60	1284.17	1247.25
105000	1721.00	1609.18	1521.66	1451.76	1395.03	1348.38	1309.62
110000	1802.96	1685.81	1594.12	1520.89	1461.46	1412.59	1371.98
120000	1966.86	1839.07	1739.04	1659.15	1594.32	1541.01	1496.70
130000	2130.77	1992.32	1883.96	1797.41	1727.18	1669.42	1621.43
140000	2294.67	2145.58	2028.88	1935.68	1860.04	1797.84	1746.16
150000	2458.58	2298.83	2173.80	2073.94	1992.89	1926.26	1870.88
175000	2868.34	2681.97	2536.10	2419.60	2325.04	2247.30	2182.69
200000	3278.10	3065.11	2898.40	2765.25	2657.19	2568.35	2494.51
225000	3687.87	3448.25	3260.70	3110.91	2989.34	2889.39	2806.32
250000	4097.63	3831.39	3623.00	3456.56	3321.49	3210.43	3118.13

12¼%

Monthly Payments

necessary to amortize a loan

AMOUNT	15 YEARS	16 YEARS	17 YEARS	18 YEARS	19 YEARS	20 YEARS	21 YEARS
100	1.22	1.19	1.17	1.15	1.13	1.12	1.11
200	2.43	2.38	2.34	2.30	2.27	2.24	2.21
500	6.08	5.95	5.84	5.74	5.66	5.59	5.53
1000	12.16	11.90	11.68	11.49	11.33	11.19	11.06
2000	24.33	23.80	23.36	22.98	22.65	22.37	22.13
5000	60.81	59.51	58.40	57.45	56.63	55.93	55.32
6000	72.98	71.41	70.08	68.94	67.96	67.11	66.38
7000	85.14	83.31	81.75	80.42	79.28	78.30	77.45
8000	97.30	95.21	93.43	91.91	90.61	89.49	88.51
9000	109.47	107.11	105.11	103.40	101.94	100.67	99.58
10000	121.63	119.02	116.79	114.89	113.26	111.86	110.64
15000	182.44	178.52	175.19	172.34	169.89	167.78	165.96
20000	243.26	238.03	233.58	229.79	226.52	223.71	221.28
25000	304.07	297.54	291.98	287.23	283.15	279.64	276.60
30000	364.89	357.05	350.38	344.68	339.79	335.57	331.92
35000	425.70	416.55	408.77	402.12	396.42	391.50	387.24
36000	437.87	428.45	420.45	413.61	407.74	402.68	398.31
37000	450.03	440.36	432.13	425.10	419.07	413.87	409.37
38000	462.19	452.26	443.81	436.59	430.40	425.05	420.44
39000	474.36	464.16	455.49	448.08	441.72	436.24	431.50
40000	486.52	476.06	467.17	459.57	453.05	447.43	442.56
41000	498.68	487.96	478.85	471.06	464.37	458.61	453.63
42000	510.85	499.86	490.53	482.55	475.70	469.80	464.69
43000	523.01	511.76	502.21	494.04	487.03	480.98	475.76
44000	535.17	523.67	513.89	505.53	498.35	492.17	486.82
45000	547.33	535.57	525.57	517.02	509.68	503.35	497.88
46000	559.50	547.47	537.24	528.51	521.00	514.54	508.95
47000	571.66	559.37	548.92	540.00	532.33	525.73	520.01
48000	583.82	571.27	560.60	551.49	543.66	536.91	531.08
49000	595.99	583.17	572.28	562.97	554.98	548.10	542.14
50000	608.15	595.08	583.96	574.46	566.31	559.28	553.21
51000	620.31	606.98	595.64	585.95	577.64	570.47	564.27
52000	632.48	618.88	607.32	597.44	588.96	581.65	575.33
53000	644.64	630.78	619.00	608.93	600.29	592.84	586.40
54000	656.80	642.68	630.68	620.42	611.61	604.02	597.46
55000	668.96	654.58	642.36	631.91	622.94	615.21	608.53
56000	681.13	666.48	654.04	643.40	634.27	626.40	619.59
57000	693.29	678.39	665.72	654.89	645.59	637.58	630.65
58000	705.45	690.29	677.40	666.38	656.92	648.77	641.72
59000	717.62	702.19	689.07	677.87	668.25	659.95	652.78
60000	729.78	714.09	700.75	689.36	679.57	671.14	663.85
65000	790.59	773.60	759.15	746.80	736.20	727.07	719.17
70000	851.41	833.11	817.55	804.25	792.83	783.00	774.49
75000	912.22	892.61	875.94	861.70	849.46	838.92	829.81
80000	973.04	952.12	934.34	919.14	906.10	894.85	885.13
85000	1033.85	1011.63	992.73	976.59	962.73	950.78	940.45
90000	1094.67	1071.14	1051.13	1034.03	1019.36	1006.71	995.77
95000	1155.48	1130.64	1109.53	1091.48	1075.99	1062.64	1051.09
100000	1216.30	1190.15	1167.92	1148.93	1132.62	1118.56	1106.41
105000	1277.11	1249.66	1226.32	1206.37	1189.25	1174.49	1161.73
110000	1337.93	1309.17	1284.71	1263.82	1245.88	1230.42	1217.05
120000	1459.56	1428.18	1401.51	1378.71	1359.14	1342.28	1327.69
130000	1581.19	1547.20	1518.30	1493.61	1472.41	1454.13	1438.33
140000	1702.82	1666.21	1635.09	1608.50	1585.67	1565.99	1548.97
150000	1824.45	1785.23	1751.88	1723.39	1698.93	1677.85	1659.62
175000	2128.52	2082.76	2043.86	2010.62	1982.08	1957.49	1936.22
200000	2432.60	2380.30	2335.85	2297.85	2265.24	2237.13	2212.82
225000	2736.67	2677.84	2627.83	2585.09	2548.39	2516.77	2489.42
250000	3040.75	2975.38	2919.81	2872.32	2831.55	2796.41	2766.03

Monthly Payments 12¼%

necessary to amortize a loan

AMOUNT	22 YEARS	23 YEARS	24 YEARS	25 YEARS	30 YEARS	35 YEARS	40 YEARS
100	1.10	1.09	1.08	1.07	1.05	1.04	1.03
200	2.19	2.17	2.16	2.14	2.10	2.07	2.06
500	5.48	5.43	5.39	5.36	5.24	5.18	5.14
1000	10.96	10.87	10.79	10.72	10.48	10.35	10.29
2000	21.92	21.73	21.57	21.43	20.96	20.71	20.57
5000	54.79	54.34	53.94	53.59	52.39	51.77	51.43
6000	65.75	65.20	64.72	64.30	62.87	62.12	61.72
7000	76.71	76.07	75.51	75.02	73.35	72.48	72.01
8000	87.67	86.94	86.30	85.74	83.83	82.83	82.29
9000	98.63	97.80	97.08	96.46	94.31	93.18	92.58
10000	109.59	108.67	107.87	107.17	104.79	103.54	102.87
15000	164.38	163.01	161.81	160.76	157.18	155.31	154.30
20000	219.17	217.34	215.74	214.35	209.58	207.07	205.74
25000	273.97	271.68	269.68	267.94	261.97	258.84	257.17
30000	328.76	326.01	323.62	321.52	314.37	310.61	308.61
35000	383.55	380.35	377.55	375.11	366.76	362.38	360.04
36000	394.51	391.21	388.34	385.83	377.24	372.73	370.33
37000	405.47	402.08	399.13	396.55	387.72	383.09	380.61
38000	416.43	412.95	409.91	407.26	398.20	393.44	390.90
39000	427.39	423.81	420.70	417.98	408.68	403.79	401.19
40000	438.35	434.68	431.49	428.70	419.16	414.15	411.47
41000	449.31	445.55	442.27	439.41	429.64	424.50	421.76
42000	460.27	456.42	453.06	450.13	440.12	434.86	432.05
43000	471.22	467.28	463.85	460.85	450.60	445.21	442.34
44000	482.18	478.15	474.64	471.57	461.07	455.56	452.62
45000	493.14	489.02	485.42	482.28	471.55	465.92	462.91
46000	504.10	499.88	496.21	493.00	482.03	476.27	473.20
47000	515.06	510.75	507.00	503.72	492.51	486.62	483.48
48000	526.02	521.62	517.78	514.44	502.99	496.98	493.77
49000	536.98	532.48	528.57	525.15	513.47	507.33	504.06
50000	547.93	543.35	539.36	535.87	523.95	517.69	514.34
51000	558.89	554.22	550.15	546.59	534.43	528.04	524.63
52000	569.85	565.09	560.93	557.31	544.91	538.39	534.92
53000	580.81	575.95	571.72	568.02	555.39	548.75	545.20
54000	591.77	586.82	582.51	578.74	565.86	559.10	555.49
55000	602.73	597.69	593.29	589.46	576.34	569.45	565.78
56000	613.69	608.55	604.08	600.18	586.82	579.81	576.06
57000	624.65	619.42	614.87	610.89	597.30	590.16	586.35
58000	635.60	630.29	625.66	621.61	607.78	600.52	596.64
59000	646.56	641.16	636.44	632.33	618.26	610.87	606.92
60000	657.52	652.02	647.23	643.05	628.74	621.22	617.21
65000	712.31	706.36	701.17	696.63	681.13	672.99	668.65
70000	767.11	760.69	755.10	750.22	733.53	724.76	720.08
75000	821.90	815.03	809.04	803.81	785.92	776.53	771.51
80000	876.70	869.36	862.97	857.40	838.32	828.30	822.95
85000	931.49	923.70	916.91	910.98	890.71	880.07	874.38
90000	986.28	978.03	970.85	964.57	943.11	931.83	925.82
95000	1041.08	1032.37	1024.78	1018.16	995.50	983.60	977.25
100000	1095.87	1086.70	1078.72	1071.74	1047.90	1035.37	1028.69
105000	1150.66	1141.04	1132.65	1125.33	1100.29	1087.14	1080.12
110000	1205.46	1195.37	1186.59	1178.92	1152.69	1138.91	1131.55
120000	1315.04	1304.04	1294.46	1286.09	1257.48	1242.45	1234.42
130000	1424.63	1412.71	1402.33	1393.27	1362.27	1345.98	1337.29
140000	1534.22	1521.39	1510.20	1500.44	1467.06	1449.52	1440.16
150000	1643.80	1630.06	1618.08	1607.62	1571.84	1553.06	1543.03
175000	1917.77	1901.73	1887.75	1875.55	1833.82	1811.90	1800.20
200000	2191.74	2173.41	2157.43	2143.49	2095.79	2070.74	2057.37
225000	2465.71	2445.08	2427.11	2411.42	2357.77	2329.59	2314.54
250000	2739.67	2716.76	2696.79	2679.36	2619.74	2588.43	2571.72

12½% Monthly Payments

necessary to amortize a loan

AMOUNT	1 YEAR	2 YEARS	3 YEARS	4 YEARS	5 YEARS	6 YEARS	7 YEARS
100	8.91	4.73	3.35	2.66	2.25	1.98	1.79
200	17.82	9.46	6.69	5.32	4.50	3.96	3.58
500	44.54	23.65	16.73	13.29	11.25	9.91	8.96
1000	89.08	47.31	33.45	26.58	22.50	19.81	17.92
2000	178.17	94.61	66.91	53.16	45.00	39.62	35.84
5000	445.41	236.54	167.27	132.90	112.49	99.06	89.61
6000	534.50	283.84	200.72	159.48	134.99	118.87	107.53
7000	623.58	331.15	234.18	186.06	157.49	138.68	125.45
8000	712.66	378.46	267.63	212.64	179.98	158.49	143.37
9000	801.75	425.77	301.08	239.22	202.48	178.30	161.29
10000	890.83	473.07	334.54	265.80	224.98	198.11	179.21
15000	1336.24	709.61	501.80	398.70	337.47	297.17	268.82
20000	1781.66	946.15	669.07	531.60	449.96	396.22	358.42
25000	2227.07	1182.68	836.34	664.50	562.45	495.28	448.03
30000	2672.49	1419.22	1003.61	797.40	674.94	594.34	537.64
35000	3117.90	1655.76	1170.88	930.30	787.43	693.39	627.24
36000	3206.98	1703.06	1204.33	956.88	809.93	713.20	645.16
37000	3296.07	1750.37	1237.78	983.46	832.42	733.01	663.09
38000	3385.15	1797.68	1271.24	1010.04	854.92	752.82	681.01
39000	3474.23	1844.99	1304.69	1036.62	877.42	772.64	698.93
40000	3563.31	1892.29	1338.15	1063.20	899.92	792.45	716.85
41000	3652.40	1939.60	1371.60	1089.78	922.42	812.26	734.77
42000	3741.48	1986.91	1405.05	1116.36	944.91	832.07	752.69
43000	3830.56	2034.21	1438.51	1142.94	967.41	851.88	770.61
44000	3919.65	2081.52	1471.96	1169.52	989.91	871.69	788.53
45000	4008.73	2128.83	1505.41	1196.10	1012.41	891.50	806.46
46000	4097.81	2176.14	1538.87	1222.68	1034.91	911.31	824.38
47000	4186.89	2223.44	1572.32	1249.26	1057.40	931.13	842.30
48000	4275.98	2270.75	1605.77	1275.84	1079.90	950.94	860.22
49000	4365.06	2318.06	1639.23	1302.42	1102.40	970.75	878.14
50000	4454.14	2365.37	1672.68	1329.00	1124.90	990.56	896.06
51000	4543.23	2412.67	1706.13	1355.58	1147.39	1010.37	913.98
52000	4632.31	2459.98	1739.59	1382.16	1169.89	1030.18	931.90
53000	4721.39	2507.29	1773.04	1408.74	1192.39	1049.99	949.83
54000	4810.47	2554.59	1806.50	1435.32	1214.89	1069.80	967.75
55000	4899.56	2601.90	1839.95	1461.90	1237.39	1089.61	985.67
56000	4988.64	2649.21	1873.40	1488.48	1259.88	1109.43	1003.59
57000	5077.72	2696.52	1906.86	1515.06	1282.38	1129.24	1021.51
58000	5166.81	2743.82	1940.31	1541.64	1304.88	1149.05	1039.43
59000	5255.89	2791.13	1973.76	1568.22	1327.38	1168.86	1057.35
60000	5344.97	2838.44	2007.22	1594.80	1349.88	1188.67	1075.27
65000	5790.39	3074.98	2174.49	1727.70	1462.37	1287.73	1164.88
70000	6235.80	3311.51	2341.75	1860.60	1574.86	1386.78	1254.49
75000	6681.21	3548.05	2509.02	1993.50	1687.35	1485.84	1344.09
80000	7126.63	3784.58	2676.29	2126.40	1799.84	1584.89	1433.70
85000	7572.04	4021.12	2843.56	2259.30	1912.32	1683.95	1523.31
90000	8017.46	4257.66	3010.83	2392.20	2024.81	1783.01	1612.91
95000	8462.87	4494.19	3178.09	2525.10	2137.30	1882.06	1702.52
100000	8908.29	4730.73	3345.36	2658.00	2249.79	1981.12	1792.12
105000	9353.70	4967.27	3512.63	2790.90	2362.28	2080.17	1881.73
110000	9799.11	5203.80	3679.90	2923.80	2474.77	2179.23	1971.34
120000	10689.94	5676.88	4014.44	3189.60	2699.75	2377.34	2150.55
130000	11580.77	6149.95	4348.97	3455.40	2924.73	2575.45	2329.76
140000	12471.60	6623.02	4683.51	3721.20	3149.71	2773.57	2508.97
150000	13362.43	7096.10	5018.04	3987.00	3374.69	2971.68	2688.19
175000	15589.50	8278.78	5854.38	4651.50	3937.14	3466.96	3136.22
200000	17816.57	9461.46	6690.73	5316.00	4499.59	3962.24	3584.25
225000	20043.64	10644.14	7527.07	5980.50	5062.04	4457.52	4032.28
250000	22270.72	11826.83	8363.41	6645.00	5624.48	4952.79	4480.31

Monthly Payments 12½%

necessary to amortize a loan

AMOUNT	8 YEARS	9 YEARS	10 YEARS	11 YEARS	12 YEARS	13 YEARS	14 YEARS
100	1.65	1.55	1.46	1.40	1.34	1.30	1.26
200	3.31	3.09	2.93	2.80	2.69	2.60	2.53
500	8.26	7.73	7.32	6.99	6.72	6.50	6.32
1000	16.53	15.47	14.64	13.98	13.44	13.00	12.63
2000	33.06	30.94	29.28	27.95	26.88	26.00	25.26
5000	82.64	77.34	73.19	69.88	67.19	64.99	63.16
6000	99.17	92.81	87.83	83.85	80.63	77.99	75.79
7000	115.70	108.27	102.46	97.83	94.07	90.98	88.42
8000	132.23	123.74	117.10	111.80	107.51	103.98	101.05
9000	148.76	139.21	131.74	125.78	120.95	116.98	113.69
10000	165.29	154.68	146.38	139.75	134.39	129.98	126.32
15000	247.93	232.01	219.56	209.63	201.58	194.96	189.48
20000	330.58	309.35	292.75	279.51	268.77	259.95	252.63
25000	413.22	386.69	365.94	349.39	335.96	324.94	315.79
30000	495.86	464.03	439.13	419.26	403.16	389.93	378.95
35000	578.51	541.36	512.32	489.14	470.35	454.92	442.11
36000	595.04	556.83	526.95	503.12	483.79	467.92	454.74
37000	611.57	572.30	541.59	517.09	497.23	480.91	467.37
38000	628.09	587.77	556.23	531.07	510.67	493.91	480.00
39000	644.62	603.23	570.87	545.04	524.10	506.91	492.64
40000	661.15	618.70	585.50	559.02	537.54	519.91	505.27
41000	677.68	634.17	600.14	572.99	550.98	532.90	517.90
42000	694.21	649.64	614.78	586.97	564.42	545.90	530.53
43000	710.74	665.10	629.42	600.94	577.86	558.90	543.16
44000	727.27	680.57	644.06	614.92	591.30	571.90	555.79
45000	743.80	696.04	658.69	628.89	604.74	584.89	568.43
46000	760.33	711.51	673.33	642.87	618.17	597.89	581.06
47000	776.85	726.97	687.97	656.85	631.61	610.89	593.69
48000	793.38	742.44	702.61	670.82	645.05	623.89	606.32
49000	809.91	757.91	717.24	684.80	658.49	636.89	618.95
50000	826.44	773.38	731.88	698.77	671.93	649.88	631.58
51000	842.97	788.85	746.52	712.75	685.37	662.88	644.22
52000	859.50	804.31	761.16	726.72	698.81	675.88	656.85
53000	876.03	819.78	775.79	740.70	712.24	688.88	669.48
54000	892.56	835.25	790.43	754.67	725.68	701.87	682.11
55000	909.08	850.72	805.07	768.65	739.12	714.87	694.74
56000	925.61	866.18	819.71	782.62	752.56	727.87	707.37
57000	942.14	881.65	834.34	796.60	766.00	740.87	720.01
58000	958.67	897.12	848.98	810.57	779.44	753.86	732.64
59000	975.20	912.59	863.62	824.55	792.88	766.86	745.27
60000	991.73	928.05	878.26	838.53	806.31	779.86	757.90
65000	1074.37	1005.39	951.45	908.40	873.51	844.85	821.06
70000	1157.02	1082.73	1024.63	978.28	940.70	909.84	884.22
75000	1239.66	1160.07	1097.82	1048.16	1007.89	974.82	947.38
80000	1322.30	1237.40	1171.01	1118.03	1075.09	1039.81	1010.53
85000	1404.95	1314.74	1244.20	1187.91	1142.28	1104.80	1073.69
90000	1487.50	1392.08	1317.39	1257.79	1209.47	1169.79	1136.85
95000	1570.24	1469.42	1390.57	1327.67	1276.66	1234.78	1200.01
100000	1652.88	1546.76	1463.76	1397.54	1343.86	1299.77	1263.17
105000	1735.52	1624.09	1536.95	1467.42	1411.05	1364.75	1326.33
110000	1818.17	1701.43	1610.14	1537.30	1478.24	1429.74	1389.49
120000	1983.46	1856.11	1756.51	1677.05	1612.63	1559.72	1515.80
130000	2148.75	2010.78	1902.89	1816.81	1747.01	1689.70	1642.12
140000	2314.03	2165.46	2049.27	1956.56	1881.40	1819.67	1768.44
150000	2479.32	2320.13	2195.64	2096.31	2015.79	1949.65	1894.75
175000	2892.54	2706.82	2561.58	2445.70	2351.75	2274.59	2210.54
200000	3305.76	3093.51	2927.52	2795.09	2687.71	2599.53	2526.34
225000	3718.98	3480.20	3293.46	3144.47	3023.68	2924.47	2842.13
250000	4132.20	3866.89	3659.40	3493.86	3359.64	3249.42	3157.92

12½% Monthly Payments

necessary to amortize a loan

AMOUNT	15 YEARS	16 YEARS	17 YEARS	18 YEARS	19 YEARS	20 YEARS	21 YEARS
100	1.23	1.21	1.18	1.17	1.15	1.14	1.12
200	2.47	2.41	2.37	2.33	2.30	2.27	2.25
500	6.16	6.03	5.92	5.83	5.75	5.68	5.62
1000	12.33	12.07	11.85	11.66	11.50	11.36	11.24
2000	24.65	24.13	23.69	23.32	23.00	22.72	22.48
5000	61.63	60.33	59.24	58.30	57.50	56.81	56.21
6000	73.95	72.40	71.08	69.96	69.00	68.17	67.45
7000	86.28	84.47	82.93	81.62	80.50	79.53	78.70
8000	98.60	96.53	94.78	93.28	92.00	90.89	89.94
9000	110.93	108.60	106.63	104.94	103.50	102.25	101.18
10000	123.25	120.67	118.47	116.60	115.00	113.61	112.42
15000	184.88	181.00	177.71	174.90	172.49	170.42	168.63
20000	246.50	241.33	236.95	233.20	229.99	227.23	224.84
25000	308.13	301.67	296.18	291.50	287.49	284.04	281.05
30000	369.76	362.00	355.42	349.80	344.99	340.84	337.27
35000	431.38	422.33	414.65	408.10	402.48	397.65	393.48
36000	443.71	434.40	426.50	419.76	413.98	409.01	404.72
37000	456.03	446.47	438.35	431.42	425.48	420.37	415.96
38000	468.36	458.53	450.20	443.08	436.98	431.73	427.20
39000	480.68	470.60	462.04	454.74	448.48	443.09	438.45
40000	493.01	482.67	473.89	466.40	459.98	454.46	449.69
41000	505.33	494.73	485.74	478.06	471.48	465.82	460.93
42000	517.66	506.80	497.58	489.72	482.98	477.18	472.17
43000	529.98	518.87	509.43	501.38	494.48	488.54	483.41
44000	542.31	530.93	521.28	513.04	505.98	499.90	494.66
45000	554.63	543.00	533.13	524.70	517.48	511.26	505.90
46000	566.96	555.07	544.97	536.36	528.98	522.62	517.14
47000	579.29	567.13	556.82	548.02	540.48	533.99	528.38
48000	591.61	579.20	568.67	559.68	551.98	545.35	539.62
49000	603.94	591.27	580.52	571.34	563.48	556.71	550.87
50000	616.26	603.33	592.36	583.00	574.98	568.07	562.11
51000	628.59	615.40	604.21	594.66	586.47	579.43	573.35
52000	640.91	627.47	616.06	606.32	597.97	590.79	584.59
53000	653.24	639.53	627.90	617.98	609.47	602.15	595.84
54000	665.56	651.60	639.75	629.64	620.97	613.52	607.08
55000	677.89	663.67	651.60	641.30	632.47	624.88	618.32
56000	690.21	675.74	663.45	652.96	643.97	636.24	629.56
57000	702.54	687.80	675.29	664.62	655.47	647.60	640.80
58000	714.86	699.87	687.14	676.28	666.97	658.96	652.05
59000	727.19	711.94	698.99	687.94	678.47	670.32	663.29
60000	739.51	724.00	710.84	699.60	689.97	681.68	674.53
65000	801.14	784.34	770.07	757.90	747.47	738.49	730.74
70000	862.77	844.67	829.31	816.20	804.97	795.30	786.95
75000	924.39	905.00	888.54	874.50	862.46	852.11	843.16
80000	986.02	965.34	947.78	932.80	919.96	908.91	899.37
85000	1047.64	1025.67	1007.02	991.10	977.46	965.72	955.59
90000	1109.27	1086.00	1066.25	1049.40	1034.96	1022.53	1011.80
95000	1170.90	1146.34	1125.49	1107.70	1092.45	1079.33	1068.01
100000	1232.52	1206.67	1184.73	1166.00	1149.95	1136.14	1124.22
105000	1294.15	1267.00	1243.96	1224.30	1207.45	1192.95	1180.43
110000	1355.77	1327.34	1303.20	1282.60	1264.95	1249.75	1236.64
120000	1479.03	1448.00	1421.67	1399.20	1379.94	1363.37	1349.06
130000	1602.28	1568.67	1540.14	1515.80	1494.94	1476.98	1461.48
140000	1725.53	1689.34	1658.62	1632.40	1609.93	1590.60	1573.91
150000	1848.78	1810.00	1777.09	1749.00	1724.93	1704.21	1686.33
175000	2156.91	2111.67	2073.27	2040.50	2012.41	1988.25	1967.38
200000	2465.04	2413.34	2369.45	2332.00	2299.90	2272.28	2248.44
225000	2773.17	2715.01	2665.63	2623.50	2587.39	2556.32	2529.49
250000	3081.31	3016.67	2961.81	2915.00	2874.88	2840.35	2810.55

Monthly Payments 12½%

necessary to amortize a loan

AMOUNT	22 YEARS	23 YEARS	24 YEARS	25 YEARS	30 YEARS	35 YEARS	40 YEARS
100	1.11	1.10	1.10	1.09	1.07	1.06	1.05
200	2.23	2.21	2.19	2.18	2.13	2.11	2.10
500	5.57	5.52	5.49	5.45	5.34	5.28	5.24
1000	11.14	11.05	10.97	10.90	10.67	10.55	10.49
2000	22.28	22.10	21.94	21.81	21.35	21.11	20.98
5000	55.69	55.25	54.86	54.52	53.36	52.76	52.45
6000	66.83	66.30	65.83	65.42	64.04	63.32	62.94
7000	77.97	77.35	76.80	76.32	74.71	73.87	73.42
8000	89.11	88.39	87.77	87.23	85.38	84.42	83.91
9000	100.25	99.44	98.74	98.13	96.05	94.97	94.40
10000	111.39	110.49	109.71	109.04	106.73	105.53	104.89
15000	167.08	165.74	164.57	163.55	160.09	158.29	157.34
20000	222.78	220.99	219.43	218.07	213.45	211.05	209.78
25000	278.47	276.23	274.29	272.59	266.81	263.81	262.23
30000	334.17	331.48	329.14	327.11	320.18	316.58	314.68
35000	389.86	386.73	384.00	381.62	373.54	369.34	367.12
36000	401.00	397.78	394.97	392.53	384.21	379.89	377.61
37000	412.14	408.83	405.94	403.43	394.89	390.44	388.10
38000	423.28	419.88	416.91	414.33	405.56	401.00	398.59
39000	434.42	430.93	427.89	425.24	416.23	411.55	409.08
40000	445.56	441.97	438.86	436.14	426.90	422.10	419.57
41000	456.70	453.02	449.83	447.05	437.58	432.65	430.06
42000	467.84	464.07	460.80	457.95	448.25	443.21	440.55
43000	478.98	475.12	471.77	468.85	458.92	453.76	451.04
44000	490.11	486.17	482.74	479.76	469.59	464.31	461.52
45000	501.25	497.22	493.72	490.66	480.27	474.86	472.01
46000	512.39	508.27	504.69	501.56	490.94	485.42	482.50
47000	523.53	519.32	515.66	512.47	501.61	495.97	492.99
48000	534.67	530.37	526.63	523.37	512.28	506.52	503.48
49000	545.81	541.42	537.60	534.27	522.96	517.07	513.97
50000	556.95	552.47	548.57	545.18	533.63	527.63	524.46
51000	568.09	563.52	559.54	556.08	544.30	538.18	534.95
52000	579.23	574.57	570.52	566.98	554.97	548.73	545.44
53000	590.36	585.62	581.49	577.89	565.65	559.28	555.93
54000	601.50	596.67	592.46	588.79	576.32	569.84	566.42
55000	612.64	607.72	603.43	599.69	586.99	580.39	576.91
56000	623.78	618.76	614.40	610.60	597.66	590.94	587.39
57000	634.92	629.81	625.37	621.50	608.34	601.50	597.88
58000	646.06	640.86	636.34	632.41	619.01	612.05	608.37
59000	657.20	651.91	647.32	643.31	629.68	622.60	618.86
60000	668.34	662.96	658.29	654.21	640.35	633.15	629.35
65000	724.03	718.21	713.14	708.73	693.72	685.92	681.80
70000	779.73	773.46	768.00	763.25	747.08	738.68	734.24
75000	835.42	828.70	822.86	817.77	800.44	791.44	786.69
80000	891.12	883.95	877.72	872.28	853.81	844.20	839.14
85000	946.81	939.20	932.57	926.80	907.17	896.97	891.58
90000	1002.51	994.44	987.43	981.32	960.53	949.73	944.03
95000	1058.20	1049.69	1042.29	1035.84	1013.89	1002.49	996.47
100000	1113.90	1104.94	1097.14	1090.35	1067.26	1055.25	1048.92
105000	1169.59	1160.18	1152.00	1144.87	1120.62	1108.02	1101.37
110000	1225.29	1215.43	1206.86	1199.39	1173.98	1160.78	1153.81
120000	1336.67	1325.92	1316.57	1308.42	1280.71	1266.31	1258.70
130000	1448.06	1436.42	1426.29	1417.46	1387.44	1371.83	1363.60
140000	1559.45	1546.91	1536.00	1526.50	1494.16	1477.36	1468.49
150000	1670.84	1657.41	1645.72	1635.53	1600.89	1582.88	1573.38
175000	1949.32	1933.64	1920.00	1908.12	1867.70	1846.70	1835.61
200000	2227.79	2209.87	2194.29	2180.71	2134.52	2110.51	2097.84
225000	2506.27	2486.11	2468.58	2453.30	2401.33	2374.32	2360.07
250000	2784.74	2762.34	2742.86	2725.89	2668.14	2638.14	2622.30

12¾%

Monthly Payments

necessary to amortize a loan

AMOUNT	1 YEAR	2 YEARS	3 YEARS	4 YEARS	5 YEARS	6 YEARS	7 YEARS
100	8.92	4.74	3.36	2.67	2.26	1.99	1.81
200	17.84	9.48	6.71	5.34	4.53	3.99	3.61
500	44.60	23.71	16.79	13.35	11.31	9.97	9.03
1000	89.20	47.42	33.57	26.70	22.63	19.94	18.06
2000	178.40	94.85	67.15	53.41	45.25	39.88	36.11
5000	446.00	237.12	167.87	133.52	113.13	99.71	90.28
6000	535.20	284.55	201.44	160.22	135.75	119.65	108.34
7000	624.40	331.97	235.02	186.93	158.38	139.60	126.39
8000	713.60	379.40	268.59	213.63	181.00	159.54	144.45
9000	802.80	426.82	302.16	240.33	203.63	179.48	162.51
10000	892.00	474.24	335.74	267.04	226.25	199.42	180.56
15000	1338.00	711.37	503.60	400.55	339.38	299.14	270.84
20000	1784.00	948.49	671.47	534.07	452.51	398.85	361.13
25000	2230.00	1185.61	839.34	667.59	565.63	498.56	451.41
30000	2676.00	1422.73	1007.21	801.11	678.76	598.27	541.69
35000	3122.00	1659.86	1175.08	934.63	791.89	697.98	631.97
36000	3211.20	1707.28	1208.65	961.33	814.51	717.93	650.03
37000	3300.40	1754.71	1242.23	988.03	837.14	737.87	668.08
38000	3389.60	1802.13	1275.80	1014.74	859.76	757.81	686.14
39000	3478.80	1849.55	1309.37	1041.44	882.39	777.75	704.20
40000	3568.00	1896.98	1342.95	1068.14	905.01	797.70	722.25
41000	3657.20	1944.40	1376.52	1094.85	927.64	817.64	740.31
42000	3746.40	1991.83	1410.09	1121.55	950.26	837.58	758.37
43000	3835.60	2039.25	1443.67	1148.25	972.89	857.52	776.42
44000	3924.80	2086.68	1477.24	1174.96	995.51	877.47	794.48
45000	4014.00	2134.10	1510.81	1201.66	1018.14	897.41	812.53
46000	4103.20	2181.53	1544.39	1228.36	1040.76	917.35	830.59
47000	4192.40	2228.95	1577.96	1255.07	1063.39	937.29	848.65
48000	4281.60	2276.38	1611.54	1281.77	1086.01	957.24	866.70
49000	4370.80	2323.80	1645.11	1308.48	1108.64	977.18	884.76
50000	4460.00	2371.22	1678.68	1335.18	1131.27	997.12	902.82
51000	4549.20	2418.65	1712.26	1361.88	1153.89	1017.06	920.87
52000	4638.40	2466.07	1745.83	1388.59	1176.52	1037.00	938.93
53000	4727.60	2513.50	1779.40	1415.29	1199.14	1056.95	956.99
54000	4816.80	2560.92	1812.98	1441.99	1221.77	1076.89	975.04
55000	4906.00	2608.35	1846.55	1468.70	1244.39	1096.83	993.10
56000	4995.20	2655.77	1880.13	1495.40	1267.02	1116.77	1011.15
57000	5084.40	2703.20	1913.70	1522.10	1289.64	1136.72	1029.21
58000	5173.60	2750.62	1947.27	1548.81	1312.27	1156.66	1047.27
59000	5262.80	2798.04	1980.85	1575.51	1334.89	1176.60	1065.32
60000	5352.00	2845.47	2014.42	1602.21	1357.52	1196.54	1083.38
65000	5798.00	3082.59	2182.29	1735.73	1470.64	1296.26	1173.66
70000	6244.00	3319.71	2350.16	1869.25	1583.77	1395.97	1263.94
75000	6690.00	3556.84	2518.02	2002.77	1696.90	1495.68	1354.22
80000	7136.00	3793.96	2685.89	2136.29	1810.02	1595.39	1444.51
85000	7582.00	4031.08	2853.76	2269.80	1923.15	1695.10	1534.79
90000	8028.00	4268.20	3021.63	2403.32	2036.28	1794.82	1625.07
95000	8474.00	4505.33	3189.50	2536.84	2149.40	1894.53	1715.35
100000	8920.00	4742.45	3357.37	2670.36	2262.53	1994.24	1805.63
105000	9366.00	4979.57	3525.23	2803.88	2375.66	2093.95	1895.91
110000	9812.00	5216.69	3693.10	2937.39	2488.78	2193.66	1986.20
120000	10704.00	5690.94	4028.84	3204.43	2715.04	2393.09	2166.76
130000	11596.00	6165.18	4364.58	3471.47	2941.29	2592.51	2347.32
140000	12488.00	6639.43	4700.31	3738.50	3167.54	2791.94	2527.89
150000	13380.00	7113.67	5036.05	4005.54	3393.80	2991.36	2708.45
175000	15610.00	8299.28	5875.39	4673.13	3959.43	3489.92	3159.86
200000	17840.01	9484.90	6714.73	5340.72	4525.06	3988.48	3611.26
225000	20070.01	10670.51	7554.07	6008.31	5090.69	4487.04	4062.67
250000	22300.01	11856.12	8393.42	6675.90	5656.33	4985.60	4514.08

Monthly Payments 12¾%

necessary to amortize a loan

AMOUNT	8 YEARS	9 YEARS	10 YEARS	11 YEARS	12 YEARS	13 YEARS	14 YEARS
100	1.67	1.56	1.48	1.41	1.36	1.32	1.28
200	3.33	3.12	2.96	2.83	2.72	2.63	2.56
500	8.33	7.81	7.39	7.06	6.80	6.58	6.40
1000	16.67	15.61	14.78	14.13	13.59	13.15	12.79
2000	33.34	31.22	29.57	28.25	27.18	26.31	25.58
5000	83.34	78.05	73.92	70.63	67.96	65.77	63.96
6000	100.01	93.66	88.70	84.75	81.55	78.93	76.75
7000	116.67	109.27	103.49	98.88	95.14	92.08	89.54
8000	133.34	124.88	118.27	113.00	108.74	105.24	102.33
9000	150.01	140.49	133.06	127.13	122.33	118.39	115.13
10000	166.68	156.10	147.84	141.25	135.92	131.54	127.92
15000	250.02	234.15	221.76	211.88	203.88	197.32	191.88
20000	333.35	312.20	295.68	282.51	271.84	263.09	255.83
25000	416.69	390.26	369.60	353.13	339.80	328.86	319.79
30000	500.03	468.31	443.52	423.76	407.76	394.63	383.75
35000	583.37	546.36	517.44	494.39	475.72	460.41	447.71
36000	600.04	561.97	532.22	508.51	489.31	473.56	460.50
37000	616.71	577.58	547.01	522.64	502.90	486.71	473.29
38000	633.37	593.19	561.79	536.76	516.50	499.87	486.09
39000	650.04	608.80	576.58	550.89	530.09	513.02	498.88
40000	666.71	624.41	591.36	565.02	543.68	526.18	511.67
41000	683.38	640.02	606.14	579.14	557.27	539.33	524.46
42000	700.04	655.63	620.93	593.27	570.86	552.49	537.25
43000	716.71	671.24	635.71	607.39	584.46	565.64	550.04
44000	733.38	686.85	650.50	621.52	598.05	578.80	562.84
45000	750.05	702.46	665.28	635.64	611.64	591.95	575.63
46000	766.72	718.07	680.06	649.77	625.23	605.10	588.42
47000	783.38	733.68	694.85	663.89	638.82	618.26	601.21
48000	800.05	749.29	709.63	678.02	652.42	631.41	614.00
49000	816.72	764.90	724.42	692.14	666.01	644.57	626.79
50000	833.39	780.51	739.20	706.27	679.60	657.72	639.59
51000	850.05	796.12	753.98	720.39	693.19	670.88	652.38
52000	866.72	811.73	768.77	734.52	706.78	684.03	665.17
53000	883.39	827.34	783.55	748.65	720.38	697.19	677.96
54000	900.06	842.95	798.33	762.77	733.97	710.34	690.75
55000	916.72	858.56	813.12	776.90	747.56	723.50	703.54
56000	933.39	874.17	827.90	791.02	761.15	736.65	716.34
57000	950.06	889.78	842.69	805.15	774.74	749.80	729.13
58000	966.73	905.39	857.47	819.27	788.34	762.96	741.92
59000	983.40	921.00	872.28	833.40	801.93	776.11	754.71
60000	1000.06	936.61	887.04	847.52	815.52	789.27	767.50
65000	1083.40	1014.67	960.96	918.15	883.48	855.04	831.46
70000	1166.74	1092.72	1034.88	988.78	951.44	920.81	895.42
75000	1250.08	1170.77	1108.80	1059.40	1019.40	986.58	959.38
80000	1333.42	1248.82	1182.72	1130.03	1087.36	1052.36	1023.34
85000	1416.76	1326.87	1256.64	1200.66	1155.32	1118.13	1087.30
90000	1500.10	1404.92	1330.56	1271.28	1223.28	1183.90	1151.25
95000	1583.43	1482.97	1404.48	1341.91	1291.24	1249.67	1215.21
100000	1666.77	1561.02	1478.40	1412.54	1359.20	1315.45	1279.17
105000	1750.11	1639.07	1552.32	1483.16	1427.16	1381.22	1343.13
110000	1833.45	1717.13	1626.24	1553.79	1495.12	1446.99	1407.09
120000	2000.13	1873.23	1774.08	1695.05	1631.04	1578.53	1535.01
130000	2166.80	2029.33	1921.92	1836.30	1766.96	1710.08	1662.92
140000	2333.48	2185.43	2069.76	1977.55	1902.88	1841.62	1790.84
150000	2500.16	2341.53	2217.60	2118.81	2038.80	1973.17	1918.76
175000	2916.85	2731.79	2587.20	2471.94	2378.60	2302.03	2238.55
200000	3333.54	3122.05	2956.80	2825.08	2718.40	2630.89	2558.34
225000	3750.24	3512.30	3326.40	3178.21	3058.20	2959.75	2878.14
250000	4166.93	3902.56	3696.00	3531.35	3398.00	3288.61	3197.93

12¾% Monthly Payments
necessary to amortize a loan

AMOUNT	15 YEARS	16 YEARS	17 YEARS	18 YEARS	19 YEARS	20 YEARS	21 YEARS
100	1.25	1.22	1.20	1.18	1.17	1.15	1.14
200	2.50	2.45	2.40	2.37	2.33	2.31	2.28
500	6.24	6.12	6.01	5.92	5.84	5.77	5.71
1000	12.49	12.23	12.02	11.83	11.67	11.54	11.42
2000	24.98	24.47	24.03	23.66	23.35	23.08	22.84
5000	62.44	61.16	60.08	59.16	58.37	57.69	57.11
6000	74.93	73.40	72.10	70.99	70.04	69.23	68.53
7000	87.42	85.63	84.11	82.82	81.72	80.77	79.95
8000	99.91	97.86	96.13	94.65	93.39	92.30	91.37
9000	112.40	110.10	108.15	106.49	105.06	103.84	102.79
10000	124.88	122.33	120.16	118.32	116.74	115.38	114.21
15000	187.33	183.49	180.24	177.48	175.11	173.07	171.32
20000	249.77	244.66	240.32	236.63	233.48	230.76	228.42
25000	312.21	305.82	300.41	295.79	291.84	288.45	285.53
30000	374.65	366.98	360.49	354.95	350.21	346.14	342.64
35000	437.09	428.15	420.57	414.11	408.58	403.83	399.74
36000	449.58	440.38	432.58	425.94	420.26	415.37	411.16
37000	462.07	452.61	444.60	437.77	431.93	426.91	422.58
38000	474.56	464.85	456.62	449.60	443.60	438.45	434.01
39000	487.05	477.08	468.63	461.44	455.28	449.99	445.43
40000	499.53	489.31	480.65	473.27	466.95	461.52	456.85
41000	512.02	501.55	492.67	485.10	478.62	473.06	468.27
42000	524.51	513.78	504.68	496.93	490.30	484.60	479.69
43000	537.00	526.01	516.70	508.76	501.97	496.14	491.11
44000	549.49	538.24	528.71	520.59	513.65	507.68	502.53
45000	561.98	550.48	540.73	532.43	525.32	519.22	513.95
46000	574.47	562.71	552.75	544.26	536.99	530.75	525.38
47000	586.95	574.94	564.76	556.09	548.67	542.29	536.80
48000	599.44	587.18	576.78	567.92	560.34	553.83	548.22
49000	611.93	599.41	588.80	579.75	572.02	565.37	559.64
50000	624.42	611.64	600.81	591.58	583.69	576.91	571.06
51000	636.91	623.87	612.83	603.42	595.36	588.44	582.48
52000	649.40	636.11	624.84	615.25	607.04	599.98	593.90
53000	661.88	648.34	636.86	627.08	618.71	611.52	605.32
54000	674.37	660.57	648.88	638.91	630.38	623.06	616.74
55000	686.86	672.81	660.89	650.74	642.06	634.60	628.17
56000	699.35	685.04	672.91	662.58	653.73	646.13	639.59
57000	711.84	697.27	684.93	674.41	665.41	657.67	651.01
58000	724.33	709.50	696.94	686.24	677.08	669.21	662.43
59000	736.81	721.74	708.96	698.07	688.75	680.75	673.85
60000	749.30	733.97	720.97	709.90	700.43	692.29	685.27
65000	811.74	795.13	781.06	769.06	758.80	749.98	742.38
70000	874.19	856.30	841.14	828.22	817.16	807.67	799.48
75000	936.63	917.46	901.22	887.38	875.53	865.36	856.59
80000	999.07	978.63	961.30	946.54	933.90	923.05	913.70
85000	1061.51	1039.79	1021.38	1005.69	992.27	980.74	970.80
90000	1123.95	1100.95	1081.46	1064.85	1050.64	1038.43	1027.91
95000	1186.40	1162.12	1141.54	1124.01	1109.01	1096.12	1085.01
100000	1248.84	1223.28	1201.62	1183.17	1167.38	1153.81	1142.12
105000	1311.28	1284.45	1261.70	1242.33	1225.75	1211.50	1199.23
110000	1373.72	1345.61	1321.79	1301.49	1284.12	1269.19	1256.33
120000	1498.60	1467.94	1441.95	1419.80	1400.85	1384.57	1370.54
130000	1623.49	1590.27	1562.11	1538.12	1517.59	1499.96	1484.76
140000	1748.37	1712.60	1682.27	1656.44	1634.33	1615.34	1598.97
150000	1873.26	1834.92	1802.44	1774.75	1751.07	1730.72	1713.18
175000	2185.46	2140.74	2102.84	2070.55	2042.91	2019.17	1998.71
200000	2497.67	2446.57	2403.25	2366.34	2334.76	2307.62	2284.24
225000	2809.88	2752.39	2703.65	2662.13	2626.60	2596.08	2569.77
250000	3122.09	3058.21	3004.06	2957.92	2918.44	2884.53	2855.30

Monthly Payments 12¾%

necessary to amortize a loan

AMOUNT	22 YEARS	23 YEARS	24 YEARS	25 YEARS	30 YEARS	35 YEARS	40 YEARS
100	1.13	1.12	1.12	1.11	1.09	1.08	1.07
200	2.26	2.25	2.23	2.22	2.17	2.15	2.14
500	5.66	5.62	5.58	5.55	5.43	5.38	5.35
1000	11.32	11.23	11.16	11.09	10.87	10.75	10.69
2000	22.64	22.47	22.31	22.18	21.73	21.50	21.38
5000	56.60	56.16	55.78	55.45	54.33	53.76	53.46
6000	67.92	67.40	66.94	66.54	65.20	64.51	64.15
7000	79.24	78.63	78.10	77.63	76.07	75.26	74.84
8000	90.56	89.86	89.25	88.72	86.94	86.02	85.54
9000	101.88	101.09	100.41	99.81	97.80	96.77	96.23
10000	113.20	112.33	111.57	110.91	108.67	107.52	106.92
15000	169.80	168.49	167.35	166.36	163.00	161.28	160.38
20000	226.40	224.65	223.13	221.81	217.34	215.04	213.84
25000	283.00	280.82	278.92	277.26	271.67	268.80	267.30
30000	339.60	336.98	334.70	332.72	326.01	322.56	320.76
35000	396.21	393.14	390.48	388.17	380.34	376.32	374.22
36000	407.53	404.37	401.64	399.26	391.21	387.07	384.91
37000	418.85	415.61	412.79	410.35	402.08	397.82	395.60
38000	430.17	426.84	423.95	421.44	412.94	408.57	406.29
39000	441.49	438.07	435.11	432.53	423.81	419.33	416.99
40000	452.81	449.30	446.26	443.62	434.68	430.08	427.68
41000	464.13	460.54	457.42	454.71	445.54	440.83	438.37
42000	475.45	471.77	468.58	465.80	456.41	451.58	449.06
43000	486.77	483.00	479.73	476.89	467.28	462.33	459.75
44000	498.09	494.24	490.89	487.98	478.15	473.09	470.45
45000	509.41	505.47	502.05	499.07	489.01	483.84	481.14
46000	520.73	516.70	513.20	510.16	499.88	494.59	491.83
47000	532.05	527.93	524.36	521.25	510.75	505.34	502.52
48000	543.37	539.17	535.52	532.35	521.61	516.09	513.21
49000	554.69	550.40	546.67	543.44	532.48	526.85	523.91
50000	566.01	561.63	557.83	554.53	543.35	537.60	534.60
51000	577.33	572.86	568.99	565.62	554.21	548.35	545.29
52000	588.65	584.10	580.14	576.71	565.08	559.10	555.98
53000	599.97	595.33	591.30	587.80	575.95	569.85	566.67
54000	611.29	606.56	602.46	598.89	586.81	580.61	577.37
55000	622.61	617.79	613.61	609.98	597.68	591.36	588.06
56000	633.93	629.03	624.77	621.07	608.55	602.11	598.75
57000	645.25	640.26	635.93	632.16	610.42	612.86	609.44
58000	656.57	651.49	647.08	643.25	630.28	623.61	620.13
59000	667.89	662.72	658.24	654.34	641.15	634.37	630.83
60000	679.21	673.96	669.40	665.43	652.02	645.12	641.52
65000	735.81	730.12	725.18	720.88	706.35	698.88	694.98
70000	792.41	786.28	780.96	776.34	760.69	752.64	748.44
75000	849.01	842.45	836.75	831.79	815.02	806.40	801.90
80000	905.61	898.61	892.53	887.24	869.35	860.16	855.36
85000	962.21	954.77	948.31	942.69	923.69	913.92	908.82
90000	1018.81	1010.94	1004.10	998.15	978.02	967.60	962.28
95000	1075.41	1067.10	1059.88	1053.60	1032.36	1021.44	1015.74
100000	1132.02	1123.26	1115.66	1109.05	1086.69	1075.20	1069.20
105000	1188.62	1179.42	1171.45	1164.50	1141.03	1128.96	1122.66
110000	1245.22	1235.59	1227.23	1219.96	1195.36	1182.72	1176.12
120000	1358.42	1347.91	1338.79	1330.86	1304.03	1290.24	1283.04
130000	1471.62	1460.24	1450.36	1441.77	1412.70	1397.75	1389.96
140000	1584.82	1572.57	1561.93	1552.67	1521.37	1505.27	1496.87
150000	1698.02	1684.89	1673.49	1663.58	1630.04	1612.79	1603.79
175000	1981.03	1965.71	1952.41	1940.84	1901.71	1881.59	1871.09
200000	2264.03	2246.52	2231.32	2218.10	2173.39	2150.39	2138.39
225000	2547.04	2527.34	2510.24	2495.37	2445.06	2419.19	2405.69
250000	2830.04	2808.15	2789.16	2772.63	2716.73	2687.99	2672.99

13% Monthly Payments

necessary to amortize a loan

AMOUNT	1 YEAR	2 YEARS	3 YEARS	4 YEARS	5 YEARS	6 YEARS	7 YEARS
100	8.93	4.75	3.37	2.68	2.28	2.01	1.82
200	17.86	9.51	6.74	5.37	4.55	4.01	3.64
500	44.66	23.77	16.85	13.41	11.38	10.04	9.10
1000	89.32	47.54	33.69	26.83	22.75	20.07	18.19
2000	178.63	95.08	67.39	53.65	45.51	40.15	36.38
5000	446.59	237.71	168.47	134.14	113.77	100.37	90.96
6000	535.90	285.25	202.16	160.96	136.52	120.44	109.15
7000	625.22	332.79	235.86	187.79	159.27	140.52	127.34
8000	714.54	380.33	269.55	214.62	182.02	160.59	145.54
9000	803.86	427.88	303.25	241.45	204.78	180.67	163.73
10000	893.17	475.42	336.94	268.27	227.53	200.74	181.92
15000	1339.76	713.13	505.41	402.41	341.30	301.11	272.88
20000	1786.35	950.84	673.88	536.55	455.06	401.48	363.84
25000	2232.93	1188.55	842.35	670.69	568.83	501.85	454.80
30000	2679.52	1426.25	1010.82	804.82	682.59	602.22	545.76
35000	3126.10	1663.96	1179.29	938.96	796.36	702.59	636.72
36000	3215.42	1711.51	1212.98	965.79	819.11	722.67	654.91
37000	3304.74	1759.05	1246.68	992.62	841.86	742.74	673.10
38000	3394.06	1806.59	1280.37	1019.44	864.62	762.82	691.29
39000	3483.37	1854.13	1314.06	1046.27	887.37	782.89	709.49
40000	3572.69	1901.67	1347.76	1073.10	910.12	802.96	727.68
41000	3662.01	1949.21	1381.45	1099.93	932.88	823.04	745.87
42000	3751.33	1996.76	1415.15	1126.75	955.63	843.11	764.06
43000	3840.64	2044.30	1448.84	1153.58	978.38	863.19	782.25
44000	3929.96	2091.84	1482.53	1180.41	1001.14	883.26	800.45
45000	4019.28	2139.38	1516.23	1207.24	1023.89	903.33	818.64
46000	4108.59	2186.92	1549.92	1234.06	1046.64	923.41	836.83
47000	4197.91	2234.47	1583.62	1260.89	1069.39	943.48	855.02
48000	4287.23	2282.01	1617.31	1287.72	1092.15	963.56	873.21
49000	4376.55	2329.55	1651.00	1314.55	1114.90	983.63	891.41
50000	4465.86	2377.09	1684.70	1341.37	1137.65	1003.71	909.60
51000	4555.18	2424.63	1718.39	1368.20	1160.41	1023.78	927.79
52000	4644.50	2472.17	1752.09	1395.03	1183.16	1043.85	945.98
53000	4733.82	2519.72	1785.78	1421.86	1205.91	1063.93	964.17
54000	4823.13	2567.26	1819.47	1448.68	1228.67	1084.00	982.37
55000	4912.45	2614.80	1853.17	1475.51	1251.42	1104.08	1000.56
56000	5001.77	2662.34	1886.86	1502.34	1274.17	1124.15	1018.75
57000	5091.08	2709.88	1920.56	1529.17	1296.93	1144.22	1036.94
58000	5180.40	2757.43	1954.25	1555.99	1319.68	1164.30	1055.13
59000	5269.72	2804.97	1987.94	1582.82	1342.43	1184.37	1073.33
60000	5359.04	2852.51	2021.64	1609.65	1365.18	1204.45	1091.52
65000	5805.62	3090.22	2190.11	1743.79	1478.95	1304.82	1182.48
70000	6252.21	3327.93	2358.58	1877.92	1592.72	1405.19	1273.44
75000	6698.80	3565.64	2527.05	2012.06	1706.48	1505.56	1364.40
80000	7145.38	3803.35	2695.52	2146.20	1820.25	1605.93	1455.36
85000	7591.97	4041.05	2863.99	2280.34	1934.01	1706.30	1546.32
90000	8038.55	4278.76	3032.46	2414.47	2047.78	1806.67	1637.28
95000	8485.14	4516.47	3200.93	2548.61	2161.54	1907.04	1728.24
100000	8931.73	4754.18	3369.40	2682.75	2275.31	2007.41	1819.20
105000	9378.31	4991.89	3537.86	2816.89	2389.07	2107.78	1910.16
110000	9824.90	5229.60	3706.33	2951.02	2502.84	2208.15	2001.12
120000	10718.07	5705.02	4043.27	3219.30	2730.37	2408.89	2183.04
130000	11611.25	6180.44	4380.21	3487.57	2957.90	2609.63	2364.96
140000	12504.42	6655.86	4717.15	3755.85	3185.43	2810.37	2546.87
150000	13397.59	7131.27	5054.09	4024.12	3412.96	3011.12	2728.79
175000	15630.52	8319.82	5896.44	4694.81	3981.79	3512.97	3183.59
200000	17863.46	9508.36	6738.79	5365.50	4550.61	4014.82	3638.39
225000	20096.39	10696.91	7581.14	6036.19	5119.44	4516.67	4093.19
250000	22329.32	11885.46	8423.49	6706.87	5688.27	5018.53	4547.99

Monthly Payments 13%

necessary to amortize a loan

AMOUNT	8 YEARS	9 YEARS	10 YEARS	11 YEARS	12 YEARS	13 YEARS	14 YEARS
100	1.68	1.58	1.49	1.43	1.37	1.33	1.30
200	3.36	3.15	2.99	2.86	2.75	2.66	2.59
500	8.40	7.88	7.47	7.14	6.87	6.66	6.48
1000	16.81	15.75	14.93	14.28	13.75	13.31	12.95
2000	33.61	31.51	29.86	28.55	27.40	26.62	25.91
5000	84.04	78.77	74.66	71.38	68.73	66.56	64.76
6000	100.84	94.52	89.59	85.66	82.48	79.87	77.72
7000	117.65	110.28	104.52	99.93	96.22	93.18	90.67
8000	134.46	126.03	119.45	114.21	109.97	106.50	103.62
9000	151.27	141.78	134.38	128.48	123.72	119.81	116.57
10000	168.07	157.54	149.31	142.76	137.46	133.12	129.53
15000	252.11	236.30	223.97	214.14	206.19	199.68	194.29
20000	336.15	315.07	298.62	285.52	274.93	266.24	259.05
25000	420.18	393.84	373.28	356.90	343.66	332.80	323.82
30000	504.22	472.61	447.93	428.28	412.39	399.36	388.58
35000	588.25	551.38	522.59	499.66	481.12	465.92	453.34
36000	605.06	567.13	537.52	513.94	494.87	479.24	466.29
37000	621.87	582.88	552.45	528.22	508.61	492.55	479.25
38000	638.68	598.64	567.38	542.49	522.36	505.86	492.20
39000	655.48	614.39	582.31	556.77	536.10	519.17	505.15
40000	672.29	630.14	597.24	571.04	549.85	532.48	518.11
41000	689.10	645.90	612.17	585.32	563.60	545.80	531.06
42000	705.90	661.65	627.11	599.60	577.34	559.11	544.01
43000	722.71	677.40	642.04	613.87	591.09	572.42	556.96
44000	739.52	693.16	656.97	628.15	604.84	585.73	569.92
45000	756.33	708.91	671.90	642.42	618.58	599.04	582.87
46000	773.13	724.67	686.83	656.70	632.33	612.36	595.82
47000	789.94	740.42	701.76	670.98	646.07	625.67	608.77
48000	806.75	756.17	716.69	685.25	659.82	638.98	621.73
49000	823.56	771.93	731.62	699.53	673.57	652.29	634.68
50000	840.36	787.68	746.55	713.81	687.31	665.61	647.63
51000	857.17	803.43	761.48	728.08	701.06	678.92	660.58
52000	873.98	819.19	776.42	742.36	714.81	692.23	673.54
53000	890.78	834.94	791.35	756.63	728.55	705.54	686.49
54000	907.59	850.69	806.28	770.91	742.30	718.85	699.44
55000	924.40	866.45	821.21	785.19	756.04	732.17	712.39
56000	941.21	882.20	836.14	799.46	769.79	745.48	725.35
57000	958.01	897.95	851.07	813.74	783.54	758.79	738.30
58000	974.82	913.71	866.00	828.01	797.28	772.10	751.25
59000	991.63	929.46	880.93	842.29	811.03	785.41	704.21
60000	1008.44	945.22	895.86	856.57	824.78	798.73	777.16
65000	1092.47	1023.98	970.52	927.95	893.51	865.29	841.92
70000	1176.51	1102.75	1045.18	999.33	962.24	931.85	906.68
75000	1260.54	1181.52	1119.83	1070.71	1030.97	998.41	971.45
80000	1344.58	1260.29	1194.49	1142.09	1099.70	1064.97	1036.21
85000	1428.62	1339.05	1269.14	1213.47	1168.43	1131.53	1100.97
90000	1512.65	1417.82	1343.80	1284.85	1237.16	1198.09	1165.74
95000	1596.69	1496.59	1418.45	1356.23	1305.89	1264.65	1230.50
100000	1680.73	1575.36	1493.11	1427.61	1374.63	1331.21	1295.26
105000	1764.76	1654.13	1567.76	1498.99	1443.36	1397.77	1360.03
110000	1848.80	1732.89	1642.42	1570.37	1512.09	1464.33	1424.79
120000	2016.87	1890.43	1791.73	1713.13	1649.55	1597.45	1554.32
130000	2184.94	2047.97	1941.04	1855.89	1787.01	1730.57	1683.84
140000	2353.02	2205.50	2090.35	1998.66	1924.48	1863.69	1813.37
150000	2521.09	2363.04	2239.66	2141.42	2061.94	1996.82	1942.90
175000	2941.27	2756.88	2612.94	2498.32	2405.59	2329.62	2266.71
200000	3361.45	3150.72	2986.21	2855.22	2749.25	2662.47	2590.53
225000	3781.63	3544.56	3359.49	3212.12	3092.91	2995.22	2914.34
250000	4201.81	3938.40	3732.77	3569.03	3436.56	3328.03	3238.16

13%

Monthly Payments

necessary to amortize a loan

AMOUNT	15 YEARS	16 YEARS	17 YEARS	18 YEARS	19 YEARS	20 YEARS	21 YEARS
100	1.27	1.24	1.22	1.20	1.18	1.17	1.16
200	2.53	2.48	2.44	2.40	2.37	2.34	2.32
500	6.33	6.20	6.09	6.00	5.92	5.86	5.80
1000	12.65	12.40	12.19	12.00	11.85	11.72	11.60
2000	25.30	24.80	24.37	24.01	23.70	23.43	23.20
5000	63.26	62.00	60.93	60.02	59.24	58.58	58.01
6000	75.91	74.40	73.12	72.03	71.09	70.29	69.61
7000	88.57	86.80	85.30	84.03	82.94	82.01	81.21
8000	101.22	99.20	97.49	96.03	94.79	93.73	92.81
9000	113.87	111.60	109.68	108.04	106.64	105.44	104.41
10000	126.52	124.00	121.86	120.04	118.49	117.16	116.01
15000	189.79	186.00	182.79	180.06	177.73	175.74	174.02
20000	253.05	248.00	243.72	240.09	236.98	234.32	232.02
25000	316.31	310.00	304.65	300.11	296.22	292.89	290.03
30000	379.57	372.00	365.58	360.13	355.47	351.47	348.03
35000	442.83	434.00	426.52	420.15	414.71	410.05	406.04
36000	455.49	446.40	438.70	432.16	426.56	421.77	417.64
37000	468.14	458.80	450.89	444.16	438.41	433.48	429.24
38000	480.79	471.20	463.07	456.16	450.26	445.20	440.84
39000	493.44	483.60	475.26	468.17	462.11	456.91	452.44
40000	506.10	496.00	487.45	480.17	473.96	468.63	464.05
41000	518.75	508.40	499.63	492.18	485.81	480.35	475.65
42000	531.40	520.79	511.82	504.18	497.66	492.06	487.25
43000	544.05	533.19	524.00	516.19	509.51	503.78	498.85
44000	556.71	545.59	536.19	528.19	521.36	515.49	510.45
45000	569.36	557.99	548.38	540.19	533.20	527.21	522.05
46000	582.01	570.39	560.56	552.20	545.05	538.92	533.65
47000	594.66	582.79	572.75	564.20	556.90	550.64	545.25
48000	607.32	595.19	584.93	576.21	568.75	562.36	556.85
49000	619.97	607.59	597.12	588.21	580.60	574.07	568.46
50000	632.62	619.99	609.31	600.22	592.45	585.79	580.06
51000	645.27	632.39	621.49	612.22	604.30	597.50	591.66
52000	657.93	644.79	633.68	624.22	616.15	609.22	603.26
53000	670.58	657.19	645.87	636.23	628.00	620.94	614.86
54000	683.23	669.59	658.05	648.23	639.84	632.65	626.46
55000	695.88	681.99	670.24	660.24	651.69	644.37	638.06
56000	708.54	694.39	682.42	672.24	663.54	656.08	649.66
57000	721.19	706.79	694.61	684.25	675.39	667.80	661.27
58000	733.84	719.19	706.80	696.25	687.24	679.51	672.87
59000	746.49	731.59	718.98	708.26	699.09	691.23	684.47
60000	759.15	743.99	731.17	720.26	710.94	702.95	696.07
65000	822.41	805.99	792.10	780.28	770.18	761.52	754.07
70000	885.67	867.99	853.03	840.30	829.43	820.10	812.08
75000	948.93	929.99	913.96	900.32	888.67	878.68	870.09
80000	1012.19	991.99	974.89	960.35	947.92	937.26	928.09
85000	1075.46	1053.99	1035.82	1020.37	1007.16	995.84	986.10
90000	1138.72	1115.99	1096.75	1080.39	1066.41	1054.42	1044.10
95000	1201.98	1177.99	1157.68	1140.41	1125.65	1113.00	1102.11
100000	1265.24	1239.99	1218.61	1200.43	1184.90	1171.58	1160.11
105000	1328.50	1301.99	1279.55	1260.45	1244.14	1230.15	1218.12
110000	1391.77	1363.99	1340.48	1320.48	1303.39	1288.73	1276.13
120000	1518.29	1487.99	1462.34	1440.52	1421.88	1405.89	1392.14
130000	1644.81	1611.98	1584.20	1560.56	1540.37	1523.05	1508.15
140000	1771.34	1735.98	1706.06	1680.61	1658.86	1640.21	1624.16
150000	1897.86	1859.98	1827.92	1800.65	1777.35	1757.36	1740.17
175000	2214.17	2169.98	2132.58	2100.76	2073.57	2050.26	2030.20
200000	2530.48	2479.98	2437.23	2400.87	2369.80	2343.15	2320.23
225000	2846.79	2789.97	2741.88	2700.97	2666.02	2636.05	2610.26
250000	3163.11	3099.97	3046.54	3001.08	2962.24	2928.94	2900.29

Monthly Payments 13%

necessary to amortize a loan

AMOUNT	22 YEARS	23 YEARS	24 YEARS	25 YEARS	30 YEARS	35 YEARS	40 YEARS
100	1.15	1.14	1.13	1.13	1.11	1.10	1.09
200	2.30	2.28	2.27	2.26	2.21	2.19	2.18
500	5.75	5.71	5.67	5.64	5.53	5.48	5.45
1000	11.50	11.42	11.34	11.28	11.06	10.95	10.90
2000	23.00	22.83	22.69	22.56	22.12	21.90	21.79
5000	57.51	57.08	56.71	56.39	55.31	54.76	54.48
6000	69.01	68.50	68.06	67.67	66.37	65.71	65.37
7000	80.52	79.92	79.40	78.95	77.43	76.66	76.27
8000	92.02	91.33	90.74	90.23	88.50	87.62	87.16
9000	103.52	102.75	102.08	101.51	99.56	98.57	98.06
10000	115.02	114.17	113.43	112.78	110.62	109.52	108.95
15000	172.53	171.25	170.14	169.18	165.93	164.28	163.43
20000	230.05	228.34	226.85	225.57	221.24	219.04	217.90
25000	287.56	285.42	283.57	281.96	276.55	273.80	272.38
30000	345.07	342.50	340.28	338.35	331.86	328.56	326.85
35000	402.58	399.59	396.99	394.74	387.17	383.32	381.33
36000	414.08	411.00	408.34	406.02	398.23	394.27	392.23
37000	425.58	422.42	419.68	417.30	409.29	405.22	403.12
38000	437.09	433.84	431.02	428.58	420.36	416.17	414.02
39000	448.59	445.25	442.36	439.86	431.42	427.13	424.91
40000	460.09	456.67	453.71	451.13	442.48	438.08	435.81
41000	471.59	468.09	465.05	462.41	453.54	449.03	446.70
42000	483.10	479.50	476.39	473.69	464.60	459.98	457.60
43000	494.60	490.92	487.73	484.97	475.67	470.93	468.49
44000	506.10	502.34	499.08	496.25	486.73	481.88	479.39
45000	517.60	513.75	510.42	507.53	497.79	492.84	490.28
46000	529.10	525.17	521.76	518.80	508.85	503.79	501.18
47000	540.61	536.59	533.11	530.08	519.91	514.74	512.07
48000	552.11	548.00	544.45	541.36	530.98	525.69	522.97
49000	563.61	559.42	555.79	552.64	542.04	536.64	533.86
50000	575.11	570.84	567.13	563.92	553.10	547.60	544.76
51000	586.62	582.25	578.48	575.20	564.16	558.55	555.65
52000	598.12	593.67	589.82	586.47	575.22	569.50	566.55
53000	609.62	605.09	601.16	597.75	586.29	580.45	577.44
54000	621.12	616.50	612.50	609.03	597.35	591.40	588.34
55000	632.62	627.92	623.85	620.31	608.41	602.36	599.23
56000	644.13	639.34	635.19	631.59	619.47	613.31	610.13
57000	655.63	650.76	646.53	642.87	630.53	624.26	621.02
58000	667.13	662.17	657.87	654.14	641.60	635.21	631.92
59000	678.63	673.59	669.22	665.42	652.66	646.16	642.81
60000	690.14	685.01	680.56	676.70	663.72	657.12	653.71
65000	747.65	742.09	737.27	733.09	719.03	711.88	708.18
70000	805.16	799.17	793.99	789.48	774.34	766.64	762.66
75000	862.67	856.26	850.70	845.88	829.65	821.39	817.14
80000	920.18	913.34	907.41	902.27	884.96	876.15	871.61
85000	977.69	970.42	904.13	958.66	940.27	930.91	926.09
90000	1035.20	1027.51	1020.84	1015.05	995.58	985.07	980.56
95000	1092.72	1084.59	1077.55	1071.44	1050.89	1040.43	1035.04
100000	1150.23	1141.68	1134.27	1127.84	1106.20	1095.19	1089.51
105000	1207.74	1198.76	1190.98	1184.23	1161.51	1149.95	1143.99
110000	1265.25	1255.84	1247.69	1240.62	1216.82	1204.71	1198.47
120000	1380.27	1370.01	1361.12	1353.40	1327.44	1314.23	1307.42
130000	1495.29	1484.18	1474.55	1466.19	1438.06	1423.75	1416.37
140000	1610.32	1598.35	1587.97	1578.97	1548.68	1533.27	1525.32
150000	1725.34	1712.51	1701.40	1691.75	1659.30	1642.79	1634.27
175000	2012.90	1997.93	1984.97	1973.71	1935.85	1916.59	1906.65
200000	2300.45	2283.35	2268.53	2255.67	2212.40	2190.39	2179.03
225000	2588.01	2568.77	2552.10	2537.63	2488.95	2464.18	2451.41
250000	2875.57	2854.19	2835.67	2819.59	2765.50	2737.98	2723.79

13¼%

Monthly Payments
necessary to amortize a loan

AMOUNT	1 YEAR	2 YEARS	3 YEARS	4 YEARS	5 YEARS	6 YEARS	7 YEARS
100	8.94	4.77	3.38	2.70	2.29	2.02	1.83
200	17.89	9.53	6.76	5.39	4.58	4.04	3.67
500	44.72	23.83	16.91	13.48	11.44	10.10	9.16
1000	89.43	47.66	33.81	26.95	22.88	20.21	18.33
2000	178.87	95.32	67.63	53.90	45.76	40.41	36.66
5000	447.17	238.30	169.07	134.76	114.41	101.03	91.64
6000	536.61	285.96	202.89	161.71	137.29	121.24	109.97
7000	626.04	333.62	236.70	188.66	160.17	141.44	128.30
8000	715.48	381.27	270.52	215.61	183.05	161.65	146.63
9000	804.91	428.93	304.33	242.57	205.93	181.86	164.95
10000	894.35	476.59	338.14	269.52	228.81	202.06	183.28
15000	1341.52	714.89	507.22	404.28	343.22	303.09	274.92
20000	1788.69	953.19	676.29	539.03	457.63	404.13	366.56
25000	2235.87	1191.48	845.36	673.79	572.03	505.16	458.20
30000	2683.04	1429.78	1014.43	808.55	686.44	606.19	549.84
35000	3130.21	1668.08	1183.51	943.31	800.84	707.22	641.49
36000	3219.65	1715.74	1217.32	970.26	823.73	727.43	659.81
37000	3309.08	1763.40	1251.14	997.21	846.61	747.63	678.14
38000	3398.52	1811.05	1284.95	1024.17	869.49	767.84	696.47
39000	3487.95	1858.71	1318.77	1051.12	892.37	788.05	714.80
40000	3577.38	1906.37	1352.58	1078.07	915.25	808.25	733.13
41000	3666.82	1954.03	1386.39	1105.02	938.13	828.46	751.45
42000	3756.25	2001.69	1420.21	1131.97	961.01	848.66	769.78
43000	3845.69	2049.35	1454.02	1158.92	983.89	868.87	788.11
44000	3935.12	2097.01	1487.84	1185.88	1006.78	889.08	806.44
45000	4024.56	2144.67	1521.65	1212.83	1029.66	909.28	824.77
46000	4113.99	2192.33	1555.47	1239.78	1052.54	929.49	843.10
47000	4203.43	2239.99	1589.28	1266.73	1075.42	949.70	861.42
48000	4292.86	2287.65	1623.10	1293.68	1098.30	969.90	879.75
49000	4382.30	2335.31	1656.91	1320.64	1121.18	990.11	898.08
50000	4471.73	2382.97	1690.72	1347.59	1144.06	1010.31	916.41
51000	4561.17	2430.63	1724.54	1374.54	1166.94	1030.52	934.74
52000	4650.60	2478.29	1758.35	1401.49	1189.83	1050.73	953.06
53000	4740.03	2525.94	1792.17	1428.44	1212.71	1070.93	971.39
54000	4829.47	2573.60	1825.98	1455.39	1235.59	1091.14	989.72
55000	4918.90	2621.26	1859.80	1482.35	1258.47	1111.35	1008.05
56000	5008.34	2668.92	1893.61	1509.30	1281.35	1131.55	1026.38
57000	5097.77	2716.58	1927.43	1536.25	1304.23	1151.76	1044.70
58000	5187.21	2764.24	1961.24	1563.20	1327.11	1171.96	1063.03
59000	5276.64	2811.90	1995.06	1590.15	1349.99	1192.17	1081.36
60000	5366.08	2859.56	2028.87	1617.10	1372.88	1212.38	1099.69
65000	5813.25	3097.86	2197.94	1751.86	1487.28	1313.41	1191.33
70000	6260.42	3336.15	2367.01	1886.62	1601.69	1414.44	1282.97
75000	6707.60	3574.45	2536.09	2021.38	1716.09	1515.47	1374.61
80000	7154.77	3812.75	2705.16	2156.14	1830.50	1616.50	1466.25
85000	7601.94	4051.04	2874.23	2290.90	1944.91	1717.53	1557.89
90000	8049.11	4289.34	3043.30	2425.66	2059.31	1818.57	1649.53
95000	8496.29	4527.64	3212.38	2560.42	2173.72	1919.60	1741.17
100000	8943.46	4765.93	3381.45	2695.17	2288.13	2020.63	1832.82
105000	9390.63	5004.23	3550.52	2829.93	2402.53	2121.66	1924.46
110000	9837.81	5242.53	3719.59	2964.69	2516.94	2222.69	2016.10
120000	10732.15	5719.12	4057.74	3234.21	2745.75	2424.76	2199.38
130000	11626.50	6195.71	4395.88	3503.73	2974.56	2626.82	2382.66
140000	12520.85	6672.31	4734.03	3773.24	3203.38	2828.88	2565.94
150000	13415.19	7148.90	5072.17	4042.76	3432.19	3030.94	2749.22
175000	15651.06	8340.38	5917.54	4716.56	4004.22	3536.10	3207.43
200000	17886.92	9531.87	6762.90	5390.35	4576.25	4041.26	3665.63
225000	20122.79	10723.35	7608.26	6064.14	5148.28	4546.42	4123.83
250000	22358.65	11914.83	8453.62	6737.94	5720.31	5051.57	4582.04

Monthly Payments 13¼%

necessary to amortize a loan

AMOUNT	8 YEARS	9 YEARS	10 YEARS	11 YEARS	12 YEARS	13 YEARS	14 YEARS
100	1.69	1.59	1.51	1.44	1.39	1.35	1.31
200	3.39	3.18	3.02	2.89	2.78	2.69	2.62
500	8.47	7.95	7.54	7.21	6.95	6.74	6.56
1000	16.95	15.90	15.08	14.43	13.90	13.47	13.11
2000	33.89	31.80	30.16	28.86	27.80	26.94	26.23
5000	84.74	79.49	75.39	72.14	69.51	67.35	65.57
6000	101.68	95.39	90.47	86.57	83.41	80.82	78.69
7000	118.63	111.28	105.55	100.99	97.31	94.29	91.80
8000	135.58	127.18	120.63	115.42	111.21	107.76	104.92
9000	152.53	143.08	135.71	129.85	125.11	121.24	118.03
10000	169.47	158.98	150.79	144.28	139.01	134.71	131.14
15000	254.21	238.46	226.18	216.41	208.52	202.06	196.72
20000	338.95	317.95	301.58	288.55	278.03	269.41	262.29
25000	423.69	397.44	376.97	360.69	347.53	336.76	327.86
30000	508.42	476.93	452.37	432.83	417.04	404.12	393.43
35000	593.16	556.42	527.76	504.97	486.55	471.47	459.00
36000	610.11	572.31	542.84	519.39	500.45	484.94	472.12
37000	627.05	588.21	557.92	533.82	514.35	498.41	485.23
38000	644.00	604.11	573.00	548.25	528.25	511.88	498.35
39000	660.95	620.01	588.08	562.68	542.15	525.35	511.46
40000	677.90	635.90	603.16	577.10	556.05	538.82	524.58
41000	694.84	651.80	618.23	591.53	569.95	552.29	537.69
42000	711.79	667.70	633.31	605.96	583.86	565.76	550.81
43000	728.74	683.60	648.39	620.39	597.76	579.24	563.92
44000	745.69	699.50	663.47	634.81	611.66	592.71	577.03
45000	762.63	715.39	678.55	649.24	625.56	606.18	590.15
46000	779.58	731.29	693.63	663.67	639.46	619.65	603.26
47000	796.53	747.19	708.71	678.10	653.36	633.12	616.38
48000	813.48	763.09	723.79	692.53	667.26	646.59	629.49
49000	830.42	778.98	738.87	706.95	681.16	660.06	642.61
50000	847.37	794.88	753.94	721.38	695.07	673.53	655.72
51000	864.32	810.78	769.02	735.81	708.97	687.00	668.84
52000	881.26	826.68	784.10	750.24	722.87	700.47	681.95
53000	898.21	842.57	799.18	764.66	736.77	713.94	695.06
54000	915.16	858.47	814.26	779.09	750.67	727.41	708.18
55000	932.11	874.37	829.34	793.52	764.57	740.88	721.29
56000	949.05	890.27	844.42	807.95	778.47	754.35	734.41
57000	966.00	906.16	859.50	822.37	792.37	767.82	747.52
58000	982.95	922.06	874.58	836.80	806.28	781.29	760.64
59000	999.90	937.96	889.65	851.23	820.18	794.76	773.75
60000	1016.84	953.86	904.73	865.66	834.08	808.24	786.87
65000	1101.58	1033.35	980.13	937.79	903.59	875.59	852.44
70000	1186.32	1112.83	1055.52	1009.93	973.09	942.94	918.01
75000	1271.06	1192.32	1130.92	1082.07	1042.60	1010.29	983.58
80000	1355.79	1271.81	1206.31	1154.21	1112.10	1077.65	1049.15
85000	1440.53	1351.30	1281.71	1226.35	1181.61	1145.00	1114.73
90000	1525.27	1430.79	1357.10	1298.48	1251.12	1212.35	1180.30
95000	1610.00	1510.27	1432.49	1370.62	1320.62	1279.71	1245.87
100000	1694.74	1589.76	1507.89	1442.76	1390.13	1347.06	1311.44
105000	1779.48	1669.25	1583.28	1514.90	1459.64	1414.41	1377.01
110000	1864.21	1748.74	1658.68	1587.04	1529.14	1481.77	1442.59
120000	2033.69	1907.71	1809.47	1731.31	1668.16	1616.47	1573.73
130000	2203.16	2066.69	1960.26	1875.59	1807.17	1751.18	1704.87
140000	2372.64	2225.67	2111.04	2019.86	1946.18	1885.88	1836.02
150000	2542.11	2384.64	2261.83	2164.14	2085.20	2020.59	1967.16
175000	2965.80	2782.08	2638.81	2524.83	2432.73	2357.35	2295.02
200000	3389.48	3179.52	3015.78	2885.52	2780.26	2694.12	2622.88
225000	3813.17	3576.96	3392.75	3246.21	3127.79	3030.88	2950.75
250000	4236.85	3974.40	3769.72	3606.90	3475.33	3367.65	3278.61

13¼%

Monthly Payments
necessary to amortize a loan

AMOUNT	15 YEARS	16 YEARS	17 YEARS	18 YEARS	19 YEARS	20 YEARS	21 YEARS
100	1.28	1.26	1.24	1.22	1.20	1.19	1.18
200	2.56	2.51	2.47	2.44	2.41	2.38	2.36
500	6.41	6.28	6.18	6.09	6.01	5.95	5.89
1000	12.82	12.57	12.36	12.18	12.03	11.89	11.78
2000	25.63	25.14	24.71	24.36	24.05	23.79	23.56
5000	64.09	62.84	61.78	60.89	60.13	59.47	58.91
6000	76.90	75.41	74.14	73.07	72.15	71.37	70.69
7000	89.72	87.97	86.50	85.25	84.18	83.26	82.47
8000	102.54	100.54	98.86	97.42	96.20	95.15	94.26
9000	115.36	113.11	111.21	109.60	108.23	107.05	106.04
10000	128.17	125.68	123.57	121.78	120.25	118.94	117.82
15000	192.26	188.52	185.35	182.67	180.38	178.41	176.73
20000	256.35	251.36	247.14	243.56	240.50	237.89	235.64
25000	320.43	314.20	308.92	304.45	300.63	297.36	294.55
30000	384.52	377.04	370.71	365.34	360.75	356.83	353.46
35000	448.61	439.87	432.49	426.23	420.88	416.30	412.37
36000	461.43	452.44	444.85	438.40	432.90	428.20	424.15
37000	474.24	465.01	457.21	450.58	444.93	440.09	435.93
38000	487.06	477.58	469.56	462.76	456.95	451.98	447.72
39000	499.88	490.15	481.92	474.94	468.98	463.88	459.50
40000	512.69	502.71	494.28	487.11	481.00	475.77	471.28
41000	525.51	515.28	506.64	499.29	493.03	487.67	483.06
42000	538.33	527.85	518.99	511.47	505.05	499.56	494.84
43000	551.15	540.42	531.35	523.65	517.08	511.46	506.63
44000	563.96	552.98	543.71	535.83	529.10	523.35	518.41
45000	576.78	565.55	556.06	548.00	541.13	535.24	530.19
46000	589.60	578.12	568.42	560.18	553.15	547.14	541.97
47000	602.42	590.69	580.78	572.36	565.18	559.03	553.75
48000	615.23	603.26	593.13	584.54	577.20	570.93	565.54
49000	628.05	615.82	605.49	596.72	589.23	582.82	577.32
50000	640.87	628.39	617.85	608.89	601.25	594.72	589.10
51000	653.69	640.96	630.21	621.07	613.28	606.61	600.88
52000	666.50	653.53	642.56	633.25	625.31	618.50	612.66
53000	679.32	666.10	654.92	645.43	637.33	630.40	624.45
54000	692.14	678.66	667.28	657.60	649.36	642.29	636.23
55000	704.96	691.23	679.63	669.78	661.38	654.19	648.01
56000	717.77	703.80	691.99	681.96	673.41	666.08	659.79
57000	730.59	716.37	704.35	694.14	685.43	677.98	671.57
58000	743.41	728.93	716.70	706.32	697.46	689.87	683.35
59000	756.22	741.50	729.06	718.49	709.48	701.76	695.14
60000	769.04	754.07	741.42	730.67	721.51	713.66	706.92
65000	833.13	816.91	803.20	791.56	781.63	773.13	765.83
70000	897.22	879.75	864.99	852.45	841.76	832.60	824.74
75000	961.30	942.59	926.77	913.34	901.88	892.07	883.65
80000	1025.39	1005.43	988.56	974.23	962.01	951.54	942.56
85000	1089.48	1068.27	1050.34	1035.12	1022.13	1011.02	1001.47
90000	1153.56	1131.11	1112.13	1096.01	1082.26	1070.49	1060.38
95000	1217.65	1193.94	1173.91	1156.90	1142.38	1129.96	1119.29
100000	1281.74	1256.78	1235.70	1217.79	1202.51	1189.43	1178.20
105000	1345.82	1319.62	1297.48	1278.68	1262.64	1248.90	1237.11
110000	1409.91	1382.46	1359.27	1339.57	1322.76	1308.37	1296.02
120000	1538.08	1508.14	1482.84	1461.34	1443.01	1427.32	1413.84
130000	1666.26	1633.82	1606.41	1583.12	1563.26	1546.26	1531.66
140000	1794.43	1759.50	1729.98	1704.90	1683.51	1665.20	1649.48
150000	1922.60	1885.18	1853.55	1826.68	1803.76	1784.15	1767.30
175000	2243.04	2199.37	2162.47	2131.13	2104.39	2081.50	2061.85
200000	2563.47	2513.57	2471.39	2435.57	2405.02	2378.86	2356.40
225000	2883.91	2827.76	2780.32	2740.02	2705.65	2676.22	2650.95
250000	3204.34	3141.96	3089.24	3044.47	3006.27	2973.58	2945.50

Monthly Payments 13¼%

necessary to amortize a loan

AMOUNT	22 YEARS	23 YEARS	24 YEARS	25 YEARS	30 YEARS	35 YEARS	40 YEARS
100	1.17	1.16	1.15	1.15	1.13	1.12	1.11
200	2.34	2.32	2.31	2.29	2.25	2.23	2.22
500	5.84	5.80	5.76	5.73	5.63	5.58	5.55
1000	11.69	11.60	11.53	11.47	11.26	11.15	11.10
2000	23.37	23.20	23.06	22.93	22.52	22.30	22.20
5000	58.43	58.01	57.65	57.34	56.29	55.76	55.49
6000	70.11	69.61	69.18	68.80	67.55	66.91	66.59
7000	81.80	81.21	80.71	80.27	78.80	78.07	77.69
8000	93.48	92.81	92.24	91.74	90.06	89.22	88.79
9000	105.17	104.42	103.77	103.20	101.32	100.37	99.89
10000	116.85	116.02	115.30	114.67	112.58	111.52	110.99
15000	175.28	174.03	172.94	172.01	168.87	167.29	166.48
20000	233.71	232.04	230.59	229.34	225.15	223.05	221.97
25000	292.13	290.04	288.24	286.68	281.44	278.81	277.47
30000	350.56	348.05	345.89	344.01	337.73	334.57	332.96
35000	408.98	406.06	403.53	401.35	394.02	390.33	388.45
36000	420.67	417.66	415.06	412.81	405.28	401.49	399.55
37000	432.35	429.27	426.59	424.28	416.54	412.64	410.65
38000	444.04	440.87	438.12	435.75	427.79	423.79	421.75
39000	455.72	452.47	449.65	447.21	439.05	434.94	432.85
40000	467.41	464.07	461.18	458.68	450.31	446.10	443.95
41000	479.10	475.67	472.71	470.15	461.57	457.25	455.05
42000	490.78	487.27	484.24	481.61	472.82	468.40	466.15
43000	502.47	498.88	495.77	493.08	484.08	479.55	477.24
44000	514.15	510.48	507.30	504.55	495.34	490.71	488.34
45000	525.84	522.08	518.83	516.02	506.60	501.86	499.44
46000	537.52	533.68	530.36	527.48	517.86	513.01	510.54
47000	549.21	545.28	541.89	538.95	529.11	524.16	521.64
48000	560.89	556.88	553.42	550.42	540.37	535.32	532.74
49000	572.58	568.49	564.95	561.88	551.63	546.47	543.84
50000	584.26	580.09	576.48	573.35	562.89	557.62	554.93
51000	595.95	591.69	588.01	584.82	574.14	568.77	566.03
52000	607.63	603.29	599.54	596.28	585.40	579.93	577.13
53000	619.32	614.89	611.07	607.75	596.66	591.08	588.23
54000	631.00	626.50	622.60	619.22	607.92	602.23	599.33
55000	642.69	638.10	634.13	630.69	619.18	613.38	610.43
56000	654.37	649.70	645.66	642.15	630.43	624.54	621.53
57000	666.06	661.30	657.18	653.62	641.69	635.69	632.63
58000	677.74	672.90	668.71	665.09	652.95	646.84	643.72
59000	689.43	684.50	680.24	676.55	664.21	657.99	654.82
60000	701.12	696.11	691.77	688.02	675.46	669.15	665.92
65000	759.54	754.11	749.42	745.36	731.75	724.91	721.42
70000	817.97	812.12	807.07	802.69	788.04	780.67	776.91
75000	876.39	870.13	864.72	860.03	844.33	836.43	832.40
80000	934.82	928.14	922.36	917.36	900.62	892.19	887.90
85000	993.25	986.15	980.01	974.70	956.91	947.96	943.39
90000	1051.67	1044.16	1037.66	1032.03	1013.20	1003.72	998.88
95000	1110.10	1102.17	1095.31	1089.37	1069.48	1059.48	1054.38
100000	1168.53	1160.18	1152.96	1146.70	1125.77	1115.24	1109.87
105000	1226.95	1218.19	1210.60	1204.04	1182.06	1171.00	1165.36
110000	1285.38	1276.19	1268.25	1261.37	1238.35	1226.77	1220.86
120000	1402.23	1392.21	1383.55	1376.04	1350.93	1338.29	1331.84
130000	1519.08	1508.23	1498.84	1490.71	1463.51	1449.81	1442.83
140000	1635.94	1624.25	1614.14	1605.38	1576.08	1561.34	1553.82
150000	1752.79	1740.26	1729.43	1720.05	1688.66	1672.86	1664.80
175000	2044.92	2030.31	2017.67	2006.73	1970.10	1951.67	1942.27
200000	2337.05	2320.35	2305.91	2293.40	2251.55	2230.48	2219.74
225000	2629.18	2610.40	2594.15	2580.08	2532.99	2509.30	2497.21
250000	2921.31	2900.44	2882.39	2866.75	2814.43	2788.11	2774.67

13½%

Monthly Payments
necessary to amortize a loan

AMOUNT	1 YEAR	2 YEARS	3 YEARS	4 YEARS	5 YEARS	6 YEARS	7 YEARS
100	8.96	4.78	3.39	2.71	2.30	2.03	1.85
200	17.91	9.56	6.79	5.42	4.60	4.07	3.69
500	44.78	23.89	16.97	13.54	11.50	10.17	9.23
1000	89.55	47.78	33.94	27.08	23.01	20.34	18.46
2000	179.10	95.55	67.87	54.15	46.02	40.68	36.93
5000	447.76	238.89	169.68	135.38	115.05	101.69	92.32
6000	537.31	286.66	203.61	162.46	138.06	122.03	110.79
7000	626.86	334.44	237.55	189.53	161.07	142.37	129.25
8000	716.42	382.22	271.48	216.61	184.08	162.71	147.72
9000	805.97	429.99	305.42	243.69	207.09	183.05	166.18
10000	895.52	477.77	339.35	270.76	230.10	203.39	184.65
15000	1343.28	716.66	509.03	406.14	345.15	305.08	276.97
20000	1791.04	955.54	678.71	541.53	460.20	406.78	369.30
25000	2238.80	1194.43	848.38	676.91	575.25	508.47	461.62
30000	2686.56	1433.31	1018.06	812.29	690.30	610.17	553.95
35000	3134.32	1672.20	1187.74	947.67	805.34	711.86	646.27
36000	3223.87	1719.97	1221.67	974.75	828.35	732.20	664.74
37000	3313.43	1767.75	1255.61	1001.82	851.36	752.54	683.20
38000	3402.98	1815.53	1289.54	1028.90	874.37	772.88	701.67
39000	3492.53	1863.30	1323.48	1055.98	897.38	793.22	720.13
40000	3582.08	1911.08	1357.41	1083.05	920.39	813.56	738.60
41000	3671.63	1958.86	1391.35	1110.13	943.40	833.90	757.06
42000	3761.19	2006.63	1425.28	1137.21	966.41	854.24	775.53
43000	3850.74	2054.41	1459.22	1164.28	989.42	874.58	793.99
44000	3940.29	2102.19	1493.15	1191.36	1012.43	894.91	812.46
45000	4029.84	2149.97	1527.09	1218.43	1035.44	915.25	830.92
46000	4119.39	2197.74	1561.02	1245.51	1058.45	935.59	849.39
47000	4208.95	2245.52	1594.96	1272.59	1081.46	955.93	867.85
48000	4298.50	2293.30	1628.89	1299.66	1104.47	976.27	886.31
49000	4388.05	2341.07	1662.83	1326.74	1127.48	996.61	904.78
50000	4477.60	2388.85	1696.76	1353.82	1150.49	1016.95	923.24
51000	4567.15	2436.63	1730.70	1380.89	1173.50	1037.29	941.71
52000	4656.71	2484.40	1764.63	1407.97	1196.51	1057.63	960.17
53000	4746.26	2532.18	1798.57	1435.05	1219.52	1077.96	978.64
54000	4835.81	2579.96	1832.51	1462.12	1242.53	1098.30	997.10
55000	4925.36	2627.74	1866.44	1489.20	1265.54	1118.64	1015.57
56000	5014.91	2675.51	1900.38	1516.27	1288.55	1138.98	1034.03
57000	5104.47	2723.29	1934.31	1543.35	1311.56	1159.32	1052.50
58000	5194.02	2771.07	1968.25	1570.43	1334.57	1179.66	1070.96
59000	5283.57	2818.84	2002.18	1597.50	1357.58	1200.00	1089.43
60000	5373.12	2866.62	2036.12	1624.58	1380.59	1220.34	1107.89
65000	5820.88	3105.51	2205.79	1759.96	1495.64	1322.03	1200.22
70000	6268.64	3344.39	2375.47	1895.34	1610.69	1423.73	1292.54
75000	6716.40	3583.28	2545.15	2030.72	1725.74	1525.42	1384.87
80000	7164.16	3822.16	2714.82	2166.11	1840.79	1627.12	1477.19
85000	7611.92	4061.05	2884.50	2301.49	1955.84	1728.81	1569.52
90000	8059.68	4299.93	3054.18	2436.87	2070.89	1830.51	1661.84
95000	8507.44	4538.82	3223.85	2572.25	2185.94	1932.20	1754.16
100000	8955.20	4777.70	3393.53	2707.63	2300.98	2033.90	1846.49
105000	9402.96	5016.59	3563.21	2843.01	2416.03	2135.59	1938.81
110000	9850.72	5255.47	3732.88	2978.40	2531.08	2237.29	2031.14
120000	10746.24	5733.24	4072.23	3249.16	2761.18	2440.68	2215.79
130000	11641.76	6211.01	4411.59	3519.92	2991.28	2644.07	2400.44
140000	12537.28	6688.78	4750.94	3790.69	3221.38	2847.45	2585.08
150000	13432.80	7166.55	5090.29	4061.45	3451.48	3050.84	2769.73
175000	15671.60	8360.98	5938.68	4738.36	4026.72	3559.32	3231.36
200000	17910.41	9555.40	6787.06	5415.26	4601.97	4067.79	3692.98
225000	20149.21	10749.83	7635.44	6092.17	5177.22	4576.27	4154.60
250000	22388.01	11944.25	8483.82	6769.08	5752.46	5084.74	4616.22

Monthly Payments 13½%

necessary to amortize a loan

AMOUNT	8 YEARS	9 YEARS	10 YEARS	11 YEARS	12 YEARS	13 YEARS	14 YEARS
100	1.71	1.60	1.52	1.46	1.41	1.36	1.33
200	3.42	3.21	3.05	2.92	2.81	2.73	2.66
500	8.54	8.02	7.61	7.29	7.03	6.81	6.64
1000	17.09	16.04	15.23	14.58	14.06	13.63	13.28
2000	34.18	32.08	30.45	29.16	20.11	27.26	26.55
5000	85.44	80.21	76.14	72.90	70.29	68.15	66.39
6000	102.53	96.25	91.36	87.48	84.34	81.78	79.66
7000	119.62	112.30	106.59	102.06	98.40	95.41	92.94
8000	136.71	128.34	121.82	116.64	112.46	109.04	106.22
9000	153.79	144.38	137.05	131.22	126.51	122.67	119.49
10000	170.88	160.42	152.27	145.80	140.57	136.30	132.77
15000	256.32	240.63	228.41	218.70	210.86	204.45	199.16
20000	341.76	320.85	304.55	291.60	281.14	272.60	265.54
25000	427.20	401.06	380.69	364.50	351.43	340.75	331.93
30000	512.64	481.27	456.82	437.40	421.72	408.90	398.31
35000	598.09	561.48	532.96	510.30	492.00	477.05	464.70
36000	615.17	577.52	548.19	524.88	506.06	490.68	477.97
37000	632.26	593.57	563.41	539.46	520.12	504.31	491.25
38000	649.35	609.61	578.64	554.03	534.17	517.94	504.53
39000	666.44	625.65	593.87	568.61	548.23	531.57	517.81
40000	683.53	641.69	609.10	583.19	562.29	545.20	531.08
41000	700.61	657.73	624.32	597.77	576.34	558.83	544.36
42000	717.70	673.78	639.55	612.35	590.40	572.46	557.64
43000	734.79	689.82	654.78	626.93	604.46	586.09	570.91
44000	751.88	705.86	670.01	641.51	618.52	599.72	584.19
45000	768.97	721.90	685.23	656.09	632.57	613.35	597.47
46000	786.06	737.95	700.46	670.67	646.63	626.98	610.75
47000	803.14	753.99	715.69	685.25	660.69	640.61	624.02
48000	820.23	770.03	730.92	699.83	674.74	654.24	637.30
49000	837.32	786.07	746.14	714.41	688.80	667.87	650.58
50000	854.41	802.12	761.37	728.99	702.86	681.50	663.85
51000	871.50	818.16	776.60	743.57	716.92	695.13	677.13
52000	888.58	834.20	791.83	758.15	730.97	708.76	690.41
53000	905.67	850.24	807.05	772.73	745.03	722.39	703.68
54000	922.76	866.28	822.28	787.31	759.09	736.02	716.96
55000	939.86	882.33	837.51	801.89	773.14	749.65	730.24
56000	956.94	898.37	852.74	816.47	787.20	763.28	743.52
57000	974.03	914.41	867.96	831.05	801.26	776.91	756.79
58000	991.11	930.45	883.19	845.63	815.32	790.54	770.07
59000	1008.20	946.50	898.42	860.21	829.37	804.17	783.35
60000	1025.29	962.54	913.65	874.79	843.43	817.80	796.62
65000	1110.73	1042.75	989.78	947.69	913.72	885.94	863.01
70000	1196.17	1122.96	1065.92	1020.59	984.00	954.09	929.39
75000	1281.61	1203.17	1142.06	1093.49	1054.29	1022.24	995.78
80000	1367.05	1283.39	1218.19	1166.39	1124.57	1090.39	1062.17
85000	1452.49	1363.60	1294.33	1239.29	1194.86	1158.54	1128.55
90000	1537.93	1443.81	1370.47	1312.19	1265.15	1226.69	1194.94
95000	1623.38	1524.02	1446.61	1385.09	1335.43	1294.84	1261.32
100000	1708.82	1604.23	1522.74	1457.99	1405.72	1362.99	1327.71
105000	1794.26	1684.44	1598.88	1530.89	1476.00	1431.14	1394.09
110000	1879.70	1764.65	1675.02	1603.79	1546.29	1499.29	1460.48
120000	2050.58	1925.08	1827.29	1749.58	1686.86	1635.59	1593.25
130000	2221.46	2085.50	1979.57	1895.38	1827.43	1771.89	1726.02
140000	2392.34	2245.92	2131.84	2041.18	1968.00	1908.19	1858.79
150000	2563.22	2406.35	2284.11	2186.98	2108.58	2044.49	1991.56
175000	2990.43	2807.40	2664.80	2551.48	2460.01	2385.24	2323.49
200000	3417.63	3208.46	3045.49	2915.97	2811.43	2725.98	2655.41
225000	3844.84	3609.52	3426.17	3280.47	3162.86	3066.73	2987.34
250000	4272.04	4010.58	3806.86	3644.97	3514.29	3407.48	3319.27

13½%

Monthly Payments
necessary to amortize a loan

AMOUNT	15 YEARS	16 YEARS	17 YEARS	18 YEARS	19 YEARS	20 YEARS	21 YEARS
100	1.30	1.27	1.25	1.24	1.22	1.21	1.20
200	2.60	2.55	2.51	2.47	2.44	2.41	2.39
500	6.49	6.37	6.26	6.18	6.10	6.04	5.98
1000	12.98	12.74	12.53	12.35	12.20	12.07	11.96
2000	25.97	25.47	25.06	24.70	24.40	24.15	23.93
5000	64.92	63.68	62.64	61.76	61.01	60.37	59.82
6000	77.90	76.42	75.17	74.11	73.21	72.44	71.78
7000	90.88	89.16	87.70	86.47	85.41	84.52	83.75
8000	103.87	101.89	100.23	98.82	97.62	96.59	95.71
9000	116.85	114.63	112.76	111.17	109.82	108.66	107.67
10000	129.83	127.37	125.29	123.52	122.02	120.74	119.64
15000	194.75	191.05	187.93	185.28	183.03	181.11	179.46
20000	259.66	254.73	250.57	247.05	244.04	241.47	239.27
25000	324.58	318.42	313.22	308.81	305.05	301.84	299.09
30000	389.50	382.10	375.86	370.57	366.06	362.21	358.91
35000	454.41	445.78	438.50	432.33	427.07	422.58	418.73
36000	467.39	458.52	451.03	444.68	439.28	434.65	430.69
37000	480.38	471.26	463.56	457.04	451.48	446.73	442.66
38000	493.36	483.99	476.09	469.39	463.68	458.80	454.62
39000	506.34	496.73	488.62	481.74	475.88	470.88	466.58
40000	519.33	509.47	501.15	494.09	488.08	482.95	478.55
41000	532.31	522.20	513.68	506.44	500.29	495.02	490.51
42000	545.29	534.94	526.20	518.80	512.49	507.10	502.48
43000	558.28	547.68	538.73	531.15	524.69	519.17	514.44
44000	571.26	560.41	551.26	543.50	536.89	531.24	526.40
45000	584.24	573.15	563.79	555.85	549.10	543.32	538.37
46000	597.23	585.89	576.32	568.21	561.30	555.39	550.33
47000	610.21	598.62	588.85	580.56	573.50	567.47	562.29
48000	623.19	611.36	601.38	592.91	585.70	579.54	574.26
49000	636.18	624.10	613.91	605.26	597.90	591.61	586.22
50000	649.16	636.83	626.43	617.62	610.11	603.69	598.18
51000	662.14	649.57	638.96	629.97	622.31	615.76	610.15
52000	675.13	662.31	651.49	642.32	634.51	627.83	622.11
53000	688.11	675.04	664.02	654.67	646.71	639.91	634.08
54000	701.09	687.78	676.55	667.02	658.91	651.98	646.04
55000	714.08	700.52	689.08	679.38	671.12	664.06	658.00
56000	727.06	713.25	701.61	691.73	683.32	676.13	669.97
57000	740.04	725.99	714.14	704.08	695.52	688.20	681.93
58000	753.02	738.73	726.66	716.43	707.72	700.28	693.89
59000	766.01	751.46	739.19	728.79	719.92	712.35	705.86
60000	778.99	764.20	751.72	741.14	732.13	724.42	717.82
65000	843.91	827.88	814.36	802.90	793.14	784.79	777.64
70000	908.82	891.57	877.01	864.66	854.15	845.16	837.46
75000	973.74	955.25	939.65	926.42	915.16	905.53	897.28
80000	1038.65	1018.93	1002.30	988.19	976.17	965.90	957.10
85000	1103.57	1082.62	1064.94	1049.95	1037.18	1026.27	1016.91
90000	1168.49	1146.30	1127.58	1111.71	1098.19	1086.64	1076.73
95000	1233.40	1209.98	1190.23	1173.47	1159.20	1147.01	1136.55
100000	1298.32	1273.67	1252.87	1235.23	1220.21	1207.37	1196.37
105000	1363.23	1337.35	1315.51	1200.99	1281.22	1267.74	1256.19
110000	1428.15	1401.03	1378.16	1358.75	1342.23	1328.11	1316.01
120000	1557.98	1528.40	1503.44	1482.28	1464.25	1448.85	1435.64
130000	1687.81	1655.77	1628.73	1605.80	1586.27	1569.59	1555.28
140000	1817.65	1783.14	1754.02	1729.32	1708.30	1690.32	1674.92
150000	1947.48	1910.50	1879.30	1852.85	1830.32	1811.06	1794.55
175000	2272.06	2228.92	2192.52	2161.65	2135.37	2112.91	2093.65
200000	2596.64	2547.34	2505.74	2470.46	2440.42	2414.75	2392.74
225000	2921.22	2865.75	2818.95	2779.27	2745.48	2716.59	2691.83
250000	3245.80	3184.17	3132.17	3088.08	3050.53	3018.44	2990.92

Monthly Payments 13½%

necessary to amortize a loan

AMOUNT	22 YEARS	23 YEARS	24 YEARS	25 YEARS	30 YEARS	35 YEARS	40 YEARS
100	1.19	1.18	1.17	1.17	1.15	1.14	1.13
200	2.37	2.36	2.34	2.33	2.29	2.27	2.26
500	5.93	5.89	5.86	5.83	5.73	5.68	5.65
1000	11.87	11.79	11.72	11.66	11.45	11.35	11.30
2000	23.74	23.58	23.43	23.31	22.91	22.71	22.61
5000	59.35	58.94	58.59	58.28	57.27	56.77	56.51
6000	71.21	70.73	70.30	69.94	68.72	68.12	67.82
7000	83.08	82.51	82.02	81.60	80.18	79.47	79.12
8000	94.95	94.30	93.74	93.25	91.63	90.83	90.42
9000	106.82	106.09	105.46	104.91	103.09	102.18	101.72
10000	118.69	117.88	117.17	116.56	114.54	113.53	113.03
15000	178.04	176.81	175.76	174.85	171.81	170.30	169.54
20000	237.38	235.75	234.35	233.13	229.08	227.07	226.05
25000	296.73	294.69	292.93	291.41	286.35	283.84	282.57
30000	356.07	353.63	351.52	349.69	343.62	340.60	339.08
35000	415.42	412.57	410.10	407.98	400.89	397.37	395.59
36000	427.29	424.35	421.82	419.63	412.35	408.72	406.89
37000	439.16	436.14	433.54	431.29	423.80	420.08	418.20
38000	451.03	447.93	445.26	442.95	435.26	431.43	429.50
39000	462.90	459.72	456.97	454.60	446.71	442.78	440.80
40000	474.76	471.50	468.69	466.26	458.16	454.14	452.10
41000	486.63	483.29	480.41	477.91	469.62	465.49	463.41
42000	498.50	495.08	492.13	489.57	481.07	476.84	474.71
43000	510.37	506.87	503.84	501.23	492.53	488.20	486.01
44000	522.24	518.66	515.56	512.88	503.98	499.55	497.31
45000	534.11	530.44	527.28	524.54	515.44	510.90	508.62
46000	545.98	542.23	538.99	536.20	526.89	522.26	519.92
47000	557.85	554.02	550.71	547.85	538.34	533.61	531.22
48000	569.72	565.81	562.43	559.51	549.80	544.96	542.53
49000	581.59	577.59	574.15	571.17	561.25	556.32	553.83
50000	593.46	589.38	585.86	582.82	572.71	567.67	565.13
51000	605.32	601.17	597.58	594.48	584.16	579.02	576.43
52000	617.19	612.96	609.30	606.14	595.61	590.38	587.74
53000	629.06	624.74	621.02	617.79	607.07	601.73	599.04
54000	640.93	636.53	632.73	629.45	618.52	613.08	610.34
55000	652.80	648.32	644.45	641.10	629.98	624.44	621.64
56000	664.07	660.11	656.17	652.76	641.43	635.79	632.95
57000	676.54	671.89	667.88	664.42	652.88	647.14	644.25
58000	688.41	683.68	670.60	676.07	664.34	658.50	655.55
59000	700.28	695.47	691.32	687.73	675.79	660.85	666.85
60000	712.15	707.26	703.04	699.39	687.25	681.20	678.16
65000	771.49	766.19	761.62	757.67	744.52	737.97	734.67
70000	830.84	825.13	820.21	815.95	801.79	794.74	791.18
75000	890.18	884.07	878.80	874.23	859.06	851.51	847.70
80000	949.53	943.01	937.38	932.52	916.33	908.27	904.21
85000	1008.87	1001.95	995.97	990.80	973.60	965.04	960.72
90000	1068.22	1060.89	1054.55	1049.08	1030.87	1021.81	1017.24
95000	1127.57	1119.82	1113.14	1107.36	1088.14	1078.57	1073.75
100000	1186.91	1178.76	1171.73	1165.64	1145.41	1135.34	1130.26
105000	1246.26	1237.70	1230.31	1223.93	1202.68	1192.11	1186.77
110000	1305.60	1296.64	1288.90	1282.21	1259.95	1248.87	1243.29
120000	1424.29	1414.51	1406.07	1398.77	1374.49	1362.41	1356.31
130000	1542.98	1532.39	1523.25	1515.34	1489.04	1475.94	1469.34
140000	1661.67	1650.27	1640.42	1631.90	1603.58	1589.48	1582.37
150000	1780.37	1768.14	1757.59	1748.47	1718.12	1703.01	1695.39
175000	2077.09	2062.83	2050.52	2039.88	2004.47	1986.85	1977.96
200000	2373.82	2357.52	2343.45	2331.29	2290.82	2270.68	2260.52
225000	2670.55	2652.21	2636.39	2622.70	2577.18	2554.52	2543.09
250000	2967.28	2946.90	2929.32	2914.11	2863.53	2838.35	2825.65

13¾%

Monthly Payments

necessary to amortize a loan

AMOUNT	1 YEAR	2 YEARS	3 YEARS	4 YEARS	5 YEARS	6 YEARS	7 YEARS
100	8.97	4.79	3.41	2.72	2.31	2.05	1.86
200	17.93	9.58	6.81	5.44	4.63	4.09	3.72
500	44.83	23.95	17.03	13.60	11.57	10.24	9.30
1000	89.67	47.89	34.06	27.20	23.14	20.47	18.60
2000	179.34	95.79	68.11	54.40	46.28	40.94	37.20
5000	448.35	239.47	170.28	136.01	115.69	102.36	93.01
6000	538.02	287.37	204.34	163.21	138.83	122.83	111.61
7000	627.69	335.26	238.39	190.41	161.97	143.30	130.22
8000	717.36	383.16	272.45	217.61	185.11	163.78	148.82
9000	807.03	431.05	306.51	244.81	208.25	184.25	167.42
10000	896.70	478.95	340.56	272.01	231.39	204.72	186.02
15000	1345.04	718.42	510.84	408.02	347.08	307.08	279.03
20000	1793.39	957.90	681.13	544.02	462.78	409.44	372.04
25000	2241.74	1197.37	851.41	680.03	578.47	511.80	465.05
30000	2690.09	1436.85	1021.69	816.04	694.17	614.16	558.07
35000	3138.43	1676.32	1191.97	952.04	809.86	716.52	651.08
36000	3228.10	1724.22	1226.03	979.24	833.00	737.00	669.68
37000	3317.77	1772.11	1260.08	1006.45	856.14	757.47	688.28
38000	3407.44	1820.00	1294.14	1033.65	879.28	777.94	706.88
39000	3497.11	1867.90	1328.20	1060.85	902.41	798.41	725.49
40000	3586.78	1915.79	1362.25	1088.05	925.55	818.88	744.09
41000	3676.45	1963.69	1396.31	1115.25	948.69	839.36	762.69
42000	3766.12	2011.58	1430.37	1142.45	971.83	859.83	781.29
43000	3855.79	2059.48	1464.42	1169.65	994.97	880.30	799.89
44000	3945.46	2107.37	1498.48	1196.85	1018.11	900.77	818.50
45000	4035.13	2155.27	1532.53	1224.06	1041.25	921.25	837.10
46000	4124.80	2203.16	1566.59	1251.26	1064.39	941.72	855.70
47000	4214.47	2251.06	1600.65	1278.46	1087.53	962.19	874.30
48000	4304.14	2298.95	1634.70	1305.66	1110.66	982.66	892.90
49000	4393.81	2346.85	1668.76	1332.86	1133.80	1003.13	911.51
50000	4483.48	2394.74	1702.82	1360.06	1156.94	1023.61	930.11
51000	4573.15	2442.64	1736.87	1387.26	1180.08	1044.08	948.71
52000	4662.82	2490.53	1770.93	1414.46	1203.22	1064.55	967.31
53000	4752.49	2538.43	1804.99	1441.67	1226.36	1085.02	985.92
54000	4842.15	2586.32	1839.04	1468.87	1249.50	1105.49	1004.52
55000	4931.82	2634.22	1873.10	1496.07	1272.64	1125.97	1023.12
56000	5021.49	2682.11	1907.15	1523.27	1295.78	1146.44	1041.72
57000	5111.16	2730.01	1941.21	1550.47	1318.91	1166.91	1060.32
58000	5200.83	2777.90	1975.27	1577.67	1342.05	1187.38	1078.93
59000	5290.50	2825.80	2009.32	1604.87	1365.19	1207.85	1097.53
60000	5380.17	2873.69	2043.38	1632.07	1388.33	1228.33	1116.13
65000	5828.52	3113.17	2213.66	1768.08	1504.02	1330.69	1209.14
70000	6276.87	3352.64	2383.94	1904.09	1619.72	1433.05	1302.15
75000	6725.21	3592.11	2554.22	2040.09	1735.41	1535.41	1395.16
80000	7173.56	3831.59	2724.51	2176.10	1851.11	1637.77	1488.17
85000	7621.91	4071.06	2894.79	2312.10	1966.80	1740.13	1581.19
90000	8070.26	4310.54	3065.07	2448.11	2082.50	1842.49	1674.20
95000	8518.61	4550.01	3235.35	2584.12	2198.19	1944.85	1767.21
100000	8966.95	4789.49	3405.63	2720.12	2313.88	2047.21	1860.22
105000	9415.30	5028.96	3575.91	2856.13	2429.58	2149.57	1953.23
110000	9863.65	5268.44	3746.20	2992.14	2545.27	2251.93	2046.24
120000	10760.34	5747.38	4086.76	3264.15	2776.66	2456.65	2232.26
130000	11657.04	6226.33	4427.32	3536.16	3008.05	2661.37	2418.28
140000	12553.73	6705.28	4767.89	3808.17	3239.44	2866.10	2604.31
150000	13450.43	7184.23	5108.45	4080.19	3470.83	3070.82	2790.33
175000	15692.17	8381.60	5959.86	4760.22	4049.30	3582.62	3255.38
200000	17933.91	9578.97	6811.27	5440.25	4627.77	4094.42	3720.44
225000	20175.64	10776.34	7662.67	6120.28	5206.24	4606.23	4185.49
250000	22417.38	11973.72	8514.08	6800.31	5784.71	5118.03	4650.54

Monthly Payments

necessary to amortize a loan

13¾%

AMOUNT	8 YEARS	9 YEARS	10 YEARS	11 YEARS	12 YEARS	13 YEARS	14 YEARS
100	1.72	1.62	1.54	1.47	1.42	1.38	1.34
200	3.45	3.24	3.08	2.95	2.84	2.76	2.69
500	8.61	8.09	7.69	7.37	7.11	6.90	6.72
1000	17.23	16.19	15.38	14.73	14.21	13.79	13.44
2000	34.46	32.38	30.75	29.47	28.43	27.58	26.88
5000	86.15	80.94	76.88	73.66	71.07	68.95	67.20
6000	103.38	97.13	92.26	88.40	85.28	82.74	80.64
7000	120.61	113.31	107.64	103.13	99.50	96.53	94.08
8000	137.84	129.50	123.01	117.86	113.71	110.32	107.52
9000	155.07	145.69	138.39	132.60	127.92	124.11	120.97
10000	172.30	161.88	153.77	147.33	142.14	137.90	134.41
15000	258.44	242.82	230.65	220.99	213.21	206.85	201.61
20000	344.59	323.75	307.53	294.66	284.28	275.80	268.81
25000	430.74	404.69	384.42	368.32	355.35	344.75	336.01
30000	516.89	485.63	461.30	441.99	426.41	413.70	403.22
35000	603.03	566.57	538.18	515.65	497.48	482.65	470.42
36000	620.26	582.76	553.56	530.38	511.70	496.44	483.86
37000	637.49	598.94	568.94	545.12	525.91	510.23	497.30
38000	654.72	615.13	584.31	559.85	540.13	524.02	510.74
39000	671.95	631.32	599.69	574.58	554.34	537.81	524.18
40000	689.18	647.51	615.07	589.32	568.55	551.60	537.62
41000	706.41	663.69	630.44	604.05	582.77	565.39	551.06
42000	723.64	679.88	645.82	618.78	596.98	579.18	564.50
43000	740.87	696.07	661.20	633.51	611.19	592.97	577.94
44000	758.10	712.26	676.57	648.25	625.41	606.76	591.38
45000	775.33	728.45	691.95	662.98	639.62	620.55	604.83
46000	792.56	744.63	707.33	677.71	653.84	634.34	618.27
47000	809.79	760.82	722.70	692.45	668.05	648.13	631.71
48000	827.02	777.01	738.08	707.18	682.26	661.92	645.15
49000	844.25	793.20	753.46	721.91	696.48	675.71	658.59
50000	861.48	809.38	768.83	736.64	710.69	689.50	672.03
51000	878.71	825.57	784.21	751.38	724.91	703.29	685.47
52000	895.94	841.76	799.59	766.11	739.12	717.08	698.91
53000	913.16	857.95	814.96	780.84	753.33	730.87	712.35
54000	930.39	874.13	830.34	795.58	767.55	744.66	725.79
55000	947.62	890.32	845.72	810.31	781.76	758.45	739.23
56000	964.85	906.51	861.09	825.04	795.97	772.24	752.67
57000	982.08	922.70	876.47	839.77	810.19	786.03	766.11
58000	999.31	938.89	891.86	854.51	824.40	799.82	779.55
59000	1016.54	955.07	907.22	869.24	838.62	813.61	792.99
60000	1033.77	971.26	922.60	883.97	852.83	827.40	806.43
65000	1119.92	1052.20	999.48	957.64	923.90	896.35	873.64
70000	1206.07	1133.14	1076.37	1031.30	994.07	965.30	940.84
75000	1292.21	1214.08	1153.25	1104.97	1066.04	1034.25	1008.04
80000	1378.36	1295.01	1230.13	1178.63	1137.11	1103.21	1075.25
85000	1464.51	1375.95	1307.02	1252.30	1208.18	1172.16	1142.45
90000	1550.66	1456.89	1383.90	1325.96	1279.24	1241.11	1209.66
95000	1636.81	1537.83	1460.78	1399.62	1350.31	1310.06	1276.85
100000	1722.95	1618.77	1537.67	1473.29	1421.38	1379.01	1344.06
105000	1809.10	1699.71	1614.55	1546.95	1492.45	1447.96	1411.26
110000	1895.25	1780.64	1691.43	1620.62	1563.52	1516.91	1478.46
120000	2067.54	1942.52	1845.20	1767.95	1705.66	1654.81	1612.87
130000	2239.84	2104.40	1998.97	1915.28	1847.80	1792.71	1747.27
140000	2412.13	2266.27	2152.74	2062.60	1989.94	1930.61	1881.68
150000	2584.43	2428.15	2306.50	2209.93	2132.07	2068.51	2016.08
175000	3015.17	2832.84	2690.92	2578.26	2487.42	2413.26	2352.10
200000	3445.91	3237.54	3075.34	2946.58	2842.77	2758.01	2688.11
225000	3876.64	3642.23	3459.75	3314.90	3198.11	3102.76	3024.13
250000	4307.38	4046.92	3844.17	3683.22	3553.46	3447.52	3360.14

13¾%

Monthly Payments
necessary to amortize a loan

AMOUNT	15 YEARS	16 YEARS	17 YEARS	18 YEARS	19 YEARS	20 YEARS	21 YEARS
100	1.31	1.29	1.27	1.25	1.24	1.23	1.21
200	2.63	2.58	2.54	2.51	2.48	2.45	2.43
500	6.57	6.45	6.35	6.26	6.19	6.13	6.07
1000	13.15	12.91	12.70	12.53	12.38	12.25	12.15
2000	26.30	25.81	25.40	25.06	24.76	24.51	24.29
5000	65.75	64.53	63.51	62.64	61.90	61.27	60.73
6000	78.90	77.44	76.21	75.17	74.28	73.52	72.88
7000	92.05	90.34	88.91	87.69	86.66	85.78	85.02
8000	105.20	103.25	101.61	100.22	99.04	98.03	97.17
9000	118.35	116.16	114.31	112.75	111.42	110.29	109.32
10000	131.50	129.06	127.01	125.28	123.80	122.54	121.46
15000	197.25	193.60	190.52	187.91	185.70	183.81	182.19
20000	263.00	258.13	254.03	250.55	247.60	245.08	242.93
25000	328.75	322.66	317.53	313.19	309.50	306.35	303.66
30000	394.50	387.19	381.04	375.83	371.40	367.62	364.39
35000	460.25	451.72	444.55	438.47	433.30	428.89	425.12
36000	473.40	464.63	457.25	451.00	445.68	441.15	437.27
37000	486.55	477.54	469.95	463.52	458.06	453.40	449.41
38000	499.70	490.44	482.65	476.05	470.44	465.65	461.56
39000	512.85	503.35	495.35	488.58	482.82	477.91	473.70
40000	525.99	516.26	508.05	501.11	495.20	490.16	485.85
41000	539.14	529.16	520.75	513.63	507.58	502.42	498.00
42000	552.29	542.07	533.45	526.16	519.96	514.67	510.14
43000	565.44	554.98	546.16	538.69	532.34	526.92	522.29
44000	578.59	567.88	558.86	551.22	544.72	539.18	534.44
45000	591.74	580.79	571.56	563.74	557.10	551.43	546.58
46000	604.89	593.69	584.26	576.27	569.48	563.69	558.73
47000	618.04	606.60	596.96	588.80	581.86	575.94	570.87
48000	631.19	619.51	609.66	601.33	594.24	588.19	583.02
49000	644.34	632.41	622.36	613.85	606.62	600.45	595.17
50000	657.49	645.32	635.06	626.38	619.00	612.70	607.31
51000	670.64	658.23	647.77	638.91	631.38	624.96	619.46
52000	683.79	671.13	660.47	651.44	643.76	637.21	631.61
53000	696.94	684.04	673.17	663.96	656.14	649.46	643.75
54000	710.09	696.95	685.87	676.49	668.52	661.72	655.90
55000	723.24	709.85	698.57	689.02	680.90	673.97	668.04
56000	736.39	722.76	711.27	701.55	693.28	686.23	680.19
57000	749.54	735.67	723.97	714.08	705.66	698.48	692.34
58000	762.69	748.57	736.67	726.60	718.04	710.74	704.48
59000	775.84	761.48	749.38	739.13	730.42	722.99	716.63
60000	788.99	774.38	762.08	751.66	742.80	735.24	728.78
65000	854.74	838.92	825.58	814.30	804.70	796.51	789.51
70000	920.49	903.45	889.09	876.93	866.60	857.78	850.24
75000	986.24	967.98	952.60	939.57	928.50	919.05	910.97
80000	1051.99	1032.51	1016.10	1002.21	990.40	980.32	971.70
85000	1117.74	1097.04	1079.61	1064.85	1052.30	1041.59	1032.43
90000	1183.49	1161.58	1143.12	1127.49	1114.20	1102.86	1093.16
95000	1249.24	1226.11	1206.62	1190.13	1176.10	1164.14	1153.90
100000	1314.99	1290.64	1270.13	1252.76	1238.00	1225.41	1214.63
105000	1380.74	1355.17	1333.64	1315.40	1299.90	1286.68	1275.36
110000	1446.49	1419.70	1397.14	1378.04	1361.80	1347.95	1336.09
120000	1577.98	1548.77	1524.15	1503.32	1485.60	1470.49	1457.55
130000	1709.48	1677.83	1651.17	1628.59	1609.40	1593.03	1579.01
140000	1840.98	1806.90	1778.18	1753.87	1733.20	1715.57	1700.48
150000	1972.48	1935.96	1905.19	1879.15	1857.00	1838.11	1821.94
175000	2301.23	2258.62	2222.73	2192.34	2166.50	2144.46	2125.60
200000	2629.97	2581.28	2540.26	2505.53	2476.00	2450.81	2429.25
225000	2958.72	2903.94	2857.79	2818.72	2785.50	2757.16	2732.91
250000	3287.47	3226.60	3175.32	3131.91	3095.00	3063.51	3036.57

Monthly Payments 13¾%

necessary to amortize a loan

AMOUNT	22 YEARS	23 YEARS	24 YEARS	25 YEARS	30 YEARS	35 YEARS	40 YEARS
100	1.21	1.20	1.19	1.18	1.17	1.16	1.15
200	2.41	2.39	2.38	2.37	2.33	2.31	2.30
500	6.03	5.99	5.95	5.92	5.83	5.78	5.75
1000	12.05	11.97	11.91	11.85	11.65	11.55	11.51
2000	24.11	23.95	23.81	23.69	23.30	23.11	23.01
5000	60.27	59.87	59.53	59.23	58.26	57.77	57.53
6000	72.32	71.85	71.43	71.08	69.91	69.33	69.04
7000	84.38	83.82	83.34	82.93	81.56	80.88	80.55
8000	96.43	95.79	95.25	94.77	93.21	92.44	92.05
9000	108.48	107.77	107.15	106.62	104.86	103.99	103.56
10000	120.54	119.74	119.06	118.47	116.51	115.55	115.07
15000	180.81	179.61	178.59	177.70	174.77	173.32	172.60
20000	241.08	239.49	238.12	236.93	233.02	231.10	230.14
25000	301.34	299.36	297.64	296.17	291.28	288.87	287.67
30000	361.61	359.23	357.17	355.40	349.53	346.65	345.21
35000	421.88	419.10	416.70	414.63	407.79	404.42	402.74
36000	433.94	431.07	428.61	426.48	419.44	415.97	414.25
37000	445.99	443.05	440.51	438.33	431.09	427.53	425.75
38000	458.04	455.02	452.42	450.17	442.74	439.08	437.26
39000	470.10	467.00	464.33	462.02	454.39	450.64	448.77
40000	482.15	478.97	476.23	473.87	466.05	462.19	460.27
41000	494.21	490.95	488.14	485.71	477.70	473.75	471.78
42000	506.26	502.92	500.04	497.56	489.35	485.30	483.29
43000	518.31	514.89	511.95	509.41	501.00	496.86	494.79
44000	530.37	526.87	523.85	521.25	512.65	508.41	506.30
45000	542.42	538.84	535.76	533.10	524.30	519.97	517.81
46000	554.47	550.82	547.67	544.95	535.95	531.52	529.32
47000	566.53	562.79	559.57	556.79	547.60	543.08	540.82
48000	578.58	574.77	571.48	568.64	559.25	554.63	552.33
49000	590.64	586.74	583.38	580.49	570.91	566.19	563.84
50000	602.69	598.71	595.29	592.33	582.56	577.74	575.34
51000	614.74	610.69	607.19	604.18	594.21	589.30	586.85
52000	626.80	622.66	619.10	616.03	605.86	600.85	598.36
53000	638.85	634.64	631.01	627.87	617.51	612.41	609.86
54000	650.90	646.61	642.91	639.72	629.16	623.96	621.37
55000	662.96	658.59	654.82	651.57	640.81	635.52	632.88
56000	675.01	670.56	666.72	663.41	652.46	647.07	644.38
57000	687.07	682.53	678.63	675.26	664.11	658.63	655.89
58000	699.12	694.51	690.53	687.11	675.77	670.18	667.40
59000	711.17	706.48	702.44	698.95	687.42	681.74	678.90
60000	723.23	718.46	714.35	710.80	699.07	693.29	690.41
65000	783.50	778.33	773.88	770.03	757.32	751.07	747.95
70000	843.77	838.20	833.40	829.27	815.58	808.84	805.48
75000	904.03	898.07	892.93	888.50	873.83	866.61	863.01
80000	964.30	957.94	952.46	947.73	932.09	924.39	920.55
85000	1024.57	1017.81	1011.08	1006.97	990.35	982.16	978.08
90000	1084.84	1077.68	1071.52	1066.20	1048.60	1039.94	1035.62
95000	1145.11	1137.56	1131.05	1125.43	1106.86	1097.71	1093.15
100000	1205.38	1197.43	1190.58	1184.67	1165.11	1155.49	1150.69
105000	1265.65	1257.30	1250.11	1243.90	1223.37	1213.26	1208.22
110000	1325.92	1317.17	1309.64	1303.13	1281.62	1271.03	1265.75
120000	1446.46	1436.91	1428.69	1421.60	1398.14	1386.58	1380.82
130000	1566.99	1556.66	1547.75	1540.07	1514.65	1502.13	1495.89
140000	1687.53	1676.40	1666.81	1658.53	1631.16	1617.68	1610.96
150000	1808.07	1796.14	1785.87	1777.00	1747.67	1733.23	1726.03
175000	2109.41	2095.50	2083.51	2073.17	2038.95	2022.10	2013.70
200000	2410.76	2394.86	2381.15	2369.33	2330.23	2310.97	2301.37
225000	2712.10	2694.21	2678.80	2665.50	2621.50	2599.84	2589.04
250000	3013.45	2993.57	2976.44	2961.66	2912.78	2888.71	2876.71

14% Monthly Payments

necessary to amortize a loan

AMOUNT	1 YEAR	2 YEARS	3 YEARS	4 YEARS	5 YEARS	6 YEARS	7 YEARS
100	8.98	4.80	3.42	2.73	2.33	2.06	1.87
200	17.96	9.60	6.84	5.47	4.65	4.12	3.75
500	44.89	24.01	17.09	13.66	11.63	10.30	9.37
1000	89.79	48.01	34.18	27.33	23.27	20.61	18.74
2000	179.57	96.03	68.36	54.65	46.54	41.21	37.48
5000	448.94	240.06	170.89	136.63	116.34	103.03	93.70
6000	538.72	288.08	205.07	163.96	139.61	123.63	112.44
7000	628.51	336.09	239.24	191.29	162.88	144.24	131.18
8000	718.30	384.10	273.42	218.61	186.15	164.85	149.92
9000	808.08	432.12	307.60	245.94	209.41	185.45	168.66
10000	897.87	480.13	341.78	273.26	232.68	206.06	187.40
15000	1346.81	720.19	512.66	409.90	349.02	309.09	281.10
20000	1795.74	960.26	683.55	546.53	465.37	412.11	374.80
25000	2244.68	1200.32	854.44	683.16	581.71	515.14	468.50
30000	2693.61	1440.39	1025.33	819.79	698.05	618.17	562.20
35000	3142.55	1680.45	1196.22	956.43	814.39	721.20	655.90
36000	3232.34	1728.46	1230.39	983.75	837.66	741.81	674.64
37000	3322.12	1776.48	1264.57	1011.08	860.93	762.41	693.38
38000	3411.91	1824.49	1298.75	1038.41	884.19	783.02	712.12
39000	3501.70	1872.50	1332.93	1065.73	907.46	803.62	730.86
40000	3591.48	1920.52	1367.11	1093.06	930.73	824.23	749.60
41000	3681.27	1968.53	1401.28	1120.39	954.00	844.84	768.34
42000	3771.06	2016.54	1435.46	1147.71	977.27	865.44	787.08
43000	3860.85	2064.55	1469.64	1175.04	1000.53	886.05	805.82
44000	3950.63	2112.57	1503.82	1202.36	1023.80	906.65	824.56
45000	4040.42	2160.58	1537.99	1229.69	1047.07	927.26	843.30
46000	4130.21	2208.59	1572.17	1257.02	1070.34	947.86	862.04
47000	4219.99	2256.61	1606.35	1284.34	1093.61	968.47	880.78
48000	4309.78	2304.62	1640.53	1311.67	1116.88	989.08	899.52
49000	4399.57	2352.63	1674.70	1339.00	1140.14	1009.68	918.26
50000	4489.36	2400.64	1708.88	1366.32	1163.41	1030.29	937.00
51000	4579.14	2448.66	1743.06	1393.65	1186.68	1050.89	955.74
52000	4668.93	2496.67	1777.24	1420.98	1209.95	1071.50	974.48
53000	4758.72	2544.68	1811.41	1448.30	1233.22	1092.10	993.22
54000	4848.50	2592.70	1845.59	1475.63	1256.49	1112.71	1011.96
55000	4938.29	2640.71	1879.77	1502.96	1279.75	1133.32	1030.70
56000	5028.08	2688.72	1913.95	1530.28	1303.02	1153.92	1049.44
57000	5117.87	2736.73	1948.12	1557.61	1326.29	1174.53	1068.18
58000	5207.65	2784.75	1982.30	1584.94	1349.56	1195.13	1086.92
59000	5297.44	2832.76	2016.48	1612.26	1372.83	1215.74	1105.66
60000	5387.23	2880.77	2050.66	1639.59	1396.10	1236.34	1124.40
65000	5836.16	3120.84	2221.55	1776.22	1512.44	1339.37	1218.10
70000	6285.10	3360.90	2392.43	1912.85	1628.78	1442.40	1311.80
75000	6734.03	3600.97	2563.32	2049.49	1745.12	1545.43	1405.50
80000	7182.97	3841.03	2734.21	2186.12	1861.46	1648.46	1499.20
85000	7631.90	4081.10	2905.10	2322.75	1977.80	1751.49	1592.90
90000	8080.84	4321.16	3075.99	2459.38	2094.14	1854.52	1686.60
95000	8529.78	4561.22	3246.87	2596.02	2210.48	1957.55	1780.30
100000	8978.71	4801.29	3417.76	2732.65	2326.83	2060.57	1874.00
105000	9427.65	5041.35	3588.65	2869.28	2443.17	2163.60	1967.70
110000	9876.58	5281.42	3759.54	3005.91	2559.51	2266.63	2061.40
120000	10774.45	5761.55	4101.32	3279.18	2792.19	2472.69	2248.80
130000	11672.33	6241.67	4443.09	3552.44	3024.87	2678.75	2436.20
140000	12570.20	6721.80	4784.87	3825.71	3257.56	2884.80	2623.60
150000	13468.07	7201.93	5126.64	4098.97	3490.24	3090.86	2811.00
175000	15712.75	8402.25	5981.09	4782.13	4071.94	3606.00	3279.50
200000	17957.42	9602.58	6835.53	5465.30	4653.65	4121.15	3748.00
225000	20202.10	10802.90	7689.97	6148.46	5235.36	4636.29	4216.50
250000	22446.78	12003.22	8544.41	6831.62	5817.06	5151.43	4685.00

Monthly Payments

necessary to amortize a loan

14%

AMOUNT	8 YEARS	9 YEARS	10 YEARS	11 YEARS	12 YEARS	13 YEARS	14 YEARS
100	1.74	1.63	1.55	1.49	1.44	1.40	1.36
200	3.47	3.27	3.11	2.98	2.87	2.79	2.72
500	8.69	8.17	7.76	7.44	7.19	6.98	6.80
1000	17.37	16.33	15.53	14.89	14.37	13.95	13.60
2000	34.74	32.67	31.05	29.77	28.74	27.90	27.21
5000	86.86	81.67	77.63	74.43	71.86	69.76	68.02
6000	104.23	98.00	93.16	89.32	86.23	83.71	81.63
7000	121.60	114.34	108.69	104.21	100.60	97.66	95.23
8000	138.97	130.67	124.21	119.09	114.97	111.61	108.84
9000	156.34	147.00	139.74	133.98	129.34	125.56	122.44
10000	173.72	163.34	155.27	148.87	143.71	139.51	136.05
15000	260.57	245.01	232.90	223.30	215.57	209.27	204.07
20000	347.43	326.67	310.53	297.73	287.43	279.02	272.10
25000	434.29	408.34	388.17	372.17	359.28	348.78	340.12
30000	521.15	490.01	465.80	446.60	431.14	418.53	408.15
35000	608.00	571.68	543.43	521.03	502.99	488.29	476.17
36000	625.37	588.01	558.96	535.92	517.37	502.24	489.78
37000	642.75	604.35	574.49	550.81	531.74	516.19	503.38
38000	660.12	620.68	590.01	565.69	546.11	530.14	516.99
39000	677.49	637.01	605.54	580.58	560.48	544.09	530.59
40000	694.86	653.35	621.07	595.47	574.85	558.04	544.20
41000	712.23	669.68	636.59	610.35	589.22	571.99	557.80
42000	729.60	686.02	652.12	625.24	603.59	585.94	571.41
43000	746.97	702.35	667.65	640.13	617.96	599.89	585.01
44000	764.35	718.68	683.17	655.01	632.34	613.85	598.62
45000	781.72	735.02	698.70	669.90	646.71	627.80	612.22
46000	799.09	751.35	714.23	684.79	661.08	641.75	625.83
47000	816.46	767.68	729.75	699.67	675.45	655.70	639.43
48000	833.83	784.02	745.28	714.56	689.82	669.65	653.04
49000	851.20	800.35	760.81	729.45	704.19	683.60	666.64
50000	868.58	816.69	776.33	744.33	718.56	697.55	680.24
51000	885.95	833.02	791.86	759.22	732.93	711.50	693.85
52000	903.32	849.35	807.39	774.11	747.31	725.45	707.45
53000	920.69	865.69	822.91	788.99	761.68	739.40	721.06
54000	938.06	882.02	838.44	803.88	776.05	753.36	734.66
55000	955.43	898.35	853.97	818.77	790.42	767.31	748.27
56000	972.80	914.69	869.49	833.65	804.79	781.26	761.87
57000	990.18	931.02	885.02	848.54	819.16	795.21	775.48
58000	1007.55	947.35	900.55	863.43	833.53	809.16	789.08
59000	1024.92	963.69	916.07	878.31	047.00	823.11	802.69
60000	1042.29	980.02	931.60	893.20	862.28	837.06	816.29
65000	1129.15	1061.69	1009.23	967.63	934.13	906.82	884.32
70000	1216.01	1143.30	1006.87	1042.07	1005.99	976.57	952.34
75000	1302.86	1225.03	1164.50	1116.50	1077.85	1046.33	1020.37
80000	1389.72	1306.70	1242.13	1190.93	1149.70	1116.08	1088.39
85000	1476.58	1388.36	1319.76	1265.37	1221.56	1185.84	1156.42
90000	1563.44	1470.03	1397.40	1339.80	1293.41	1255.50	1224.44
95000	1650.29	1551.70	1475.03	1414.23	1365.27	1325.35	1292.47
100000	1737.15	1633.37	1552.66	1488.67	1437.13	1395.10	1360.49
105000	1824.01	1715.04	1630.30	1563.10	1508.98	1464.86	1428.51
110000	1910.87	1796.71	1707.93	1637.53	1580.84	1534.61	1496.54
120000	2084.58	1960.04	1863.20	1786.40	1724.55	1674.12	1632.59
130000	2258.30	2123.38	2018.46	1935.27	1868.27	1813.63	1768.64
140000	2432.01	2286.72	2173.73	2084.13	2011.98	1953.14	1904.69
150000	2605.73	2450.06	2329.00	2233.00	2155.69	2092.65	2040.73
175000	3040.01	2858.40	2717.16	2605.17	2514.97	2441.43	2380.86
200000	3474.30	3266.74	3105.33	2977.33	2874.25	2790.21	2720.98
225000	3908.59	3675.08	3493.49	3349.50	3233.54	3138.98	3061.10
250000	4342.88	4083.43	3881.66	3721.67	3592.82	3487.76	3401.22

14% Monthly Payments

necessary to amortize a loan

AMOUNT	15 YEARS	16 YEARS	17 YEARS	18 YEARS	19 YEARS	20 YEARS	21 YEARS
100	1.33	1.31	1.29	1.27	1.26	1.24	1.23
200	2.66	2.62	2.57	2.54	2.51	2.49	2.47
500	6.66	6.54	6.44	6.35	6.28	6.22	6.16
1000	13.32	13.08	12.87	12.70	12.56	12.44	12.33
2000	26.63	26.15	25.75	25.41	25.12	24.87	24.66
5000	66.59	65.38	64.37	63.52	62.79	62.18	61.65
6000	79.90	78.46	77.25	76.22	75.35	74.61	73.98
7000	93.22	91.54	90.12	88.93	87.91	87.05	86.31
8000	106.54	104.62	103.00	101.63	100.47	99.48	98.64
9000	119.86	117.69	115.87	114.33	113.03	111.92	110.97
10000	133.17	130.77	128.75	127.04	125.59	124.35	123.30
15000	199.76	196.15	193.12	190.56	188.38	186.53	184.95
20000	266.35	261.54	257.50	254.08	251.18	248.70	246.59
25000	332.94	326.92	321.87	317.60	313.97	310.88	308.24
30000	399.52	392.31	386.24	381.11	376.76	373.06	369.89
35000	466.11	457.69	450.62	444.63	439.56	435.23	431.54
36000	479.43	470.77	463.49	457.34	452.12	447.67	443.87
37000	492.74	483.85	476.37	470.04	464.67	460.10	456.20
38000	506.06	496.93	489.24	482.75	477.23	472.54	468.53
39000	519.38	510.00	502.12	495.45	489.79	484.97	480.86
40000	532.70	523.08	514.99	508.15	502.35	497.41	493.19
41000	546.01	536.16	527.87	520.86	514.91	509.84	505.52
42000	559.33	549.23	540.74	533.56	527.47	522.28	517.85
43000	572.65	562.31	553.61	546.26	540.03	534.71	530.18
44000	585.97	575.39	566.49	558.97	552.59	547.15	542.51
45000	599.28	588.46	579.36	571.67	565.14	559.58	554.84
46000	612.60	601.54	592.24	584.38	577.70	572.02	567.16
47000	625.92	614.62	605.11	597.08	590.26	584.45	579.49
48000	639.24	627.70	617.99	609.78	602.82	596.89	591.82
49000	652.55	640.77	630.86	622.49	615.38	609.33	604.15
50000	665.87	653.85	643.74	635.19	627.94	621.76	616.48
51000	679.19	666.93	656.61	647.90	640.50	634.20	628.81
52000	692.51	680.00	669.49	660.60	653.06	646.63	641.14
53000	705.82	693.08	682.36	673.30	665.61	659.07	653.47
54000	719.14	706.16	695.24	686.01	678.17	671.50	665.80
55000	732.46	719.23	708.11	698.71	690.73	683.94	678.13
56000	745.78	732.31	720.99	711.41	703.29	696.37	690.46
57000	759.09	745.39	733.86	724.12	715.85	708.81	702.79
58000	772.41	758.47	746.74	736.82	728.41	721.24	715.12
59000	785.73	771.54	759.61	749.53	740.97	733.68	727.45
60000	799.04	784.62	772.49	762.23	753.53	746.11	739.78
65000	865.63	850.00	836.86	825.75	816.32	808.29	801.43
70000	932.22	915.39	901.23	889.27	879.11	870.46	863.08
75000	998.81	980.77	965.61	952.79	941.91	932.64	924.73
80000	1065.39	1046.16	1029.98	1016.31	1004.70	994.82	986.37
85000	1131.98	1111.54	1094.35	1079.83	1067.49	1056.99	1048.02
90000	1198.57	1176.93	1158.73	1143.34	1130.29	1119.17	1109.67
95000	1265.15	1242.31	1223.10	1206.86	1193.08	1181.34	1171.32
100000	1331.74	1307.70	1287.48	1270.38	1255.88	1243.52	1232.97
105000	1398.33	1373.08	1351.85	1333.90	1318.67	1305.70	1294.62
110000	1464.92	1438.47	1416.22	1397.42	1381.46	1367.87	1356.26
120000	1598.09	1569.24	1544.97	1524.46	1507.05	1492.22	1479.56
130000	1731.26	1700.01	1673.72	1651.50	1632.64	1616.58	1602.86
140000	1864.44	1830.78	1802.47	1778.54	1758.23	1740.93	1726.15
150000	1997.61	1961.55	1931.21	1905.57	1883.81	1865.28	1849.45
175000	2330.55	2288.47	2253.08	2223.17	2197.78	2176.16	2157.69
200000	2663.48	2615.40	2574.95	2540.77	2511.75	2487.04	2465.93
225000	2996.42	2942.32	2896.82	2858.36	2825.72	2797.92	2774.18
250000	3329.35	3269.25	3218.69	3175.96	3139.69	3108.80	3082.42

Monthly Payments 14%

necessary to amortize a loan

AMOUNT	22 YEARS	23 YEARS	24 YEARS	25 YEARS	30 YEARS	35 YEARS	40 YEARS
100	1.22	1.22	1.21	1.20	1.18	1.18	1.17
200	2.45	2.43	2.42	2.41	2.37	2.35	2.34
500	6.12	6.08	6.05	6.02	5.92	5.88	5.86
1000	12.24	12.16	12.10	12.04	11.85	11.76	11.71
2000	24.48	24.32	24.19	24.08	23.70	23.51	23.42
5000	61.20	60.81	60.48	60.19	59.24	58.78	58.56
6000	73.44	72.97	72.57	72.23	71.09	70.54	70.27
7000	85.68	85.13	84.67	84.26	82.94	82.30	81.98
8000	97.91	97.29	96.76	96.30	94.79	94.05	93.69
9000	110.15	109.46	108.86	108.34	106.64	105.81	105.40
10000	122.39	121.62	120.95	120.38	118.49	117.57	117.11
15000	183.59	182.43	181.43	180.56	177.73	176.35	175.67
20000	244.79	243.23	241.90	240.75	236.97	235.13	234.23
25000	305.98	304.04	302.38	300.94	296.22	293.92	292.79
30000	367.18	364.85	362.85	361.13	355.46	352.70	351.34
35000	428.38	425.66	423.33	421.32	414.71	411.49	409.90
36000	440.61	437.82	435.42	433.35	426.55	423.24	421.61
37000	452.85	449.98	447.52	445.39	438.40	435.00	433.32
38000	465.09	462.15	459.61	457.43	450.25	446.76	445.03
39000	477.33	474.31	471.71	469.47	462.10	458.51	456.74
40000	489.57	486.47	483.80	481.50	473.95	470.27	468.46
41000	501.81	498.63	495.90	493.54	485.80	482.03	480.17
42000	514.05	510.79	507.99	505.58	497.65	493.78	491.88
43000	526.29	522.95	520.09	517.62	509.49	505.54	503.59
44000	538.53	535.12	532.18	529.65	521.34	517.30	515.30
45000	550.77	547.28	544.28	541.69	533.19	529.05	527.01
46000	563.01	559.44	556.37	553.73	545.04	540.81	538.72
47000	575.25	571.60	568.47	565.77	556.89	552.57	550.44
48000	587.49	583.76	580.56	577.81	568.74	564.32	562.15
49000	599.73	595.92	592.66	589.84	580.59	576.08	573.86
50000	611.96	608.09	604.75	601.88	592.44	587.84	585.57
51000	624.20	620.25	616.85	613.92	604.28	599.59	597.28
52000	636.44	632.41	628.94	625.96	616.13	611.35	608.99
53000	648.68	644.57	641.04	637.99	627.98	623.11	620.70
54000	660.92	656.73	653.13	650.03	639.83	634.86	632.42
55000	673.16	668.90	665.23	662.07	651.68	646.62	644.13
56000	685.40	681.06	677.32	674.11	663.53	658.38	655.84
57000	697.64	603.22	689.42	686.14	675.38	670.13	667.55
58000	709.88	705.38	701.51	698.18	687.23	681.89	679.26
59000	722.12	717.54	713.61	710.22	600.07	693.65	690.97
60000	734.36	729.70	725.70	722.26	710.92	705.40	702.68
65000	795.55	790.51	786.18	782.44	770.17	764.19	761.24
70000	856.75	851.32	846.65	842.63	829.41	822.97	819.80
75000	917.95	912.13	907.13	902.82	888.65	881.75	878.36
80000	979.14	972.94	967.60	963.01	947.90	940.54	936.91
85000	1040.34	1033.75	1028.08	1023.20	1007.14	999.32	995.47
90000	1101.54	1094.56	1088.55	1083.38	1066.38	1050.11	1064.03
95000	1162.73	1155.36	1149.03	1143.57	1125.63	1116.89	1112.58
100000	1223.93	1216.17	1209.50	1203.76	1184.87	1175.67	1171.14
105000	1285.13	1276.98	1269.98	1263.95	1244.12	1234.46	1229.70
110000	1346.32	1337.79	1330.45	1324.14	1303.36	1293.24	1288.25
120000	1468.72	1459.41	1451.41	1444.51	1421.85	1410.81	1405.37
130000	1591.11	1581.03	1572.36	1564.89	1540.33	1528.38	1522.48
140000	1713.50	1702.64	1693.31	1685.27	1658.82	1645.94	1639.60
150000	1835.89	1824.26	1814.26	1805.64	1777.31	1763.51	1756.71
175000	2141.88	2128.30	2116.63	2106.58	2073.53	2057.43	2049.50
200000	2447.86	2432.35	2419.01	2407.52	2369.74	2351.35	2342.28
225000	2753.84	2736.39	2721.38	2708.46	2665.96	2645.26	2635.07
250000	3059.82	3040.43	3023.76	3009.40	2962.18	2939.18	2927.85

14¼%

Monthly Payments
necessary to amortize a loan

AMOUNT	1 YEAR	2 YEARS	3 YEARS	4 YEARS	5 YEARS	6 YEARS	7 YEARS
100	8.99	4.81	3.43	2.75	2.34	2.07	1.89
200	17.98	9.63	6.86	5.49	4.68	4.15	3.78
500	44.95	24.07	17.15	13.73	11.70	10.37	9.44
1000	89.90	48.13	34.30	27.45	23.40	20.74	18.88
2000	179.81	96.26	68.60	54.90	46.80	41.48	37.76
5000	449.52	240.66	171.50	137.26	116.99	103.70	94.39
6000	539.43	288.79	205.80	164.71	140.39	124.44	113.27
7000	629.33	336.92	240.09	192.16	163.79	145.18	132.15
8000	719.24	385.05	274.39	219.62	187.18	165.92	151.03
9000	809.14	433.18	308.69	247.07	210.58	186.66	169.91
10000	899.05	481.31	342.99	274.52	233.98	207.40	188.78
15000	1348.57	721.97	514.49	411.78	350.97	311.10	283.18
20000	1798.10	962.62	685.98	549.04	467.96	414.80	377.57
25000	2247.62	1203.28	857.48	686.30	584.95	518.50	471.96
30000	2697.14	1443.93	1028.98	823.56	701.94	622.20	566.35
35000	3146.67	1684.59	1200.47	960.82	818.93	725.89	660.74
36000	3236.57	1732.72	1234.77	988.27	842.33	746.63	679.62
37000	3326.48	1780.85	1269.07	1015.73	865.73	767.37	698.50
38000	3416.38	1828.98	1303.37	1043.18	889.13	788.11	717.38
39000	3506.29	1877.11	1337.67	1070.63	912.52	808.85	736.26
40000	3596.19	1925.24	1371.97	1098.08	935.92	829.59	755.14
41000	3686.10	1973.37	1406.27	1125.53	959.32	850.33	774.01
42000	3776.00	2021.50	1440.57	1152.99	982.72	871.07	792.89
43000	3865.91	2069.64	1474.86	1180.44	1006.12	891.81	811.77
44000	3955.81	2117.77	1509.16	1207.89	1029.51	912.55	830.65
45000	4045.72	2165.90	1543.46	1235.34	1052.91	933.29	849.53
46000	4135.62	2214.03	1577.76	1262.79	1076.31	954.03	868.41
47000	4225.53	2262.16	1612.06	1290.25	1099.71	974.77	887.28
48000	4315.43	2310.29	1646.36	1317.70	1123.11	995.51	906.16
49000	4405.33	2358.42	1680.66	1345.15	1146.51	1016.25	925.04
50000	4495.24	2406.55	1714.96	1372.60	1169.90	1036.99	943.92
51000	4585.14	2454.68	1749.26	1400.05	1193.30	1057.73	962.80
52000	4675.05	2502.82	1783.56	1427.51	1216.70	1078.47	981.68
53000	4764.95	2550.95	1817.86	1454.96	1240.10	1099.21	1000.55
54000	4854.86	2599.08	1852.16	1482.41	1263.50	1119.95	1019.43
55000	4944.76	2647.21	1886.45	1509.86	1286.89	1140.69	1038.31
56000	5034.67	2695.34	1920.75	1537.31	1310.29	1161.43	1057.19
57000	5124.57	2743.47	1955.05	1564.77	1333.69	1182.17	1076.07
58000	5214.48	2791.60	1989.35	1592.22	1357.09	1202.91	1094.95
59000	5304.38	2839.73	2023.65	1619.67	1380.49	1223.65	1113.82
60000	5394.29	2887.86	2057.95	1647.12	1403.88	1244.39	1132.70
65000	5843.81	3128.52	2229.45	1784.38	1520.87	1348.09	1227.10
70000	6293.34	3369.17	2400.94	1921.64	1637.86	1451.79	1321.49
75000	6742.86	3609.83	2572.44	2058.90	1754.85	1555.49	1415.88
80000	7192.38	3850.49	2743.93	2196.16	1871.85	1659.19	1510.27
85000	7641.91	4091.14	2915.43	2333.42	1988.84	1762.89	1604.66
90000	8091.43	4331.80	3086.93	2470.68	2105.83	1866.59	1699.05
95000	8540.96	4572.45	3258.42	2607.94	2222.82	1970.29	1793.45
100000	8990.48	4813.11	3429.92	2745.20	2339.81	2073.98	1887.84
105000	9440.00	5053.76	3601.41	2882.47	2456.80	2177.68	1982.23
110000	9889.53	5294.42	3772.91	3019.73	2573.79	2281.38	2076.62
120000	10788.57	5775.73	4115.90	3294.25	2807.77	2488.78	2265.41
130000	11687.62	6257.04	4458.89	3568.77	3041.75	2696.18	2454.19
140000	12586.67	6738.35	4801.88	3843.29	3275.73	2903.58	2642.97
150000	13485.72	7219.66	5144.88	4117.81	3509.71	3110.98	2831.76
175000	15733.34	8422.94	6002.36	4804.11	4094.66	3629.47	3303.72
200000	17980.96	9626.21	6859.84	5490.41	4679.61	4147.97	3775.68
225000	20228.58	10829.49	7717.32	6176.71	5264.56	4666.47	4247.64
250000	22476.20	12032.77	8574.79	6863.01	5849.52	5184.96	4719.60

Monthly Payments 14¼%

necessary to amortize a loan

AMOUNT	8 YEARS	9 YEARS	10 YEARS	11 YEARS	12 YEARS	13 YEARS	14 YEARS
100	1.75	1.65	1.57	1.50	1.45	1.41	1.38
200	3.50	3.30	3.14	3.01	2.91	2.82	2.75
500	8.76	8.24	7.84	7.52	7.26	7.06	6.89
1000	17.51	16.48	15.68	15.04	14.53	14.11	13.77
2000	35.03	32.96	31.35	30.08	29.06	28.23	27.54
5000	87.57	82.40	78.39	75.21	72.65	70.56	68.85
6000	105.08	98.88	94.06	90.25	87.18	84.68	82.62
7000	122.60	115.36	109.74	105.29	101.71	98.79	96.39
8000	140.11	131.84	125.42	120.33	116.24	112.90	110.16
9000	157.63	148.32	141.10	135.37	130.77	127.02	123.93
10000	175.14	164.80	156.77	150.41	145.29	141.13	137.70
15000	262.71	247.21	235.16	225.62	217.94	211.69	206.55
20000	350.28	329.61	313.55	300.82	290.59	282.26	275.40
25000	437.85	412.01	391.93	376.03	363.24	352.82	344.25
30000	525.42	494.41	470.32	451.24	435.88	423.38	413.10
35000	612.99	576.81	548.71	526.44	508.53	493.95	481.95
36000	630.51	593.29	564.38	541.48	523.06	508.06	495.72
37000	648.02	609.77	580.06	556.52	537.59	522.17	509.49
38000	665.53	626.25	595.74	571.56	552.12	536.29	523.26
39000	683.05	642.73	611.42	586.61	566.65	550.40	537.03
40000	700.56	659.22	627.09	601.65	581.18	564.51	550.80
41000	718.08	675.70	642.77	616.69	595.71	578.63	564.57
42000	735.59	692.18	658.45	631.73	610.24	592.74	578.34
43000	753.11	708.66	674.12	646.77	624.77	606.85	592.11
44000	770.62	725.14	689.80	661.81	639.30	620.96	605.88
45000	788.13	741.62	705.48	676.85	653.83	635.08	619.65
46000	805.65	758.10	721.16	691.89	668.36	649.19	633.42
47000	823.16	774.58	736.83	706.94	682.89	663.30	647.19
48000	840.68	791.06	752.51	721.98	697.42	677.41	660.96
49000	858.19	807.54	768.19	737.02	711.95	691.53	674.73
50000	875.70	824.02	783.87	752.06	726.47	705.64	688.50
51000	893.22	840.50	799.54	767.10	741.00	719.75	702.27
52000	910.73	856.98	815.22	782.14	755.53	733.87	716.04
53000	928.25	873.46	830.90	797.18	770.06	747.98	729.81
54000	945.76	889.94	846.57	812.22	784.59	762.09	743.58
55000	963.27	906.42	862.25	827.26	799.12	776.20	757.35
56000	980.79	922.90	877.93	842.31	813.65	790.32	771.12
57000	998.30	939.38	893.61	857.35	828.18	804.43	784.89
58000	1015.82	955.86	909.28	872.39	842.71	818.54	798.66
59000	1033.33	972.34	924.96	887.43	857.24	832.66	812.43
60000	1050.84	988.82	940.64	902.47	871.77	846.77	826.20
65000	1138.42	1071.22	1019.03	977.68	944.42	917.33	895.05
70000	1225.99	1153.63	1097.41	1052.88	1017.06	987.90	963.90
75000	1313.56	1236.03	1175.80	1128.09	1089.71	1058.46	1032.75
80000	1401.13	1318.43	1254.18	1203.29	1162.36	1129.02	1101.60
85000	1488.70	1400.83	1332.57	1278.50	1235.01	1199.59	1170.45
90000	1576.27	1483.23	1410.96	1353.71	1307.65	1270.15	1239.31
95000	1663.84	1565.64	1489.34	1428.91	1380.30	1340.72	1308.16
100000	1751.41	1648.04	1567.73	1504.12	1452.95	1411.28	1377.01
105000	1838.98	1730.44	1646.12	1579.32	1525.60	1481.84	1445.86
110000	1926.55	1812.84	1724.50	1654.53	1598.24	1552.41	1514.71
120000	2101.69	1977.65	1881.28	1804.94	1743.54	1693.54	1652.41
130000	2276.83	2142.45	2038.05	1955.35	1888.83	1834.66	1790.11
140000	2451.97	2307.25	2194.82	2105.77	2034.13	1975.79	1927.81
150000	2627.11	2472.06	2351.60	2256.18	2179.42	2116.92	2065.51
175000	3064.96	2884.07	2743.53	2632.21	2542.66	2469.74	2409.76
200000	3502.82	3296.08	3135.46	3008.24	2905.90	2822.56	2754.01
225000	3940.67	3708.09	3527.39	3384.27	3269.14	3175.38	3098.26
250000	4378.52	4120.10	3919.33	3760.29	3632.37	3528.20	3442.51

14¼%

Monthly Payments

necessary to amortize a loan

AMOUNT	15 YEARS	16 YEARS	17 YEARS	18 YEARS	19 YEARS	20 YEARS	21 YEARS
100	1.35	1.32	1.30	1.29	1.27	1.26	1.25
200	2.70	2.65	2.61	2.58	2.55	2.52	2.50
500	6.74	6.62	6.52	6.44	6.37	6.31	6.26
1000	13.49	13.25	13.05	12.88	12.74	12.62	12.51
2000	26.97	26.50	26.10	25.76	25.48	25.23	25.03
5000	67.43	66.24	65.25	64.40	63.69	63.09	62.57
6000	80.91	79.49	78.29	77.29	76.43	75.70	75.08
7000	94.40	92.74	91.34	90.17	89.17	88.32	87.60
8000	107.89	105.99	104.39	103.05	101.91	100.94	100.11
9000	121.37	119.24	117.44	115.93	114.65	113.55	112.62
10000	134.86	132.48	130.49	128.81	127.38	126.17	125.14
15000	202.29	198.73	195.74	193.21	191.08	189.26	187.71
20000	269.72	264.97	260.98	257.62	254.77	252.34	250.28
25000	337.14	331.21	326.23	322.02	318.46	315.43	312.85
30000	404.57	397.45	391.47	386.43	382.15	378.52	375.42
35000	472.00	463.70	456.72	450.83	445.84	441.60	437.99
36000	485.49	476.94	469.77	463.71	458.58	454.22	450.50
37000	498.97	490.19	482.82	476.59	471.32	466.84	463.01
38000	512.46	503.44	495.87	489.47	484.06	479.45	475.53
39000	525.95	516.69	508.91	502.35	496.80	492.07	488.04
40000	539.43	529.94	521.96	515.23	509.53	504.69	500.56
41000	552.92	543.19	535.01	528.12	522.27	517.30	513.07
42000	566.40	556.43	548.06	541.00	535.01	529.92	525.58
43000	579.89	569.68	561.11	553.88	547.75	542.54	538.10
44000	593.38	582.93	574.16	566.76	560.49	555.16	550.61
45000	606.86	596.18	587.21	579.64	573.23	567.77	563.12
46000	620.35	609.43	600.26	592.52	585.96	580.39	575.64
47000	633.83	622.68	613.31	605.40	598.70	593.01	588.15
48000	647.32	635.92	626.36	618.28	611.44	605.63	600.67
49000	660.80	649.17	639.41	631.16	624.18	618.24	613.18
50000	674.29	662.42	652.45	644.04	636.92	630.86	625.69
51000	687.78	675.67	665.50	656.92	649.66	643.48	638.21
52000	701.26	688.92	678.55	669.81	662.39	656.09	650.72
53000	714.75	702.17	691.60	682.69	675.13	668.71	663.24
54000	728.23	715.42	704.65	695.57	687.87	681.33	675.75
55000	741.72	728.66	717.70	708.45	700.61	693.95	688.26
56000	755.20	741.91	730.75	721.33	713.35	706.56	700.78
57000	768.69	755.16	743.80	734.21	726.09	719.18	713.29
58000	782.18	768.41	756.85	747.09	738.82	731.80	725.81
59000	795.66	781.66	769.90	759.97	751.56	744.41	738.32
60000	809.15	794.91	782.95	772.85	764.30	757.03	750.83
65000	876.58	861.15	848.19	837.26	827.99	820.12	813.40
70000	944.01	927.39	913.44	901.66	891.68	883.20	875.97
75000	1011.43	993.63	978.68	966.07	955.38	946.29	938.54
80000	1078.86	1059.87	1043.93	1030.47	1019.07	1009.38	1001.11
85000	1146.29	1126.12	1109.17	1094.87	1082.76	1072.46	1063.68
90000	1213.72	1192.36	1174.42	1159.28	1146.45	1135.55	1126.25
95000	1281.15	1258.60	1239.66	1223.68	1210.14	1198.63	1188.82
100000	1348.58	1324.84	1304.91	1288.09	1273.84	1261.72	1251.39
105000	1416.01	1391.09	1370.15	1352.49	1337.53	1324.80	1313.96
110000	1483.44	1457.33	1435.40	1416.90	1401.22	1387.89	1376.53
120000	1618.30	1589.81	1565.89	1545.70	1528.60	1514.06	1501.67
130000	1753.15	1722.30	1696.38	1674.51	1655.99	1640.23	1626.80
140000	1888.01	1854.78	1826.87	1803.32	1783.37	1766.41	1751.94
150000	2022.87	1987.26	1957.36	1932.13	1910.75	1892.58	1877.08
175000	2360.01	2318.48	2283.59	2254.15	2229.21	2208.01	2189.93
200000	2697.16	2649.69	2609.82	2576.17	2547.67	2523.44	2502.78
225000	3034.30	2980.90	2936.04	2898.20	2866.13	2838.87	2815.62
250000	3371.45	3312.11	3262.27	3220.22	3184.59	3154.30	3128.47

Monthly Payments

necessary to amortize a loan

14¼%

AMOUNT	22 YEARS	23 YEARS	24 YEARS	25 YEARS	30 YEARS	35 YEARS	40 YEARS
100	1.24	1.23	1.23	1.22	1.20	1.20	1.19
200	2.49	2.47	2.46	2.45	2.41	2.39	2.38
500	6.21	6.17	6.14	6.11	6.02	5.98	5.96
1000	12.43	12.35	12.29	12.23	12.05	11.96	11.92
2000	24.85	24.70	24.57	24.46	24.09	23.92	23.83
5000	62.13	61.75	61.43	61.15	60.23	59.80	59.58
6000	74.55	74.10	73.71	73.38	72.28	71.75	71.50
7000	86.98	86.45	86.00	85.60	84.33	83.71	83.41
8000	99.40	98.80	98.28	97.83	96.37	95.67	95.33
9000	111.83	111.15	110.57	110.06	108.42	107.63	107.25
10000	124.26	123.50	122.85	122.29	120.47	119.59	119.16
15000	186.38	185.25	184.28	183.44	180.70	179.39	178.74
20000	248.51	247.00	245.70	244.59	240.94	239.18	238.32
25000	310.64	308.75	307.13	305.73	301.17	298.98	297.91
30000	372.77	370.50	368.55	366.88	361.41	358.77	357.49
35000	434.90	432.25	429.98	428.02	421.64	418.57	417.07
36000	447.32	444.60	442.26	440.25	433.69	430.52	428.98
37000	459.75	456.95	454.55	452.48	445.73	442.48	440.90
38000	472.17	469.30	466.83	464.71	457.78	454.44	452.82
39000	484.60	481.65	479.12	476.94	469.83	466.40	464.73
40000	497.02	494.00	491.40	489.17	481.87	478.36	476.65
41000	509.45	506.35	503.69	501.40	493.92	490.32	488.57
42000	521.87	518.70	515.97	513.63	505.97	502.28	500.48
43000	534.30	531.05	528.26	525.86	518.02	514.24	512.40
44000	546.73	543.40	540.54	538.09	530.06	526.20	524.31
45000	559.15	555.75	552.83	550.32	542.11	538.16	536.23
46000	571.58	568.10	565.11	562.55	554.16	550.12	548.15
47000	584.00	580.45	577.40	574.78	566.20	562.07	560.06
48000	596.43	592.80	589.68	587.01	578.25	574.03	571.98
49000	608.85	605.15	601.97	599.23	590.30	585.99	583.90
50000	621.28	617.50	614.25	611.46	602.34	597.95	595.81
51000	633.70	629.85	626.54	623.69	614.39	609.91	607.73
52000	646.13	642.20	638.82	635.92	626.44	621.87	619.64
53000	658.56	654.55	651.11	648.15	638.48	633.83	631.56
54000	670.98	666.90	663.39	660.38	650.53	645.79	643.48
55000	683.41	679.25	675.68	672.61	662.58	657.75	655.39
56000	695.83	691.60	687.96	684.84	674.62	669.71	667.31
57000	708.26	703.95	700.25	697.07	686.67	681.66	679.23
58000	720.68	716.30	712.53	709.30	698.72	693.62	691.14
59000	733.11	728.65	724.82	721.53	710.77	705.58	703.06
60000	745.54	741.00	737.10	733.76	722.81	717.54	714.97
65000	807.66	802.75	798.53	794.90	783.05	777.34	774.56
70000	869.79	864.50	859.95	856.05	843.28	837.13	834.14
75000	931.92	926.25	921.38	917.20	903.52	896.93	893.72
80000	994.05	988.00	982.80	978.34	963.75	956.72	953.30
85000	1056.17	1049.75	1044.23	1039.49	1023.98	1016.52	1012.88
90000	1118.30	1111.50	1105.65	1100.63	1084.22	1076.31	1072.46
95000	1180.43	1173.25	1167.08	1161.78	1144.45	1136.11	1132.04
100000	1242.56	1235.00	1228.51	1222.93	1204.69	1195.90	1191.62
105000	1304.69	1296.75	1289.93	1284.07	1264.92	1255.70	1251.20
110000	1366.81	1358.49	1351.36	1345.22	1325.16	1315.49	1310.79
120000	1491.07	1481.99	1474.21	1467.51	1445.62	1435.08	1429.95
130000	1615.33	1605.49	1597.06	1589.81	1566.09	1554.67	1549.11
140000	1739.58	1728.99	1719.91	1712.10	1686.56	1674.26	1668.27
150000	1863.84	1852.49	1842.76	1834.39	1807.03	1793.85	1787.43
175000	2174.48	2161.24	2149.88	2140.12	2108.20	2092.83	2085.34
200000	2485.12	2469.99	2457.01	2445.86	2409.37	2391.81	2383.25
225000	2795.76	2778.74	2764.14	2751.59	2710.55	2690.78	2681.15
250000	3106.40	3087.49	3071.26	3057.32	3011.72	2989.76	2979.06

14½%

Monthly Payments
necessary to amortize a loan

AMOUNT	1 YEAR	2 YEARS	3 YEARS	4 YEARS	5 YEARS	6 YEARS	7 YEARS
100	9.00	4.82	3.44	2.76	2.35	2.09	1.90
200	18.00	9.65	6.88	5.52	4.71	4.17	3.80
500	45.01	24.12	17.21	13.79	11.76	10.44	9.51
1000	90.02	48.25	34.42	27.58	23.53	20.87	19.02
2000	180.05	96.50	68.84	55.16	47.06	41.75	38.03
5000	450.11	241.25	172.10	137.89	117.64	104.37	95.09
6000	540.14	289.50	206.53	165.47	141.17	125.25	114.10
7000	630.16	337.75	240.95	193.05	164.70	146.12	133.12
8000	720.18	386.00	275.37	220.62	188.23	167.00	152.14
9000	810.20	434.24	309.79	248.20	211.75	187.87	171.16
10000	900.23	482.49	344.21	275.78	235.28	208.74	190.17
15000	1350.34	723.74	516.31	413.67	352.92	313.12	285.26
20000	1800.45	964.99	688.42	551.56	470.57	417.49	380.35
25000	2250.56	1206.24	860.52	689.45	588.21	521.86	475.43
30000	2700.68	1447.48	1032.63	827.34	705.85	626.23	570.52
35000	3150.79	1688.73	1204.73	965.23	823.49	730.60	665.61
36000	3240.81	1736.98	1239.16	992.81	847.02	751.48	684.62
37000	3330.83	1785.23	1273.58	1020.38	870.55	772.35	703.64
38000	3420.86	1833.48	1308.00	1047.96	894.07	793.23	722.66
39000	3510.88	1881.73	1342.42	1075.54	917.60	814.10	741.67
40000	3600.90	1929.98	1376.84	1103.12	941.13	834.98	760.69
41000	3690.92	1978.23	1411.26	1130.70	964.66	855.85	779.71
42000	3780.95	2026.48	1445.68	1158.27	988.19	876.73	798.73
43000	3870.97	2074.73	1480.10	1185.85	1011.72	897.60	817.74
44000	3960.99	2122.97	1514.52	1213.43	1035.24	918.47	836.76
45000	4051.01	2171.22	1548.94	1241.01	1058.77	939.35	855.78
46000	4141.04	2219.47	1583.36	1268.59	1082.30	960.22	874.80
47000	4231.06	2267.72	1617.79	1296.16	1105.83	981.10	893.81
48000	4321.08	2315.97	1652.21	1323.74	1129.36	1001.97	912.83
49000	4411.10	2364.22	1686.63	1351.32	1152.89	1022.85	931.85
50000	4501.13	2412.47	1721.05	1378.90	1176.41	1043.72	950.87
51000	4591.15	2460.72	1755.47	1406.48	1199.94	1064.60	969.88
52000	4681.17	2508.97	1789.89	1434.05	1223.47	1085.47	988.90
53000	4771.19	2557.22	1824.31	1461.63	1247.00	1106.34	1007.92
54000	4861.22	2605.47	1858.73	1489.21	1270.53	1127.22	1026.93
55000	4951.24	2653.72	1893.15	1516.79	1294.06	1148.09	1045.95
56000	5041.26	2701.97	1927.57	1544.37	1317.58	1168.97	1064.97
57000	5131.29	2750.22	1962.00	1571.94	1341.11	1189.84	1083.99
58000	5221.31	2798.47	1996.42	1599.52	1364.64	1210.72	1103.00
59000	5311.33	2846.72	2030.84	1627.10	1388.17	1231.59	1122.02
60000	5401.35	2894.97	2065.26	1654.68	1411.70	1252.47	1141.04
65000	5851.47	3136.21	2237.36	1792.57	1529.34	1356.84	1236.12
70000	6301.58	3377.46	2409.47	1930.46	1646.98	1461.21	1331.21
75000	6751.69	3618.71	2581.57	2068.35	1764.62	1565.58	1426.30
80000	7201.80	3859.95	2753.68	2206.24	1882.26	1669.95	1521.38
85000	7651.92	4101.20	2925.70	2344.13	1999.90	1774.33	1616.47
90000	8102.03	4342.45	3097.89	2482.02	2117.55	1878.70	1711.56
95000	8552.14	4583.70	3269.99	2619.91	2235.19	1983.07	1806.64
100000	9002.25	4824.94	3442.10	2757.80	2352.83	2087.44	1901.73
105000	9452.37	5066.19	3614.20	2895.69	2470.47	2191.81	1996.82
110000	9902.48	5307.44	3786.31	3033.57	2588.11	2296.19	2091.90
120000	10802.71	5789.93	4130.52	3309.35	2823.39	2504.93	2282.08
130000	11702.93	6272.43	4474.73	3585.13	3058.68	2713.68	2472.25
140000	12603.16	6754.92	4818.94	3860.91	3293.96	2922.42	2662.42
150000	13503.38	7237.41	5163.15	4136.69	3529.24	3131.16	2852.60
175000	15753.95	8443.65	6023.67	4826.14	4117.45	3653.02	3328.03
200000	18004.51	9649.89	6884.20	5515.59	4705.66	4174.89	3803.46
225000	20255.07	10856.12	7744.72	6205.04	5293.86	4696.75	4278.89
250000	22505.64	12062.36	8605.24	6894.49	5882.07	5218.61	4754.33

Monthly Payments 14½%

necessary to amortize a loan

AMOUNT	8 YEARS	9 YEARS	10 YEARS	11 YEARS	12 YEARS	13 YEARS	14 YEARS
100	1.77	1.66	1.58	1.52	1.47	1.43	1.39
200	3.53	3.33	3.17	3.04	2.94	2.86	2.79
500	8.83	8.31	7.91	7.60	7.34	7.14	6.97
1000	17.66	16.63	15.83	15.20	14.69	14.28	13.94
2000	35.31	33.26	31.66	30.39	29.38	28.55	27.87
5000	88.29	83.14	79.14	75.98	73.44	71.38	69.68
6000	105.94	99.77	94.97	91.18	88.13	85.65	83.62
7000	123.60	116.39	110.80	106.38	102.82	99.93	97.55
8000	141.26	133.02	126.63	121.57	117.51	114.20	111.49
9000	158.92	149.65	142.46	136.77	132.20	128.48	125.42
10000	176.57	166.28	158.29	151.96	146.88	142.75	139.36
15000	264.86	249.42	237.43	227.95	220.33	214.13	209.04
20000	353.15	332.55	316.57	303.93	293.77	285.51	278.72
25000	441.43	415.69	395.72	379.91	367.21	356.88	348.40
30000	529.72	498.83	474.86	455.89	440.65	428.26	418.08
35000	618.00	581.97	554.00	531.88	514.10	499.64	487.76
36000	635.66	598.60	569.83	547.07	528.79	513.91	501.70
37000	653.32	615.23	585.66	562.27	543.47	528.19	515.63
38000	670.98	631.85	601.49	577.46	558.16	542.46	529.57
39000	688.63	648.48	617.32	592.66	572.85	556.74	543.51
40000	706.29	665.11	633.15	607.86	587.54	571.02	557.44
41000	723.95	681.74	648.98	623.05	602.23	585.29	571.38
42000	741.60	698.36	664.80	638.25	616.92	599.57	585.31
43000	759.26	714.99	680.63	653.45	631.61	613.84	599.25
44000	776.92	731.62	696.46	668.64	646.29	628.12	613.19
45000	794.58	748.25	712.29	683.84	660.98	642.39	627.12
46000	812.23	764.88	728.12	699.04	675.67	656.67	641.06
47000	829.89	781.50	743.95	714.23	690.36	670.94	654.99
48000	847.55	798.13	759.78	729.43	705.05	685.22	668.93
49000	865.21	814.76	775.61	744.63	719.74	699.49	682.87
50000	882.86	831.39	791.43	759.82	734.42	713.77	696.80
51000	900.52	848.01	807.26	775.02	749.11	728.04	710.74
52000	918.18	864.64	823.09	790.21	763.80	742.32	724.67
53000	935.83	881.27	838.92	805.41	778.49	756.59	738.61
54000	953.49	897.90	854.75	820.61	793.18	770.87	752.55
55000	971.15	914.52	870.58	835.80	807.87	785.15	766.48
56000	988.81	931.15	886.41	851.00	822.56	799.42	780.42
57000	1006.46	947.78	902.23	866.20	837.24	813.70	794.35
58000	1024.12	964.41	918.06	881.39	851.93	827.97	808.29
59000	1041.78	981.04	933.09	896.60	866.62	842.25	822.23
60000	1059.44	997.66	949.72	911.79	881.31	856.52	836.16
65000	1147.72	1080.80	1028.86	987.77	954.75	927.90	905.84
70000	1236.01	1163.94	1108.01	1063.75	1028.19	999.28	975.52
75000	1324.29	1247.08	1187.15	1139.73	1101.64	1070.65	1045.20
80000	1412.58	1330.22	1266.29	1215.72	1175.08	1142.03	1114.88
85000	1500.87	1413.36	1345.44	1291.70	1248.52	1213.41	1184.56
90000	1589.15	1496.49	1424.58	1367.68	1321.96	1284.78	1254.24
95000	1677.44	1579.63	1503.72	1443.66	1395.41	1356.16	1323.92
100000	1765.73	1662.77	1582.87	1519.64	1468.85	1427.54	1393.60
105000	1854.01	1745.91	1662.01	1595.63	1542.29	1498.91	1463.28
110000	1942.30	1829.05	1741.15	1671.61	1615.73	1570.29	1532.96
120000	2118.87	1995.33	1899.44	1823.57	1762.62	1713.05	1672.32
130000	2295.44	2161.60	2057.73	1975.54	1909.50	1855.80	1811.68
140000	2472.02	2327.88	2216.02	2127.50	2056.39	1998.55	1951.04
150000	2648.59	2494.16	2374.30	2279.47	2203.27	2141.31	2090.41
175000	3090.02	2909.85	2770.02	2659.38	2570.49	2498.19	2438.81
200000	3531.45	3325.54	3165.74	3039.29	2937.70	2855.08	2787.21
225000	3972.88	3741.24	3561.45	3419.20	3304.91	3211.96	3136.61
250000	4414.31	4156.93	3957.17	3799.11	3672.12	3568.84	3484.01

14½%

Monthly Payments
necessary to amortize a loan

AMOUNT	15 YEARS	16 YEARS	17 YEARS	18 YEARS	19 YEARS	20 YEARS	21 YEARS
100	1.37	1.34	1.32	1.31	1.29	1.28	1.27
200	2.73	2.68	2.64	2.61	2.58	2.56	2.54
500	6.83	6.71	6.61	6.53	6.46	6.40	6.35
1000	13.66	13.42	13.22	13.06	12.92	12.80	12.70
2000	27.31	26.84	26.45	26.12	25.84	25.60	25.40
5000	68.28	67.10	66.12	65.29	64.59	64.00	63.49
6000	81.93	80.52	79.35	78.35	77.51	76.80	76.19
7000	95.59	93.94	92.57	91.41	90.43	89.60	88.89
8000	109.24	107.37	105.79	104.47	103.35	102.40	101.59
9000	122.90	120.79	119.02	117.53	116.27	115.20	114.29
10000	136.55	134.21	132.24	130.59	129.19	128.00	126.99
15000	204.83	201.31	198.36	195.88	193.78	192.00	190.48
20000	273.10	268.41	264.48	261.17	258.38	256.00	253.98
25000	341.38	335.52	330.61	326.47	322.97	320.00	317.47
30000	409.65	402.62	396.73	391.76	387.56	384.00	380.97
35000	477.93	469.72	462.85	457.06	452.16	448.00	444.46
36000	491.58	483.15	476.07	470.11	465.08	460.80	457.16
37000	505.24	496.57	489.30	483.17	477.99	473.60	469.86
38000	518.89	509.99	502.52	496.23	490.91	486.40	482.56
39000	532.55	523.41	515.75	509.29	503.83	499.20	495.26
40000	546.20	536.83	528.97	522.35	516.75	512.00	507.96
41000	559.86	550.25	542.19	535.41	529.67	524.80	520.65
42000	573.51	563.67	555.42	548.47	542.59	537.60	533.35
43000	587.17	577.09	568.64	561.53	555.51	550.40	546.05
44000	600.82	590.51	581.87	574.58	568.43	563.20	558.75
45000	614.48	603.93	595.09	587.64	581.34	576.00	571.45
46000	628.13	617.35	608.32	600.70	594.26	588.80	584.15
47000	641.79	630.77	621.54	613.76	607.18	601.60	596.85
48000	655.44	644.19	634.76	626.82	620.10	614.40	609.55
49000	669.10	657.61	647.99	639.88	633.02	627.20	622.25
50000	682.75	671.04	661.21	652.94	645.94	640.00	634.94
51000	696.41	684.46	674.44	666.00	658.86	652.80	647.64
52000	710.06	697.88	687.66	679.05	671.78	665.60	660.34
53000	723.72	711.30	700.88	692.11	684.69	678.40	673.04
54000	737.37	724.72	714.11	705.17	697.61	691.20	685.74
55000	751.03	738.14	727.33	718.23	710.53	704.00	698.44
56000	764.68	751.56	740.56	731.29	723.45	716.80	711.14
57000	778.34	764.98	753.78	744.35	736.37	729.60	723.84
58000	791.99	778.40	767.01	757.41	749.29	742.40	736.54
59000	805.65	791.82	780.23	770.47	762.21	755.20	749.23
60000	819.30	805.24	793.45	783.52	775.13	768.00	761.93
65000	887.58	872.35	859.58	848.82	839.72	832.00	825.43
70000	955.85	939.45	925.70	914.11	904.31	896.00	888.92
75000	1024.13	1006.55	991.82	979.41	968.91	960.00	952.42
80000	1092.40	1073.66	1057.94	1044.70	1033.50	1024.00	1015.91
85000	1160.68	1140.76	1124.06	1109.99	1098.09	1088.00	1079.41
90000	1228.95	1207.86	1190.18	1175.29	1162.69	1152.00	1142.90
95000	1297.23	1274.97	1256.30	1240.58	1227.28	1216.00	1206.39
100000	1365.50	1342.07	1322.42	1305.87	1291.88	1280.00	1269.89
105000	1433.78	1409.17	1388.55	1371.17	1356.47	1344.00	1333.38
110000	1502.05	1476.28	1454.67	1436.46	1421.06	1408.00	1396.88
120000	1638.60	1610.48	1586.91	1567.05	1550.25	1536.00	1523.87
130000	1775.15	1744.69	1719.15	1697.64	1679.44	1664.00	1650.86
140000	1911.70	1878.90	1851.39	1828.22	1808.63	1792.00	1777.84
150000	2048.25	2013.11	1983.64	1958.81	1937.81	1920.00	1904.83
175000	2389.63	2348.62	2314.24	2285.28	2260.78	2240.00	2222.30
200000	2731.00	2684.14	2644.85	2611.75	2583.75	2560.00	2539.78
225000	3072.38	3019.66	2975.45	2938.22	2906.72	2879.99	2857.25
250000	3413.75	3355.18	3306.06	3264.69	3229.69	3199.99	3174.72

Monthly Payments 14½%

necessary to amortize a loan

AMOUNT	22 YEARS	23 YEARS	24 YEARS	25 YEARS	30 YEARS	35 YEARS	40 YEARS
100	1.26	1.25	1.25	1.24	1.22	1.22	1.21
200	2.52	2.51	2.50	2.48	2.45	2.43	2.42
500	6.31	6.27	6.24	6.21	6.12	6.08	6.06
1000	12.61	12.54	12.48	12.42	12.25	12.16	12.12
2000	25.23	25.08	24.95	24.84	24.49	24.32	24.24
5000	63.06	62.69	62.38	62.11	61.23	60.81	60.61
6000	75.68	75.23	74.85	74.53	73.47	72.97	72.73
7000	88.29	87.77	87.33	86.95	85.72	85.13	84.85
8000	100.90	100.31	99.81	99.37	97.96	97.29	96.97
9000	113.51	112.85	112.28	111.79	110.21	109.46	109.09
10000	126.13	125.39	124.76	124.22	122.46	121.62	121.21
15000	189.19	188.08	187.14	186.32	183.68	182.43	181.82
20000	252.25	250.78	249.52	248.43	244.91	243.23	242.43
25000	315.32	313.47	311.89	310.54	306.14	304.04	303.03
30000	378.38	376.17	374.27	372.65	367.37	364.85	363.64
35000	441.44	438.86	436.65	434.76	428.59	425.66	424.25
36000	454.06	451.40	449.13	447.18	440.84	437.82	436.37
37000	466.67	463.94	461.60	459.60	453.09	449.98	448.49
38000	479.28	476.48	474.08	472.02	465.33	462.14	460.61
39000	491.89	489.02	486.56	484.44	477.58	474.31	472.73
40000	504.51	501.56	499.03	496.87	489.82	486.47	484.85
41000	517.12	514.10	511.51	509.29	502.07	498.63	496.97
42000	529.73	526.63	523.98	521.71	514.31	510.79	509.10
43000	542.34	539.17	536.46	534.13	526.56	522.95	521.22
44000	554.96	551.71	548.93	546.55	538.80	535.12	533.34
45000	567.57	564.25	561.41	558.97	551.05	547.28	545.46
46000	580.18	576.79	573.89	571.39	563.30	559.44	557.58
47000	592.79	589.33	586.36	583.82	575.54	571.60	569.70
48000	605.41	601.87	598.84	596.24	587.79	583.76	581.82
49000	618.02	614.41	611.31	608.66	600.03	595.92	593.95
50000	630.63	626.95	623.79	621.08	612.28	608.09	606.07
51000	643.24	639.48	636.26	633.50	624.52	620.25	618.19
52000	655.86	652.02	648.74	645.92	636.77	632.41	630.31
53000	668.47	664.56	661.22	658.35	649.01	644.57	642.43
54000	681.08	677.10	673.69	670.77	661.26	656.73	654.55
55000	693.70	689.64	686.17	683.19	673.51	668.89	666.67
56000	706.31	702.18	698.64	695.61	685.75	681.06	678.79
57000	718.92	714.72	711.12	708.03	698.00	693.22	690.92
58000	731.53	727.26	723.60	720.45	710.24	705.38	703.04
59000	744.16	739.80	736.07	732.08	722.49	717.54	715.16
60000	756.76	752.34	748.55	745.30	734.73	729.70	727.28
65000	819.82	815.03	810.93	807.41	795.96	790.51	787.89
70000	882.89	877.72	873.30	869.51	857.19	851.32	848.49
75000	945.95	940.42	935.68	931.02	918.42	912.13	909.10
80000	1009.01	1003.11	998.06	993.73	979.64	972.94	969.71
85000	1072.07	1065.81	1060.44	1055.84	1040.87	1033.74	1030.31
90000	1135.14	1128.50	1122.82	1117.95	1102.10	1094.55	1090.92
95000	1198.20	1191.20	1185.20	1180.05	1163.33	1155.36	1151.53
100000	1261.26	1253.89	1247.58	1242.16	1224.56	1216.17	1212.13
105000	1324.33	1316.59	1309.96	1304.27	1285.78	1276.98	1272.74
110000	1387.39	1379.28	1372.34	1366.38	1347.01	1337.79	1333.35
120000	1513.52	1504.67	1497.09	1490.60	1469.47	1459.40	1454.56
130000	1639.64	1630.06	1621.85	1614.81	1591.92	1581.02	1575.77
140000	1765.77	1755.45	1746.61	1739.03	1714.38	1702.64	1696.99
150000	1891.90	1880.84	1871.37	1863.24	1836.83	1824.26	1818.20
175000	2207.21	2194.31	2183.26	2173.79	2142.97	2128.30	2121.23
200000	2522.53	2507.78	2495.16	2484.33	2449.11	2432.34	2424.27
225000	2837.84	2821.26	2807.05	2794.87	2755.25	2736.38	2727.30
250000	3153.16	3134.73	3118.95	3105.41	3061.39	3040.43	3030.33

14¾% Monthly Payments

necessary to amortize a loan

AMOUNT	1 YEAR	2 YEARS	3 YEARS	4 YEARS	5 YEARS	6 YEARS	7 YEARS
100	9.01	4.84	3.45	2.77	2.37	2.10	1.92
200	18.03	9.67	6.91	5.54	4.73	4.20	3.83
500	45.07	24.18	17.27	13.85	11.83	10.50	9.58
1000	90.14	48.37	34.54	27.70	23.66	21.01	19.16
2000	180.28	96.74	69.09	55.41	47.32	42.02	38.31
5000	450.70	241.84	172.72	138.52	118.29	105.05	95.78
6000	540.84	290.21	207.26	166.23	141.95	126.06	114.94
7000	630.98	338.58	241.80	193.93	165.61	147.07	134.10
8000	721.12	386.94	276.34	221.63	189.27	168.08	153.25
9000	811.26	435.31	310.89	249.34	212.93	189.09	172.41
10000	901.40	483.68	345.43	277.04	236.59	210.09	191.57
15000	1352.11	725.52	518.15	415.56	354.88	315.14	287.35
20000	1802.81	967.36	690.86	554.08	473.18	420.19	383.14
25000	2253.51	1209.20	863.58	692.60	591.47	525.24	478.92
30000	2704.21	1451.04	1036.29	831.13	709.77	630.28	574.70
35000	3154.91	1692.88	1209.01	969.65	828.06	735.33	670.49
36000	3245.05	1741.25	1243.55	997.35	851.72	756.34	689.64
37000	3335.19	1789.61	1278.09	1025.05	875.38	777.35	708.80
38000	3425.33	1837.98	1312.64	1052.76	899.04	798.36	727.96
39000	3515.48	1886.35	1347.18	1080.46	922.70	819.37	747.11
40000	3605.62	1934.72	1381.72	1108.17	946.36	840.38	766.27
41000	3695.76	1983.09	1416.26	1135.87	970.02	861.39	785.43
42000	3785.90	2031.45	1450.81	1163.58	993.67	882.40	804.58
43000	3876.04	2079.82	1485.35	1191.28	1017.33	903.41	823.74
44000	3966.18	2128.19	1519.89	1218.98	1040.99	924.42	842.90
45000	4056.32	2176.56	1554.44	1246.69	1064.65	945.43	862.05
46000	4146.46	2224.93	1588.98	1274.39	1088.31	966.44	881.21
47000	4236.60	2273.29	1623.52	1302.10	1111.97	987.45	900.37
48000	4326.74	2321.66	1658.07	1329.80	1135.63	1008.46	919.52
49000	4416.88	2370.03	1692.61	1357.51	1159.29	1029.46	938.68
50000	4507.02	2418.40	1727.15	1385.21	1182.95	1050.47	957.84
51000	4597.16	2466.77	1761.69	1412.91	1206.60	1071.48	976.99
52000	4687.30	2515.13	1796.24	1440.62	1230.26	1092.49	996.15
53000	4777.44	2563.50	1830.78	1468.32	1253.92	1113.50	1015.31
54000	4867.58	2611.87	1865.32	1496.03	1277.58	1134.51	1034.47
55000	4957.72	2660.24	1899.87	1523.73	1301.24	1155.52	1053.62
56000	5047.86	2708.61	1934.41	1551.43	1324.90	1176.53	1072.78
57000	5138.00	2756.97	1968.95	1579.14	1348.56	1197.54	1091.94
58000	5228.14	2805.34	2003.50	1606.84	1372.22	1218.55	1111.09
59000	5318.28	2853.71	2038.04	1634.55	1395.88	1239.56	1130.25
60000	5408.42	2902.08	2072.58	1662.25	1419.53	1260.57	1149.41
65000	5859.13	3143.92	2245.30	1800.77	1537.83	1365.62	1245.19
70000	6309.83	3385.76	2418.01	1939.29	1656.12	1470.66	1340.97
75000	6760.53	3627.60	2590.73	2077.81	1774.42	1575.71	1436.76
80000	7211.23	3869.44	2763.44	2216.33	1892.71	1680.76	1532.54
85000	7661.93	4111.28	2936.16	2354.86	2011.01	1785.81	1628.32
90000	8112.63	4353.12	3108.87	2493.38	2129.30	1890.85	1724.11
95000	8563.34	4594.96	3281.59	2631.90	2247.60	1995.90	1819.89
100000	9014.04	4836.80	3454.30	2770.42	2365.89	2100.95	1915.68
105000	9464.74	5078.64	3627.02	2908.94	2484.18	2206.00	2011.46
110000	9915.44	5320.47	3799.73	3047.46	2602.48	2311.04	2107.24
120000	10816.85	5804.15	4145.16	3324.50	2839.07	2521.14	2298.81
130000	11718.25	6287.83	4490.59	3601.54	3075.66	2731.23	2490.38
140000	12619.65	6771.51	4836.02	3878.59	3312.25	2941.33	2681.95
150000	13521.06	7255.19	5181.45	4155.63	3548.84	3151.42	2873.51
175000	15774.57	8464.39	6045.03	4848.23	4140.31	3676.66	3352.43
200000	18028.08	9673.59	6908.61	5540.84	4731.78	4201.90	3831.35
225000	20281.59	10882.79	7772.18	6233.44	5323.25	4727.13	4310.27
250000	22535.10	12091.99	8635.76	6926.05	5914.73	5252.37	4789.19

Monthly Payments 14¾%

necessary to amortize a loan

AMOUNT	8 YEARS	9 YEARS	10 YEARS	11 YEARS	12 YEARS	13 YEARS	14 YEARS
100	1.78	1.68	1.60	1.54	1.48	1.44	1.41
200	3.56	3.36	3.20	3.07	2.97	2.89	2.82
500	8.90	8.39	7.99	7.68	7.42	7.22	7.05
1000	17.80	16.78	15.98	15.35	14.85	14.44	14.10
2000	35.60	33.55	31.96	30.70	29.70	28.88	28.21
5000	89.01	83.88	79.90	76.76	74.24	72.19	70.51
6000	106.81	100.65	95.88	92.11	89.09	86.63	84.62
7000	124.61	117.43	111.87	107.47	103.94	101.07	98.72
8000	142.41	134.21	127.85	122.82	118.79	115.51	112.82
9000	160.21	150.98	143.83	138.17	133.63	129.95	126.93
10000	178.01	167.76	159.81	153.52	148.48	144.39	141.03
15000	267.02	251.64	239.71	230.29	222.72	216.58	211.54
20000	356.02	335.51	319.61	307.05	296.97	288.77	282.06
25000	445.03	419.39	399.52	383.81	371.21	360.97	352.57
30000	534.03	503.27	479.42	460.57	445.45	433.16	423.08
35000	623.04	587.15	559.33	537.34	519.69	505.36	493.60
36000	640.84	603.93	575.31	552.69	534.54	519.79	507.70
37000	658.64	620.70	591.29	568.04	549.39	534.23	521.80
38000	676.44	637.48	607.27	583.39	564.23	548.67	535.91
39000	694.24	654.25	623.25	598.74	579.08	563.11	550.01
40000	712.04	671.03	639.23	614.10	593.93	577.55	564.11
41000	729.84	687.80	655.21	629.45	608.78	591.99	578.22
42000	747.64	704.58	671.19	644.80	623.63	606.43	592.32
43000	765.44	721.36	687.17	660.15	638.47	620.87	606.42
44000	783.25	738.13	703.15	675.51	653.32	635.30	620.52
45000	801.05	754.91	719.13	690.86	668.17	649.74	634.63
46000	818.85	771.68	735.11	706.21	683.02	664.18	648.73
47000	836.65	788.46	751.09	721.56	697.87	678.62	662.83
48000	854.45	805.23	767.08	736.92	712.72	693.06	676.94
49000	872.25	822.01	783.06	752.27	727.56	707.50	691.04
50000	890.05	838.79	799.04	767.62	742.41	721.94	705.14
51000	907.85	855.56	815.02	782.97	757.26	736.38	719.24
52000	925.65	872.34	831.00	798.33	772.11	750.81	733.35
53000	943.45	889.11	846.98	813.68	786.96	765.25	747.45
54000	961.26	905.89	862.96	829.03	801.81	779.69	761.55
55000	979.06	922.66	878.94	844.38	816.65	794.13	775.65
56000	996.86	939.44	894.92	859.74	831.50	808.57	789.76
57000	1014.66	956.22	910.90	875.09	846.35	823.01	803.86
58000	1032.46	972.99	926.88	890.44	861.20	837.45	817.96
60000	1050.26	989.77	942.86	905.79	876.05	851.89	832.07
60000	1068.06	1006.54	958.84	921.15	890.90	866.32	846.17
65000	1157.07	1090.42	1038.75	997.91	965.14	938.52	916.68
70000	1246.07	1174.30	1118.65	1074.67	1039.38	1010.71	987.20
75000	1335.08	1258.18	1198.56	1151.43	1113.62	1082.91	1057.71
80000	1424.08	1342.06	1278.46	1228.19	1187.86	1155.10	1128.23
85000	1513.09	1425.93	1358.36	1304.96	1262.10	1227.29	1198.74
90000	1602.09	1509.81	1438.27	1381.72	1336.34	1299.49	1269.25
95000	1691.10	1593.69	1518.17	1458.48	1410.58	1371.68	1339.77
100000	1780.10	1677.57	1598.07	1535.24	1484.83	1443.87	1410.28
105000	1869.11	1761.45	1677.98	1612.01	1559.07	1516.07	1480.80
110000	1958.11	1845.33	1757.88	1688.77	1633.31	1588.26	1551.31
120000	2136.12	2013.08	1917.69	1842.29	1781.79	1732.65	1692.34
130000	2314.13	2180.84	2077.50	1995.82	1930.27	1877.04	1833.37
140000	2492.14	2348.60	2237.30	2149.34	2078.76	2021.42	1974.39
150000	2670.16	2516.36	2397.11	2302.86	2227.24	2165.81	2115.42
175000	3115.18	2935.75	2796.63	2686.68	2598.44	2526.78	2467.99
200000	3560.21	3355.14	3196.15	3070.49	2969.65	2887.75	2820.56
225000	4005.23	3774.53	3595.67	3454.30	3340.86	3248.72	3173.13
250000	4450.26	4193.93	3995.19	3838.11	3712.06	3609.68	3525.70

14¾% Monthly Payments

necessary to amortize a loan

AMOUNT	15 YEARS	16 YEARS	17 YEARS	18 YEARS	19 YEARS	20 YEARS	21 YEARS
100	1.38	1.36	1.34	1.32	1.31	1.30	1.29
200	2.77	2.72	2.68	2.65	2.62	2.60	2.58
500	6.91	6.80	6.70	6.62	6.55	6.49	6.44
1000	13.83	13.59	13.40	13.24	13.10	12.98	12.88
2000	27.65	27.19	26.80	26.47	26.20	25.97	25.77
5000	69.13	67.97	67.00	66.19	65.50	64.92	64.42
6000	82.95	81.56	80.40	79.42	78.60	77.90	77.31
7000	96.78	95.16	93.80	92.66	91.70	90.88	90.19
8000	110.60	108.75	107.20	105.90	104.80	103.87	103.08
9000	124.43	122.34	120.60	119.14	117.90	116.85	115.96
10000	138.25	135.94	134.00	132.37	131.00	129.84	128.85
15000	207.38	203.91	201.00	198.56	196.50	194.75	193.27
20000	276.50	271.88	268.00	264.75	262.00	259.67	257.69
25000	345.63	339.84	335.01	330.94	327.50	324.59	322.12
30000	414.75	407.81	402.01	397.12	393.00	389.51	386.54
35000	483.88	475.78	469.01	463.31	458.50	454.42	450.96
36000	497.70	489.38	482.41	476.55	471.60	467.41	463.85
37000	511.53	502.97	495.81	489.78	484.70	480.39	476.73
38000	525.35	516.56	509.21	503.02	497.80	493.38	489.62
39000	539.18	530.16	522.61	516.26	510.90	506.36	502.50
40000	553.00	543.75	536.01	529.50	524.00	519.34	515.39
41000	566.83	557.35	549.41	542.73	537.10	532.33	528.27
42000	580.65	570.94	562.81	555.97	550.20	545.31	541.16
43000	594.48	584.53	576.21	569.21	563.30	558.29	554.04
44000	608.30	598.13	589.61	582.45	576.40	571.28	566.92
45000	622.13	611.72	603.01	595.68	589.50	584.26	579.81
46000	635.95	625.31	616.41	608.92	602.60	597.24	592.69
47000	649.78	638.91	629.81	622.16	615.70	610.23	605.58
48000	663.60	652.50	643.21	635.40	628.80	623.21	618.46
49000	677.43	666.10	656.61	648.63	641.90	636.19	631.35
50000	691.25	679.69	670.01	661.87	655.00	649.18	644.23
51000	705.08	693.28	683.41	675.11	668.10	662.16	657.12
52000	718.90	706.88	696.81	688.35	681.20	675.14	670.00
53000	732.73	720.47	710.21	701.58	694.30	688.13	682.89
54000	746.55	734.06	723.61	714.82	707.40	701.11	695.77
55000	760.38	747.66	737.01	728.06	720.50	714.10	708.66
56000	774.20	761.25	750.41	741.30	733.60	727.08	721.54
57000	788.03	774.85	763.81	754.53	746.70	740.06	734.43
58000	801.85	788.44	777.21	767.77	759.80	753.05	747.31
59000	815.68	802.03	790.61	781.01	772.90	766.03	760.19
60000	829.50	815.63	804.01	794.25	786.00	779.01	773.08
65000	898.63	883.60	871.01	860.43	851.50	843.93	837.50
70000	967.75	951.57	938.02	926.62	917.00	908.85	901.93
75000	1036.88	1019.53	1005.02	992.81	982.50	973.77	966.35
80000	1106.00	1087.50	1072.02	1058.99	1048.00	1038.68	1030.77
85000	1175.13	1155.47	1139.02	1125.18	1113.50	1103.60	1095.20
90000	1244.25	1223.44	1206.02	1191.37	1179.00	1168.52	1159.62
95000	1313.38	1291.41	1273.02	1257.56	1244.50	1233.44	1224.04
100000	1382.50	1359.38	1340.02	1323.74	1310.00	1298.36	1288.47
105000	1451.63	1427.35	1407.02	1389.93	1375.50	1363.27	1352.89
110000	1520.75	1495.32	1474.02	1456.12	1441.00	1428.19	1417.31
120000	1659.00	1631.26	1608.03	1588.49	1572.00	1558.03	1546.16
130000	1797.25	1767.19	1742.03	1720.87	1703.00	1687.86	1675.01
140000	1935.51	1903.13	1876.03	1853.24	1834.00	1817.70	1803.85
150000	2073.76	2039.07	2010.03	1985.61	1965.00	1947.53	1932.70
175000	2419.38	2378.91	2345.04	2316.55	2292.50	2272.12	2254.81
200000	2765.01	2718.76	2680.04	2647.49	2620.00	2596.71	2576.93
225000	3110.63	3058.60	3015.05	2978.42	2947.50	2921.30	2899.05
250000	3456.26	3398.45	3350.06	3309.36	3275.00	3245.89	3221.16

Monthly Payments 14¾%

necessary to amortize a loan

AMOUNT	22 YEARS	23 YEARS	24 YEARS	25 YEARS	30 YEARS	35 YEARS	40 YEARS
100	1.28	1.27	1.27	1.26	1.24	1.24	1.23
200	2.56	2.55	2.53	2.52	2.49	2.47	2.47
500	6.40	6.36	6.33	6.31	6.22	6.18	6.16
1000	12.80	12.73	12.67	12.61	12.44	12.36	12.33
2000	25.60	25.46	25.33	25.23	24.89	24.73	24.65
5000	64.00	63.64	63.34	63.07	62.22	61.82	61.63
6000	76.80	76.37	76.00	75.69	74.67	74.19	73.96
7000	89.60	89.10	88.67	88.30	87.11	86.55	86.29
8000	102.40	101.83	101.34	100.92	99.56	98.92	98.61
9000	115.20	114.56	114.00	113.53	112.00	111.28	110.94
10000	128.00	127.29	126.67	126.15	124.45	123.65	123.27
15000	192.01	190.93	190.01	189.22	186.67	185.47	184.90
20000	256.01	254.57	253.34	252.29	248.90	247.29	246.53
25000	320.01	318.22	316.68	315.37	311.12	309.12	308.17
30000	384.01	381.86	380.02	378.44	373.34	370.94	369.80
35000	448.02	445.50	443.35	441.51	435.57	432.77	431.43
36000	460.82	458.23	456.02	454.13	448.01	445.13	443.76
37000	473.62	470.96	468.69	466.74	460.46	457.50	456.09
38000	486.42	483.69	481.35	479.36	472.90	469.86	468.41
39000	499.22	496.42	494.02	491.97	485.35	482.23	480.74
40000	512.02	509.14	506.69	504.59	497.79	494.59	493.07
41000	524.82	521.87	519.36	517.20	510.24	506.95	505.39
42000	537.62	534.60	532.02	529.82	522.68	519.32	517.72
43000	550.42	547.33	544.69	542.43	535.12	531.68	530.05
44000	563.22	560.06	557.36	555.04	547.57	544.05	542.37
45000	576.02	572.79	570.02	567.66	560.01	556.41	554.70
46000	588.82	585.52	582.69	580.27	572.46	568.78	567.03
47000	601.62	598.24	595.36	592.89	584.90	581.14	579.35
48000	614.42	610.97	608.03	605.50	597.35	593.51	591.68
49000	627.22	623.70	620.69	618.12	609.79	605.87	604.01
50000	640.02	636.43	633.36	630.73	622.24	618.24	616.33
51000	652.82	649.16	646.03	643.35	634.68	630.60	628.66
52000	665.62	661.89	658.69	655.96	647.13	642.97	640.99
53000	678.42	674.62	671.36	668.58	659.57	655.33	653.31
54000	691.22	687.34	684.03	681.19	672.02	667.70	665.64
55000	704.02	700.07	696.70	693.81	684.46	680.06	677.97
56000	716.83	712.80	709.36	706.42	696.91	692.43	690.29
57000	729.63	725.53	722.03	719.03	709.35	704.79	702.62
58000	742.43	738.26	734.70	731.65	721.80	717.16	714.95
59000	755.23	750.99	747.36	744.26	734.24	729.52	727.27
60000	768.03	763.72	760.03	756.88	746.69	741.88	739.60
65000	832.03	827.36	823.37	819.95	808.91	803.71	801.23
70000	896.03	891.00	886.70	883.03	871.13	865.53	862.87
75000	960.03	954.65	950.04	946.10	933.36	927.36	924.50
80000	1024.04	1018.29	1013.38	1009.17	995.58	989.18	986.13
85000	1088.04	1081.93	1076.71	1072.25	1057.80	1051.00	1047.77
90000	1152.04	1145.57	1140.05	1135.32	1120.03	1112.83	1109.40
95000	1216.04	1209.22	1203.38	1198.39	1182.25	1174.65	1171.03
100000	1280.04	1272.86	1266.72	1261.46	1244.48	1236.47	1232.67
105000	1344.05	1336.50	1330.06	1324.54	1306.70	1298.30	1294.30
110000	1408.05	1400.15	1393.39	1387.61	1368.92	1360.12	1355.93
120000	1536.05	1527.43	1520.06	1513.76	1493.37	1483.77	1479.20
130000	1664.06	1654.72	1646.74	1639.90	1617.82	1607.42	1602.47
140000	1792.06	1782.00	1773.41	1766.05	1742.27	1731.06	1725.73
150000	1920.07	1909.29	1900.08	1892.20	1866.71	1854.71	1849.00
175000	2240.08	2227.51	2216.76	2207.56	2177.83	2163.83	2157.17
200000	2560.09	2545.72	2533.44	2522.93	2488.95	2472.95	2465.33
225000	2880.10	2863.94	2850.12	2838.30	2800.07	2782.07	2773.50
250000	3200.11	3182.15	3166.80	3153.66	3111.19	3091.19	3081.67

15%

Monthly Payments

necessary to amortize a loan

AMOUNT	1 YEAR	2 YEARS	3 YEARS	4 YEARS	5 YEARS	6 YEARS	7 YEARS
100	9.03	4.85	3.47	2.78	2.38	2.11	1.93
200	18.05	9.70	6.93	5.57	4.76	4.23	3.86
500	45.13	24.24	17.33	13.92	11.89	10.57	9.65
1000	90.26	48.49	34.67	27.83	23.79	21.15	19.30
2000	180.52	96.97	69.33	55.66	47.58	42.29	38.59
5000	451.29	242.43	173.33	139.15	118.95	105.73	96.48
6000	541.55	290.92	207.99	166.98	142.74	126.87	115.78
7000	631.81	339.41	242.66	194.82	166.53	148.02	135.08
8000	722.07	387.89	277.32	222.65	190.32	169.16	154.37
9000	812.32	436.38	311.99	250.48	214.11	190.31	173.67
10000	902.58	484.87	346.65	278.31	237.90	211.45	192.97
15000	1353.87	727.30	519.98	417.46	356.85	317.18	289.45
20000	1805.17	969.73	693.31	556.61	475.80	422.90	385.94
25000	2256.46	1212.17	866.63	695.77	594.75	528.63	482.42
30000	2707.75	1454.60	1039.96	834.92	713.70	634.35	578.90
35000	3159.04	1697.03	1213.29	974.08	832.65	740.08	675.39
36000	3249.30	1745.52	1247.95	1001.91	856.44	761.22	694.68
37000	3339.56	1794.01	1282.62	1029.74	880.23	782.37	713.98
38000	3429.82	1842.49	1317.28	1057.57	904.02	803.51	733.28
39000	3520.07	1890.98	1351.95	1085.40	927.81	824.66	752.57
40000	3610.33	1939.47	1386.61	1113.23	951.60	845.80	771.87
41000	3700.59	1987.95	1421.28	1141.06	975.39	866.95	791.17
42000	3790.85	2036.44	1455.94	1168.89	999.18	888.09	810.46
43000	3881.11	2084.93	1490.61	1196.72	1022.97	909.24	829.76
44000	3971.37	2133.41	1525.27	1224.55	1046.76	930.38	849.06
45000	4061.62	2181.90	1559.94	1252.38	1070.55	951.53	868.35
46000	4151.88	2230.39	1594.61	1280.21	1094.34	972.67	887.65
47000	4242.14	2278.87	1629.27	1308.05	1118.13	993.82	906.95
48000	4332.40	2327.36	1663.94	1335.88	1141.92	1014.96	926.24
49000	4422.66	2375.85	1698.60	1363.71	1165.71	1036.11	945.54
50000	4512.92	2424.33	1733.27	1391.54	1189.50	1057.25	964.84
51000	4603.17	2472.82	1767.93	1419.37	1213.29	1078.40	984.13
52000	4693.43	2521.31	1802.60	1447.20	1237.08	1099.54	1003.43
53000	4783.69	2569.79	1837.26	1475.03	1260.87	1120.69	1022.73
54000	4873.95	2618.28	1871.93	1502.86	1284.66	1141.83	1042.02
55000	4964.21	2666.77	1906.59	1530.69	1308.45	1162.98	1061.32
56000	5054.47	2715.25	1941.26	1558.52	1332.24	1184.12	1080.62
57000	5144.72	2763.74	1975.92	1586.35	1356.03	1205.27	1099.92
58000	5234.98	2812.23	2010.59	1614.18	1379.82	1226.41	1119.21
59000	5325.24	2860.71	2045.25	1642.01	1403.61	1247.56	1138.51
60000	5415.50	2909.20	2079.92	1669.84	1427.40	1268.70	1157.81
65000	5866.79	3151.63	2253.25	1809.00	1546.35	1374.43	1254.29
70000	6318.08	3394.07	2426.57	1948.15	1665.30	1480.15	1350.77
75000	6769.37	3636.50	2599.90	2087.31	1784.24	1585.88	1447.26
80000	7220.66	3878.93	2773.23	2226.46	1903.19	1691.60	1543.74
85000	7671.96	4121.37	2946.55	2365.61	2022.14	1797.33	1640.22
90000	8123.25	4363.80	3119.88	2504.77	2141.09	1903.05	1736.71
95000	8574.54	4606.23	3293.21	2643.92	2260.04	2008.78	1833.19
100000	9025.83	4848.66	3466.53	2783.07	2378.99	2114.50	1929.68
105000	9477.12	5091.10	3639.86	2922.23	2497.94	2220.23	2026.16
110000	9928.41	5333.53	3813.19	3061.38	2616.89	2325.95	2122.64
120000	10831.00	5818.40	4159.84	3339.69	2854.79	2537.40	2315.61
130000	11733.58	6303.26	4506.49	3618.00	3092.69	2748.85	2508.58
140000	12636.16	6788.13	4853.15	3896.30	3330.59	2960.30	2701.55
150000	13538.75	7273.00	5199.80	4174.61	3568.49	3171.75	2894.51
175000	15795.20	8485.16	6066.43	4870.38	4163.24	3700.38	3376.93
200000	18051.66	9697.33	6933.07	5566.15	4757.99	4229.00	3859.35
225000	20308.12	10909.50	7799.70	6261.92	5352.73	4757.63	4341.77
250000	22564.58	12121.66	8666.33	6957.69	5947.48	5286.25	4824.19

Monthly Payments **15%**

necessary to amortize a loan

AMOUNT	8 YEARS	9 YEARS	10 YEARS	11 YEARS	12 YEARS	13 YEARS	14 YEARS
100	1.79	1.69	1.61	1.55	1.50	1.46	1.43
200	3.59	3.38	3.23	3.10	3.00	2.92	2.85
500	8.97	8.46	8.07	7.75	7.50	7.30	7.14
1000	17.95	16.92	16.13	15.51	15.01	14.60	14.27
2000	35.89	33.85	32.27	31.02	30.02	29.21	28.54
5000	89.73	84.62	80.67	77.55	75.04	73.01	71.35
6000	107.67	101.55	96.80	93.05	90.05	87.62	85.62
7000	125.62	118.47	112.93	108.56	105.06	102.22	99.89
8000	143.56	135.39	129.07	124.07	120.07	116.82	114.16
9000	161.51	152.32	145.20	139.58	135.08	131.43	128.43
10000	179.45	169.24	161.33	155.09	150.09	146.03	142.70
15000	269.18	253.87	242.00	232.64	225.13	219.04	214.06
20000	358.91	338.49	322.67	310.18	300.18	292.06	285.41
25000	448.64	423.11	403.34	387.73	375.22	365.07	356.76
30000	538.36	507.73	484.00	465.27	450.26	438.09	428.11
35000	628.09	592.35	564.67	542.82	525.31	511.10	499.46
36000	646.03	609.28	580.81	558.33	540.32	525.70	513.73
37000	663.98	626.20	596.94	573.84	555.32	540.31	528.00
38000	681.93	643.12	613.07	589.35	570.33	554.91	542.28
39000	699.87	660.05	629.21	604.86	585.34	569.51	556.55
40000	717.82	676.97	645.34	620.37	600.35	584.11	570.82
41000	735.76	693.90	661.47	635.88	615.36	598.72	585.09
42000	753.71	710.82	677.61	651.38	630.37	613.32	599.36
43000	771.65	727.75	693.74	666.89	645.38	627.92	613.63
44000	789.60	744.67	709.87	682.40	660.39	642.53	627.90
45000	807.54	761.60	726.01	697.91	675.39	657.13	642.17
46000	825.49	778.52	742.14	713.42	690.40	671.73	656.44
47000	843.43	795.44	758.27	728.93	705.41	686.34	670.71
48000	861.38	812.37	774.41	744.44	720.42	700.94	684.98
49000	879.32	829.29	790.54	759.95	735.43	715.54	699.25
50000	897.27	846.22	806.67	775.46	750.44	730.14	713.52
51000	915.22	863.14	822.81	790.97	765.45	744.75	727.79
52000	933.16	880.07	838.94	806.48	780.46	759.35	742.06
53000	951.11	896.99	855.08	821.98	795.46	773.95	756.33
54000	969.05	913.91	871.21	837.49	810.47	788.56	770.60
55000	987.00	930.84	887.34	853.00	825.48	803.16	784.87
56000	1004.94	947.76	903.48	868.51	840.49	817.76	799.14
57000	1022.89	964.69	919.61	884.02	855.50	832.36	813.41
58000	1040.83	981.61	935.74	899.53	870.51	846.97	827.68
59000	1058.78	998.54	951.88	915.04	885.52	861.57	841.95
60000	1076.72	1015.46	968.01	930.55	900.53	876.17	856.22
65000	1166.45	1100.08	1048.68	1008.09	975.57	949.19	927.58
70000	1256.18	1184.70	1129.34	1085.64	1050.61	1022.20	998.93
75000	1345.91	1269.33	1210.01	1163.19	1125.66	1095.22	1070.28
80000	1435.63	1353.95	1290.68	1240.73	1200.70	1168.23	1141.63
85000	1525.36	1438.57	1371.35	1318.28	1275.75	1241.24	1212.98
90000	1615.09	1523.19	1452.01	1395.82	1350.79	1314.26	1284.34
95000	1704.81	1607.81	1532.68	1473.37	1425.83	1387.27	1355.69
100000	1794.54	1692.43	1613.35	1550.91	1500.88	1460.29	1427.04
105000	1884.27	1777.06	1694.02	1628.46	1575.92	1533.30	1498.39
110000	1973.99	1861.68	1774.68	1706.01	1650.96	1606.32	1569.74
120000	2153.45	2030.92	1936.02	1861.10	1801.05	1752.34	1712.45
130000	2332.90	2200.16	2097.35	2016.19	1951.14	1898.37	1855.15
140000	2512.36	2369.41	2258.69	2171.28	2101.23	2044.40	1997.86
150000	2691.81	2538.65	2420.02	2326.37	2251.32	2190.43	2140.56
175000	3140.45	2961.76	2823.36	2714.10	2626.53	2555.50	2497.32
200000	3589.08	3384.87	3226.70	3101.83	3001.75	2920.57	2854.08
225000	4037.72	3807.98	3630.04	3489.56	3376.97	3285.65	3210.84
250000	4486.35	4231.08	4033.37	3877.29	3752.19	3650.72	3567.60

15%

Monthly Payments

necessary to amortize a loan

AMOUNT	15 YEARS	16 YEARS	17 YEARS	18 YEARS	19 YEARS	20 YEARS	21 YEARS
100	1.40	1.38	1.36	1.34	1.33	1.32	1.31
200	2.80	2.75	2.72	2.68	2.66	2.63	2.61
500	7.00	6.88	6.79	6.71	6.64	6.58	6.54
1000	14.00	13.77	13.58	13.42	13.28	13.17	13.07
2000	27.99	27.54	27.15	26.83	26.56	26.34	26.14
5000	69.98	68.84	67.89	67.08	66.41	65.84	65.36
6000	83.98	82.61	81.46	80.50	79.69	79.01	78.43
7000	97.97	96.37	95.04	93.92	92.97	92.18	91.50
8000	111.97	110.14	108.62	107.34	106.26	105.34	104.57
9000	125.96	123.91	122.19	120.75	119.54	118.51	117.64
10000	139.96	137.68	135.77	134.17	132.82	131.68	130.71
15000	209.94	206.52	203.66	201.25	199.23	197.52	196.07
20000	279.92	275.35	271.54	268.34	265.64	263.36	261.42
25000	349.90	344.19	339.43	335.42	332.05	329.20	326.78
30000	419.88	413.03	407.31	402.51	398.46	395.04	392.14
35000	489.86	481.87	475.20	469.59	464.87	460.88	457.49
36000	503.85	495.64	488.77	483.01	478.15	474.04	470.56
37000	517.85	509.40	502.35	496.43	491.43	487.21	483.63
38000	531.84	523.17	515.93	509.84	504.72	500.38	496.70
39000	545.84	536.94	529.50	523.26	518.00	513.55	509.78
40000	559.83	550.71	543.08	536.68	531.28	526.72	522.85
41000	573.83	564.48	556.66	550.09	544.56	539.88	535.92
42000	587.83	578.24	570.23	563.51	557.84	553.05	548.99
43000	601.82	592.01	583.81	576.93	571.13	566.22	562.06
44000	615.82	605.78	597.39	590.34	584.41	579.39	575.13
45000	629.81	619.55	610.97	603.76	597.69	592.56	588.20
46000	643.81	633.31	624.54	617.18	610.97	605.72	601.27
47000	657.81	647.08	638.12	630.59	624.25	618.89	614.35
48000	671.80	660.85	651.70	644.01	637.54	632.06	627.42
49000	685.80	674.62	665.27	657.43	650.82	645.23	640.49
50000	699.79	688.38	678.85	670.85	664.10	658.39	653.56
51000	713.79	702.15	692.43	684.26	677.38	671.56	666.63
52000	727.79	715.92	706.00	697.68	690.66	684.73	679.70
53000	741.78	729.69	719.58	711.10	703.94	697.90	692.77
54000	755.78	743.46	733.16	724.51	717.23	711.07	705.84
55000	769.77	757.22	746.74	737.93	730.51	724.23	718.91
56000	783.77	770.99	760.31	751.35	743.79	737.40	731.99
57000	797.76	784.76	773.89	764.76	757.07	750.57	745.06
58000	811.76	798.53	787.47	778.18	770.35	763.74	758.13
59000	825.76	812.29	801.04	791.60	783.64	776.91	771.20
60000	839.75	826.06	814.62	805.01	796.92	790.07	784.27
65000	909.73	894.90	882.51	872.10	863.33	855.91	849.63
70000	979.71	963.74	950.39	939.18	929.74	921.75	914.98
75000	1049.69	1032.58	1018.28	1006.27	996.15	987.59	980.34
80000	1119.67	1101.42	1086.16	1073.35	1062.56	1053.43	1045.69
85000	1189.65	1170.25	1154.05	1140.44	1128.97	1119.27	1111.05
90000	1259.63	1239.09	1221.93	1207.52	1195.38	1185.11	1176.41
95000	1329.61	1307.93	1289.82	1274.61	1261.79	1250.95	1241.76
100000	1399.59	1376.77	1357.70	1341.69	1328.20	1316.79	1307.12
105000	1469.57	1445.61	1425.59	1408.78	1394.61	1382.63	1372.47
110000	1539.55	1514.45	1493.47	1475.86	1461.02	1448.47	1437.83
120000	1679.50	1652.12	1629.24	1610.03	1593.84	1580.15	1568.54
130000	1819.46	1789.80	1765.01	1744.20	1726.66	1711.83	1699.25
140000	1959.42	1927.48	1900.78	1878.37	1859.48	1843.51	1829.96
150000	2099.38	2065.15	2036.55	2012.54	1992.30	1975.18	1960.68
175000	2449.28	2409.35	2375.98	2347.96	2324.35	2304.38	2287.46
200000	2799.17	2753.54	2715.40	2683.38	2656.40	2633.58	2614.23
225000	3149.07	3097.73	3054.83	3018.80	2988.45	2962.78	2941.01
250000	3498.97	3441.92	3394.25	3354.23	3320.49	3291.97	3267.79

Monthly Payments 15%

necessary to amortize a loan

AMOUNT	22 YEARS	23 YEARS	24 YEARS	25 YEARS	30 YEARS	35 YEARS	40 YEARS
100	1.30	1.29	1.29	1.28	1.26	1.26	1.25
200	2.60	2.58	2.57	2.56	2.53	2.51	2.51
500	6.49	6.46	6.43	6.40	6.32	6.28	6.27
1000	12.99	12.92	12.86	12.81	12.64	12.57	12.53
2000	25.98	25.84	25.72	25.62	25.29	25.14	25.06
5000	64.94	64.59	64.30	64.04	63.22	62.84	62.66
6000	77.93	77.51	77.16	76.85	75.87	75.41	75.19
7000	90.92	90.43	90.02	89.66	88.51	87.98	87.73
8000	103.91	103.35	102.87	102.47	101.16	100.55	100.26
9000	116.90	116.27	115.73	115.27	113.80	113.11	112.79
10000	129.89	129.19	128.59	128.08	126.44	125.68	125.32
15000	194.83	193.78	192.89	192.12	189.67	188.52	187.98
20000	259.78	258.38	257.19	256.17	252.89	251.36	250.64
25000	324.72	322.97	321.48	320.21	316.11	314.20	313.31
30000	389.67	387.57	385.78	384.25	379.33	377.04	375.97
35000	454.61	452.16	450.08	448.29	442.56	439.88	438.63
36000	467.60	465.08	462.93	461.10	455.20	452.45	451.16
37000	480.59	478.00	475.79	473.91	467.84	465.02	463.69
38000	493.58	490.92	488.65	486.72	480.49	477.59	476.23
39000	506.57	503.84	501.51	499.52	493.13	490.16	488.76
40000	519.56	516.76	514.37	512.33	505.78	502.73	501.29
41000	532.55	529.68	527.23	525.14	518.42	515.29	513.82
42000	545.54	542.60	540.09	537.95	531.07	527.86	526.35
43000	558.53	555.52	552.95	550.76	543.71	540.43	538.89
44000	571.51	568.44	565.81	563.57	556.36	553.00	551.42
45000	584.50	581.35	578.67	576.37	569.00	565.57	563.95
46000	597.49	594.27	591.53	589.18	581.64	578.13	576.48
47000	610.48	607.19	604.39	601.99	594.29	590.70	589.02
48000	623.47	620.11	617.25	614.80	606.93	603.27	601.55
49000	636.46	633.03	630.11	627.61	619.58	615.84	614.08
50000	649.45	645.95	642.96	640.42	632.22	628.41	626.61
51000	662.44	658.87	655.82	653.22	644.87	640.97	639.14
52000	675.43	671.79	668.68	666.03	657.51	653.54	651.68
53000	688.42	684.71	681.54	678.84	670.16	666.11	664.21
54000	701.40	697.63	694.40	691.65	682.80	678.68	676.74
55000	714.39	710.54	707.26	704.46	695.44	691.25	689.27
56000	727.38	723.46	720.12	717.27	708.09	703.82	701.81
57000	740.37	736.38	732.98	730.07	720.73	716.38	714.34
58000	753.30	749.30	745.84	742.88	733.38	728.95	726.87
59000	766.35	762.22	758.70	755.00	746.02	741.52	739.40
60000	779.34	775.14	771.56	768.50	758.67	754.09	751.93
65000	844.28	839.73	835.85	832.54	821.89	816.93	814.60
70000	909.23	904.33	900.15	896.58	885.11	879.77	877.26
75000	974.17	968.92	964.45	960.62	948.33	942.61	939.92
80000	1039.12	1033.52	1028.74	1024.66	1011.56	1005.45	1002.58
85000	1104.06	1098.11	1093.04	1088.71	1074.78	1068.29	1065.24
90000	1169.01	1162.71	1157.34	1152.75	1138.00	1131.13	1127.90
95000	1233.95	1227.30	1221.63	1216.79	1201.22	1193.97	1190.56
100000	1298.90	1291.90	1285.93	1280.83	1264.44	1256.81	1253.22
105000	1363.84	1356.49	1350.23	1344.87	1327.67	1319.65	1315.89
110000	1428.79	1421.09	1414.52	1408.91	1390.89	1382.49	1378.55
120000	1558.68	1550.28	1543.12	1537.00	1517.33	1508.18	1503.87
130000	1688.57	1679.47	1671.71	1665.08	1643.78	1633.86	1629.19
140000	1818.46	1808.66	1800.30	1793.16	1770.22	1759.54	1754.51
150000	1948.35	1937.85	1928.89	1921.25	1896.67	1885.22	1879.84
175000	2273.07	2260.82	2250.38	2241.45	2212.78	2199.42	2193.14
200000	2597.79	2583.80	2571.86	2561.66	2528.89	2513.63	2506.45
225000	2922.52	2906.77	2893.34	2881.87	2845.00	2827.83	2819.76
250000	3247.24	3229.75	3214.82	3202.08	3161.11	3142.03	3133.06

15¼% Monthly Payments

necessary to amortize a loan

AMOUNT	1 YEAR	2 YEARS	3 YEARS	4 YEARS	5 YEARS	6 YEARS	7 YEARS
100	9.04	4.86	3.48	2.80	2.39	2.13	1.94
200	18.08	9.72	6.96	5.59	4.78	4.26	3.89
500	45.19	24.30	17.39	13.98	11.96	10.64	9.72
1000	90.38	48.61	34.79	27.96	23.92	21.28	19.44
2000	180.75	97.21	69.58	55.92	47.84	42.56	38.87
5000	451.88	243.03	173.94	139.79	119.61	106.41	97.19
6000	542.26	291.63	208.73	167.75	143.53	127.69	116.62
7000	632.63	340.24	243.52	195.70	167.45	148.97	136.06
8000	723.01	388.84	278.30	223.66	191.37	170.25	155.50
9000	813.39	437.45	313.09	251.62	215.29	191.53	174.94
10000	903.76	486.06	347.88	279.58	239.21	212.81	194.37
15000	1355.64	729.08	521.82	419.36	358.82	319.22	291.56
20000	1807.53	972.11	695.76	559.15	478.43	425.62	388.75
25000	2259.41	1215.14	869.70	698.94	598.03	532.03	485.93
30000	2711.29	1458.17	1043.64	838.73	717.64	638.43	583.12
35000	3163.17	1701.19	1217.58	978.52	837.25	744.84	680.30
36000	3253.55	1749.80	1252.36	1006.48	861.17	766.12	699.74
37000	3343.92	1798.40	1287.15	1034.43	885.09	787.40	719.18
38000	3434.30	1847.01	1321.94	1062.39	909.01	808.68	738.62
39000	3524.68	1895.61	1356.73	1090.35	932.93	829.96	758.05
40000	3615.05	1944.22	1391.52	1118.31	956.85	851.24	777.49
41000	3705.43	1992.83	1426.30	1146.26	980.78	872.52	796.93
42000	3795.81	2041.43	1461.09	1174.22	1004.70	893.80	816.37
43000	3886.18	2090.04	1495.88	1202.18	1028.62	915.08	835.80
44000	3976.56	2138.64	1530.67	1230.14	1052.54	936.36	855.24
45000	4066.93	2187.25	1565.45	1258.09	1076.46	957.65	874.68
46000	4157.31	2235.85	1600.24	1286.05	1100.38	978.93	894.12
47000	4247.69	2284.46	1635.03	1314.01	1124.30	1000.21	913.55
48000	4338.06	2333.06	1669.82	1341.97	1148.23	1021.49	932.99
49000	4428.44	2381.67	1704.61	1369.92	1172.15	1042.77	952.43
50000	4518.82	2430.28	1739.39	1397.88	1196.07	1064.05	971.86
51000	4609.19	2478.88	1774.18	1425.84	1219.99	1085.33	991.30
52000	4699.57	2527.49	1808.97	1453.80	1243.91	1106.61	1010.74
53000	4789.95	2576.09	1843.76	1481.75	1267.83	1127.89	1030.18
54000	4880.32	2624.70	1878.55	1509.71	1291.75	1149.17	1049.61
55000	4970.70	2673.30	1913.33	1537.67	1315.67	1170.46	1069.05
56000	5061.07	2721.91	1948.12	1565.63	1339.60	1191.74	1088.49
57000	5151.45	2770.51	1982.91	1593.59	1363.52	1213.02	1107.93
58000	5241.83	2819.12	2017.70	1621.54	1387.44	1234.30	1127.36
59000	5332.20	2867.73	2052.48	1649.50	1411.36	1255.58	1146.80
60000	5422.58	2916.33	2087.27	1677.46	1435.28	1276.86	1166.24
65000	5874.46	3159.36	2261.21	1817.25	1554.89	1383.27	1263.42
70000	6326.34	3402.39	2435.15	1957.03	1674.50	1489.67	1360.61
75000	6778.22	3645.41	2609.09	2096.82	1794.10	1596.08	1457.80
80000	7230.11	3888.44	2783.03	2236.61	1913.71	1702.48	1554.98
85000	7681.99	4131.47	2956.97	2376.40	2033.32	1808.89	1652.17
90000	8133.87	4374.50	3130.91	2516.19	2152.92	1915.29	1749.36
95000	8585.75	4617.52	3304.85	2655.98	2272.53	2021.70	1846.54
100000	9037.63	4860.55	3478.79	2795.76	2392.14	2128.10	1943.73
105000	9489.51	5103.58	3652.73	2935.55	2511.74	2234.51	2040.91
110000	9941.40	5346.61	3826.67	3075.34	2631.35	2340.91	2138.10
120000	10845.16	5832.66	4174.55	3354.92	2870.56	2553.72	2332.47
130000	11748.92	6318.72	4522.42	3634.49	3109.78	2766.53	2526.85
140000	12652.69	6804.77	4870.30	3914.07	3348.99	2979.34	2721.22
150000	13556.45	7290.83	5218.18	4193.65	3588.20	3192.15	2915.59
175000	15815.86	8505.96	6087.88	4892.59	4186.24	3724.18	3401.52
200000	18075.26	9721.10	6957.58	5591.53	4784.27	4256.20	3887.46
225000	20334.67	10936.24	7827.27	6290.47	5382.31	4788.23	4373.39
250000	22594.08	12151.38	8696.97	6989.41	5980.34	5320.25	4859.32

Monthly Payments 15¼%

necessary to amortize a loan

AMOUNT	8 YEARS	9 YEARS	10 YEARS	11 YEARS	12 YEARS	13 YEARS	14 YEARS
100	1.81	1.71	1.63	1.57	1.52	1.48	1.44
200	3.62	3.41	3.26	3.13	3.03	2.95	2.89
500	9.05	8.54	8.14	7.83	7.59	7.38	7.22
1000	18.09	17.07	16.29	15.67	15.17	14.77	14.44
2000	36.18	34.15	32.57	31.33	30.34	29.54	28.88
5000	90.45	85.37	81.43	78.33	75.85	73.84	72.19
6000	108.54	102.44	97.72	94.00	91.02	88.61	86.63
7000	126.63	119.52	114.01	109.67	106.19	103.37	101.07
8000	144.72	136.59	130.30	125.33	121.36	118.14	115.51
9000	162.81	153.66	146.58	141.00	136.53	132.91	129.95
10000	180.90	170.74	162.87	156.67	151.70	147.68	144.39
15000	271.36	256.10	244.30	235.00	227.55	221.52	216.58
20000	361.81	341.47	325.74	313.33	303.40	295.36	288.78
25000	452.26	426.84	407.17	391.66	379.25	369.19	360.97
30000	542.71	512.21	488.61	470.00	455.10	443.03	433.16
35000	633.16	597.58	570.04	548.33	530.95	516.87	505.36
36000	651.25	614.65	586.33	564.00	546.12	531.64	519.80
37000	669.34	631.72	602.62	579.66	561.29	546.41	534.23
38000	687.43	648.80	618.90	595.33	576.46	561.18	548.67
39000	705.52	665.87	635.19	611.00	591.63	575.94	563.11
40000	723.61	682.94	651.48	626.66	606.80	590.71	577.55
41000	741.71	700.02	667.76	642.33	621.97	605.48	591.99
42000	759.80	717.09	684.05	658.00	637.14	620.25	606.43
43000	777.89	734.17	700.34	673.66	652.31	635.01	620.87
44000	795.98	751.24	716.63	689.33	667.48	649.78	635.31
45000	814.07	768.31	732.91	705.00	682.65	664.55	649.74
46000	832.16	785.39	749.20	720.66	697.82	679.32	664.18
47000	850.25	802.46	765.49	736.33	712.99	694.09	678.62
48000	868.34	819.53	781.77	752.00	728.16	708.85	693.06
49000	886.43	836.61	798.06	767.66	743.33	723.62	707.50
50000	904.52	853.68	814.35	783.33	758.50	738.39	721.94
51000	922.61	870.75	830.63	799.00	773.67	753.10	736.38
52000	940.70	887.83	846.92	814.66	788.84	767.92	750.82
53000	958.79	904.90	863.21	830.33	804.01	782.69	765.25
54000	976.88	921.98	879.49	846.00	819.18	797.46	779.69
55000	994.97	939.05	895.78	861.66	834.35	812.23	794.13
56000	1013.06	956.12	912.07	877.33	849.52	827.00	808.57
57000	1031.15	973.20	928.36	893.00	864.69	841.76	823.01
58000	1049.24	990.27	944.64	908.66	879.86	856.53	837.45
59000	1067.33	1007.34	960.93	924.33	895.03	871.30	851.89
60000	1085.42	1024.42	977.22	940.00	910.20	886.07	866.33
65000	1175.87	1109.78	1058.65	1018.33	986.05	959.91	938.52
70000	1266.33	1195.15	1140.09	1096.66	1061.90	1033.74	1010.71
75000	1356.78	1280.52	1221.52	1174.99	1137.75	1107.58	1082.91
80000	1447.23	1365.89	1302.95	1253.33	1213.60	1181.42	1155.10
85000	1537.68	1451.26	1384.39	1331.66	1289.45	1255.26	1227.29
90000	1628.13	1536.63	1465.82	1409.99	1365.30	1329.10	1299.49
95000	1718.59	1621.99	1547.26	1488.33	1441.15	1402.94	1371.68
100000	1809.04	1707.36	1628.69	1566.66	1517.00	1476.78	1443.88
105000	1899.49	1792.73	1710.13	1644.99	1592.85	1550.62	1516.07
110000	1989.94	1878.10	1791.56	1723.32	1668.70	1624.46	1588.26
120000	2170.84	2048.83	1954.43	1879.99	1820.40	1772.13	1732.65
130000	2351.75	2219.57	2117.30	2036.66	1972.10	1919.81	1877.04
140000	2532.65	2390.31	2280.17	2193.32	2123.80	2067.49	2021.43
150000	2713.56	2561.04	2443.04	2349.99	2275.51	2215.17	2165.81
175000	3165.81	2987.88	2850.21	2741.65	2654.76	2584.36	2526.78
200000	3618.07	3414.72	3257.39	3133.32	3034.01	2953.56	2887.75
225000	4070.33	3841.56	3664.56	3524.98	3413.26	3322.75	3248.72
250000	4522.59	4268.40	4071.73	3916.65	3792.51	3691.95	3609.69

15¼% Monthly Payments

necessary to amortize a loan

AMOUNT	15 YEARS	16 YEARS	17 YEARS	18 YEARS	19 YEARS	20 YEARS	21 YEARS
100	1.42	1.39	1.38	1.36	1.35	1.34	1.33
200	2.83	2.79	2.75	2.72	2.69	2.67	2.65
500	7.08	6.97	6.88	6.80	6.73	6.68	6.63
1000	14.17	13.94	13.75	13.60	13.46	13.35	13.26
2000	28.33	27.88	27.51	27.19	26.93	26.71	26.52
5000	70.84	69.71	68.77	67.99	67.32	66.76	66.29
6000	85.00	83.65	82.53	81.58	80.79	80.12	79.55
7000	99.17	97.60	96.28	95.18	94.25	93.47	92.81
8000	113.34	111.54	110.04	108.78	107.72	106.82	106.07
9000	127.51	125.48	123.79	122.37	121.18	120.18	119.33
10000	141.67	139.42	137.55	135.97	134.65	133.53	132.58
15000	212.51	209.14	206.32	203.96	201.97	200.29	198.88
20000	283.35	278.85	275.09	271.94	269.29	267.06	265.17
25000	354.19	348.56	343.86	339.93	336.62	333.82	331.46
30000	425.02	418.27	412.64	407.92	403.94	400.59	397.75
35000	495.86	487.98	481.41	475.90	471.27	467.35	464.04
36000	510.03	501.93	495.16	489.50	484.73	480.71	477.30
37000	524.20	515.87	508.92	503.10	498.20	494.06	490.56
38000	538.36	529.81	522.67	516.69	511.66	507.41	503.82
39000	552.53	543.75	536.43	530.29	525.13	520.77	517.08
40000	566.70	557.70	550.18	543.89	538.59	534.12	530.34
41000	580.87	571.64	563.94	557.48	552.05	547.47	543.60
42000	595.03	585.58	577.69	571.08	565.52	560.83	556.85
43000	609.20	599.52	591.45	584.68	578.98	574.18	570.11
44000	623.37	613.47	605.20	598.28	592.45	587.53	583.37
45000	637.54	627.41	618.96	611.87	605.91	600.88	596.63
46000	651.70	641.35	632.71	625.47	619.38	614.24	609.89
47000	665.87	655.29	646.47	639.07	632.84	627.59	623.15
48000	680.04	669.23	660.22	652.66	646.31	640.94	636.40
49000	694.21	683.18	673.97	666.26	659.77	654.30	649.66
50000	708.37	697.12	687.73	679.86	673.24	667.65	662.92
51000	722.54	711.06	701.48	693.46	686.70	681.00	676.18
52000	736.71	725.00	715.24	707.05	700.17	694.36	689.44
53000	750.88	738.95	728.99	720.65	713.63	707.71	702.70
54000	765.04	752.89	742.75	734.25	727.10	721.06	715.95
55000	779.21	766.83	756.50	747.84	740.56	734.41	729.21
56000	793.38	780.77	770.26	761.44	754.03	747.77	742.47
57000	807.55	794.72	784.01	775.04	767.49	761.12	755.73
58000	821.71	808.66	797.77	788.64	780.96	774.47	768.99
59000	835.88	822.60	811.52	802.23	794.42	787.83	782.25
60000	850.05	836.54	825.27	815.83	807.88	801.18	795.50
65000	920.89	906.26	894.05	883.82	875.21	867.94	861.80
70000	991.72	975.97	962.82	951.80	942.53	934.71	928.09
75000	1062.56	1045.68	1031.59	1019.79	1009.86	1001.47	994.38
80000	1133.40	1115.39	1100.37	1087.77	1077.18	1068.24	1060.67
85000	1204.24	1185.10	1169.14	1155.76	1144.50	1135.00	1126.97
90000	1275.07	1254.82	1237.91	1223.75	1211.83	1201.77	1193.26
95000	1345.91	1324.53	1306.68	1291.73	1279.15	1268.53	1259.55
100000	1416.75	1394.24	1375.46	1359.72	1346.47	1335.30	1325.84
105000	1487.59	1463.95	1444.23	1427.70	1413.80	1402.06	1392.13
110000	1558.42	1533.66	1513.00	1495.69	1481.12	1468.83	1458.43
120000	1700.10	1673.09	1650.55	1631.66	1615.77	1602.36	1591.01
130000	1841.77	1812.51	1788.10	1767.63	1750.42	1735.89	1723.59
140000	1983.45	1951.93	1925.64	1903.60	1885.06	1869.42	1856.18
150000	2125.12	2091.36	2063.19	2039.58	2019.71	2002.95	1988.76
175000	2479.31	2439.92	2407.05	2379.50	2356.33	2336.77	2320.22
200000	2833.50	2788.48	2750.92	2719.43	2692.95	2670.60	2651.68
225000	3187.69	3137.04	3094.78	3059.36	3029.57	3004.42	2983.14
250000	3541.87	3485.60	3438.64	3399.29	3366.19	3338.25	3314.60

Monthly Payments 15¼%

necessary to amortize a loan

AMOUNT	22 YEARS	23 YEARS	24 YEARS	25 YEARS	30 YEARS	35 YEARS	40 YEARS
100	1.32	1.31	1.31	1.30	1.28	1.28	1.27
200	2.64	2.62	2.61	2.60	2.57	2.55	2.55
500	6.59	6.56	6.53	6.50	6.42	6.39	6.37
1000	13.18	13.11	13.05	13.00	12.84	12.77	12.74
2000	26.36	26.22	26.10	26.01	25.69	25.54	25.48
5000	65.89	65.55	65.26	65.01	64.22	63.86	63.69
6000	79.07	78.66	78.31	78.02	77.07	76.63	76.43
7000	92.25	91.77	91.36	91.02	89.91	89.40	89.17
8000	105.43	104.88	104.42	104.02	102.76	102.17	101.90
9000	118.60	117.99	117.47	117.02	115.60	114.95	114.64
10000	131.78	131.10	130.52	130.03	128.45	127.72	127.38
15000	197.67	196.65	195.78	195.04	192.67	191.58	191.07
20000	263.56	262.20	261.04	260.05	256.89	255.44	254.76
25000	329.46	327.75	326.30	325.06	321.11	319.30	318.45
30000	395.35	393.30	391.56	390.08	385.34	383.16	382.14
35000	461.24	458.85	456.82	455.09	449.56	447.01	445.83
36000	474.42	471.96	469.87	468.09	462.41	459.79	458.57
37000	487.59	485.07	482.93	481.10	475.25	472.56	471.31
38000	500.77	498.18	495.98	494.10	488.09	485.33	484.04
39000	513.95	511.29	509.03	507.10	500.94	498.10	496.78
40000	527.13	524.40	522.08	520.10	513.78	510.87	509.52
41000	540.31	537.51	535.13	533.11	526.63	523.65	522.26
42000	553.48	550.62	548.19	546.11	539.47	536.42	535.00
43000	566.66	563.73	561.24	559.11	552.32	549.19	547.73
44000	579.84	576.84	574.29	572.11	565.16	561.96	560.47
45000	593.02	589.95	587.34	585.12	578.01	574.73	573.21
46000	606.20	603.06	600.39	598.12	590.85	587.50	585.95
47000	619.38	616.17	613.45	611.12	603.70	600.28	598.69
48000	632.55	629.28	626.50	624.12	616.54	613.05	611.43
49000	645.73	642.39	639.55	637.13	629.38	625.82	624.16
50000	658.91	655.50	652.60	650.13	642.23	638.59	636.90
51000	672.09	668.61	665.65	663.13	655.07	651.36	649.64
52000	685.27	681.72	678.71	676.13	667.92	664.14	662.38
53000	698.44	694.83	691.76	689.14	680.76	676.91	675.12
54000	711.62	707.94	704.81	702.14	693.61	689.68	687.85
55000	724.80	721.05	717.86	715.14	706.45	702.45	700.59
56000	737.98	734.16	730.91	728.14	719.30	715.22	713.33
57000	751.16	747.27	743.97	741.15	732.14	727.99	726.07
58000	764.34	760.38	757.02	754.15	744.99	740.77	738.81
59000	777.51	773.49	770.07	767.15	757.83	753.54	751.54
60000	790.69	786.60	783.12	780.15	770.68	766.31	764.28
65000	856.58	852.15	848.38	845.17	834.90	830.17	827.97
70000	922.47	917.70	913.64	910.18	899.12	894.03	891.66
75000	988.37	983.25	978.90	975.19	963.34	957.89	955.35
80000	1054.26	1048.80	1044.16	1040.21	1027.57	1021.75	1019.04
85000	1120.15	1114.35	1109.42	1105.22	1091.79	1085.61	1082.73
90000	1186.04	1179.90	1174.68	1170.23	1156.01	1149.47	1146.42
95000	1251.93	1245.45	1239.94	1235.25	1220.24	1213.32	1210.11
100000	1317.82	1311.00	1305.20	1300.26	1284.46	1277.18	1273.80
105000	1383.71	1376.55	1370.46	1365.27	1348.68	1341.04	1337.49
110000	1449.60	1442.10	1435.72	1430.28	1412.90	1404.90	1401.18
120000	1581.38	1573.21	1566.24	1560.31	1541.35	1532.62	1528.56
130000	1713.17	1704.31	1696.76	1690.34	1669.80	1660.34	1655.94
140000	1844.95	1835.41	1827.28	1820.36	1798.24	1788.06	1783.32
150000	1976.73	1966.51	1957.80	1950.39	1926.69	1915.78	1910.70
175000	2306.19	2294.26	2284.11	2275.45	2247.80	2235.07	2229.15
200000	2635.64	2622.01	2610.41	2600.52	2568.92	2554.37	2547.60
225000	2965.10	2949.76	2936.71	2925.58	2890.03	2873.66	2866.06
250000	3294.55	3277.51	3263.01	3250.65	3211.15	3192.96	3184.51

15½% Monthly Payments

necessary to amortize a loan

AMOUNT	1 YEAR	2 YEARS	3 YEARS	4 YEARS	5 YEARS	6 YEARS	7 YEARS
100	9.05	4.87	3.49	2.81	2.41	2.14	1.96
200	18.10	9.74	6.98	5.62	4.81	4.28	3.92
500	45.25	24.36	17.46	14.04	12.03	10.71	9.79
1000	90.49	48.72	34.91	28.08	24.05	21.42	19.58
2000	180.99	97.45	69.82	56.17	48.11	42.83	39.16
5000	452.47	243.62	174.55	140.42	120.27	107.09	97.89
6000	542.97	292.35	209.46	168.51	144.32	128.50	117.47
7000	633.46	341.07	244.37	196.59	168.37	149.92	137.05
8000	723.96	389.80	279.29	224.68	192.43	171.34	156.63
9000	814.45	438.52	314.20	252.76	216.48	192.76	176.21
10000	904.94	487.25	349.11	280.85	240.53	214.17	195.78
15000	1357.42	730.87	523.66	421.27	360.80	321.26	293.68
20000	1809.89	974.49	698.21	561.70	481.06	428.35	391.57
25000	2262.36	1218.11	872.77	702.12	601.33	535.44	489.46
30000	2714.83	1461.74	1047.32	842.55	721.60	642.52	587.35
35000	3167.30	1705.36	1221.87	982.97	841.86	749.61	685.24
36000	3257.80	1754.08	1256.78	1011.05	865.91	771.03	704.82
37000	3348.29	1802.81	1291.70	1039.14	889.97	792.45	724.40
38000	3438.79	1851.53	1326.61	1067.22	914.02	813.86	743.98
39000	3529.28	1900.26	1361.52	1095.31	938.07	835.28	763.56
40000	3619.78	1948.98	1396.43	1123.39	962.13	856.70	783.13
41000	3710.27	1997.71	1431.34	1151.48	986.18	878.12	802.71
42000	3800.77	2046.43	1466.25	1179.56	1010.23	899.53	822.29
43000	3891.26	2095.16	1501.16	1207.65	1034.29	920.95	841.87
44000	3981.75	2143.88	1536.07	1235.73	1058.34	942.37	861.45
45000	4072.25	2192.60	1570.98	1263.82	1082.39	963.79	881.03
46000	4162.74	2241.33	1605.89	1291.90	1106.45	985.20	900.60
47000	4253.24	2290.05	1640.80	1319.99	1130.50	1006.62	920.18
48000	4343.73	2338.78	1675.71	1348.07	1154.55	1028.04	939.76
49000	4434.23	2387.50	1710.62	1376.16	1178.61	1049.46	959.34
50000	4524.72	2436.23	1745.53	1404.24	1202.66	1070.87	978.92
51000	4615.22	2484.95	1780.44	1432.33	1226.71	1092.29	998.50
52000	4705.71	2533.68	1815.36	1460.41	1250.77	1113.71	1018.07
53000	4796.20	2582.40	1850.27	1488.50	1274.82	1135.13	1037.65
54000	4886.70	2631.13	1885.18	1516.58	1298.87	1156.54	1057.23
55000	4977.19	2679.85	1920.09	1544.67	1322.93	1177.96	1076.81
56000	5067.69	2728.57	1955.00	1572.75	1346.98	1199.38	1096.39
57000	5158.18	2777.30	1989.91	1600.84	1371.03	1220.80	1115.97
58000	5248.68	2826.02	2024.82	1628.92	1395.09	1242.21	1135.54
59000	5339.17	2874.75	2059.73	1657.01	1419.14	1263.63	1155.12
60000	5429.66	2923.47	2094.64	1685.09	1443.19	1285.05	1174.70
65000	5882.14	3167.10	2269.19	1825.52	1563.46	1392.14	1272.59
70000	6334.61	3410.72	2443.75	1965.94	1683.72	1499.22	1370.48
75000	6787.08	3654.34	2618.30	2106.36	1803.99	1606.31	1468.38
80000	7239.55	3897.96	2792.85	2246.79	1924.26	1713.40	1566.27
85000	7692.03	4141.59	2967.41	2387.21	2044.52	1820.49	1664.16
90000	8144.50	4385.21	3141.96	2527.64	2164.79	1927.57	1762.05
95000	8596.97	4628.83	3316.51	2668.06	2285.05	2034.66	1859.94
100000	9049.44	4872.45	3491.07	2808.49	2405.32	2141.75	1957.83
105000	9501.91	5116.08	3665.62	2948.91	2525.59	2248.84	2055.73
110000	9954.39	5359.70	3840.17	3089.33	2645.85	2355.92	2153.62
120000	10859.33	5846.95	4189.28	3370.18	2886.38	2570.10	2349.40
130000	11764.27	6334.19	4538.39	3651.03	3126.91	2784.27	2545.19
140000	12669.22	6821.44	4887.50	3931.88	3367.45	2998.45	2740.97
150000	13574.16	7308.68	5236.60	4212.73	3607.98	3212.62	2936.75
175000	15836.52	8526.79	6109.37	4914.85	4209.31	3748.06	3426.21
200000	18098.88	9744.91	6982.14	5616.97	4810.64	4283.50	3915.67
225000	20361.24	10963.02	7854.90	6319.09	5411.97	4818.93	4405.13
250000	22623.60	12181.14	8727.67	7021.21	6013.30	5354.37	4894.59

Monthly Payments 15½%

necessary to amortize a loan

AMOUNT	8 YEARS	9 YEARS	10 YEARS	11 YEARS	12 YEARS	13 YEARS	14 YEARS
100	1.82	1.72	1.64	1.58	1.53	1.49	1.46
200	3.65	3.44	3.29	3.16	3.07	2.99	2.92
500	9.12	8.61	8.22	7.91	7.67	7.47	7.30
1000	18.24	17.22	16.44	15.82	15.33	14.93	14.61
2000	36.47	34.45	32.88	31.65	30.66	29.87	29.22
5000	91.18	86.12	82.21	79.12	76.66	74.67	73.04
6000	109.42	103.34	98.65	94.95	91.99	89.60	87.65
7000	127.65	120.56	115.09	110.77	107.32	104.53	102.26
8000	145.89	137.79	131.53	126.60	122.66	119.47	116.86
9000	164.12	155.01	147.97	142.42	137.99	134.40	131.47
10000	182.36	172.24	164.41	158.25	153.32	149.33	146.08
15000	273.54	258.35	246.62	237.37	229.98	224.00	219.12
20000	364.72	344.47	328.82	316.49	306.64	298.67	292.16
25000	455.90	430.59	411.03	395.62	383.30	373.34	365.20
30000	547.08	516.71	493.23	474.74	459.96	448.00	438.24
35000	638.26	602.82	575.44	553.87	536.62	522.67	511.28
36000	656.49	620.05	591.88	569.69	551.95	537.60	525.88
37000	674.73	637.27	608.32	585.52	567.29	552.54	540.49
38000	692.97	654.49	624.76	601.34	582.62	567.47	555.10
39000	711.20	671.72	641.20	617.17	597.95	582.40	569.71
40000	729.44	688.94	657.64	632.99	613.28	597.34	584.32
41000	747.67	706.16	674.08	648.81	628.61	612.27	598.92
42000	765.91	723.39	690.52	664.64	643.95	627.21	613.53
43000	784.14	740.61	706.97	680.46	659.28	642.14	628.14
44000	802.38	757.84	723.41	696.29	674.61	657.07	642.75
45000	820.62	775.06	739.85	712.11	689.94	672.01	657.36
46000	838.85	792.28	756.29	727.94	705.27	686.94	671.96
47000	857.09	809.51	772.73	743.76	720.61	701.87	686.57
48000	875.32	826.73	789.17	759.59	735.94	716.81	701.18
49000	893.56	843.95	805.61	775.41	751.27	731.74	715.79
50000	911.80	861.18	822.05	791.24	766.60	746.67	730.39
51000	930.03	878.40	838.49	807.06	781.93	761.61	745.00
52000	948.27	895.62	854.93	822.89	797.27	776.54	759.61
53000	966.50	912.85	871.38	838.71	812.60	791.47	774.22
54000	984.74	930.07	887.82	854.54	827.93	806.41	788.83
55000	1002.98	947.29	904.26	870.36	843.26	821.34	803.43
56000	1021.21	964.52	920.70	886.19	858.59	836.27	818.04
57000	1039.45	981.74	937.14	902.01	873.93	851.21	832.65
58000	1057.68	998.96	953.58	917.04	889.26	866.14	847.26
59000	1075.92	1016.19	970.02	933.66	904.59	881.07	861.87
60000	1094.16	1033.41	986.46	949.48	919.92	896.01	876.47
65000	1185.33	1119.53	1068.67	1028.61	996.58	970.67	949.51
70000	1276.51	1205.65	1150.87	1107.73	1073.24	1045.34	1022.55
75000	1367.09	1291.76	1233.08	1186.86	1149.90	1120.01	1095.59
80000	1458.87	1377.88	1315.28	1265.98	1226.56	1194.68	1168.63
85000	1550.05	1464.00	1397.49	1345.10	1303.22	1269.34	1241.67
90000	1641.23	1550.12	1479.69	1424.23	1379.88	1344.01	1314.71
95000	1732.41	1636.23	1561.90	1503.35	1456.54	1418.68	1387.75
100000	1823.59	1722.35	1644.11	1582.47	1533.20	1493.35	1460.79
105000	1914.77	1808.47	1726.31	1661.60	1609.86	1568.01	1533.83
110000	2005.95	1894.59	1808.52	1740.72	1686.52	1642.68	1606.87
120000	2188.31	2066.82	1972.93	1898.97	1839.85	1792.01	1752.95
130000	2370.67	2239.06	2137.34	2057.22	1993.17	1941.35	1899.03
140000	2553.03	2411.29	2301.75	2215.46	2146.49	2090.68	2045.11
150000	2735.39	2583.53	2466.16	2373.71	2299.81	2240.02	2191.18
175000	3191.29	3014.12	2877.18	2769.33	2683.11	2613.35	2556.38
200000	3647.18	3444.71	3288.21	3164.95	3066.41	2986.69	2921.58
225000	4103.08	3875.29	3699.24	3560.57	3449.71	3360.03	3286.78
250000	4558.98	4305.88	4110.26	3956.19	3833.01	3733.30	3651.97

15½%

Monthly Payments
necessary to amortize a loan

AMOUNT	15 YEARS	16 YEARS	17 YEARS	18 YEARS	19 YEARS	20 YEARS	21 YEARS
100	1.43	1.41	1.39	1.38	1.36	1.35	1.34
200	2.87	2.82	2.79	2.76	2.73	2.71	2.69
500	7.17	7.06	6.97	6.89	6.82	6.77	6.72
1000	14.34	14.12	13.93	13.78	13.65	13.54	13.45
2000	28.68	28.24	27.87	27.56	27.30	27.08	26.89
5000	71.70	70.59	69.66	68.89	68.24	67.69	67.23
6000	86.04	84.71	83.60	82.67	81.89	81.23	80.68
7000	100.38	98.83	97.53	96.45	95.54	94.77	94.12
8000	114.72	112.94	111.46	110.23	109.19	108.31	107.57
9000	129.06	127.06	125.40	124.00	122.83	121.85	121.02
10000	143.40	141.18	139.33	137.78	136.48	135.39	134.46
15000	215.10	211.77	208.99	206.67	204.72	203.08	201.70
20000	286.80	282.36	278.66	275.56	272.97	270.78	268.93
25000	358.50	352.95	348.32	344.45	341.21	338.47	336.16
30000	430.20	423.54	417.99	413.35	409.45	406.16	403.39
35000	501.90	494.13	487.65	482.24	477.69	473.86	470.62
36000	516.24	508.24	501.59	496.02	491.34	487.40	484.07
37000	530.58	522.36	515.52	509.79	504.99	500.94	497.52
38000	544.92	536.48	529.45	523.57	518.63	514.47	510.96
39000	559.26	550.60	543.38	537.35	532.28	528.01	524.41
40000	573.60	564.71	557.32	551.13	545.93	541.55	537.85
41000	587.94	578.83	571.25	564.91	559.58	555.09	551.30
42000	602.28	592.95	585.18	578.68	573.23	568.63	564.75
43000	616.62	607.07	599.12	592.46	586.88	582.17	578.19
44000	630.96	621.19	613.05	606.24	600.52	595.71	591.64
45000	645.30	635.30	626.98	620.02	614.17	609.25	605.09
46000	659.64	649.42	640.91	633.80	627.82	622.79	618.53
47000	673.98	663.54	654.85	647.58	641.47	636.32	631.98
48000	688.32	677.66	668.78	661.35	655.12	649.86	645.43
49000	702.66	691.78	682.71	675.13	668.76	663.40	658.87
50000	717.00	705.89	696.65	688.91	682.41	676.94	672.32
51000	731.34	720.01	710.58	702.69	696.06	690.48	685.76
52000	745.67	734.13	724.51	716.47	709.71	704.02	699.21
53000	760.01	748.25	738.45	730.24	723.36	717.56	712.66
54000	774.35	762.36	752.38	744.02	737.01	731.10	726.10
55000	788.69	776.48	766.31	757.80	750.65	744.63	739.55
56000	803.03	790.60	780.24	771.58	764.30	758.17	753.00
57000	817.37	804.72	794.18	785.36	777.95	771.71	766.44
58000	831.71	818.84	808.11	799.14	791.60	785.25	779.89
59000	846.05	832.95	822.04	812.91	805.25	798.79	793.34
60000	860.39	847.07	835.98	826.69	818.90	812.33	806.78
65000	932.09	917.66	905.64	895.58	887.14	880.02	874.01
70000	1003.79	988.25	975.30	964.47	955.38	947.72	941.25
75000	1075.49	1058.84	1044.97	1033.36	1023.62	1015.41	1008.48
80000	1147.19	1129.43	1114.63	1102.26	1091.86	1083.10	1075.71
85000	1218.89	1200.02	1184.30	1171.15	1160.10	1150.80	1142.94
90000	1290.59	1270.61	1253.96	1240.04	1228.34	1218.49	1210.17
95000	1362.29	1341.20	1323.63	1308.93	1296.58	1286.19	1277.40
100000	1433.99	1411.79	1393.29	1377.82	1364.83	1353.88	1344.64
105000	1505.69	1482.38	1462.96	1446.71	1433.07	1421.57	1411.87
110000	1577.39	1552.97	1532.62	1515.60	1501.31	1489.27	1479.10
120000	1720.79	1694.14	1671.95	1653.38	1637.79	1624.66	1613.56
130000	1864.19	1835.32	1811.28	1791.17	1774.27	1760.04	1748.03
140000	2007.59	1976.50	1950.61	1928.95	1910.76	1895.43	1882.49
150000	2150.99	2117.68	2089.94	2066.73	2047.24	2030.82	2016.95
175000	2509.48	2470.63	2438.26	2411.18	2388.45	2369.29	2353.11
200000	2867.98	2823.57	2786.58	2755.64	2729.65	2707.76	2689.27
225000	3226.48	3176.52	3134.91	3100.09	3070.86	3046.23	3025.43
250000	3584.98	3529.47	3483.23	3444.55	3412.07	3384.70	3361.59

Monthly Payments 15½%

necessary to amortize a loan

AMOUNT	22 YEARS	23 YEARS	24 YEARS	25 YEARS	30 YEARS	35 YEARS	40 YEARS
100	1.34	1.33	1.32	1.32	1.30	1.30	1.29
200	2.67	2.66	2.65	2.64	2.61	2.60	2.59
500	6.68	6.65	6.62	6.60	6.52	6.49	6.47
1000	13.37	13.30	13.25	13.20	13.05	12.98	12.94
2000	26.74	26.60	26.49	26.39	26.09	25.95	25.89
5000	66.84	66.51	66.23	65.99	65.23	64.88	64.72
6000	80.21	79.81	79.47	79.18	78.27	77.86	77.66
7000	93.58	93.11	92.72	92.38	91.32	90.83	90.61
8000	106.94	106.41	105.96	105.58	104.36	103.81	103.55
9000	120.31	119.72	119.21	118.78	117.41	116.78	116.50
10000	133.68	133.02	132.45	131.97	130.45	129.76	129.44
15000	200.52	199.53	198.68	197.96	195.68	194.64	194.16
20000	267.36	266.04	264.91	263.95	260.90	259.52	258.88
25000	334.20	332.54	331.13	329.94	326.13	324.40	323.60
30000	401.04	399.05	397.36	395.92	391.36	389.28	388.32
35000	467.88	465.56	463.59	461.91	456.58	454.15	453.04
36000	481.25	478.86	476.83	475.11	469.63	467.13	465.98
37000	494.62	492.17	490.08	488.31	482.67	480.11	478.93
38000	507.99	505.47	503.32	501.50	495.72	493.08	491.87
39000	521.36	518.77	516.57	514.70	508.76	506.06	504.82
40000	534.72	532.07	529.82	527.90	521.81	519.03	517.76
41000	548.09	545.37	543.06	541.10	534.85	532.01	530.70
42000	561.46	558.67	556.31	554.29	547.90	544.99	543.65
43000	574.83	571.98	569.55	567.49	560.94	557.96	556.59
44000	588.20	585.28	582.80	580.69	573.99	570.94	569.54
45000	601.57	598.58	596.04	593.89	587.03	583.91	582.48
46000	614.93	611.88	609.29	607.08	600.08	596.89	595.42
47000	628.30	625.18	622.53	620.28	613.12	609.86	608.37
48000	641.67	638.48	635.78	633.48	626.17	622.84	621.31
49000	655.04	651.79	649.02	646.68	639.21	635.82	634.26
50000	668.41	665.09	662.27	659.87	652.26	648.79	647.20
51000	681.77	678.39	675.52	673.07	665.30	661.77	660.14
52000	695.14	691.69	688.76	686.27	678.35	674.74	673.09
53000	708.51	704.99	702.01	699.46	691.39	687.72	686.03
54000	721.88	718.29	715.25	712.66	704.44	700.70	698.98
55000	735.25	731.60	728.50	725.86	717.48	713.67	711.92
56000	748.61	744.90	741.74	739.06	730.53	726.65	724.86
57000	761.98	758.20	754.99	752.25	743.57	739.62	737.81
58000	775.35	771.50	768.23	765.45	756.62	752.60	750.75
59000	788.72	784.80	781.48	778.65	769.66	765.57	763.70
60000	802.09	798.11	794.72	791.85	782.71	778.55	776.64
65000	868.93	864.61	860.95	857.83	847.94	843.43	841.36
70000	935.77	931.12	927.18	923.82	913.16	908.31	906.08
75000	1002.61	997.62	993.40	989.81	978.39	973.19	970.80
80000	1069.45	1064.14	1059.63	1055.80	1043.61	1038.07	1035.52
85000	1136.29	1130.65	1125.86	1121.78	1108.84	1102.95	1100.24
90000	1203.13	1197.16	1192.09	1187.77	1174.07	1167.83	1164.96
95000	1269.97	1263.67	1258.31	1253.76	1239.29	1232.71	1229.68
100000	1336.81	1330.18	1324.54	1319.75	1304.52	1297.58	1294.40
105000	1403.65	1396.68	1390.77	1385.73	1369.74	1362.46	1359.12
110000	1470.49	1463.19	1456.99	1451.72	1434.97	1427.34	1423.84
120000	1604.17	1596.21	1589.45	1583.69	1565.42	1557.10	1553.28
130000	1737.86	1729.23	1721.90	1715.67	1695.87	1686.86	1682.72
140000	1871.54	1862.25	1854.36	1847.64	1826.32	1816.62	1812.16
150000	2005.22	1995.26	1986.81	1979.62	1956.78	1946.38	1941.60
175000	2339.42	2327.81	2317.94	2309.55	2282.90	2270.77	2265.20
200000	2673.62	2660.35	2649.08	2639.49	2609.03	2595.17	2588.80
225000	3007.83	2992.90	2980.21	2969.43	2935.16	2919.57	2912.40
250000	3342.03	3325.44	3311.35	3299.36	3261.29	3243.96	3236.00

15¾%

Monthly Payments
necessary to amortize a loan

AMOUNT	1 YEAR	2 YEARS	3 YEARS	4 YEARS	5 YEARS	6 YEARS	7 YEARS
100	9.06	4.88	3.50	2.82	2.42	2.16	1.97
200	18.12	9.77	7.01	5.64	4.84	4.31	3.94
500	45.31	24.42	17.52	14.11	12.09	10.78	9.86
1000	90.61	48.84	35.03	28.21	24.19	21.55	19.72
2000	181.23	97.69	70.07	56.42	48.37	43.11	39.44
5000	453.06	244.22	175.17	141.06	120.93	107.77	98.60
6000	543.68	293.06	210.20	169.27	145.11	129.33	118.32
7000	634.29	341.91	245.24	197.49	169.30	150.88	138.04
8000	724.90	390.75	280.27	225.70	193.48	172.44	157.76
9000	815.51	439.59	315.30	253.91	217.67	193.99	177.48
10000	906.13	488.44	350.34	282.12	241.85	215.54	197.20
15000	1359.19	732.66	525.51	423.19	362.78	323.32	295.80
20000	1812.25	976.87	700.67	564.25	483.71	431.09	394.40
25000	2265.31	1221.09	875.84	705.31	604.64	538.86	493.00
30000	2718.38	1465.31	1051.01	846.37	725.56	646.63	591.60
35000	3171.44	1709.53	1226.18	987.43	846.49	754.41	690.20
36000	3262.05	1758.37	1261.21	1015.65	870.68	775.96	709.92
37000	3352.67	1807.22	1296.25	1043.86	894.86	797.51	729.64
38000	3443.28	1856.06	1331.28	1072.07	919.05	819.07	749.36
39000	3533.89	1904.91	1366.32	1100.28	943.23	840.62	769.08
40000	3624.50	1953.75	1401.35	1128.50	967.42	862.18	788.80
41000	3715.12	2002.59	1436.38	1156.71	991.60	883.73	808.52
42000	3805.73	2051.44	1471.42	1184.92	1015.79	905.29	828.24
43000	3896.34	2100.28	1506.45	1213.13	1039.97	926.84	847.96
44000	3986.95	2149.12	1541.48	1241.35	1064.16	948.39	867.68
45000	4077.57	2197.97	1576.52	1269.56	1088.34	969.95	887.40
46000	4168.18	2246.81	1611.55	1297.77	1112.53	991.50	907.12
47000	4258.79	2295.66	1646.59	1325.98	1136.71	1013.06	926.84
48000	4349.40	2344.50	1681.62	1354.20	1160.90	1034.61	946.56
49000	4440.02	2393.34	1716.65	1382.41	1185.09	1056.17	966.28
50000	4530.63	2442.19	1751.69	1410.62	1209.27	1077.72	986.00
51000	4621.24	2491.03	1786.72	1438.83	1233.46	1099.28	1005.72
52000	4711.85	2539.87	1821.75	1467.05	1257.64	1120.83	1025.44
53000	4802.47	2588.72	1856.79	1495.26	1281.83	1142.38	1045.16
54000	4893.08	2637.56	1891.82	1523.47	1306.01	1163.94	1064.88
55000	4983.69	2686.41	1926.86	1551.68	1330.20	1185.49	1084.60
56000	5074.31	2735.25	1961.89	1579.89	1354.38	1207.05	1104.32
57000	5164.92	2784.09	1996.92	1608.11	1378.57	1228.60	1124.04
58000	5255.53	2832.94	2031.96	1636.32	1402.75	1250.16	1143.76
59000	5346.14	2881.78	2066.99	1664.53	1426.94	1271.71	1163.48
60000	5436.76	2930.62	2102.02	1692.74	1451.13	1293.27	1183.20
65000	5889.82	3174.84	2277.19	1833.81	1572.05	1401.04	1281.80
70000	6342.88	3419.06	2452.36	1974.87	1692.98	1508.81	1380.40
75000	6795.94	3663.28	2627.53	2115.93	1813.91	1616.58	1479.00
80000	7249.01	3907.50	2802.70	2256.99	1934.83	1724.35	1577.60
85000	7702.07	4151.72	2977.87	2398.05	2055.76	1832.13	1676.19
90000	8155.13	4395.94	3153.04	2539.12	2176.69	1939.90	1774.79
95000	8608.20	4640.16	3328.20	2680.18	2297.62	2047.67	1873.39
100000	9061.26	4884.37	3503.37	2821.24	2418.54	2155.44	1971.99
105000	9514.32	5128.59	3678.54	2962.30	2539.47	2263.22	2070.59
110000	9967.39	5372.81	3853.71	3103.36	2660.40	2370.99	2169.19
120000	10873.51	5861.25	4204.05	3385.49	2902.25	2586.53	2366.39
130000	11779.64	6349.69	4554.39	3667.61	3144.11	2802.08	2563.59
140000	12685.76	6838.12	4904.72	3949.74	3385.96	3017.62	2760.79
150000	13591.89	7326.56	5255.06	4231.86	3627.81	3233.16	2957.99
175000	15857.20	8547.65	6130.90	4937.17	4232.45	3772.03	3450.99
200000	18122.52	9768.75	7006.75	5642.48	4837.08	4310.89	3943.99
225000	20387.83	10989.84	7882.59	6347.79	5441.72	4849.75	4436.99
250000	22653.15	12210.94	8758.43	7053.10	6046.36	5388.61	4929.99

Monthly Payments 15¾%

necessary to amortize a loan

AMOUNT	8 YEARS	9 YEARS	10 YEARS	11 YEARS	12 YEARS	13 YEARS	14 YEARS
100	1.84	1.74	1.66	1.60	1.55	1.51	1.48
200	3.68	3.47	3.32	3.20	3.10	3.02	2.96
500	9.19	8.69	8.30	7.99	7.75	7.55	7.39
1000	18.38	17.37	16.60	15.98	15.49	15.10	14.78
2000	36.76	34.75	33.19	31.97	30.99	30.20	29.56
5000	91.91	86.87	82.98	79.92	77.47	75.50	73.89
6000	110.29	104.24	99.58	95.90	92.97	90.60	88.67
7000	128.67	121.62	116.17	111.89	108.46	105.70	103.44
8000	147.06	138.99	132.77	127.87	123.96	120.80	118.22
9000	165.44	156.37	149.36	143.85	139.45	135.90	133.00
10000	183.82	173.74	165.96	159.84	154.95	151.00	147.78
15000	275.73	260.61	248.94	239.75	232.42	226.50	221.67
20000	367.64	347.48	331.92	319.67	309.90	302.00	295.56
25000	459.55	434.35	414.90	399.59	387.37	377.50	369.45
30000	551.46	521.22	497.88	479.51	464.84	453.00	443.33
35000	643.37	608.09	580.85	559.43	542.32	528.50	517.22
36000	661.75	625.47	597.45	575.41	557.81	543.60	532.00
37000	680.14	642.84	614.05	591.39	573.31	558.70	546.78
38000	698.52	660.21	630.64	607.38	588.80	573.80	561.56
39000	716.90	677.59	647.24	623.36	604.30	588.90	576.33
40000	735.28	694.96	663.83	639.34	619.79	604.00	591.11
41000	753.66	712.34	680.43	655.33	635.29	619.10	605.89
42000	772.05	729.71	697.03	671.31	650.78	634.19	620.67
43000	790.43	747.09	713.62	687.30	666.28	649.29	635.45
44000	808.81	764.46	730.22	703.28	681.77	664.39	650.22
45000	827.19	781.83	746.81	719.26	697.27	679.49	665.00
46000	845.57	799.21	763.41	735.25	712.76	694.59	679.78
47000	863.96	816.58	780.00	751.23	728.25	709.69	694.56
48000	882.34	833.96	796.60	767.21	743.75	724.79	709.33
49000	900.72	851.33	813.20	783.20	759.24	739.89	724.11
50000	919.10	868.70	829.79	799.18	774.74	754.99	738.89
51000	937.49	886.08	846.39	815.16	790.23	770.09	753.67
52000	955.87	903.45	862.98	831.15	805.73	785.19	768.45
53000	974.25	920.83	879.58	847.13	821.22	800.29	783.22
54000	992.63	938.20	896.18	863.11	836.72	815.39	798.00
55000	1011.01	955.57	912.77	879.10	852.21	830.49	812.78
56000	1029.40	972.95	929.37	895.08	867.71	845.59	827.56
57000	1047.78	990.32	945.96	911.07	883.20	860.69	842.33
58000	1066.16	1007.70	962.56	927.05	898.70	875.79	857.11
59000	1084.54	1025.07	979.16	943.03	914.19	890.89	871.89
60000	1102.92	1042.44	995.75	959.02	929.69	905.99	886.67
65000	1194.83	1129.31	1078.73	1038.93	1007.16	981.49	960.56
70000	1286.74	1216.19	1161.71	1118.85	1084.63	1056.99	1034.45
75000	1378.65	1303.06	1244.69	1198.77	1162.11	1132.49	1108.34
80000	1470.57	1389.93	1327.67	1278.69	1239.58	1207.99	1182.22
85000	1562.48	1476.80	1410.65	1358.61	1317.06	1283.49	1256.11
90000	1654.39	1563.67	1493.63	1438.52	1394.53	1358.99	1330.00
95000	1746.30	1650.54	1576.61	1518.44	1472.00	1434.49	1403.89
100000	1838.21	1737.41	1659.58	1598.36	1549.48	1509.99	1477.78
105000	1930.12	1824.28	1742.56	1678.28	1626.95	1585.49	1551.67
110000	2022.03	1911.15	1825.54	1758.20	1704.43	1660.99	1625.56
120000	2205.85	2084.89	1991.50	1918.03	1859.37	1811.99	1773.34
130000	2389.67	2258.63	2157.46	2077.87	2014.32	1962.98	1921.11
140000	2573.49	2432.37	2323.42	2237.71	2169.27	2113.98	2068.89
150000	2757.31	2606.11	2489.38	2397.54	2324.22	2264.98	2216.67
175000	3216.86	3040.46	2904.27	2797.13	2711.59	2642.48	2586.12
200000	3676.41	3474.81	3319.17	3196.72	3098.96	3019.98	2955.56
225000	4135.96	3909.17	3734.07	3596.31	3486.33	3397.47	3325.01
250000	4595.52	4343.52	4148.96	3995.90	3873.70	3774.97	3694.45

15¾%

Monthly Payments
necessary to amortize a loan

AMOUNT	15 YEARS	16 YEARS	17 YEARS	18 YEARS	19 YEARS	20 YEARS	21 YEARS
100	1.45	1.43	1.41	1.40	1.38	1.37	1.36
200	2.90	2.86	2.82	2.79	2.77	2.75	2.73
500	7.26	7.15	7.06	6.98	6.92	6.86	6.82
1000	14.51	14.29	14.11	13.96	13.83	13.73	13.64
2000	29.03	28.59	28.22	27.92	27.67	27.45	27.27
5000	72.57	71.47	70.56	69.80	69.16	68.63	68.18
6000	87.08	85.76	84.67	83.76	83.00	82.35	81.81
7000	101.59	100.06	98.78	97.72	96.83	96.08	95.45
8000	116.10	114.35	112.90	111.68	110.66	109.80	109.08
9000	130.62	128.65	127.01	125.64	124.49	123.53	122.72
10000	145.13	142.94	141.12	139.60	138.33	137.25	136.35
15000	217.70	214.41	211.68	209.40	207.49	205.88	204.53
20000	290.26	285.88	282.24	279.20	276.65	274.51	272.70
25000	362.83	357.35	352.80	349.00	345.81	343.13	340.88
30000	435.39	428.82	423.36	418.80	414.98	411.76	409.05
35000	507.96	500.29	493.92	488.60	484.14	480.39	477.23
36000	522.47	514.59	508.03	502.56	497.97	494.11	490.86
37000	536.98	528.88	522.15	516.52	511.80	507.84	504.50
38000	551.50	543.18	536.26	530.48	525.64	521.56	518.13
39000	566.01	557.47	550.37	544.44	539.47	535.29	531.77
40000	580.52	571.76	564.48	558.40	553.30	549.01	545.40
41000	595.04	586.06	578.59	572.36	567.13	562.74	559.04
42000	609.55	600.35	592.71	586.32	580.97	576.46	572.67
43000	624.06	614.65	606.82	600.28	594.80	590.19	586.31
44000	638.58	628.94	620.93	614.24	608.63	603.91	599.94
45000	653.09	643.23	635.04	628.20	622.46	617.64	613.58
46000	667.60	657.53	649.15	642.16	636.30	631.37	627.21
47000	682.11	671.82	663.27	656.12	650.13	645.09	640.85
48000	696.63	686.12	677.38	670.08	663.96	658.82	654.48
49000	711.14	700.41	691.49	684.04	677.79	672.54	668.12
50000	725.65	714.71	705.60	698.00	691.63	686.27	681.75
51000	740.17	729.00	719.71	711.96	705.46	699.99	695.39
52000	754.68	743.29	733.83	725.92	719.29	713.72	709.02
53000	769.19	757.59	747.94	739.88	733.12	727.44	722.66
54000	783.71	771.88	762.05	753.84	746.96	741.17	736.29
55000	798.22	786.18	776.16	767.80	760.79	754.89	749.93
56000	812.73	800.47	790.27	781.76	774.62	768.62	763.56
57000	827.25	814.76	804.39	795.72	788.45	782.34	777.20
58000	841.76	829.06	818.50	809.68	802.29	796.07	790.83
59000	856.27	843.35	832.61	823.64	816.12	809.79	804.47
60000	870.78	857.65	846.72	837.60	829.95	823.52	818.10
65000	943.35	929.12	917.28	907.40	899.11	892.15	886.28
70000	1015.92	1000.59	987.84	977.20	968.28	960.77	954.45
75000	1088.48	1072.06	1058.40	1047.00	1037.44	1029.40	1022.63
80000	1161.05	1143.53	1128.96	1116.80	1106.60	1098.03	1090.80
85000	1233.61	1215.00	1199.52	1186.60	1175.76	1166.65	1158.98
90000	1306.18	1286.47	1270.08	1256.40	1244.93	1235.28	1227.15
95000	1378.74	1357.94	1340.64	1326.20	1314.09	1303.91	1295.33
100000	1451.31	1429.41	1411.20	1396.00	1383.25	1372.53	1363.50
105000	1523.87	1500.88	1481.76	1465.80	1452.41	1441.16	1431.68
110000	1596.44	1572.35	1552.32	1535.60	1521.58	1509.79	1499.85
120000	1741.57	1715.29	1693.44	1675.20	1659.90	1647.04	1636.20
130000	1886.70	1858.23	1834.56	1814.80	1798.23	1784.29	1772.55
140000	2031.83	2001.18	1975.68	1954.40	1936.55	1921.55	1908.90
150000	2176.96	2144.12	2116.80	2094.00	2074.88	2058.80	2045.25
175000	2539.79	2501.47	2469.61	2442.99	2420.69	2401.93	2386.13
200000	2902.62	2858.82	2822.41	2791.99	2766.50	2745.07	2727.00
225000	3265.44	3216.17	3175.21	3140.99	3112.31	3088.20	3067.88
250000	3628.27	3573.53	3528.01	3489.99	3458.13	3431.33	3408.75

Monthly Payments 15¾%
necessary to amortize a loan

AMOUNT	22 YEARS	23 YEARS	24 YEARS	25 YEARS	30 YEARS	35 YEARS	40 YEARS
100	1.36	1.35	1.34	1.34	1.32	1.32	1.32
200	2.71	2.70	2.69	2.68	2.65	2.64	2.63
500	6.78	6.75	6.72	6.70	6.62	6.59	6.58
1000	13.56	13.49	13.44	13.39	13.25	13.18	13.15
2000	27.12	26.99	26.88	26.79	26.49	26.36	26.30
5000	67.79	67.47	67.20	66.96	66.23	65.90	65.75
6000	81.35	80.96	80.64	80.36	79.48	79.08	78.90
7000	94.91	94.46	94.08	93.75	92.72	92.26	92.05
8000	108.47	107.95	107.51	107.14	105.97	105.44	105.20
9000	122.03	121.45	120.95	120.54	119.22	118.62	118.35
10000	135.59	134.94	134.39	133.93	132.46	131.80	131.50
15000	203.38	202.41	201.59	200.89	198.69	197.70	197.25
20000	271.17	269.88	268.79	267.86	264.92	263.60	263.00
25000	338.97	337.35	335.98	334.82	331.15	329.50	328.75
30000	406.76	404.82	403.18	401.79	397.39	395.40	394.50
35000	474.55	472.29	470.38	468.75	463.62	461.30	460.26
36000	488.11	485.79	483.82	482.14	476.86	474.48	473.41
37000	501.67	499.28	497.26	495.54	490.11	487.67	486.56
38000	515.23	512.78	510.70	508.93	503.35	500.85	499.71
39000	528.79	526.27	524.13	522.32	516.60	514.03	512.86
40000	542.35	539.76	537.57	535.72	529.85	527.21	526.01
41000	555.91	553.26	551.01	549.11	543.09	540.39	539.16
42000	569.46	566.75	564.45	562.50	556.34	553.57	552.31
43000	583.02	580.25	577.89	575.89	569.59	566.75	565.46
44000	596.58	593.74	591.33	589.29	582.83	579.93	578.61
45000	610.14	607.23	604.77	602.68	596.08	593.11	591.76
46000	623.70	620.73	618.21	616.07	609.32	606.29	604.91
47000	637.26	634.22	631.65	629.47	622.57	619.47	618.06
48000	650.82	647.72	645.09	642.86	635.82	632.65	631.21
49000	664.38	661.21	658.53	656.25	649.06	645.83	644.36
50000	677.93	674.71	671.97	669.64	662.31	659.01	657.51
51000	691.49	688.20	685.41	683.04	675.55	672.19	670.66
52000	705.05	701.69	698.85	696.43	688.80	685.37	683.81
53000	718.61	715.19	712.29	709.82	702.05	698.55	696.96
54000	732.17	728.68	725.73	723.22	715.29	711.73	710.11
55000	745.73	742.18	739.16	736.61	728.54	724.91	723.26
56000	759.29	755.67	752.60	750.00	741.79	738.09	736.41
57000	772.85	769.16	766.04	763.40	755.03	751.27	749.56
58000	786.40	782.66	779.48	776.79	768.28	764.45	762.71
59000	799.96	796.15	792.92	790.18	781.52	777.63	775.86
60000	813.52	809.65	806.36	803.57	794.77	790.81	789.01
65000	881.31	877.12	873.56	870.54	861.00	856.71	854.76
70000	949.11	944.59	940.76	937.50	927.23	922.61	920.51
75000	1016.90	1012.06	1007.95	1004.47	993.46	988.51	986.26
80000	1084.70	1079.53	1075.15	1071.43	1059.69	1054.41	1052.01
85000	1152.49	1147.00	1142.35	1138.40	1125.92	1120.31	1117.76
90000	1220.28	1214.47	1209.54	1205.36	1192.16	1186.21	1183.51
95000	1288.08	1281.94	1276.74	1272.33	1258.39	1252.11	1249.27
100000	1355.87	1349.41	1343.94	1339.29	1324.62	1318.01	1315.02
105000	1423.66	1416.88	1411.13	1406.25	1390.85	1383.91	1380.77
110000	1491.46	1484.35	1478.33	1473.22	1457.08	1449.82	1446.52
120000	1627.04	1619.29	1612.72	1607.15	1589.54	1581.62	1578.02
130000	1762.63	1754.23	1747.12	1741.08	1722.00	1713.42	1709.52
140000	1898.22	1889.17	1881.51	1875.01	1854.46	1845.22	1841.02
150000	2033.80	2024.12	2015.90	2008.93	1986.93	1977.02	1972.52
175000	2372.77	2361.47	2351.89	2343.76	2318.08	2306.52	2301.28
200000	2711.74	2698.82	2687.87	2678.58	2649.23	2636.03	2630.03
225000	3050.70	3036.17	3023.86	3013.40	2980.39	2965.53	2958.79
250000	3389.67	3373.53	3359.84	3348.22	3311.54	3295.03	3287.54

16% Monthly Payments

necessary to amortize a loan

AMOUNT	1 YEAR	2 YEARS	3 YEARS	4 YEARS	5 YEARS	6 YEARS	7 YEARS
100	9.07	4.90	3.52	2.83	2.43	2.17	1.99
200	18.15	9.79	7.03	5.67	4.86	4.34	3.97
500	45.37	24.48	17.58	14.17	12.16	10.85	9.93
1000	90.73	48.96	35.16	28.34	24.32	21.69	19.86
2000	181.46	97.93	70.31	56.68	48.64	43.38	39.72
5000	453.65	244.82	175.79	141.70	121.59	108.46	99.31
6000	544.39	293.78	210.94	170.04	145.91	130.15	119.17
7000	635.12	342.74	246.10	198.38	170.23	151.84	139.03
8000	725.85	391.70	281.26	226.72	194.54	173.53	158.90
9000	816.58	440.67	316.41	255.06	218.86	195.23	178.76
10000	907.31	489.63	351.57	283.40	243.18	216.92	198.62
15000	1360.96	734.45	527.36	425.10	364.77	325.38	297.93
20000	1814.62	979.26	703.14	566.81	486.36	433.84	397.24
25000	2268.27	1224.08	878.93	708.51	607.95	542.30	496.55
30000	2721.93	1468.89	1054.71	850.21	729.54	650.76	595.86
35000	3175.58	1713.71	1230.50	991.91	851.13	759.21	695.17
36000	3266.31	1762.67	1265.65	1020.25	875.45	780.91	715.03
37000	3357.04	1811.64	1300.81	1048.59	899.77	802.60	734.90
38000	3447.77	1860.60	1335.97	1076.93	924.09	824.29	754.76
39000	3538.50	1909.56	1371.12	1105.27	948.40	845.98	774.62
40000	3629.23	1958.52	1406.28	1133.61	972.72	867.67	794.48
41000	3719.97	2007.49	1441.44	1161.95	997.04	889.37	814.34
42000	3810.70	2056.45	1476.60	1190.29	1021.36	911.06	834.21
43000	3901.43	2105.41	1511.75	1218.63	1045.68	932.75	854.07
44000	3992.16	2154.38	1546.91	1246.97	1069.99	954.44	873.93
45000	4082.89	2203.34	1582.07	1275.31	1094.31	976.13	893.79
46000	4173.62	2252.30	1617.22	1303.65	1118.63	997.82	913.65
47000	4264.35	2301.27	1652.38	1331.99	1142.95	1019.52	933.52
48000	4355.08	2350.23	1687.54	1360.33	1167.27	1041.21	953.38
49000	4445.81	2399.19	1722.69	1388.67	1191.58	1062.90	973.24
50000	4536.54	2448.16	1757.85	1417.01	1215.90	1084.59	993.10
51000	4627.27	2497.12	1793.01	1445.35	1240.22	1106.28	1012.97
52000	4718.00	2546.08	1828.17	1473.69	1264.54	1127.98	1032.83
53000	4808.74	2595.04	1863.32	1502.03	1288.86	1149.67	1052.69
54000	4899.47	2644.01	1898.48	1530.38	1313.18	1171.36	1072.55
55000	4990.20	2692.97	1933.64	1558.72	1337.49	1193.05	1092.41
56000	5080.93	2741.93	1968.79	1587.06	1361.81	1214.74	1112.28
57000	5171.66	2790.90	2003.95	1615.40	1386.13	1236.43	1132.14
58000	5262.39	2839.86	2039.11	1643.74	1410.45	1258.13	1152.00
59000	5353.12	2888.82	2074.26	1672.08	1434.77	1279.82	1171.86
60000	5443.85	2937.79	2109.42	1700.42	1459.08	1301.51	1191.72
65000	5897.51	3182.60	2285.21	1842.12	1580.67	1409.97	1291.03
70000	6351.16	3427.42	2460.99	1983.82	1702.26	1518.43	1390.34
75000	6804.81	3672.23	2636.78	2125.52	1823.85	1626.89	1489.65
80000	7258.47	3917.05	2812.56	2267.22	1945.44	1735.35	1588.97
85000	7712.12	4161.86	2988.35	2408.92	2067.03	1843.81	1688.28
90000	8165.78	4406.68	3164.13	2550.63	2188.63	1952.27	1787.59
95000	8619.43	4651.50	3339.92	2692.33	2310.22	2060.72	1886.90
100000	9073.09	4896.31	3515.70	2834.03	2431.81	2169.18	1986.21
105000	9526.74	5141.13	3691.49	2975.73	2553.40	2277.64	2085.52
110000	9980.39	5385.94	3867.27	3117.43	2674.99	2386.10	2184.83
120000	10887.70	5875.57	4218.84	3400.83	2918.17	2603.02	2383.45
130000	11795.01	6365.20	4570.41	3684.24	3161.35	2819.94	2582.07
140000	12702.32	6854.84	4921.98	3967.64	3404.53	3036.86	2780.69
150000	13609.63	7344.47	5273.55	4251.04	3647.71	3253.78	2979.31
175000	15877.90	8568.54	6152.48	4959.55	4255.66	3796.07	3475.86
200000	18146.17	9792.62	7031.41	5668.06	4863.61	4338.37	3972.41
225000	20414.44	11016.70	7910.33	6376.56	5471.56	4880.66	4468.96
250000	22682.71	12240.78	8789.26	7085.07	6079.51	5422.96	4965.52

Monthly Payments **16%**

necessary to amortize a loan

AMOUNT	8 YEARS	9 YEARS	10 YEARS	11 YEARS	12 YEARS	13 YEARS	14 YEARS
100	1.85	1.75	1.68	1.61	1.57	1.53	1.49
200	3.71	3.51	3.35	3.23	3.13	3.05	2.99
500	9.26	8.76	8.38	8.07	7.83	7.63	7.47
1000	18.53	17.53	16.75	16.14	15.66	15.27	14.95
2000	37.06	35.05	33.50	32.29	31.32	30.53	29.90
5000	92.64	87.63	83.76	80.72	78.29	76.34	74.74
6000	111.17	105.15	100.51	96.86	93.95	91.60	89.69
7000	129.70	122.68	117.26	113.00	109.61	106.87	104.64
8000	148.23	140.20	134.01	129.15	125.27	122.14	119.59
9000	166.76	157.73	150.76	145.29	140.92	137.40	134.54
10000	185.29	175.25	167.51	161.43	156.58	152.67	149.48
15000	277.93	262.88	251.27	242.15	234.87	229.01	224.23
20000	370.58	350.51	335.03	322.86	313.17	305.34	298.97
25000	463.22	438.13	418.78	403.58	391.46	381.68	373.71
30000	555.86	525.76	502.54	484.30	469.75	458.01	448.45
35000	648.51	613.38	586.30	565.01	548.04	534.35	523.20
36000	667.04	630.91	603.05	581.15	563.70	549.61	538.14
37000	685.57	648.43	619.80	597.30	579.36	564.88	553.09
38000	704.09	665.96	636.55	613.44	595.01	580.15	568.04
39000	722.62	683.48	653.30	629.58	610.67	595.41	582.99
40000	741.15	701.01	670.05	645.73	626.33	610.68	597.94
41000	759.68	718.54	686.80	661.87	641.99	625.95	612.89
42000	778.21	736.06	703.56	678.01	657.65	641.22	627.84
43000	796.74	753.59	720.31	694.16	673.30	656.48	642.78
44000	815.27	771.11	737.06	710.30	688.96	671.75	657.73
45000	833.80	788.64	753.81	726.44	704.62	687.02	672.68
46000	852.32	806.16	770.56	742.59	720.28	702.28	687.63
47000	870.85	823.69	787.31	758.73	735.94	717.55	702.58
48000	889.38	841.21	804.06	774.87	751.60	732.82	717.53
49000	907.91	858.74	820.81	791.02	767.25	748.09	732.47
50000	926.44	876.26	837.57	807.16	782.91	763.35	747.42
51000	944.97	893.79	854.32	823.30	798.57	778.62	762.37
52000	963.50	911.31	871.07	839.44	814.23	793.89	777.32
53000	982.03	928.84	887.82	855.59	829.89	809.15	792.27
54000	1000.55	946.36	904.57	871.73	845.55	824.42	807.22
55000	1019.08	963.89	921.32	887.87	861.20	839.69	822.16
56000	1037.61	981.41	938.07	904.02	876.86	854.95	837.11
57000	1056.14	998.94	954.82	920.16	892.52	870.22	852.06
58000	1074.67	1016.46	971.58	936.30	908.18	885.49	867.01
59000	1093.20	1033.99	988.33	952.45	923.84	900.76	881.96
60000	1111.73	1051.52	1005.08	968.59	939.50	910.02	896.91
65000	1204.37	1139.14	1088.84	1049.31	1017.79	992.36	971.65
70000	1297.02	1226.77	1172.59	1130.02	1096.08	1068.69	1046.39
75000	1389.66	1314.39	1256.35	1210.74	1174.37	1145.03	1121.13
80000	1482.30	1402.02	1340.10	1291.45	1252.66	1221.30	1106.88
85000	1574.95	1489.65	1423.86	1372.17	1330.95	1207.70	1270.62
90000	1667.59	1577.27	1507.62	1452.89	1409.24	1374.03	1345.36
95000	1760.23	1664.90	1591.37	1533.60	1487.53	1450.37	1420.10
100000	1852.88	1752.53	1675.13	1614.32	1565.83	1526.70	1494.85
105000	1945.52	1840.15	1758.89	1695.03	1644.12	1603.04	1569.59
110000	2038.17	1927.78	1842.64	1775.75	1722.41	1679.37	1644.33
120000	2223.45	2103.03	2010.16	1937.18	1878.99	1832.05	1793.81
130000	2408.74	2278.28	2177.67	2098.61	2035.57	1984.72	1943.30
140000	2594.03	2453.54	2345.18	2260.04	2192.16	2137.39	2092.78
150000	2779.32	2628.79	2512.70	2421.48	2348.74	2290.06	2242.27
175000	3242.54	3066.92	2931.48	2825.06	2740.19	2671.73	2615.98
200000	3705.76	3505.05	3350.26	3228.63	3131.65	3053.41	2989.69
225000	4168.98	3943.18	3769.05	3632.21	3523.11	3435.09	3363.40
250000	4632.20	4381.31	4187.83	4035.79	3914.56	3816.76	3737.11

16% Monthly Payments

necessary to amortize a loan

AMOUNT	15 YEARS	16 YEARS	17 YEARS	18 YEARS	19 YEARS	20 YEARS	21 YEARS
100	1.47	1.45	1.43	1.41	1.40	1.39	1.38
200	2.94	2.89	2.86	2.83	2.80	2.78	2.76
500	7.34	7.24	7.15	7.07	7.01	6.96	6.91
1000	14.69	14.47	14.29	14.14	14.02	13.91	13.82
2000	29.37	28.94	28.58	28.28	28.03	27.83	27.65
5000	73.44	72.36	71.46	70.71	70.09	69.56	69.12
6000	88.12	86.83	85.75	84.85	84.10	83.48	82.95
7000	102.81	101.30	100.04	99.00	98.12	97.39	96.77
8000	117.50	115.77	114.34	113.14	112.14	111.30	110.59
9000	132.18	130.24	128.63	127.28	126.16	125.21	124.42
10000	146.87	144.71	142.92	141.42	140.17	139.13	138.24
15000	220.31	217.07	214.38	212.14	210.26	208.69	207.36
20000	293.74	289.42	285.84	282.85	280.35	278.25	276.49
25000	367.18	361.78	357.30	353.56	350.44	347.81	345.61
30000	440.61	434.13	428.76	424.27	420.52	417.38	414.73
35000	514.05	506.49	500.22	494.99	490.61	486.94	483.85
36000	528.73	520.96	514.51	509.13	504.63	500.85	497.67
37000	543.42	535.43	528.80	523.27	518.65	514.76	511.50
38000	558.11	549.90	543.09	537.41	532.66	528.68	525.32
39000	572.79	564.37	557.38	551.56	546.68	542.59	539.15
40000	587.48	578.84	571.68	565.70	560.70	556.50	552.97
41000	602.17	593.32	585.97	579.84	574.72	570.41	566.80
42000	616.85	607.79	600.26	593.98	588.73	584.33	580.62
43000	631.54	622.26	614.55	608.13	602.75	598.24	594.45
44000	646.23	636.73	628.84	622.27	616.77	612.15	608.27
45000	660.92	651.20	643.13	636.41	630.79	626.07	622.09
46000	675.60	665.67	657.43	650.55	644.80	639.98	635.92
47000	690.29	680.14	671.72	664.70	658.82	653.89	649.74
48000	704.98	694.61	686.01	678.84	672.84	667.80	663.57
49000	719.66	709.08	700.30	692.98	686.86	681.72	677.39
50000	734.35	723.56	714.59	707.12	700.87	695.63	691.22
51000	749.04	738.03	728.89	721.27	714.89	709.54	705.04
52000	763.72	752.50	743.18	735.41	728.91	723.45	718.86
53000	778.41	766.97	757.47	749.55	742.93	737.37	732.69
54000	793.10	781.44	771.76	763.69	756.94	751.28	746.51
55000	807.79	795.91	786.05	777.84	770.96	765.19	760.34
56000	822.47	810.38	800.35	791.98	784.98	779.10	774.16
57000	837.16	824.85	814.64	806.12	799.00	793.02	787.99
58000	851.85	839.32	828.93	820.26	813.01	806.93	801.81
59000	866.53	853.80	843.22	834.41	827.03	820.84	815.63
60000	881.22	868.27	857.51	848.55	841.05	834.75	829.46
65000	954.66	940.62	928.97	919.26	911.14	904.32	898.58
70000	1028.09	1012.98	1000.43	989.97	981.22	973.88	967.70
75000	1101.53	1085.33	1071.89	1060.69	1051.31	1043.44	1036.82
80000	1174.96	1157.69	1143.35	1131.40	1121.40	1113.00	1105.94
85000	1248.40	1230.04	1214.81	1202.11	1191.48	1182.57	1175.07
90000	1321.83	1302.40	1286.27	1272.82	1261.57	1252.13	1244.19
95000	1395.27	1374.75	1357.73	1343.53	1331.66	1321.69	1313.31
100000	1468.70	1447.11	1429.19	1414.25	1401.75	1391.26	1382.43
105000	1542.14	1519.47	1500.65	1484.96	1471.83	1460.82	1451.55
110000	1615.57	1591.82	1572.11	1555.67	1541.92	1530.38	1520.67
120000	1762.44	1736.53	1715.03	1697.10	1682.10	1669.51	1658.92
130000	1909.31	1881.24	1857.94	1838.52	1822.27	1808.63	1797.16
140000	2056.18	2025.95	2000.86	1979.95	1962.44	1947.76	1935.40
150000	2203.05	2170.67	2143.78	2121.37	2102.62	2086.88	2073.65
175000	2570.23	2532.44	2501.08	2474.93	2453.06	2434.70	2419.25
200000	2937.40	2894.22	2858.38	2828.49	2803.49	2782.51	2764.86
225000	3304.58	3256.00	3215.67	3182.06	3153.93	3130.33	3110.47
250000	3671.75	3617.78	3572.97	3535.62	3504.37	3478.14	3456.08

Monthly Payments **16%**

necessary to amortize a loan

AMOUNT	22 YEARS	23 YEARS	24 YEARS	25 YEARS	30 YEARS	35 YEARS	40 YEARS
100	1.37	1.37	1.36	1.36	1.34	1.34	1.34
200	2.75	2.74	2.73	2.72	2.69	2.68	2.67
500	6.87	6.84	6.82	6.79	6.72	6.69	6.68
1000	13.75	13.69	13.63	13.59	13.45	13.38	13.36
2000	27.50	27.37	27.27	27.18	26.90	26.77	26.71
5000	68.75	68.44	68.17	67.94	67.24	66.92	66.78
6000	82.50	82.12	81.80	81.53	80.69	80.31	80.14
7000	96.25	95.81	95.44	95.12	94.13	93.69	93.50
8000	110.00	109.50	109.07	108.71	107.58	107.08	106.85
9000	123.75	123.18	122.71	122.30	121.03	120.46	120.21
10000	137.50	136.87	136.34	135.89	134.48	133.85	133.56
15000	206.25	205.31	204.51	203.83	201.71	200.77	200.35
20000	275.00	273.74	272.68	271.78	268.95	267.69	267.13
25000	343.75	342.18	340.85	339.72	336.19	334.62	333.91
30000	412.50	410.61	409.02	407.67	403.43	401.54	400.69
35000	481.25	479.05	477.19	475.61	470.66	468.46	467.48
36000	495.00	492.73	490.82	489.20	484.11	481.85	480.83
37000	508.75	506.42	504.45	502.79	497.56	495.23	494.19
38000	522.50	520.11	518.09	516.38	511.01	508.62	507.55
39000	536.25	533.80	531.72	529.97	524.46	522.00	520.90
40000	550.00	547.48	545.36	543.56	537.90	535.39	534.26
41000	563.75	561.17	558.99	557.14	551.35	548.77	547.62
42000	577.50	574.86	572.62	570.73	564.80	562.16	560.97
43000	591.25	588.54	586.26	584.32	578.25	575.54	574.33
44000	605.00	602.23	599.89	597.91	591.69	588.93	587.69
45000	618.75	615.92	613.53	611.50	605.14	602.31	601.04
46000	632.50	629.60	627.16	625.09	618.59	615.70	614.40
47000	646.25	643.29	640.79	638.68	632.04	629.08	627.75
48000	660.00	656.98	654.43	652.27	645.48	642.47	641.11
49000	673.75	670.67	668.06	665.86	658.93	655.85	654.47
50000	687.50	684.35	681.70	679.44	672.38	669.23	667.82
51000	701.24	698.04	695.33	693.03	685.83	682.62	681.18
52000	714.99	711.73	708.96	706.62	699.27	696.00	694.54
53000	728.74	725.41	722.60	720.21	712.72	709.39	707.89
54000	742.49	739.10	736.23	733.80	726.17	722.77	721.25
55000	756.24	752.79	749.86	747.39	739.62	736.16	734.61
56000	769.99	766.48	763.50	760.98	753.06	749.54	747.96
57000	783.74	780.16	777.13	774.57	766.51	762.93	761.32
58000	797.49	793.85	790.77	788.16	779.96	776.31	774.68
59000	811.24	807.54	804.40	801.74	793.41	789.70	788.03
60000	824.99	821.22	818.03	815.33	806.85	803.08	801.39
65000	893.74	889.66	886.20	883.28	874.00	870.01	868.17
70000	962.49	958.09	954.37	951.22	941.33	936.03	934.96
75000	1031.24	1026.53	1022.54	1019.17	1008.57	1003.85	1001.74
80000	1099.99	1094.96	1090.71	1087.11	1075.81	1070.78	1068.52
85000	1168.74	1163.40	1158.88	1155.06	1143.04	1137.70	1135.30
90000	1237.49	1231.84	1227.05	1223.00	1210.28	1204.62	1202.08
95000	1306.24	1300.27	1295.22	1290.94	1277.52	1271.55	1268.87
100000	1374.99	1368.71	1363.39	1358.89	1344.76	1338.47	1335.65
105000	1443.74	1437.14	1431.56	1426.83	1411.99	1405.39	1402.43
110000	1512.49	1505.58	1499.73	1494.78	1479.23	1472.32	1469.21
120000	1649.99	1642.45	1636.07	1630.67	1613.71	1606.16	1602.78
130000	1787.49	1779.32	1772.41	1766.56	1748.18	1740.01	1736.34
140000	1924.99	1916.19	1908.75	1902.44	1882.66	1873.86	1869.91
150000	2062.49	2053.06	2045.09	2038.33	2017.14	2007.70	2003.47
175000	2406.23	2395.24	2385.93	2378.06	2353.32	2342.32	2337.38
200000	2749.98	2737.41	2726.78	2717.78	2689.51	2676.94	2671.30
225000	3093.73	3079.59	3067.63	3057.50	3025.70	3011.56	3005.21
250000	3437.48	3421.76	3408.48	3397.22	3361.89	3346.17	3339.12

16¼%

Monthly Payments
necessary to amortize a loan

AMOUNT	1 YEAR	2 YEARS	3 YEARS	4 YEARS	5 YEARS	6 YEARS	7 YEARS
100	9.08	4.91	3.53	2.85	2.45	2.18	2.00
200	18.17	9.82	7.06	5.69	4.89	4.37	4.00
500	45.42	24.54	17.64	14.23	12.23	10.91	10.00
1000	90.85	49.08	35.28	28.47	24.45	21.83	20.00
2000	181.70	98.17	70.56	56.94	48.90	43.66	40.01
5000	454.25	245.41	176.40	142.34	122.26	109.15	100.02
6000	545.10	294.50	211.68	170.81	146.71	130.98	120.03
7000	635.94	343.58	246.96	199.28	171.16	152.81	140.03
8000	726.79	392.66	282.24	227.75	195.61	174.64	160.04
9000	817.64	441.74	317.53	256.22	220.06	196.47	180.04
10000	908.49	490.83	352.81	284.68	244.51	218.30	200.05
15000	1362.74	736.24	529.21	427.03	366.77	327.45	300.07
20000	1816.98	981.65	705.61	569.37	489.02	436.59	400.09
25000	2271.23	1227.07	882.01	711.71	611.28	545.74	500.12
30000	2725.48	1472.48	1058.42	854.05	733.53	654.89	600.14
35000	3179.72	1717.89	1234.82	996.40	855.79	764.04	700.16
36000	3270.57	1766.98	1270.10	1024.87	880.24	785.87	720.17
37000	3361.42	1816.06	1305.38	1053.33	904.69	807.70	740.17
38000	3452.27	1865.14	1340.66	1081.80	929.14	829.53	760.18
39000	3543.12	1914.22	1375.94	1110.27	953.59	851.36	780.18
40000	3633.97	1963.31	1411.22	1138.74	978.04	873.19	800.19
41000	3724.82	2012.39	1446.50	1167.21	1002.49	895.02	820.19
42000	3815.67	2061.47	1481.78	1195.68	1026.95	916.85	840.20
43000	3906.52	2110.55	1517.07	1224.14	1051.40	938.68	860.20
44000	3997.37	2159.64	1552.35	1252.61	1075.85	960.51	880.21
45000	4088.21	2208.72	1587.63	1281.08	1100.30	982.34	900.21
46000	4179.06	2257.80	1622.91	1309.55	1124.75	1004.17	920.22
47000	4269.91	2306.88	1658.19	1338.02	1149.20	1026.00	940.22
48000	4360.76	2355.97	1693.47	1366.49	1173.65	1047.83	960.23
49000	4451.61	2405.05	1728.75	1394.96	1198.10	1069.66	980.23
50000	4542.46	2454.13	1764.03	1423.42	1222.55	1091.49	1000.24
51000	4633.31	2503.21	1799.31	1451.89	1247.01	1113.32	1020.24
52000	4724.16	2552.30	1834.59	1480.36	1271.46	1135.15	1040.25
53000	4815.01	2601.38	1869.87	1508.83	1295.91	1156.98	1060.25
54000	4905.86	2650.46	1905.15	1537.30	1320.36	1178.80	1080.25
55000	4996.71	2699.55	1940.43	1565.77	1344.81	1200.63	1100.26
56000	5087.56	2748.63	1975.71	1594.24	1369.26	1222.46	1120.26
57000	5178.40	2797.71	2010.99	1622.70	1393.71	1244.29	1140.27
58000	5269.25	2846.79	2046.27	1651.17	1418.16	1266.12	1160.27
59000	5360.10	2895.88	2081.55	1679.64	1442.61	1287.95	1180.28
60000	5450.95	2944.96	2116.83	1708.11	1467.07	1309.78	1200.28
65000	5905.20	3190.37	2293.24	1850.45	1589.32	1418.93	1300.31
70000	6359.44	3435.79	2469.64	1992.79	1711.58	1528.08	1400.33
75000	6813.69	3681.20	2646.04	2135.14	1833.83	1637.23	1500.35
80000	7267.94	3926.61	2822.45	2277.48	1956.09	1746.38	1600.38
85000	7722.18	4172.02	2998.85	2419.82	2078.34	1855.53	1700.40
90000	8176.43	4417.44	3175.25	2562.16	2200.60	1964.67	1800.42
95000	8630.67	4662.85	3351.66	2704.51	2322.85	2073.82	1900.45
100000	9084.92	4908.26	3528.06	2846.85	2445.11	2182.97	2000.47
105000	9539.17	5153.68	3704.46	2989.19	2567.36	2292.12	2100.49
110000	9993.41	5399.09	3880.86	3131.53	2689.62	2401.27	2200.52
120000	10901.90	5889.92	4233.67	3416.22	2934.13	2619.57	2400.57
130000	11810.40	6380.74	4586.48	3700.90	3178.64	2837.86	2600.61
140000	12718.89	6871.57	4939.28	3985.59	3423.15	3056.16	2800.66
150000	13627.38	7362.40	5292.09	4270.27	3667.66	3274.46	3000.71
175000	15898.61	8589.46	6174.10	4981.98	4278.94	3820.20	3500.82
200000	18169.84	9816.53	7056.12	5693.70	4890.22	4365.94	4000.94
225000	20441.07	11043.60	7938.13	6405.41	5501.50	4911.69	4501.06
250000	22712.30	12270.66	8820.15	7117.12	6112.77	5457.43	5001.18

Monthly Payments 16¼%

necessary to amortize a loan

AMOUNT	8 YEARS	9 YEARS	10 YEARS	11 YEARS	12 YEARS	13 YEARS	14 YEARS
100	1.87	1.77	1.69	1.63	1.58	1.54	1.51
200	3.74	3.54	3.38	3.26	3.16	3.09	3.02
500	9.34	8.84	8.45	8.15	7.91	7.72	7.56
1000	18.68	17.68	16.91	16.30	15.82	15.43	15.12
2000	37.35	35.35	33.81	32.61	31.64	30.87	30.24
5000	93.38	88.39	84.54	81.52	79.11	77.17	75.60
6000	112.06	106.06	101.44	97.82	94.93	92.61	90.72
7000	130.73	123.74	118.35	114.12	110.76	108.04	105.84
8000	149.41	141.42	135.26	130.43	126.58	123.48	120.96
9000	168.08	159.09	152.17	146.73	142.40	138.91	136.08
10000	186.76	176.77	169.07	163.03	158.22	154.35	151.20
15000	280.14	265.16	253.61	244.55	237.34	231.52	226.80
20000	373.52	353.54	338.15	326.07	316.45	308.70	302.40
25000	466.90	441.93	422.69	407.59	395.56	385.87	378.00
30000	560.28	530.31	507.22	489.10	474.67	463.05	453.60
35000	653.66	618.70	591.76	570.62	553.79	540.22	529.19
36000	672.34	636.37	608.67	586.92	569.61	555.66	544.31
37000	691.02	654.05	625.58	603.23	585.43	571.09	559.43
38000	709.69	671.73	642.48	619.53	601.25	586.53	574.55
39000	728.37	689.41	659.39	635.83	617.08	601.96	589.67
40000	747.04	707.08	676.30	652.14	632.90	617.40	604.79
41000	765.72	724.76	693.21	668.44	648.72	632.83	619.91
42000	784.40	742.44	710.11	684.74	664.54	648.27	635.03
43000	803.07	760.11	727.02	701.05	680.36	663.70	650.15
44000	821.75	777.79	743.93	717.35	696.19	679.14	665.27
45000	840.42	795.47	760.83	733.65	712.01	694.57	680.39
46000	859.10	813.14	777.74	749.96	727.83	710.01	695.51
47000	877.78	830.82	794.65	766.26	743.65	725.44	710.63
48000	896.45	848.50	811.56	782.56	759.48	740.88	725.75
49000	915.13	866.18	828.46	798.87	775.30	756.31	740.87
50000	933.80	883.85	845.37	815.17	791.12	771.75	755.99
51000	952.48	901.53	862.28	831.48	806.94	787.18	771.11
52000	971.16	919.21	879.19	847.78	822.77	802.62	786.23
53000	989.83	936.88	896.09	864.08	838.59	818.05	801.35
54000	1008.51	954.56	913.00	880.39	854.41	833.49	816.47
55000	1027.18	972.24	929.91	896.69	870.23	848.92	831.59
56000	1045.86	989.92	946.82	912.99	886.06	864.36	846.71
57000	1064.54	1007.59	963.72	929.30	901.88	879.79	861.83
58000	1083.21	1025.27	980.63	945.60	917.70	895.23	876.95
59000	1101.89	1042.95	997.54	961.90	933.52	910.66	892.07
60000	1120.57	1060.62	1014.45	978.21	949.35	926.10	907.19
65000	1213.95	1149.01	1098.98	1059.72	1028.46	1003.27	982.79
70000	1307.33	1237.39	1183.52	1141.24	1107.57	1080.45	1058.39
75000	1400.71	1325.78	1268.06	1222.76	1186.68	1157.62	1133.99
80000	1494.09	1414.16	1352.60	1304.27	1265.80	1234.80	1209.59
85000	1587.47	1502.55	1437.13	1385.79	1344.91	1311.97	1285.19
90000	1680.85	1590.93	1521.67	1467.31	1424.02	1389.15	1360.79
95000	1774.23	1679.32	1606.21	1548.83	1503.13	1466.32	1436.39
100000	1867.61	1767.71	1690.74	1630.34	1582.24	1543.49	1511.99
105000	1960.99	1856.09	1775.28	1711.86	1661.36	1620.67	1587.58
110000	2054.37	1944.48	1859.82	1793.38	1740.47	1697.84	1663.18
120000	2241.13	2121.25	2028.89	1956.41	1898.69	1852.19	1814.38
130000	2427.89	2298.02	2197.97	2119.45	2056.92	2006.54	1965.58
140000	2614.65	2474.79	2367.04	2282.48	2215.14	2160.89	2116.78
150000	2801.41	2651.56	2536.12	2445.51	2373.37	2315.24	2267.98
175000	3268.32	3093.48	2958.80	2853.10	2768.93	2701.12	2645.97
200000	3735.22	3535.41	3381.49	3260.69	3164.49	3086.99	3023.97
225000	4202.12	3977.34	3804.17	3668.27	3560.05	3472.86	3401.97
250000	4669.02	4419.26	4226.86	4075.86	3955.61	3858.74	3779.96

16¼%

Monthly Payments

necessary to amortize a loan

AMOUNT	15 YEARS	16 YEARS	17 YEARS	18 YEARS	19 YEARS	20 YEARS	21 YEARS
100	1.49	1.46	1.45	1.43	1.42	1.41	1.40
200	2.97	2.93	2.89	2.87	2.84	2.82	2.80
500	7.43	7.32	7.24	7.16	7.10	7.05	7.01
1000	14.86	14.65	14.47	14.33	14.20	14.10	14.01
2000	29.72	29.30	28.94	28.65	28.41	28.20	28.03
5000	74.31	73.24	72.36	71.63	71.02	70.50	70.07
6000	89.17	87.89	86.83	85.95	85.22	84.60	84.09
7000	104.03	102.54	101.31	100.28	99.42	98.70	98.10
8000	118.89	117.19	115.78	114.61	113.62	112.80	112.11
9000	133.76	131.84	130.25	128.93	127.83	126.90	126.13
10000	148.62	146.49	144.72	143.26	142.03	141.00	140.14
15000	222.93	219.73	217.09	214.89	213.05	211.51	210.21
20000	297.23	292.98	289.45	286.51	284.06	282.01	280.29
25000	371.54	366.22	361.81	358.14	355.08	352.51	350.36
30000	445.85	439.47	434.17	429.77	426.09	423.01	420.43
35000	520.16	512.71	506.54	501.40	497.11	493.52	490.50
36000	535.02	527.36	521.01	515.72	511.31	507.62	504.51
37000	549.88	542.01	535.48	530.05	525.52	521.72	518.53
38000	564.74	556.66	549.95	544.38	539.72	535.82	532.54
39000	579.61	571.30	564.43	558.70	553.92	549.92	546.56
40000	594.47	585.95	578.90	573.03	568.12	564.02	560.57
41000	609.33	600.60	593.37	587.35	582.33	578.12	574.58
42000	624.19	615.25	607.84	601.68	596.53	592.22	588.60
43000	639.05	629.90	622.32	616.00	610.73	606.32	602.61
44000	653.91	644.55	636.79	630.33	624.94	620.42	616.63
45000	668.78	659.20	651.26	644.66	639.14	634.52	630.64
46000	683.64	673.85	665.73	658.98	653.34	648.62	644.66
47000	698.50	688.50	680.21	673.31	667.55	662.72	658.67
48000	713.36	703.14	694.68	687.63	681.75	676.82	672.68
49000	728.22	717.79	709.15	701.96	695.95	690.92	686.70
50000	743.08	732.44	723.62	716.28	710.16	705.02	700.71
51000	757.95	747.09	738.10	730.61	724.36	719.12	714.73
52000	772.81	761.74	752.57	744.94	738.56	733.22	728.74
53000	787.67	776.39	767.04	759.26	752.77	747.32	742.76
54000	802.53	791.04	781.51	773.59	766.97	761.42	756.77
55000	817.39	805.69	795.99	787.91	781.17	775.53	770.78
56000	832.25	820.33	810.46	802.24	795.37	789.63	784.80
57000	847.12	834.98	824.93	816.56	809.58	803.73	798.81
58000	861.98	849.63	839.40	830.89	823.78	817.83	812.83
59000	876.84	864.28	853.88	845.22	837.98	831.93	826.84
60000	891.70	878.93	868.35	859.54	852.19	846.03	840.86
65000	966.01	952.17	940.71	931.17	923.20	916.53	910.93
70000	1040.32	1025.42	1013.07	1002.80	994.22	987.03	981.00
75000	1114.63	1098.66	1085.43	1074.43	1065.23	1057.53	1051.07
80000	1188.93	1171.91	1157.80	1146.06	1136.25	1128.04	1121.14
85000	1263.24	1245.15	1230.16	1217.68	1207.26	1198.54	1191.21
90000	1337.55	1318.40	1302.52	1289.31	1278.28	1269.04	1261.28
95000	1411.86	1391.64	1374.88	1360.94	1349.30	1339.54	1331.35
100000	1486.17	1464.88	1447.25	1432.57	1420.31	1410.05	1401.43
105000	1560.48	1538.13	1519.61	1504.20	1491.33	1480.55	1471.50
110000	1634.78	1611.37	1591.97	1575.83	1562.34	1551.05	1541.57
120000	1783.40	1757.86	1736.70	1719.08	1704.37	1692.05	1681.71
130000	1932.02	1904.35	1881.42	1862.34	1846.41	1833.06	1821.85
140000	2080.64	2050.84	2026.14	2005.60	1988.44	1974.06	1962.00
150000	2229.25	2197.33	2170.87	2148.85	2130.47	2115.07	2102.14
175000	2600.79	2563.55	2532.68	2507.00	2485.55	2467.58	2452.50
200000	2972.34	2929.77	2894.49	2865.14	2840.62	2820.09	2802.85
225000	3343.88	3295.99	3256.30	3223.28	3195.70	3172.60	3153.21
250000	3715.42	3662.21	3618.12	3581.42	3550.78	3525.11	3503.56

Monthly Payments 16¼%

necessary to amortize a loan

AMOUNT	22 YEARS	23 YEARS	24 YEARS	25 YEARS	30 YEARS	35 YEARS	40 YEARS
100	1.39	1.39	1.38	1.38	1.36	1.36	1.36
200	2.79	2.78	2.77	2.76	2.73	2.72	2.71
500	6.97	6.94	6.91	6.89	6.82	6.79	6.78
1000	13.94	13.88	13.83	13.79	13.65	13.59	13.56
2000	27.88	27.76	27.66	27.57	27.30	27.18	27.13
5000	69.71	69.40	69.15	68.93	68.25	67.95	67.81
6000	83.65	83.28	82.97	82.71	81.90	81.54	81.38
7000	97.59	97.16	96.80	96.50	95.55	95.13	94.94
8000	111.53	111.04	110.63	110.28	109.19	108.72	108.50
9000	125.48	124.93	124.46	124.07	122.84	122.31	122.07
10000	139.42	138.81	138.29	137.85	136.49	135.89	135.63
15000	209.13	208.21	207.44	206.78	204.74	203.84	203.44
20000	278.83	277.61	276.58	275.71	272.99	271.79	271.26
25000	348.54	347.02	345.73	344.64	341.23	339.74	339.07
30000	418.25	416.42	414.87	413.56	409.48	407.68	406.89
35000	487.96	485.82	484.02	482.49	477.73	475.63	474.70
36000	501.90	499.70	497.84	496.27	491.38	489.22	488.27
37000	515.84	513.58	511.67	510.06	505.03	502.81	501.83
38000	529.79	527.46	525.50	523.85	518.68	516.40	515.39
39000	543.73	541.34	539.33	537.63	532.32	529.99	528.96
40000	557.67	555.22	553.16	551.42	545.97	543.58	542.52
41000	571.61	569.10	566.99	565.20	559.62	557.17	556.08
42000	585.55	582.99	580.82	578.99	573.27	570.76	569.64
43000	599.49	596.87	594.65	592.77	586.92	584.35	583.21
44000	613.44	610.75	608.48	606.56	600.57	597.94	596.77
45000	627.38	624.63	622.31	620.34	614.22	611.53	610.33
46000	641.32	638.51	636.13	634.13	627.87	625.12	623.90
47000	655.26	652.39	649.96	647.91	641.52	638.71	637.46
48000	669.20	666.27	663.79	661.70	655.17	652.30	651.02
49000	683.14	680.15	677.62	675.49	668.82	665.89	664.59
50000	697.09	694.03	691.45	689.27	682.47	679.47	678.15
51000	711.03	707.91	705.28	703.06	696.12	693.06	691.71
52000	724.97	721.79	719.11	716.84	709.77	706.65	705.27
53000	738.91	735.67	732.94	730.63	723.42	720.24	718.84
54000	752.85	749.55	746.77	744.41	737.06	733.83	732.40
55000	766.80	763.43	760.60	758.20	750.71	747.42	745.96
56000	780.74	777.31	774.42	771.98	764.36	761.01	759.53
57000	794.68	791.19	788.25	785.77	778.01	774.60	773.09
58000	808.62	805.08	802.08	799.55	791.66	788.19	786.65
59000	822.50	818.06	816.01	813.34	805.31	801.78	800.22
60000	836.50	832.84	829.74	827.12	818.96	815.37	813.78
65000	906.21	902.24	898.89	896.05	887.21	883.32	881.59
70000	975.92	971.64	968.03	964.98	955.45	951.26	949.41
75000	1045.63	1041.05	1037.18	1033.91	1023.70	1019.21	1017.22
80000	1115.34	1110.45	1106.32	1102.83	1091.95	1087.16	1085.04
85000	1185.05	1179.85	1175.47	1171.76	1160.19	1155.11	1152.85
90000	1254.76	1249.25	1244.61	1240.69	1228.44	1223.06	1220.67
95000	1324.46	1318.66	1313.76	1309.61	1296.69	1291.00	1288.48
100000	1394.17	1388.06	1382.90	1378.54	1364.93	1358.95	1356.30
105000	1463.88	1457.46	1452.05	1447.47	1433.18	1426.90	1424.11
110000	1533.59	1526.87	1521.19	1516.40	1501.43	1494.84	1491.93
120000	1673.01	1665.67	1659.48	1654.25	1637.92	1630.74	1627.56
130000	1812.43	1804.48	1797.77	1792.10	1774.42	1766.63	1763.19
140000	1951.84	1943.29	1936.06	1929.96	1910.91	1902.53	1898.82
150000	2091.26	2082.09	2074.35	2067.81	2047.40	2038.42	2034.45
175000	2439.80	2429.11	2420.08	2412.45	2388.64	2378.16	2373.52
200000	2788.35	2776.12	2765.80	2757.08	2729.87	2717.90	2712.59
225000	3136.89	3123.14	3111.53	3101.72	3071.10	3057.64	3051.67
250000	3485.43	3470.15	3457.25	3446.35	3412.34	3397.37	3390.74

16½%

Monthly Payments

necessary to amortize a loan

AMOUNT	1 YEAR	2 YEARS	3 YEARS	4 YEARS	5 YEARS	6 YEARS	7 YEARS
100	9.10	4.92	3.54	2.86	2.46	2.20	2.01
200	18.19	9.84	7.08	5.72	4.92	4.39	4.03
500	45.48	24.60	17.70	14.30	12.29	10.98	10.07
1000	90.97	49.20	35.40	28.60	24.58	21.97	20.15
2000	181.94	98.40	70.81	57.19	49.17	43.94	40.30
5000	454.84	246.01	177.02	142.99	122.92	109.84	100.74
6000	545.81	295.21	212.43	171.58	147.51	131.81	120.89
7000	636.77	344.42	247.83	200.18	172.09	153.78	141.04
8000	727.74	393.62	283.24	228.78	196.68	175.74	161.18
9000	818.71	442.82	318.64	257.37	221.26	197.71	181.33
10000	909.68	492.02	354.04	285.97	245.85	219.68	201.48
15000	1364.51	738.04	531.07	428.96	368.77	329.52	302.22
20000	1819.35	984.05	708.09	571.94	491.69	439.36	402.96
25000	2274.19	1230.06	885.11	714.93	614.61	549.20	503.70
30000	2729.03	1476.07	1062.13	857.91	737.54	659.04	604.44
35000	3183.87	1722.08	1239.15	1000.90	860.46	768.88	705.18
36000	3274.83	1771.28	1274.56	1029.49	885.04	790.85	725.32
37000	3365.80	1820.49	1309.96	1058.09	909.63	812.82	745.47
38000	3456.77	1869.69	1345.37	1086.69	934.21	834.79	765.62
39000	3547.74	1918.89	1380.77	1115.28	958.80	856.75	785.77
40000	3638.71	1968.09	1416.18	1143.88	983.38	878.72	805.92
41000	3729.67	2017.30	1451.58	1172.48	1007.97	900.69	826.06
42000	3820.64	2066.50	1486.98	1201.07	1032.55	922.66	846.21
43000	3911.61	2115.70	1522.39	1229.67	1057.13	944.63	866.36
44000	4002.58	2164.90	1557.79	1258.27	1081.72	966.59	886.51
45000	4093.54	2214.11	1593.20	1286.87	1106.30	988.56	906.66
46000	4184.51	2263.31	1628.60	1315.46	1130.89	1010.53	926.80
47000	4275.48	2312.51	1664.01	1344.06	1155.47	1032.50	946.95
48000	4366.45	2361.71	1699.41	1372.66	1180.06	1054.47	967.10
49000	4457.41	2410.92	1734.81	1401.25	1204.64	1076.43	987.25
50000	4548.38	2460.12	1770.22	1429.85	1229.23	1098.40	1007.39
51000	4639.35	2509.32	1805.62	1458.45	1253.81	1120.37	1027.54
52000	4730.32	2558.52	1841.03	1487.04	1278.40	1142.34	1047.69
53000	4821.28	2607.72	1876.43	1515.64	1302.98	1164.31	1067.84
54000	4912.25	2656.93	1911.84	1544.24	1327.56	1186.28	1087.99
55000	5003.22	2706.13	1947.24	1572.84	1352.15	1208.24	1108.13
56000	5094.19	2755.33	1982.65	1601.43	1376.73	1230.21	1128.28
57000	5185.16	2804.53	2018.05	1630.03	1401.32	1252.18	1148.43
58000	5276.12	2853.74	2053.45	1658.63	1425.90	1274.15	1168.58
59000	5367.09	2902.94	2088.86	1687.22	1450.49	1296.12	1188.73
60000	5458.06	2952.14	2124.26	1715.82	1475.07	1318.08	1208.87
65000	5912.90	3198.15	2301.28	1858.81	1597.99	1427.92	1309.61
70000	6367.73	3444.16	2478.31	2001.79	1720.92	1537.76	1410.35
75000	6822.57	3690.18	2655.33	2144.78	1843.84	1647.60	1511.09
80000	7277.41	3936.19	2832.35	2287.76	1966.76	1757.44	1611.83
85000	7732.25	4182.20	3009.37	2430.75	2089.68	1867.28	1712.57
90000	8187.09	4428.21	3186.39	2573.73	2212.61	1977.13	1813.31
95000	8641.93	4674.22	3363.42	2716.72	2335.53	2086.97	1914.05
100000	9096.76	4920.24	3540.44	2859.70	2458.45	2196.81	2014.79
105000	9551.60	5166.25	3717.46	3002.69	2581.37	2306.65	2115.53
110000	10006.44	5412.26	3894.48	3145.67	2704.30	2416.49	2216.27
120000	10916.12	5904.28	4248.53	3431.64	2950.14	2636.17	2417.75
130000	11825.79	6396.31	4602.57	3717.61	3195.99	2855.85	2619.23
140000	12735.47	6888.33	4956.61	4003.58	3441.83	3075.53	2820.70
150000	13645.15	7380.35	5310.66	4289.55	3687.68	3295.21	3022.18
175000	15919.34	8610.41	6195.77	5004.48	4302.29	3844.41	3525.88
200000	18193.53	9840.47	7080.88	5719.40	4916.90	4393.61	4029.58
225000	20467.72	11070.53	7965.99	6434.33	5531.52	4942.81	4533.28
250000	22741.91	12300.59	8851.10	7149.25	6146.13	5492.01	5036.97

Monthly Payments 16½%

necessary to amortize a loan

AMOUNT	8 YEARS	9 YEARS	10 YEARS	11 YEARS	12 YEARS	13 YEARS	14 YEARS
100	1.88	1.78	1.71	1.65	1.60	1.56	1.53
200	3.76	3.57	3.41	3.29	3.20	3.12	3.06
500	9.41	8.91	8.53	8.23	7.99	7.80	7.65
1000	18.82	17.83	17.06	16.46	15.99	15.60	15.29
2000	37.65	35.66	34.13	32.93	31.97	31.21	30.58
5000	94.12	89.15	85.32	82.32	79.94	78.02	76.46
6000	112.94	106.98	102.39	98.79	95.92	93.62	91.75
7000	131.77	124.81	119.45	115.25	111.91	109.22	107.04
8000	150.59	142.64	136.51	131.72	127.90	124.83	122.34
9000	169.42	160.47	153.58	148.18	143.89	140.43	137.63
10000	188.24	178.29	170.64	164.64	159.87	156.04	152.92
15000	282.36	267.44	255.96	246.97	239.81	234.05	229.38
20000	376.48	356.59	341.28	329.29	319.75	312.07	305.84
25000	470.60	445.74	426.61	411.61	399.68	390.09	382.30
30000	564.72	534.88	511.93	493.93	479.62	468.11	458.76
35000	658.84	624.03	597.25	576.25	559.56	546.12	535.22
36000	677.66	641.86	614.31	592.72	575.54	561.73	550.51
37000	696.49	659.69	631.38	609.18	591.53	577.33	565.80
38000	715.31	677.52	648.44	625.65	607.52	592.94	581.10
39000	734.13	695.35	665.50	642.11	623.51	608.54	596.39
40000	752.96	713.18	682.57	658.58	639.49	624.14	611.68
41000	771.78	731.01	699.63	675.04	655.48	639.75	626.97
42000	790.61	748.84	716.70	691.50	671.47	655.35	642.26
43000	809.43	766.67	733.76	707.97	687.46	670.95	657.56
44000	828.25	784.50	750.83	724.43	703.44	686.56	672.85
45000	847.08	802.33	767.89	740.90	719.43	702.16	688.14
46000	865.90	820.16	784.95	757.36	735.42	717.76	703.43
47000	884.73	837.99	802.02	773.83	751.40	733.37	718.72
48000	903.55	855.82	819.08	790.29	767.39	748.97	734.01
49000	922.37	873.64	836.15	806.75	783.38	764.57	749.31
50000	941.20	891.47	853.21	823.22	799.37	780.18	764.60
51000	960.02	909.30	870.28	839.68	815.35	795.78	779.89
52000	978.85	927.13	887.34	856.15	831.34	811.39	795.18
53000	997.67	944.96	904.40	872.61	847.33	826.99	810.47
54000	1016.49	962.79	921.47	889.08	863.32	842.59	825.77
55000	1035.32	980.62	938.53	905.54	879.30	858.20	841.06
56000	1054.14	998.45	955.60	922.01	895.29	873.80	856.35
57000	1072.97	1016.28	972.66	938.47	911.28	889.40	871.64
58000	1091.79	1034.11	989.73	954.93	927.27	905.01	886.93
59000	1110.61	1051.94	1006.79	971.40	943.25	920.61	902.23
60000	1129.44	1069.77	1023.85	987.86	959.24	936.21	917.52
65000	1223.56	1158.92	1109.17	1070.18	1039.18	1014.23	993.98
70000	1317.68	1248.06	1194.50	1152.51	1119.11	1092.25	1070.44
75000	1411.80	1337.21	1279.82	1234.83	1199.05	1170.27	1146.90
80000	1505.92	1426.36	1365.14	1317.15	1278.99	1248.29	1223.36
85000	1600.04	1515.51	1450.46	1399.47	1358.92	1326.30	1299.82
90000	1694.16	1604.65	1535.78	1481.79	1438.86	1404.32	1376.28
95000	1788.28	1693.80	1621.10	1564.12	1518.80	1482.34	1452.74
100000	1882.40	1782.95	1706.42	1646.44	1598.73	1560.36	1529.20
105000	1976.52	1872.10	1791.74	1728.76	1678.67	1638.37	1605.66
110000	2070.64	1961.24	1877.07	1811.08	1758.61	1716.39	1682.12
120000	2258.88	2139.54	2047.71	1975.73	1918.48	1872.43	1835.04
130000	2447.12	2317.83	2218.35	2140.37	2078.35	2028.46	1987.96
140000	2635.36	2496.13	2388.99	2305.01	2238.23	2184.50	2140.88
150000	2823.60	2674.42	2559.63	2469.66	2398.10	2340.54	2293.80
175000	3294.19	3120.16	2986.24	2881.27	2797.78	2730.62	2676.10
200000	3764.79	3565.90	3412.85	3292.88	3197.47	3120.71	3058.40
225000	4235.39	4011.63	3839.45	3704.49	3597.15	3510.80	3440.69
250000	4705.99	4457.37	4266.06	4116.10	3996.83	3900.89	3822.99

16½%

Monthly Payments
necessary to amortize a loan

AMOUNT	15 YEARS	16 YEARS	17 YEARS	18 YEARS	19 YEARS	20 YEARS	21 YEARS
100	1.50	1.48	1.47	1.45	1.44	1.43	1.42
200	3.01	2.97	2.93	2.90	2.88	2.86	2.84
500	7.52	7.41	7.33	7.25	7.19	7.14	7.10
1000	15.04	14.83	14.65	14.51	14.39	14.29	14.20
2000	30.07	29.65	29.31	29.02	28.78	28.58	28.41
5000	75.19	74.14	73.27	72.55	71.95	71.45	71.02
6000	90.22	88.96	87.92	87.06	86.34	85.73	85.23
7000	105.26	103.79	102.58	101.57	100.73	100.02	99.43
8000	120.30	118.62	117.23	116.08	115.12	114.31	113.64
9000	135.33	133.45	131.88	130.59	129.51	128.60	127.84
10000	150.37	148.27	146.54	145.10	143.89	142.89	142.05
15000	225.56	222.41	219.81	217.64	215.84	214.34	213.07
20000	300.74	296.55	293.08	290.19	287.79	285.78	284.10
25000	375.93	370.68	366.34	362.74	359.74	357.23	355.12
30000	451.11	444.82	439.61	435.29	431.68	428.67	426.15
35000	526.30	518.96	512.88	507.84	503.63	500.12	497.17
36000	541.34	533.78	527.54	522.35	518.02	514.40	511.37
37000	556.37	548.61	542.19	536.86	532.41	528.69	525.58
38000	571.41	563.44	556.84	551.37	546.80	542.98	539.78
39000	586.45	578.26	571.50	565.87	561.19	557.27	553.99
40000	601.48	593.09	586.15	580.38	575.58	571.56	568.19
41000	616.52	607.92	600.80	594.89	589.97	585.85	582.40
42000	631.56	622.75	615.46	609.40	604.36	600.14	596.60
43000	646.59	637.57	630.11	623.91	618.75	614.43	610.81
44000	661.63	652.40	644.77	638.42	633.14	628.72	625.01
45000	676.67	667.23	659.42	652.93	647.53	643.01	639.22
46000	691.71	682.06	674.07	667.44	661.91	657.29	653.42
47000	706.74	696.88	688.73	681.95	676.30	671.58	667.63
48000	721.78	711.71	703.38	696.46	690.69	685.87	681.83
49000	736.82	726.54	718.03	710.97	705.08	700.16	696.04
50000	751.85	741.36	732.69	725.48	719.47	714.45	710.24
51000	766.89	756.19	747.34	739.99	733.86	728.74	724.45
52000	781.93	771.02	762.00	754.50	748.25	743.03	738.65
53000	796.97	785.85	776.65	769.01	762.64	757.32	752.86
54000	812.00	800.67	791.30	783.52	777.03	771.61	767.06
55000	827.04	815.50	805.96	798.03	791.42	785.90	781.27
56000	842.08	830.33	820.61	812.54	805.81	800.18	795.47
57000	857.11	845.16	835.26	827.05	820.20	814.47	809.68
58000	872.15	859.98	849.92	841.56	834.59	828.76	823.88
59000	887.19	874.81	864.57	856.07	848.98	843.05	838.09
60000	902.23	889.64	879.23	870.58	863.37	857.34	852.29
65000	977.41	963.77	952.49	943.12	935.31	928.79	923.31
70000	1052.60	1037.91	1025.76	1015.67	1007.26	1000.23	994.34
75000	1127.78	1112.05	1099.03	1088.22	1079.21	1071.68	1065.36
80000	1202.97	1186.18	1172.30	1160.77	1151.16	1143.12	1136.39
85000	1278.15	1260.32	1245.57	1233.32	1223.10	1214.57	1207.41
90000	1353.34	1334.46	1318.84	1305.86	1295.05	1286.01	1278.44
95000	1428.52	1408.59	1392.11	1378.41	1367.00	1357.46	1349.46
100000	1503.71	1482.73	1465.38	1450.96	1438.94	1428.90	1420.48
105000	1578.89	1556.87	1538.64	1523.51	1510.89	1500.35	1491.51
110000	1654.08	1631.00	1611.91	1596.06	1582.84	1571.79	1562.53
120000	1804.45	1779.28	1758.45	1741.15	1726.73	1714.68	1704.58
130000	1954.82	1927.55	1904.99	1886.25	1870.63	1857.57	1846.63
140000	2105.19	2075.82	2051.53	2031.34	2014.52	2000.46	1988.68
150000	2255.56	2224.09	2198.06	2176.44	2158.42	2143.35	2130.73
175000	2631.49	2594.78	2564.41	2539.18	2518.15	2500.58	2485.85
200000	3007.42	2965.46	2930.75	2901.92	2877.89	2857.80	2840.97
225000	3383.34	3336.14	3297.10	3264.66	3237.63	3215.03	3196.09
250000	3759.27	3706.82	3663.44	3627.40	3597.36	3572.25	3551.21

Monthly Payments 16½%

necessary to amortize a loan

AMOUNT	22 YEARS	23 YEARS	24 YEARS	25 YEARS	30 YEARS	35 YEARS	40 YEARS
100	1.41	1.41	1.40	1.40	1.39	1.38	1.38
200	2.83	2.81	2.80	2.80	2.77	2.76	2.75
500	7.07	7.04	7.01	6.99	6.93	6.90	6.88
1000	14.13	14.07	14.02	13.98	13.85	13.79	13.77
2000	28.27	28.16	28.05	27.96	27.70	27.59	27.54
5000	70.67	70.37	70.12	69.91	69.26	68.97	68.85
6000	84.81	84.45	84.15	83.89	83.11	82.77	82.62
7000	98.94	98.52	98.17	97.88	96.96	96.56	96.39
8000	113.07	112.60	112.20	111.86	110.81	110.36	110.16
9000	127.21	126.67	126.22	125.84	124.66	124.15	123.93
10000	141.34	140.75	140.25	139.82	138.51	137.95	137.70
15000	212.01	211.12	210.37	209.74	207.77	206.92	206.54
20000	282.68	281.49	280.49	279.65	277.03	275.89	275.39
25000	353.35	351.87	350.62	349.56	346.29	344.86	344.24
30000	424.03	422.24	420.74	419.47	415.54	413.84	413.09
35000	494.70	492.62	490.86	489.39	484.80	482.81	481.94
36000	508.83	506.69	504.89	503.37	498.65	496.60	495.71
37000	522.96	520.76	518.91	517.35	512.50	510.40	509.47
38000	537.10	534.84	532.94	531.33	526.36	524.19	523.24
39000	551.23	548.91	546.96	545.32	540.21	537.99	537.01
40000	565.37	562.99	560.99	559.30	554.06	551.78	550.78
41000	579.50	577.06	575.01	573.28	567.91	565.58	564.55
42000	593.64	591.14	589.04	587.26	581.76	579.37	578.32
43000	607.77	605.21	603.06	601.25	595.61	593.17	592.09
44000	621.90	619.29	617.09	615.23	609.47	606.96	605.86
45000	636.04	633.36	631.11	629.21	623.32	620.75	619.63
46000	650.17	647.44	645.13	643.19	637.17	634.55	633.40
47000	664.31	661.51	659.16	657.17	651.02	648.34	647.17
48000	678.44	675.59	673.18	671.16	664.87	662.14	660.94
49000	692.57	689.66	687.21	685.14	678.72	675.93	674.71
50000	706.71	703.74	701.23	600.12	692.57	689.73	688.48
51000	720.84	717.81	715.26	713.10	706.43	703.52	702.25
52000	734.98	731.89	729.28	727.09	720.28	717.32	716.02
53000	749.11	745.96	743.31	741.07	734.13	731.11	729.79
54000	763.25	760.04	757.33	755.05	747.98	744.91	743.56
55000	777.38	774.11	771.36	769.03	761.83	758.70	757.33
56000	791.51	788.18	785.38	783.02	775.68	772.49	771.10
57000	805.65	802.26	799.41	797.00	789.53	786.29	784.87
58000	819.78	816.33	813.43	810.98	803.39	800.08	798.64
59000	833.92	830.41	827.46	824.96	817.24	813.88	812.41
60000	848.05	844.48	841.48	838.95	831.09	827.67	826.18
65000	918.72	914.86	911.60	908.86	900.35	896.65	895.02
70000	989.39	985.23	981.73	970.77	969.60	965.62	963.87
75000	1060.06	1055.60	1051.85	1048.68	1038.86	1034.59	1032.72
80000	1130.73	1125.98	1121.97	1118.60	1108.12	1103.56	1101.57
85000	1201.40	1196.35	1192.10	1188.51	1177.38	1172.54	1170.42
90000	1272.08	1266.73	1262.22	1258.42	1246.63	1241.51	1239.26
95000	1342.75	1337.10	1332.34	1328.33	1315.89	1310.48	1308.11
100000	1413.42	1407.47	1402.47	1398.24	1385.15	1379.45	1376.96
105000	1484.09	1477.85	1472.59	1468.16	1454.41	1448.43	1445.81
110000	1554.76	1548.22	1542.71	1538.07	1523.66	1517.40	1514.66
120000	1696.10	1688.97	1682.96	1677.89	1662.18	1655.34	1652.35
130000	1837.44	1829.71	1823.21	1817.72	1800.69	1793.29	1790.05
140000	1978.78	1970.46	1963.45	1957.54	1939.21	1931.24	1927.74
150000	2120.13	2111.21	2103.70	2097.37	2077.72	2069.18	2065.44
175000	2473.48	2463.08	2454.32	2446.93	2424.01	2414.04	2409.68
200000	2826.83	2814.95	2804.93	2796.49	2770.30	2758.91	2753.92
225000	3180.19	3166.81	3155.55	3146.05	3116.58	3103.77	3098.16
250000	3533.54	3518.68	3506.17	3495.61	3462.87	3448.63	3442.40

16¾%

Monthly Payments

necessary to amortize a loan

AMOUNT	1 YEAR	2 YEARS	3 YEARS	4 YEARS	5 YEARS	6 YEARS	7 YEARS
100	9.11	4.93	3.55	2.87	2.47	2.21	2.03
200	18.22	9.86	7.11	5.75	4.94	4.42	4.06
500	45.54	24.66	17.76	14.36	12.36	11.05	10.15
1000	91.09	49.32	35.53	28.73	24.72	22.11	20.29
2000	182.17	98.64	71.06	57.45	49.44	44.21	40.58
5000	455.43	246.61	177.64	143.63	123.59	110.53	101.46
6000	546.52	295.93	213.17	172.36	148.31	132.64	121.75
7000	637.60	345.26	248.70	201.08	173.03	154.75	142.04
8000	728.69	394.58	284.23	229.81	197.75	176.85	162.33
9000	819.78	443.90	319.76	258.53	222.47	198.96	182.62
10000	910.86	493.22	355.28	287.26	247.18	221.07	202.92
15000	1366.29	739.83	532.93	430.89	370.78	331.60	304.37
20000	1821.72	986.44	710.57	574.52	494.37	442.14	405.83
25000	2277.15	1233.06	888.21	718.15	617.96	552.67	507.29
30000	2732.58	1479.67	1065.85	861.78	741.55	663.21	608.75
35000	3188.02	1726.28	1243.50	1005.41	865.14	773.74	710.21
36000	3279.10	1775.60	1279.02	1034.13	889.86	795.85	730.50
37000	3370.19	1824.92	1314.55	1062.86	914.58	817.95	750.79
38000	3461.27	1874.24	1350.08	1091.58	939.30	840.06	771.08
39000	3552.36	1923.57	1385.61	1120.31	964.02	862.17	791.37
40000	3643.45	1972.89	1421.14	1149.03	988.73	884.27	811.66
41000	3734.53	2022.21	1456.67	1177.76	1013.45	906.38	831.96
42000	3825.62	2071.53	1492.19	1206.49	1038.17	928.49	852.25
43000	3916.70	2120.86	1527.72	1235.21	1062.89	950.60	872.54
44000	4007.79	2170.18	1563.25	1263.94	1087.61	972.70	892.83
45000	4098.88	2219.50	1598.78	1292.66	1112.33	994.81	913.12
46000	4189.96	2268.82	1634.31	1321.39	1137.04	1016.92	933.41
47000	4281.05	2318.14	1669.84	1350.12	1161.76	1039.02	953.70
48000	4372.14	2367.47	1705.36	1378.84	1186.48	1061.13	974.00
49000	4463.22	2416.79	1740.89	1407.57	1211.20	1083.24	994.29
50000	4554.31	2466.11	1776.42	1436.29	1235.92	1105.34	1014.58
51000	4645.39	2515.43	1811.95	1465.02	1260.64	1127.45	1034.87
52000	4736.48	2564.76	1847.48	1493.74	1285.35	1149.56	1055.16
53000	4827.57	2614.08	1883.01	1522.47	1310.07	1171.66	1075.45
54000	4918.65	2663.40	1918.54	1551.20	1334.79	1193.77	1095.75
55000	5009.74	2712.72	1954.06	1579.92	1359.51	1215.88	1116.04
56000	5100.82	2762.04	1989.59	1608.65	1384.23	1237.98	1136.33
57000	5191.91	2811.37	2025.12	1637.37	1408.95	1260.09	1156.62
58000	5283.00	2860.69	2060.65	1666.10	1433.66	1282.20	1176.91
59000	5374.08	2910.01	2096.18	1694.83	1458.38	1304.30	1197.20
60000	5465.17	2959.33	2131.71	1723.55	1483.10	1326.41	1217.50
65000	5920.60	3205.94	2309.35	1867.18	1606.69	1436.95	1318.95
70000	6376.03	3452.56	2486.99	2010.81	1730.28	1547.48	1420.41
75000	6831.46	3699.17	2664.63	2154.44	1853.88	1658.01	1521.87
80000	7286.89	3945.78	2842.27	2298.07	1977.47	1768.55	1623.33
85000	7742.32	4192.39	3019.92	2441.70	2101.06	1879.08	1724.78
90000	8197.75	4439.00	3197.56	2585.33	2224.65	1989.62	1826.24
95000	8653.18	4685.61	3375.20	2728.96	2348.24	2100.15	1927.70
100000	9108.62	4932.22	3552.84	2872.59	2471.84	2210.69	2029.16
105000	9564.05	5178.83	3730.49	3016.22	2595.43	2321.22	2130.62
110000	10019.48	5425.44	3908.13	3159.84	2719.02	2431.76	2232.07
120000	10930.34	5918.67	4263.41	3447.10	2966.20	2652.82	2434.99
130000	11841.20	6411.89	4618.70	3734.36	3213.39	2873.89	2637.91
140000	12752.06	6905.11	4973.98	4021.62	3460.57	3094.96	2840.82
150000	13662.92	7398.33	5329.26	4308.88	3707.75	3316.03	3043.74
175000	15940.08	8631.39	6217.48	5027.03	4325.71	3868.70	3551.03
200000	18217.23	9864.44	7105.69	5745.17	4943.67	4421.37	4058.32
225000	20494.38	11097.50	7993.90	6463.32	5561.63	4974.04	4565.61
250000	22771.54	12330.56	8882.11	7181.47	6179.59	5526.72	5072.90

Monthly Payments

necessary to amortize a loan

16¾%

AMOUNT	8 YEARS	9 YEARS	10 YEARS	11 YEARS	12 YEARS	13 YEARS	14 YEARS
100	1.90	1.80	1.72	1.66	1.62	1.58	1.55
200	3.79	3.60	3.44	3.33	3.23	3.15	3.09
500	9.49	8.99	8.61	8.31	8.08	7.89	7.73
1000	18.97	17.98	17.22	16.63	16.15	15.77	15.46
2000	37.94	35.97	34.44	33.25	32.31	31.55	30.93
5000	94.86	89.91	86.11	83.13	80.76	78.86	77.32
6000	113.83	107.90	103.33	99.76	96.92	94.64	92.79
7000	132.81	125.88	120.55	116.38	113.07	110.41	108.25
8000	151.78	143.86	137.77	133.01	129.22	126.18	123.72
9000	170.75	161.84	155.00	149.63	145.38	141.96	139.18
10000	189.72	179.83	172.22	166.26	161.53	157.73	154.65
15000	284.59	269.74	258.33	249.39	242.29	236.59	231.97
20000	379.45	359.65	344.43	332.52	323.06	315.46	309.30
25000	474.31	449.56	430.54	415.65	403.82	394.32	386.62
30000	569.17	539.48	516.65	498.78	484.59	473.19	463.94
35000	664.03	629.39	602.76	581.91	565.35	552.05	541.27
36000	683.01	647.37	619.98	598.54	581.51	567.82	556.73
37000	701.98	665.35	637.20	615.16	597.66	583.60	572.20
38000	720.95	683.34	654.42	631.79	613.81	599.37	587.66
39000	739.92	701.32	671.65	648.41	629.96	615.14	603.13
40000	758.90	719.30	688.87	665.04	646.12	630.92	618.59
41000	777.87	737.28	706.09	681.67	662.27	646.69	634.06
42000	796.84	755.27	723.31	698.29	678.42	662.46	649.52
43000	815.81	773.25	740.53	714.92	694.58	678.24	664.99
44000	834.79	791.23	757.75	731.54	710.73	694.01	680.45
45000	853.76	809.21	774.98	748.17	726.88	709.78	695.92
46000	872.73	827.20	792.20	764.80	743.04	725.55	711.38
47000	891.70	845.18	809.42	781.42	759.19	741.33	726.85
48000	910.68	863.16	826.64	798.05	775.34	757.10	742.31
49000	929.65	881.14	843.86	814.67	791.49	772.87	757.78
50000	948.62	899.13	861.00	831.30	807.65	788.65	773.24
51000	967.59	917.11	878.31	847.93	823.80	804.42	788.71
52000	986.57	935.09	895.53	864.55	839.95	820.19	804.17
53000	1005.54	953.07	912.75	881.18	856.11	835.96	819.64
54000	1024.51	971.06	929.97	897.80	872.26	851.74	835.10
55000	1043.48	989.04	947.19	914.43	888.41	867.51	850.57
56000	1062.46	1007.02	964.41	931.06	904.56	883.28	866.03
57000	1081.43	1025.00	981.64	947.68	920.72	899.06	881.50
58000	1100.40	1042.99	998.86	964.31	936.87	914.83	896.96
59000	1119.37	1060.97	1016.08	900.03	953.02	930.60	912.42
60000	1138.35	1078.95	1033.30	997.56	969.18	946.37	927.89
65000	1233.21	1168.86	1119.41	1080.69	1049.94	1025.24	1005.21
70000	1328.07	1258.78	1205.52	1163.82	1130.71	1104.10	1082.54
75000	1422.93	1348.69	1291.63	1246.95	1211.47	1182.97	1159.86
80000	1517.79	1438.60	1377.73	1330.08	1292.23	1261.83	1237.19
85000	1612.66	1528.51	1463.84	1413.21	1373.00	1340.70	1314.51
90000	1707.52	1618.43	1549.95	1496.34	1453.76	1419.56	1391.83
95000	1802.38	1708.34	1636.06	1579.47	1534.53	1498.43	1469.16
100000	1897.24	1798.25	1722.17	1662.60	1615.29	1577.29	1546.48
105000	1992.10	1888.17	1808.28	1745.73	1696.06	1656.16	1623.81
110000	2086.97	1978.08	1894.38	1828.86	1776.82	1735.02	1701.13
120000	2276.69	2157.90	2066.60	1995.12	1938.35	1892.75	1855.78
130000	2466.42	2337.73	2238.82	2161.38	2099.88	2050.48	2010.43
140000	2656.14	2517.55	2411.03	2327.64	2261.41	2208.21	2165.08
150000	2845.86	2697.38	2583.25	2493.90	2422.94	2365.94	2319.72
175000	3320.17	3146.94	3013.79	2909.55	2826.76	2760.26	2706.34
200000	3794.49	3596.51	3444.33	3325.20	3230.59	3154.58	3092.96
225000	4268.80	4046.07	3874.88	3740.85	3634.41	3548.90	3479.59
250000	4743.11	4495.63	4305.42	4156.50	4038.23	3943.23	3866.21

16¾% Monthly Payments

necessary to amortize a loan

AMOUNT	15 YEARS	16 YEARS	17 YEARS	18 YEARS	19 YEARS	20 YEARS	21 YEARS
100	1.52	1.50	1.48	1.47	1.46	1.45	1.44
200	3.04	3.00	2.97	2.94	2.92	2.90	2.88
500	7.61	7.50	7.42	7.35	7.29	7.24	7.20
1000	15.21	15.01	14.84	14.69	14.58	14.48	14.40
2000	30.43	30.01	29.67	29.39	29.15	28.96	28.79
5000	76.07	75.03	74.18	73.47	72.88	72.39	71.98
6000	91.28	90.04	89.01	88.17	87.46	86.87	86.38
7000	106.49	105.05	103.85	102.86	102.04	101.35	100.77
8000	121.71	120.05	118.69	117.55	116.61	115.83	115.17
9000	136.92	135.06	133.52	132.25	131.19	130.30	129.56
10000	152.13	150.06	148.36	146.94	145.76	144.78	143.96
15000	228.20	225.10	222.54	220.41	218.65	217.17	215.94
20000	304.26	300.13	296.72	293.88	291.53	289.56	287.92
25000	380.33	375.16	370.89	367.36	364.41	361.95	359.90
30000	456.40	450.19	445.07	440.83	437.29	434.35	431.88
35000	532.46	525.23	519.25	514.30	510.18	506.74	503.86
36000	547.68	540.23	534.09	528.99	524.75	521.22	518.26
37000	562.89	555.24	548.92	543.69	539.33	535.69	532.65
38000	578.10	570.25	563.76	558.38	553.90	550.17	547.05
39000	593.32	585.25	578.59	573.07	568.48	564.65	561.45
40000	608.53	600.26	593.43	587.77	583.06	579.13	575.84
41000	623.74	615.27	608.27	602.46	597.63	593.61	590.24
42000	638.95	630.27	623.10	617.16	612.21	608.08	604.63
43000	654.17	645.28	637.94	631.85	626.79	622.56	619.03
44000	669.38	660.28	652.77	646.55	641.36	637.04	633.43
45000	684.59	675.29	667.61	661.24	655.94	651.52	647.82
46000	699.81	690.30	682.44	675.93	670.52	666.00	662.22
47000	715.02	705.30	697.28	690.63	685.09	680.48	676.61
48000	730.23	720.31	712.12	705.32	699.67	694.95	691.01
49000	745.45	735.32	726.95	720.02	714.25	709.43	705.41
50000	760.66	750.32	741.79	734.71	728.82	723.91	719.80
51000	775.87	765.33	756.62	749.40	743.40	738.39	734.20
52000	791.09	780.34	771.46	764.10	757.98	752.87	748.59
53000	806.30	795.34	786.29	778.79	772.55	767.34	762.99
54000	821.51	810.35	801.13	793.49	787.13	781.82	777.39
55000	836.73	825.36	815.97	808.18	801.70	796.30	791.78
56000	851.94	840.36	830.80	822.88	816.28	810.78	806.18
57000	867.15	855.37	845.64	837.57	830.86	825.26	820.57
58000	882.37	870.38	860.47	852.26	845.43	839.74	834.97
59000	897.58	885.38	875.31	866.96	860.01	854.21	849.37
60000	912.79	900.39	890.15	881.65	874.59	868.69	863.76
65000	988.86	975.42	964.32	955.12	947.47	941.08	935.74
70000	1064.92	1050.45	1038.50	1028.59	1020.35	1013.47	1007.72
75000	1140.99	1125.49	1112.68	1102.07	1093.23	1085.86	1079.70
80000	1217.06	1200.52	1186.86	1175.54	1166.12	1158.26	1151.68
85000	1293.12	1275.55	1261.04	1249.01	1239.00	1230.65	1223.66
90000	1369.19	1350.58	1335.22	1322.48	1311.88	1303.04	1295.64
95000	1445.26	1425.61	1409.40	1395.95	1384.76	1375.43	1367.62
100000	1521.32	1500.65	1483.58	1469.42	1457.64	1447.82	1439.60
105000	1597.39	1575.68	1557.75	1542.89	1530.53	1520.21	1511.58
110000	1673.45	1650.71	1631.93	1616.36	1603.41	1592.60	1583.56
120000	1825.59	1800.78	1780.29	1763.30	1749.17	1737.38	1727.52
130000	1977.72	1950.84	1928.65	1910.25	1894.94	1882.17	1871.48
140000	2129.85	2100.91	2077.01	2057.19	2040.70	2026.95	2015.44
150000	2281.98	2250.97	2225.36	2204.13	2186.47	2171.73	2159.40
175000	2662.31	2626.13	2596.26	2571.49	2550.88	2533.68	2519.31
200000	3042.64	3001.29	2967.15	2938.84	2915.29	2895.64	2879.21
225000	3422.97	3376.46	3338.04	3306.20	3279.70	3257.59	3239.11
250000	3803.30	3751.62	3708.94	3673.55	3644.11	3619.55	3599.01

Monthly Payments 16¾%

necessary to amortize a loan

AMOUNT	22 YEARS	23 YEARS	24 YEARS	25 YEARS	30 YEARS	35 YEARS	40 YEARS
100	1.43	1.43	1.42	1.42	1.41	1.40	1.40
200	2.87	2.85	2.84	2.84	2.81	2.80	2.80
500	7.16	7.13	7.11	7.09	7.03	7.00	6.99
1000	14.33	14.27	14.22	14.18	14.05	14.00	13.98
2000	28.65	28.54	28.44	28.36	28.11	28.00	27.95
5000	71.64	71.35	71.10	70.90	70.27	70.00	69.88
6000	85.96	85.62	85.33	85.08	84.32	84.00	83.86
7000	100.29	99.89	99.55	99.26	98.38	98.00	97.83
8000	114.62	114.16	113.77	113.44	112.43	112.00	111.81
9000	128.94	128.42	127.99	127.62	126.49	126.00	125.79
10000	143.27	142.69	142.21	141.80	140.54	140.00	139.76
15000	214.91	214.04	213.31	212.70	210.81	210.00	209.65
20000	286.54	285.39	284.42	283.60	281.08	280.00	279.53
25000	358.18	356.74	355.52	354.50	351.35	349.99	349.41
30000	429.82	428.08	426.63	425.40	421.62	419.99	419.29
35000	501.45	499.43	497.73	496.30	491.89	489.99	489.17
36000	515.78	513.70	511.95	510.48	505.94	503.99	503.15
37000	530.11	527.97	526.17	524.66	520.00	517.99	517.13
38000	544.43	542.24	540.39	538.84	534.05	531.99	531.10
39000	558.76	556.51	554.61	553.02	548.10	545.99	545.08
40000	573.09	570.78	568.83	567.20	562.16	559.99	559.05
41000	587.41	585.05	583.05	581.38	576.21	573.99	573.03
42000	601.74	599.31	597.28	595.56	590.27	587.99	587.01
43000	616.07	613.58	611.50	609.74	604.32	601.99	600.98
44000	630.40	627.85	625.72	623.92	618.37	615.99	614.96
45000	644.72	642.12	639.94	638.10	632.43	629.99	628.94
46000	659.05	656.39	654.16	652.28	646.48	643.99	642.91
47000	673.38	670.66	668.38	666.46	660.54	657.99	656.89
48000	687.70	684.93	682.60	680.64	674.59	671.99	670.86
49000	702.03	699.20	696.82	694.82	688.64	685.99	684.84
50000	716.36	713.47	711.04	709.00	702.70	699.99	698.82
51000	730.69	727.74	725.26	723.18	716.75	713.99	712.79
52000	745.01	742.01	739.48	737.36	730.81	727.99	726.77
53000	759.34	756.28	753.70	751.54	744.86	741.99	740.75
54000	773.67	770.55	767.93	765.72	758.91	755.99	754.72
55000	788.00	784.82	782.15	779.90	772.97	769.99	768.70
56000	802.32	799.09	796.37	794.08	787.02	783.99	782.68
57000	816.65	813.36	810.59	808.26	801.08	797.99	796.65
58000	830.98	827.63	824.81	822.44	815.13	811.99	810.63
59000	845.30	841.89	839.03	836.62	829.18	825.99	824.60
60000	859.63	856.16	853.25	850.80	843.24	839.99	838.58
65000	931.27	927.51	924.35	921.70	913.51	909.99	908.46
70000	1002.90	998.86	995.46	992.00	983.78	979.99	978.34
75000	1074.54	1070.21	1066.56	1063.50	1054.05	1049.98	1048.23
80000	1146.17	1141.55	1137.67	1134.40	1124.32	1119.98	1118.11
85000	1217.81	1212.90	1208.77	1205.30	1194.59	1189.98	1187.99
90000	1289.45	1284.25	1279.88	1276.20	1264.86	1259.98	1257.87
95000	1361.08	1355.59	1350.98	1347.10	1335.13	1329.98	1327.75
100000	1432.72	1426.94	1422.08	1418.00	1405.40	1399.98	1397.64
105000	1504.35	1498.29	1493.19	1488.90	1475.67	1469.98	1467.52
110000	1575.99	1569.63	1564.29	1559.80	1545.94	1539.98	1537.40
120000	1719.26	1712.33	1706.50	1701.60	1686.47	1679.98	1677.16
130000	1862.53	1855.02	1848.71	1843.40	1827.01	1819.97	1816.93
140000	2005.81	1997.72	1990.92	1985.20	1967.55	1959.97	1956.69
150000	2149.08	2140.41	2133.13	2127.00	2108.09	2099.97	2096.45
175000	2507.26	2497.16	2488.65	2481.49	2459.44	2449.96	2445.86
200000	2865.44	2853.88	2844.17	2835.99	2810.79	2799.96	2795.27
225000	3223.62	3210.62	3199.69	3190.49	3162.14	3149.95	3144.68
250000	3581.80	3567.35	3555.21	3544.99	3513.49	3499.95	3494.09

17%

Monthly Payments

necessary to amortize a loan

AMOUNT	1 YEAR	2 YEARS	3 YEARS	4 YEARS	5 YEARS	6 YEARS	7 YEARS
100	9.12	4.94	3.57	2.89	2.49	2.22	2.04
200	18.24	9.89	7.13	5.77	4.97	4.45	4.09
500	45.60	24.72	17.83	14.43	12.43	11.12	10.22
1000	91.20	49.44	35.65	28.86	24.85	22.25	20.44
2000	182.41	98.88	71.31	57.71	49.71	44.49	40.87
5000	456.02	247.21	178.26	144.28	124.26	111.23	102.18
6000	547.23	296.65	213.92	173.13	149.12	133.48	122.61
7000	638.43	346.10	249.57	201.99	173.97	155.72	143.05
8000	729.64	395.54	285.22	230.84	198.82	177.97	163.49
9000	820.84	444.98	320.87	259.70	223.67	200.22	183.92
10000	912.05	494.42	356.53	288.55	248.53	222.46	204.36
15000	1368.07	741.63	534.79	432.83	372.79	333.69	306.54
20000	1824.10	988.85	713.05	577.10	497.05	444.92	408.72
25000	2280.12	1236.06	891.32	721.38	621.31	556.15	510.90
30000	2736.14	1483.27	1069.58	865.65	745.58	667.38	613.07
35000	3192.17	1730.48	1247.85	1009.93	869.84	778.61	715.25
36000	3283.37	1779.92	1283.50	1038.78	894.69	800.86	735.69
37000	3374.58	1829.36	1319.15	1067.64	919.55	823.11	756.12
38000	3465.78	1878.81	1354.80	1096.49	944.40	845.35	776.56
39000	3556.99	1928.25	1390.46	1125.35	969.25	867.60	797.00
40000	3648.19	1977.69	1426.11	1154.20	994.10	889.85	817.43
41000	3739.39	2027.13	1461.76	1183.06	1018.96	912.09	837.87
42000	3830.60	2076.58	1497.41	1211.91	1043.81	934.34	858.30
43000	3921.80	2126.02	1533.07	1240.77	1068.66	956.58	878.74
44000	4013.01	2175.46	1568.72	1269.62	1093.51	978.83	899.18
45000	4104.21	2224.90	1604.37	1298.48	1118.37	1001.08	919.61
46000	4195.42	2274.34	1640.03	1327.33	1143.22	1023.32	940.05
47000	4286.62	2323.79	1675.68	1356.19	1168.07	1045.57	960.48
48000	4377.83	2373.23	1711.33	1385.04	1192.92	1067.81	980.92
49000	4469.03	2422.67	1746.98	1413.90	1217.78	1090.06	1001.35
50000	4560.24	2472.11	1782.64	1442.75	1242.63	1112.31	1021.79
51000	4651.44	2521.56	1818.29	1471.61	1267.48	1134.55	1042.23
52000	4742.65	2571.00	1853.94	1500.46	1292.33	1156.80	1062.66
53000	4833.85	2620.44	1889.59	1529.32	1317.19	1179.04	1083.10
54000	4925.06	2669.88	1925.25	1558.17	1342.04	1201.29	1103.53
55000	5016.26	2719.32	1960.90	1587.03	1366.89	1223.54	1123.97
56000	5107.47	2768.77	1996.55	1615.88	1391.74	1245.78	1144.41
57000	5198.67	2818.21	2032.21	1644.74	1416.60	1268.03	1164.84
58000	5289.88	2867.65	2067.86	1673.59	1441.45	1290.28	1185.28
59000	5381.08	2917.09	2103.51	1702.45	1466.30	1312.52	1205.71
60000	5472.29	2966.54	2139.16	1731.30	1491.15	1334.77	1226.15
65000	5928.31	3213.75	2317.43	1875.58	1615.42	1446.00	1328.33
70000	6384.33	3460.96	2495.69	2019.85	1739.68	1557.23	1430.51
75000	6840.36	3708.17	2673.95	2164.13	1863.94	1668.46	1532.69
80000	7296.38	3955.38	2852.22	2308.40	1988.21	1779.69	1634.86
85000	7752.40	4202.59	3030.48	2452.68	2112.47	1890.92	1737.04
90000	8208.43	4449.80	3208.75	2596.95	2236.73	2002.15	1839.22
95000	8664.45	4697.02	3387.01	2741.23	2360.99	2113.38	1941.40
100000	9120.48	4944.23	3565.27	2885.50	2485.26	2224.61	2043.58
105000	9576.50	5191.44	3743.54	3029.78	2609.52	2335.84	2145.76
110000	10032.52	5438.65	3921.80	3174.05	2733.78	2447.07	2247.94
120000	10944.57	5933.07	4278.33	3462.61	2982.31	2669.54	2452.30
130000	11856.62	6427.49	4634.85	3751.16	3230.83	2892.00	2656.65
140000	12768.67	6921.92	4991.38	4039.71	3479.36	3114.46	2861.01
150000	13680.71	7416.34	5347.91	4328.26	3727.89	3336.92	3065.37
175000	15960.83	8652.40	6239.23	5049.63	4349.20	3893.07	3576.27
200000	18240.95	9888.45	7130.55	5771.01	4970.52	4449.23	4087.16
225000	20521.07	11124.51	8021.86	6492.38	5591.83	5005.38	4598.06
250000	22801.19	12360.57	8913.18	7213.76	6213.14	5561.53	5108.95

Monthly Payments 17%

necessary to amortize a loan

AMOUNT	8 YEARS	9 YEARS	10 YEARS	11 YEARS	12 YEARS	13 YEARS	14 YEARS
100	1.91	1.81	1.74	1.68	1.63	1.59	1.56
200	3.82	3.63	3.48	3.36	3.26	3.19	3.13
500	9.56	9.07	8.69	8.39	8.16	7.97	7.82
1000	19.12	18.14	17.38	16.79	16.32	15.94	15.64
2000	38.24	36.27	34.76	33.58	32.64	31.89	31.28
5000	95.61	90.68	86.90	83.94	81.60	79.71	78.19
6000	114.73	108.82	104.28	100.73	97.92	95.66	93.83
7000	133.85	126.95	121.66	117.52	114.23	111.60	109.47
8000	152.97	145.09	139.04	134.31	130.55	127.54	125.11
9000	172.09	163.23	156.42	151.09	146.87	143.49	140.75
10000	191.21	181.36	173.80	167.88	163.19	159.43	156.38
15000	286.82	272.04	260.70	251.82	244.79	239.14	234.58
20000	382.43	362.72	347.60	335.77	326.38	318.86	312.77
25000	478.04	453.40	434.49	419.71	407.98	398.57	390.96
30000	573.64	544.09	521.39	503.65	489.58	478.29	469.15
35000	669.25	634.77	608.29	587.59	571.17	558.00	547.34
36000	688.37	652.90	625.67	604.38	587.49	573.95	562.98
37000	707.49	671.04	643.05	621.17	603.81	589.89	578.62
38000	726.62	689.18	660.43	637.96	620.13	605.83	594.26
39000	745.74	707.31	677.81	654.74	636.45	621.78	609.90
40000	764.86	725.45	695.19	671.53	652.77	637.72	625.54
41000	783.98	743.58	712.57	688.32	669.09	653.66	641.17
42000	803.10	761.72	729.95	705.11	685.41	669.60	656.81
43000	822.22	779.86	747.33	721.90	701.73	685.55	672.45
44000	841.34	797.99	764.71	738.69	718.05	701.49	688.09
45000	860.47	816.13	782.09	755.47	734.37	717.43	703.73
46000	879.59	834.26	799.47	772.26	750.68	733.38	719.37
47000	898.71	852.40	816.85	789.05	767.00	749.32	735.00
48000	917.83	870.54	834.23	805.84	783.32	765.26	750.64
49000	936.95	888.67	851.61	822.63	799.64	781.20	766.28
50000	956.07	906.81	868.99	839.42	815.96	797.15	781.92
51000	975.19	924.95	886.37	856.20	832.28	813.09	797.56
52000	994.32	943.08	903.75	872.99	848.60	829.03	813.20
53000	1013.44	961.22	921.13	889.78	864.92	844.98	828.83
54000	1032.56	979.35	938.51	906.57	881.24	860.92	844.47
55000	1051.68	997.49	955.89	923.36	897.56	876.86	860.11
56000	1070.80	1015.63	973.27	940.15	913.88	892.81	875.75
57000	1089.92	1033.76	990.65	956.93	930.20	908.75	891.39
58000	1109.04	1051.90	1008.03	973.72	946.52	924.69	907.03
59000	1128.17	1070.04	1025.41	990.51	962.83	940.63	922.66
60000	1147.29	1088.17	1042.79	1007.30	979.15	956.58	938.30
65000	1242.00	1178.85	1129.68	1091.24	1060.75	1036.29	1016.49
70000	1338.50	1269.53	1216.60	1175.18	1142.35	1116.01	1094.69
75000	1434.11	1360.21	1303.48	1259.12	1223.94	1195.72	1172.88
80000	1529.72	1450.90	1390.38	1343.07	1305.64	1275.44	1251.07
85000	1625.32	1541.58	1477.28	1427.01	1387.13	1355.15	1329.26
90000	1720.93	1632.26	1564.18	1510.95	1468.73	1434.87	1407.45
95000	1816.54	1722.94	1651.08	1594.89	1550.33	1514.58	1485.65
100000	1912.15	1813.62	1737.98	1678.83	1631.92	1594.30	1563.84
105000	2007.75	1904.30	1824.88	1762.77	1713.52	1674.01	1642.03
110000	2103.36	1994.98	1911.77	1846.72	1795.12	1753.72	1720.22
120000	2294.57	2176.34	2085.57	2014.60	1958.31	1913.15	1876.61
130000	2485.79	2357.70	2259.37	2182.48	2121.50	2072.58	2032.99
140000	2677.00	2539.07	2433.17	2350.36	2284.69	2232.01	2189.37
150000	2868.22	2720.43	2606.96	2518.25	2447.88	2391.44	2345.76
175000	3346.25	3173.83	3041.46	2937.96	2855.87	2790.02	2736.72
200000	3824.29	3627.24	3475.95	3357.66	3263.85	3188.59	3127.68
225000	4302.33	4080.64	3910.45	3777.37	3671.83	3587.16	3518.64
250000	4780.36	4534.05	4344.94	4197.08	4079.81	3985.74	3909.60

17%

Monthly Payments
necessary to amortize a loan

AMOUNT	15 YEARS	16 YEARS	17 YEARS	18 YEARS	19 YEARS	20 YEARS	21 YEARS
100	1.54	1.52	1.50	1.49	1.48	1.47	1.46
200	3.08	3.04	3.00	2.98	2.95	2.93	2.92
500	7.70	7.59	7.51	7.44	7.38	7.33	7.29
1000	15.39	15.19	15.02	14.88	14.76	14.67	14.59
2000	30.78	30.37	30.04	29.76	29.53	29.34	29.18
5000	76.95	75.93	75.09	74.40	73.82	73.34	72.94
6000	92.34	91.12	90.11	89.28	88.58	88.01	87.53
7000	107.73	106.30	105.13	104.16	103.35	102.68	102.11
8000	123.12	121.49	120.15	119.04	118.11	117.34	116.70
9000	138.51	136.68	135.17	133.92	132.88	132.01	131.29
10000	153.90	151.86	150.18	148.79	147.64	146.68	145.88
15000	230.85	227.80	225.28	223.19	221.46	220.02	218.82
20000	307.80	303.73	300.37	297.59	295.28	293.36	291.76
25000	384.75	379.66	375.46	371.99	369.10	366.70	364.70
30000	461.70	455.59	450.55	446.38	442.92	440.04	437.63
35000	538.65	531.52	525.65	520.78	516.74	513.38	510.57
36000	554.04	546.71	540.66	535.66	531.51	528.05	525.16
37000	569.43	561.89	555.68	550.54	546.27	542.72	539.75
38000	584.82	577.08	570.70	565.42	561.04	557.38	554.34
39000	600.21	592.27	585.72	580.30	575.80	572.05	568.92
40000	615.60	607.45	600.74	595.18	590.56	586.72	583.51
41000	630.99	622.64	615.76	610.06	605.33	601.39	598.10
42000	646.38	637.83	630.77	624.94	620.09	616.06	612.69
43000	661.77	653.01	645.79	639.82	634.86	630.72	627.28
44000	677.16	668.20	660.81	654.70	649.62	645.39	641.86
45000	692.55	683.39	675.83	669.58	664.38	660.06	656.45
46000	707.94	698.57	690.85	684.46	679.15	674.73	671.04
47000	723.33	713.76	705.87	699.34	693.91	689.40	685.63
48000	738.72	728.94	720.88	714.21	708.68	704.06	700.22
49000	754.11	744.13	735.90	729.09	723.44	718.73	714.80
50000	769.50	759.32	750.92	743.97	738.20	733.40	729.39
51000	784.89	774.50	765.94	758.85	752.97	748.07	743.98
52000	800.28	789.69	780.96	773.73	767.73	762.74	758.57
53000	815.67	804.88	795.98	788.61	782.50	777.40	773.15
54000	831.06	820.06	811.00	803.49	797.26	792.07	787.74
55000	846.45	835.25	826.01	818.37	812.02	806.74	802.33
56000	861.84	850.44	841.03	833.25	826.79	821.41	816.92
57000	877.23	865.62	856.05	848.13	841.55	836.08	831.51
58000	892.62	880.81	871.07	863.01	856.32	850.74	846.09
59000	908.01	895.99	886.09	877.89	871.08	865.41	860.68
60000	923.40	911.18	901.11	892.77	885.85	880.08	875.27
65000	1000.35	987.11	976.20	967.17	959.67	953.42	948.21
70000	1077.30	1063.04	1051.29	1041.56	1033.49	1026.76	1021.15
75000	1154.25	1138.98	1126.38	1115.96	1107.31	1100.10	1094.09
80000	1231.20	1214.91	1201.47	1190.36	1181.13	1173.44	1167.03
85000	1308.15	1290.84	1276.57	1264.76	1254.95	1246.78	1239.96
90000	1385.10	1366.77	1351.66	1339.15	1328.77	1320.12	1312.90
95000	1462.05	1442.70	1426.75	1413.55	1402.59	1393.46	1385.84
100000	1539.00	1518.63	1501.84	1487.95	1476.41	1466.80	1458.78
105000	1615.95	1594.57	1576.94	1562.34	1550.23	1540.14	1531.72
110000	1692.90	1670.50	1652.03	1636.74	1624.05	1613.48	1604.66
120000	1846.81	1822.36	1802.21	1785.54	1771.69	1760.16	1750.54
130000	2000.71	1974.22	1952.40	1934.33	1919.33	1906.84	1896.42
140000	2154.61	2126.09	2102.58	2083.13	2066.97	2053.52	2042.29
150000	2308.51	2277.95	2252.77	2231.92	2214.61	2200.20	2188.17
175000	2693.26	2657.61	2628.23	2603.91	2583.71	2566.90	2552.87
200000	3078.01	3037.27	3003.69	2975.89	2952.82	2933.60	2917.56
225000	3462.76	3416.93	3379.15	3347.88	3321.92	3300.30	3282.26
250000	3847.51	3796.59	3754.61	3719.87	3691.02	3667.00	3646.95

Monthly Payments **17%**

necessary to amortize a loan

AMOUNT	22 YEARS	23 YEARS	24 YEARS	25 YEARS	30 YEARS	35 YEARS	40 YEARS
100	1.45	1.45	1.44	1.44	1.43	1.42	1.42
200	2.90	2.89	2.88	2.88	2.85	2.84	2.84
500	7.26	7.23	7.21	7.19	7.13	7.10	7.09
1000	14.52	14.46	14.42	14.38	14.26	14.21	14.18
2000	29.04	28.93	28.84	28.76	28.51	28.41	28.37
5000	72.60	72.32	72.09	71.89	71.28	71.03	70.92
6000	87.12	86.79	86.51	86.27	85.54	85.23	85.10
7000	101.65	101.25	100.92	100.65	99.80	99.44	99.28
8000	116.17	115.72	115.34	115.02	114.05	113.64	113.47
9000	130.69	130.18	129.76	129.40	128.31	127.85	127.65
10000	145.21	144.65	144.18	143.78	142.57	142.05	141.83
15000	217.81	216.97	216.26	215.67	213.85	213.08	212.75
20000	290.42	289.29	288.35	287.56	285.14	284.11	283.66
25000	363.02	361.62	360.44	359.45	356.42	355.13	354.58
30000	435.62	433.94	432.53	431.34	427.70	426.16	425.50
35000	508.23	506.26	504.61	503.23	498.99	497.18	496.41
36000	522.75	520.73	519.03	517.61	513.24	511.39	510.60
37000	537.27	535.19	533.45	531.98	527.50	525.59	524.78
38000	551.79	549.66	547.87	546.36	541.76	539.80	538.96
39000	566.31	564.12	562.28	560.74	556.01	554.01	553.15
40000	580.83	578.58	576.70	575.12	570.27	568.21	567.33
41000	595.35	593.05	591.12	589.50	584.53	582.42	581.51
42000	609.87	607.51	605.54	603.87	598.78	596.62	595.70
43000	624.39	621.98	619.95	618.25	613.04	610.83	609.88
44000	638.91	636.44	634.37	632.63	627.30	625.03	624.06
45000	653.43	650.91	648.79	647.01	641.55	639.24	638.25
46000	667.96	665.37	663.21	661.39	655.81	653.44	652.43
47000	682.48	679.84	677.62	675.76	670.07	667.65	666.61
48000	697.00	694.30	692.04	690.14	684.32	681.85	680.80
49000	711.52	708.77	706.46	704.52	698.58	696.06	694.98
50000	726.04	723.23	720.88	718.90	712.84	710.26	709.16
51000	740.56	737.70	735.29	733.28	727.09	724.47	723.35
52000	755.08	752.16	749.71	747.65	741.35	738.67	737.53
53000	769.60	766.62	764.13	762.03	755.61	752.88	751.71
54000	784.12	781.09	778.55	776.41	769.86	767.08	765.89
55000	798.64	795.55	792.96	790.79	784.12	781.29	780.08
56000	813.16	810.02	807.38	805.17	798.38	795.49	794.26
57000	827.68	824.48	821.80	819.54	812.63	809.70	808.44
58000	842.20	838.95	836.22	833.92	826.89	823.91	822.63
59000	856.73	853.41	850.63	848.30	841.15	838.11	836.81
60000	871.25	867.88	865.05	862.68	855.41	852.32	850.99
65000	943.85	940.20	937.14	934.57	926.69	923.34	921.91
70000	1016.45	1012.52	1009.23	1006.46	997.97	994.37	992.83
75000	1089.06	1084.85	1081.31	1078.35	1069.20	1065.39	1063.74
80000	1161.66	1157.17	1153.40	1150.24	1140.54	1136.42	1134.66
85000	1234.27	1229.49	1225.49	1222.13	1211.82	1207.45	1205.58
90000	1306.87	1301.81	1297.58	1294.02	1283.11	1278.47	1276.49
95000	1379.47	1374.14	1369.66	1365.91	1354.39	1349.50	1347.41
100000	1452.08	1446.46	1441.75	1437.80	1425.68	1420.53	1418.32
105000	1524.68	1518.78	1513.84	1509.69	1496.96	1491.55	1489.24
110000	1597.28	1591.11	1585.93	1581.58	1568.24	1562.58	1560.16
120000	1742.49	1735.75	1730.10	1725.36	1710.81	1704.63	1701.99
130000	1887.70	1880.40	1874.28	1869.14	1853.38	1846.68	1843.82
140000	2032.91	2025.05	2018.45	2012.92	1995.95	1988.74	1985.65
150000	2178.11	2169.69	2162.63	2156.69	2138.51	2130.79	2127.49
175000	2541.13	2531.31	2523.06	2516.14	2494.93	2485.92	2482.07
200000	2904.15	2892.92	2883.50	2875.59	2851.35	2841.05	2836.65
225000	3267.17	3254.54	3243.94	3235.04	3207.77	3196.18	3191.23
250000	3630.19	3616.15	3604.38	3594.49	3564.19	3551.32	3545.81

17¼% Monthly Payments

necessary to amortize a loan

AMOUNT	1 YEAR	2 YEARS	3 YEARS	4 YEARS	5 YEARS	6 YEARS	7 YEARS
100	9.13	4.96	3.58	2.90	2.50	2.24	2.06
200	18.26	9.91	7.16	5.80	5.00	4.48	4.12
500	45.66	24.78	17.89	14.49	12.49	11.19	10.29
1000	91.32	49.56	35.78	28.98	24.99	22.39	20.58
2000	182.65	99.12	71.55	57.97	49.97	44.77	41.16
5000	456.62	247.81	178.89	144.92	124.94	111.93	102.90
6000	547.94	297.37	214.66	173.91	149.92	134.32	123.48
7000	639.26	346.94	250.44	202.89	174.91	156.70	144.06
8000	730.59	396.50	286.22	231.88	199.90	179.09	164.64
9000	821.91	446.06	322.00	260.86	224.88	201.47	185.22
10000	913.23	495.62	357.77	289.85	249.87	223.86	205.81
15000	1369.85	743.44	536.66	434.77	374.81	335.79	308.71
20000	1826.47	991.25	715.55	579.69	499.74	447.72	411.61
25000	2283.09	1239.06	894.43	724.61	624.68	559.65	514.51
30000	2739.70	1486.87	1073.32	869.54	749.62	671.58	617.42
35000	3196.32	1734.69	1252.20	1014.46	874.55	783.51	720.32
36000	3287.64	1784.25	1287.98	1043.44	899.54	805.89	740.90
37000	3378.97	1833.81	1323.76	1072.43	924.53	828.28	761.48
38000	3470.29	1883.37	1359.54	1101.41	949.51	850.66	782.06
39000	3561.61	1932.94	1395.31	1130.40	974.50	873.05	802.64
40000	3652.94	1982.50	1431.09	1159.38	999.49	895.43	823.22
41000	3744.26	2032.06	1466.87	1188.37	1024.48	917.82	843.80
42000	3835.58	2081.62	1502.65	1217.35	1049.46	940.21	864.38
43000	3926.91	2131.19	1538.42	1246.34	1074.45	962.59	884.96
44000	4018.23	2180.75	1574.20	1275.32	1099.44	984.98	905.54
45000	4109.55	2230.31	1609.98	1304.30	1124.42	1007.36	926.12
46000	4200.88	2279.87	1645.75	1333.29	1149.41	1029.75	946.70
47000	4292.20	2329.44	1681.53	1362.27	1174.40	1052.14	967.29
48000	4383.52	2379.00	1717.31	1391.26	1199.39	1074.52	987.87
49000	4474.85	2428.56	1753.09	1420.24	1224.37	1096.91	1008.45
50000	4566.17	2478.12	1788.86	1449.23	1249.36	1119.29	1029.03
51000	4657.50	2527.69	1824.64	1478.21	1274.35	1141.68	1049.61
52000	4748.82	2577.25	1860.42	1507.20	1299.33	1164.06	1070.19
53000	4840.14	2626.81	1896.20	1536.18	1324.32	1186.45	1090.77
54000	4931.47	2676.37	1931.97	1565.17	1349.31	1208.84	1111.35
55000	5022.79	2725.94	1967.75	1594.15	1374.30	1231.22	1131.93
56000	5114.11	2775.50	2003.53	1623.13	1399.28	1253.61	1152.51
57000	5205.44	2825.06	2039.30	1652.12	1424.27	1275.99	1173.09
58000	5296.76	2874.62	2075.08	1681.10	1449.26	1298.38	1193.67
59000	5388.08	2924.19	2110.86	1710.09	1474.24	1320.77	1214.25
60000	5479.41	2973.75	2146.64	1739.07	1499.23	1343.15	1234.83
65000	5936.02	3221.56	2325.52	1884.00	1624.17	1455.08	1337.74
70000	6392.64	3469.37	2504.41	2028.92	1749.10	1567.01	1440.64
75000	6849.26	3717.19	2683.30	2173.84	1874.04	1678.94	1543.54
80000	7305.87	3965.00	2862.18	2318.76	1998.98	1790.87	1646.44
85000	7762.49	4212.81	3041.07	2463.69	2123.91	1902.80	1749.35
90000	8219.11	4460.62	3219.95	2608.61	2248.85	2014.73	1852.25
95000	8675.73	4708.43	3398.84	2753.53	2373.78	2126.66	1955.15
100000	9132.34	4956.25	3577.73	2898.45	2498.72	2238.59	2058.05
105000	9588.96	5204.06	3756.61	3043.38	2623.66	2350.52	2160.96
110000	10045.58	5451.87	3935.50	3188.30	2748.59	2462.44	2263.86
120000	10958.81	5947.50	4293.27	3478.15	2998.46	2686.30	2469.66
130000	11872.05	6443.12	4651.05	3767.99	3248.34	2910.16	2675.47
140000	12785.28	6938.75	5008.82	4057.84	3498.21	3134.02	2881.28
150000	13698.52	7434.37	5366.59	4347.68	3748.08	3357.88	3087.08
175000	15981.60	8673.43	6261.02	5072.30	4372.76	3917.53	3601.59
200000	18264.69	9912.49	7155.45	5796.91	4997.44	4477.17	4116.11
225000	20547.77	11151.56	8049.89	6521.52	5622.12	5036.82	4630.62
250000	22830.86	12390.62	8944.32	7246.14	6246.80	5596.46	5145.14

Monthly Payments 17¼%

necessary to amortize a loan

AMOUNT	8 YEARS	9 YEARS	10 YEARS	11 YEARS	12 YEARS	13 YEARS	14 YEARS
100	1.93	1.83	1.75	1.70	1.65	1.61	1.58
200	3.85	3.66	3.51	3.39	3.30	3.22	3.16
500	9.64	9.15	8.77	8.48	8.24	8.06	7.91
1000	19.27	18.29	17.54	16.95	16.49	16.11	15.81
2000	38.54	36.58	35.08	33.90	32.97	32.23	31.63
5000	96.36	91.45	87.69	84.76	82.43	80.57	79.06
6000	115.63	109.74	105.23	101.71	98.92	96.68	94.88
7000	134.90	128.03	122.77	118.66	115.40	112.80	110.69
8000	154.17	146.32	140.31	135.61	131.89	128.91	126.50
9000	173.44	164.61	157.85	152.56	148.38	145.02	142.31
10000	192.71	182.90	175.39	169.51	164.86	161.14	158.13
15000	289.07	274.36	263.08	254.27	247.29	241.71	237.19
20000	385.42	365.81	350.77	339.03	329.72	322.27	316.25
25000	481.78	457.26	438.46	423.78	412.16	402.84	395.32
30000	578.13	548.71	526.16	508.54	494.59	483.41	474.38
35000	674.49	640.17	613.85	593.30	577.02	563.98	553.44
36000	693.76	658.46	631.39	610.25	593.50	580.09	569.26
37000	713.03	676.75	648.92	627.20	609.99	596.21	585.07
38000	732.30	695.04	666.46	644.15	626.48	612.32	600.88
39000	751.57	713.33	684.00	661.10	642.96	628.43	616.69
40000	770.84	731.62	701.54	678.05	659.45	644.55	632.51
41000	790.11	749.91	719.08	695.00	675.93	660.66	648.32
42000	809.38	768.20	736.62	711.95	692.42	676.78	664.13
43000	828.66	786.49	754.16	728.91	708.91	692.89	679.94
44000	847.93	804.78	771.69	745.86	725.39	709.00	695.76
45000	867.20	823.07	789.23	762.81	741.88	725.12	711.57
46000	886.47	841.36	806.77	779.76	758.37	741.23	727.38
47000	905.74	859.65	824.31	796.71	774.85	757.34	743.19
48000	925.01	877.94	841.85	813.66	791.34	773.46	759.01
49000	944.28	896.23	859.39	830.61	807.82	789.57	774.82
50000	963.55	914.52	876.93	847.56	824.31	805.68	790.63
51000	982.82	932.81	894.46	864.52	840.80	821.80	806.44
52000	1002.09	951.10	912.00	881.47	857.28	837.91	822.26
53000	1021.37	969.39	929.54	898.42	873.77	854.03	838.07
54000	1040.64	987.68	947.08	915.37	890.26	870.14	853.88
55000	1059.91	1005.98	964.62	932.32	906.74	886.25	869.70
56000	1079.18	1024.27	982.16	949.27	923.23	902.37	885.51
57000	1098.46	1042.56	999.69	966.22	939.71	918.48	901.32
58000	1117.72	1060.85	1017.23	983.18	956.20	934.59	917.13
59000	1136.99	1079.14	1034.77	1000.10	972.69	950.71	932.95
60000	1156.26	1097.43	1052.31	1017.08	989.17	966.82	948.76
65000	1252.62	1188.88	1140.00	1101.83	1071.60	1047.39	1027.82
70000	1348.97	1280.33	1227.70	1186.59	1154.03	1127.96	1106.88
75000	1445.33	1371.78	1315.39	1271.35	1236.47	1208.53	1185.95
80000	1541.68	1463.24	1403.08	1356.10	1318.90	1289.10	1265.01
85000	1638.04	1554.69	1480.77	1440.86	1401.33	1369.66	1344.07
90000	1734.39	1646.14	1578.47	1525.62	1483.76	1450.23	1423.14
95000	1830.75	1737.59	1666.16	1610.37	1566.19	1530.80	1502.20
100000	1927.10	1829.05	1753.85	1695.13	1648.62	1611.37	1581.26
105000	2023.46	1920.50	1841.54	1779.89	1731.05	1691.94	1660.33
110000	2119.82	2011.95	1929.24	1864.64	1813.48	1772.51	1739.39
120000	2312.53	2194.85	2104.62	2034.16	1978.35	1933.64	1897.52
130000	2505.24	2377.76	2280.01	2203.67	2143.21	2094.78	2055.64
140000	2697.95	2560.66	2455.39	2373.18	2308.07	2255.92	2213.77
150000	2890.66	2743.57	2630.78	2542.69	2472.93	2417.05	2371.90
175000	3372.43	3200.83	3069.24	2966.48	2885.09	2819.90	2767.21
200000	3854.21	3658.09	3507.70	3390.26	3297.24	3222.74	3162.53
225000	4335.99	4115.35	3946.16	3814.04	3709.40	3625.58	3557.84
250000	4817.76	4572.61	4384.63	4237.82	4121.55	4028.42	3953.16

17¼%

Monthly Payments
necessary to amortize a loan

AMOUNT	15 YEARS	16 YEARS	17 YEARS	18 YEARS	19 YEARS	20 YEARS	21 YEARS
100	1.56	1.54	1.52	1.51	1.50	1.49	1.48
200	3.11	3.07	3.04	3.01	2.99	2.97	2.96
500	7.78	7.68	7.60	7.53	7.48	7.43	7.39
1000	15.57	15.37	15.20	15.07	14.95	14.86	14.78
2000	31.14	30.73	30.40	30.13	29.90	29.72	29.56
5000	77.84	76.83	76.01	75.33	74.76	74.29	73.90
6000	93.41	92.20	91.21	90.39	89.71	89.15	88.68
7000	108.97	107.57	106.41	105.46	104.67	104.01	103.46
8000	124.54	122.94	121.61	120.52	119.62	118.87	118.24
9000	140.11	138.30	136.82	135.59	134.57	133.73	133.02
10000	155.68	153.67	152.02	150.65	149.52	148.58	147.80
15000	233.51	230.50	228.03	225.98	224.29	222.88	221.70
20000	311.35	307.34	304.04	301.31	299.05	297.17	295.60
25000	389.19	384.17	380.04	376.63	373.81	371.46	369.50
30000	467.03	461.01	456.05	451.96	448.57	445.75	443.41
35000	544.86	537.84	532.06	527.29	523.33	520.04	517.31
36000	560.43	553.21	547.26	542.35	538.28	534.90	532.09
37000	576.00	568.58	562.47	557.42	553.24	549.76	546.87
38000	591.57	583.94	577.67	572.48	568.19	564.62	561.65
39000	607.14	599.31	592.87	587.55	583.14	579.48	576.43
40000	622.70	614.68	608.07	602.62	598.09	594.34	591.21
41000	638.27	630.04	623.27	617.68	613.05	609.20	605.99
42000	653.84	645.41	638.48	632.75	628.00	624.05	620.77
43000	669.41	660.78	653.68	647.81	642.95	638.91	635.55
44000	684.97	676.14	668.88	662.88	657.90	653.77	650.33
45000	700.54	691.51	684.08	677.94	672.86	668.63	665.11
46000	716.11	706.88	699.28	693.01	687.81	683.49	679.89
47000	731.68	722.24	714.48	708.07	702.76	698.35	694.67
48000	747.24	737.61	729.69	723.14	717.71	713.20	709.45
49000	762.81	752.98	744.89	738.20	732.67	728.06	724.23
50000	778.38	768.34	760.09	753.27	747.62	742.92	739.01
51000	793.95	783.71	775.29	768.34	762.57	757.78	753.79
52000	809.51	799.08	790.49	783.40	777.52	772.64	768.57
53000	825.08	814.45	805.69	798.47	792.47	787.50	783.35
54000	840.65	829.81	820.90	813.53	807.43	802.35	798.13
55000	856.22	845.18	836.10	828.60	822.38	817.21	812.91
56000	871.78	860.55	851.30	843.66	837.33	832.07	827.69
57000	887.35	875.91	866.50	858.73	852.28	846.93	842.47
58000	902.92	891.28	881.70	873.79	867.24	861.79	857.25
59000	918.49	906.65	896.91	888.86	882.19	876.65	872.03
60000	934.05	922.01	912.11	903.92	897.14	891.51	886.81
65000	1011.89	998.85	988.12	979.25	971.90	965.80	960.71
70000	1089.73	1075.68	1064.13	1054.58	1046.66	1040.09	1034.61
75000	1167.57	1152.52	1140.13	1129.90	1121.43	1114.38	1108.51
80000	1245.41	1229.35	1216.14	1205.23	1196.19	1188.67	1182.41
85000	1323.24	1306.19	1292.15	1280.56	1270.95	1262.97	1256.32
90000	1401.08	1383.02	1368.16	1355.89	1345.71	1337.26	1330.22
95000	1478.92	1459.86	1444.17	1431.21	1420.47	1411.55	1404.12
100000	1556.76	1536.69	1520.18	1506.54	1495.24	1485.84	1478.02
105000	1634.59	1613.52	1596.19	1581.87	1570.00	1560.13	1551.92
110000	1712.43	1690.36	1672.20	1657.19	1644.76	1634.43	1625.82
120000	1868.11	1844.03	1824.21	1807.85	1794.28	1783.01	1773.62
130000	2023.78	1997.70	1976.23	1958.50	1943.81	1931.59	1921.42
140000	2179.46	2151.37	2128.25	2109.16	2093.33	2080.18	2069.23
150000	2335.14	2305.03	2280.27	2259.81	2242.85	2228.76	2217.03
175000	2724.32	2689.21	2660.31	2636.44	2616.66	2600.22	2586.53
200000	3113.51	3073.38	3040.36	3013.08	2990.47	2971.68	2956.04
225000	3502.70	3457.55	3420.40	3389.71	3364.28	3343.14	3325.54
250000	3891.89	3841.72	3800.45	3766.35	3738.09	3714.60	3695.05

Monthly Payments 17¼%

necessary to amortize a loan

AMOUNT	22 YEARS	23 YEARS	24 YEARS	25 YEARS	30 YEARS	35 YEARS	40 YEARS
100	1.47	1.47	1.46	1.46	1.45	1.44	1.44
200	2.94	2.93	2.92	2.92	2.89	2.88	2.88
500	7.36	7.33	7.31	7.29	7.23	7.21	7.20
1000	14.71	14.66	14.61	14.58	14.46	14.41	14.39
2000	29.43	29.32	29.23	29.15	28.92	28.82	28.78
5000	73.57	73.30	73.07	72.88	72.30	72.05	71.95
6000	88.29	87.96	87.69	87.46	86.76	86.47	86.34
7000	103.00	102.62	102.30	102.03	101.22	100.88	100.73
8000	117.72	117.28	116.92	116.61	115.68	115.29	115.12
9000	132.43	131.94	131.53	131.19	130.14	129.70	129.51
10000	147.15	146.60	146.15	145.76	144.60	144.11	143.90
15000	220.72	219.90	219.22	218.65	216.90	216.16	215.85
20000	294.30	293.21	292.29	291.53	289.20	288.22	287.80
25000	367.87	366.51	365.37	364.41	361.50	360.27	359.76
30000	441.45	439.81	438.44	437.29	433.80	432.33	431.71
35000	515.02	513.11	511.51	510.17	506.10	504.38	503.66
36000	529.74	527.77	526.13	524.75	520.55	518.79	518.05
37000	544.45	542.43	540.74	539.33	535.01	533.20	532.44
38000	559.17	557.09	555.36	553.90	549.47	547.61	546.83
39000	573.88	571.75	569.97	568.48	563.93	562.03	561.22
40000	588.60	586.41	584.59	583.06	578.39	576.44	575.61
41000	603.31	601.07	599.20	597.63	592.85	590.85	590.00
42000	618.03	615.73	613.82	612.21	607.31	605.26	604.39
43000	632.74	630.39	628.43	626.79	621.77	619.67	618.78
44000	647.46	645.05	643.05	641.36	636.23	634.08	633.17
45000	662.17	659.71	657.66	655.94	650.69	648.49	647.56
46000	676.89	674.38	672.27	670.52	665.15	662.90	661.95
47000	691.60	689.04	686.89	685.09	679.61	677.31	676.34
48000	706.31	703.70	701.50	699.67	694.07	691.72	690.73
49000	721.03	718.36	716.12	714.24	708.53	706.13	705.12
50000	735.74	733.02	730.73	720.82	722.99	720.55	719.51
51000	750.46	747.68	745.35	743.40	737.45	734.96	733.00
52000	765.17	762.34	759.96	757.97	751.91	749.37	748.29
53000	779.89	777.00	774.58	772.55	766.37	763.78	762.68
54000	794.60	791.66	789.19	787.13	780.83	778.19	777.07
55000	809.32	806.32	803.81	801.70	795.29	792.60	791.46
56000	824.03	820.98	818.42	816.28	809.75	807.01	805.85
57000	838.75	835.64	833.04	830.86	824.21	821.42	820.24
58000	853.40	850.30	847.65	845.43	838.67	835.83	834.63
59000	868.18	864.96	862.27	860.01	853.13	850.24	849.02
60000	882.89	879.62	876.88	874.58	867.59	864.66	863.41
65000	950.47	952.92	949.95	947.47	939.89	936.71	935.37
70000	1030.04	1026.22	1023.03	1020.35	1012.19	1008.76	1007.32
75000	1103.62	1099.52	1096.10	1093.23	1084.49	1080.82	1070.27
80000	1177.19	1172.83	1169.17	1166.11	1156.79	1152.87	1151.22
85000	1250.77	1246.13	1242.26	1239.00	1229.09	1224.93	1223.17
90000	1324.34	1319.43	1315.32	1311.88	1301.39	1206.98	1295.12
95000	1397.91	1392.73	1388.39	1384.76	1373.69	1369.04	1367.07
100000	1471.49	1466.03	1461.47	1457.64	1445.99	1441.09	1439.02
105000	1545.06	1539.33	1534.54	1530.52	1518.29	1513.15	1510.97
110000	1618.64	1612.64	1607.61	1603.41	1590.58	1585.20	1582.93
120000	1765.79	1759.24	1753.76	1749.17	1735.18	1729.31	1726.83
130000	1912.94	1905.84	1899.91	1894.93	1879.78	1873.42	1870.73
140000	2060.09	2052.45	2046.05	2040.70	2024.38	2017.53	2014.63
150000	2207.23	2199.05	2192.20	2186.46	2168.98	2161.64	2158.53
175000	2575.11	2565.56	2557.57	2550.87	2530.48	2521.91	2518.29
200000	2942.98	2932.07	2922.93	2915.28	2891.97	2882.18	2878.05
225000	3310.85	3298.57	3288.30	3279.69	3253.47	3242.46	3237.80
250000	3678.72	3665.08	3653.67	3644.10	3614.96	3602.73	3597.56

17½%

Monthly Payments

necessary to amortize a loan

AMOUNT	1 YEAR	2 YEARS	3 YEARS	4 YEARS	5 YEARS	6 YEARS	7 YEARS
100	9.14	4.97	3.59	2.91	2.51	2.25	2.07
200	18.29	9.94	7.18	5.82	5.02	4.51	4.15
500	45.72	24.84	17.95	14.56	12.56	11.26	10.36
1000	91.44	49.68	35.90	29.11	25.12	22.53	20.73
2000	182.88	99.37	71.80	58.23	50.24	45.05	41.45
5000	457.21	248.41	179.51	145.57	125.61	112.63	103.63
6000	548.65	298.10	215.41	174.69	150.73	135.16	124.35
7000	640.10	347.78	251.31	203.80	175.86	157.68	145.08
8000	731.54	397.46	287.22	232.91	200.98	180.21	165.81
9000	822.98	447.15	323.12	262.03	226.10	202.73	186.53
10000	914.42	496.83	359.02	291.14	251.22	225.26	207.26
15000	1371.63	745.24	538.53	436.72	376.83	337.89	310.89
20000	1828.84	993.66	718.04	582.29	502.44	450.52	414.52
25000	2286.06	1242.07	897.55	727.86	628.06	563.15	518.14
30000	2743.27	1490.49	1077.06	873.43	753.67	675.78	621.77
35000	3200.48	1738.90	1256.57	1019.00	879.28	788.41	725.40
36000	3291.92	1788.58	1292.47	1048.12	904.40	810.94	746.13
37000	3383.36	1838.27	1328.38	1077.23	929.52	833.46	766.85
38000	3474.80	1887.95	1364.28	1106.35	954.64	855.99	787.58
39000	3566.25	1937.63	1400.18	1135.46	979.77	878.52	808.31
40000	3657.69	1987.31	1436.08	1164.57	1004.89	901.04	829.03
41000	3749.13	2037.00	1471.98	1193.69	1030.01	923.57	849.76
42000	3840.57	2086.68	1507.89	1222.80	1055.13	946.09	870.48
43000	3932.01	2136.36	1543.79	1251.92	1080.26	968.62	891.21
44000	4023.46	2186.05	1579.69	1281.03	1105.38	991.15	911.93
45000	4114.90	2235.73	1615.59	1310.15	1130.50	1013.67	932.66
46000	4206.34	2285.41	1651.50	1339.26	1155.62	1036.20	953.39
47000	4297.78	2335.09	1687.40	1368.38	1180.74	1058.72	974.11
48000	4389.23	2384.78	1723.30	1397.49	1205.87	1081.25	994.84
49000	4480.67	2434.46	1759.20	1426.60	1230.99	1103.78	1015.56
50000	4572.11	2484.14	1795.10	1455.72	1256.11	1126.30	1036.29
51000	4663.55	2533.83	1831.01	1484.83	1281.23	1148.83	1057.02
52000	4754.99	2583.51	1866.91	1513.95	1306.36	1171.35	1077.74
53000	4846.44	2633.19	1902.81	1543.06	1331.48	1193.88	1098.47
54000	4937.88	2682.87	1938.71	1572.18	1356.60	1216.41	1119.19
55000	5029.32	2732.56	1974.61	1601.29	1381.72	1238.93	1139.92
56000	5120.76	2782.24	2010.52	1630.40	1406.84	1261.46	1160.64
57000	5212.21	2831.92	2046.42	1659.52	1431.97	1283.98	1181.37
58000	5303.65	2881.61	2082.32	1688.63	1457.09	1306.51	1202.10
59000	5395.09	2931.29	2118.22	1717.75	1482.21	1329.04	1222.82
60000	5486.53	2980.97	2154.12	1746.86	1507.33	1351.56	1243.55
65000	5943.74	3229.39	2333.63	1892.43	1632.94	1464.19	1347.18
70000	6400.95	3477.80	2513.14	2038.01	1758.55	1576.82	1450.81
75000	6858.17	3726.21	2692.65	2183.58	1884.17	1689.45	1554.43
80000	7315.38	3974.63	2872.17	2329.15	2009.78	1802.08	1658.06
85000	7772.59	4223.04	3051.68	2474.72	2135.39	1914.71	1761.69
90000	8229.80	4471.46	3231.19	2620.29	2261.00	2027.34	1865.32
95000	8687.01	4719.87	3410.70	2765.87	2386.61	2139.97	1968.95
100000	9144.22	4968.28	3590.21	2911.44	2512.22	2252.60	2072.58
105000	9601.43	5216.70	3769.72	3057.01	2637.83	2365.23	2176.21
110000	10058.64	5465.11	3949.23	3202.58	2763.44	2477.87	2279.84
120000	10973.06	5961.94	4308.25	3493.72	3014.67	2703.13	2487.10
130000	11887.49	6458.77	4667.27	3784.87	3265.89	2928.39	2694.35
140000	12801.91	6955.60	5026.29	4076.01	3517.11	3153.65	2901.61
150000	13716.33	7452.43	5385.31	4367.16	3768.33	3378.91	3108.87
175000	16002.39	8694.50	6282.86	5095.02	4396.39	3942.06	3627.01
200000	18288.44	9936.57	7180.41	5822.87	5024.44	4505.21	4145.16
225000	20574.50	11178.64	8077.96	6550.73	5652.50	5068.36	4663.30
250000	22860.55	12420.71	8975.52	7278.59	6280.55	5631.51	5181.45

Monthly Payments 17½%

necessary to amortize a loan

AMOUNT	8 YEARS	9 YEARS	10 YEARS	11 YEARS	12 YEARS	13 YEARS	14 YEARS
100	1.94	1.84	1.77	1.71	1.67	1.63	1.60
200	3.88	3.69	3.54	3.42	3.33	3.26	3.20
500	9.71	9.22	8.85	8.56	8.33	8.14	7.99
1000	19.42	18.45	17.70	17.11	16.65	16.29	15.99
2000	38.84	36.89	35.40	34.23	33.31	32.57	31.98
5000	97.11	92.23	88.49	85.57	83.27	81.43	79.94
6000	116.53	110.67	106.19	102.69	99.92	97.71	95.93
7000	135.95	129.12	123.89	119.80	116.58	114.00	111.91
8000	155.37	147.56	141.58	136.92	133.23	130.28	127.90
9000	174.79	166.01	159.28	154.03	149.88	146.57	143.89
10000	194.21	184.45	176.98	171.15	166.54	162.85	159.88
15000	291.32	276.68	265.47	256.72	249.81	244.28	239.81
20000	388.42	368.91	353.96	342.30	333.08	325.70	319.75
25000	485.53	461.13	442.45	427.87	416.35	407.13	399.69
30000	582.64	553.36	530.94	513.45	499.62	488.55	479.63
35000	679.74	645.59	619.43	599.02	582.89	569.98	559.57
36000	699.16	664.03	637.12	616.14	599.54	586.26	575.55
37000	718.58	682.48	654.82	633.25	616.19	602.55	591.54
38000	738.01	700.92	672.52	650.37	632.85	618.83	607.53
39000	757.43	719.37	690.22	667.48	649.50	635.12	623.52
40000	776.85	737.81	707.92	684.60	666.15	651.40	639.50
41000	796.27	756.26	725.61	701.71	682.81	667.69	655.49
42000	815.69	774.70	743.31	718.83	699.46	683.98	671.48
43000	835.11	793.15	761.01	735.94	716.12	700.26	687.47
44000	854.53	811.59	778.71	753.06	732.77	716.55	703.45
45000	873.95	830.04	796.40	770.17	749.42	732.83	719.44
46000	893.38	848.49	814.10	787.29	766.08	749.12	735.43
47000	912.80	866.93	831.80	804.40	782.73	765.40	751.42
48000	932.22	885.38	849.50	821.52	799.39	781.69	767.40
49000	951.64	903.82	867.20	838.63	816.04	797.97	783.39
50000	971.06	922.27	884.89	855.75	832.69	814.26	799.38
51000	990.48	940.71	902.59	872.86	849.35	830.54	815.37
52000	1009.90	959.16	920.29	889.98	866.00	846.83	831.35
53000	1029.32	977.60	937.99	907.09	882.66	863.11	847.34
54000	1048.75	996.05	955.69	924.21	899.31	879.40	863.33
55000	1068.17	1014.49	973.38	941.32	915.96	895.68	879.32
56000	1087.59	1032.94	991.08	958.44	932.62	911.97	895.30
57000	1107.01	1051.38	1008.78	975.55	949.27	928.25	911.29
58000	1126.43	1069.83	1026.40	992.67	965.92	944.54	927.28
59000	1145.85	1088.27	1044.17	1009.78	982.58	960.82	943.27
60000	1165.27	1106.72	1061.87	1026.90	999.23	977.11	959.26
65000	1262.38	1198.95	1150.36	1112.47	1082.50	1058.53	1039.19
70000	1359.48	1291.17	1238.85	1198.05	1165.77	1139.96	1119.13
75000	1456.59	1383.40	1327.34	1283.62	1249.04	1221.38	1199.07
80000	1553.70	1475.63	1415.83	1369.19	1332.31	1302.81	1279.01
85000	1650.80	1567.85	1504.32	1454.77	1415.58	1384.24	1358.94
90000	1747.91	1660.08	1592.81	1540.34	1498.85	1465.66	1438.88
95000	1845.01	1752.31	1681.30	1625.92	1582.12	1547.09	1518.82
100000	1942.12	1844.53	1769.79	1711.49	1665.39	1628.51	1598.76
105000	2039.23	1936.76	1858.28	1797.07	1748.66	1709.94	1678.70
110000	2136.33	2028.99	1946.77	1882.64	1831.93	1791.36	1758.63
120000	2330.55	2213.44	2123.75	2053.79	1998.46	1954.21	1918.51
130000	2524.76	2397.89	2300.72	2224.94	2165.00	2117.07	2078.39
140000	2718.97	2582.35	2477.70	2396.09	2331.54	2279.92	2238.26
150000	2913.18	2766.80	2654.68	2567.24	2498.08	2442.77	2398.14
175000	3398.71	3227.93	3097.13	2995.11	2914.43	2849.90	2797.83
200000	3884.24	3689.07	3539.58	3422.99	3330.77	3257.02	3197.52
225000	4369.77	4150.20	3982.02	3850.86	3747.12	3664.15	3597.21
250000	4855.30	4611.33	4424.47	4278.73	4163.47	4071.28	3996.90

17½%

Monthly Payments
necessary to amortize a loan

AMOUNT	15 YEARS	16 YEARS	17 YEARS	18 YEARS	19 YEARS	20 YEARS	21 YEARS
100	1.57	1.55	1.54	1.53	1.51	1.50	1.50
200	3.15	3.11	3.08	3.05	3.03	3.01	2.99
500	7.87	7.77	7.69	7.63	7.57	7.52	7.49
1000	15.75	15.55	15.39	15.25	15.14	15.05	14.97
2000	31.49	31.10	30.77	30.50	30.28	30.10	29.95
5000	78.73	77.74	76.93	76.26	75.71	75.25	74.87
6000	94.47	93.29	92.31	91.51	90.85	90.30	89.84
7000	110.22	108.84	107.70	106.76	105.99	105.35	104.81
8000	125.97	124.39	123.09	122.02	121.13	120.40	119.78
9000	141.71	139.93	138.47	137.27	136.27	135.44	134.76
10000	157.46	155.48	153.86	152.52	151.41	150.49	149.73
15000	236.19	233.22	230.79	228.78	227.12	225.74	224.60
20000	314.92	310.96	307.72	305.04	302.82	300.99	299.46
25000	393.64	388.70	384.64	381.30	378.53	376.24	374.33
30000	472.37	466.44	461.57	457.56	454.24	451.48	449.19
35000	551.10	544.18	538.50	533.82	529.94	526.73	524.06
36000	566.85	559.73	553.89	549.07	545.08	541.78	539.03
37000	582.59	575.28	569.27	564.32	560.23	556.83	554.00
38000	598.34	590.83	584.66	579.57	575.37	571.88	568.98
39000	614.09	606.38	600.05	594.83	590.51	586.93	583.95
40000	629.83	621.93	615.43	610.08	605.65	601.98	598.92
41000	645.58	637.47	630.82	625.33	620.79	617.03	613.90
42000	661.32	653.02	646.20	640.58	635.93	632.08	628.87
43000	677.07	668.57	661.59	655.83	651.07	647.13	643.84
44000	692.81	684.12	676.97	671.09	666.21	662.17	658.82
45000	708.56	699.67	692.36	686.34	681.36	677.22	673.79
46000	724.31	715.21	707.75	701.59	696.50	692.27	688.76
47000	740.05	730.76	723.13	716.84	711.64	707.32	703.74
48000	755.80	746.31	738.52	732.09	726.78	722.37	718.71
49000	771.54	761.86	753.90	747.35	741.92	737.42	733.68
50000	787.29	777.41	769.29	762.60	757.06	752.47	748.66
51000	803.03	792.95	784.68	777.85	772.20	767.52	763.63
52000	818.78	808.50	800.06	793.10	787.34	782.57	778.60
53000	834.53	824.05	815.45	808.35	802.49	797.62	793.57
54000	850.27	839.60	830.83	823.61	817.63	812.67	808.55
55000	866.02	855.15	846.22	838.86	832.77	827.72	823.52
56000	881.76	870.70	861.60	854.11	847.91	842.77	838.49
57000	897.51	886.24	876.99	869.36	863.05	857.82	853.47
58000	913.26	901.79	892.38	884.61	878.19	872.87	868.44
59000	929.00	917.34	907.76	899.87	893.33	887.92	883.41
60000	944.75	932.89	923.15	915.12	908.47	902.97	898.39
65000	1023.48	1010.63	1000.08	991.38	984.18	978.21	973.25
70000	1102.20	1088.37	1077.01	1067.64	1059.89	1053.46	1048.12
75000	1180.93	1166.11	1153.93	1143.90	1135.59	1128.71	1122.98
80000	1259.66	1243.85	1230.86	1220.16	1211.30	1203.95	1197.85
85000	1338.39	1321.59	1307.79	1296.42	1287.01	1279.20	1272.71
90000	1417.12	1399.33	1384.72	1372.68	1362.71	1354.45	1347.58
95000	1495.85	1477.07	1461.65	1448.94	1438.42	1429.69	1422.44
100000	1574.58	1554.81	1538.58	1525.19	1514.12	1504.94	1497.31
105000	1653.31	1632.55	1615.51	1601.45	1589.83	1580.19	1572.18
110000	1732.04	1710.29	1692.44	1677.71	1665.54	1655.44	1647.04
120000	1889.49	1865.78	1846.30	1830.23	1816.95	1805.93	1796.77
130000	2046.95	2021.26	2000.15	1982.75	1968.36	1956.42	1946.50
140000	2204.41	2176.74	2154.01	2135.27	2119.77	2106.92	2096.23
150000	2361.87	2332.22	2307.87	2287.79	2271.19	2257.41	2245.97
175000	2755.51	2720.92	2692.51	2669.09	2649.72	2633.65	2620.29
200000	3149.16	3109.63	3077.16	3050.39	3028.25	3009.88	2994.62
225000	3542.80	3498.33	3461.80	3431.69	3406.78	3386.12	3368.95
250000	3936.45	3887.03	3846.45	3812.99	3785.31	3762.35	3743.28

Monthly Payments

necessary to amortize a loan

17½%

AMOUNT	22 YEARS	23 YEARS	24 YEARS	25 YEARS	30 YEARS	35 YEARS	40 YEARS
100	1.49	1.49	1.48	1.48	1.47	1.46	1.46
200	2.98	2.97	2.96	2.96	2.93	2.92	2.92
500	7.45	7.43	7.41	7.39	7.33	7.31	7.30
1000	14.91	14.86	14.81	14.78	14.66	14.62	14.60
2000	29.82	29.71	29.62	29.55	29.33	29.23	29.19
5000	74.55	74.28	74.06	73.88	73.32	73.08	72.99
6000	89.46	89.14	88.87	88.65	87.98	87.70	87.58
7000	104.37	104.00	103.69	103.43	102.64	102.32	102.18
8000	119.28	118.85	118.50	118.20	117.31	116.93	116.78
9000	134.19	133.71	133.31	132.98	131.97	131.55	131.38
10000	149.10	148.57	148.12	147.75	146.63	146.17	145.97
15000	223.64	222.85	222.18	221.63	219.95	219.25	218.96
20000	298.19	297.13	296.25	295.51	293.27	292.34	291.95
25000	372.74	371.41	370.31	369.38	366.58	365.42	364.93
30000	447.29	445.70	444.37	443.26	439.90	438.50	437.92
35000	521.83	519.98	518.43	517.14	513.21	511.59	510.91
36000	536.74	534.84	533.24	531.91	527.88	526.20	525.50
37000	551.65	549.69	548.05	546.69	542.54	540.82	540.10
38000	566.56	564.55	562.87	561.46	557.20	555.44	554.70
39000	581.47	579.41	577.68	576.24	571.87	570.05	569.30
40000	596.38	594.26	592.49	591.01	586.53	584.67	583.89
41000	611.29	609.12	607.30	605.79	601.19	599.29	598.49
42000	626.20	623.98	622.12	620.56	615.86	613.90	613.09
43000	641.11	638.83	636.93	635.34	630.52	628.52	627.69
44000	656.02	653.69	651.74	650.11	645.18	643.14	642.28
45000	670.93	668.54	666.55	664.89	659.85	657.75	656.88
46000	685.84	683.40	681.37	679.66	674.51	672.37	671.48
47000	700.75	698.26	696.18	694.44	689.17	686.99	686.07
48000	715.66	713.11	710.99	709.21	703.84	701.60	700.67
49000	730.57	727.97	725.80	723.99	718.50	716.22	715.27
50000	745.48	742.83	740.61	738.76	733.16	730.84	729.87
51000	760.39	757.68	755.43	753.54	747.83	745.45	744.46
52000	775.30	772.54	770.24	768.32	762.49	760.07	759.06
53000	790.21	787.40	785.05	783.09	777.15	774.69	773.66
54000	805.12	802.25	799.86	797.87	791.82	789.30	788.26
55000	820.03	817.11	814.68	812.64	806.48	803.92	802.85
56000	834.93	831.97	829.49	827.42	821.14	818.54	817.45
57000	849.84	846.82	844.30	842.19	835.81	833.15	832.05
58000	864.75	861.68	859.11	856.97	850.47	847.77	846.65
59000	879.66	876.54	873.93	871.74	865.13	862.39	861.24
60000	894.57	891.39	888.74	886.52	879.80	877.01	875.84
65000	969.12	965.68	962.80	960.39	953.11	950.09	948.83
70000	1043.67	1039.96	1036.86	1034.27	1026.43	1023.17	1021.81
75000	1118.22	1114.24	1110.92	1108.15	1099.74	1098.20	1084.80
80000	1192.76	1188.52	1184.98	1182.02	1173.06	1169.34	1167.79
85000	1267.31	1262.81	1259.04	1255.90	1246.38	1242.42	1240.77
90000	1341.86	1337.09	1333.11	1329.78	1319.69	1315.51	1313.76
95000	1416.41	1411.37	1407.17	1403.65	1393.01	1388.59	1386.75
100000	1490.95	1485.65	1481.23	1477.53	1466.33	1461.68	1459.73
105000	1565.50	1559.94	1555.29	1551.41	1539.64	1534.76	1532.72
110000	1640.05	1634.22	1629.35	1625.28	1612.96	1607.84	1605.71
120000	1789.15	1782.79	1777.48	1773.04	1759.59	1754.01	1751.68
130000	1938.24	1931.35	1925.60	1920.79	1906.22	1900.18	1897.65
140000	2087.34	2079.92	2073.72	2068.54	2052.86	2046.35	2043.63
150000	2236.43	2228.48	2221.84	2216.29	2199.49	2192.51	2189.60
175000	2609.17	2599.90	2592.15	2585.68	2566.07	2557.93	2554.53
200000	2981.91	2971.31	2962.46	2955.06	2932.65	2923.35	2919.47
225000	3354.65	3342.72	3332.77	3324.44	3299.23	3288.77	3284.40
250000	3727.39	3714.14	3703.07	3693.82	3665.81	3654.19	3649.33

17¾%

Monthly Payments
necessary to amortize a loan

AMOUNT	1 YEAR	2 YEARS	3 YEARS	4 YEARS	5 YEARS	6 YEARS	7 YEARS
100	9.16	4.98	3.60	2.92	2.53	2.27	2.09
200	18.31	9.96	7.21	5.85	5.05	4.53	4.17
500	45.78	24.90	18.01	14.62	12.63	11.33	10.44
1000	91.56	49.80	36.03	29.24	25.26	22.67	20.87
2000	183.12	99.61	72.05	58.49	50.52	45.33	41.74
5000	457.81	249.02	180.14	146.22	126.29	113.33	104.36
6000	549.37	298.82	216.16	175.47	151.55	136.00	125.23
7000	640.93	348.62	252.19	204.71	176.80	158.67	146.10
8000	732.49	398.43	288.22	233.96	202.06	181.33	166.97
9000	824.05	448.23	324.24	263.20	227.32	204.00	187.84
10000	915.61	498.03	360.27	292.45	252.58	226.67	208.72
15000	1373.42	747.05	540.41	438.67	378.86	340.00	313.07
20000	1831.22	996.07	720.54	584.89	505.15	453.33	417.43
25000	2289.03	1245.08	900.68	731.11	631.44	566.67	521.79
30000	2746.83	1494.10	1080.81	877.34	757.73	680.00	626.15
35000	3204.64	1743.12	1260.95	1023.56	884.02	793.33	730.50
36000	3296.20	1792.92	1296.98	1052.80	909.27	816.00	751.38
37000	3387.76	1842.73	1333.00	1082.05	934.53	838.67	772.25
38000	3479.32	1892.53	1369.03	1111.29	959.79	861.33	793.12
39000	3570.88	1942.33	1405.06	1140.54	985.05	884.00	813.99
40000	3662.44	1992.14	1441.08	1169.78	1010.30	906.67	834.86
41000	3754.00	2041.94	1477.11	1199.03	1035.56	929.33	855.73
42000	3845.56	2091.74	1513.14	1228.27	1060.82	952.00	876.61
43000	3937.13	2141.55	1549.17	1257.51	1086.08	974.67	897.48
44000	4028.69	2191.35	1585.19	1286.76	1111.34	997.33	918.35
45000	4120.25	2241.15	1621.22	1316.00	1136.59	1020.00	939.22
46000	4211.81	2290.96	1657.25	1345.25	1161.85	1042.67	960.09
47000	4303.37	2340.76	1693.27	1374.49	1187.11	1065.33	980.96
48000	4394.93	2390.56	1729.30	1403.74	1212.37	1088.00	1001.83
49000	4486.49	2440.37	1765.33	1432.98	1237.62	1110.67	1022.71
50000	4578.05	2490.17	1801.36	1462.23	1262.88	1133.33	1043.58
51000	4669.61	2539.97	1837.38	1491.47	1288.14	1156.00	1064.45
52000	4761.17	2589.78	1873.41	1520.72	1313.40	1178.67	1085.32
53000	4852.74	2639.58	1909.44	1549.96	1338.65	1201.33	1106.19
54000	4944.30	2689.38	1945.46	1579.20	1363.91	1224.00	1127.06
55000	5035.86	2739.19	1981.49	1608.45	1389.17	1246.67	1147.94
56000	5127.42	2788.99	2017.52	1637.69	1414.43	1269.33	1168.81
57000	5218.98	2838.79	2053.55	1666.94	1439.68	1292.00	1189.68
58000	5310.54	2888.60	2089.57	1696.18	1464.94	1314.67	1210.55
59000	5402.10	2938.40	2125.60	1725.43	1490.20	1337.33	1231.42
60000	5493.66	2988.20	2161.63	1754.67	1515.46	1360.00	1252.29
65000	5951.47	3237.22	2341.76	1900.89	1641.75	1473.33	1356.65
70000	6409.27	3486.24	2521.90	2047.12	1768.03	1586.67	1461.01
75000	6867.08	3735.25	2702.03	2193.34	1894.32	1700.00	1565.37
80000	7324.88	3984.27	2882.17	2339.56	2020.61	1813.34	1669.72
85000	7782.69	4233.29	3062.30	2485.78	2146.90	1926.67	1774.08
90000	8240.50	4482.31	3242.44	2632.01	2273.19	2040.00	1878.44
95000	8698.30	4731.32	3422.58	2778.23	2399.47	2153.34	1982.80
100000	9156.11	4980.34	3602.71	2924.45	2525.76	2266.67	2087.16
105000	9613.91	5229.36	3782.85	3070.68	2652.05	2380.00	2191.51
110000	10071.72	5478.37	3962.98	3216.90	2778.34	2493.34	2295.87
120000	10987.33	5976.41	4323.25	3509.34	3030.91	2720.00	2504.59
130000	11902.94	6474.44	4683.52	3801.79	3283.49	2946.67	2713.30
140000	12818.55	6972.47	5043.79	4094.23	3536.07	3173.34	2922.02
150000	13734.16	7470.51	5404.07	4386.68	3788.64	3400.00	3130.73
175000	16023.18	8715.59	6304.74	5117.79	4420.08	3966.67	3652.52
200000	18312.21	9960.68	7205.42	5848.91	5051.52	4533.34	4174.31
225000	20601.24	11205.76	8106.10	6580.02	5682.97	5100.01	4696.10
250000	22890.26	12450.85	9006.78	7311.13	6314.41	5666.67	5217.89

Monthly Payments 17¾%

necessary to amortize a loan

AMOUNT	8 YEARS	9 YEARS	10 YEARS	11 YEARS	12 YEARS	13 YEARS	14 YEARS
100	1.96	1.86	1.79	1.73	1.68	1.65	1.62
200	3.91	3.72	3.57	3.46	3.36	3.29	3.23
500	9.79	9.30	8.93	8.64	8.41	8.23	8.08
1000	19.57	18.60	17.86	17.28	16.82	16.46	16.16
2000	39.14	37.20	35.72	34.56	33.64	32.91	32.33
5000	97.86	93.00	89.29	86.40	84.11	82.29	80.02
6000	117.43	111.60	107.15	103.68	100.93	98.74	96.98
7000	137.00	130.21	125.01	120.95	117.76	115.20	113.14
8000	156.58	148.81	142.86	138.23	134.58	131.66	129.31
9000	176.15	167.41	160.72	155.51	151.40	148.12	145.47
10000	195.72	186.01	178.58	172.79	168.22	164.57	161.63
15000	293.58	279.01	267.87	259.19	252.33	246.86	242.45
20000	391.44	372.02	357.16	345.58	336.44	329.14	323.26
25000	489.30	465.02	446.45	431.98	420.56	411.43	404.08
30000	587.16	558.02	535.74	518.38	504.67	493.72	484.90
35000	685.02	651.03	625.03	604.77	588.78	576.00	565.71
36000	704.59	669.63	642.88	622.05	605.60	592.46	581.88
37000	724.16	688.23	660.74	639.33	622.42	608.92	598.04
38000	743.73	706.83	678.60	656.61	639.24	625.37	614.20
39000	763.31	725.43	696.46	673.89	656.07	641.83	630.37
40000	782.88	744.03	714.32	691.17	672.89	658.29	646.53
41000	802.45	762.63	732.17	708.45	689.71	674.75	662.69
42000	822.02	781.23	750.03	725.73	706.53	691.20	678.85
43000	841.59	799.83	767.89	743.01	723.35	707.66	695.02
44000	861.17	818.44	785.75	760.29	740.18	724.12	711.18
45000	880.74	837.04	803.60	777.57	757.00	740.58	727.34
46000	900.31	855.64	821.46	794.84	773.82	757.03	743.51
47000	919.88	874.24	839.32	812.12	790.64	773.49	759.67
48000	939.45	892.84	857.18	829.40	807.47	789.95	775.83
49000	959.02	911.44	875.04	846.68	824.29	806.40	792.00
50000	978.60	930.04	892.89	863.96	841.11	822.86	808.16
51000	998.17	948.64	910.75	881.24	857.93	839.32	824.32
52000	1017.74	967.24	928.61	898.52	874.75	855.78	840.49
53000	1037.31	985.84	946.47	915.80	891.58	872.23	856.65
54000	1056.88	1004.44	964.33	933.08	908.40	888.69	872.81
55000	1076.46	1023.04	982.18	950.36	925.22	905.15	888.98
56000	1096.03	1041.65	1000.04	967.64	942.04	921.60	905.14
57000	1115.60	1060.25	1017.90	984.92	958.87	938.06	921.30
58000	1135.17	1078.85	1035.76	1002.20	975.69	954.52	937.47
59000	1154.71	1097.45	1053.62	1019.47	992.51	970.98	953.63
60000	1174.32	1116.05	1071.47	1036.75	1009.33	987.43	969.79
65000	1272.18	1209.05	1160.76	1123.15	1093.44	1069.72	1050.61
70000	1370.04	1302.06	1250.05	1209.55	1177.55	1152.01	1131.42
75000	1467.89	1395.06	1339.34	1295.94	1261.67	1234.29	1212.24
80000	1565.75	1488.06	1428.63	1382.34	1345.78	1316.58	1293.06
85000	1663.61	1581.07	1517.92	1468.73	1429.89	1398.86	1373.87
90000	1761.47	1674.07	1007.21	1555.13	1514.00	1481.15	1454.69
95000	1859.33	1767.08	1696.50	1641.53	1598.11	1563.44	1535.51
100000	1957.19	1860.08	1785.79	1727.92	1682.22	1645.72	1616.32
105000	2055.05	1953.09	1875.08	1814.32	1766.33	1728.01	1697.14
110000	2152.91	2046.09	1964.37	1900.72	1850.44	1810.30	1777.95
120000	2348.63	2232.10	2142.95	2073.51	2018.66	1974.87	1939.59
130000	2544.35	2418.11	2321.52	2246.30	2186.89	2139.44	2101.22
140000	2740.07	2604.11	2500.10	2419.09	2355.11	2304.01	2262.85
150000	2935.79	2790.12	2678.68	2591.88	2523.33	2468.58	2424.48
175000	3425.09	3255.14	3125.13	3023.87	2943.89	2880.02	2828.56
200000	3914.39	3720.16	3571.58	3455.85	3364.44	3291.45	3232.64
225000	4403.68	4185.18	4018.02	3887.83	3785.00	3702.88	3636.72
250000	4892.98	4650.20	4464.47	4319.81	4205.55	4114.31	4040.80

17¾% Monthly Payments

necessary to amortize a loan

AMOUNT	15 YEARS	16 YEARS	17 YEARS	18 YEARS	19 YEARS	20 YEARS	21 YEARS
100	1.59	1.57	1.56	1.54	1.53	1.52	1.52
200	3.18	3.15	3.11	3.09	3.07	3.05	3.03
500	7.96	7.87	7.79	7.72	7.67	7.62	7.58
1000	15.92	15.73	15.57	15.44	15.33	15.24	15.17
2000	31.85	31.46	31.14	30.88	30.66	30.48	30.33
5000	79.62	78.65	77.85	77.20	76.65	76.20	75.83
6000	95.55	94.38	93.42	92.63	91.98	91.45	91.00
7000	111.47	110.11	108.99	108.07	107.32	106.69	106.17
8000	127.40	125.84	124.56	123.51	122.65	121.93	121.33
9000	143.32	141.57	140.13	138.95	137.98	137.17	136.50
10000	159.25	157.30	155.70	154.39	153.31	152.41	151.67
15000	238.87	235.95	233.56	231.59	229.96	228.61	227.50
20000	318.49	314.60	311.41	308.78	306.61	304.82	303.33
25000	398.12	393.25	389.26	385.98	383.27	381.02	379.16
30000	477.74	471.90	467.11	463.17	459.92	457.23	455.00
35000	557.36	550.55	544.97	540.37	536.58	533.43	530.83
36000	573.29	566.28	560.54	555.81	551.91	548.68	546.00
37000	589.21	582.01	576.11	571.25	567.24	563.92	561.16
38000	605.14	597.74	591.68	586.69	582.57	579.16	576.33
39000	621.06	613.47	607.25	602.13	597.90	594.40	591.50
40000	636.99	629.20	622.82	617.57	613.23	609.64	606.66
41000	652.91	644.93	638.39	633.00	628.56	624.88	621.83
42000	668.84	660.66	653.96	648.44	643.89	640.12	637.00
43000	684.76	676.39	669.53	663.88	659.22	655.36	652.16
44000	700.69	692.12	685.10	679.32	674.55	670.60	667.33
45000	716.61	707.85	700.67	694.76	689.88	685.84	682.50
46000	732.53	723.58	716.24	710.20	705.21	701.09	697.66
47000	748.46	739.31	731.81	725.64	720.54	716.33	712.83
48000	764.38	755.04	747.38	741.08	735.87	731.57	727.99
49000	780.31	770.77	762.95	756.52	751.21	746.81	743.16
50000	796.23	786.50	778.52	771.96	766.54	762.05	758.33
51000	812.16	802.23	794.09	787.40	781.87	777.29	773.49
52000	828.08	817.96	809.66	802.83	797.20	792.53	788.66
53000	844.01	833.69	825.23	818.27	812.53	807.77	803.83
54000	859.93	849.42	840.80	833.71	827.86	823.01	818.99
55000	875.86	865.15	856.37	849.15	843.19	838.25	834.16
56000	891.78	880.88	871.95	864.59	858.52	853.50	849.33
57000	907.71	896.61	887.52	880.03	873.85	868.74	864.49
58000	923.63	912.34	903.09	895.47	889.18	883.98	879.66
59000	939.56	928.07	918.66	910.91	904.51	899.22	894.83
60000	955.48	943.80	934.23	926.35	919.84	914.46	909.99
65000	1035.10	1022.45	1012.08	1003.54	996.50	990.66	985.83
70000	1114.73	1101.10	1089.93	1080.74	1073.15	1066.87	1061.66
75000	1194.35	1179.75	1167.78	1157.93	1149.80	1143.07	1137.49
80000	1273.97	1258.40	1245.64	1235.13	1226.46	1219.28	1213.32
85000	1353.60	1337.05	1323.49	1312.33	1303.11	1295.48	1289.16
90000	1433.22	1415.70	1401.34	1389.52	1379.76	1371.69	1364.99
95000	1512.84	1494.35	1479.19	1466.72	1456.42	1447.89	1440.82
100000	1592.47	1573.00	1557.04	1543.91	1533.07	1524.10	1516.66
105000	1672.09	1651.65	1634.90	1621.11	1609.73	1600.30	1592.49
110000	1751.71	1730.30	1712.75	1698.30	1686.38	1676.51	1668.32
120000	1910.96	1887.60	1868.45	1852.70	1839.69	1828.92	1819.99
130000	2070.21	2044.90	2024.16	2007.09	1992.99	1981.33	1971.65
140000	2229.45	2202.20	2179.86	2161.48	2146.30	2133.74	2123.32
150000	2388.70	2359.50	2335.57	2315.87	2299.61	2286.15	2274.98
175000	2786.82	2752.75	2724.83	2701.85	2682.88	2667.17	2654.15
200000	3184.93	3146.00	3114.09	3087.83	3066.14	3048.20	3033.31
225000	3583.05	3539.25	3503.35	3473.80	3449.41	3429.22	3412.48
250000	3981.17	3932.50	3892.61	3859.78	3832.68	3810.25	3791.64

Monthly Payments

necessary to amortize a loan

17¾%

AMOUNT	22 YEARS	23 YEARS	24 YEARS	25 YEARS	30 YEARS	35 YEARS	40 YEARS
100	1.51	1.51	1.50	1.50	1.49	1.48	1.48
200	3.02	3.01	3.00	2.99	2.97	2.96	2.96
500	7.55	7.53	7.51	7.49	7.43	7.41	7.40
1000	15.10	15.05	15.01	14.97	14.87	14.82	14.80
2000	30.21	30.11	30.02	29.95	29.73	29.65	29.61
5000	75.52	75.27	75.05	74.87	74.33	74.11	74.02
6000	90.63	90.32	90.06	89.85	89.20	88.94	88.83
7000	105.73	105.37	105.07	104.82	104.07	103.76	103.63
8000	120.84	120.43	120.08	119.80	118.94	118.58	118.44
9000	135.94	135.48	135.09	134.77	133.80	133.40	133.24
10000	151.05	150.53	150.10	149.75	148.67	148.23	148.05
15000	226.57	225.80	225.16	224.62	223.00	222.34	222.07
20000	302.09	301.06	300.21	299.49	297.34	296.46	296.09
25000	377.62	376.33	375.26	374.36	371.67	370.57	370.11
30000	453.14	451.60	450.31	449.24	446.01	444.68	444.14
35000	528.67	526.86	525.36	524.11	520.34	518.80	518.16
36000	543.77	541.92	540.37	539.09	535.21	533.62	532.96
37000	558.87	556.97	555.38	554.06	550.08	548.44	547.77
38000	573.98	572.02	570.39	569.03	564.94	563.26	562.57
39000	589.08	587.08	585.40	584.01	579.81	578.09	577.38
40000	604.19	602.13	600.41	598.98	594.68	592.91	592.18
41000	619.29	617.18	615.42	613.96	609.54	607.73	606.99
42000	634.40	632.24	630.44	628.93	624.41	622.56	621.79
43000	649.50	647.29	645.45	643.91	639.28	637.38	636.59
44000	664.61	662.34	660.46	658.88	654.14	652.20	651.40
45000	679.71	677.40	675.47	673.86	669.01	667.02	666.20
46000	694.82	692.45	690.48	688.83	683.88	681.85	681.01
47000	709.92	707.50	705.49	703.81	698.75	696.67	695.81
48000	725.03	722.56	720.50	718.78	713.61	711.49	710.62
49000	740.13	737.61	735.51	733.76	728.48	726.32	725.42
50000	755.24	752.66	750.52	748.73	743.35	741.14	740.23
51000	770.34	767.72	765.53	763.70	758.21	755.96	755.03
52000	785.45	782.77	780.54	778.68	773.08	770.78	769.84
53000	800.55	797.82	795.55	793.65	787.95	785.61	784.64
54000	815.65	812.88	810.56	808.63	802.81	800.43	799.44
55000	830.76	827.93	825.57	823.60	817.68	815.25	814.25
56000	845.86	842.98	840.58	838.58	832.55	830.07	829.05
57000	860.97	858.04	855.59	853.55	847.41	844.90	843.86
58000	876.07	873.09	870.60	868.53	862.28	859.72	858.66
59000	891.18	888.14	885.61	883.50	877.15	874.54	873.47
60000	906.28	903.19	900.62	898.48	892.02	889.37	888.27
65000	981.81	978.46	975.67	973.35	966.35	963.48	962.29
70000	1057.33	1053.73	1050.73	1048.22	1040.68	1037.59	1036.32
75000	1132.85	1128.99	1125.70	1123.09	1115.02	1111.71	1110.34
80000	1208.38	1204.26	1200.83	1197.97	1189.35	1185.82	1184.36
85000	1283.90	1279.53	1275.88	1272.84	1263.69	1259.93	1258.39
90000	1359.42	1354.79	1350.93	1347.71	1338.02	1334.05	1332.41
95000	1434.95	1430.06	1425.98	1422.59	1412.36	1408.16	1406.43
100000	1510.47	1505.32	1501.04	1497.46	1486.69	1482.28	1480.45
105000	1586.00	1580.59	1576.09	1572.33	1561.03	1556.39	1554.48
110000	1661.52	1655.86	1651.14	1647.21	1635.36	1630.50	1628.50
120000	1812.57	1806.39	1801.24	1796.95	1784.03	1778.73	1776.54
130000	1963.61	1956.92	1951.35	1946.70	1932.70	1926.96	1924.59
140000	2114.66	2107.45	2101.45	2096.44	2081.37	2075.19	2072.63
150000	2265.71	2257.99	2251.55	2246.19	2230.04	2223.41	2220.68
175000	2643.33	2634.32	2626.81	2620.55	2601.71	2593.98	2590.79
200000	3020.94	3010.65	3002.07	2994.92	2973.38	2964.55	2960.91
225000	3398.56	3386.98	3377.33	3369.28	3345.06	3335.12	3331.02
250000	3776.18	3763.31	3752.59	3743.65	3716.73	3705.69	3701.13

18% Monthly Payments

necessary to amortize a loan

AMOUNT	1 YEAR	2 YEARS	3 YEARS	4 YEARS	5 YEARS	6 YEARS	7 YEARS
100	9.17	4.99	3.62	2.94	2.54	2.28	2.10
200	18.34	9.98	7.23	5.87	5.08	4.56	4.20
500	45.84	24.96	18.08	14.69	12.70	11.40	10.51
1000	91.68	49.92	36.15	29.37	25.39	22.81	21.02
2000	183.36	99.85	72.30	58.75	50.79	45.62	42.04
5000	458.40	249.62	180.76	146.87	126.97	114.04	105.09
6000	550.08	299.54	216.91	176.25	152.36	136.85	126.11
7000	641.76	349.47	253.07	205.62	177.75	159.65	147.12
8000	733.44	399.39	289.22	235.00	203.15	182.46	168.14
9000	825.12	449.32	325.37	264.37	228.54	205.27	189.16
10000	916.80	499.24	361.52	293.75	253.93	228.08	210.18
15000	1375.20	748.86	542.29	440.62	380.90	342.12	315.27
20000	1833.60	998.48	723.05	587.50	507.87	456.16	420.36
25000	2292.00	1248.10	903.81	734.37	634.84	570.19	525.45
30000	2750.40	1497.72	1084.57	881.25	761.80	684.23	630.54
35000	3208.80	1747.34	1265.33	1028.12	888.77	798.27	735.62
36000	3300.48	1797.27	1301.49	1057.50	914.16	821.08	756.64
37000	3392.16	1847.19	1337.64	1086.87	939.56	843.89	777.66
38000	3483.84	1897.12	1373.79	1116.25	964.95	866.70	798.68
39000	3575.52	1947.04	1409.94	1145.62	990.34	889.50	819.70
40000	3667.20	1996.96	1446.10	1175.00	1015.74	912.31	840.71
41000	3758.88	2046.89	1482.25	1204.37	1041.13	935.12	861.73
42000	3850.56	2096.81	1518.40	1233.75	1066.52	957.93	882.75
43000	3942.24	2146.74	1554.55	1263.12	1091.92	980.74	903.77
44000	4033.92	2196.66	1590.71	1292.50	1117.31	1003.54	924.78
45000	4125.60	2246.58	1626.86	1321.87	1142.70	1026.35	945.80
46000	4217.28	2296.51	1663.01	1351.25	1168.10	1049.16	966.82
47000	4308.96	2346.43	1699.16	1380.62	1193.49	1071.97	987.84
48000	4400.64	2396.36	1735.31	1410.00	1218.88	1094.77	1008.86
49000	4492.32	2446.28	1771.47	1439.37	1244.28	1117.58	1029.87
50000	4584.00	2496.21	1807.62	1468.75	1269.67	1140.39	1050.89
51000	4675.68	2546.13	1843.77	1498.12	1295.06	1163.20	1071.91
52000	4767.36	2596.06	1879.92	1527.50	1320.46	1186.01	1092.93
53000	4859.04	2645.98	1916.08	1556.87	1345.85	1208.81	1113.95
54000	4950.72	2695.90	1952.23	1586.25	1371.25	1231.62	1134.96
55000	5042.40	2745.83	1988.38	1615.62	1396.64	1254.43	1155.98
56000	5134.08	2795.75	2024.53	1645.00	1422.03	1277.24	1177.00
57000	5225.76	2845.67	2060.69	1674.37	1447.43	1300.04	1198.02
58000	5317.44	2895.60	2096.84	1703.75	1472.82	1322.85	1219.03
59000	5409.12	2945.52	2132.99	1733.12	1498.21	1345.66	1240.05
60000	5500.80	2995.45	2169.14	1762.50	1523.61	1368.47	1261.07
65000	5959.20	3245.07	2349.91	1909.37	1650.57	1482.51	1366.16
70000	6417.60	3494.69	2530.67	2056.25	1777.54	1596.55	1471.25
75000	6876.00	3744.31	2711.43	2203.12	1904.51	1710.58	1576.34
80000	7334.40	3993.93	2892.19	2350.00	2031.47	1824.62	1681.43
85000	7792.80	4243.55	3072.95	2496.87	2158.44	1938.66	1786.52
90000	8251.20	4493.17	3253.72	2643.75	2285.41	2052.70	1891.61
95000	8709.60	4742.79	3434.48	2790.62	2412.38	2166.74	1996.69
100000	9168.00	4992.41	3615.24	2937.50	2539.34	2280.78	2101.78
105000	9626.40	5242.03	3796.00	3084.37	2666.31	2394.82	2206.87
110000	10084.80	5491.65	3976.76	3231.25	2793.28	2508.86	2311.96
120000	11001.60	5990.89	4338.29	3525.00	3047.21	2736.93	2522.14
130000	11918.40	6490.13	4699.81	3818.75	3301.15	2965.01	2732.32
140000	12835.20	6989.37	5061.34	4112.50	3555.08	3193.09	2942.50
150000	13752.00	7488.62	5422.86	4406.25	3809.01	3421.17	3152.68
175000	16044.00	8736.72	6326.67	5140.62	4443.85	3991.36	3678.12
200000	18336.00	9984.82	7230.48	5875.00	5078.69	4561.56	4203.57
225000	20628.00	11232.92	8134.29	6609.37	5713.52	5131.75	4729.01
250000	22920.00	12481.03	9038.10	7343.75	6348.36	5701.95	5254.46

Monthly Payments 18%

necessary to amortize a loan

AMOUNT	8 YEARS	9 YEARS	10 YEARS	11 YEARS	12 YEARS	13 YEARS	14 YEARS
100	1.97	1.88	1.80	1.74	1.70	1.66	1.63
200	3.94	3.75	3.60	3.49	3.40	3.33	3.27
500	9.86	9.38	9.01	8.72	8.50	8.32	8.17
1000	19.72	18.76	18.02	17.44	16.99	16.63	16.34
2000	39.45	37.51	36.04	34.89	33.98	33.26	32.68
5000	98.62	93.78	90.09	87.22	84.96	83.15	81.70
6000	118.34	112.54	108.11	104.67	101.95	99.78	98.04
7000	138.06	131.30	126.13	122.11	118.94	116.41	114.38
8000	157.79	150.06	144.15	139.55	135.93	133.04	130.72
9000	177.51	168.81	162.17	157.00	152.92	149.67	147.06
10000	197.23	187.57	180.19	174.44	169.91	166.30	163.40
15000	295.85	281.35	270.28	261.66	254.87	249.45	245.09
20000	394.46	375.14	360.37	348.88	339.82	332.60	326.79
25000	493.08	468.92	450.46	436.10	424.78	415.75	408.49
30000	591.70	562.71	540.56	523.33	509.74	498.90	490.19
35000	690.31	656.49	630.65	610.55	594.69	582.05	571.88
36000	710.04	675.25	648.67	627.99	611.68	598.68	588.22
37000	729.76	694.00	666.69	645.43	628.67	615.31	604.56
38000	749.48	712.76	684.70	662.88	645.67	631.94	620.90
39000	769.21	731.52	702.72	680.32	662.66	648.57	637.24
40000	788.93	750.28	720.74	697.77	679.65	665.20	653.58
41000	808.65	769.03	738.76	715.21	696.64	681.83	669.92
42000	828.37	787.79	756.78	732.66	713.63	698.46	686.26
43000	848.10	806.55	774.80	750.10	730.62	715.09	702.60
44000	867.82	825.30	792.81	767.54	747.61	731.72	718.94
45000	887.54	844.06	810.83	784.99	764.60	748.35	735.28
46000	907.27	862.82	828.85	802.43	781.59	764.98	751.62
47000	926.99	881.57	846.87	819.88	798.59	781.61	767.96
48000	946.71	900.33	864.89	837.32	815.58	798.24	784.30
49000	966.44	919.09	882.91	854.76	832.57	814.87	800.64
50000	986.16	937.84	900.93	872.21	849.56	831.50	816.98
51000	1005.88	956.60	918.94	889.65	866.55	848.13	833.31
52000	1025.61	975.36	936.96	907.10	883.54	864.76	849.65
53000	1045.33	994.12	954.98	924.54	900.53	881.39	865.99
54000	1065.05	1012.87	973.00	941.99	917.52	898.02	882.33
55000	1084.78	1031.63	991.02	959.43	934.52	914.65	898.67
56000	1104.50	1050.39	1009.04	976.87	951.51	931.28	915.01
57000	1124.22	1069.14	1027.06	994.32	968.50	947.91	931.35
58000	1143.95	1087.90	1045.07	1011.76	985.49	964.54	947.69
59000	1163.67	1106.66	1063.09	1029.21	1002.48	981.17	964.03
60000	1183.39	1125.41	1081.11	1046.65	1019.47	997.80	980.37
65000	1282.01	1219.20	1171.20	1133.87	1104.43	1080.95	1062.07
70000	1380.02	1312.98	1261.30	1221.09	1189.38	1164.10	1143.77
75000	1479.24	1406.77	1351.39	1308.31	1274.34	1247.25	1225.46
80000	1577.86	1500.55	1441.48	1395.53	1359.30	1330.40	1307.16
85000	1676.47	1594.34	1531.57	1482.76	1444.25	1413.55	1388.86
90000	1775.09	1688.12	1621.67	1569.98	1529.21	1496.70	1470.56
95000	1873.71	1781.90	1711.76	1657.20	1614.16	1579.85	1552.25
100000	1972.32	1875.69	1801.85	1744.42	1699.12	1663.00	1633.95
105000	2070.94	1969.47	1891.94	1831.64	1784.08	1746.15	1715.65
110000	2169.55	2063.26	1982.04	1918.86	1869.03	1829.30	1797.35
120000	2366.79	2250.83	2162.22	2093.30	2038.94	1995.60	1960.74
130000	2564.02	2438.40	2342.41	2267.74	2208.86	2161.90	2124.14
140000	2761.25	2625.96	2522.59	2442.19	2378.77	2328.20	2287.53
150000	2958.48	2813.53	2702.78	2616.63	2548.68	2494.50	2450.93
175000	3451.56	3282.46	3153.24	3052.73	2973.46	2910.25	2859.41
200000	3944.64	3751.38	3603.70	3488.84	3398.24	3326.00	3267.90
225000	4437.72	4220.30	4054.17	3924.94	3823.02	3741.75	3676.39
250000	4930.80	4689.22	4504.63	4361.04	4247.80	4157.50	4084.88

18%

Monthly Payments

necessary to amortize a loan

AMOUNT	15 YEARS	16 YEARS	17 YEARS	18 YEARS	19 YEARS	20 YEARS	21 YEARS
100	1.61	1.59	1.58	1.56	1.55	1.54	1.54
200	3.22	3.18	3.15	3.13	3.10	3.09	3.07
500	8.05	7.96	7.88	7.81	7.76	7.72	7.68
1000	16.10	15.91	15.76	15.63	15.52	15.43	15.36
2000	32.21	31.83	31.51	31.25	31.04	30.87	30.72
5000	80.52	79.56	78.78	78.13	77.60	77.17	76.80
6000	96.63	95.48	94.53	93.76	93.12	92.60	92.16
7000	112.73	111.39	110.29	109.39	108.65	108.03	107.52
8000	128.83	127.30	126.05	125.02	124.17	123.46	122.88
9000	144.94	143.21	141.80	140.64	139.69	138.90	138.24
10000	161.04	159.13	157.56	156.27	155.21	154.33	153.61
15000	241.56	238.69	236.34	234.40	232.81	231.50	230.41
20000	322.08	318.25	315.11	312.54	310.42	308.66	307.21
25000	402.61	397.81	393.89	390.67	388.02	385.83	384.01
30000	483.13	477.38	472.67	468.81	465.62	462.99	460.82
35000	563.65	556.94	551.45	546.94	543.23	540.16	537.62
36000	579.75	572.85	567.21	562.57	558.75	555.59	552.98
37000	595.86	588.76	582.96	578.20	574.27	571.03	568.34
38000	611.96	604.68	598.72	593.82	589.79	586.46	583.70
39000	628.06	620.59	614.47	609.45	605.31	601.89	599.06
40000	644.17	636.50	630.23	625.08	620.83	617.32	614.42
41000	660.27	652.41	645.98	640.70	636.35	632.76	629.78
42000	676.38	668.33	661.74	656.33	651.87	648.19	645.14
43000	692.48	684.24	677.50	671.96	667.39	663.62	660.50
44000	708.59	700.15	693.25	687.58	682.91	679.06	675.86
45000	724.69	716.07	709.01	703.21	698.44	694.49	691.22
46000	740.79	731.98	724.76	718.84	713.96	709.92	706.59
47000	756.90	747.89	740.52	734.46	729.48	725.36	721.95
48000	773.00	763.80	756.27	750.09	745.00	740.79	737.31
49000	789.11	779.72	772.03	765.72	760.52	756.22	752.67
50000	805.21	795.63	787.79	781.35	776.04	771.66	768.03
51000	821.31	811.54	803.54	796.97	791.56	787.09	783.39
52000	837.42	827.45	819.30	812.60	807.08	802.52	798.75
53000	853.52	843.37	835.05	828.23	822.60	817.96	814.11
54000	869.63	859.28	850.81	843.85	838.12	833.39	829.47
55000	885.73	875.19	866.57	859.48	853.64	848.82	844.83
56000	901.84	891.10	882.32	875.11	869.16	864.25	860.19
57000	917.94	907.02	898.08	890.73	884.68	879.69	875.55
58000	934.04	922.93	913.83	906.36	900.21	895.12	890.91
59000	950.15	938.84	929.59	921.99	915.73	910.55	906.27
60000	966.25	954.75	945.34	937.61	931.25	925.99	921.63
65000	1046.77	1034.32	1024.12	1015.75	1008.85	1003.15	998.44
70000	1127.29	1113.88	1102.90	1093.88	1086.45	1080.32	1075.24
75000	1207.82	1193.44	1181.68	1172.02	1164.06	1157.40	1152.04
80000	1288.34	1273.00	1260.46	1250.15	1241.66	1234.65	1228.84
85000	1368.86	1352.57	1339.24	1328.29	1319.27	1311.81	1305.65
90000	1449.38	1432.13	1418.02	1406.42	1396.87	1388.98	1382.45
95000	1529.90	1511.69	1496.79	1484.56	1474.47	1466.15	1459.25
100000	1610.42	1591.26	1575.57	1562.69	1552.08	1543.31	1536.05
105000	1690.94	1670.82	1654.35	1640.83	1629.68	1620.48	1612.86
110000	1771.46	1750.38	1733.13	1718.96	1707.29	1697.64	1689.66
120000	1932.51	1909.51	1890.69	1875.23	1862.49	1851.97	1843.27
130000	2093.55	2068.63	2048.24	2031.50	2017.70	2006.30	1996.87
140000	2254.59	2227.76	2205.80	2187.77	2172.91	2160.64	2150.48
150000	2415.63	2386.88	2363.36	2344.04	2328.12	2314.97	2304.08
175000	2818.24	2784.70	2757.25	2734.71	2716.14	2700.80	2688.10
200000	3220.84	3182.51	3151.15	3125.38	3104.16	3086.62	3072.11
225000	3623.45	3580.33	3545.04	3516.06	3492.18	3472.45	3456.12
250000	4026.05	3978.14	3938.93	3906.73	3880.20	3858.28	3840.14

Monthly Payments — 18%

necessary to amortize a loan

AMOUNT	22 YEARS	23 YEARS	24 YEARS	25 YEARS	30 YEARS	35 YEARS	40 YEARS
100	1.53	1.53	1.52	1.52	1.51	1.50	1.50
200	3.06	3.05	3.04	3.03	3.01	3.01	3.00
500	7.65	7.63	7.60	7.59	7.54	7.51	7.51
1000	15.30	15.25	15.21	15.17	15.07	15.03	15.01
2000	30.60	30.50	30.42	30.35	30.14	30.06	30.02
5000	76.50	76.25	76.04	75.87	75.35	75.14	75.06
6000	91.80	91.50	91.25	91.05	90.43	90.17	90.07
7000	107.10	106.75	106.46	106.22	105.50	105.20	105.08
8000	122.40	122.00	121.67	121.39	120.57	120.23	120.09
9000	137.70	137.25	136.88	136.57	135.64	135.26	135.11
10000	153.00	152.50	152.09	151.74	150.71	150.29	150.12
15000	229.51	228.76	228.13	227.61	226.06	225.43	225.18
20000	306.01	305.01	304.18	303.49	301.42	300.58	300.24
25000	382.51	381.26	380.22	379.36	376.77	375.72	375.30
30000	459.01	457.51	456.27	455.23	452.13	450.87	450.35
35000	535.51	533.76	532.31	531.10	527.48	526.01	525.41
36000	550.81	549.01	547.52	546.27	542.55	541.04	540.43
37000	566.11	564.27	562.73	561.45	557.62	556.07	555.44
38000	581.41	579.52	577.94	576.62	572.69	571.10	570.45
39000	596.71	594.77	593.15	591.80	587.76	586.13	585.46
40000	612.02	610.02	608.35	606.97	602.83	601.16	600.47
41000	627.32	625.27	623.56	622.15	617.91	616.19	615.48
42000	642.62	640.52	638.77	637.32	632.98	631.21	630.50
43000	657.92	655.77	653.98	652.49	648.05	646.24	645.51
44000	673.22	671.02	669.19	667.67	663.12	661.27	660.52
45000	688.52	686.27	684.40	682.84	678.19	676.30	675.53
46000	703.82	701.52	699.61	698.02	693.26	691.33	690.54
47000	719.12	716.77	714.82	713.19	708.33	706.36	705.56
48000	734.42	732.02	730.03	728.37	723.40	721.39	720.57
49000	749.72	747.27	745.23	743.54	738.47	736.42	735.58
50000	765.02	762.52	760.44	758.71	753.54	751.45	750.59
51000	780.32	777.77	775.65	773.89	768.61	766.47	765.60
52000	795.62	793.02	790.86	789.06	783.68	781.50	780.61
53000	810.92	808.27	806.07	804.24	798.76	796.53	795.63
54000	826.22	823.52	821.28	819.41	813.83	811.56	810.64
55000	841.52	838.77	836.49	834.59	828.90	826.59	825.65
56000	856.82	854.02	851.70	849.76	843.97	841.62	840.66
57000	872.12	869.27	866.91	864.94	859.04	856.65	855.67
58000	887.42	884.52	882.11	880.11	874.11	871.68	870.69
59000	902.72	899.77	897.32	895.28	889.18	886.71	885.70
60000	918.02	915.02	912.53	910.46	904.25	901.74	900.71
65000	994.52	991.28	988.58	986.33	979.61	976.88	975.77
70000	1071.03	1067.53	1064.62	1062.20	1054.96	1052.02	1050.83
75000	1147.53	1143.78	1140.67	1138.07	1130.31	1127.17	1125.80
80000	1224.03	1220.03	1216.71	1213.94	1205.67	1202.31	1200.95
85000	1300.53	1296.28	1292.75	1289.82	1281.02	1277.46	1276.00
90000	1377.03	1372.54	1368.80	1365.69	1356.38	1352.60	1351.06
95000	1453.54	1448.79	1444.84	1441.56	1431.73	1427.75	1426.12
100000	1530.04	1525.04	1520.89	1517.43	1507.09	1502.89	1501.18
105000	1606.54	1601.29	1596.93	1593.30	1582.44	1578.04	1576.24
110000	1683.04	1677.55	1672.98	1669.17	1657.79	1653.18	1651.30
120000	1836.05	1830.05	1825.06	1820.92	1808.50	1803.47	1801.42
130000	1989.05	1982.55	1977.15	1972.66	1959.21	1953.76	1951.54
140000	2142.05	2135.06	2129.24	2124.40	2109.92	2104.05	2101.66
150000	2295.06	2287.56	2281.33	2276.14	2260.63	2254.34	2251.77
175000	2677.57	2668.82	2661.55	2655.50	2637.40	2630.06	2627.07
200000	3060.08	3050.08	3041.77	3034.86	3014.17	3005.78	3002.36
225000	3442.58	3431.34	3422.00	3414.22	3390.94	3381.51	3377.66
250000	3825.09	3812.60	3802.22	3793.57	3767.71	3757.23	3752.96

18¼%

Monthly Payments

necessary to amortize a loan

AMOUNT	1 YEAR	2 YEARS	3 YEARS	4 YEARS	5 YEARS	6 YEARS	7 YEARS
100	9.18	5.00	3.63	2.95	2.55	2.29	2.12
200	18.36	10.01	7.26	5.90	5.11	4.59	4.23
500	45.90	25.02	18.14	14.75	12.76	11.47	10.58
1000	91.80	50.04	36.28	29.51	25.53	22.95	21.16
2000	183.60	100.09	72.56	59.01	51.06	45.90	42.33
5000	459.00	250.22	181.39	147.53	127.65	114.75	105.82
6000	550.79	300.27	217.67	177.03	153.18	137.70	126.99
7000	642.59	350.31	253.95	206.54	178.71	160.65	148.15
8000	734.39	400.36	290.22	236.05	204.24	183.59	169.32
9000	826.19	450.40	326.50	265.55	229.77	206.54	190.48
10000	917.99	500.45	362.78	295.06	255.30	229.49	211.65
15000	1376.99	750.67	544.17	442.59	382.94	344.24	317.47
20000	1835.98	1000.90	725.56	590.12	510.59	458.99	423.29
25000	2294.98	1251.12	906.95	737.64	638.24	573.73	529.12
30000	2753.97	1501.35	1088.34	885.17	765.89	688.48	634.94
35000	3212.97	1751.57	1269.73	1032.70	893.54	803.23	740.76
36000	3304.76	1801.62	1306.01	1062.21	919.07	826.18	761.93
37000	3396.56	1851.66	1342.28	1091.71	944.60	849.13	783.09
38000	3488.36	1901.71	1378.56	1121.22	970.13	872.08	804.26
39000	3580.16	1951.75	1414.84	1150.73	995.66	895.02	825.42
40000	3671.96	2001.80	1451.12	1180.23	1021.18	917.97	846.59
41000	3763.76	2051.84	1487.40	1209.74	1046.71	940.92	867.75
42000	3855.56	2101.89	1523.67	1239.24	1072.24	963.87	888.91
43000	3947.36	2151.93	1559.95	1268.75	1097.77	986.82	910.08
44000	4039.16	2201.98	1596.23	1298.26	1123.30	1009.77	931.24
45000	4130.96	2252.02	1632.51	1327.76	1148.83	1032.72	952.41
46000	4222.75	2302.07	1668.78	1357.27	1174.36	1055.67	973.57
47000	4314.55	2352.11	1705.06	1386.77	1199.89	1078.62	994.74
48000	4406.35	2402.16	1741.34	1416.28	1225.42	1101.57	1015.90
49000	4498.15	2452.20	1777.62	1445.78	1250.95	1124.52	1037.07
50000	4589.95	2502.25	1813.90	1475.29	1276.48	1147.47	1058.23
51000	4681.75	2552.29	1850.17	1504.80	1302.01	1170.42	1079.40
52000	4773.55	2602.34	1886.45	1534.30	1327.54	1193.37	1100.56
53000	4865.35	2652.38	1922.73	1563.81	1353.07	1216.32	1121.73
54000	4957.15	2702.43	1959.01	1593.31	1378.60	1239.26	1142.89
55000	5048.95	2752.47	1995.29	1622.82	1404.13	1262.21	1164.05
56000	5140.74	2802.52	2031.56	1652.32	1429.66	1285.16	1185.22
57000	5232.54	2852.56	2067.84	1681.83	1455.19	1308.11	1206.38
58000	5324.34	2902.61	2104.12	1711.34	1480.72	1331.06	1227.55
59000	5416.14	2952.65	2140.40	1740.84	1506.25	1354.01	1248.71
60000	5507.94	3002.70	2176.68	1770.35	1531.78	1376.96	1269.88
65000	5966.94	3252.92	2358.07	1917.88	1659.43	1491.71	1375.70
70000	6425.93	3503.15	2539.46	2065.41	1787.07	1606.45	1481.52
75000	6884.93	3753.37	2720.84	2212.93	1814.72	1721.20	1587.35
80000	7343.92	4003.60	2902.23	2360.46	2042.37	1835.95	1693.17
85000	7802.92	4253.82	3083.62	2507.99	2170.02	1950.69	1798.99
90000	8261.91	4504.05	3265.01	2655.52	2297.67	2065.44	1904.82
95000	8720.91	4754.27	3446.40	2803.05	2425.31	2180.19	2010.64
100000	9179.90	5004.50	3627.79	2950.58	2552.96	2294.93	2116.46
105000	9638.90	5254.72	3809.18	3098.11	2680.61	2409.68	2222.29
110000	10097.89	5504.95	3990.57	3245.64	2808.26	2524.43	2328.11
120000	11015.88	6005.40	4353.35	3540.70	3063.55	2753.92	2539.76
130000	11933.87	6505.85	4716.13	3835.75	3318.85	2983.42	2751.40
140000	12851.86	7006.30	5078.91	4130.81	3574.15	3212.91	2963.05
150000	13769.85	7506.75	5441.69	4425.87	3829.44	3442.40	3174.69
175000	16064.83	8757.87	6348.64	5163.51	4467.68	4016.14	3703.81
200000	18359.80	10009.00	7255.59	5901.16	5105.92	4589.87	4232.93
225000	20654.78	11260.12	8162.53	6638.80	5744.17	5163.60	4762.04
250000	22949.75	12511.25	9069.48	7376.45	6382.41	5737.34	5291.16

Monthly Payments **18¼%**

necessary to amortize a loan

AMOUNT	8 YEARS	9 YEARS	10 YEARS	11 YEARS	12 YEARS	13 YEARS	14 YEARS
100	1.99	1.89	1.82	1.76	1.72	1.68	1.65
200	3.98	3.78	3.64	3.52	3.43	3.36	3.30
500	9.94	9.46	9.09	8.80	8.58	8.40	8.26
1000	19.88	18.91	18.18	17.61	17.16	16.80	16.52
2000	39.75	37.83	36.36	35.22	34.32	33.61	33.03
5000	99.38	94.57	90.90	88.05	85.80	84.02	82.58
6000	119.25	113.48	109.08	105.66	102.97	100.82	99.10
7000	139.13	132.39	127.26	123.27	120.13	117.62	115.62
8000	159.00	151.31	145.44	140.88	137.29	134.43	132.13
9000	178.88	170.22	163.62	158.49	154.45	151.23	148.65
10000	198.75	189.14	181.80	176.10	171.61	168.03	165.16
15000	298.13	283.70	272.70	264.15	257.41	252.05	247.75
20000	397.50	378.27	363.60	352.20	343.22	336.07	330.33
25000	496.88	472.84	454.49	440.24	429.02	420.09	412.91
30000	596.25	567.41	545.39	528.29	514.83	504.10	495.49
35000	695.63	661.97	636.29	616.34	600.63	588.12	578.08
36000	715.50	680.89	654.47	633.95	617.79	604.92	594.59
37000	735.38	699.80	672.65	651.56	634.95	621.73	611.11
38000	755.25	718.72	690.83	669.17	652.11	638.53	627.63
39000	775.13	737.63	709.01	686.78	669.27	655.33	644.14
40000	795.00	756.54	727.19	704.39	686.43	672.14	660.66
41000	814.88	775.46	745.37	722.00	703.59	688.94	677.17
42000	834.75	794.37	763.55	739.61	720.76	705.74	693.69
43000	854.63	813.28	781.73	757.22	737.92	722.55	710.21
44000	874.50	832.20	799.91	774.83	755.08	739.35	726.72
45000	894.38	851.11	818.09	792.44	772.24	756.16	743.24
46000	914.25	870.02	836.27	810.05	789.40	772.96	759.76
47000	934.13	888.94	854.45	827.66	806.56	789.76	776.27
48000	954.00	907.85	872.63	845.27	823.72	806.57	792.79
49000	973.88	926.76	890.81	862.88	840.88	823.37	809.31
50000	993.75	945.68	908.99	880.49	858.04	840.17	825.82
51000	1013.63	964.59	927.17	898.10	875.20	856.98	842.34
52000	1033.50	983.50	945.35	915.71	892.36	873.78	858.86
53000	1053.38	1002.42	963.53	933.32	909.52	890.58	875.37
54000	1073.25	1021.33	981.71	950.93	926.69	907.39	891.89
55000	1093.13	1040.25	999.89	968.54	943.85	924.19	908.40
56000	1113.00	1059.16	1018.07	986.15	961.01	940.99	924.92
57000	1132.88	1078.07	1036.25	1003.76	978.17	957.80	941.44
58000	1152.75	1096.99	1054.43	1021.37	995.33	974.60	957.95
59000	1172.63	1115.90	1072.61	1038.98	1012.49	991.40	974.47
60000	1192.50	1134.81	1090.79	1056.59	1029.65	1008.21	990.99
65000	1291.88	1229.38	1181.69	1144.63	1115.45	1092.22	1073.57
70000	1391.25	1323.95	1272.58	1232.68	1201.26	1176.24	1156.15
75000	1490.63	1418.52	1363.48	1320.73	1287.06	1260.26	1238.73
80000	1590.00	1513.08	1454.38	1408.78	1372.87	1344.28	1321.32
85000	1689.38	1607.65	1545.28	1496.83	1458.67	1428.29	1403.90
90000	1788.75	1702.22	1636.18	1584.88	1544.48	1512.31	1486.48
95000	1888.13	1796.79	1727.08	1672.93	1630.28	1596.33	1569.06
100000	1987.51	1891.36	1817.98	1760.98	1716.08	1680.34	1651.65
105000	2086.88	1985.92	1908.88	1849.03	1801.89	1764.36	1734.23
110000	2186.26	2080.49	1999.78	1937.07	1887.69	1848.38	1816.81
120000	2385.01	2269.63	2181.57	2113.17	2059.30	2016.41	1981.97
130000	2583.76	2458.76	2363.37	2289.27	2230.91	2184.45	2147.14
140000	2782.51	2647.90	2545.17	2465.37	2402.52	2352.48	2312.30
150000	2981.26	2837.03	2726.97	2641.47	2574.13	2520.52	2477.47
175000	3478.13	3309.87	3181.46	3081.71	3003.15	2940.60	2890.38
200000	3975.01	3782.71	3635.96	3521.95	3432.17	3360.69	3303.29
225000	4471.89	4255.55	4090.45	3962.20	3861.19	3780.78	3716.20
250000	4968.76	4728.39	4544.94	4402.44	4290.21	4200.86	4129.11

18¼%

Monthly Payments
necessary to amortize a loan

AMOUNT	15 YEARS	16 YEARS	17 YEARS	18 YEARS	19 YEARS	20 YEARS	21 YEARS
100	1.63	1.61	1.59	1.58	1.57	1.56	1.56
200	3.26	3.22	3.19	3.16	3.14	3.13	3.11
500	8.14	8.05	7.97	7.91	7.86	7.81	7.78
1000	16.28	16.10	15.94	15.82	15.71	15.63	15.56
2000	32.57	32.19	31.88	31.63	31.42	31.25	31.11
5000	81.42	80.48	79.71	79.08	78.56	78.13	77.78
6000	97.71	96.57	95.65	94.89	94.27	93.75	93.33
7000	113.99	112.67	111.59	110.71	109.98	109.38	108.89
8000	130.28	128.77	127.53	126.52	125.69	125.01	124.44
9000	146.56	144.86	143.47	142.34	141.40	140.63	140.00
10000	162.84	160.96	159.42	158.15	157.11	156.26	155.55
15000	244.27	241.44	239.12	237.23	235.67	234.39	233.33
20000	325.69	321.91	318.83	316.31	314.23	312.52	311.10
25000	407.11	402.39	398.54	395.38	392.79	390.64	388.88
30000	488.53	482.87	478.25	474.46	471.34	468.77	466.65
35000	569.95	563.35	557.96	553.54	549.90	546.90	544.43
36000	586.24	579.45	573.90	569.35	565.61	562.53	559.98
37000	602.52	595.54	589.84	585.17	581.32	578.15	575.54
38000	618.81	611.64	605.78	600.98	597.03	593.78	591.09
39000	635.09	627.73	621.72	616.80	612.75	609.41	606.65
40000	651.38	643.83	637.67	632.61	628.46	625.03	622.20
41000	667.66	659.92	653.61	648.43	644.17	640.66	637.76
42000	683.94	676.02	669.55	664.24	659.88	656.28	653.31
43000	700.23	692.12	685.49	680.06	675.59	671.91	668.87
44000	716.51	708.21	701.43	695.87	691.30	687.53	684.42
45000	732.80	724.31	717.37	711.69	707.01	703.16	699.98
46000	749.08	740.40	733.31	727.50	722.72	718.79	715.53
47000	765.37	756.50	749.26	743.32	738.44	734.41	731.09
48000	781.65	772.59	765.20	759.13	754.15	750.04	746.64
49000	797.94	788.69	781.14	774.95	769.86	765.66	762.20
50000	814.22	804.79	797.08	790.76	785.57	781.29	777.75
51000	830.50	820.88	813.02	806.58	801.28	796.91	793.31
52000	846.79	836.98	828.96	822.40	816.99	812.54	808.86
53000	863.07	853.07	844.91	838.21	832.70	828.17	824.42
54000	879.36	869.17	860.85	854.03	848.42	843.79	839.97
55000	895.64	885.27	876.79	869.84	864.13	859.42	855.53
56000	911.93	901.36	892.73	885.66	879.84	875.04	871.08
57000	928.21	917.46	908.67	901.47	895.55	890.67	886.64
58000	944.50	933.55	924.61	917.29	911.26	906.30	902.19
59000	960.78	949.65	940.56	933.10	926.97	921.92	917.75
60000	977.06	965.74	956.50	948.92	942.68	937.55	933.30
65000	1058.49	1046.22	1036.21	1027.99	1021.24	1015.68	1011.08
70000	1139.91	1126.70	1115.91	1107.07	1099.80	1093.80	1088.85
75000	1221.33	1207.18	1195.62	1186.15	1178.36	1171.93	1166.63
80000	1302.75	1287.66	1275.33	1265.22	1256.91	1250.06	1244.40
85000	1384.17	1368.14	1355.04	1344.30	1335.47	1328.19	1322.18
90000	1465.60	1448.62	1434.75	1423.38	1414.03	1406.32	1399.95
95000	1547.02	1529.09	1514.45	1502.45	1492.58	1484.45	1477.73
100000	1628.44	1609.57	1594.16	1581.53	1571.14	1562.58	1555.50
105000	1709.86	1690.05	1673.87	1660.61	1649.70	1640.71	1633.28
110000	1791.28	1770.53	1753.58	1739.68	1728.26	1718.84	1711.05
120000	1954.13	1931.49	1913.00	1897.84	1885.37	1875.09	1866.61
130000	2116.97	2092.44	2072.41	2055.99	2042.48	2031.35	2022.16
140000	2279.82	2253.40	2231.83	2214.14	2199.60	2187.61	2177.71
150000	2442.66	2414.36	2391.24	2372.29	2356.71	2343.87	2333.26
175000	2849.77	2816.75	2789.78	2767.68	2749.50	2734.51	2722.13
200000	3256.88	3219.15	3188.33	3163.06	3142.28	3125.16	3111.01
225000	3663.99	3621.54	3586.87	3558.44	3535.07	3515.80	3499.88
250000	4071.10	4023.93	3985.41	3953.82	3927.85	3906.44	3888.76

Monthly Payments

necessary to amortize a loan

18¼%

AMOUNT	22 YEARS	23 YEARS	24 YEARS	25 YEARS	30 YEARS	35 YEARS	40 YEARS
100	1.55	1.54	1.54	1.54	1.53	1.52	1.52
200	3.10	3.09	3.08	3.07	3.06	3.05	3.04
500	7.75	7.72	7.70	7.69	7.64	7.62	7.61
1000	15.50	15.45	15.41	15.37	15.28	15.24	15.22
2000	30.99	30.90	30.82	30.75	30.55	30.47	30.44
5000	77.48	77.24	77.04	76.87	76.38	76.18	76.10
6000	92.98	92.69	92.45	92.25	91.65	91.41	91.32
7000	108.48	108.14	107.85	107.62	106.93	106.65	106.53
8000	123.97	123.58	123.26	123.00	122.20	121.88	121.75
9000	139.47	139.03	138.67	138.37	137.48	137.12	136.97
10000	154.97	154.48	154.08	153.74	152.75	152.35	152.19
15000	232.45	231.72	231.12	230.62	229.13	228.53	228.29
20000	309.93	308.96	308.16	307.49	305.50	304.70	304.38
25000	387.41	386.20	385.19	384.36	381.88	380.88	380.48
30000	464.90	463.44	462.23	461.23	458.25	457.06	456.58
35000	542.38	540.68	539.27	538.10	534.63	533.23	532.67
36000	557.87	556.13	554.68	553.48	549.90	548.47	547.89
37000	573.37	571.58	570.09	568.85	565.18	563.70	563.11
38000	588.87	587.02	585.50	584.23	580.45	578.94	578.33
39000	604.36	602.47	600.90	599.60	595.73	594.17	593.55
40000	619.86	617.92	616.31	614.98	611.00	609.41	608.77
41000	635.36	633.37	631.72	630.35	626.28	624.64	623.99
42000	650.85	648.82	647.13	645.72	641.55	639.88	639.21
43000	666.35	664.26	662.54	661.10	656.83	655.11	654.43
44000	681.85	679.71	677.94	676.47	672.10	670.35	669.64
45000	697.34	695.16	693.35	691.85	687.38	685.59	684.86
46000	712.84	710.61	708.76	707.22	702.65	700.82	700.08
47000	728.34	726.06	724.17	722.60	717.93	716.06	715.30
48000	743.83	741.50	739.57	737.97	733.20	731.29	730.52
49000	759.33	756.95	754.98	753.34	748.48	746.53	745.74
50000	774.83	772.40	770.39	768.72	763.75	761.76	760.96
51000	790.32	787.85	785.80	784.09	779.03	777.00	776.18
52000	805.82	803.30	801.21	799.47	794.30	792.23	791.40
53000	821.32	818.75	816.61	814.84	809.58	807.47	806.62
54000	836.81	834.19	832.02	830.22	824.85	822.70	821.84
55000	852.31	849.64	847.43	845.59	840.13	837.94	837.06
56000	867.80	865.09	862.84	860.97	855.40	853.17	852.27
57000	883.30	880.54	878.24	876.34	870.68	868.41	867.49
58000	898.80	895.99	893.65	891.71	885.95	883.64	882.71
59000	914.29	911.43	909.06	907.09	901.23	898.88	897.93
60000	929.79	926.88	924.47	922.46	916.50	914.11	913.15
65000	1007.27	1004.12	1001.51	999.34	992.88	990.29	989.25
70000	1084.76	1081.36	1078.55	1076.21	1069.25	1066.47	1065.34
75000	1162.24	1158.60	1155.58	1153.08	1145.63	1142.64	1141.44
80000	1239.72	1235.84	1232.62	1229.95	1222.00	1218.82	1217.54
85000	1317.20	1313.08	1309.66	1306.82	1298.38	1294.99	1293.63
90000	1394.69	1390.32	1386.70	1383.69	1374.75	1371.17	1369.73
95000	1472.17	1467.56	1463.74	1460.57	1451.13	1447.35	1445.82
100000	1549.65	1544.80	1540.78	1537.44	1527.50	1523.52	1521.92
105000	1627.13	1622.04	1617.82	1614.31	1603.88	1599.70	1598.02
110000	1704.62	1699.28	1694.86	1691.18	1680.25	1675.88	1674.11
120000	1859.58	1853.76	1848.93	1844.93	1833.00	1828.23	1826.30
130000	2014.55	2008.24	2003.01	1998.67	1985.75	1980.58	1978.50
140000	2169.51	2162.72	2157.09	2152.41	2138.50	2132.93	2130.69
150000	2324.48	2317.20	2311.17	2306.16	2291.25	2285.28	2282.88
175000	2711.89	2703.40	2696.36	2690.52	2673.13	2666.17	2663.36
200000	3099.30	3089.60	3081.56	3074.88	3055.01	3047.05	3043.84
225000	3486.72	3475.80	3466.75	3459.24	3436.88	3427.93	3424.32
250000	3874.13	3862.01	3851.95	3843.60	3818.76	3808.81	3804.80

18½% Monthly Payments

necessary to amortize a loan

AMOUNT	1 YEAR	2 YEARS	3 YEARS	4 YEARS	5 YEARS	6 YEARS	7 YEARS
100	9.19	5.02	3.64	2.96	2.57	2.31	2.13
200	18.38	10.03	7.28	5.93	5.13	4.62	4.26
500	45.96	25.08	18.20	14.82	12.83	11.55	10.66
1000	91.92	50.17	36.40	29.64	25.67	23.09	21.31
2000	183.84	100.33	72.81	59.27	51.33	46.18	42.62
5000	459.59	250.83	182.02	148.18	128.33	115.46	106.56
6000	551.51	301.00	218.42	177.82	154.00	138.55	127.87
7000	643.43	351.16	254.83	207.46	179.66	161.64	149.18
8000	735.34	401.33	291.23	237.10	205.33	184.73	170.50
9000	827.26	451.49	327.63	266.73	231.00	207.82	191.81
10000	919.18	501.66	364.04	296.37	256.66	230.91	213.12
15000	1378.77	752.49	546.06	444.55	384.99	346.37	319.68
20000	1838.36	1003.32	728.07	592.74	513.32	461.83	426.24
25000	2297.95	1254.15	910.09	740.92	641.66	577.28	532.80
30000	2757.54	1504.98	1092.11	889.11	769.99	692.74	639.36
35000	3217.13	1755.81	1274.13	1037.29	898.32	808.20	745.92
36000	3309.05	1805.98	1310.53	1066.93	923.98	831.29	767.23
37000	3400.97	1856.14	1346.94	1096.57	949.65	854.38	788.54
38000	3492.89	1906.31	1383.34	1126.20	975.32	877.47	809.85
39000	3584.81	1956.47	1419.74	1155.84	1000.98	900.56	831.16
40000	3676.72	2006.64	1456.15	1185.48	1026.65	923.65	852.48
41000	3768.64	2056.81	1492.55	1215.11	1052.31	946.75	873.79
42000	3860.56	2106.97	1528.96	1244.75	1077.98	969.84	895.10
43000	3952.48	2157.14	1565.36	1274.39	1103.65	992.93	916.41
44000	4044.40	2207.31	1601.76	1304.02	1129.31	1016.02	937.72
45000	4136.32	2257.47	1638.17	1333.66	1154.98	1039.11	959.04
46000	4228.23	2307.64	1674.57	1363.30	1180.65	1062.20	980.35
47000	4320.15	2357.80	1710.97	1392.94	1206.31	1085.29	1001.66
48000	4412.07	2407.97	1747.38	1422.57	1231.98	1108.39	1022.97
49000	4503.99	2458.14	1783.78	1452.21	1257.64	1131.48	1044.28
50000	4595.91	2508.30	1820.19	1481.85	1283.31	1154.57	1065.60
51000	4687.82	2558.47	1856.59	1511.48	1308.98	1177.66	1086.91
52000	4779.74	2608.63	1892.99	1541.12	1334.64	1200.75	1108.22
53000	4871.66	2658.80	1929.40	1570.76	1360.31	1223.84	1129.53
54000	4963.58	2708.97	1965.80	1600.39	1385.98	1246.93	1150.84
55000	5055.50	2759.13	2002.20	1630.03	1411.64	1270.02	1172.16
56000	5147.41	2809.30	2038.61	1659.67	1437.31	1293.12	1193.47
57000	5239.33	2859.46	2075.01	1689.30	1462.97	1316.21	1214.78
58000	5331.25	2909.63	2111.42	1718.94	1488.64	1339.30	1236.09
59000	5423.17	2959.80	2147.82	1748.58	1514.31	1362.39	1257.40
60000	5515.09	3009.96	2184.22	1778.21	1539.97	1385.48	1278.72
65000	5974.68	3260.79	2366.24	1926.40	1668.30	1500.94	1385.27
70000	6434.27	3511.62	2548.26	2074.58	1796.63	1616.39	1491.83
75000	6893.86	3762.45	2730.28	2222.77	1924.97	1731.85	1598.39
80000	7353.45	4013.28	2912.30	2370.95	2053.30	1847.31	1704.95
85000	7813.04	4264.11	3094.32	2519.14	2181.63	1962.77	1811.51
90000	8272.63	4514.94	3276.33	2667.32	2309.96	2078.22	1918.07
95000	8732.22	4765.77	3458.35	2815.51	2438.29	2193.68	2024.63
100000	9191.81	5016.60	3640.37	2963.69	2566.62	2309.14	2131.19
105000	9651.40	5267.43	3822.39	3111.88	2694.95	2424.59	2237.75
110000	10110.99	5518.26	4004.41	3260.06	2823.28	2540.05	2344.31
120000	11030.17	6019.92	4368.45	3556.43	3079.95	2770.96	2557.43
130000	11949.36	6521.58	4732.48	3852.80	3336.61	3001.88	2770.55
140000	12868.54	7023.24	5096.52	4149.17	3593.27	3232.79	2983.67
150000	13787.72	7524.90	5460.56	4445.54	3849.93	3463.70	3196.79
175000	16085.67	8779.05	6370.65	5186.46	4491.59	4040.99	3729.59
200000	18383.62	10033.21	7280.74	5927.38	5133.24	4618.27	4262.38
225000	20681.58	11287.36	8190.84	6668.31	5774.90	5195.55	4795.18
250000	22979.53	12541.51	9100.93	7409.23	6416.55	5772.84	5327.98

Monthly Payments 18½%

necessary to amortize a loan

AMOUNT	8 YEARS	9 YEARS	10 YEARS	11 YEARS	12 YEARS	13 YEARS	14 YEARS
100	2.00	1.91	1.83	1.78	1.73	1.70	1.67
200	4.01	3.81	3.67	3.56	3.47	3.40	3.34
500	10.01	9.54	9.17	8.89	8.67	8.49	8.35
1000	20.03	19.07	18.34	17.78	17.33	16.98	16.69
2000	40.05	38.14	36.68	35.55	34.66	33.96	33.39
5000	100.14	95.35	91.71	88.88	86.66	84.00	83.47
6000	120.16	114.42	110.05	106.66	103.99	101.87	100.16
7000	140.19	133.50	128.39	124.43	121.32	118.84	116.86
8000	160.22	152.57	146.73	142.21	138.65	135.82	133.55
9000	180.25	171.64	165.07	159.98	155.98	152.80	150.25
10000	200.27	190.71	183.42	177.76	173.31	169.78	166.94
15000	300.41	286.06	275.12	266.64	259.97	254.66	250.41
20000	400.55	381.42	366.83	355.52	346.62	339.55	333.88
25000	500.69	476.77	458.54	444.40	433.28	424.44	417.35
30000	600.82	572.12	550.25	533.28	519.93	509.33	500.82
35000	700.96	667.48	641.96	622.16	606.59	594.21	584.29
36000	720.99	686.55	660.30	639.94	623.92	611.19	600.99
37000	741.02	705.62	678.64	657.71	641.25	628.17	617.68
38000	761.04	724.69	696.98	675.49	658.58	645.15	634.37
39000	781.07	743.76	715.32	693.26	675.91	662.12	651.07
40000	801.10	762.83	733.67	711.04	693.25	679.10	667.76
41000	821.13	781.90	752.01	728.82	710.58	696.08	684.46
42000	841.15	800.97	770.35	746.59	727.91	713.06	701.15
43000	861.18	820.05	788.69	764.37	745.24	730.03	717.84
44000	881.21	839.12	807.03	782.14	762.57	747.01	734.54
45000	901.23	858.19	825.37	799.92	779.90	763.99	751.23
46000	921.26	877.26	843.72	817.70	797.23	780.97	767.93
47000	941.29	896.33	862.06	835.47	814.56	797.94	784.62
48000	961.32	915.40	880.40	853.25	831.89	814.92	801.31
49000	981.34	934.47	898.74	871.02	849.23	831.90	818.01
50000	1001.37	953.54	917.08	888.80	866.56	848.88	834.70
51000	1021.40	972.61	935.42	906.58	883.89	865.85	851.40
52000	1041.43	991.68	953.77	924.35	901.22	882.83	868.09
53000	1061.45	1010.75	972.11	942.13	918.55	899.81	884.78
54000	1081.48	1029.82	990.45	959.90	935.88	916.79	901.48
55000	1101.51	1048.89	1008.79	977.68	953.21	933.76	918.17
56000	1121.54	1067.97	1027.13	995.46	970.54	950.74	934.87
57000	1141.56	1087.04	1045.47	1013.23	987.88	967.72	951.56
58000	1161.59	1106.11	1063.82	1031.01	1005.21	984.70	968.25
59000	1181.62	1125.18	1082.16	1048.78	1022.54	1001.67	984.95
60000	1201.65	1144.25	1100.50	1066.56	1039.87	1018.65	1001.64
65000	1301.78	1239.60	1192.21	1155.44	1126.52	1103.54	1085.11
70000	1401.92	1334.96	1283.92	1244.32	1213.18	1188.43	1168.58
75000	1502.06	1430.31	1375.62	1333.20	1299.84	1273.31	1252.05
80000	1602.20	1525.67	1467.33	1422.08	1386.49	1358.20	1335.52
85000	1702.33	1621.02	1559.04	1510.96	1473.15	1443.09	1418.99
90000	1802.47	1716.37	1650.75	1599.84	1559.80	1527.98	1502.46
95000	1902.61	1811.73	1742.46	1688.72	1646.46	1612.87	1585.93
100000	2002.74	1907.08	1834.17	1777.60	1733.11	1697.75	1669.41
105000	2102.88	2002.44	1925.87	1866.48	1819.77	1782.64	1752.88
110000	2203.02	2097.79	2017.58	1955.36	1906.43	1867.53	1836.35
120000	2403.29	2288.50	2201.00	2133.12	2079.74	2037.30	2003.29
130000	2603.57	2479.21	2384.42	2310.88	2253.05	2207.08	2170.23
140000	2803.84	2669.91	2567.83	2488.64	2426.36	2376.85	2337.17
150000	3004.12	2860.62	2751.25	2666.40	2599.67	2546.63	2504.11
175000	3504.80	3337.39	3209.79	3110.80	3032.95	2971.07	2921.46
200000	4005.49	3814.16	3668.33	3555.20	3466.23	3395.51	3338.81
225000	4506.17	4290.93	4126.87	3999.60	3899.51	3819.94	3756.16
250000	5006.86	4767.70	4585.41	4444.00	4332.79	4244.38	4173.51

18½%

Monthly Payments
necessary to amortize a loan

AMOUNT	15 YEARS	16 YEARS	17 YEARS	18 YEARS	19 YEARS	20 YEARS	21 YEARS
100	1.65	1.63	1.61	1.60	1.59	1.58	1.58
200	3.29	3.26	3.23	3.20	3.18	3.16	3.15
500	8.23	8.14	8.06	8.00	7.95	7.91	7.88
1000	16.47	16.28	16.13	16.00	15.90	15.82	15.75
2000	32.93	32.56	32.26	32.01	31.81	31.64	31.50
5000	82.33	81.40	80.64	80.02	79.51	79.09	78.75
6000	98.79	97.68	96.77	96.03	95.42	94.91	94.50
7000	115.26	113.96	112.90	112.03	111.32	110.73	110.25
8000	131.72	130.24	129.02	128.03	127.22	126.55	126.00
9000	148.19	146.52	145.15	144.04	143.12	142.37	141.75
10000	164.65	162.80	161.28	160.04	159.03	158.19	157.50
15000	246.98	244.19	241.92	240.06	238.54	237.28	236.25
20000	329.30	325.59	322.56	320.08	318.05	316.38	315.00
25000	411.63	406.99	403.20	400.11	397.56	395.47	393.75
30000	493.96	488.39	483.84	480.13	477.08	474.57	472.50
35000	576.28	569.78	564.48	560.15	556.59	553.66	551.25
36000	592.75	586.06	580.61	576.15	572.49	569.48	567.00
37000	609.21	602.34	596.74	592.16	588.40	585.30	582.75
38000	625.68	618.62	612.87	608.16	604.30	601.12	598.50
39000	642.14	634.90	629.00	624.17	620.20	616.94	614.25
40000	658.61	651.18	645.12	640.17	636.10	632.76	630.00
41000	675.07	667.46	661.25	656.17	652.01	648.58	645.75
42000	691.54	683.74	677.38	672.18	667.91	664.40	661.50
43000	708.01	700.02	693.51	688.18	683.81	680.22	677.25
44000	724.47	716.30	709.64	704.19	699.71	696.03	693.00
45000	740.94	732.58	725.77	720.19	715.62	711.85	708.75
46000	757.40	748.86	741.89	736.20	731.52	727.67	724.50
47000	773.87	765.14	758.02	752.20	747.42	743.49	740.25
48000	790.33	781.42	774.15	768.20	763.32	759.31	756.00
49000	806.80	797.70	790.28	784.21	779.23	775.13	771.75
50000	823.26	813.98	806.41	800.21	795.13	790.95	787.50
51000	839.73	830.26	822.53	816.22	811.03	806.77	803.25
52000	856.19	846.54	838.66	832.22	826.93	822.59	819.00
53000	872.66	862.81	854.79	848.23	842.84	838.41	834.75
54000	889.12	879.09	870.92	864.23	858.74	854.22	850.50
55000	905.59	895.37	887.05	880.23	874.64	870.04	866.25
56000	922.05	911.65	903.17	896.24	890.55	885.86	882.00
57000	938.52	927.93	919.30	912.24	906.45	901.68	897.75
58000	954.98	944.21	935.43	928.25	922.35	917.50	913.50
59000	971.45	960.49	951.56	944.25	938.25	933.32	929.25
60000	987.91	976.77	967.69	960.25	954.16	949.14	945.00
65000	1070.24	1058.17	1048.33	1040.28	1033.67	1028.23	1023.75
70000	1152.57	1139.57	1128.97	1120.30	1113.18	1107.33	1102.50
75000	1234.89	1220.96	1209.61	1200.32	1192.69	1186.42	1181.25
80000	1317.22	1302.36	1290.25	1280.34	1272.21	1265.52	1260.00
85000	1399.54	1383.76	1370.89	1360.36	1351.72	1344.61	1338.75
90000	1481.87	1465.16	1451.53	1440.38	1431.23	1423.71	1417.50
95000	1564.20	1546.55	1532.17	1520.40	1510.75	1502.80	1496.25
100000	1646.52	1627.95	1612.81	1600.42	1590.26	1581.90	1575.00
105000	1728.85	1709.35	1693.45	1680.45	1669.77	1660.99	1653.75
110000	1811.18	1790.75	1774.09	1760.47	1749.29	1740.09	1732.50
120000	1975.83	1953.54	1935.37	1920.51	1908.31	1898.28	1890.00
130000	2140.48	2116.34	2096.66	2080.55	2067.34	2056.47	2047.50
140000	2305.13	2279.13	2257.94	2240.59	2226.36	2214.66	2205.00
150000	2469.79	2441.93	2419.22	2400.64	2385.39	2372.84	2362.50
175000	2881.42	2848.92	2822.42	2800.74	2782.95	2768.32	2756.26
200000	3293.05	3255.90	3225.62	3200.85	3180.52	3163.79	3150.01
225000	3704.68	3662.89	3628.83	3600.96	3578.08	3559.27	3543.76
250000	4116.31	4069.88	4032.03	4001.06	3975.65	3954.74	3937.51

Monthly Payments 18½%

necessary to amortize a loan

AMOUNT	22 YEARS	23 YEARS	24 YEARS	25 YEARS	30 YEARS	35 YEARS	40 YEARS
100	1.57	1.56	1.56	1.56	1.55	1.54	1.54
200	3.14	3.13	3.12	3.11	3.10	3.09	3.09
500	7.85	7.82	7.80	7.79	7.74	7.72	7.71
1000	15.69	15.65	15.61	15.57	15.48	15.44	15.43
2000	31.39	31.29	31.21	31.15	30.96	30.88	30.85
5000	78.47	78.23	78.04	77.87	77.40	77.21	77.13
6000	94.16	93.88	93.64	93.45	92.88	92.65	92.56
7000	109.85	109.52	109.25	109.02	108.36	108.09	107.99
8000	125.54	125.17	124.86	124.60	123.84	123.53	123.41
9000	141.24	140.81	140.46	140.17	139.32	138.98	138.84
10000	156.93	156.46	156.07	155.75	154.79	154.42	154.27
15000	235.40	234.69	234.11	233.62	232.19	231.63	231.40
20000	313.86	312.92	312.14	311.50	309.59	308.83	308.53
25000	392.33	391.15	390.18	389.37	386.99	386.04	385.67
30000	470.79	469.38	468.21	467.25	464.38	463.25	462.80
35000	549.26	547.61	546.25	545.12	541.78	540.46	539.93
36000	564.95	563.26	561.86	560.69	557.26	555.90	555.36
37000	580.65	578.90	577.46	576.27	572.74	571.34	570.79
38000	596.34	594.55	593.07	591.84	588.22	586.78	586.21
39000	612.03	610.20	608.68	607.42	603.70	602.23	601.64
40000	627.72	625.84	624.28	622.99	619.18	617.67	617.07
41000	643.42	641.49	639.89	638.57	634.66	633.11	632.49
42000	659.11	657.13	655.50	654.14	650.14	648.55	647.92
43000	674.80	672.78	671.11	669.72	665.62	663.99	663.35
44000	690.50	688.43	686.71	685.29	681.10	679.43	678.77
45000	706.19	704.07	702.32	700.87	696.58	694.88	694.20
46000	721.88	719.72	717.93	716.44	712.05	710.32	709.63
47000	737.58	735.36	733.53	732.02	727.53	725.76	725.05
48000	753.27	751.01	749.14	747.59	743.01	741.20	740.48
49000	768.96	766.66	764.75	763.17	758.49	756.64	755.91
50000	784.66	782.30	780.36	778.74	773.97	772.08	771.33
51000	800.35	797.95	795.96	794.32	789.45	787.53	786.76
52000	816.04	813.60	811.57	809.89	804.93	802.97	802.19
53000	831.74	829.24	827.18	825.47	820.41	818.41	817.61
54000	847.43	844.89	842.78	841.04	835.89	833.85	833.04
55000	863.12	860.53	858.39	856.62	851.37	849.29	848.47
56000	878.81	876.18	874.00	872.19	866.85	864.73	863.89
57000	894.51	891.83	889.61	887.77	882.33	880.18	879.32
58000	910.20	907.47	905.21	903.34	897.81	895.62	894.75
59000	925.80	923.12	920.82	918.92	913.29	911.06	910.17
60000	941.59	938.76	936.43	934.49	928.77	926.50	925.60
65000	1020.05	1016.99	1014.46	1012.36	1006.16	1003.71	1002.73
70000	1098.52	1095.22	1092.50	1090.24	1083.56	1080.92	1079.87
75000	1176.98	1173.45	1170.53	1168.11	1160.96	1158.13	1157.00
80000	1255.45	1251.68	1248.57	1245.99	1238.36	1235.33	1234.13
85000	1333.91	1329.92	1326.60	1323.86	1315.75	1312.54	1311.26
90000	1412.38	1408.15	1404.64	1401.74	1393.15	1389.75	1388.40
95000	1490.85	1486.38	1482.68	1479.61	1470.55	1466.96	1465.53
100000	1569.31	1564.61	1560.71	1557.48	1547.94	1544.17	1542.66
105000	1647.78	1642.84	1638.75	1635.36	1625.34	1621.38	1619.80
110000	1726.24	1721.07	1716.78	1713.23	1702.74	1698.58	1696.93
120000	1883.17	1877.53	1872.85	1868.98	1857.53	1853.00	1851.20
130000	2040.11	2033.99	2028.92	2024.73	2012.33	2007.42	2005.46
140000	2197.04	2190.45	2185.00	2180.48	2167.12	2161.83	2159.73
150000	2353.97	2346.91	2341.07	2336.23	2321.92	2316.25	2314.00
175000	2746.30	2738.06	2731.24	2725.60	2708.90	2702.29	2699.66
200000	3138.62	3129.21	3121.42	3114.97	3095.89	3088.34	3085.33
225000	3530.95	3520.36	3511.60	3504.34	3482.88	3474.38	3470.99
250000	3923.28	3911.52	3901.78	3893.71	3869.86	3860.42	3856.66

18¾%

Monthly Payments
necessary to amortize a loan

AMOUNT	1 YEAR	2 YEARS	3 YEARS	4 YEARS	5 YEARS	6 YEARS	7 YEARS
100	9.20	5.03	3.65	2.98	2.58	2.32	2.15
200	18.41	10.06	7.31	5.95	5.16	4.65	4.29
500	46.02	25.14	18.26	14.88	12.90	11.62	10.73
1000	92.04	50.29	36.53	29.77	25.80	23.23	21.46
2000	184.07	100.57	73.06	59.54	51.61	46.47	42.92
5000	460.19	251.44	182.65	148.84	129.02	116.17	107.30
6000	552.22	301.72	219.18	178.61	154.82	139.40	128.76
7000	644.26	352.01	255.71	208.38	180.62	162.64	150.22
8000	736.30	402.30	292.24	238.15	206.43	185.87	171.68
9000	828.34	452.59	328.77	267.92	232.23	209.10	193.14
10000	920.37	502.87	365.30	297.68	258.03	232.34	214.60
15000	1380.56	754.31	547.95	446.53	387.05	348.51	321.90
20000	1840.75	1005.74	730.59	595.37	516.06	464.68	429.19
25000	2300.93	1257.18	913.24	744.21	645.08	580.85	536.49
30000	2761.12	1508.62	1095.89	893.05	774.10	697.01	643.79
35000	3221.31	1760.05	1278.54	1041.89	903.11	813.18	751.09
36000	3313.34	1810.34	1315.07	1071.66	928.91	836.42	772.55
37000	3405.38	1860.63	1351.60	1101.43	954.72	859.65	794.01
38000	3497.42	1910.92	1388.13	1131.20	980.52	882.88	815.47
39000	3589.45	1961.20	1424.66	1160.97	1006.32	906.12	836.93
40000	3681.49	2011.49	1461.19	1190.73	1032.13	929.35	858.39
41000	3773.53	2061.78	1497.72	1220.50	1057.93	952.59	879.85
42000	3865.57	2112.06	1534.25	1250.27	1083.73	975.82	901.31
43000	3957.60	2162.35	1570.78	1280.04	1109.54	999.05	922.77
44000	4049.64	2212.64	1607.31	1309.81	1135.34	1022.29	944.23
45000	4141.68	2262.93	1643.84	1339.58	1161.14	1045.52	965.69
46000	4233.72	2313.21	1680.37	1369.34	1186.95	1068.76	987.15
47000	4325.75	2363.50	1716.90	1399.11	1212.75	1091.99	1008.61
48000	4417.79	2413.79	1753.43	1428.88	1238.55	1115.22	1030.07
49000	4509.83	2464.07	1789.96	1458.65	1264.36	1138.46	1051.53
50000	4601.87	2514.36	1826.49	1488.42	1290.16	1161.69	1072.99
51000	4693.90	2564.65	1863.02	1518.19	1315.96	1184.92	1094.45
52000	4785.94	2614.94	1899.55	1547.95	1341.77	1208.16	1115.91
53000	4877.98	2665.22	1936.08	1577.72	1367.57	1231.39	1137.37
54000	4970.01	2715.51	1972.61	1607.49	1393.37	1254.63	1158.82
55000	5062.05	2765.80	2009.14	1637.26	1419.18	1277.86	1180.28
56000	5154.09	2816.09	2045.67	1667.03	1444.98	1301.09	1201.74
57000	5246.13	2866.37	2082.20	1696.80	1470.78	1324.33	1223.20
58000	5338.16	2916.66	2118.73	1726.56	1496.58	1347.56	1244.66
59000	5430.20	2966.95	2155.25	1756.33	1522.39	1370.80	1266.12
60000	5522.24	3017.23	2191.78	1786.10	1548.19	1394.03	1287.58
65000	5982.42	3268.67	2374.43	1934.94	1677.21	1510.20	1394.88
70000	6442.61	3520.11	2557.08	2083.78	1806.22	1626.37	1502.18
75000	6902.80	3771.54	2739.73	2232.63	1935.24	1742.54	1609.48
80000	7362.98	4022.98	2922.38	2381.47	2064.25	1858.71	1716.78
85000	7823.17	4274.42	3105.03	2530.31	2193.27	1974.87	1824.08
90000	8283.36	4525.85	3287.68	2679.15	2322.29	2091.04	1931.37
95000	8743.54	4777.29	3470.33	2827.99	2451.30	2207.21	2038.67
100000	9203.73	5028.72	3652.97	2976.84	2580.32	2323.38	2145.97
105000	9663.92	5280.16	3835.62	3125.68	2709.33	2439.55	2253.27
110000	10124.10	5531.60	4018.27	3274.52	2838.35	2555.72	2360.57
120000	11044.48	6034.47	4383.57	3572.20	3096.38	2788.06	2575.17
130000	11964.85	6537.34	4748.87	3869.89	3354.41	3020.40	2789.76
140000	12885.22	7040.21	5114.16	4167.57	3612.45	3252.73	3004.36
150000	13805.60	7543.09	5479.46	4465.25	3870.48	3485.07	3218.96
175000	16106.53	8800.27	6392.71	5209.46	4515.56	4065.92	3755.45
200000	18407.46	10057.45	7305.95	5953.67	5160.64	4646.76	4291.94
225000	20708.39	11314.63	8219.19	6697.88	5805.72	5227.61	4828.44
250000	23009.33	12571.81	9132.44	7442.09	6450.80	5808.45	5364.93

Monthly Payments 18¾%

necessary to amortize a loan

AMOUNT	8 YEARS	9 YEARS	10 YEARS	11 YEARS	12 YEARS	13 YEARS	14 YEARS
100	2.02	1.92	1.85	1.79	1.75	1.72	1.69
200	4.04	3.85	3.70	3.59	3.50	3.43	3.37
500	10.09	9.61	9.25	8.97	8.75	8.58	8.44
1000	20.18	19.23	18.50	17.94	17.50	17.15	16.87
2000	40.36	38.46	37.01	35.89	35.00	34.30	33.74
5000	100.90	96.14	92.52	89.71	87.51	85.76	84.36
6000	121.08	115.37	111.02	107.66	105.01	102.91	101.23
7000	141.26	134.60	129.53	125.60	122.51	120.07	118.11
8000	161.44	153.83	148.03	143.54	140.02	137.22	134.98
9000	181.62	173.06	166.54	161.49	157.52	154.37	151.85
10000	201.80	192.29	185.04	179.43	175.02	171.52	168.72
15000	302.71	288.43	277.56	269.14	262.53	257.28	253.08
20000	403.61	384.57	370.08	358.86	350.04	343.05	337.45
25000	504.51	480.72	462.60	448.57	437.55	428.81	421.81
30000	605.41	576.86	555.12	538.29	525.06	514.57	506.17
35000	706.31	673.00	647.64	628.00	612.57	600.33	590.53
36000	726.49	692.23	666.15	645.94	630.07	617.48	607.40
37000	746.67	711.46	684.65	663.89	647.58	634.63	624.27
38000	766.85	730.69	703.16	681.83	665.08	651.79	641.15
39000	787.03	749.92	721.66	699.77	682.58	668.94	658.02
40000	807.22	769.15	740.17	717.71	700.08	686.09	674.89
41000	827.40	788.38	758.67	735.66	717.59	703.24	691.76
42000	847.58	807.60	777.17	753.60	735.09	720.40	708.64
43000	867.76	826.83	795.68	771.54	752.59	737.55	725.51
44000	887.94	846.06	814.18	789.49	770.09	754.70	742.38
45000	908.12	865.29	832.69	807.43	787.59	771.85	759.25
46000	928.30	884.52	851.19	825.37	805.10	789.00	776.13
47000	948.48	903.75	869.69	843.31	822.60	806.16	793.00
48000	968.66	922.98	888.20	861.26	840.10	823.31	809.87
49000	988.84	942.20	906.70	879.20	857.60	840.46	826.74
50000	1009.02	961.43	925.21	897.14	875.10	857.61	843.61
51000	1029.20	980.66	943.71	915.09	892.61	874.77	860.49
52000	1049.38	999.89	962.22	933.03	910.11	891.92	877.36
53000	1069.56	1019.12	980.72	950.97	927.61	909.07	894.23
54000	1089.74	1038.35	999.22	968.91	945.11	926.22	911.10
55000	1109.92	1057.58	1017.73	986.86	962.61	943.37	927.98
56000	1130.10	1076.80	1036.23	1004.80	980.12	960.53	944.85
57000	1150.28	1096.03	1054.74	1022.74	997.62	977.68	961.72
58000	1170.46	1115.26	1073.24	1040.68	1015.12	994.83	978.59
59000	1190.64	1134.49	1091.74	1058.63	1032.62	1011.98	995.46
60000	1210.82	1153.72	1110.25	1076.57	1050.12	1029.14	1012.34
65000	1311.72	1249.86	1202.77	1166.29	1137.64	1114.90	1096.70
70000	1412.63	1346.01	1295.29	1256.00	1225.15	1200.66	1181.06
75000	1513.53	1442.15	1387.81	1345.71	1312.66	1286.42	1265.42
80000	1614.43	1538.29	1480.33	1435.43	1400.17	1372.18	1349.78
85000	1715.33	1634.44	1572.85	1525.14	1487.68	1457.94	1434.14
90000	1816.23	1730.58	1665.37	1614.86	1575.19	1543.70	1518.51
95000	1917.14	1826.72	1757.89	1704.57	1662.70	1629.46	1602.87
100000	2018.04	1922.87	1850.41	1794.28	1750.21	1715.23	1687.23
105000	2118.94	2019.01	1942.93	1884.00	1837.72	1800.99	1771.59
110000	2219.84	2115.15	2035.46	1973.71	1925.23	1886.75	1855.95
120000	2421.65	2307.44	2220.50	2153.14	2100.25	2058.27	2024.67
130000	2623.45	2499.73	2405.54	2332.57	2275.27	2229.79	2193.40
140000	2825.25	2692.01	2590.58	2512.00	2450.29	2401.32	2362.12
150000	3027.06	2884.30	2775.62	2691.43	2625.31	2572.84	2530.84
175000	3531.57	3365.02	3238.22	3140.00	3062.86	3001.65	2952.65
200000	4036.08	3845.73	3700.83	3588.57	3500.42	3430.45	3374.46
225000	4540.59	4326.45	4163.43	4037.14	3937.97	3859.26	3796.26
250000	5045.09	4807.16	4626.04	4485.71	4375.52	4288.07	4218.07

18¾% Monthly Payments

necessary to amortize a loan

AMOUNT	15 YEARS	16 YEARS	17 YEARS	18 YEARS	19 YEARS	20 YEARS	21 YEARS
100	1.66	1.65	1.63	1.62	1.61	1.60	1.59
200	3.33	3.29	3.26	3.24	3.22	3.20	3.19
500	8.32	8.23	8.16	8.10	8.05	8.01	7.97
1000	16.65	16.46	16.32	16.19	16.09	16.01	15.95
2000	33.29	32.93	32.63	32.39	32.19	32.03	31.89
5000	83.23	82.32	81.58	80.97	80.47	80.06	79.73
6000	99.88	98.78	97.89	97.16	96.57	96.08	95.67
7000	116.53	115.25	114.21	113.36	112.66	112.09	111.62
8000	133.17	131.71	130.52	129.55	128.75	128.10	127.56
9000	149.82	148.18	146.84	145.74	144.85	144.11	143.51
10000	166.47	164.64	163.15	161.94	160.94	160.13	159.45
15000	249.70	246.96	244.73	242.91	241.41	240.19	239.18
20000	332.93	329.28	326.30	323.88	321.89	320.25	318.91
25000	416.17	411.60	407.88	404.84	402.36	400.32	398.64
30000	499.40	493.92	489.46	485.81	482.83	480.38	478.36
35000	582.63	576.24	571.03	566.78	563.30	560.44	558.09
36000	599.28	592.70	587.35	582.98	579.40	576.46	574.04
37000	615.93	609.17	603.66	599.17	595.49	592.47	589.98
38000	632.57	625.63	619.98	615.36	611.58	608.48	605.93
39000	649.22	642.09	636.29	631.56	627.68	624.49	621.87
40000	665.87	658.56	652.61	647.75	643.77	640.51	637.82
41000	682.51	675.02	668.92	663.94	659.87	656.52	653.77
42000	699.16	691.48	685.24	680.14	675.96	672.53	669.71
43000	715.81	707.95	701.55	696.33	692.06	688.54	685.66
44000	732.45	724.41	717.87	712.53	708.15	704.56	701.60
45000	749.10	740.88	734.18	728.72	724.24	720.57	717.55
46000	765.75	757.34	750.50	744.91	740.34	736.58	733.49
47000	782.39	773.80	766.81	761.11	756.43	752.60	749.44
48000	799.04	790.27	783.13	777.30	772.53	768.61	765.38
49000	815.69	806.73	799.45	793.49	788.62	784.62	781.33
50000	832.33	823.20	815.76	809.69	804.72	800.63	797.27
51000	848.98	839.66	832.08	825.88	820.81	816.65	813.22
52000	865.63	856.12	848.39	842.08	836.90	832.66	829.17
53000	882.27	872.59	864.71	858.27	853.00	848.67	845.11
54000	898.92	889.05	881.02	874.46	869.09	864.68	861.06
55000	915.57	905.52	897.34	890.66	885.19	880.70	877.00
56000	932.21	921.98	913.65	906.85	901.28	896.71	892.95
57000	948.86	938.44	929.97	923.04	917.38	912.72	908.89
58000	965.51	954.91	946.28	939.24	933.47	928.73	924.84
59000	982.15	971.37	962.60	955.43	949.56	944.75	940.78
60000	998.80	987.84	978.91	971.63	965.66	960.76	956.73
65000	1082.03	1070.16	1060.49	1052.60	1046.13	1040.82	1036.46
70000	1165.27	1152.47	1142.06	1133.56	1126.60	1120.89	1116.18
75000	1248.50	1234.79	1223.64	1214.53	1207.07	1200.95	1195.91
80000	1331.74	1317.11	1305.22	1295.50	1287.54	1281.01	1275.64
85000	1414.97	1399.43	1386.79	1376.47	1368.02	1361.08	1355.37
90000	1498.20	1481.75	1468.37	1457.44	1448.49	1441.14	1435.09
95000	1581.44	1564.07	1549.95	1538.41	1528.96	1521.20	1514.82
100000	1664.67	1646.39	1631.52	1619.38	1609.43	1601.27	1594.55
105000	1747.90	1728.71	1713.10	1700.35	1689.90	1681.33	1674.28
110000	1831.14	1811.03	1794.67	1781.31	1770.37	1761.39	1754.00
120000	1997.60	1975.67	1957.83	1943.25	1931.32	1921.52	1913.46
130000	2164.07	2140.31	2120.98	2105.19	2092.26	2081.65	2072.91
140000	2330.54	2304.95	2284.13	2267.13	2253.20	2241.77	2232.37
150000	2497.00	2469.59	2447.28	2429.07	2414.15	2401.90	2391.82
175000	2913.17	2881.19	2855.16	2833.91	2816.50	2802.22	2790.46
200000	3329.34	3292.79	3263.04	3238.75	3218.86	3202.53	3189.10
225000	3745.51	3704.38	3670.92	3643.60	3621.22	3602.85	3587.74
250000	4161.67	4115.98	4078.80	4048.44	4023.58	4003.17	3986.37

Monthly Payments 18¾%

necessary to amortize a loan

AMOUNT	22 YEARS	23 YEARS	24 YEARS	25 YEARS	30 YEARS	35 YEARS	40 YEARS
100	1.59	1.58	1.58	1.58	1.57	1.56	1.56
200	3.18	3.17	3.16	3.16	3.14	3.13	3.13
500	7.95	7.92	7.90	7.89	7.84	7.82	7.82
1000	15.89	15.84	15.81	15.78	15.68	15.65	15.63
2000	31.78	31.69	31.61	31.55	31.37	31.30	31.27
5000	79.45	79.22	79.03	78.88	78.42	78.24	78.17
6000	95.34	95.07	94.84	94.65	94.10	93.89	93.80
7000	111.23	110.91	110.65	110.43	109.79	109.54	109.44
8000	127.12	126.76	126.45	126.21	125.47	125.19	125.07
9000	143.01	142.60	142.26	141.98	141.16	140.83	140.71
10000	158.90	158.45	158.07	157.76	156.84	156.48	156.34
15000	238.35	237.67	237.10	236.63	235.26	234.72	234.51
20000	317.80	316.89	316.14	315.51	313.68	312.97	312.68
25000	397.25	396.11	395.17	394.39	392.10	391.21	390.85
30000	476.70	475.34	474.20	473.27	470.52	469.45	469.02
35000	556.16	554.56	553.24	552.15	548.94	547.69	547.20
36000	572.05	570.40	569.05	567.92	564.63	563.34	562.83
37000	587.94	586.25	584.85	583.70	580.31	578.99	578.46
38000	603.83	602.09	600.66	599.47	596.00	594.63	594.10
39000	619.72	617.94	616.47	615.25	611.68	610.28	609.73
40000	635.61	633.78	632.27	631.03	627.36	625.93	625.37
41000	651.50	649.63	648.08	646.80	643.05	641.58	641.00
42000	667.39	665.47	663.89	662.58	658.73	657.23	656.63
43000	683.28	681.31	679.69	678.35	674.42	672.87	672.27
44000	699.17	697.16	695.50	694.13	690.10	688.52	687.90
45000	715.06	713.00	711.31	709.90	705.78	704.17	703.54
46000	730.95	728.85	727.11	725.68	721.47	719.82	719.17
47000	746.84	744.69	742.92	741.46	737.15	735.47	734.81
48000	762.73	760.54	758.73	757.23	752.84	751.12	750.44
49000	778.62	776.38	774.53	773.01	768.52	766.76	766.07
50000	794.51	792.23	790.34	788.78	784.20	782.41	781.71
51000	810.40	808.07	806.15	804.56	799.89	798.06	797.34
52000	826.29	823.91	821.95	820.33	815.57	813.71	812.98
53000	842.18	839.76	837.76	836.11	831.26	829.36	828.61
54000	858.07	855.60	853.57	851.89	846.94	845.01	844.24
55000	873.96	871.45	869.37	867.66	862.62	860.65	859.88
56000	889.85	887.29	885.18	883.44	878.31	876.30	875.51
57000	905.74	903.14	900.99	899.21	893.99	891.95	891.15
58000	921.63	918.98	916.80	914.99	909.68	907.60	906.78
59000	937.52	934.83	932.60	930.76	925.36	923.25	922.42
60000	953.41	950.67	948.41	946.54	941.04	938.90	938.05
65000	1032.86	1029.89	1027.44	1025.42	1019.47	1017.14	1016.22
70000	1112.31	1109.12	1106.48	1104.30	1097.89	1095.38	1094.39
75000	1191.76	1188.34	1185.51	1183.17	1176.31	1173.62	1172.56
80000	1271.21	1267.56	1264.55	1262.05	1254.73	1251.86	1250.73
85000	1350.66	1346.78	1343.58	1340.93	1333.15	1330.10	1328.90
90000	1430.11	1426.01	1422.61	1419.81	1411.57	1408.34	1407.07
95000	1509.57	1505.23	1501.65	1498.69	1489.99	1486.58	1485.25
100000	1589.02	1584.45	1580.68	1577.57	1568.41	1564.83	1563.42
105000	1668.47	1663.67	1659.72	1656.44	1646.83	1643.07	1641.59
110000	1747.92	1742.90	1738.75	1735.32	1725.25	1721.31	1719.76
120000	1906.82	1901.34	1896.82	1893.08	1882.09	1877.79	1876.10
130000	2065.72	2059.79	2054.89	2050.83	2038.93	2034.27	2032.44
140000	2224.62	2218.23	2212.95	2208.59	2195.77	2190.76	2188.78
150000	2383.52	2376.68	2371.02	2366.35	2352.61	2347.24	2345.12
175000	2780.78	2772.79	2766.19	2760.74	2744.71	2738.44	2735.98
200000	3178.03	3168.90	3161.36	3155.13	3136.82	3129.65	3126.83
225000	3575.29	3565.02	3556.53	3549.52	3528.92	3520.86	3517.69
250000	3972.54	3961.13	3951.70	3943.91	3921.02	3912.06	3908.54

19%

Monthly Payments

necessary to amortize a loan

AMOUNT	1 YEAR	2 YEARS	3 YEARS	4 YEARS	5 YEARS	6 YEARS	7 YEARS
100	9.22	5.04	3.67	2.99	2.59	2.34	2.16
200	18.43	10.08	7.33	5.98	5.19	4.68	4.32
500	46.08	25.20	18.33	14.95	12.97	11.69	10.80
1000	92.16	50.41	36.66	29.90	25.94	23.38	21.61
2000	184.31	100.82	73.31	59.80	51.88	46.75	43.22
5000	460.78	252.04	183.28	149.50	129.70	116.88	108.04
6000	552.94	302.45	219.94	179.40	155.64	140.26	129.65
7000	645.10	352.86	256.59	209.30	181.58	163.64	151.26
8000	737.25	403.27	293.25	239.20	207.52	187.01	172.86
9000	829.41	453.68	329.90	269.10	233.46	210.39	194.47
10000	921.57	504.09	366.56	299.00	259.41	233.77	216.08
15000	1382.35	756.13	549.84	448.50	389.11	350.65	324.12
20000	1843.13	1008.17	733.12	598.00	518.81	467.53	432.16
25000	2303.91	1260.22	916.40	747.50	648.51	584.42	540.20
30000	2764.70	1512.26	1099.68	897.00	778.22	701.30	648.24
35000	3225.48	1764.30	1282.96	1046.50	907.92	818.19	756.28
36000	3317.64	1814.71	1319.62	1076.40	933.86	841.56	777.89
37000	3409.79	1865.12	1356.27	1106.30	959.80	864.94	799.50
38000	3501.95	1915.53	1392.93	1136.20	985.74	888.32	821.10
39000	3594.11	1965.94	1429.58	1166.10	1011.68	911.69	842.71
40000	3686.26	2016.34	1466.24	1196.00	1037.62	935.07	864.32
41000	3778.42	2066.75	1502.90	1225.90	1063.56	958.45	885.93
42000	3870.58	2117.16	1539.55	1255.80	1089.50	981.82	907.54
43000	3962.73	2167.57	1576.21	1285.71	1115.44	1005.20	929.14
44000	4054.89	2217.98	1612.86	1315.61	1141.38	1028.58	950.75
45000	4147.05	2268.39	1649.52	1345.51	1167.32	1051.95	972.36
46000	4239.20	2318.80	1686.18	1375.41	1193.27	1075.33	993.97
47000	4331.36	2369.21	1722.83	1405.31	1219.21	1098.71	1015.58
48000	4423.52	2419.61	1759.49	1435.21	1245.15	1122.08	1037.18
49000	4515.67	2470.02	1796.14	1465.11	1271.09	1145.46	1058.79
50000	4607.83	2520.43	1832.80	1495.01	1297.03	1168.84	1080.40
51000	4699.99	2570.84	1869.46	1524.91	1322.97	1192.21	1102.01
52000	4792.14	2621.25	1906.11	1554.81	1348.91	1215.59	1123.62
53000	4884.30	2671.66	1942.77	1584.71	1374.85	1238.97	1145.23
54000	4976.46	2722.07	1979.43	1614.61	1400.79	1262.34	1166.83
55000	5068.61	2772.47	2016.08	1644.51	1426.73	1285.72	1188.44
56000	5160.77	2822.88	2052.74	1674.41	1452.67	1309.10	1210.05
57000	5252.92	2873.29	2089.39	1704.31	1478.61	1332.47	1231.66
58000	5345.08	2923.70	2126.05	1734.21	1504.55	1355.85	1253.27
59000	5437.24	2974.11	2162.71	1764.11	1530.49	1379.23	1274.87
60000	5529.39	3024.52	2199.36	1794.01	1556.43	1402.60	1296.48
65000	5990.18	3276.56	2382.64	1943.51	1686.14	1519.49	1404.52
70000	6450.96	3528.60	2565.92	2093.01	1815.84	1636.37	1512.56
75000	6911.74	3780.65	2749.20	2242.51	1945.54	1753.25	1620.60
80000	7372.53	4032.69	2932.40	2392.01	2075.24	1870.14	1728.64
85000	7833.31	4284.73	3115.76	2541.51	2204.95	1987.02	1836.68
90000	8294.09	4536.78	3299.04	2691.01	2334.65	2103.91	1944.72
95000	8754.87	4788.82	3482.32	2840.51	2464.35	2220.79	2052.76
100000	9215.66	5040.86	3665.60	2990.01	2594.06	2337.67	2160.80
105000	9676.44	5292.90	3848.88	3139.51	2723.76	2454.56	2268.84
110000	10137.22	5544.95	4032.16	3289.01	2853.46	2571.44	2376.88
120000	11058.79	6049.03	4398.72	3588.01	3112.87	2805.21	2592.96
130000	11980.36	6553.12	4765.28	3887.02	3372.27	3038.97	2809.04
140000	12901.92	7057.21	5131.84	4186.02	3631.68	3272.74	3025.12
150000	13823.49	7561.29	5498.40	4485.02	3891.08	3506.51	3241.20
175000	16127.40	8821.51	6414.80	5232.52	4539.60	4090.93	3781.40
200000	18431.32	10081.72	7331.20	5980.02	5188.11	4675.34	4321.60
225000	20735.23	11341.94	8247.60	6727.53	5836.62	5259.76	4861.80
250000	23039.14	12602.15	9164.01	7475.03	6485.14	5844.18	5402.00

Monthly Payments 19%

necessary to amortize a loan

AMOUNT	8 YEARS	9 YEARS	10 YEARS	11 YEARS	12 YEARS	13 YEARS	14 YEARS
100	2.03	1.94	1.87	1.81	1.77	1.73	1.71
200	4.07	3.88	3.73	3.62	3.53	3.47	3.41
500	10.17	9.69	9.33	9.06	8.84	8.66	8.53
1000	20.33	19.39	18.67	18.11	17.67	17.33	17.05
2000	40.67	38.77	37.33	36.22	35.35	34.66	34.10
5000	101.67	96.94	93.34	90.55	88.37	86.64	85.26
6000	122.00	116.32	112.00	108.66	106.04	103.97	102.31
7000	142.34	135.71	130.67	126.77	123.72	121.29	119.36
8000	162.67	155.10	149.34	144.88	141.39	138.62	136.41
9000	183.00	174.48	168.01	162.99	159.06	155.95	153.46
10000	203.34	193.87	186.67	181.10	176.74	173.28	170.51
15000	305.01	290.81	280.01	271.65	265.10	259.91	255.77
20000	406.68	387.74	373.34	362.21	353.47	346.55	341.02
25000	508.35	484.68	466.68	452.76	441.84	433.19	426.28
30000	610.02	581.61	560.02	543.31	530.21	519.83	511.53
35000	711.69	678.55	653.35	633.86	618.58	606.47	596.79
36000	732.02	697.93	672.02	651.97	636.25	623.79	613.84
37000	752.35	717.32	690.69	670.08	653.92	641.12	630.89
38000	772.69	736.71	709.35	688.19	671.60	658.45	647.94
39000	793.02	756.10	728.02	706.30	689.27	675.78	664.99
40000	813.35	775.48	746.69	724.41	706.95	693.10	682.05
41000	833.69	794.87	765.36	742.52	724.62	710.43	699.10
42000	854.02	814.26	784.02	760.63	742.29	727.76	716.15
43000	874.36	833.64	802.69	778.74	759.97	745.09	733.20
44000	894.69	853.03	821.36	796.85	777.64	762.42	750.25
45000	915.02	872.42	840.03	814.96	795.31	779.74	767.30
46000	935.36	891.81	858.69	833.07	812.99	797.07	784.35
47000	955.69	911.19	877.36	851.19	830.66	814.40	801.40
48000	976.03	930.58	896.03	869.30	848.34	831.73	818.45
49000	996.36	949.97	914.69	887.41	866.01	849.05	835.51
50000	1016.69	969.35	933.36	905.52	883.68	866.38	852.56
51000	1037.03	988.74	952.03	923.63	901.36	883.71	869.61
52000	1057.36	1008.13	970.70	941.74	919.03	901.04	886.66
53000	1077.69	1027.52	989.36	959.85	936.70	918.36	903.71
54000	1098.03	1046.90	1008.03	977.96	954.38	935.69	920.76
55000	1118.36	1066.29	1026.70	996.07	972.05	953.02	937.81
56000	1138.70	1085.68	1045.37	1014.18	989.72	970.35	954.86
57000	1159.03	1105.06	1064.03	1032.29	1007.40	987.67	971.92
58000	1179.36	1124.45	1082.70	1050.40	1025.07	1005.00	988.97
59000	1199.70	1143.84	1101.37	1068.51	1042.78	1022.33	1006.02
60000	1220.03	1163.22	1120.03	1086.62	1060.42	1039.66	1023.07
65000	1321.70	1260.16	1213.37	1177.17	1148.79	1126.30	1108.32
70000	1423.37	1357.10	1306.71	1267.72	1237.16	1212.93	1193.58
75000	1525.04	1454.03	1400.04	1358.27	1325.52	1299.57	1278.84
80000	1626.71	1550.97	1493.38	1448.83	1413.89	1386.21	1364.09
85000	1728.38	1647.90	1586.72	1539.38	1502.26	1472.85	1449.35
90000	1830.05	1744.84	1680.05	1629.93	1590.63	1559.49	1534.60
95000	1931.72	1841.77	1773.39	1720.48	1679.00	1646.12	1619.86
100000	2033.39	1938.71	1866.72	1811.03	1767.36	1732.76	1705.11
105000	2135.06	2035.64	1960.06	1901.58	1855.73	1819.40	1790.37
110000	2236.73	2132.58	2053.40	1992.14	1944.10	1906.04	1875.63
120000	2440.06	2326.45	2240.07	2173.24	2120.84	2079.31	2046.14
130000	2643.40	2520.32	2426.74	2354.34	2297.57	2252.59	2216.65
140000	2846.74	2714.19	2613.41	2535.45	2474.31	2425.87	2387.16
150000	3050.08	2908.06	2800.09	2716.55	2651.05	2599.14	2557.67
175000	3558.43	3392.74	3266.77	3169.31	3092.89	3032.33	2983.95
200000	4066.77	3877.42	3733.45	3622.07	3534.73	3465.52	3410.23
225000	4575.12	4362.09	4200.13	4074.82	3976.57	3898.72	3836.51
250000	5083.47	4846.77	4666.81	4527.58	4418.41	4331.91	4262.79

19%

Monthly Payments

necessary to amortize a loan

AMOUNT	15 YEARS	16 YEARS	17 YEARS	18 YEARS	19 YEARS	20 YEARS	21 YEARS
100	1.68	1.66	1.65	1.64	1.63	1.62	1.61
200	3.37	3.33	3.30	3.28	3.26	3.24	3.23
500	8.41	8.32	8.25	8.19	8.14	8.10	8.07
1000	16.83	16.65	16.50	16.38	16.29	16.21	16.14
2000	33.66	33.30	33.01	32.77	32.57	32.41	32.28
5000	84.14	83.24	82.51	81.92	81.43	81.03	80.71
6000	100.97	99.89	99.02	98.30	97.72	97.24	96.85
7000	117.80	116.54	115.52	114.69	114.01	113.45	112.99
8000	134.63	133.19	132.02	131.07	130.29	129.65	129.13
9000	151.46	149.84	148.53	147.45	146.58	145.86	145.27
10000	168.29	166.49	165.03	163.84	162.87	162.07	161.41
15000	252.43	249.73	247.54	245.76	244.30	243.10	242.12
20000	336.58	332.98	330.06	327.68	325.73	324.14	322.83
25000	420.72	416.22	412.57	409.60	407.16	405.17	403.54
30000	504.86	499.47	495.09	491.52	488.60	486.21	484.24
35000	589.01	582.71	577.60	573.43	570.03	567.24	564.95
36000	605.84	599.36	594.10	589.82	586.32	583.45	581.09
37000	622.66	616.01	610.61	606.20	602.60	599.65	597.23
38000	639.49	632.66	627.11	622.59	618.89	615.86	613.37
39000	656.32	649.31	643.61	638.97	635.18	632.07	629.52
40000	673.15	665.96	660.12	655.35	651.46	648.27	645.66
41000	689.98	682.61	676.62	671.74	667.75	664.48	661.80
42000	706.81	699.25	693.12	688.12	684.04	680.69	677.94
43000	723.64	715.90	709.62	704.51	700.32	696.89	694.08
44000	740.47	732.55	726.13	720.89	716.61	713.10	710.22
45000	757.29	749.20	742.63	737.27	732.89	729.31	726.36
46000	774.12	765.85	759.13	753.66	749.18	745.52	742.51
47000	790.95	782.50	775.64	770.04	765.47	761.72	758.65
48000	807.78	799.15	792.14	786.42	781.75	777.93	774.79
49000	824.61	815.80	808.64	802.81	798.04	794.14	790.93
50000	841.44	832.45	825.14	819.19	814.33	810.34	807.07
51000	858.27	849.10	841.65	835.58	830.61	826.55	823.21
52000	875.10	865.74	858.16	851.96	846.90	842.76	839.35
53000	891.92	882.39	874.65	868.34	863.19	858.96	855.50
54000	908.75	899.04	891.16	884.73	879.47	875.17	871.64
55000	925.58	915.69	907.66	901.11	895.76	891.38	887.78
56000	942.41	932.34	924.16	917.50	912.05	907.58	903.92
57000	959.24	948.99	940.66	933.88	928.33	923.79	920.06
58000	976.07	965.64	957.17	950.26	944.62	940.00	936.20
59000	992.90	982.29	973.67	966.65	960.91	956.20	952.34
60000	1009.73	998.94	990.17	983.03	977.19	972.41	968.49
65000	1093.87	1082.18	1072.69	1064.95	1058.63	1053.45	1049.19
70000	1178.01	1165.42	1155.20	1146.87	1140.06	1134.48	1129.90
75000	1262.16	1248.67	1237.72	1228.79	1221.49	1215.51	1210.61
80000	1346.30	1331.91	1320.23	1310.71	1302.92	1296.55	1291.31
85000	1430.44	1415.16	1402.74	1392.63	1384.36	1377.58	1372.02
90000	1514.59	1498.40	1485.26	1474.55	1465.79	1458.62	1452.73
95000	1598.73	1581.65	1567.77	1556.47	1547.22	1539.65	1533.44
100000	1682.88	1664.89	1650.29	1638.38	1628.66	1620.68	1614.14
105000	1767.02	1748.14	1732.80	1720.30	1710.09	1701.72	1694.85
110000	1851.16	1831.38	1815.32	1802.22	1791.52	1782.75	1775.56
120000	2019.45	1997.87	1980.35	1966.06	1954.39	1944.82	1936.97
130000	2187.74	2164.36	2145.37	2129.90	2117.25	2106.89	2098.39
140000	2356.03	2330.85	2310.40	2293.74	2280.12	2268.96	2259.80
150000	2524.31	2497.34	2475.43	2457.58	2442.98	2431.03	2421.21
175000	2945.03	2913.56	2888.00	2867.17	2850.15	2836.20	2824.75
200000	3365.75	3329.79	3300.58	3276.77	3257.31	3241.37	3228.29
225000	3786.47	3746.01	3713.15	3686.36	3664.47	3646.54	3631.82
250000	4207.19	4162.23	4125.72	4095.96	4071.64	4051.71	4035.36

Monthly Payments 19%

necessary to amortize a loan

AMOUNT	22 YEARS	23 YEARS	24 YEARS	25 YEARS	30 YEARS	35 YEARS	40 YEARS
100	1.61	1.60	1.60	1.60	1.59	1.59	1.58
200	3.22	3.21	3.20	3.20	3.18	3.17	3.17
500	8.04	8.02	8.00	7.99	7.94	7.93	7.92
1000	16.09	16.04	16.01	15.98	15.89	15.85	15.84
2000	32.18	32.09	32.01	31.95	31.78	31.71	31.68
5000	00.44	80.22	80.03	79.88	79.44	79.27	79.21
6000	96.53	96.26	96.04	95.86	95.33	95.13	95.05
7000	112.61	112.30	112.05	111.84	111.22	110.98	110.89
8000	128.70	128.35	128.06	127.81	127.11	126.84	126.73
9000	144.79	144.39	144.06	143.79	143.00	142.69	142.58
10000	160.88	160.43	160.07	159.77	158.89	158.55	158.42
15000	241.31	240.65	240.10	239.65	238.33	237.82	237.63
20000	321.75	320.87	320.14	319.54	317.78	317.10	316.83
25000	402.19	401.08	400.17	399.42	397.22	396.37	396.04
30000	482.63	481.30	480.21	479.30	476.67	475.65	475.25
35000	563.07	561.52	560.24	559.19	556.11	554.92	554.46
36000	579.16	577.56	576.25	575.16	572.00	570.78	570.30
37000	595.24	593.60	592.25	591.14	587.89	586.63	586.14
38000	611.33	609.65	608.26	607.12	603.78	602.49	601.99
39000	627.42	625.69	624.27	623.10	619.67	618.34	617.83
40000	643.51	641.73	640.28	639.07	635.56	634.20	633.67
41000	659.59	657.78	656.28	655.05	651.45	650.05	649.51
42000	675.68	673.82	672.29	671.03	667.33	665.91	665.35
43000	691.77	689.86	688.30	687.00	683.22	681.76	681.20
44000	707.86	705.91	704.30	702.98	699.11	697.62	697.04
45000	723.94	721.95	720.31	718.96	715.00	713.47	712.88
46000	740.03	738.00	736.32	734.93	730.89	729.33	728.72
47000	756.12	754.04	752.32	750.91	746.78	745.18	744.56
48000	772.21	770.08	768.33	766.89	762.67	761.04	760.40
49000	788.29	786.13	784.34	782.86	778.56	776.89	776.25
50000	804.38	802.17	800.34	798.84	794.45	792.75	792.09
51000	820.47	818.21	816.35	814.82	810.34	808.60	807.93
52000	836.56	834.26	832.36	830.79	826.22	824.46	823.77
53000	852.65	850.30	848.37	846.77	842.11	840.31	839.61
54000	868.73	866.34	864.37	862.75	858.00	856.17	855.45
55000	884.82	882.39	880.38	878.72	873.89	872.02	871.30
56000	900.91	898.43	896.39	894.70	889.78	887.88	887.14
57000	917.00	914.47	912.39	910.68	905.67	903.73	902.98
58000	933.08	930.52	928.40	926.65	921.56	919.59	918.82
59000	949.17	946.56	944.41	942.63	937.45	935.44	934.66
60000	965.26	962.60	960.41	958.61	953.34	951.30	950.50
65000	1045.70	1042.82	1040.45	1038.49	1032.78	1030.57	1029.71
70000	1126.14	1123.04	1120.48	1118.38	1112.22	1109.85	1108.92
75000	1206.57	1203.25	1200.52	1108.26	1191.67	1189.12	1188.13
80000	1287.01	1283.47	1280.55	1278.14	1271.11	1268.40	1267.34
85000	1367.45	1363.69	1360.59	1358.03	1350.56	1347.67	1346.55
90000	1447.89	1443.90	1440.62	1437.91	1430.00	1426.05	1425.76
95000	1520.33	1524.12	1520.65	1517.80	1509.45	1506.22	1504.97
100000	1608.76	1604.34	1600.69	1597.68	1588.89	1585.49	1584.17
105000	1689.20	1684.55	1680.72	1677.56	1668.34	1664.77	1663.38
110000	1769.64	1764.77	1760.76	1757.45	1747.78	1744.04	1742.59
120000	1930.52	1925.20	1920.83	1917.22	1906.67	1902.59	1901.01
130000	2091.39	2085.64	2080.90	2076.98	2065.56	2061.14	2059.43
140000	2252.27	2246.07	2240.96	2236.75	2224.45	2219.69	2217.84
150000	2413.15	2406.51	2401.03	2396.52	2383.34	2378.24	2376.26
175000	2815.34	2807.59	2801.21	2795.94	2780.56	2774.62	2772.31
200000	3217.53	3208.67	3201.38	3195.36	3177.78	3170.99	3168.35
225000	3619.72	3609.76	3601.55	3594.78	3575.01	3567.36	3564.39
250000	4021.91	4010.84	4001.72	3994.20	3972.23	3963.74	3960.44

19¼%

Monthly Payments
necessary to amortize a loan

AMOUNT	1 YEAR	2 YEARS	3 YEARS	4 YEARS	5 YEARS	6 YEARS	7 YEARS
100	9.23	5.05	3.68	3.00	2.61	2.35	2.18
200	18.46	10.11	7.36	6.01	5.22	4.70	4.35
500	46.14	25.27	18.39	15.02	13.04	11.76	10.88
1000	92.28	50.53	36.78	30.03	26.08	23.52	21.76
2000	184.55	101.06	73.57	60.06	52.16	47.04	43.51
5000	461.38	252.65	183.91	150.16	130.39	117.60	108.78
6000	553.66	303.18	220.70	180.19	156.47	141.12	130.54
7000	645.93	353.71	257.48	210.23	182.55	164.64	152.30
8000	738.21	404.24	294.26	240.26	208.63	188.16	174.05
9000	830.48	454.77	331.04	270.29	234.70	211.68	195.81
10000	922.76	505.30	367.83	300.32	260.78	235.20	217.57
15000	1384.14	757.95	551.74	450.48	391.17	352.80	326.35
20000	1845.52	1010.60	735.65	600.64	521.57	470.40	435.14
25000	2306.90	1263.25	919.56	750.81	651.96	588.00	543.92
30000	2768.28	1515.90	1103.48	900.97	782.35	705.60	652.70
35000	3229.66	1768.56	1287.39	1051.13	912.74	823.20	761.49
36000	3321.93	1819.09	1324.17	1081.16	938.82	846.72	783.25
37000	3414.21	1869.62	1360.95	1111.19	964.90	870.24	805.00
38000	3506.49	1920.15	1397.74	1141.22	990.98	893.76	826.76
39000	3598.76	1970.68	1434.52	1171.26	1017.05	917.28	848.52
40000	3691.04	2021.21	1471.30	1201.29	1043.13	940.80	870.27
41000	3783.31	2071.74	1508.08	1231.32	1069.21	964.32	892.03
42000	3875.59	2122.27	1544.87	1261.35	1095.29	987.84	913.79
43000	3967.87	2172.80	1581.65	1291.38	1121.37	1011.36	935.54
44000	4060.14	2223.33	1618.43	1321.42	1147.45	1034.88	957.30
45000	4152.42	2273.86	1655.21	1351.45	1173.52	1058.40	979.06
46000	4244.69	2324.39	1692.00	1381.48	1199.60	1081.92	1000.81
47000	4336.97	2374.92	1728.78	1411.51	1225.68	1105.44	1022.57
48000	4429.24	2425.45	1765.56	1441.55	1251.76	1128.96	1044.33
49000	4521.52	2475.98	1802.34	1471.58	1277.84	1152.48	1066.08
50000	4613.80	2526.51	1839.13	1501.61	1303.92	1176.00	1087.84
51000	4706.07	2577.04	1875.91	1531.64	1329.99	1199.52	1109.60
52000	4798.35	2627.57	1912.69	1561.67	1356.07	1223.04	1131.35
53000	4890.62	2678.10	1949.47	1591.71	1382.15	1246.56	1153.11
54000	4982.90	2728.63	1986.26	1621.74	1408.23	1270.08	1174.87
55000	5075.18	2779.16	2023.04	1651.77	1434.31	1293.60	1196.63
56000	5167.45	2829.69	2059.82	1681.80	1460.39	1317.12	1218.38
57000	5259.73	2880.22	2096.60	1711.84	1486.46	1340.64	1240.14
58000	5352.00	2930.75	2133.39	1741.87	1512.54	1364.16	1261.90
59000	5444.28	2981.28	2170.17	1771.90	1538.62	1387.68	1283.65
60000	5536.56	3031.81	2206.95	1801.93	1564.70	1411.20	1305.41
65000	5997.94	3284.46	2390.87	1952.09	1695.09	1528.81	1414.19
70000	6459.32	3537.11	2574.78	2102.25	1825.48	1646.41	1522.98
75000	6920.70	3789.76	2758.69	2252.42	1955.87	1764.01	1631.76
80000	7382.07	4042.41	2942.60	2402.58	2086.26	1881.61	1740.55
85000	7843.45	4295.06	3126.52	2552.74	2216.66	1999.21	1849.33
90000	8304.83	4547.71	3310.43	2702.90	2347.05	2116.81	1958.11
95000	8766.21	4800.37	3494.34	2853.06	2477.44	2234.41	2066.90
100000	9227.59	5053.02	3678.25	3003.22	2607.83	2352.01	2175.68
105000	9688.97	5305.67	3862.17	3153.38	2738.22	2469.61	2284.47
110000	10150.35	5558.32	4046.08	3303.54	2868.61	2587.21	2393.25
120000	11073.11	6063.62	4413.91	3603.86	3129.40	2822.41	2610.82
130000	11995.87	6568.92	4781.73	3904.19	3390.18	3057.61	2828.39
140000	12918.63	7074.22	5149.56	4204.51	3650.96	3292.81	3045.95
150000	13841.39	7579.52	5517.38	4504.83	3911.75	3528.01	3263.52
175000	16148.29	8842.78	6436.94	5255.64	4563.70	4116.01	3807.44
200000	18455.19	10106.03	7356.51	6006.44	5215.66	4704.02	4351.36
225000	20762.09	11369.29	8276.07	6757.25	5867.62	5292.02	4895.28
250000	23068.98	12632.54	9195.64	7508.05	6519.58	5880.02	5439.21

Monthly Payments 19¼%

necessary to amortize a loan

AMOUNT	8 YEARS	9 YEARS	10 YEARS	11 YEARS	12 YEARS	13 YEARS	14 YEARS
100	2.05	1.95	1.88	1.83	1.78	1.75	1.72
200	4.10	3.91	3.77	3.66	3.57	3.50	3.45
500	10.24	9.77	9.42	9.14	8.92	8.75	8.62
1000	20.49	19.55	18.83	18.28	17.85	17.50	17.23
2000	40.98	39.09	37.66	36.56	35.69	35.01	34.46
5000	102.44	97.73	94.15	91.39	89.23	87.52	86.15
6000	122.93	117.28	112.99	109.67	107.08	105.02	103.38
7000	143.42	136.82	131.82	127.95	124.92	122.53	120.61
8000	163.90	156.37	150.65	146.23	142.77	140.03	137.84
9000	184.39	175.91	169.48	164.51	160.61	157.53	155.08
10000	204.88	195.46	188.31	182.78	178.46	175.04	172.31
15000	307.32	293.19	282.46	274.18	267.69	262.55	258.46
20000	409.76	390.92	376.62	365.57	356.92	350.07	344.61
25000	512.20	488.65	470.77	456.96	446.15	437.59	430.77
30000	614.64	586.38	564.93	548.35	535.38	525.11	516.92
35000	717.08	684.11	659.08	639.74	624.60	612.63	603.07
36000	737.56	703.66	677.91	658.02	642.45	630.13	620.30
37000	758.05	723.21	696.74	676.30	660.30	647.63	637.53
38000	778.54	742.75	715.58	694.58	678.14	665.14	654.76
39000	799.03	762.30	734.41	712.86	695.99	682.64	671.99
40000	819.52	781.84	753.24	731.14	713.83	700.14	689.22
41000	840.00	801.39	772.07	749.42	731.68	717.65	706.46
42000	860.49	820.94	790.90	767.69	749.53	735.15	723.69
43000	880.98	840.48	809.73	785.97	767.37	752.66	740.92
44000	901.47	860.03	828.56	804.25	785.22	770.16	758.15
45000	921.96	879.57	847.39	822.53	803.06	787.66	775.38
46000	942.44	899.12	866.22	840.81	820.91	805.17	792.61
47000	962.93	918.67	885.05	859.09	838.75	822.67	809.84
48000	983.42	938.21	903.88	877.36	856.60	840.17	827.07
49000	1003.91	957.76	922.72	895.64	874.45	857.68	844.30
50000	1024.39	977.30	941.55	913.92	892.29	875.18	861.53
51000	1044.88	996.85	960.38	932.20	910.14	892.68	878.76
52000	1065.37	1016.40	979.21	950.48	927.98	910.19	895.99
53000	1085.86	1035.94	998.04	968.76	945.83	927.69	913.22
54000	1106.35	1055.49	1016.87	987.03	963.68	945.19	930.45
55000	1126.83	1075.03	1035.70	1005.31	981.52	962.70	947.68
56000	1147.32	1094.58	1054.53	1023.59	999.37	980.20	964.91
57000	1167.81	1114.13	1073.36	1041.87	1017.21	997.71	982.15
58000	1188.30	1133.67	1092.19	1060.15	1035.06	1015.21	999.38
59000	1208.79	1153.22	1111.02	1078.43	1052.00	1032.71	1016.61
60000	1229.27	1172.77	1129.86	1096.71	1070.75	1050.22	1033.84
65000	1331.71	1270.50	1224.01	1188.10	1159.98	1137.73	1119.99
70000	1434.15	1368.23	1318.17	1279.49	1249.21	1225.25	1206.14
75000	1536.59	1465.96	1412.32	1370.88	1338.44	1312.77	1292.30
80000	1639.03	1563.69	1506.47	1462.27	1427.67	1400.29	1378.45
85000	1741.47	1661.42	1600.63	1553.67	1516.90	1487.81	1464.60
90000	1843.91	1759.15	1694.78	1645.06	1606.13	1575.32	1650.76
95000	1946.35	1856.88	1788.94	1736.45	1695.35	1662.84	1636.91
100000	2048.79	1954.61	1883.09	1827.84	1784.58	1750.36	1723.06
105000	2151.23	2052.34	1977.25	1919.23	1873.81	1837.88	1809.22
110000	2253.67	2150.07	2071.40	2010.63	1963.04	1925.40	1895.37
120000	2458.55	2345.53	2259.71	2193.41	2141.50	2100.43	2067.67
130000	2663.43	2540.99	2448.02	2376.19	2319.96	2275.47	2239.98
140000	2868.30	2736.45	2636.33	2558.98	2498.42	2450.51	2412.29
150000	3073.18	2931.91	2824.64	2741.76	2676.88	2625.54	2584.59
175000	3585.38	3420.56	3295.41	3198.72	3123.02	3063.13	3015.36
200000	4097.58	3909.22	3766.19	3655.68	3569.17	3500.72	3446.12
225000	4609.78	4397.87	4236.96	4112.64	4015.31	3938.31	3876.89
250000	5121.97	4886.52	4707.73	4569.61	4461.46	4375.90	4307.66

19¼%

Monthly Payments
necessary to amortize a loan

AMOUNT	15 YEARS	16 YEARS	17 YEARS	18 YEARS	19 YEARS	20 YEARS	21 YEARS
100	1.70	1.68	1.67	1.66	1.65	1.64	1.63
200	3.40	3.37	3.34	3.31	3.30	3.28	3.27
500	8.51	8.42	8.35	8.29	8.24	8.20	8.17
1000	17.01	16.83	16.69	16.57	16.48	16.40	16.34
2000	34.02	33.67	33.38	33.15	32.96	32.80	32.68
5000	85.06	84.17	83.46	82.87	82.40	82.01	81.69
6000	102.07	101.01	100.15	99.45	98.88	98.41	98.03
7000	119.08	117.84	116.84	116.02	115.36	114.81	114.36
8000	136.09	134.68	133.53	132.60	131.83	131.21	130.70
9000	153.10	151.51	150.22	149.17	148.31	147.61	147.04
10000	170.11	168.35	166.91	165.74	164.79	164.02	163.38
15000	255.17	252.52	250.37	248.62	247.19	246.02	245.07
20000	340.23	336.69	333.82	331.49	329.59	328.03	326.76
25000	425.29	420.86	417.28	414.36	411.98	410.04	408.45
30000	510.34	505.04	500.73	497.23	494.38	492.05	490.13
35000	595.40	589.21	584.19	580.11	576.78	574.05	571.82
36000	612.41	606.04	600.88	596.68	593.25	590.45	588.16
37000	629.42	622.88	617.57	613.25	609.73	606.86	604.50
38000	646.43	639.71	634.26	629.83	626.21	623.26	620.84
39000	663.45	656.55	650.95	646.40	642.69	639.66	637.17
40000	680.46	673.38	667.64	662.98	659.17	656.06	653.51
41000	697.47	690.22	684.34	679.55	675.65	672.46	669.85
42000	714.48	707.05	701.03	696.13	692.13	688.86	686.19
43000	731.49	723.88	717.72	712.70	708.61	705.27	702.53
44000	748.50	740.72	734.41	729.28	725.09	721.67	718.86
45000	765.51	757.55	751.10	745.85	741.57	738.07	735.20
46000	782.53	774.39	767.79	762.42	758.05	754.47	751.54
47000	799.54	791.22	784.48	779.00	774.53	770.87	767.88
48000	816.55	808.06	801.17	795.57	791.01	787.27	784.21
49000	833.56	824.89	817.86	812.15	807.49	803.67	800.55
50000	850.57	841.73	834.56	828.72	823.97	820.08	816.89
51000	867.58	858.56	851.25	845.30	840.44	836.48	833.23
52000	884.59	875.39	867.94	861.87	856.92	852.88	849.57
53000	901.61	892.23	884.63	878.45	873.40	869.28	865.90
54000	918.62	909.06	901.32	895.02	889.88	885.68	882.24
55000	935.63	925.90	918.01	911.59	906.36	902.08	898.58
56000	952.64	942.73	934.70	928.17	922.84	918.48	914.92
57000	969.65	959.57	951.39	944.74	939.32	934.89	931.25
58000	986.66	976.40	968.08	961.32	955.80	951.29	947.59
59000	1003.67	993.24	984.77	977.89	972.28	967.69	963.93
60000	1020.69	1010.07	1001.47	994.47	988.76	984.09	980.27
65000	1105.74	1094.24	1084.92	1077.34	1071.15	1066.10	1061.96
70000	1190.80	1178.42	1168.38	1160.21	1153.55	1148.11	1143.65
75000	1275.86	1262.59	1251.83	1243.08	1235.95	1230.11	1225.34
80000	1360.91	1346.76	1335.29	1325.96	1318.34	1312.12	1307.02
85000	1445.97	1430.93	1418.74	1408.83	1400.74	1394.13	1388.71
90000	1531.03	1515.11	1502.20	1491.70	1483.14	1476.14	1470.40
95000	1616.09	1599.28	1585.65	1574.57	1565.53	1558.14	1552.09
100000	1701.14	1683.45	1669.11	1657.45	1647.93	1640.15	1633.78
105000	1786.20	1767.62	1752.57	1740.32	1730.33	1722.16	1715.47
110000	1871.26	1851.80	1836.02	1823.19	1812.72	1804.17	1797.16
120000	2041.37	2020.14	2002.93	1988.93	1977.52	1968.18	1960.54
130000	2211.49	2188.49	2169.84	2154.68	2142.31	2132.20	2123.91
140000	2381.60	2356.83	2336.75	2320.42	2307.10	2296.21	2287.29
150000	2551.72	2525.18	2503.67	2486.17	2471.90	2460.23	2450.67
175000	2977.00	2946.04	2920.94	2900.53	2883.88	2870.27	2859.12
200000	3402.29	3366.90	3338.22	3314.89	3295.86	3280.30	3267.56
225000	3827.57	3787.77	3755.50	3729.25	3707.84	3690.34	3676.01
250000	4252.86	4208.63	4172.78	4143.61	4119.83	4100.38	4084.45

Monthly Payments 19¼%

necessary to amortize a loan

AMOUNT	22 YEARS	23 YEARS	24 YEARS	25 YEARS	30 YEARS	35 YEARS	40 YEARS
100	1.63	1.62	1.62	1.62	1.61	1.61	1.60
200	3.26	3.25	3.24	3.24	3.22	3.21	3.21
500	8.14	8.12	8.10	8.09	8.05	8.03	8.02
1000	16.29	16.24	16.21	16.18	16.09	16.06	16.05
2000	32.57	32.49	32.41	32.36	32.19	32.12	32.10
5000	81.43	81.21	81.04	80.89	80.47	80.31	80.25
6000	97.71	97.46	97.24	97.07	96.56	96.37	96.30
7000	114.00	113.70	113.45	113.25	112.66	112.43	112.35
8000	130.28	129.94	129.66	129.43	128.75	128.49	128.40
9000	146.57	146.18	145.87	145.60	144.85	144.56	144.44
10000	162.86	162.43	162.07	161.78	160.94	160.62	160.49
15000	244.28	243.64	243.11	242.67	241.41	240.93	240.74
20000	325.71	324.85	324.15	323.57	321.88	321.24	320.99
25000	407.14	406.07	405.18	404.46	402.35	401.54	401.23
30000	488.57	487.28	486.22	485.35	482.82	481.85	481.48
35000	569.99	568.49	567.26	566.24	563.29	562.16	561.73
36000	586.28	584.73	583.46	582.42	579.38	578.22	577.78
37000	602.56	600.98	599.67	598.60	595.48	594.28	593.83
38000	618.85	617.22	615.88	614.77	611.57	610.35	609.88
39000	635.14	633.46	632.09	630.95	627.66	626.41	625.93
40000	651.42	649.70	648.29	647.13	643.76	642.47	641.98
41000	667.71	665.95	664.50	663.31	659.85	658.53	658.03
42000	683.99	682.19	680.71	679.49	675.95	674.59	674.07
43000	700.28	698.43	696.91	695.67	692.04	690.66	690.12
44000	716.56	714.67	713.12	711.84	708.13	706.72	706.17
45000	732.85	730.92	729.33	728.02	724.23	722.78	722.22
46000	749.13	747.16	745.54	744.20	740.32	738.84	738.27
47000	765.42	763.40	761.74	760.38	756.42	754.90	754.32
48000	781.71	779.65	777.95	776.56	772.51	770.96	770.37
49000	797.99	795.89	794.16	792.74	788.60	787.03	786.42
50000	814.28	812.13	810.37	808.91	804.70	803.09	802.47
51000	830.56	828.37	826.57	825.09	820.79	810.15	818.52
52000	846.85	844.62	842.78	841.27	836.89	835.21	834.57
53000	863.13	860.86	858.99	857.45	852.98	851.27	850.62
54000	879.42	877.10	875.20	873.63	869.07	867.33	866.67
55000	895.70	893.34	891.40	889.81	885.17	883.40	882.72
56000	911.99	909.59	907.61	905.98	901.26	899.46	898.77
57000	928.28	925.83	923.82	922.16	917.36	915.52	914.82
58000	944.56	942.07	940.02	938.34	933.45	931.58	930.86
59000	960.85	958.31	956.23	954.52	949.54	947.64	940.91
60000	977.13	974.56	972.44	970.70	965.64	963.71	962.96
65000	1058.56	1055.77	1053.48	1051.59	1046.11	1044.01	1043.21
70000	1139.99	1136.98	1134.51	1132.48	1126.58	1124.32	1123.46
75000	1221.42	1218.20	1215.55	1213.37	1207.05	1204.63	1203.70
80000	1302.84	1299.41	1296.59	1294.26	1287.52	1284.94	1283.95
85000	1384.27	1380.62	1377.62	1375.15	1367.99	1365.25	1364.20
90000	1465.70	1461.84	1458.66	1456.04	1448.46	1445.56	1444.45
95000	1547.13	1543.05	1539.70	1536.94	1528.93	1525.87	1524.69
100000	1628.55	1624.26	1620.73	1617.83	1609.40	1606.18	1604.94
105000	1709.98	1705.47	1701.77	1698.72	1689.87	1686.48	1685.19
110000	1791.41	1786.69	1782.80	1779.61	1770.34	1766.79	1765.43
120000	1954.26	1949.11	1944.88	1941.39	1931.28	1927.41	1925.93
130000	2117.12	2111.54	2106.95	2103.18	2092.22	2088.03	2086.42
140000	2279.98	2273.97	2269.02	2264.96	2253.16	2248.65	2246.91
150000	2442.83	2436.39	2431.10	2426.74	2414.10	2409.26	2407.41
175000	2849.97	2842.46	2836.28	2831.20	2816.44	2810.81	2808.64
200000	3257.11	3248.52	3241.46	3235.65	3218.79	3212.35	3209.88
225000	3664.25	3654.59	3646.65	3640.11	3621.14	3613.89	3611.11
250000	4071.38	4060.65	4051.83	4044.57	4023.49	4015.44	4012.35

19½%

Monthly Payments
necessary to amortize a loan

AMOUNT	1 YEAR	2 YEARS	3 YEARS	4 YEARS	5 YEARS	6 YEARS	7 YEARS
100	9.24	5.07	3.69	3.02	2.62	2.37	2.19
200	18.48	10.13	7.38	6.03	5.24	4.73	4.38
500	46.20	25.33	18.45	15.08	13.11	11.83	10.95
1000	92.40	50.65	36.91	30.16	26.22	23.66	21.91
2000	184.79	101.30	73.82	60.33	52.43	47.33	43.81
5000	461.98	253.26	184.55	150.82	131.08	118.32	109.53
6000	554.37	303.91	221.46	180.99	157.30	141.98	131.44
7000	646.77	354.56	258.37	211.15	183.52	165.65	153.34
8000	739.16	405.22	295.27	241.32	209.73	189.31	175.25
9000	831.56	455.87	332.18	271.48	235.95	212.97	197.16
10000	923.95	506.52	369.09	301.65	262.16	236.64	219.06
15000	1385.93	759.78	553.64	452.47	393.25	354.96	328.59
20000	1847.91	1013.04	738.19	603.29	524.33	473.28	438.12
25000	2309.88	1266.30	922.73	754.12	655.41	591.60	547.65
30000	2771.86	1519.56	1107.28	904.94	786.49	709.92	657.18
35000	3233.84	1772.82	1291.83	1055.76	917.58	828.24	766.71
36000	3326.23	1823.47	1328.74	1085.93	943.79	851.90	788.62
37000	3418.63	1874.12	1365.64	1116.09	970.01	875.56	810.53
38000	3511.02	1924.77	1402.55	1146.25	996.22	899.23	832.43
39000	3603.42	1975.42	1439.46	1176.42	1022.44	922.89	854.34
40000	3695.81	2026.08	1476.37	1206.58	1048.66	946.56	876.24
41000	3788.21	2076.73	1513.28	1236.75	1074.87	970.22	898.15
42000	3880.61	2127.38	1550.19	1266.91	1101.09	993.88	920.06
43000	3973.00	2178.03	1587.10	1297.08	1127.31	1017.55	941.96
44000	4065.40	2228.68	1624.01	1327.24	1153.52	1041.21	963.87
45000	4157.79	2279.33	1660.92	1357.41	1179.74	1064.87	985.78
46000	4250.19	2329.99	1697.83	1387.57	1205.96	1088.54	1007.68
47000	4342.58	2380.64	1734.74	1417.74	1232.17	1112.20	1029.59
48000	4434.98	2431.29	1771.65	1447.90	1258.39	1135.87	1051.49
49000	4527.37	2481.94	1808.56	1478.07	1284.61	1159.53	1073.40
50000	4619.77	2532.59	1845.47	1508.23	1310.82	1183.19	1095.31
51000	4712.16	2583.25	1882.37	1538.39	1337.04	1206.86	1117.21
52000	4804.56	2633.90	1919.28	1568.56	1363.26	1230.52	1139.12
53000	4896.95	2684.55	1956.19	1598.72	1389.47	1254.19	1161.02
54000	4989.35	2735.20	1993.10	1628.89	1415.69	1277.85	1182.93
55000	5081.75	2785.85	2030.01	1659.05	1441.90	1301.51	1204.84
56000	5174.14	2836.51	2066.92	1689.22	1468.12	1325.18	1226.74
57000	5266.54	2887.16	2103.83	1719.38	1494.34	1348.84	1248.65
58000	5358.93	2937.81	2140.74	1749.55	1520.55	1372.51	1270.55
59000	5451.33	2988.46	2177.65	1779.71	1546.77	1396.17	1292.46
60000	5543.72	3039.11	2214.56	1809.88	1572.99	1419.83	1314.37
65000	6005.70	3292.37	2399.11	1960.70	1704.07	1538.15	1423.90
70000	6467.68	3545.63	2583.65	2111.52	1835.15	1656.47	1533.43
75000	6929.65	3798.89	2768.20	2262.35	1966.23	1774.79	1642.96
80000	7391.63	4052.15	2952.74	2413.17	2097.32	1893.11	1752.49
85000	7853.61	4305.41	3137.29	2563.99	2228.40	2011.43	1862.02
90000	8315.58	4558.67	3321.84	2714.81	2359.48	2129.75	1971.55
95000	8777.56	4811.93	3506.38	2865.64	2490.56	2248.07	2081.08
100000	9239.54	5065.19	3690.93	3016.46	2621.64	2366.39	2190.61
105000	9701.51	5318.45	3875.48	3167.28	2752.73	2484.71	2300.14
110000	10163.49	5571.71	4060.02	3318.11	2883.81	2603.03	2409.67
120000	11087.44	6078.23	4429.12	3619.75	3145.97	2839.67	2628.73
130000	12011.40	6584.74	4798.21	3921.40	3408.14	3076.30	2847.80
140000	12935.35	7091.26	5167.30	4223.04	3670.30	3312.94	3066.86
150000	13859.31	7597.78	5536.40	4524.69	3932.47	3549.58	3285.92
175000	16169.19	8864.08	6459.13	5278.81	4587.88	4141.18	3833.57
200000	18479.07	10130.38	7381.86	6032.92	5243.29	4732.78	4381.22
225000	20788.96	11396.67	8304.59	6787.04	5898.70	5324.37	4928.88
250000	23098.84	12662.97	9227.33	7541.15	6554.11	5915.97	5476.53

Monthly Payments 19½%

necessary to amortize a loan

AMOUNT	8 YEARS	9 YEARS	10 YEARS	11 YEARS	12 YEARS	13 YEARS	14 YEARS
100	2.06	1.97	1.90	1.84	1.80	1.77	1.74
200	4.13	3.94	3.80	3.69	3.60	3.54	3.48
500	10.32	9.85	9.50	9.22	9.01	8.84	8.71
1000	20.64	19.71	19.00	18.45	18.02	17.68	17.41
2000	41.28	39.41	37.99	36.89	36.04	35.36	34.82
5000	103.21	98.53	94.98	92.24	90.09	88.40	87.05
6000	123.85	118.23	113.97	110.68	108.11	106.08	104.46
7000	144.50	137.94	132.97	129.13	126.13	123.76	121.87
8000	165.14	157.65	151.96	147.58	144.15	141.44	139.29
9000	185.78	177.35	170.96	166.02	162.17	159.12	156.70
10000	206.42	197.06	189.95	184.47	180.19	176.80	174.11
15000	309.64	295.58	284.93	276.71	270.28	265.20	261.16
20000	412.85	394.11	379.90	368.94	360.37	353.60	348.21
25000	516.06	492.64	474.88	461.18	450.47	442.01	435.27
30000	619.27	591.17	569.86	553.41	540.56	530.41	522.32
35000	722.49	689.70	664.83	645.65	630.65	618.81	609.37
36000	743.13	709.40	683.83	664.10	648.67	636.49	626.79
37000	763.77	729.11	702.82	682.54	666.69	654.17	644.20
38000	784.41	748.81	721.82	700.99	684.71	671.85	661.61
39000	805.06	768.52	740.81	719.44	702.73	689.53	679.02
40000	825.70	788.23	759.81	737.89	720.75	707.21	696.43
41000	846.34	807.93	778.80	756.33	738.76	724.89	713.84
42000	866.98	827.64	797.80	774.78	756.78	742.57	731.25
43000	887.63	847.34	816.79	793.23	774.80	760.25	748.66
44000	908.27	867.05	835.79	811.67	792.82	777.93	766.07
45000	928.91	886.75	854.78	830.12	810.84	795.61	783.48
46000	949.55	906.46	873.78	848.57	828.86	813.29	800.89
47000	970.20	926.17	892.78	867.01	846.88	830.97	818.30
48000	990.84	945.87	911.77	885.46	864.90	848.65	835.71
49000	1011.48	965.58	930.77	903.91	882.91	866.33	853.12
50000	1032.12	985.28	949.76	922.36	900.93	884.01	870.54
51000	1052.77	1004.99	968.76	940.80	918.95	901.69	887.95
52000	1073.41	1024.69	987.75	959.25	936.97	919.37	905.36
53000	1094.05	1044.40	1006.75	977.70	954.99	937.05	922.77
54000	1114.69	1064.11	1025.74	996.14	973.01	954.73	940.18
55000	1135.34	1083.81	1044.74	1014.59	991.03	972.41	957.59
56000	1155.98	1103.52	1063.73	1033.04	1009.04	990.09	975.00
57000	1176.62	1123.22	1082.73	1051.49	1027.06	1007.77	992.41
58000	1197.26	1142.93	1101.72	1069.93	1045.08	1025.45	1009.82
59000	1217.91	1162.63	1120.72	1088.38	1063.10	1043.13	1027.23
60000	1238.55	1182.34	1139.71	1106.83	1081.12	1060.81	1044.64
65000	1341.76	1280.87	1234.69	1199.06	1171.21	1149.21	1131.70
70000	1444.97	1379.40	1329.67	1291.30	1261.31	1237.61	1218.75
75000	1548.18	1477.92	1424.64	1383.53	1351.40	1326.02	1305.80
80000	1651.40	1576.45	1519.62	1475.77	1441.49	1414.42	1392.86
85000	1754.61	1674.98	1614.59	1568.01	1531.59	1502.82	1479.91
90000	1857.82	1773.51	1709.57	1660.24	1621.68	1591.22	1566.96
95000	1961.03	1872.04	1804.55	1752.48	1711.77	1679.62	1654.02
100000	2064.25	1970.57	1899.52	1844.71	1801.86	1768.02	1741.07
105000	2167.46	2069.09	1994.50	1936.95	1891.96	1856.42	1828.12
110000	2270.67	2167.62	2089.47	2029.18	1982.05	1944.82	1915.18
120000	2477.10	2364.68	2279.43	2213.66	2162.24	2121.63	2089.28
130000	2683.52	2561.74	2469.38	2398.13	2342.42	2298.43	2263.39
140000	2889.94	2758.79	2659.33	2582.60	2522.61	2475.23	2437.50
150000	3096.37	2955.85	2849.28	2767.07	2702.80	2652.03	2611.61
175000	3612.43	3448.49	3324.16	3228.25	3153.26	3094.04	3046.87
200000	4128.49	3941.13	3799.04	3689.43	3603.73	3536.04	3482.14
225000	4644.55	4433.77	4273.92	4150.60	4054.20	3978.05	3917.41
250000	5160.62	4926.41	4748.81	4611.78	4504.66	4420.05	4352.68

19½%

Monthly Payments

necessary to amortize a loan

AMOUNT	15 YEARS	16 YEARS	17 YEARS	18 YEARS	19 YEARS	20 YEARS	21 YEARS
100	1.72	1.70	1.69	1.68	1.67	1.66	1.65
200	3.44	3.40	3.38	3.35	3.33	3.32	3.31
500	8.60	8.51	8.44	8.38	8.34	8.30	8.27
1000	17.19	17.02	16.88	16.77	16.67	16.60	16.53
2000	34.39	34.04	33.76	33.53	33.35	33.19	33.07
5000	85.97	85.10	84.40	83.83	83.36	82.98	82.67
6000	103.17	102.12	101.28	100.59	100.04	99.58	99.21
7000	120.36	119.14	118.16	117.36	116.71	116.18	115.74
8000	137.56	136.17	135.04	134.12	133.38	132.77	132.28
9000	154.75	153.19	151.92	150.89	150.05	149.37	148.81
10000	171.95	170.21	168.80	167.66	166.73	165.97	165.35
15000	257.92	255.31	253.20	251.48	250.09	248.95	248.02
20000	343.89	340.41	337.60	335.31	333.45	331.93	330.69
25000	429.87	425.52	422.00	419.14	416.81	414.92	413.37
30000	515.84	510.62	506.40	502.97	500.18	497.90	496.04
35000	601.81	595.72	590.80	586.80	583.54	580.88	578.71
36000	619.01	612.74	607.68	603.56	600.21	597.48	595.25
37000	636.20	629.76	624.56	620.33	616.88	614.08	611.78
38000	653.40	646.79	641.44	637.09	633.56	630.67	628.32
39000	670.59	663.81	658.32	653.86	650.23	647.27	644.85
40000	687.79	680.83	675.20	670.62	666.90	663.87	661.38
41000	704.98	697.85	692.07	687.39	683.57	680.46	677.92
42000	722.18	714.87	708.95	704.15	700.25	697.06	694.45
43000	739.37	731.89	725.83	720.92	716.92	713.66	710.99
44000	756.57	748.91	742.71	737.69	733.59	730.25	727.52
45000	773.76	765.93	759.59	754.45	750.26	746.85	744.06
46000	790.96	782.95	776.47	771.22	766.94	763.45	760.59
47000	808.15	799.97	793.35	787.98	783.61	780.04	777.13
48000	825.35	816.99	810.23	804.75	800.28	796.64	793.66
49000	842.54	834.01	827.11	821.51	816.95	813.24	810.20
50000	859.74	851.03	843.99	838.28	833.63	829.83	826.73
51000	876.93	868.05	860.87	855.04	850.30	846.43	843.27
52000	894.12	885.07	877.75	871.81	866.97	863.03	859.80
53000	911.32	902.10	894.63	888.58	883.64	879.62	876.33
54000	928.51	919.12	911.51	905.34	900.32	896.22	892.87
55000	945.71	936.14	928.39	922.11	916.99	912.82	909.40
56000	962.90	953.16	945.27	938.87	933.66	929.41	925.94
57000	980.10	970.18	962.15	955.64	950.34	946.01	942.47
58000	997.29	987.20	979.03	972.40	967.01	962.61	959.01
59000	1014.49	1004.22	995.91	989.17	983.68	979.20	975.54
60000	1031.68	1021.24	1012.79	1005.93	1000.35	995.80	992.08
65000	1117.66	1106.34	1097.19	1089.76	1083.72	1078.78	1074.75
70000	1203.63	1191.45	1181.59	1173.59	1167.08	1161.77	1157.42
75000	1289.60	1276.55	1265.99	1257.42	1250.44	1244.75	1240.10
80000	1375.58	1361.65	1350.39	1341.25	1333.80	1327.73	1322.77
85000	1461.55	1446.76	1434.79	1425.07	1417.17	1410.71	1405.44
90000	1547.52	1531.86	1519.19	1508.90	1500.53	1493.70	1488.12
95000	1633.50	1616.96	1603.59	1592.73	1583.89	1576.68	1570.79
100000	1719.47	1702.07	1687.99	1676.56	1667.25	1659.66	1653.46
105000	1805.44	1787.17	1772.39	1760.39	1750.62	1742.65	1736.13
110000	1891.42	1872.27	1856.79	1844.21	1833.98	1825.63	1818.81
120000	2063.36	2042.48	2025.59	2011.87	2000.71	1991.60	1984.15
130000	2235.31	2212.69	2194.38	2179.53	2167.43	2157.56	2149.50
140000	2407.26	2382.89	2363.18	2347.18	2334.16	2323.53	2314.85
150000	2579.21	2553.10	2531.98	2514.84	2500.88	2489.50	2480.19
175000	3009.07	2978.62	2953.98	2933.98	2917.70	2904.41	2893.56
200000	3438.94	3404.13	3375.98	3353.12	3334.51	3319.33	3306.92
225000	3868.81	3829.65	3797.97	3772.26	3751.32	3734.25	3720.29
250000	4298.68	4255.17	4219.97	4191.40	4168.14	4149.16	4133.65

Monthly Payments 19½%

necessary to amortize a loan

AMOUNT	22 YEARS	23 YEARS	24 YEARS	25 YEARS	30 YEARS	35 YEARS	40 YEARS
100	1.65	1.64	1.64	1.64	1.63	1.63	1.63
200	3.30	3.29	3.28	3.28	3.26	3.25	3.25
500	8.24	8.22	8.20	8.19	8.15	8.13	8.13
1000	16.48	16.44	16.41	16.38	16.30	16.27	16.26
2000	32.97	32.88	32.82	32.76	32.60	32.54	32.51
5000	82.42	82.21	82.04	81.90	81.50	81.34	81.29
6000	98.90	98.65	98.45	98.28	97.80	97.61	97.54
7000	115.39	115.10	114.86	114.66	114.09	113.88	113.80
8000	131.87	131.54	131.26	131.04	130.39	130.15	130.06
9000	148.35	147.98	147.67	147.42	146.69	146.42	146.31
10000	164.84	164.42	164.08	163.80	162.99	162.69	162.57
15000	247.26	246.63	246.12	245.70	244.49	244.03	243.86
20000	329.68	328.84	328.16	327.60	325.98	325.37	325.14
25000	412.10	411.06	410.20	409.50	407.48	406.72	406.43
30000	494.52	493.27	492.24	491.40	488.98	488.06	487.71
35000	576.93	575.48	574.28	573.30	570.47	569.40	569.00
36000	593.42	591.92	590.69	589.68	586.77	585.67	585.26
37000	609.90	608.36	607.10	606.06	603.07	601.94	601.51
38000	626.39	624.80	623.51	622.44	619.37	618.21	617.77
39000	642.87	641.25	639.92	638.82	635.67	634.48	634.03
40000	659.35	657.69	656.32	655.20	651.97	650.75	650.28
41000	675.84	674.13	672.73	671.58	668.27	667.02	666.54
42000	692.32	690.57	689.14	687.96	684.57	683.28	682.80
43000	708.80	707.02	705.55	704.34	700.87	699.55	699.05
44000	725.29	723.46	721.96	720.72	717.16	715.82	715.31
45000	741.77	739.90	738.36	737.10	733.46	732.09	731.57
46000	758.26	756.34	754.77	753.48	749.76	748.36	747.83
47000	774.74	772.78	771.18	769.86	766.06	764.63	764.08
48000	791.22	789.23	787.59	786.24	782.36	780.90	780.34
49000	807.71	805.67	804.00	802.62	798.66	797.16	796.60
50000	824.19	822.11	820.40	819.00	814.96	813.43	812.85
51000	840.68	838.55	836.81	835.38	831.26	829.70	829.11
52000	857.16	855.00	853.22	851.76	847.56	845.97	845.37
53000	873.64	871.44	869.63	868.14	863.86	862.24	861.63
54000	890.13	887.88	886.04	884.52	880.16	878.51	877.88
55000	906.61	904.32	902.44	900.90	896.46	894.78	894.14
56000	923.09	920.76	918.85	917.28	912.76	911.05	910.40
57000	939.58	937.21	935.26	933.66	929.05	927.31	926.65
58000	956.06	953.66	951.67	950.04	945.35	943.58	942.91
59000	972.55	970.09	968.08	966.42	961.65	959.85	959.17
60000	989.03	986.53	984.49	982.80	977.95	976.12	975.43
65000	1071.45	1068.74	1066.53	1064.70	1059.45	1057.46	1056.71
70000	1153.87	1150.96	1148.57	1146.60	1140.94	1138.81	1138.00
75000	1236.29	1233.17	1230.61	1228.50	1222.44	1220.15	1219.28
80000	1318.71	1315.38	1312.65	1310.40	1303.94	1301.49	1300.57
85000	1401.13	1397.59	1394.69	1392.31	1385.43	1382.84	1381.85
90000	1483.55	1479.80	1476.73	1474.21	1466.93	1464.18	1463.14
95000	1566.06	1562.01	1558.77	1556.11	1548.42	1545.52	1544.42
100000	1648.38	1644.22	1640.81	1638.01	1629.92	1626.87	1625.71
105000	1730.80	1726.43	1722.85	1719.91	1711.42	1708.21	1706.99
110000	1813.22	1808.64	1804.89	1801.81	1792.91	1789.55	1788.28
120000	1978.06	1973.07	1968.97	1965.61	1955.90	1952.24	1950.85
130000	2142.90	2137.49	2133.05	2129.41	2118.90	2114.93	2113.42
140000	2307.74	2301.91	2297.13	2293.21	2281.89	2277.61	2275.99
150000	2472.58	2466.33	2461.21	2457.01	2444.88	2440.30	2438.56
175000	2884.67	2877.39	2871.42	2866.51	2852.36	2847.02	2844.99
200000	3296.77	3288.44	3281.62	3276.01	3259.84	3253.73	3251.42
225000	3708.86	3699.50	3691.82	3685.51	3667.32	3660.45	3657.85
250000	4120.96	4110.56	4102.02	4095.02	4074.80	4067.17	4064.27

19¾% Monthly Payments

necessary to amortize a loan

AMOUNT	1 YEAR	2 YEARS	3 YEARS	4 YEARS	5 YEARS	6 YEARS	7 YEARS
100	9.25	5.08	3.70	3.03	2.64	2.38	2.21
200	18.50	10.15	7.41	6.06	5.27	4.76	4.41
500	46.26	25.39	18.52	15.15	13.18	11.90	11.03
1000	92.51	50.77	37.04	30.30	26.35	23.81	22.06
2000	185.03	101.55	74.07	60.59	52.71	47.62	44.11
5000	462.57	253.87	185.18	151.49	131.77	119.04	110.28
6000	555.09	304.64	222.22	181.78	158.13	142.85	132.34
7000	647.60	355.42	259.25	212.08	184.48	166.66	154.39
8000	740.12	406.19	296.29	242.38	210.84	190.47	176.45
9000	832.63	456.96	333.33	272.68	237.19	214.27	198.50
10000	925.15	507.74	370.36	302.97	263.55	238.08	220.56
15000	1387.72	761.61	555.54	454.46	395.32	357.12	330.84
20000	1850.30	1015.48	740.73	605.95	527.10	476.16	441.12
25000	2312.87	1269.34	925.91	757.43	658.87	595.20	551.40
30000	2775.45	1523.21	1111.09	908.92	790.65	714.24	661.68
35000	3238.02	1777.08	1296.27	1060.41	922.42	833.28	771.96
36000	3330.54	1827.86	1333.31	1090.70	948.78	857.09	794.01
37000	3423.05	1878.63	1370.34	1121.00	975.13	880.90	816.07
38000	3515.57	1929.40	1407.38	1151.30	1001.49	904.71	838.12
39000	3608.08	1980.18	1444.42	1181.60	1027.84	928.52	860.18
40000	3700.60	2030.95	1481.45	1211.89	1054.20	952.33	882.24
41000	3793.11	2081.72	1518.49	1242.19	1080.55	976.13	904.29
42000	3885.63	2132.50	1555.53	1272.49	1106.91	999.94	926.35
43000	3978.14	2183.27	1592.56	1302.78	1133.26	1023.75	948.40
44000	4070.66	2234.05	1629.60	1333.08	1159.62	1047.56	970.46
45000	4163.17	2284.82	1666.63	1363.38	1185.97	1071.37	992.52
46000	4255.69	2335.59	1703.67	1393.68	1212.33	1095.17	1014.57
47000	4348.20	2386.37	1740.71	1423.97	1238.68	1118.98	1036.63
48000	4440.72	2437.14	1777.74	1454.27	1265.04	1142.79	1058.68
49000	4533.23	2487.91	1814.78	1484.57	1291.39	1166.60	1080.74
50000	4625.74	2538.69	1851.82	1514.87	1317.75	1190.41	1102.80
51000	4718.26	2589.46	1888.85	1545.16	1344.10	1214.21	1124.85
52000	4810.77	2640.24	1925.89	1575.46	1370.46	1238.02	1146.91
53000	4903.29	2691.01	1962.93	1605.76	1396.81	1261.83	1168.96
54000	4995.80	2741.78	1999.96	1636.06	1423.17	1285.64	1191.02
55000	5088.32	2792.56	2037.00	1666.35	1449.52	1309.45	1213.08
56000	5180.83	2843.33	2074.03	1696.65	1475.88	1333.26	1235.13
57000	5273.35	2894.10	2111.07	1726.95	1502.23	1357.06	1257.19
58000	5365.86	2944.88	2148.11	1757.24	1528.59	1380.87	1279.24
59000	5458.38	2995.65	2185.14	1787.54	1554.94	1404.68	1301.30
60000	5550.89	3046.43	2222.18	1817.84	1581.30	1428.49	1323.35
65000	6013.47	3300.29	2407.36	1969.33	1713.07	1547.53	1433.63
70000	6476.04	3554.16	2592.54	2120.81	1844.85	1666.57	1543.91
75000	6938.62	3808.03	2777.72	2272.30	1976.62	1785.61	1654.19
80000	7401.19	4061.90	2962.91	2423.79	2108.40	1904.65	1764.47
85000	7863.77	4315.77	3148.09	2575.27	2240.17	2023.69	1874.75
90000	8326.34	4569.64	3333.27	2726.76	2371.95	2142.73	1985.03
95000	8788.92	4823.51	3518.45	2878.25	2503.72	2261.77	2095.31
100000	9251.49	5077.38	3703.63	3029.73	2635.50	2380.81	2205.59
105000	9714.06	5331.24	3888.81	3181.22	2767.27	2499.85	2315.87
110000	10176.64	5585.11	4074.00	3332.71	2899.05	2618.89	2426.15
120000	11101.79	6092.85	4444.36	3635.68	3162.60	2856.98	2646.71
130000	12026.94	6600.59	4814.72	3938.65	3426.15	3095.06	2867.27
140000	12952.09	7108.33	5185.09	4241.63	3689.70	3333.14	3087.83
150000	13877.23	7616.06	5555.45	4544.60	3953.25	3571.22	3308.39
175000	16190.11	8885.41	6481.36	5302.03	4612.12	4166.42	3859.78
200000	18502.98	10154.75	7407.26	6059.46	5270.99	4761.63	4411.18
225000	20815.85	11424.10	8333.17	6816.90	5929.87	5356.83	4962.58
250000	23128.72	12693.44	9259.08	7574.33	6588.74	5952.03	5513.98

Monthly Payments 19¾%

necessary to amortize a loan

AMOUNT	8 YEARS	9 YEARS	10 YEARS	11 YEARS	12 YEARS	13 YEARS	14 YEARS
100	2.08	1.99	1.92	1.86	1.82	1.79	1.76
200	4.16	3.97	3.83	3.72	3.64	3.57	3.52
500	10.40	9.93	9.58	9.31	9.10	8.93	8.80
1000	20.80	19.87	19.16	18.62	18.19	17.86	17.59
2000	41.60	39.73	38.32	37.23	36.38	35.71	35.18
5000	103.99	99.33	95.80	93.08	90.96	89.29	87.96
6000	124.79	119.19	114.96	111.70	109.15	107.14	105.55
7000	145.58	139.06	134.12	130.32	127.34	125.00	123.14
8000	166.38	158.93	153.28	148.93	145.54	142.86	140.73
9000	187.18	178.79	172.44	167.55	163.73	160.72	158.32
10000	207.98	198.66	191.60	186.16	181.92	178.57	175.91
15000	311.96	297.99	287.40	279.25	272.88	267.86	263.87
20000	415.95	397.32	383.20	372.33	363.84	357.15	351.83
25000	519.94	496.64	479.00	465.41	454.80	446.44	439.78
30000	623.93	595.97	574.80	558.49	545.76	535.72	527.74
35000	727.91	695.30	670.60	651.58	636.72	625.01	615.70
36000	748.71	715.17	689.76	670.19	654.91	642.87	633.29
37000	769.51	735.03	708.92	688.81	673.11	660.72	650.88
38000	790.31	754.90	728.08	707.42	691.30	678.58	668.47
39000	811.10	774.77	747.24	726.04	709.49	696.44	686.06
40000	831.90	794.63	766.40	744.66	727.68	714.30	703.66
41000	852.70	814.50	785.56	763.27	745.87	732.15	721.25
42000	873.50	834.36	804.72	781.89	764.07	750.01	738.84
43000	894.30	854.23	823.88	800.51	782.26	767.87	756.43
44000	915.09	874.10	843.04	819.12	800.45	785.73	774.02
45000	935.89	893.96	862.20	837.74	818.64	803.58	791.61
46000	956.69	913.83	881.36	856.36	836.84	821.44	809.20
47000	977.49	933.69	900.52	874.97	855.03	839.30	826.80
48000	998.28	953.56	919.68	893.59	873.22	857.16	844.39
49000	1019.08	973.42	938.84	912.21	891.41	875.01	861.98
50000	1039.88	993.29	958.01	930.82	909.60	892.87	879.57
51000	1060.68	1013.16	977.17	949.44	927.80	910.73	897.16
52000	1081.47	1033.02	996.33	968.05	945.99	928.59	914.75
53000	1102.27	1052.89	1015.49	986.67	964.18	946.44	932.34
54000	1123.07	1072.75	1034.65	1005.29	982.37	964.30	949.93
55000	1143.87	1092.62	1053.81	1023.90	1000.56	982.16	967.53
56000	1164.66	1112.48	1072.97	1042.52	1018.76	1000.02	985.12
57000	1185.46	1132.35	1092.13	1061.14	1036.95	1017.87	1002.71
58000	1206.26	1152.22	1111.29	1079.75	1055.14	1035.73	1020.30
59000	1227.06	1172.08	1130.45	1098.37	1073.33	1053.59	1037.89
60000	1247.85	1191.95	1149.61	1116.99	1091.52	1071.45	1055.48
65000	1351.84	1291.28	1245.41	1210.07	1182.48	1160.73	1143.44
70000	1455.83	1390.61	1341.21	1303.15	1273.44	1250.02	1231.40
75000	1559.82	1489.93	1437.01	1396.23	1364.41	1339.31	1319.35
80000	1663.81	1589.26	1532.81	1489.31	1455.37	1428.59	1407.31
85000	1767.79	1688.59	1628.61	1582.40	1546.33	1517.88	1495.27
90000	1871.78	1787.92	1724.41	1675.48	1637.29	1607.17	1583.22
95000	1975.77	1887.25	1820.21	1768.56	1728.25	1696.45	1671.18
100000	2079.76	1986.58	1916.01	1861.64	1819.21	1785.74	1759.14
105000	2183.74	2085.91	2011.81	1954.73	1910.17	1875.03	1847.10
110000	2287.73	2185.24	2107.61	2047.81	2001.13	1964.32	1935.05
120000	2495.71	2383.90	2299.21	2233.97	2183.05	2142.89	2110.97
130000	2703.68	2582.55	2490.81	2420.14	2364.97	2321.46	2286.88
140000	2911.66	2781.21	2682.41	2606.30	2546.89	2500.04	2462.79
150000	3119.63	2979.87	2874.02	2792.47	2728.81	2678.61	2638.71
175000	3639.57	3476.51	3353.02	3257.88	3183.61	3125.05	3078.49
200000	4159.51	3973.16	3832.02	3723.29	3638.41	3571.48	3518.28
225000	4679.45	4469.80	4311.02	4188.70	4093.22	4017.92	3958.06
250000	5199.39	4966.45	4790.03	4654.11	4548.02	4464.35	4397.85

19¾%

Monthly Payments
necessary to amortize a loan

AMOUNT	15 YEARS	16 YEARS	17 YEARS	18 YEARS	19 YEARS	20 YEARS	21 YEARS
100	1.74	1.72	1.71	1.70	1.69	1.68	1.67
200	3.48	3.44	3.41	3.39	3.37	3.36	3.35
500	8.69	8.60	8.53	8.48	8.43	8.40	8.37
1000	17.38	17.21	17.07	16.96	16.87	16.79	16.73
2000	34.76	34.41	34.14	33.91	33.73	33.58	33.46
5000	86.89	86.04	85.35	84.79	84.33	83.96	83.66
6000	104.27	103.24	102.42	101.74	101.20	100.75	100.39
7000	121.65	120.45	119.48	118.70	118.06	117.55	117.12
8000	139.03	137.66	136.55	135.66	134.93	134.34	133.85
9000	156.41	154.87	153.62	152.62	151.80	151.13	150.59
10000	173.79	172.07	170.69	169.57	168.66	167.92	167.32
15000	260.68	258.11	256.04	254.36	252.99	251.88	250.98
20000	347.57	344.15	341.38	339.14	337.33	335.84	334.64
25000	434.46	430.18	426.73	423.93	421.66	419.81	418.30
30000	521.36	516.22	512.08	508.72	505.99	503.77	501.96
35000	608.25	602.26	597.42	593.50	590.32	587.73	585.61
36000	625.63	619.47	614.49	610.46	607.19	604.52	602.35
37000	643.01	636.67	631.56	627.42	624.05	621.31	619.08
38000	660.38	653.88	648.63	644.37	640.92	638.10	635.81
39000	677.76	671.09	665.70	661.33	657.78	654.90	652.54
40000	695.14	688.30	682.77	678.29	674.65	671.69	669.27
41000	712.52	705.50	699.84	695.25	691.52	688.48	686.01
42000	729.90	722.71	716.91	712.20	708.38	705.27	702.74
43000	747.28	739.92	733.98	729.16	725.25	722.07	719.47
44000	764.66	757.13	751.04	746.12	742.12	738.86	736.20
45000	782.03	774.33	768.11	763.08	758.98	755.65	752.93
46000	799.41	791.54	785.18	780.03	775.85	772.44	769.66
47000	816.79	808.75	802.25	796.99	792.71	789.23	786.40
48000	834.17	825.95	819.32	813.95	809.58	806.03	803.13
49000	851.55	843.16	836.39	830.90	826.45	822.82	819.86
50000	868.93	860.37	853.46	847.86	843.31	839.61	836.59
51000	886.31	877.58	870.53	864.82	860.18	856.40	853.32
52000	903.68	894.78	887.60	881.78	877.05	873.20	870.06
53000	921.06	911.99	904.67	898.73	893.91	889.99	886.79
54000	938.44	929.20	921.74	915.69	910.78	906.78	903.52
55000	955.82	946.41	938.81	932.65	927.64	923.57	920.25
56000	973.20	963.61	955.87	949.60	944.51	940.36	936.98
57000	990.58	980.82	972.94	966.56	961.38	957.16	953.71
58000	1007.96	998.03	990.01	983.52	978.24	973.95	970.45
59000	1025.33	1015.24	1007.08	1000.48	995.11	990.74	987.18
60000	1042.71	1032.44	1024.15	1017.43	1011.98	1007.53	1003.91
65000	1129.61	1118.48	1109.50	1102.22	1096.31	1091.49	1087.57
70000	1216.50	1204.52	1194.84	1187.01	1180.64	1175.46	1171.23
75000	1303.39	1290.55	1280.19	1271.79	1264.97	1259.42	1254.89
80000	1390.28	1376.59	1365.54	1356.58	1349.30	1343.38	1338.55
85000	1477.18	1462.63	1450.88	1441.36	1433.63	1427.34	1422.21
90000	1564.07	1548.67	1536.23	1526.15	1517.96	1511.30	1505.87
95000	1650.96	1634.70	1621.57	1610.94	1602.30	1595.26	1589.52
100000	1737.85	1720.74	1706.92	1695.72	1686.63	1679.22	1673.18
105000	1824.75	1806.78	1792.26	1780.51	1770.96	1763.18	1756.84
110000	1911.64	1892.81	1877.61	1865.29	1855.29	1847.15	1840.50
120000	2085.43	2064.89	2048.30	2034.87	2023.95	2015.07	2007.82
130000	2259.21	2236.96	2218.99	2204.44	2192.62	2182.99	2175.14
140000	2433.00	2409.03	2389.69	2374.01	2361.28	2350.91	2342.46
150000	2606.78	2581.11	2560.38	2543.58	2529.94	2518.83	2509.78
175000	3041.25	3011.29	2987.11	2967.51	2951.60	2938.64	2928.07
200000	3475.71	3441.48	3413.84	3391.44	3373.25	3358.45	3346.37
225000	3910.17	3871.66	3840.57	3815.38	3794.91	3778.25	3764.66
250000	4344.64	4301.85	4267.30	4239.31	4216.57	4198.06	4182.96

Monthly Payments
necessary to amortize a loan

19¾%

AMOUNT	22 YEARS	23 YEARS	24 YEARS	25 YEARS	30 YEARS	35 YEARS	40 YEARS
100	1.67	1.66	1.66	1.66	1.65	1.65	1.65
200	3.34	3.33	3.32	3.32	3.30	3.30	3.29
500	8.34	8.32	8.30	8.29	8.25	8.24	8.23
1000	16.68	16.64	16.61	16.58	16.50	16.48	16.46
2000	33.37	33.28	33.22	33.16	33.01	32.95	32.93
5000	83.41	83.21	83.05	82.91	82.52	82.38	82.32
6000	100.10	99.85	99.66	99.49	99.03	98.85	98.79
7000	116.78	116.50	116.26	116.08	115.53	115.33	115.25
8000	133.46	133.14	132.87	132.66	132.04	131.81	131.72
9000	150.14	149.78	149.48	149.24	148.54	148.28	148.18
10000	166.83	166.42	166.09	165.82	165.05	164.76	164.65
15000	250.24	249.63	249.14	248.73	247.57	247.14	246.97
20000	333.65	332.84	332.18	331.64	330.09	329.51	329.30
25000	417.06	416.05	415.23	414.55	412.62	411.89	411.62
30000	500.48	499.27	498.28	497.46	495.14	494.27	493.95
35000	583.89	582.48	581.32	580.38	577.66	576.65	576.27
36000	600.57	599.12	597.93	596.96	594.17	593.12	592.73
37000	617.25	615.76	614.54	613.54	610.67	609.60	609.20
38000	633.94	632.40	631.15	630.12	627.18	626.08	625.66
39000	650.62	649.05	647.76	646.70	643.68	642.55	642.13
40000	667.30	665.69	664.37	663.29	660.18	659.03	658.59
41000	683.98	682.33	680.98	679.87	676.69	675.50	675.06
42000	700.67	698.97	697.59	696.45	693.19	691.98	691.52
43000	717.35	715.61	714.19	713.03	709.70	708.45	707.99
44000	734.03	732.26	730.80	729.61	726.20	724.93	724.45
45000	750.71	748.90	747.41	746.20	742.71	741.41	740.92
46000	767.40	765.54	764.02	762.78	759.21	757.88	757.38
47000	784.08	782.18	780.63	779.36	775.72	774.36	773.85
48000	800.76	798.83	797.24	795.94	792.22	790.83	790.31
49000	817.44	815.47	813.85	812.53	808.73	807.31	806.78
50000	834.13	832.11	830.46	829.11	825.23	823.78	823.24
51000	850.81	848.75	847.07	845.69	841.74	840.26	839.71
52000	867.49	865.39	863.68	862.27	858.24	856.74	856.17
53000	884.17	882.04	880.29	878.85	874.74	873.21	872.64
54000	900.86	898.68	896.90	895.44	891.25	889.69	889.10
55000	917.54	915.32	913.51	912.02	907.75	906.16	905.57
56000	934.22	931.96	930.11	928.60	924.26	922.64	922.03
57000	950.90	948.60	946.72	945.18	940.76	939.11	938.50
58000	967.59	965.25	963.33	961.76	957.27	955.59	954.96
59000	984.27	981.89	979.94	978.35	973.77	972.07	971.43
60000	1000.95	998.53	996.55	994.93	990.28	988.54	987.89
65000	1084.36	1081.74	1079.60	1077.84	1072.80	1070.92	1070.21
70000	1167.78	1164.95	1162.64	1160.75	1155.32	1153.30	1152.54
75000	1251.19	1248.16	1245.69	1243.66	1237.85	1235.68	1234.86
80000	1334.60	1331.38	1328.73	1326.57	1320.37	1318.05	1317.19
85000	1418.01	1414.59	1411.78	1409.48	1402.89	1400.43	1399.51
90000	1501.43	1497.80	1494.83	1492.39	1485.41	1482.81	1481.84
95000	1584.84	1581.01	1577.87	1575.30	1567.94	1565.19	1564.16
100000	1668.25	1664.22	1660.92	1658.21	1650.46	1647.57	1646.48
105000	1751.66	1747.43	1743.96	1741.13	1732.98	1729.95	1728.81
110000	1835.08	1830.64	1827.01	1824.04	1815.51	1812.32	1811.13
120000	2001.90	1997.06	1993.10	1989.86	1980.55	1977.08	1975.78
130000	2168.73	2163.49	2159.19	2155.68	2145.60	2141.84	2140.43
140000	2335.55	2329.91	2325.29	2321.50	2310.65	2306.60	2305.08
150000	2502.38	2496.33	2491.38	2487.32	2475.69	2471.35	2469.73
175000	2919.44	2912.38	2906.61	2901.88	2888.31	2883.24	2881.35
200000	3336.50	3328.44	3321.84	3316.43	3300.92	3295.14	3292.97
225000	3753.57	3744.49	3737.07	3730.98	3713.54	3707.03	3704.59
250000	4170.63	4160.66	4152.30	4145.54	4126.15	4118.92	4116.21

20%

Monthly Payments

necessary to amortize a loan

AMOUNT	1 YEAR	2 YEARS	3 YEARS	4 YEARS	5 YEARS	6 YEARS	7 YEARS
100	9.26	5.09	3.72	3.04	2.65	2.40	2.22
200	18.53	10.18	7.43	6.09	5.30	4.79	4.44
500	46.32	25.45	18.58	15.22	13.25	11.98	11.10
1000	92.63	50.90	37.16	30.43	26.49	23.95	22.21
2000	185.27	101.79	74.33	60.86	52.99	47.91	44.41
5000	463.17	254.48	185.82	152.15	132.47	119.76	111.03
6000	555.81	305.37	222.98	182.58	158.96	143.72	133.24
7000	648.44	356.27	260.15	213.01	185.46	167.67	155.44
8000	741.08	407.17	297.31	243.44	211.95	191.62	177.65
9000	833.71	458.06	334.47	273.87	238.44	215.58	199.86
10000	926.35	508.96	371.64	304.30	264.94	239.53	222.06
15000	1389.52	763.44	557.45	456.46	397.41	359.29	333.09
20000	1852.69	1017.92	743.27	608.61	529.88	479.06	444.12
25000	2315.86	1272.40	929.09	760.76	662.35	598.82	555.15
30000	2779.04	1526.87	1114.91	912.91	794.82	718.58	666.19
35000	3242.21	1781.35	1300.73	1065.06	927.29	838.35	777.22
36000	3334.84	1832.25	1337.89	1095.49	953.78	862.30	799.42
37000	3427.48	1883.14	1375.05	1125.92	980.27	886.25	821.63
38000	3520.11	1934.04	1412.22	1156.35	1006.77	910.21	843.84
39000	3612.75	1984.94	1449.38	1186.78	1033.26	934.16	866.04
40000	3705.38	2035.83	1486.54	1217.21	1059.76	958.11	888.25
41000	3798.01	2086.73	1523.71	1247.64	1086.25	982.07	910.45
42000	3890.65	2137.62	1560.87	1278.08	1112.74	1006.02	932.66
43000	3983.28	2188.52	1598.03	1308.51	1139.24	1029.97	954.87
44000	4075.92	2239.42	1635.20	1338.94	1165.73	1053.92	977.07
45000	4168.55	2290.31	1672.36	1369.37	1192.22	1077.88	999.28
46000	4261.19	2341.21	1709.52	1399.80	1218.72	1101.83	1021.49
47000	4353.82	2392.10	1746.69	1430.23	1245.21	1125.78	1043.69
48000	4446.46	2443.00	1783.85	1460.66	1271.71	1149.74	1065.90
49000	4539.09	2493.89	1821.02	1491.09	1298.20	1173.69	1088.10
50000	4631.73	2544.79	1858.18	1521.52	1324.69	1197.64	1110.31
51000	4724.36	2595.69	1895.34	1551.95	1351.19	1221.59	1132.52
52000	4816.99	2646.58	1932.51	1582.38	1377.68	1245.55	1154.72
53000	4909.63	2697.48	1969.67	1612.81	1404.18	1269.60	1176.93
54000	5002.26	2748.37	2006.83	1643.24	1430.67	1293.45	1199.13
55000	5094.90	2799.27	2044.00	1673.67	1457.16	1317.41	1221.34
56000	5187.53	2850.16	2081.16	1704.10	1483.66	1341.36	1243.55
57000	5280.17	2901.06	2118.32	1734.53	1510.15	1365.31	1265.75
58000	5372.80	2951.96	2155.49	1764.96	1536.65	1389.26	1287.96
59000	5465.44	3002.85	2192.65	1795.39	1563.14	1413.22	1310.17
60000	5558.07	3053.75	2229.82	1825.82	1589.63	1437.17	1332.37
65000	6021.24	3308.23	2415.63	1977.97	1722.10	1556.93	1443.40
70000	6484.42	3562.71	2601.45	2130.13	1854.57	1676.70	1554.43
75000	6947.59	3817.19	2787.27	2282.28	1987.04	1796.46	1665.46
80000	7410.76	4071.66	2973.09	2434.43	2119.51	1916.23	1776.50
85000	7873.93	4326.14	3158.90	2586.58	2251.98	2035.99	1887.53
90000	8337.11	4580.62	3344.72	2738.73	2384.45	2155.75	1998.56
95000	8800.28	4835.10	3530.54	2890.88	2516.92	2275.52	2109.59
100000	9263.45	5089.58	3716.36	3043.04	2649.39	2395.28	2220.62
105000	9726.62	5344.06	3902.18	3195.19	2781.86	2515.05	2331.65
110000	10189.80	5598.54	4087.99	3347.34	2914.33	2634.81	2442.68
120000	11116.14	6107.50	4459.63	3651.64	3179.27	2874.34	2664.74
130000	12042.49	6616.45	4831.27	3955.95	3444.20	3113.87	2886.81
140000	12968.83	7125.41	5202.90	4260.25	3709.14	3353.40	3108.87
150000	13895.18	7634.37	5574.54	4564.55	3974.08	3592.92	3330.93
175000	16211.04	8906.77	6503.63	5325.31	4636.43	4191.74	3886.08
200000	18526.90	10179.16	7432.72	6086.07	5298.78	4790.57	4441.24
225000	20842.76	11451.56	8361.81	6846.83	5961.12	5389.39	4996.39
250000	23158.63	12723.95	9290.90	7607.59	6623.47	5988.21	5551.55

Monthly Payments 20%

necessary to amortize a loan

AMOUNT	8 YEARS	9 YEARS	10 YEARS	11 YEARS	12 YEARS	13 YEARS	14 YEARS
100	2.10	2.00	1.93	1.88	1.84	1.80	1.78
200	4.19	4.01	3.87	3.76	3.67	3.61	3.55
500	10.48	10.01	9.66	9.39	9.18	9.02	8.89
1000	20.95	20.03	19.33	18.79	18.37	18.04	17.77
2000	41.91	40.05	38.65	37.57	36.73	36.07	35.55
5000	104.77	100.13	96.63	93.93	91.83	00.10	88.86
6000	125.72	120.16	115.95	112.72	110.20	108.21	106.64
7000	146.67	140.19	135.28	131.50	128.56	126.25	124.41
8000	167.63	160.21	154.60	150.29	146.93	144.28	142.18
9000	188.58	180.24	173.93	169.08	165.29	162.32	159.95
10000	209.53	200.27	193.26	187.86	183.66	180.35	177.73
15000	314.30	300.40	289.88	281.80	275.49	270.53	266.59
20000	419.06	400.53	386.51	375.73	367.32	360.70	355.45
25000	523.83	500.66	483.14	469.66	459.15	450.88	444.32
30000	628.60	600.80	579.77	563.59	550.98	541.06	533.18
35000	733.36	700.93	676.39	657.52	642.81	631.23	622.04
36000	754.32	720.95	695.72	676.31	661.18	649.27	639.82
37000	775.27	740.98	715.05	695.09	679.55	667.30	657.59
38000	796.22	761.01	734.37	713.88	697.91	685.34	675.36
39000	817.17	781.03	753.70	732.67	716.28	703.37	693.13
40000	838.13	801.06	773.02	751.45	734.64	721.41	710.91
41000	859.08	821.09	792.35	770.24	753.01	739.44	728.68
42000	880.03	841.11	811.67	789.03	771.38	757.48	746.45
43000	900.99	861.14	831.00	807.81	789.74	775.51	764.22
44000	921.94	881.17	850.32	826.60	808.11	793.55	782.00
45000	942.89	901.19	869.65	845.39	826.47	811.58	799.77
46000	963.85	921.22	888.98	864.17	844.84	829.62	817.54
47000	984.80	941.25	908.30	882.96	863.21	847.66	835.31
48000	1005.75	961.27	927.63	901.74	881.57	865.69	853.09
49000	1026.71	981.30	946.95	920.53	899.94	883.73	870.86
50000	1047.66	1001.33	966.28	939.32	918.30	901.76	888.63
51000	1068.61	1021.35	985.60	958.10	936.67	919.80	906.41
52000	1089.57	1041.38	1004.93	976.89	955.04	937.83	924.18
53000	1110.52	1061.40	1024.26	995.68	973.40	955.87	941.95
54000	1131.47	1081.43	1043.58	1014.46	991.77	973.90	959.72
55000	1152.43	1101.46	1062.91	1033.25	1010.13	991.94	977.50
56000	1173.38	1121.48	1082.23	1052.04	1028.50	1009.97	995.27
57000	1194.33	1141.51	1101.56	1070.82	1046.87	1028.01	1013.04
58000	1215.29	1161.54	1120.88	1089.61	1065.23	1046.04	1030.81
59000	1236.24	1181.56	1140.21	1108.30	1083.60	1064.08	1048.59
60000	1257.19	1201.59	1160.00	1127.18	1101.97	1082.11	1066.36
65000	1361.96	1301.72	1256.16	1221.11	1193.80	1172.29	1155.22
70000	1466.72	1401.86	1352.79	1315.04	1285.63	1262.47	1244.09
75000	1571.49	1501.99	1449.42	1408.98	1377.46	1352.64	1332.95
80000	1676.26	1602.12	1546.05	1502.91	1469.29	1442.82	1421.81
85000	1781.02	1702.25	1642.67	1596.84	1561.12	1532.99	1510.68
90000	1885.79	1802.39	1739.30	1690.77	1652.95	1623.17	1599.54
95000	1990.55	1902.52	1835.93	1784.70	1744.78	1713.35	1688.40
100000	2095.32	2002.65	1932.56	1878.63	1836.61	1803.52	1777.27
105000	2200.09	2102.78	2029.18	1972.57	1928.44	1893.70	1866.13
110000	2304.85	2202.92	2125.81	2066.50	2020.27	1983.87	1954.99
120000	2514.38	2403.18	2319.07	2254.36	2203.93	2164.23	2132.72
130000	2723.92	2603.45	2512.32	2442.22	2387.59	2344.58	2310.44
140000	2933.45	2803.71	2705.58	2630.09	2571.25	2524.93	2488.17
150000	3142.98	3003.98	2898.84	2817.95	2754.91	2705.28	2665.90
175000	3666.81	3504.64	3381.97	3287.61	3214.06	3156.16	3110.21
200000	4190.64	4005.30	3865.11	3757.27	3673.22	3607.04	3554.53
225000	4714.47	4505.96	4348.25	4226.93	4132.37	4057.92	3998.85
250000	5238.30	5006.63	4831.39	4696.59	4591.52	4508.81	4443.16

20% Monthly Payments

necessary to amortize a loan

AMOUNT	15 YEARS	16 YEARS	17 YEARS	18 YEARS	19 YEARS	20 YEARS	21 YEARS
100	1.76	1.74	1.73	1.71	1.71	1.70	1.69
200	3.51	3.48	3.45	3.43	3.41	3.40	3.39
500	8.78	8.70	8.63	8.57	8.53	8.49	8.46
1000	17.56	17.39	17.26	17.15	17.06	16.99	16.93
2000	35.13	34.79	34.52	34.30	34.12	33.98	33.86
5000	87.81	86.97	86.30	85.75	85.30	84.94	84.65
6000	105.38	104.37	103.55	102.90	102.36	101.93	101.58
7000	122.94	121.76	120.81	120.05	119.42	118.92	118.51
8000	140.50	139.16	138.07	137.19	136.48	135.91	135.44
9000	158.07	156.55	155.33	154.34	153.54	152.89	152.37
10000	175.63	173.95	172.59	171.49	170.60	169.88	169.29
15000	263.44	260.92	258.89	257.24	255.91	254.82	253.94
20000	351.26	347.89	345.18	342.99	341.21	339.76	338.59
25000	439.07	434.87	431.48	428.73	426.51	424.71	423.24
30000	526.89	521.84	517.77	514.48	511.81	509.65	507.88
35000	614.70	608.81	604.07	600.23	597.12	594.59	592.53
36000	632.27	626.21	621.32	617.38	614.18	611.58	609.46
37000	649.83	643.60	638.58	634.53	631.24	628.57	626.39
38000	667.39	661.00	655.84	651.68	648.30	645.55	643.32
39000	684.96	678.39	673.10	668.83	665.36	662.54	660.25
40000	702.52	695.79	690.36	685.97	682.42	679.53	677.18
41000	720.08	713.18	707.62	703.12	699.48	696.52	694.11
42000	737.64	730.58	724.88	720.27	716.54	713.51	711.04
43000	755.21	747.97	742.14	737.42	733.60	730.49	727.97
44000	772.77	765.37	759.40	754.57	750.66	747.48	744.90
45000	790.33	782.76	776.66	771.72	767.72	764.47	761.83
46000	807.90	800.15	793.92	788.87	784.78	781.46	778.76
47000	825.46	817.55	811.17	806.02	801.84	798.45	795.69
48000	843.02	834.94	828.43	823.17	818.90	815.44	812.61
49000	860.59	852.34	845.69	840.32	835.96	832.42	829.54
50000	878.15	869.73	862.95	857.47	853.02	849.41	846.47
51000	895.71	887.13	880.21	874.62	870.08	866.40	863.40
52000	913.27	904.52	897.47	891.77	887.14	883.39	880.33
53000	930.84	921.92	914.73	908.92	904.20	900.38	897.26
54000	948.40	939.31	931.99	926.07	921.27	917.37	914.19
55000	965.96	956.71	949.25	943.21	938.33	934.35	931.12
56000	983.53	974.10	966.51	960.36	955.39	951.34	948.05
57000	1001.09	991.50	983.76	977.51	972.45	968.33	964.98
58000	1018.65	1008.89	1001.02	994.66	989.51	985.32	981.91
59000	1036.21	1026.28	1018.28	1011.81	1006.57	1002.31	998.84
60000	1053.78	1043.68	1035.54	1028.96	1023.63	1019.29	1015.77
65000	1141.59	1130.65	1121.84	1114.71	1108.93	1104.24	1100.42
70000	1229.41	1217.63	1208.13	1200.46	1194.23	1189.18	1185.06
75000	1317.22	1304.60	1294.43	1286.20	1279.53	1274.12	1269.71
80000	1405.04	1391.57	1380.72	1371.95	1364.84	1359.06	1354.36
85000	1492.85	1478.55	1467.02	1457.70	1450.14	1444.00	1439.01
90000	1580.67	1565.52	1553.31	1543.44	1535.44	1528.94	1523.65
95000	1668.48	1652.49	1639.61	1629.19	1620.74	1613.88	1608.30
100000	1756.30	1739.47	1725.90	1714.94	1706.05	1698.82	1692.95
105000	1844.11	1826.44	1812.20	1800.68	1791.35	1783.77	1777.59
110000	1931.93	1913.41	1898.49	1886.43	1876.65	1868.71	1862.24
120000	2107.56	2087.36	2071.08	2057.92	2047.26	2038.59	2031.54
130000	2283.19	2261.31	2243.67	2229.42	2217.86	2208.47	2200.83
140000	2458.82	2435.25	2416.26	2400.91	2388.47	2378.35	2370.13
150000	2634.44	2609.20	2588.85	2572.40	2559.07	2548.24	2539.42
175000	3073.52	3044.07	3020.33	3001.14	2985.58	2972.94	2962.66
200000	3512.59	3478.93	3451.81	3429.87	3412.09	3397.65	3385.90
225000	3951.67	3913.80	3883.28	3858.61	3838.60	3822.36	3809.13
250000	4390.74	4348.67	4314.76	4287.34	4265.12	4247.06	4232.37

Monthly Payments 20%

necessary to amortize a loan

AMOUNT	22 YEARS	23 YEARS	24 YEARS	25 YEARS	30 YEARS	35 YEARS	40 YEARS
100	1.69	1.68	1.68	1.68	1.67	1.67	1.67
200	3.38	3.37	3.36	3.36	3.34	3.34	3.33
500	8.44	8.42	8.41	8.39	8.36	8.34	8.34
1000	16.88	16.84	16.81	16.78	16.71	16.68	16.67
2000	33.76	33.69	33.62	33.57	33.42	33.37	33.35
5000	84.41	84.21	84.05	83.92	83.55	83.41	83.36
6000	101.29	101.06	100.86	100.71	100.26	100.10	100.04
7000	118.17	117.90	117.67	117.49	116.97	116.78	116.71
8000	135.05	134.74	134.48	134.28	133.68	133.46	133.38
9000	151.93	151.58	151.30	151.06	150.39	150.15	150.05
10000	168.82	168.43	168.11	167.85	167.10	166.83	166.73
15000	253.22	252.64	252.16	251.77	250.65	250.24	250.09
20000	337.63	336.85	336.21	335.69	334.20	333.66	333.45
25000	422.04	421.06	420.26	419.61	417.75	417.07	416.82
30000	506.45	505.28	504.32	503.54	501.31	500.48	500.18
35000	590.86	589.49	588.37	587.46	584.86	583.90	583.54
36000	607.74	606.33	605.18	604.24	601.57	600.58	600.22
37000	624.62	623.17	621.99	621.03	618.28	617.26	616.89
38000	641.50	640.02	638.80	637.81	634.99	633.95	633.56
39000	658.38	656.86	655.61	654.60	651.70	650.63	650.23
40000	675.26	673.70	672.42	671.38	668.41	667.31	666.91
41000	692.14	690.54	689.23	688.17	685.12	683.99	683.58
42000	709.03	707.39	706.05	704.95	701.83	700.68	700.25
43000	725.91	724.23	722.86	721.73	718.54	717.36	716.92
44000	742.79	741.07	739.67	738.52	735.25	734.04	733.60
45000	759.67	757.91	756.48	755.30	751.96	750.73	750.27
46000	776.55	774.76	773.29	772.09	768.67	767.41	766.94
47000	793.43	791.60	790.10	788.87	785.38	784.09	783.61
48000	810.32	808.44	806.91	805.66	802.09	800.77	800.29
49000	827.20	825.28	823.72	822.44	818.80	817.46	816.96
50000	844.08	842.13	840.53	839.23	835.51	834.14	833.63
51000	860.96	858.97	857.34	856.01	852.22	850.82	850.30
52000	877.84	875.81	874.15	872.79	868.93	867.50	866.98
53000	894.72	892.65	890.96	889.58	885.64	884.19	883.65
54000	911.61	909.50	907.77	906.36	902.35	900.87	900.32
55000	928.49	926.34	924.58	923.15	919.06	917.55	917.00
56000	945.37	943.18	941.39	939.93	935.77	934.24	933.67
57000	962.25	960.02	958.20	956.72	952.48	950.92	950.34
58000	979.13	976.87	975.01	973.50	969.19	967.60	967.01
59000	996.01	993.71	991.83	990.29	985.90	984.28	983.69
60000	1012.90	1010.55	1008.64	1007.07	1002.61	1000.97	1000.36
65000	1097.30	1094.76	1092.69	1090.99	1086.16	1084.38	1083.72
70000	1181.71	1178.98	1176.74	1174.92	1169.71	1167.79	1167.08
75000	1266.12	1263.19	1260.79	1258.84	1253.26	1251.21	1250.45
80000	1350.53	1347.40	1344.85	1342.76	1336.81	1334.62	1333.81
85000	1434.93	1431.61	1428.90	1426.68	1420.37	1418.04	1417.17
90000	1519.34	1515.83	1512.95	1510.61	1503.92	1501.45	1500.54
95000	1603.75	1600.04	1597.01	1594.53	1587.47	1584.86	1583.90
100000	1688.16	1684.25	1681.06	1678.45	1671.02	1668.28	1667.26
105000	1772.57	1768.46	1765.11	1762.37	1754.57	1751.69	1750.63
110000	1856.97	1852.68	1849.17	1846.30	1838.12	1835.11	1833.99
120000	2025.79	2021.10	2017.27	2014.14	2005.22	2001.93	2000.72
130000	2194.61	2189.53	2185.38	2181.99	2172.32	2168.76	2167.44
140000	2363.42	2357.95	2353.48	2349.83	2339.43	2335.59	2334.17
150000	2532.24	2526.38	2521.59	2517.68	2506.53	2502.42	2500.90
175000	2954.28	2947.44	2941.85	2937.29	2924.28	2919.49	2917.71
200000	3376.32	3368.50	3362.12	3356.90	3342.04	3336.56	3334.53
225000	3798.36	3789.56	3782.38	3776.52	3759.79	3753.63	3751.34
250000	4220.40	4210.63	4202.65	4196.13	4177.55	4170.70	4168.16

20¼% Monthly Payments

necessary to amortize a loan

AMOUNT	1 YEAR	2 YEARS	3 YEARS	4 YEARS	5 YEARS	6 YEARS	7 YEARS
100	9.28	5.10	3.73	3.06	2.66	2.41	2.24
200	18.55	10.20	7.46	6.11	5.33	4.82	4.47
500	46.38	25.51	18.65	15.28	13.32	12.05	11.18
1000	92.75	51.02	37.29	30.56	26.63	24.10	22.36
2000	185.51	102.04	74.58	61.13	53.27	48.20	44.71
5000	463.77	255.09	186.46	152.82	133.17	120.49	111.78
6000	556.53	306.11	223.75	183.38	159.80	144.59	134.14
7000	649.28	357.13	261.04	213.95	186.43	168.69	156.50
8000	742.03	408.14	298.33	244.51	213.07	192.78	178.86
9000	834.79	459.16	335.62	275.07	239.70	216.88	201.21
10000	927.54	510.18	372.91	305.64	266.33	240.98	223.57
15000	1391.31	765.27	559.37	458.46	399.50	361.47	335.35
20000	1855.08	1020.36	745.82	611.27	532.66	481.96	447.14
25000	2318.85	1275.45	932.28	764.09	665.83	602.45	558.92
30000	2782.63	1530.54	1118.73	916.91	799.00	722.94	670.71
35000	3246.40	1785.63	1305.19	1069.73	932.16	843.43	782.49
36000	3339.15	1836.65	1342.48	1100.29	958.79	867.53	804.85
37000	3431.91	1887.67	1379.77	1130.86	985.43	891.62	827.21
38000	3524.66	1938.68	1417.06	1161.42	1012.06	915.72	849.57
39000	3617.41	1989.70	1454.35	1191.99	1038.69	939.82	871.92
40000	3710.17	2040.72	1491.64	1222.55	1065.33	963.92	894.28
41000	3802.92	2091.74	1528.93	1253.11	1091.96	988.02	916.64
42000	3895.68	2142.76	1566.23	1283.68	1118.59	1012.11	938.99
43000	3988.43	2193.77	1603.52	1314.24	1145.23	1036.21	961.35
44000	4081.18	2244.79	1640.81	1344.80	1171.86	1060.31	983.71
45000	4173.94	2295.81	1678.10	1375.37	1198.49	1084.41	1006.06
46000	4266.69	2346.83	1715.39	1405.93	1225.13	1108.51	1028.42
47000	4359.45	2397.85	1752.68	1436.49	1251.76	1132.60	1050.78
48000	4452.20	2448.86	1789.97	1467.06	1278.39	1156.70	1073.13
49000	4544.96	2499.88	1827.26	1497.62	1305.03	1180.80	1095.49
50000	4637.71	2550.90	1864.55	1528.19	1331.66	1204.90	1117.85
51000	4730.46	2601.92	1901.85	1558.75	1358.29	1229.00	1140.21
52000	4823.22	2652.94	1939.14	1589.31	1384.93	1253.09	1162.56
53000	4915.97	2703.95	1976.43	1619.88	1411.56	1277.19	1184.92
54000	5008.73	2754.97	2013.72	1650.44	1438.19	1301.29	1207.28
55000	5101.48	2805.99	2051.01	1681.00	1464.82	1325.39	1229.63
56000	5194.24	2857.01	2088.30	1711.57	1491.46	1349.49	1251.99
57000	5286.99	2908.03	2125.59	1742.13	1518.09	1373.58	1274.35
58000	5379.74	2959.04	2162.88	1772.70	1544.72	1397.68	1296.70
59000	5472.50	3010.06	2200.17	1803.26	1571.36	1421.78	1319.06
60000	5565.25	3061.08	2237.47	1833.82	1597.99	1445.88	1341.42
65000	6029.02	3316.17	2423.92	1986.64	1731.16	1566.37	1453.20
70000	6492.79	3571.26	2610.38	2139.46	1864.32	1686.86	1564.99
75000	6956.56	3826.35	2796.83	2292.28	1997.49	1807.35	1676.77
80000	7420.34	4081.44	2983.29	2445.10	2130.65	1927.84	1788.56
85000	7884.11	4336.53	3169.74	2597.92	2263.82	2048.33	1900.34
90000	8347.88	4591.62	3356.20	2750.73	2396.99	2168.82	2012.13
95000	8811.65	4846.71	3542.65	2903.55	2530.15	2289.31	2123.91
100000	9275.42	5101.80	3729.11	3056.37	2663.32	2409.80	2235.70
105000	9739.19	5356.89	3915.56	3209.19	2796.48	2530.29	2347.48
110000	10202.96	5611.98	4102.02	3362.01	2929.65	2650.78	2459.27
120000	11130.50	6122.16	4474.93	3667.65	3195.98	2891.76	2682.84
130000	12058.05	6632.34	4847.84	3973.28	3462.31	3132.73	2906.41
140000	12985.59	7142.52	5220.75	4278.92	3728.65	3373.71	3129.98
150000	13913.13	7652.70	5593.66	4584.56	3994.98	3614.69	3353.55
175000	16231.98	8928.15	6525.94	5348.65	4660.81	4217.14	3912.47
200000	18550.84	10203.60	7458.22	6112.74	5326.64	4819.59	4471.40
225000	20869.69	11479.05	8390.49	6876.84	5992.47	5422.04	5030.32
250000	23188.55	12754.50	9322.77	7640.93	6658.29	6024.49	5589.24

Monthly Payments 20¼%

necessary to amortize a loan

AMOUNT	8 YEARS	9 YEARS	10 YEARS	11 YEARS	12 YEARS	13 YEARS	14 YEARS
100	2.11	2.02	1.95	1.90	1.85	1.82	1.80
200	4.22	4.04	3.90	3.79	3.71	3.64	3.59
500	10.55	10.09	9.75	9.48	9.27	9.11	8.98
1000	21.11	20.19	19.49	18.96	18.54	18.21	17.95
2000	42.22	40.38	38.98	37.91	37.08	36.43	35.91
5000	105.55	100.94	97.46	94.78	92.70	91.07	89.77
6000	126.66	121.13	116.95	113.74	111.24	109.28	107.73
7000	147.77	141.31	136.44	132.70	129.78	127.50	125.68
8000	168.87	161.50	155.93	151.65	148.33	145.71	143.64
9000	189.98	181.69	175.42	170.61	166.87	163.92	161.59
10000	211.09	201.88	194.92	189.57	185.41	182.14	179.54
15000	316.64	302.82	292.37	284.35	278.11	273.20	269.32
20000	422.19	403.76	389.83	379.14	370.81	364.27	359.09
25000	527.73	504.69	487.29	473.92	463.52	455.34	448.86
30000	633.28	605.63	584.75	568.71	556.22	546.41	538.63
35000	738.83	706.57	682.21	663.49	648.92	637.48	628.41
36000	759.94	726.76	701.70	682.45	667.47	655.69	646.36
37000	781.05	746.95	721.19	701.40	686.01	673.90	664.32
38000	802.16	767.14	740.68	720.36	704.55	692.12	682.27
39000	823.27	787.32	760.17	739.32	723.09	710.33	700.23
40000	844.37	807.51	779.66	758.27	741.63	728.54	718.18
41000	865.48	827.70	799.16	777.23	760.17	746.76	736.13
42000	886.59	847.89	818.65	796.19	778.71	764.97	754.09
43000	907.70	868.07	838.14	815.14	797.25	783.19	772.04
44000	928.81	888.26	857.63	834.10	815.79	801.40	790.00
45000	949.92	908.45	877.12	853.06	834.33	819.61	807.95
46000	971.03	928.64	896.61	872.01	852.87	837.83	825.91
47000	992.14	948.82	916.11	890.97	871.41	856.04	843.86
48000	1013.25	969.01	935.60	909.93	889.95	874.25	861.82
49000	1034.36	989.20	955.09	928.88	908.49	892.47	879.77
50000	1055.47	1009.39	974.58	947.84	927.03	910.68	897.72
51000	1076.58	1029.58	994.07	966.80	945.58	928.89	915.68
52000	1097.69	1049.76	1013.56	985.76	964.12	947.11	933.63
53000	1118.80	1069.95	1033.06	1004.71	982.66	965.32	951.59
54000	1139.91	1090.14	1052.55	1023.67	1001.20	983.54	969.54
55000	1161.02	1110.33	1072.04	1042.63	1019.74	1001.75	987.50
56000	1182.12	1130.51	1091.53	1061.58	1038.28	1019.96	1005.45
57000	1203.23	1150.70	1111.02	1080.54	1056.82	1038.18	1023.41
58000	1224.34	1170.89	1130.51	1099.50	1075.36	1056.39	1041.36
59000	1245.45	1191.08	1150.01	1118.45	1093.90	1074.60	1059.32
60000	1266.66	1211.27	1169.50	1137.41	1112.44	1092.82	1077.27
65000	1372.11	1312.20	1266.95	1232.19	1205.15	1183.88	1167.04
70000	1477.66	1413.14	1364.41	1326.98	1297.85	1274.95	1256.81
75000	1583.20	1514.08	1461.87	1421.76	1390.55	1366.02	1346.59
80000	1688.75	1615.02	1559.33	1516.55	1483.26	1457.09	1436.36
85000	1794.30	1715.96	1656.79	1611.33	1575.96	1548.16	1526.13
90000	1899.84	1816.90	1754.25	1706.12	1668.66	1639.23	1615.90
95000	2005.39	1917.84	1851.70	1800.90	1761.37	1730.29	1705.68
100000	2110.94	2018.78	1949.16	1895.68	1854.07	1821.36	1795.45
105000	2216.48	2119.72	2046.62	1990.47	1946.77	1912.43	1885.22
110000	2322.03	2220.65	2144.08	2085.25	2039.48	2003.50	1974.99
120000	2533.12	2422.53	2338.99	2274.82	2224.88	2185.63	2154.54
130000	2744.22	2624.41	2533.91	2464.39	2410.29	2367.77	2334.08
140000	2955.31	2826.29	2728.83	2653.96	2595.70	2549.91	2513.63
150000	3166.40	3028.16	2923.74	2843.53	2781.10	2732.04	2693.17
175000	3694.14	3532.86	3411.03	3317.45	3244.62	3187.38	3142.04
200000	4221.87	4037.55	3898.32	3791.37	3708.14	3642.72	3590.90
225000	4749.61	4542.25	4385.61	4265.29	4171.66	4098.06	4039.76
250000	5277.34	5046.94	4872.90	4739.21	4635.17	4553.40	4488.62

20¼%

Monthly Payments
necessary to amortize a loan

AMOUNT	15 YEARS	16 YEARS	17 YEARS	18 YEARS	19 YEARS	20 YEARS	21 YEARS
100	1.77	1.76	1.74	1.73	1.73	1.72	1.71
200	3.55	3.52	3.49	3.47	3.45	3.44	3.43
500	8.87	8.79	8.72	8.67	8.63	8.59	8.56
1000	17.75	17.58	17.45	17.34	17.26	17.18	17.13
2000	35.50	35.16	34.90	34.68	34.51	34.37	34.26
5000	88.74	87.91	87.25	86.71	86.28	85.92	85.64
6000	106.49	105.49	104.70	104.05	103.53	103.11	102.77
7000	124.24	123.08	122.15	121.39	120.79	120.29	119.89
8000	141.98	140.66	139.60	138.74	138.04	137.48	137.02
9000	159.73	158.24	157.04	156.08	155.30	154.66	154.15
10000	177.48	175.82	174.49	173.42	172.55	171.85	171.28
15000	266.22	263.74	261.74	260.13	258.83	257.77	256.91
20000	354.96	351.65	348.99	346.84	345.10	343.69	342.55
25000	443.70	439.56	436.23	433.55	431.38	429.62	428.19
30000	532.44	527.47	523.48	520.26	517.65	515.54	513.83
35000	621.18	615.39	610.73	606.97	603.93	601.46	599.46
36000	638.93	632.97	628.18	624.31	621.18	618.65	616.59
37000	656.67	650.55	645.63	641.65	638.44	635.83	633.72
38000	674.42	668.13	663.08	659.00	655.69	653.02	650.85
39000	692.17	685.72	680.53	676.34	672.95	670.20	667.97
40000	709.92	703.30	697.98	693.68	690.20	687.39	685.10
41000	727.67	720.88	715.42	711.02	707.46	704.57	702.23
42000	745.41	738.46	732.87	728.36	724.71	721.76	719.36
43000	763.16	756.05	750.32	745.71	741.97	738.94	736.48
44000	780.91	773.63	767.77	763.05	759.22	756.13	753.61
45000	798.66	791.21	785.22	780.39	776.48	773.31	770.74
46000	816.41	808.79	802.67	797.73	793.74	790.50	787.87
47000	834.15	826.38	820.12	815.07	810.99	807.68	804.99
48000	851.90	843.96	837.57	832.42	828.25	824.87	822.12
49000	869.65	861.54	855.02	849.76	845.50	842.05	839.25
50000	887.40	879.12	872.47	867.10	862.76	859.23	856.38
51000	905.15	896.71	889.92	884.44	880.01	876.42	873.50
52000	922.89	914.29	907.37	901.78	897.27	893.60	890.63
53000	940.64	931.87	924.82	919.13	914.52	910.79	907.76
54000	958.39	949.45	942.27	936.47	931.78	927.97	924.89
55000	976.14	967.04	959.72	953.81	949.03	945.16	942.01
56000	993.88	984.62	977.17	971.15	966.29	962.34	959.14
57000	1011.63	1002.20	994.61	988.49	983.54	979.53	976.27
58000	1029.38	1019.78	1012.06	1005.84	1000.80	996.71	993.40
59000	1047.13	1037.37	1029.51	1023.18	1018.05	1013.90	1010.52
60000	1064.88	1054.95	1046.96	1040.52	1035.31	1031.08	1027.65
65000	1153.62	1142.86	1134.21	1127.23	1121.58	1117.00	1113.29
70000	1242.36	1230.77	1221.46	1213.94	1207.86	1202.93	1198.93
75000	1331.10	1318.69	1308.70	1300.65	1294.13	1288.85	1284.56
80000	1419.84	1406.60	1395.95	1387.36	1380.41	1374.78	1370.20
85000	1508.58	1494.51	1483.20	1474.07	1466.68	1460.70	1455.84
90000	1597.31	1582.42	1570.44	1560.78	1552.96	1546.62	1541.48
95000	1686.05	1670.33	1657.69	1647.49	1639.24	1632.55	1627.11
100000	1774.79	1758.25	1744.94	1734.20	1725.51	1718.47	1712.75
105000	1863.53	1846.16	1832.18	1820.91	1811.79	1804.39	1798.39
110000	1952.27	1934.07	1919.43	1907.62	1898.06	1890.32	1884.03
120000	2129.75	2109.90	2093.93	2081.04	2070.61	2062.16	2055.30
130000	2307.23	2285.72	2268.42	2254.46	2243.16	2234.01	2226.58
140000	2484.71	2461.55	2442.91	2427.88	2415.72	2405.86	2397.85
150000	2662.19	2637.37	2617.41	2601.30	2588.27	2577.70	2569.13
175000	3105.89	3076.93	3053.64	3034.85	3019.64	3007.32	2997.31
200000	3549.59	3516.49	3489.88	3468.40	3451.02	3436.94	3425.50
225000	3993.29	3956.06	3926.11	3901.95	3882.40	3866.55	3853.69
250000	4436.99	4395.62	4362.34	4335.50	4313.78	4296.17	4281.88

Monthly Payments

necessary to amortize a loan

20¼%

AMOUNT	22 YEARS	23 YEARS	24 YEARS	25 YEARS	30 YEARS	35 YEARS	40 YEARS
100	1.71	1.70	1.70	1.70	1.69	1.69	1.69
200	3.42	3.41	3.40	3.40	3.38	3.38	3.38
500	8.54	8.52	8.51	8.49	8.46	8.44	8.44
1000	17.08	17.04	17.01	16.99	16.92	16.89	16.88
2000	34.16	34.09	34.02	33.97	33.83	33.78	33.76
5000	85.41	85.22	85.06	84.94	84.58	84.45	84.40
6000	102.49	102.26	102.07	101.92	101.50	101.34	101.28
7000	119.57	119.30	119.09	118.91	118.41	118.23	118.16
8000	136.65	136.35	136.10	135.90	135.33	135.12	135.04
9000	153.73	153.39	153.11	152.88	152.24	152.01	151.92
10000	170.81	170.43	170.12	169.87	169.16	168.90	168.80
15000	256.22	255.65	255.18	254.81	253.74	253.35	253.21
20000	341.62	340.86	340.25	339.74	338.32	337.80	337.61
25000	427.03	426.08	425.31	424.68	422.90	422.25	422.01
30000	512.43	511.29	510.37	509.61	507.48	506.70	506.41
35000	597.84	596.51	595.43	594.55	592.06	591.15	590.82
36000	614.92	613.55	612.44	611.54	608.97	608.04	607.70
37000	632.00	630.60	629.46	628.53	625.89	624.93	624.58
38000	649.08	647.64	646.47	645.51	642.81	641.82	641.46
39000	666.16	664.68	663.48	662.50	659.72	658.71	658.34
40000	683.24	681.73	680.49	679.49	676.64	675.60	675.22
41000	700.32	698.77	697.50	696.47	693.55	692.49	692.10
42000	717.40	715.81	714.52	713.46	710.47	709.38	708.98
43000	734.48	732.86	731.53	730.45	727.38	726.27	725.86
44000	751.56	749.90	748.54	747.44	744.30	743.16	742.74
45000	768.65	766.94	765.55	764.42	761.22	760.05	759.62
46000	785.73	783.98	782.57	781.41	778.13	776.94	776.50
47000	802.81	801.03	799.58	798.40	795.05	793.83	793.38
48000	819.89	818.07	816.59	815.38	811.96	810.72	810.26
49000	836.97	835.11	833.60	832.37	828.88	827.61	827.14
50000	854.05	852.16	850.62	849.36	845.80	844.50	844.02
51000	871.13	869.20	867.63	866.35	862.71	861.39	860.90
52000	888.21	886.24	884.64	883.33	879.63	878.28	877.79
53000	905.29	903.29	901.65	900.32	896.54	895.17	894.67
54000	922.37	920.33	918.66	917.31	913.46	912.06	911.55
55000	939.46	937.37	935.68	934.29	930.38	928.95	928.43
56000	956.54	954.42	952.69	951.28	947.29	945.84	945.31
57000	973.62	971.46	969.70	968.27	964.21	962.73	962.19
58000	990.70	988.50	986.71	985.26	981.12	979.62	979.07
59000	1007.78	1005.55	1003.73	1002.24	998.04	996.51	995.95
60000	1024.00	1022.59	1020.74	1019.23	1014.96	1013.40	1012.83
65000	1110.27	1107.80	1105.80	1104.17	1099.54	1097.85	1097.23
70000	1195.67	1193.02	1190.86	1189.10	1184.11	1182.30	1181.63
75000	1281.08	1278.24	1275.92	1274.04	1268.69	1266.75	1266.04
80000	1366.48	1363.45	1360.98	1358.97	1353.27	1351.20	1350.44
85000	1451.89	1448.67	1446.05	1443.91	1437.85	1435.65	1434.84
90000	1537.29	1533.88	1531.11	1528.84	1522.43	1520.10	1519.24
95000	1622.70	1619.10	1616.17	1613.78	1007.01	1604.55	1603.65
100000	1708.10	1704.32	1701.23	1698.72	1691.59	1689.00	1688.05
105000	1793.51	1789.53	1786.29	1783.65	1776.17	1773.45	1772.45
110000	1878.91	1874.75	1871.35	1868.59	1860.75	1857.90	1856.85
120000	2049.72	2045.18	2041.48	2038.46	2029.91	2026.80	2025.66
130000	2220.53	2215.61	2211.60	2208.33	2199.07	2195.70	2194.46
140000	2391.34	2386.04	2381.72	2378.20	2368.23	2364.60	2363.27
150000	2562.15	2556.47	2551.85	2548.07	2537.39	2533.50	2532.07
175000	2989.18	2982.55	2977.15	2972.75	2960.29	2955.74	2954.08
200000	3416.20	3408.63	3402.46	3397.43	3383.18	3377.99	3376.10
225000	3843.23	3834.71	3827.77	3822.11	3806.08	3800.24	3798.11
250000	4270.25	4260.79	4253.08	4246.79	4228.98	4222.49	4220.12

20½%

Monthly Payments
necessary to amortize a loan

AMOUNT	1 YEAR	2 YEARS	3 YEARS	4 YEARS	5 YEARS	6 YEARS	7 YEARS
100	9.29	5.11	3.74	3.07	2.68	2.42	2.25
200	18.57	10.23	7.48	6.14	5.35	4.85	4.50
500	46.44	25.57	18.71	15.35	13.39	12.12	11.25
1000	92.87	51.14	37.42	30.70	26.77	24.24	22.51
2000	185.75	102.28	74.84	61.39	53.55	48.49	45.02
5000	464.37	255.70	187.09	153.49	133.86	121.22	112.54
6000	557.24	306.84	224.51	184.18	160.64	145.46	135.05
7000	650.12	357.98	261.93	214.88	187.41	169.70	157.56
8000	742.99	409.12	299.35	245.58	214.18	193.95	180.07
9000	835.87	460.26	336.77	276.28	240.96	218.19	202.57
10000	928.74	511.40	374.19	306.97	267.73	242.44	225.08
15000	1393.11	767.11	561.28	460.46	401.59	363.65	337.62
20000	1857.48	1022.81	748.38	613.95	535.46	484.87	450.16
25000	2321.85	1278.51	935.47	767.43	669.32	606.09	562.71
30000	2786.22	1534.21	1122.57	920.92	803.19	727.31	675.25
35000	3250.59	1789.91	1309.66	1074.41	937.05	848.52	787.79
36000	3343.46	1841.05	1347.08	1105.11	963.82	872.77	810.30
37000	3436.34	1892.19	1384.50	1135.80	990.60	897.01	832.80
38000	3529.21	1943.33	1421.92	1166.50	1017.37	921.25	855.31
39000	3622.08	1994.48	1459.33	1197.20	1044.14	945.50	877.82
40000	3714.96	2045.62	1496.75	1227.90	1070.91	969.74	900.33
41000	3807.83	2096.76	1534.17	1258.59	1097.69	993.98	922.84
42000	3900.71	2147.90	1571.59	1289.29	1124.46	1018.23	945.35
43000	3993.58	2199.04	1609.01	1319.99	1151.23	1042.47	967.85
44000	4086.45	2250.18	1646.43	1350.69	1178.01	1066.72	990.36
45000	4179.33	2301.32	1683.85	1381.38	1204.78	1090.96	1012.87
46000	4272.20	2352.46	1721.27	1412.08	1231.55	1115.20	1035.38
47000	4365.08	2403.60	1758.69	1442.78	1258.32	1139.45	1057.89
48000	4457.95	2454.74	1796.10	1473.47	1285.10	1163.69	1080.40
49000	4550.82	2505.88	1833.52	1504.17	1311.87	1187.93	1102.90
50000	4643.70	2557.02	1870.94	1534.87	1338.64	1212.18	1125.41
51000	4736.57	2608.16	1908.36	1565.57	1365.42	1236.42	1147.92
52000	4829.45	2659.30	1945.78	1596.26	1392.19	1260.66	1170.43
53000	4922.32	2710.44	1983.20	1626.96	1418.96	1284.91	1192.94
54000	5015.19	2761.58	2020.62	1657.66	1445.73	1309.15	1215.45
55000	5108.07	2812.72	2058.04	1688.36	1472.51	1333.39	1237.95
56000	5200.94	2863.86	2095.45	1719.05	1499.28	1357.64	1260.46
57000	5293.82	2915.00	2132.87	1749.75	1526.05	1381.88	1282.97
58000	5386.69	2966.14	2170.29	1780.45	1552.83	1406.12	1305.48
59000	5479.56	3017.28	2207.71	1811.15	1579.60	1430.37	1327.99
60000	5572.44	3068.42	2245.13	1841.84	1606.37	1454.61	1350.49
65000	6036.81	3324.13	2432.22	1995.33	1740.24	1575.83	1463.04
70000	6501.18	3579.83	2619.32	2148.82	1874.10	1697.05	1575.58
75000	6965.55	3835.53	2806.41	2302.30	2007.96	1818.27	1688.12
80000	7429.92	4091.23	2993.51	2455.79	2141.83	1939.48	1800.66
85000	7894.29	4346.93	3180.60	2609.28	2275.69	2060.70	1913.20
90000	8358.66	4602.64	3367.70	2762.77	2409.56	2181.92	2025.74
95000	8823.03	4858.34	3554.79	2916.25	2543.42	2303.14	2138.28
100000	9287.40	5114.04	3741.88	3069.74	2677.29	2424.35	2250.82
105000	9751.77	5369.74	3928.98	3223.23	2811.15	2545.57	2363.37
110000	10216.14	5625.44	4116.07	3376.71	2945.01	2666.79	2475.91
120000	11144.88	6136.85	4490.26	3683.69	3212.74	2909.22	2700.99
130000	12073.62	6648.25	4864.45	3990.66	3480.47	3151.66	2926.07
140000	13002.36	7159.66	5238.64	4297.64	3748.20	3394.09	3151.15
150000	13931.10	7671.06	5612.83	4604.61	4015.93	3636.53	3376.24
175000	16252.95	8949.57	6548.30	5372.04	4685.25	4242.62	3938.94
200000	18574.79	10228.08	7483.77	6139.48	5354.57	4848.71	4501.65
225000	20896.64	11506.59	8419.24	6906.91	6023.89	5454.80	5064.35
250000	23218.49	12785.10	9354.71	7674.35	6693.21	6060.88	5627.06

Monthly Payments 20½%

necessary to amortize a loan

AMOUNT	8 YEARS	9 YEARS	10 YEARS	11 YEARS	12 YEARS	13 YEARS	14 YEARS
100	2.13	2.03	1.97	1.91	1.87	1.84	1.81
200	4.25	4.07	3.93	3.83	3.74	3.68	3.63
500	10.63	10.17	9.83	9.56	9.36	9.20	9.07
1000	21.27	20.35	19.66	19.13	18.72	18.39	18.14
2000	42.53	40.70	39.32	38.26	37.43	36.79	36.27
5000	106.33	101.75	98.29	95.64	93.58	91.86	00.68
6000	127.60	122.10	117.95	114.77	112.30	110.36	108.82
7000	148.86	142.45	137.61	133.90	131.01	128.75	126.96
8000	170.13	162.80	157.27	153.02	149.73	147.14	145.10
9000	191.39	183.15	176.92	172.15	168.44	165.53	163.23
10000	212.66	203.50	196.58	191.28	187.16	183.93	181.37
15000	318.99	305.24	294.87	286.92	280.74	275.89	272.05
20000	425.32	406.99	393.16	382.56	374.32	367.85	362.74
25000	531.65	508.74	491.46	478.20	467.90	459.81	453.42
30000	637.98	610.49	589.75	573.84	561.48	551.78	544.11
35000	744.31	712.24	688.04	669.48	655.06	643.74	634.79
36000	765.58	732.59	707.70	688.60	673.77	662.13	652.93
37000	786.84	752.93	727.35	707.73	692.49	680.53	671.07
38000	808.11	773.28	747.01	726.86	711.20	698.92	689.20
39000	829.38	793.63	766.67	745.99	729.92	717.31	707.34
40000	850.64	813.98	786.33	765.12	748.64	735.70	725.48
41000	871.91	834.33	805.99	784.24	767.35	754.10	743.61
42000	893.17	854.68	825.65	803.37	786.07	772.49	761.75
43000	914.44	875.03	845.30	822.50	804.78	790.88	779.89
44000	935.71	895.38	864.96	841.63	823.50	809.27	798.02
45000	956.97	915.73	884.62	860.76	842.22	827.67	816.16
46000	978.24	936.08	904.28	879.88	860.93	846.06	834.30
47000	999.50	956.43	923.94	899.01	879.65	864.45	852.43
48000	1020.77	976.78	943.60	918.14	898.36	882.84	870.57
49000	1042.04	997.13	963.25	937.27	917.08	901.24	888.71
50000	1063.30	1017.48	982.91	956.40	935.79	919.63	906.85
51000	1084.57	1037.83	1002.57	975.52	954.51	938.02	924.98
52000	1105.84	1058.18	1022.23	994.65	973.23	956.41	943.12
53000	1127.10	1078.53	1041.89	1013.78	991.94	974.81	961.26
54000	1148.37	1098.88	1061.54	1032.91	1010.66	993.20	979.39
55000	1169.63	1119.23	1081.20	1052.04	1029.37	1011.59	997.53
56000	1190.90	1139.58	1100.86	1071.16	1048.09	1029.98	1015.67
57000	1212.17	1159.93	1120.52	1090.29	1066.81	1048.38	1033.80
58000	1233.43	1180.28	1140.18	1109.42	1085.52	1066.77	1051.94
59000	1254.70	1200.63	1159.84	1128.55	1104.24	1085.16	1070.08
60000	1275.96	1220.98	1179.49	1147.67	1122.95	1103.56	1088.21
65000	1382.29	1322.72	1277.78	1243.31	1216.53	1195.52	1178.90
70000	1488.62	1424.47	1376.08	1338.95	1310.11	1287.48	1269.58
75000	1594.95	1526.22	1474.37	1434.59	1403.69	1379.44	1360.27
80000	1701.28	1627.97	1672.66	1530.23	1497.27	1471.41	1450.95
85000	1807.62	1729.71	1670.95	1625.87	1590.85	1563.37	1541.64
90000	1913.95	1831.46	1769.24	1721.51	1684.43	1655.33	1632.32
95000	2020.28	1933.21	1867.53	1817.15	1778.01	1747.30	1723.01
100000	2126.61	2034.96	1965.82	1912.79	1871.59	1839.26	1813.69
105000	2232.94	2136.71	2064.11	2008.43	1965.17	1931.22	1904.38
110000	2339.27	2238.45	2162.41	2104.07	2058.75	2023.18	1995.06
120000	2551.93	2441.95	2358.99	2295.35	2245.91	2207.11	2176.43
130000	2764.59	2645.45	2555.57	2486.63	2433.07	2391.04	2357.80
140000	2977.25	2848.94	2752.15	2677.91	2620.23	2574.96	2539.17
150000	3189.91	3052.44	2948.73	2869.19	2807.38	2758.89	2720.54
175000	3721.56	3561.18	3440.19	3347.39	3275.28	3218.70	3173.96
200000	4253.21	4069.92	3931.65	3825.58	3743.18	3678.52	3627.38
225000	4784.86	4578.66	4423.10	4303.78	4211.08	4138.33	4080.80
250000	5316.51	5087.40	4914.56	4781.98	4678.97	4598.15	4534.23

20½%

Monthly Payments
necessary to amortize a loan

AMOUNT	15 YEARS	16 YEARS	17 YEARS	18 YEARS	19 YEARS	20 YEARS	21 YEARS
100	1.79	1.78	1.76	1.75	1.75	1.74	1.73
200	3.59	3.55	3.53	3.51	3.49	3.48	3.47
500	8.97	8.89	8.82	8.77	8.73	8.69	8.66
1000	17.93	17.77	17.64	17.54	17.45	17.38	17.33
2000	35.87	35.54	35.28	35.07	34.90	34.76	34.65
5000	89.67	88.85	88.20	87.68	87.25	86.91	86.63
6000	107.60	106.62	105.84	105.21	104.70	104.29	103.96
7000	125.53	124.40	123.48	122.75	122.15	121.67	121.28
8000	143.47	142.17	141.12	140.28	139.60	139.05	138.61
9000	161.40	159.94	158.76	157.82	157.05	156.43	155.93
10000	179.33	177.71	176.40	175.35	174.50	173.82	173.26
15000	269.00	266.56	264.60	263.03	261.75	260.72	259.89
20000	358.67	355.42	352.80	350.70	349.00	347.63	346.52
25000	448.34	444.27	441.01	438.38	436.26	434.54	433.15
30000	538.00	533.12	529.21	526.05	523.51	521.45	519.78
35000	627.67	621.98	617.41	613.73	610.76	608.35	606.41
36000	645.60	639.75	635.05	631.26	628.21	625.74	623.73
37000	663.54	657.52	652.69	648.80	645.66	643.12	641.06
38000	681.47	675.29	670.33	666.33	663.11	660.50	658.38
39000	699.41	693.06	687.97	683.87	680.56	677.88	675.71
40000	717.34	710.83	705.61	701.40	698.01	695.26	693.04
41000	735.27	728.60	723.25	718.94	715.46	712.64	710.36
42000	753.21	746.37	740.89	736.47	732.91	730.02	727.69
43000	771.14	764.14	758.53	754.01	750.36	747.41	745.01
44000	789.07	781.92	776.17	771.54	767.81	764.79	762.34
45000	807.01	799.69	793.81	789.08	785.26	782.17	779.67
46000	824.94	817.46	811.45	806.61	802.71	799.55	796.99
47000	842.87	835.23	829.09	824.15	820.16	816.93	814.32
48000	860.81	853.00	846.73	841.68	837.61	834.31	831.64
49000	878.74	870.77	864.37	859.22	855.06	851.70	848.97
50000	896.67	888.54	882.01	876.75	872.51	869.08	866.30
51000	914.61	906.31	899.65	894.29	889.96	886.46	883.62
52000	932.54	924.08	917.29	911.82	907.41	903.84	900.95
53000	950.47	941.85	934.93	929.36	924.86	921.22	918.27
54000	968.41	959.62	952.57	946.89	942.31	938.60	935.60
55000	986.34	977.39	970.21	964.43	959.76	955.98	952.93
56000	1004.27	995.16	987.85	981.96	977.21	973.37	970.25
57000	1022.21	1012.94	1005.49	999.50	994.66	990.75	987.58
58000	1040.14	1030.71	1023.13	1017.03	1012.11	1008.13	1004.90
59000	1058.07	1048.48	1040.77	1034.57	1029.56	1025.51	1022.23
60000	1076.01	1066.25	1058.41	1052.10	1047.01	1042.89	1039.55
65000	1165.68	1155.10	1146.61	1139.78	1134.26	1129.80	1126.18
70000	1255.34	1243.96	1234.82	1227.46	1221.51	1216.71	1212.81
75000	1345.01	1332.81	1323.02	1315.13	1308.77	1303.62	1299.44
80000	1434.68	1421.66	1411.22	1402.81	1396.02	1390.52	1386.07
85000	1524.34	1510.52	1499.42	1490.48	1483.27	1477.43	1472.70
90000	1614.01	1599.37	1587.62	1578.16	1570.52	1564.34	1559.33
95000	1703.68	1688.23	1675.82	1665.83	1657.77	1651.25	1645.96
100000	1793.35	1777.08	1764.02	1753.51	1745.02	1738.15	1732.59
105000	1883.01	1865.93	1852.22	1841.18	1832.27	1825.06	1819.22
110000	1972.68	1954.79	1940.42	1928.86	1919.52	1911.97	1905.85
120000	2152.02	2132.50	2116.83	2104.21	2094.02	2085.78	2079.11
130000	2331.35	2310.20	2293.23	2279.56	2268.53	2259.60	2252.37
140000	2510.69	2487.91	2469.63	2454.91	2443.03	2433.42	2425.63
150000	2690.02	2665.62	2646.03	2630.26	2617.53	2607.23	2598.89
175000	3138.36	3109.89	3087.04	3068.64	3053.79	3041.77	3032.03
200000	3586.69	3554.16	3528.04	3507.02	3490.04	3476.31	3465.18
225000	4035.03	3998.43	3969.05	3945.39	3926.30	3910.85	3898.33
250000	4483.37	4442.70	4410.06	4383.77	4362.55	4345.39	4331.48

Monthly Payments 20½%

necessary to amortize a loan

AMOUNT	22 YEARS	23 YEARS	24 YEARS	25 YEARS	30 YEARS	35 YEARS	40 YEARS
100	1.73	1.72	1.72	1.72	1.71	1.71	1.71
200	3.46	3.45	3.44	3.44	3.42	3.42	3.42
500	8.64	8.62	8.61	8.60	8.56	8.55	8.54
1000	17.28	17.24	17.21	17.19	17.12	17.10	17.09
2000	34.56	34.49	34.43	34.38	34.24	34.19	34.18
5000	86.40	86.22	86.07	85.95	85.61	85.49	85.44
6000	103.68	103.46	103.29	103.14	102.73	102.58	102.53
7000	120.97	120.71	120.50	120.33	119.85	119.68	119.62
8000	138.25	137.95	137.71	137.52	136.97	136.78	136.71
9000	155.53	155.20	154.93	154.71	154.10	153.88	153.80
10000	172.81	172.44	172.14	171.90	171.22	170.97	170.88
15000	259.21	258.66	258.21	257.85	256.83	256.46	256.33
20000	345.62	344.88	344.29	343.80	342.44	341.94	341.77
25000	432.02	431.10	430.36	429.75	428.05	427.43	427.21
30000	518.42	517.32	516.43	515.70	513.65	512.92	512.65
35000	604.83	603.54	602.50	601.65	599.26	598.40	598.09
36000	622.11	620.79	619.72	618.84	616.39	615.50	615.18
37000	639.39	638.03	636.93	636.03	633.51	632.60	632.27
38000	656.67	655.28	654.14	653.22	650.63	649.70	649.36
39000	673.95	672.52	671.36	670.41	667.75	666.79	666.45
40000	691.23	689.76	688.57	687.60	684.87	683.89	683.53
41000	708.51	707.01	705.79	704.79	701.99	700.99	700.62
42000	725.79	724.25	723.00	721.98	719.12	718.08	717.71
43000	743.07	741.50	740.22	739.17	736.24	735.18	734.80
44000	760.35	758.74	757.43	756.36	753.36	752.28	751.89
45000	777.63	775.99	774.64	773.55	770.48	769.38	768.98
46000	794.92	793.23	791.86	790.74	787.60	786.47	786.06
47000	812.20	810.47	809.07	807.93	804.73	803.57	803.15
48000	829.48	827.72	826.29	825.12	821.85	820.67	820.24
49000	846.76	844.96	843.50	842.31	838.97	837.76	837.33
50000	864.04	862.21	860.72	859.50	856.09	854.86	854.42
51000	881.32	879.45	877.93	876.69	873.21	871.96	871.51
52000	898.60	896.69	895.14	893.88	890.33	889.06	888.59
53000	915.88	913.94	912.36	911.07	907.46	906.15	905.68
54000	933.16	931.18	929.57	928.26	924.58	923.25	922.77
55000	950.44	948.43	946.79	945.45	941.70	940.35	939.86
56000	967.72	965.67	964.00	962.64	958.82	957.45	956.95
57000	985.00	982.91	981.22	979.83	975.94	974.54	974.04
58000	1002.28	1000.16	998.43	997.02	993.06	991.64	991.13
59000	1019.57	1017.40	1015.64	1014.21	1010.19	1008.74	1008.21
60000	1036.85	1034.65	1032.86	1031.40	1027.31	1025.83	1025.30
65000	1123.25	1120.87	1118.93	1117.35	1112.92	1111.32	1110.74
70000	1209.65	1207.09	1205.00	1203.30	1198.53	1196.81	1196.19
75000	1296.06	1293.31	1291.07	1289.26	1284.14	1282.29	1281.63
80000	1382.46	1379.53	1377.15	1375.21	1369.74	1367.78	1367.07
85000	1468.87	1465.75	1463.22	1461.16	1455.35	1453.27	1452.51
90000	1555.27	1551.97	1549.29	1547.11	1540.96	1538.75	1537.95
95000	1641.67	1638.19	1635.36	1633.06	1626.57	1624.24	1623.39
100000	1728.08	1724.41	1721.43	1719.01	1712.18	1709.72	1708.84
105000	1814.48	1810.63	1807.50	1804.96	1797.79	1795.21	1794.28
110000	1900.89	1896.85	1893.57	1890.91	1883.40	1880.70	1879.72
120000	2073.69	2069.29	2065.72	2062.81	2054.62	2051.67	2050.60
130000	2246.50	2241.73	2237.86	2234.71	2225.84	2222.64	2221.49
140000	2419.31	2414.18	2410.00	2406.61	2397.05	2393.61	2392.37
150000	2592.12	2586.62	2582.15	2578.51	2568.27	2564.59	2563.25
175000	3024.14	3017.72	3012.50	3008.26	2996.32	2992.02	2990.46
200000	3456.15	3448.82	3442.86	3438.01	3424.36	3419.45	3417.67
225000	3888.17	3879.93	3873.22	3867.77	3852.41	3846.88	3844.88
250000	4320.19	4311.03	4303.58	4297.52	4280.45	4274.31	4272.09

20¾%

Monthly Payments
necessary to amortize a loan

AMOUNT	1 YEAR	2 YEARS	3 YEARS	4 YEARS	5 YEARS	6 YEARS	7 YEARS
100	9.30	5.13	3.75	3.08	2.69	2.44	2.27
200	18.60	10.25	7.51	6.17	5.38	4.88	4.53
500	46.50	25.63	18.77	15.42	13.46	12.19	11.33
1000	92.99	51.26	37.55	30.83	26.91	24.39	22.66
2000	185.99	102.53	75.09	61.66	53.83	48.78	45.32
5000	464.97	256.31	187.73	154.16	134.56	121.95	113.30
6000	557.96	307.58	225.28	184.99	161.48	146.34	135.96
7000	650.96	358.84	262.83	215.82	188.39	170.73	158.62
8000	743.95	410.10	300.37	246.65	215.30	195.12	181.28
9000	836.94	461.37	337.92	277.48	242.22	219.51	203.94
10000	929.94	512.63	375.47	308.31	269.13	243.90	226.60
15000	1394.91	768.94	563.20	462.47	403.69	365.84	339.90
20000	1859.88	1025.26	750.94	616.63	538.26	487.79	453.20
25000	2324.85	1281.57	938.67	770.78	672.82	609.74	566.50
30000	2789.81	1537.89	1126.40	924.94	807.39	731.69	679.80
35000	3254.78	1794.20	1314.14	1079.10	941.95	853.63	793.10
36000	3347.78	1845.47	1351.69	1109.93	968.87	878.02	815.76
37000	3440.77	1896.73	1389.23	1140.76	995.78	902.41	838.42
38000	3533.77	1947.99	1426.78	1171.59	1022.69	926.80	861.08
39000	3626.76	1999.25	1464.33	1202.42	1049.60	951.19	883.74
40000	3719.75	2050.52	1501.87	1233.26	1076.52	975.58	906.40
41000	3812.75	2101.78	1539.42	1264.09	1103.43	999.97	929.06
42000	3905.74	2153.04	1576.97	1294.92	1130.34	1024.36	951.72
43000	3998.73	2204.31	1614.51	1325.75	1157.26	1048.75	974.38
44000	4091.73	2255.57	1652.06	1356.58	1184.17	1073.14	997.04
45000	4184.72	2306.83	1689.61	1387.41	1211.08	1097.53	1019.70
46000	4277.72	2358.10	1727.15	1418.24	1237.99	1121.92	1042.36
47000	4370.71	2409.36	1764.70	1449.08	1264.91	1146.31	1065.02
48000	4463.70	2460.62	1802.25	1479.91	1291.82	1170.70	1087.68
49000	4556.70	2511.88	1839.79	1510.74	1318.73	1195.09	1110.34
50000	4649.69	2563.15	1877.34	1541.57	1345.65	1219.48	1133.00
51000	4742.69	2614.41	1914.89	1572.40	1372.56	1243.87	1155.66
52000	4835.68	2665.67	1952.44	1603.23	1399.47	1268.26	1178.32
53000	4928.67	2716.94	1989.98	1634.06	1426.38	1292.65	1200.98
54000	5021.67	2768.20	2027.53	1664.89	1453.30	1317.04	1223.64
55000	5114.66	2819.46	2065.08	1695.73	1480.21	1341.43	1246.30
56000	5207.65	2870.72	2102.62	1726.56	1507.12	1365.81	1268.96
57000	5300.65	2921.99	2140.17	1757.39	1534.04	1390.20	1291.62
58000	5393.64	2973.25	2177.72	1788.22	1560.95	1414.59	1314.28
59000	5486.64	3024.51	2215.26	1819.05	1587.86	1438.98	1336.94
60000	5579.63	3075.78	2252.81	1849.88	1614.78	1463.37	1359.60
65000	6044.60	3332.09	2440.54	2004.04	1749.34	1585.32	1472.90
70000	6509.57	3588.41	2628.28	2158.20	1883.90	1707.27	1586.20
75000	6974.54	3844.72	2816.01	2312.35	2018.47	1829.22	1699.50
80000	7439.51	4101.04	3003.75	2466.51	2153.03	1951.16	1812.80
85000	7904.48	4357.35	3191.48	2620.67	2287.60	2073.11	1926.10
90000	8369.44	4613.66	3379.21	2774.82	2422.16	2195.06	2039.40
95000	8834.41	4869.98	3566.95	2928.98	2556.73	2317.01	2152.70
100000	9299.38	5126.29	3754.68	3083.14	2691.29	2438.95	2266.00
105000	9764.35	5382.61	3942.42	3237.30	2825.86	2560.90	2379.30
110000	10229.32	5638.92	4130.15	3391.45	2960.42	2682.85	2492.60
120000	11159.26	6151.55	4505.62	3699.77	3229.55	2926.75	2719.20
130000	12089.20	6664.18	4881.09	4008.08	3498.68	3170.64	2945.80
140000	13019.14	7176.81	5256.56	4316.39	3767.81	3414.54	3172.40
150000	13949.07	7689.44	5632.02	4624.71	4036.94	3658.43	3399.00
175000	16273.92	8971.01	6570.70	5395.49	4709.76	4268.17	3965.50
200000	18598.77	10252.59	7509.37	6166.28	5382.58	4877.91	4532.00
225000	20923.61	11534.16	8448.04	6937.06	6055.41	5487.65	5098.50
250000	23248.46	12815.73	9386.71	7707.85	6728.23	6097.39	5665.00

Monthly Payments 20¾%

necessary to amortize a loan

AMOUNT	8 YEARS	9 YEARS	10 YEARS	11 YEARS	12 YEARS	13 YEARS	14 YEARS
100	2.14	2.05	1.98	1.93	1.89	1.86	1.83
200	4.28	4.10	3.97	3.86	3.78	3.71	3.66
500	10.71	10.26	9.91	9.65	9.45	9.29	9.16
1000	21.42	20.51	19.83	19.30	18.89	18.57	18.32
2000	42.85	41.02	39.65	38.60	37.78	37.14	36.64
5000	107.12	102.56	99.13	96.50	94.46	92.86	91.60
6000	128.54	123.07	118.95	115.80	113.35	111.43	109.92
7000	149.96	143.58	138.78	135.10	132.24	130.00	128.24
8000	171.39	164.10	158.60	154.40	151.13	148.58	146.56
9000	192.81	184.61	178.43	173.70	170.03	167.15	164.88
10000	214.23	205.12	198.25	193.00	188.92	185.72	183.20
15000	321.35	307.68	297.38	289.49	283.38	278.58	274.80
20000	428.47	410.24	396.51	385.99	377.83	371.44	366.40
25000	535.58	512.80	495.64	482.49	472.29	464.30	458.00
30000	642.70	615.36	594.76	578.99	566.75	557.16	549.60
35000	749.81	717.92	693.89	675.49	661.21	650.02	641.20
36000	771.24	738.43	713.72	694.78	680.10	668.60	659.52
37000	792.66	758.94	733.54	714.08	698.99	687.17	677.84
38000	814.08	779.45	753.37	733.38	717.88	705.74	696.16
39000	835.51	799.97	773.19	752.68	736.78	724.31	714.48
40000	856.93	820.48	793.02	771.98	755.67	742.89	732.79
41000	878.35	840.99	812.84	791.28	774.56	761.46	751.11
42000	899.78	861.50	832.67	810.58	793.45	780.03	769.43
43000	921.20	882.01	852.49	829.88	812.34	798.60	787.75
44000	942.62	902.53	872.32	849.18	831.23	817.17	806.07
45000	964.05	923.04	892.14	868.48	850.13	835.75	824.39
46000	985.47	943.55	911.97	887.78	869.02	854.32	842.71
47000	1006.89	964.06	931.79	907.08	887.91	872.89	861.03
48000	1028.32	984.57	951.62	926.38	906.80	891.46	879.35
49000	1049.74	1005.09	971.45	945.68	925.69	910.03	897.67
50000	1071.16	1025.60	991.27	964.98	944.58	928.61	915.99
51000	1092.59	1046.11	1011.10	984.28	963.48	947.18	934.31
52000	1114.01	1066.62	1030.92	1003.58	982.37	965.75	952.63
53000	1135.43	1087.13	1050.75	1022.88	1001.26	984.32	970.95
54000	1156.86	1107.65	1070.57	1042.18	1020.15	1002.89	989.27
55000	1178.28	1128.16	1090.40	1061.48	1039.04	1021.47	1007.59
56000	1199.70	1148.67	1110.22	1080.78	1057.93	1040.04	1025.91
57000	1221.13	1169.18	1130.05	1100.08	1076.83	1058.61	1044.23
58000	1242.55	1189.69	1149.87	1119.38	1095.72	1077.18	1062.55
59000	1263.97	1210.21	1169.70	1138.67	1114.61	1095.76	1080.87
60000	1285.40	1230.72	1189.53	1157.97	1133.50	1114.33	1099.19
65000	1392.51	1333.28	1288.65	1254.47	1227.96	1207.19	1190.79
70000	1499.63	1435.84	1387.78	1350.97	1322.42	1300.05	1282.39
75000	1606.75	1538.40	1486.91	1447.47	1416.88	1392.91	1373.99
80000	1713.86	1640.96	1586.03	1543.97	1511.33	1485.77	1465.59
85000	1820.98	1743.52	1685.16	1640.46	1605.79	1578.63	1557.19
90000	1928.09	1846.08	1784.29	1736.96	1700.25	1671.49	1648.79
95000	2035.21	1948.64	1883.41	1833.46	1794.71	1764.35	1740.39
100000	2142.33	2051.20	1982.54	1929.96	1889.17	1857.21	1831.99
105000	2249.44	2153.76	2081.67	2026.46	1983.63	1950.07	1923.59
110000	2356.56	2256.31	2180.80	2122.95	2078.08	2042.93	2015.19
120000	2570.79	2461.43	2379.05	2315.95	2267.00	2228.66	2198.38
130000	2785.03	2666.55	2577.30	2508.94	2455.92	2414.38	2381.58
140000	2999.26	2871.67	2775.56	2701.94	2644.83	2600.10	2564.78
150000	3213.49	3076.79	2973.81	2894.94	2833.75	2785.82	2747.98
175000	3749.07	3589.59	3469.45	3377.43	3306.04	3250.12	3205.98
200000	4284.65	4102.39	3965.08	3859.91	3778.33	3714.43	3663.97
225000	4820.24	4615.19	4460.72	4342.40	4250.63	4178.73	4121.97
250000	5355.82	5127.99	4956.35	4824.89	4722.92	4643.03	4579.97

20¾% Monthly Payments

necessary to amortize a loan

AMOUNT	15 YEARS	16 YEARS	17 YEARS	18 YEARS	19 YEARS	20 YEARS	21 YEARS
100	1.81	1.80	1.78	1.77	1.76	1.76	1.75
200	3.62	3.59	3.57	3.55	3.53	3.52	3.50
500	9.06	8.98	8.92	8.86	8.82	8.79	8.76
1000	18.12	17.96	17.83	17.73	17.65	17.58	17.52
2000	36.24	35.92	35.66	35.46	35.29	35.16	35.05
5000	90.60	89.80	89.16	88.64	88.23	87.89	87.62
6000	108.72	107.76	106.99	106.37	105.87	105.47	105.15
7000	126.84	125.72	124.82	124.10	123.52	123.05	122.67
8000	144.96	143.68	142.65	141.83	141.17	140.63	140.20
9000	163.08	161.64	160.48	159.56	158.81	158.21	157.72
10000	181.20	179.60	178.32	177.29	176.46	175.79	175.25
15000	271.79	269.39	267.47	265.93	264.69	263.68	262.87
20000	362.39	359.19	356.63	354.57	352.91	351.58	350.49
25000	452.99	448.99	445.79	443.22	441.14	439.47	438.12
30000	543.59	538.79	534.95	531.86	529.37	527.36	525.74
35000	634.18	628.59	624.10	620.50	617.60	615.26	613.36
36000	652.30	646.55	641.94	638.23	635.25	632.84	630.89
37000	670.42	664.51	659.77	655.96	652.89	650.42	648.41
38000	688.54	682.47	677.60	673.69	670.54	667.99	665.94
39000	706.66	700.43	695.43	691.42	688.18	685.57	683.46
40000	724.78	718.39	713.26	709.15	705.83	703.15	700.99
41000	742.90	736.35	731.09	726.87	723.47	720.73	718.51
42000	761.02	754.31	748.93	744.60	741.12	738.31	736.04
43000	779.14	772.26	766.76	762.33	758.77	755.89	753.56
44000	797.26	790.22	784.59	780.06	776.41	773.47	771.09
45000	815.38	808.18	802.42	797.79	794.06	791.05	788.61
46000	833.50	826.14	820.25	815.52	811.70	808.62	806.14
47000	851.62	844.10	838.08	833.25	829.35	826.20	823.66
48000	869.74	862.06	855.92	850.97	846.99	843.78	841.18
49000	887.86	880.02	873.75	868.70	864.64	861.36	858.71
50000	905.98	897.98	891.58	886.43	882.29	878.94	876.23
51000	924.10	915.94	909.41	904.16	899.93	896.52	893.76
52000	942.22	933.90	927.24	921.89	917.58	914.10	911.28
53000	960.34	951.86	945.07	939.62	935.22	931.68	928.81
54000	978.45	969.82	962.90	957.35	952.87	949.25	946.33
55000	996.57	987.78	980.74	975.07	970.51	966.83	963.86
56000	1014.69	1005.74	998.57	992.80	988.16	984.41	981.38
57000	1032.81	1023.70	1016.40	1010.53	1005.81	1001.99	998.91
58000	1050.93	1041.66	1034.23	1028.26	1023.45	1019.57	1016.43
59000	1069.05	1059.62	1052.06	1045.99	1041.10	1037.15	1033.96
60000	1087.17	1077.58	1069.89	1063.72	1058.74	1054.73	1051.48
65000	1177.77	1167.38	1159.05	1152.36	1146.97	1142.62	1139.10
70000	1268.37	1257.18	1248.21	1241.00	1235.20	1230.52	1226.73
75000	1358.96	1346.97	1337.37	1329.65	1323.43	1318.41	1314.35
80000	1449.56	1436.77	1426.53	1418.29	1411.66	1406.30	1401.97
85000	1540.16	1526.57	1515.68	1506.93	1499.89	1494.20	1489.60
90000	1630.76	1616.37	1604.84	1595.58	1588.11	1582.09	1577.22
95000	1721.36	1706.17	1694.00	1684.22	1676.34	1669.99	1664.84
100000	1811.95	1795.96	1783.16	1772.86	1764.57	1757.88	1752.47
105000	1902.55	1885.76	1872.31	1861.51	1852.80	1845.77	1840.09
110000	1993.15	1975.56	1961.47	1950.15	1941.03	1933.67	1927.72
120000	2174.34	2155.16	2139.79	2127.44	2117.49	2109.46	2102.96
130000	2355.54	2334.75	2318.10	2304.72	2293.94	2285.24	2278.21
140000	2536.73	2514.35	2496.42	2482.01	2470.40	2461.03	2453.46
150000	2717.93	2693.95	2674.73	2659.30	2646.86	2636.82	2628.70
175000	3170.92	3142.94	3120.52	3102.51	3088.00	3076.29	3066.82
200000	3623.91	3591.93	3566.31	3545.73	3529.14	3515.76	3504.94
225000	4076.89	4040.92	4012.10	3988.94	3970.29	3955.23	3943.05
250000	4529.88	4489.91	4457.89	4432.16	4411.43	4394.70	4381.17

Monthly Payments 20¾%

necessary to amortize a loan

AMOUNT	22 YEARS	23 YEARS	24 YEARS	25 YEARS	30 YEARS	35 YEARS	40 YEARS
100	1.75	1.74	1.74	1.74	1.73	1.73	1.73
200	3.50	3.49	3.48	3.48	3.47	3.46	3.46
500	8.74	8.72	8.71	8.70	8.66	8.65	8.65
1000	17.48	17.45	17.42	17.39	17.33	17.30	17.30
2000	34.96	34.89	34.83	34.79	34.66	34.61	34.59
5000	87.40	87.23	87.08	86.97	86.64	86.52	86.48
6000	104.89	104.67	104.50	104.36	103.97	103.83	103.78
7000	122.37	122.12	121.92	121.75	121.29	121.13	121.07
8000	139.85	139.56	139.33	139.15	138.62	138.44	138.37
9000	157.33	157.01	156.75	156.54	155.95	155.74	155.67
10000	174.81	174.45	174.17	173.93	173.28	173.05	172.96
15000	262.21	261.68	261.25	260.90	259.92	259.57	259.44
20000	349.62	348.91	348.33	347.86	346.56	346.09	345.93
25000	437.02	436.13	435.41	434.83	433.20	432.61	432.41
30000	524.43	523.36	522.50	521.80	519.84	519.14	518.89
35000	611.83	610.59	609.58	608.76	606.47	605.66	605.37
36000	629.31	628.03	627.00	626.16	623.80	622.96	622.67
37000	646.79	645.48	644.41	643.55	641.13	640.27	639.96
38000	664.27	662.92	661.83	660.94	658.46	657.57	657.26
39000	681.75	680.37	679.25	678.34	675.79	674.88	674.55
40000	699.24	697.82	696.66	695.73	693.11	692.18	691.85
41000	716.72	715.26	714.08	713.12	710.44	709.49	709.15
42000	734.20	732.71	731.50	730.52	727.77	726.79	726.44
43000	751.68	750.15	748.91	747.91	745.10	744.10	743.74
44000	769.16	767.60	766.33	765.30	762.42	761.40	761.04
45000	786.64	785.04	783.75	782.70	779.75	778.71	778.33
46000	804.12	802.49	801.16	800.09	797.08	796.01	795.63
47000	821.60	819.93	818.58	817.48	814.41	813.32	812.93
48000	839.08	837.38	836.00	834.88	831.74	830.62	830.22
49000	856.56	854.82	853.41	852.27	849.06	847.92	847.52
50000	874.04	872.27	870.83	869.66	866.39	865.23	864.81
51000	891.52	889.71	888.25	887.05	883.72	882.53	882.11
52000	909.01	907.16	905.66	904.45	901.05	899.84	899.41
53000	926.49	924.61	923.08	921.84	918.38	917.14	916.70
54000	943.97	942.05	940.50	939.23	935.70	934.45	934.00
55000	961.45	959.50	957.91	956.63	953.03	951.75	951.30
56000	978.93	976.94	975.33	974.02	970.36	969.06	968.59
57000	996.41	994.39	992.75	991.41	987.69	986.36	985.89
58000	1013.89	1011.83	1010.16	1008.81	1005.01	1003.67	1003.18
59000	1031.37	1029.28	1027.58	1026.20	1022.34	1020.97	1020.48
60000	1048.86	1046.72	1045.00	1043.60	1039.07	1038.27	1037.78
65000	1136.26	1133.95	1132.08	1130.56	1126.31	1124.80	1124.26
70000	1223.66	1221.18	1219.16	1217.53	1212.95	1211.32	1210.74
75000	1311.07	1308.40	1306.24	1304.49	1299.59	1297.84	1297.22
80000	1398.47	1395.63	1393.33	1391.46	1386.23	1384.37	1383.70
85000	1485.87	1482.86	1480.41	1478.42	1472.87	1470.89	1470.18
90000	1573.28	1570.08	1567.49	1565.39	1559.51	1557.41	1556.67
95000	1660.68	1657.31	1654.58	1652.36	1646.14	1643.94	1643.16
100000	1748.09	1744.54	1741.66	1739.32	1732.78	1730.46	1729.63
105000	1835.49	1831.77	1828.74	1826.29	1819.42	1816.98	1816.11
110000	1922.90	1918.99	1915.83	1913.26	1906.06	1903.50	1902.59
120000	2097.71	2093.45	2089.99	2087.19	2079.34	2076.55	2075.55
130000	2272.51	2267.90	2264.16	2261.12	2252.62	2249.60	2248.52
140000	2447.32	2442.35	2438.32	2435.05	2425.90	2422.64	2421.48
150000	2622.13	2616.81	2612.49	2608.98	2599.18	2595.69	2594.44
175000	3059.15	3052.94	3047.90	3043.82	3032.37	3028.30	3026.85
200000	3496.18	3489.08	3483.32	3478.65	3465.57	3460.92	3459.26
225000	3933.20	3925.21	3918.73	3913.48	3898.76	3893.53	3891.66
250000	4370.22	4361.35	4354.15	4348.31	4331.96	4326.15	4324.07

21%

Monthly Payments

necessary to amortize a loan

AMOUNT	1 YEAR	2 YEARS	3 YEARS	4 YEARS	5 YEARS	6 YEARS	7 YEARS
100	9.31	5.14	3.77	3.10	2.71	2.45	2.28
200	18.62	10.28	7.54	6.19	5.41	4.91	4.56
500	46.56	25.69	18.84	15.48	13.53	12.27	11.41
1000	93.11	51.39	37.68	30.97	27.05	24.54	22.81
2000	186.23	102.77	75.35	61.93	54.11	49.07	45.62
5000	465.57	256.93	188.38	154.83	135.27	122.68	114.06
6000	558.68	308.31	226.05	185.79	162.32	147.22	136.87
7000	651.80	359.70	263.73	216.76	189.37	171.75	159.69
8000	744.91	411.09	301.40	247.73	216.43	196.29	182.50
9000	838.02	462.47	339.08	278.69	243.48	220.82	205.31
10000	931.14	513.86	376.75	309.66	270.53	245.36	228.12
15000	1396.71	770.78	565.13	464.49	405.80	368.04	342.18
20000	1862.28	1027.71	753.50	619.31	541.07	490.72	456.24
25000	2327.84	1284.64	941.88	774.14	676.33	613.40	570.31
30000	2793.41	1541.57	1130.25	928.97	811.60	736.08	684.37
35000	3258.98	1798.50	1318.63	1083.80	946.87	858.76	798.43
36000	3352.10	1849.88	1356.30	1114.77	973.92	883.30	821.24
37000	3445.21	1901.27	1393.98	1145.73	1000.97	907.83	844.05
38000	3538.32	1952.65	1431.65	1176.70	1028.03	932.37	866.86
39000	3631.44	2004.04	1469.33	1207.66	1055.08	956.90	889.68
40000	3724.55	2055.43	1507.00	1238.63	1082.13	981.44	912.49
41000	3817.66	2106.81	1544.68	1269.59	1109.19	1005.98	935.30
42000	3910.78	2158.20	1582.35	1300.56	1136.24	1030.51	958.11
43000	4003.89	2209.58	1620.03	1331.52	1163.29	1055.05	980.93
44000	4097.01	2260.97	1657.70	1362.49	1190.35	1079.58	1003.74
45000	4190.12	2312.35	1695.38	1393.46	1217.40	1104.12	1026.55
46000	4283.23	2363.74	1733.05	1424.42	1244.45	1128.66	1049.36
47000	4376.35	2415.13	1770.73	1455.39	1271.51	1153.19	1072.17
48000	4469.46	2466.51	1808.40	1486.35	1298.56	1177.73	1094.99
49000	4562.57	2517.90	1846.08	1517.32	1325.61	1202.26	1117.80
50000	4655.69	2569.28	1883.75	1548.28	1352.67	1226.80	1140.61
51000	4748.80	2620.67	1921.43	1579.25	1379.72	1251.34	1163.42
52000	4841.92	2672.05	1959.10	1610.22	1406.77	1275.87	1186.24
53000	4935.03	2723.44	1996.78	1641.18	1433.83	1300.41	1209.05
54000	5028.14	2774.83	2034.45	1672.15	1460.88	1324.94	1231.86
55000	5121.26	2826.21	2072.13	1703.11	1487.93	1349.48	1254.67
56000	5214.37	2877.60	2109.80	1734.08	1514.99	1374.02	1277.48
57000	5307.49	2928.98	2147.48	1765.04	1542.04	1398.55	1300.30
58000	5400.60	2980.37	2185.15	1796.01	1569.09	1423.09	1323.11
59000	5493.71	3031.75	2222.83	1826.98	1596.15	1447.62	1345.92
60000	5586.83	3083.14	2260.50	1857.94	1623.20	1472.16	1368.73
65000	6052.40	3340.07	2448.88	2012.77	1758.47	1594.84	1482.79
70000	6517.96	3597.00	2637.25	2167.60	1893.74	1717.52	1596.86
75000	6983.53	3853.92	2825.63	2322.43	2029.00	1840.20	1710.92
80000	7449.10	4110.85	3014.01	2477.26	2164.27	1962.88	1824.98
85000	7914.67	4367.78	3202.38	2632.08	2299.54	2085.56	1939.04
90000	8380.24	4624.71	3390.76	2786.91	2434.80	2208.24	2053.10
95000	8845.81	4881.64	3579.13	2941.74	2570.07	2330.92	2167.16
100000	9311.38	5138.57	3767.51	3096.57	2705.34	2453.60	2281.22
105000	9776.95	5395.49	3955.88	3251.40	2840.60	2576.28	2395.28
110000	10242.52	5652.42	4144.26	3406.23	2975.87	2698.96	2509.34
120000	11173.65	6166.28	4521.01	3715.88	3246.40	2944.32	2737.47
130000	12104.79	6680.13	4897.76	4025.54	3516.94	3189.68	2965.59
140000	13035.93	7193.99	5274.51	4335.20	3787.47	3435.04	3193.71
150000	13967.07	7707.85	5651.26	4644.85	4058.00	3680.40	3421.83
175000	16294.91	8992.49	6593.14	5419.00	4734.34	4293.80	3992.14
200000	18622.75	10277.13	7535.01	6193.14	5410.67	4907.20	4562.45
225000	20950.60	11561.77	8476.89	6967.28	6087.01	5520.60	5132.75
250000	23278.44	12846.41	9418.77	7741.42	6763.34	6134.00	5703.06

Monthly Payments 21%

necessary to amortize a loan

AMOUNT	8 YEARS	9 YEARS	10 YEARS	11 YEARS	12 YEARS	13 YEARS	14 YEARS
100	2.16	2.07	2.00	1.95	1.91	1.88	1.85
200	4.32	4.13	4.00	3.89	3.81	3.75	3.70
500	10.79	10.34	10.00	9.74	9.53	9.38	9.25
1000	21.58	20.67	19.99	19.47	19.07	18.75	18.50
2000	43.16	41.35	39.99	38.94	38.14	37.50	37.01
5000	107.91	103.37	99.97	97.36	95.34	93.76	92.52
6000	129.49	124.05	119.96	116.83	114.41	112.51	111.02
7000	151.07	144.72	139.95	136.30	133.48	131.27	129.52
8000	172.65	165.40	159.95	155.77	152.54	150.02	148.03
9000	194.23	186.07	179.94	175.25	171.61	168.77	166.53
10000	215.81	206.75	199.93	194.72	190.68	187.52	185.03
15000	323.72	310.12	299.90	292.08	286.02	281.28	277.55
20000	431.62	413.50	399.86	389.44	381.36	375.04	370.07
25000	539.53	516.87	499.83	486.80	476.70	468.81	462.58
30000	647.43	620.25	599.80	584.15	572.04	562.57	555.10
35000	755.34	723.62	699.76	681.51	667.38	656.33	647.62
36000	776.92	744.30	719.75	700.98	686.45	675.08	666.12
37000	798.50	764.97	739.75	720.46	705.52	693.83	684.63
38000	820.08	785.64	759.74	739.93	724.58	712.58	703.13
39000	841.66	806.32	779.73	759.40	743.65	731.34	721.63
40000	863.24	826.99	799.73	778.87	762.72	750.09	740.14
41000	884.82	847.67	819.72	798.34	781.79	768.84	758.64
42000	906.40	868.34	839.71	817.82	800.86	787.59	777.14
43000	927.98	889.02	859.71	837.29	819.92	806.35	795.65
44000	949.56	909.69	879.70	856.76	838.99	825.10	814.15
45000	971.15	930.37	899.69	876.23	858.06	843.85	832.65
46000	992.73	951.04	919.69	895.70	877.13	862.60	851.16
47000	1014.31	971.72	939.68	915.17	896.20	881.35	869.66
48000	1035.89	992.39	959.67	934.65	915.26	900.11	888.16
49000	1057.47	1013.07	979.67	954.12	934.33	918.86	906.67
50000	1079.05	1033.74	999.66	973.59	953.40	937.61	925.17
51000	1100.63	1054.42	1019.65	993.06	972.47	956.36	943.67
52000	1122.21	1075.09	1039.64	1012.53	991.54	975.12	962.18
53000	1143.79	1095.77	1059.64	1032.01	1010.60	993.87	980.68
54000	1165.37	1116.44	1079.63	1051.48	1029.67	1012.62	999.18
55000	1186.96	1137.12	1099.62	1070.95	1048.74	1031.37	1017.69
56000	1208.54	1157.79	1119.62	1090.42	1067.81	1050.12	1036.19
57000	1230.12	1178.47	1139.61	1109.89	1086.88	1068.88	1054.69
58000	1251.70	1199.14	1159.60	1129.36	1105.94	1087.63	1073.20
59000	1273.28	1219.82	1179.60	1148.84	1125.01	1106.38	1091.70
60000	1294.86	1240.49	1199.59	1168.31	1144.08	1125.13	1110.20
65000	1402.77	1343.87	1299.56	1265.67	1239.42	1218.89	1202.72
70000	1510.67	1447.24	1399.52	1363.03	1334.76	1312.66	1295.24
75000	1618.58	1550.62	1499.49	1460.39	1430.10	1406.42	1387.75
80000	1726.48	1653.99	1599.45	1557.74	1525.44	1500.18	1480.27
85000	1834.39	1757.36	1699.42	1655.10	1620.78	1593.94	1572.79
90000	1942.29	1860.74	1799.39	1752.46	1716.12	1687.70	1665.30
95000	2050.20	1964.11	1899.35	1849.82	1811.46	1781.46	1757.82
100000	2158.10	2067.49	1999.32	1947.18	1906.80	1875.22	1850.34
105000	2266.01	2170.86	2099.28	2044.54	2002.14	1968.98	1942.86
110000	2373.91	2274.24	2199.25	2141.90	2097.48	2062.75	2035.37
120000	2589.72	2480.98	2399.18	2336.62	2288.16	2250.27	2220.41
130000	2805.53	2687.73	2599.11	2531.33	2478.84	2437.79	2405.44
140000	3021.34	2894.48	2799.04	2726.05	2669.52	2625.31	2590.47
150000	3237.15	3101.23	2998.98	2920.77	2860.20	2812.83	2775.51
175000	3776.68	3618.10	3498.80	3407.57	3336.90	3281.64	3238.09
200000	4316.20	4134.97	3998.63	3894.36	3813.60	3750.45	3700.68
225000	4855.73	4651.85	4498.46	4381.16	4290.30	4219.25	4163.26
250000	5395.25	5168.72	4998.29	4867.95	4767.00	4688.06	4625.85

21%

Monthly Payments
necessary to amortize a loan

AMOUNT	15 YEARS	16 YEARS	17 YEARS	18 YEARS	19 YEARS	20 YEARS	21 YEARS
100	1.83	1.81	1.80	1.79	1.78	1.78	1.77
200	3.66	3.63	3.60	3.58	3.57	3.56	3.54
500	9.15	9.07	9.01	8.96	8.92	8.89	8.86
1000	18.31	18.15	18.02	17.92	17.84	17.78	17.72
2000	36.61	36.30	36.05	35.85	35.68	35.55	35.45
5000	91.53	90.74	90.12	89.61	89.21	88.88	88.62
6000	109.84	108.89	108.14	107.54	107.05	106.66	106.34
7000	128.14	127.04	126.16	125.46	124.89	124.44	124.07
8000	146.45	145.19	144.19	143.38	142.73	142.21	141.79
9000	164.76	163.34	162.21	161.30	160.57	159.99	159.51
10000	183.06	181.49	180.23	179.23	178.42	177.76	177.24
15000	274.59	272.23	270.35	268.84	267.62	266.65	265.86
20000	366.12	362.98	360.47	358.45	356.83	355.53	354.48
25000	457.65	453.72	450.58	448.07	446.04	444.41	443.10
30000	549.18	544.47	540.70	537.68	535.25	533.29	531.71
35000	640.71	635.21	630.82	627.29	624.46	622.18	620.33
36000	659.02	653.36	648.84	645.21	642.30	639.95	638.06
37000	677.33	671.51	666.86	663.14	660.14	657.73	655.78
38000	695.63	689.66	684.89	681.06	677.98	675.50	673.50
39000	713.94	707.81	702.91	698.98	695.82	693.28	691.23
40000	732.24	725.96	720.94	716.91	713.67	711.06	708.95
41000	750.55	744.11	738.96	734.83	731.51	728.83	726.68
42000	768.86	762.26	756.98	752.75	749.35	746.61	744.40
43000	787.16	780.41	775.01	770.67	767.19	764.39	762.12
44000	805.47	798.56	793.03	788.60	785.03	782.16	779.85
45000	823.78	816.70	811.05	806.52	802.87	799.94	797.57
46000	842.08	834.85	829.08	824.44	820.72	817.72	815.30
47000	860.39	853.00	847.10	842.36	838.56	835.49	833.02
48000	878.69	871.15	865.12	860.29	856.40	853.27	850.74
49000	897.00	889.30	883.15	878.21	874.24	871.05	868.47
50000	915.31	907.45	901.17	896.13	892.08	888.82	886.19
51000	933.61	925.60	919.19	914.05	909.92	906.60	903.91
52000	951.92	943.75	937.22	931.98	927.77	924.37	921.64
53000	970.22	961.90	955.24	949.90	945.61	942.15	939.36
54000	988.53	980.05	973.26	967.82	963.45	959.93	957.09
55000	1006.84	998.19	991.29	985.75	981.29	977.70	974.81
56000	1025.14	1016.34	1009.31	1003.67	999.13	995.48	992.53
57000	1043.45	1034.49	1027.33	1021.59	1016.97	1013.26	1010.26
58000	1061.76	1052.64	1045.36	1039.51	1034.82	1031.03	1027.98
59000	1080.06	1070.79	1063.38	1057.44	1052.66	1048.81	1045.70
60000	1098.37	1088.94	1081.40	1075.36	1070.50	1066.59	1063.43
65000	1189.90	1179.68	1171.52	1164.97	1159.71	1155.47	1152.05
70000	1281.43	1270.43	1261.64	1254.58	1248.92	1244.35	1240.67
75000	1372.96	1361.17	1351.75	1344.20	1338.12	1333.23	1329.29
80000	1464.49	1451.92	1441.87	1433.81	1427.33	1422.11	1417.90
85000	1556.02	1542.66	1531.99	1523.42	1516.54	1511.00	1506.52
90000	1647.55	1633.41	1622.10	1613.04	1605.75	1599.88	1595.14
95000	1739.08	1724.15	1712.22	1702.65	1694.96	1688.76	1683.76
100000	1830.61	1814.90	1802.34	1792.26	1784.17	1777.64	1772.38
105000	1922.14	1905.64	1892.45	1881.88	1873.37	1866.53	1861.00
110000	2013.67	1996.39	1982.57	1971.49	1962.58	1955.41	1949.62
120000	2196.73	2177.88	2162.81	2150.72	2141.00	2133.17	2126.86
130000	2379.80	2359.37	2343.04	2329.94	2319.42	2310.94	2304.10
140000	2562.86	2540.86	2523.27	2509.17	2497.83	2488.70	2481.33
150000	2745.92	2722.35	2703.51	2688.40	2676.25	2666.46	2658.57
175000	3203.57	3176.07	3154.09	3136.46	3122.29	3110.88	3101.67
200000	3661.22	3629.80	3604.68	3584.53	3568.33	3555.29	3544.76
225000	4118.88	4083.52	4055.26	4032.59	4014.37	3999.70	3987.86
250000	4576.53	4537.25	4505.84	4480.66	4460.41	4444.11	4430.95

Monthly Payments 21%

necessary to amortize a loan

AMOUNT	22 YEARS	23 YEARS	24 YEARS	25 YEARS	30 YEARS	35 YEARS	40 YEARS
100	1.77	1.76	1.76	1.76	1.75	1.75	1.75
200	3.54	3.53	3.52	3.52	3.51	3.50	3.50
500	8.84	8.82	8.81	8.80	8.77	8.76	8.75
1000	17.68	17.65	17.62	17.60	17.53	17.51	17.50
2000	35.36	35.29	35.24	35.19	35.07	35.02	35.01
5000	88.41	88.23	88.10	87.98	87.67	87.56	87.52
6000	106.00	105.88	105.71	105.58	105.20	105.07	105.03
7000	123.77	123.53	123.33	123.18	122.74	122.58	122.53
8000	141.45	141.18	140.95	140.77	140.27	140.10	140.03
9000	159.13	158.82	158.57	158.37	157.81	157.61	157.54
10000	176.81	176.47	176.19	175.97	175.34	175.12	175.04
15000	265.22	264.70	264.29	263.95	263.01	262.68	262.56
20000	353.63	352.94	352.38	351.93	350.68	350.24	350.08
25000	442.03	441.17	440.48	439.92	438.35	437.80	437.61
30000	530.44	529.41	528.57	527.90	526.02	525.36	525.13
35000	618.85	617.64	616.67	615.88	613.69	612.92	612.65
36000	636.53	635.29	634.29	633.48	631.22	630.43	630.15
37000	654.21	652.94	651.91	651.08	648.76	647.94	647.66
38000	671.89	670.58	669.53	668.67	666.29	665.46	665.16
39000	689.57	688.23	687.15	686.27	683.83	682.97	682.67
40000	707.25	705.88	704.77	703.87	701.36	700.48	700.17
41000	724.93	723.52	722.38	721.46	718.89	717.99	717.67
42000	742.62	741.17	740.00	739.06	736.43	735.50	735.18
43000	760.30	758.82	757.62	756.66	753.96	753.02	752.68
44000	777.98	776.47	775.24	774.25	771.50	770.53	770.19
45000	795.66	794.11	792.86	791.85	789.03	788.04	787.69
46000	813.34	811.76	810.48	809.44	806.56	805.55	805.19
47000	831.02	829.41	828.10	827.04	824.10	823.06	822.70
48000	848.70	847.05	845.72	844.64	841.63	840.58	840.20
49000	866.38	864.70	863.34	862.23	859.17	858.09	857.71
50000	884.07	882.35	880.96	879.83	876.70	875.60	875.21
51000	901.75	899.99	898.58	897.43	894.23	893.11	892.72
52000	919.43	917.64	916.20	915.02	911.77	910.62	910.22
53000	937.11	935.29	933.81	932.62	929.30	928.14	927.72
54000	954.79	952.94	951.43	950.22	946.84	945.65	945.23
55000	972.47	970.58	969.05	967.81	964.37	963.16	962.73
56000	990.15	988.23	986.67	985.41	981.90	980.67	980.24
57000	1007.83	1005.88	1004.29	1003.01	999.44	998.18	997.74
58000	1025.52	1023.52	1021.91	1020.60	1016.97	1015.70	1015.25
59000	1043.20	1041.17	1039.53	1038.20	1034.51	1033.21	1032.75
60000	1060.88	1058.82	1057.15	1055.80	1052.04	1050.72	1050.25
65000	1149.29	1147.05	1145.24	1143.78	1139.71	1138.28	1137.78
70000	1237.69	1235.29	1233.34	1231.76	1227.38	1225.84	1225.30
75000	1326.10	1323.52	1321.44	1319.75	1315.05	1313.40	1312.82
80000	1414.51	1411.76	1409.53	1407.73	1402.72	1400.90	1400.34
85000	1502.91	1499.99	1497.63	1495.71	1490.39	1488.52	1487.86
90000	1591.32	1588.23	1585.72	1583.70	1578.06	1576.08	1575.38
95000	1679.72	1676.46	1673.82	1671.68	1665.73	1663.64	1662.90
100000	1768.13	1764.70	1761.91	1759.66	1753.40	1751.20	1750.42
105000	1856.54	1852.93	1850.01	1847.65	1841.07	1838.76	1837.94
110000	1944.94	1941.16	1938.11	1935.63	1928.74	1926.32	1925.47
120000	2121.76	2117.63	2114.30	2111.60	2104.08	2101.44	2100.51
130000	2298.57	2294.10	2290.49	2287.56	2279.42	2276.56	2275.55
140000	2475.38	2470.57	2466.68	2463.53	2454.76	2451.68	2450.59
150000	2652.20	2647.04	2642.87	2639.49	2630.10	2626.80	2625.63
175000	3094.23	3088.22	3083.35	3079.41	3068.45	3064.60	3063.24
200000	3536.26	3529.39	3523.83	3519.33	3506.80	3502.40	3500.85
225000	3978.30	3970.56	3964.31	3959.24	3945.15	3940.20	3938.45
250000	4420.33	4411.74	4404.79	4399.16	4383.50	4378.00	4376.06

21¼% Monthly Payments

necessary to amortize a loan

AMOUNT	1 YEAR	2 YEARS	3 YEARS	4 YEARS	5 YEARS	6 YEARS	7 YEARS
100	9.32	5.15	3.78	3.11	2.72	2.47	2.30
200	18.65	10.30	7.56	6.22	5.44	4.94	4.59
500	46.62	25.75	18.90	15.55	13.60	12.34	11.48
1000	93.23	51.51	37.80	31.10	27.19	24.68	22.96
2000	186.47	103.02	75.61	62.20	54.39	49.37	45.93
5000	466.17	257.54	189.02	155.50	135.97	123.41	114.82
6000	559.40	309.05	226.82	186.60	163.17	148.10	137.79
7000	652.64	360.56	264.62	217.70	190.36	172.78	160.75
8000	745.87	412.07	302.43	248.80	217.55	197.46	183.72
9000	839.10	463.58	340.23	279.90	244.75	222.15	206.68
10000	932.34	515.09	378.04	311.00	271.94	246.83	229.65
15000	1398.51	772.63	567.05	466.50	407.91	370.24	344.47
20000	1864.68	1030.17	756.07	622.01	543.88	493.66	459.30
25000	2330.84	1287.71	945.09	777.51	679.85	617.07	574.12
30000	2797.01	1545.26	1134.11	933.01	815.83	740.49	688.95
35000	3263.18	1802.80	1323.12	1088.51	951.80	863.90	803.77
36000	3356.42	1854.31	1360.93	1119.61	978.99	888.58	826.74
37000	3449.65	1905.82	1398.73	1150.71	1006.18	913.27	849.70
38000	3542.88	1957.32	1436.53	1181.81	1033.38	937.95	872.67
39000	3636.12	2008.83	1474.34	1212.91	1060.57	962.63	895.63
40000	3729.35	2060.34	1512.14	1244.01	1087.77	987.32	918.60
41000	3822.59	2111.85	1549.95	1275.11	1114.96	1012.00	941.56
42000	3915.82	2163.36	1587.75	1306.21	1142.16	1036.68	964.53
43000	4009.05	2214.87	1625.55	1337.31	1169.35	1061.36	987.49
44000	4102.29	2266.38	1663.36	1368.41	1196.54	1086.05	1010.46
45000	4195.52	2317.88	1701.16	1399.51	1223.74	1110.73	1033.42
46000	4288.75	2369.39	1738.96	1430.61	1250.93	1135.41	1056.39
47000	4381.99	2420.90	1776.77	1461.71	1278.13	1160.10	1079.35
48000	4475.22	2472.41	1814.57	1492.82	1305.32	1184.78	1102.32
49000	4568.46	2523.92	1852.37	1523.92	1332.51	1209.46	1125.28
50000	4661.69	2575.43	1890.18	1555.02	1359.71	1234.14	1148.25
51000	4754.92	2626.93	1927.98	1586.12	1386.90	1258.83	1171.21
52000	4848.16	2678.44	1965.78	1617.22	1414.10	1283.51	1194.18
53000	4941.39	2729.95	2003.59	1648.32	1441.29	1308.19	1217.14
54000	5034.63	2781.46	2041.39	1679.42	1468.49	1332.88	1240.11
55000	5127.86	2832.97	2079.20	1710.52	1495.68	1357.56	1263.07
56000	5221.09	2884.48	2117.00	1741.62	1522.87	1382.24	1286.04
57000	5314.33	2935.99	2154.80	1772.72	1550.07	1406.92	1309.00
58000	5407.56	2987.49	2192.61	1803.82	1577.26	1431.61	1331.97
59000	5500.79	3039.00	2230.41	1834.92	1604.46	1456.29	1354.93
60000	5594.03	3090.51	2268.21	1866.02	1631.65	1480.97	1377.90
65000	6060.20	3348.05	2457.23	2021.52	1767.62	1604.39	1492.72
70000	6526.37	3605.60	2646.25	2177.02	1903.59	1727.80	1607.55
75000	6992.53	3863.14	2835.27	2332.52	2039.56	1851.22	1722.37
80000	7458.70	4120.68	3024.28	2488.03	2175.53	1974.63	1837.20
85000	7924.87	4378.22	3213.30	2643.53	2311.51	2098.04	1952.02
90000	8391.04	4635.77	3402.32	2799.03	2447.48	2221.46	2066.84
95000	8857.21	4893.31	3591.34	2954.53	2583.45	2344.87	2181.67
100000	9323.38	5150.85	3780.35	3110.03	2719.42	2468.29	2296.49
105000	9789.55	5408.40	3969.37	3265.53	2855.39	2591.70	2411.32
110000	10255.72	5665.94	4158.39	3421.04	2991.36	2715.12	2526.14
120000	11188.06	6181.02	4536.43	3732.04	3263.30	2961.95	2755.79
130000	12120.39	6696.11	4914.46	4043.04	3535.24	3208.77	2985.44
140000	13052.73	7211.19	5292.50	4354.04	3807.19	3455.60	3215.09
150000	13985.07	7726.28	5670.53	4665.05	4079.13	3702.43	3444.74
175000	16315.91	9013.99	6615.62	5442.56	4758.98	4319.50	4018.86
200000	18646.76	10301.71	7560.71	6220.06	5438.84	4936.58	4592.99
225000	20977.60	11589.42	8505.80	6997.57	6118.69	5553.65	5167.11
250000	23308.45	12877.13	9450.89	7775.08	6798.55	6170.72	5741.24

Monthly Payments 21¼%

necessary to amortize a loan

AMOUNT	8 YEARS	9 YEARS	10 YEARS	11 YEARS	12 YEARS	13 YEARS	14 YEARS
100	2.17	2.08	2.02	1.96	1.92	1.89	1.87
200	4.35	4.17	4.03	3.93	3.85	3.79	3.74
500	10.87	10.42	10.08	9.82	9.62	9.47	9.34
1000	21.74	20.84	20.16	19.64	19.24	18.93	18.69
2000	43.48	41.68	40.32	39.29	38.49	37.87	37.37
5000	108.70	104.19	100.81	98.22	96.22	94.66	93.44
6000	130.44	125.03	120.97	117.87	115.47	113.60	112.12
7000	152.17	145.87	141.13	137.51	134.71	132.53	130.81
8000	173.91	166.71	161.29	157.16	153.96	151.46	149.50
9000	195.65	187.54	181.45	176.80	173.20	170.40	168.19
10000	217.39	208.38	201.61	196.45	192.45	189.33	186.87
15000	326.09	312.57	302.42	294.67	288.67	283.99	280.31
20000	434.79	416.77	403.23	392.89	384.90	378.66	373.75
25000	543.48	520.96	504.04	491.11	481.12	473.32	467.19
30000	652.18	625.15	604.84	589.34	577.35	567.99	560.62
35000	760.87	729.34	705.65	687.56	673.57	662.65	654.06
36000	782.61	750.18	725.81	707.21	692.82	681.58	672.75
37000	804.35	771.02	745.97	726.85	712.06	700.52	691.44
38000	826.09	791.86	766.14	746.49	731.31	719.45	710.12
39000	847.83	812.69	786.30	766.14	750.55	738.38	728.81
40000	869.57	833.53	806.46	785.78	769.80	757.32	747.50
41000	891.31	854.37	826.62	805.43	789.04	776.25	766.19
42000	913.05	875.21	846.78	825.07	808.29	795.18	784.87
43000	934.79	896.05	866.94	844.72	827.53	814.11	803.56
44000	956.53	916.89	887.10	864.36	846.78	833.05	822.25
45000	978.27	937.72	907.27	884.01	866.02	851.98	840.93
46000	1000.01	958.56	927.43	903.65	885.27	870.91	859.62
47000	1021.75	979.40	947.59	923.30	904.51	889.85	878.31
48000	1043.48	1000.24	967.75	942.94	923.76	908.78	897.00
49000	1065.22	1021.08	987.91	962.59	943.00	927.71	915.68
50000	1086.96	1041.92	1008.07	982.23	962.25	946.64	934.37
51000	1108.70	1062.75	1028.24	1001.87	981.49	965.58	953.06
52000	1130.44	1083.59	1048.40	1021.52	1000.74	984.51	971.75
53000	1152.18	1104.43	1068.56	1041.16	1019.98	1003.44	990.43
54000	1173.92	1125.27	1088.72	1060.81	1039.23	1022.38	1009.12
55000	1195.66	1146.11	1108.88	1080.45	1058.47	1041.31	1027.81
56000	1217.40	1166.95	1129.04	1100.10	1077.72	1060.24	1046.50
57000	1239.14	1187.78	1149.20	1119.74	1096.96	1079.17	1065.18
58000	1260.88	1208.62	1169.37	1139.39	1116.21	1098.11	1083.87
59000	1282.62	1229.46	1189.53	1159.03	1135.45	1117.04	1102.56
60000	1304.36	1250.30	1209.69	1178.68	1154.70	1135.97	1121.25
65000	1413.05	1354.49	1310.50	1276.90	1250.92	1230.64	1214.68
70000	1521.75	1458.68	1411.30	1375.12	1347.14	1325.30	1308.12
75000	1630.44	1562.87	1512.11	1473.34	1443.37	1419.97	1401.56
80000	1739.14	1667.07	1612.92	1571.57	1539.60	1514.63	1495.00
85000	1847.84	1771.26	1713.73	1669.79	1635.82	1609.30	1588.43
90000	1956.53	1875.45	1814.53	1768.01	1732.04	1703.96	1681.87
95000	2065.23	1979.64	1915.34	1866.24	1828.27	1798.62	1775.31
100000	2173.93	2083.83	2016.15	1964.46	1924.49	1893.29	1868.74
105000	2282.62	2188.02	2116.95	2062.68	2020.72	1987.95	1962.18
110000	2391.32	2292.22	2217.76	2160.91	2116.94	2082.62	2055.62
120000	2608.71	2500.60	2419.38	2357.35	2309.39	2271.95	2242.49
130000	2826.10	2708.98	2620.99	2553.80	2501.84	2461.28	2429.37
140000	3043.50	2917.37	2822.61	2750.24	2694.29	2650.60	2616.24
150000	3260.89	3125.75	3024.22	2946.69	2886.74	2839.93	2803.12
175000	3804.37	3646.71	3528.26	3437.80	3367.86	3313.25	3270.30
200000	4347.85	4167.66	4032.29	3928.92	3848.98	3786.58	3737.49
225000	4891.33	4688.62	4536.33	4420.03	4330.11	4259.90	4204.67
250000	5434.82	5209.58	5040.37	4911.15	4811.23	4733.22	4671.86

21¼%

Monthly Payments

necessary to amortize a loan

AMOUNT	15 YEARS	16 YEARS	17 YEARS	18 YEARS	19 YEARS	20 YEARS	21 YEARS
100	1.85	1.83	1.82	1.81	1.80	1.80	1.79
200	3.70	3.67	3.64	3.62	3.61	3.59	3.58
500	9.25	9.17	9.11	9.06	9.02	8.99	8.96
1000	18.49	18.34	18.22	18.12	18.04	17.97	17.92
2000	36.99	36.68	36.43	36.23	36.08	35.95	35.85
5000	92.47	91.69	91.08	90.59	90.19	89.87	89.62
6000	110.96	110.03	109.29	108.70	108.23	107.85	107.54
7000	129.45	128.37	127.51	126.82	126.27	125.82	125.46
8000	147.95	146.71	145.73	144.94	144.30	143.80	143.39
9000	166.44	165.05	163.94	163.05	162.34	161.77	161.31
10000	184.93	183.39	182.16	181.17	180.38	179.74	179.23
15000	277.40	275.08	273.23	271.76	270.57	269.62	268.85
20000	369.86	366.78	364.31	362.34	360.76	359.49	358.47
25000	462.33	458.47	455.39	452.93	450.95	449.36	448.08
30000	554.80	550.17	546.47	543.51	541.14	539.23	537.70
35000	647.26	641.86	637.55	634.10	631.33	629.11	627.31
36000	665.76	660.20	655.76	652.21	649.37	647.08	645.24
37000	684.25	678.54	673.98	670.33	667.41	665.05	663.16
38000	702.74	696.88	692.19	688.45	685.44	683.03	681.08
39000	721.24	715.21	710.41	706.57	703.48	701.00	699.01
40000	739.73	733.55	728.63	724.68	721.52	718.98	716.93
41000	758.22	751.89	746.84	742.80	739.56	736.95	734.85
42000	776.72	770.23	765.06	760.92	757.60	754.93	752.78
43000	795.21	788.57	783.27	779.03	775.63	772.90	770.70
44000	813.70	806.91	801.49	797.15	793.67	790.88	788.62
45000	832.20	825.25	819.70	815.27	811.71	808.85	806.55
46000	850.69	843.59	837.92	833.39	829.75	826.82	824.47
47000	869.18	861.93	856.14	851.50	847.79	844.80	842.39
48000	887.68	880.26	874.35	869.62	865.82	862.77	860.32
49000	906.17	898.60	892.57	887.74	883.86	880.75	878.24
50000	924.66	916.94	910.78	905.85	901.90	898.72	896.16
51000	943.15	935.28	929.00	923.97	919.94	916.70	914.09
52000	961.65	953.62	947.21	942.09	937.98	934.67	932.01
53000	980.14	971.96	965.43	960.20	956.01	952.65	949.93
54000	998.63	990.30	983.65	978.32	974.05	970.62	967.86
55000	1017.13	1008.64	1001.86	996.44	992.09	988.59	985.78
56000	1035.62	1026.98	1020.08	1014.56	1010.13	1006.57	1003.70
57000	1054.11	1045.31	1038.29	1032.67	1028.17	1024.54	1021.63
58000	1072.61	1063.65	1056.51	1050.79	1046.20	1042.52	1039.55
59000	1091.10	1081.99	1074.72	1068.91	1064.24	1060.49	1057.47
60000	1109.59	1100.33	1092.94	1087.02	1082.28	1078.47	1075.40
65000	1202.06	1192.02	1184.02	1177.61	1172.47	1168.34	1165.01
70000	1294.53	1283.72	1275.10	1268.20	1262.66	1258.21	1254.63
75000	1386.99	1375.41	1366.17	1358.78	1352.85	1348.08	1344.25
80000	1479.46	1467.11	1457.25	1449.37	1443.04	1437.96	1433.86
85000	1571.92	1558.80	1548.33	1539.95	1533.23	1527.83	1523.48
90000	1664.39	1650.50	1639.41	1630.54	1623.42	1617.70	1613.10
95000	1756.86	1742.19	1730.49	1721.12	1713.61	1707.57	1702.71
100000	1849.32	1833.88	1821.57	1811.71	1803.80	1797.44	1792.33
105000	1941.79	1925.58	1912.64	1902.29	1893.99	1887.32	1881.94
110000	2034.26	2017.27	2003.72	1992.88	1984.18	1977.19	1971.56
120000	2219.19	2200.66	2185.88	2174.05	2164.56	2156.93	2150.79
130000	2404.12	2384.05	2368.04	2355.22	2344.94	2336.68	2330.03
140000	2589.05	2567.44	2550.19	2536.39	2525.32	2516.42	2509.26
150000	2773.98	2750.83	2732.35	2717.56	2705.70	2696.17	2688.49
175000	3236.32	3209.30	3187.74	3170.49	3156.65	3145.53	3136.57
200000	3698.65	3667.77	3643.13	3623.41	3607.60	3594.89	3584.66
225000	4160.98	4126.24	4098.52	4076.34	4058.55	4044.25	4032.74
250000	4623.31	4584.71	4553.91	4529.27	4509.50	4493.61	4480.82

Monthly Payments 21¼%

necessary to amortize a loan

AMOUNT	22 YEARS	23 YEARS	24 YEARS	25 YEARS	30 YEARS	35 YEARS	40 YEARS
100	1.79	1.78	1.78	1.78	1.77	1.77	1.77
200	3.58	3.57	3.56	3.56	3.55	3.54	3.54
500	8.94	8.92	8.91	8.90	8.87	8.86	8.86
1000	17.88	17.85	17.82	17.80	17.74	17.72	17.71
2000	35.76	35.70	35.64	35.60	35.48	35.44	35.42
5000	89.41	89.24	89.11	89.00	88.70	88.60	88.56
6000	107.29	107.09	106.93	106.80	106.44	106.32	106.27
7000	125.17	124.94	124.75	124.60	124.18	124.04	123.99
8000	143.06	142.79	142.58	142.40	141.92	141.76	141.70
9000	160.94	160.64	160.40	160.20	159.66	159.48	159.41
10000	178.82	178.49	178.22	178.00	177.40	177.19	177.12
15000	268.23	267.73	267.33	267.00	266.10	265.79	265.68
20000	357.64	356.98	356.44	356.01	354.81	354.39	354.24
25000	447.05	446.22	445.55	445.01	443.51	442.99	442.81
30000	536.46	535.46	534.66	534.01	532.21	531.58	531.37
35000	625.87	624.71	623.77	623.01	620.91	620.18	619.93
36000	643.75	642.56	641.59	640.81	638.65	637.90	637.64
37000	661.64	660.41	659.41	658.61	656.39	655.62	655.35
38000	679.52	678.25	677.23	676.41	674.13	673.34	673.06
39000	697.40	696.10	695.06	694.21	691.87	691.06	690.78
40000	715.28	713.95	712.88	712.01	709.61	708.78	708.49
41000	733.16	731.80	730.70	729.81	727.35	726.50	726.20
42000	751.05	749.65	748.52	747.61	745.09	744.22	743.91
43000	768.93	767.50	766.34	765.41	762.83	761.94	761.63
44000	786.81	785.35	784.17	783.21	780.57	779.66	779.34
45000	804.69	803.20	801.99	801.01	798.31	797.38	797.05
46000	822.57	821.04	819.81	818.81	816.05	815.10	814.76
47000	840.46	838.89	837.63	836.61	833.79	832.81	832.47
48000	858.34	856.74	855.45	854.41	851.53	850.53	850.19
49000	876.22	874.59	873.28	872.21	869.27	868.25	867.90
50000	894.10	892.44	891.10	890.01	887.01	885.97	885.61
51000	911.98	910.29	908.92	907.81	904.75	903.69	903.32
52000	929.87	928.14	926.74	925.61	922.50	921.41	921.04
53000	947.75	945.99	944.56	943.41	940.24	939.13	938.75
54000	965.63	963.84	962.39	961.21	957.98	956.85	956.46
55000	983.51	981.68	980.21	979.01	975.72	974.57	974.17
56000	1001.40	999.53	998.03	996.81	993.46	992.29	991.88
57000	1019.28	1017.38	1015.85	1014.61	1011.20	1010.01	1009.60
58000	1037.16	1035.23	1033.67	1032.41	1028.94	1027.73	1027.31
59000	1055.04	1053.08	1051.49	1050.22	1046.68	1045.45	1045.02
60000	1072.92	1070.93	1069.32	1068.02	1064.42	1063.17	1062.73
65000	1162.33	1160.17	1158.43	1157.02	1153.12	1151.77	1151.29
70000	1251.74	1249.42	1247.54	1246.02	1241.82	1240.36	1239.86
75000	1341.15	1338.66	1336.65	1335.02	1330.52	1328.96	1328.42
80000	1430.56	1427.90	1425.76	1424.02	1419.22	1417.56	1416.98
85000	1519.97	1517.15	1514.87	1513.02	1507.92	1506.15	1505.54
90000	1609.39	1606.39	1603.98	1602.02	1596.63	1594.75	1594.10
95000	1698.80	1695.64	1693.09	1691.02	1685.33	1683.35	1682.66
100000	1788.21	1784.88	1782.19	1780.03	1774.03	1771.95	1771.22
105000	1877.62	1874.12	1871.30	1869.03	1862.73	1860.54	1859.78
110000	1967.03	1963.37	1960.41	1958.03	1951.43	1949.14	1948.34
120000	2145.85	2141.86	2138.63	2136.03	2128.83	2126.34	2125.47
130000	2324.67	2320.34	2316.85	2314.03	2306.24	2303.53	2302.59
140000	2503.49	2498.83	2495.07	2492.04	2483.64	2480.73	2479.71
150000	2682.31	2677.32	2673.29	2670.04	2661.04	2657.92	2656.83
175000	3129.36	3123.54	3118.84	3115.04	3104.55	3100.91	3099.64
200000	3576.41	3569.76	3564.39	3560.05	3548.06	3543.89	3542.44
225000	4023.46	4015.98	4009.94	4005.06	3991.57	3986.88	3985.25
250000	4470.51	4462.20	4455.49	4450.06	4435.07	4429.87	4428.05

21½% Monthly Payments

necessary to amortize a loan

AMOUNT	1 YEAR	2 YEARS	3 YEARS	4 YEARS	5 YEARS	6 YEARS	7 YEARS
100	9.34	5.16	3.79	3.12	2.73	2.48	2.31
200	18.67	10.33	7.59	6.25	5.47	4.97	4.62
500	46.68	25.82	18.97	15.62	13.67	12.42	11.56
1000	93.35	51.63	37.93	31.24	27.34	24.83	23.12
2000	186.71	103.26	75.86	62.47	54.67	49.66	46.24
5000	466.77	258.16	189.66	156.18	136.68	124.15	115.59
6000	560.12	309.79	227.59	187.41	164.01	148.98	138.71
7000	653.48	361.42	265.53	218.65	191.35	173.81	161.83
8000	746.83	413.05	303.46	249.88	218.68	198.64	184.95
9000	840.19	464.68	341.39	281.12	246.02	223.47	208.06
10000	933.54	516.32	379.32	312.35	273.35	248.30	231.18
15000	1400.31	774.47	568.98	468.53	410.03	372.45	346.77
20000	1867.08	1032.63	758.65	624.71	546.71	496.60	462.36
25000	2333.85	1290.79	948.31	780.88	683.38	620.75	577.95
30000	2800.62	1548.95	1137.97	937.06	820.06	744.91	693.54
35000	3267.39	1807.10	1327.63	1093.23	956.74	869.06	809.13
36000	3360.74	1858.74	1365.56	1124.47	984.07	893.89	832.25
37000	3454.09	1910.37	1403.49	1155.70	1011.41	918.72	855.37
38000	3547.45	1962.00	1441.43	1186.94	1038.74	943.55	878.49
39000	3640.80	2013.63	1479.36	1218.18	1066.08	968.38	901.61
40000	3734.16	2065.26	1517.29	1249.41	1093.42	993.21	924.73
41000	3827.51	2116.89	1555.22	1280.65	1120.75	1018.04	947.84
42000	3920.86	2168.53	1593.16	1311.88	1148.09	1042.87	970.96
43000	4014.22	2220.16	1631.09	1343.12	1175.42	1067.70	994.08
44000	4107.57	2271.79	1669.02	1374.35	1202.76	1092.53	1017.20
45000	4200.93	2323.42	1706.95	1405.59	1230.09	1117.36	1040.32
46000	4294.28	2375.05	1744.88	1436.82	1257.43	1142.19	1063.43
47000	4387.63	2426.68	1782.82	1468.06	1284.76	1167.02	1086.55
48000	4480.99	2478.32	1820.75	1499.29	1312.10	1191.85	1109.67
49000	4574.34	2529.95	1858.68	1530.53	1339.43	1216.68	1132.79
50000	4667.70	2581.58	1896.61	1561.76	1366.77	1241.51	1155.91
51000	4761.05	2633.21	1934.55	1593.00	1394.10	1266.34	1179.02
52000	4854.40	2684.84	1972.48	1624.23	1421.44	1291.17	1202.14
53000	4947.76	2736.47	2010.41	1655.47	1448.78	1316.00	1225.26
54000	5041.11	2788.10	2048.34	1686.70	1476.11	1340.83	1248.38
55000	5134.47	2839.74	2086.28	1717.94	1503.45	1365.66	1271.50
56000	5227.82	2891.37	2124.21	1749.17	1530.78	1390.49	1294.62
57000	5321.17	2943.00	2162.14	1780.41	1558.12	1415.32	1317.73
58000	5414.53	2994.63	2200.07	1811.64	1585.45	1440.15	1340.85
59000	5507.88	3046.26	2238.00	1842.88	1612.79	1464.98	1363.97
60000	5601.23	3097.89	2275.94	1874.12	1640.12	1489.81	1387.09
65000	6068.00	3356.05	2465.60	2030.29	1776.80	1613.96	1502.68
70000	6534.77	3614.21	2655.26	2186.47	1913.48	1738.11	1618.27
75000	7001.54	3872.37	2844.92	2342.64	2050.15	1862.26	1733.86
80000	7468.31	4130.53	3034.58	2498.82	2186.83	1986.42	1849.45
85000	7935.08	4388.68	3224.24	2655.00	2323.51	2110.57	1965.04
90000	8401.85	4646.84	3413.90	2811.17	2460.18	2234.72	2080.63
95000	8868.62	4905.00	3603.57	2967.35	2596.86	2358.87	2196.22
100000	9335.39	5163.16	3793.23	3123.53	2733.54	2483.02	2311.81
105000	9802.16	5421.31	3982.89	3279.70	2870.21	2607.17	2427.40
110000	10268.93	5679.47	4172.55	3435.88	3006.89	2731.32	2542.99
120000	11202.47	6195.79	4551.87	3748.23	3280.25	2979.62	2774.18
130000	12136.01	6712.10	4931.20	4060.58	3553.60	3227.93	3005.36
140000	13069.55	7228.42	5310.52	4372.94	3826.95	3476.23	3236.54
150000	14003.09	7744.74	5689.84	4685.29	4100.31	3724.53	3467.72
175000	16336.93	9035.52	6638.15	5466.17	4783.69	4345.28	4045.67
200000	18670.78	10326.31	7586.45	6247.05	5467.08	4966.04	4623.63
225000	21004.63	11617.10	8534.76	7027.93	6150.46	5586.79	5201.58
250000	23338.48	12907.89	9483.07	7808.81	6833.85	6207.55	5779.53

Monthly Payments **21½%**

necessary to amortize a loan

AMOUNT	8 YEARS	9 YEARS	10 YEARS	11 YEARS	12 YEARS	13 YEARS	14 YEARS
100	2.19	2.10	2.03	1.98	1.94	1.91	1.89
200	4.38	4.20	4.07	3.96	3.88	3.82	3.77
500	10.95	10.50	10.17	9.91	9.71	9.56	9.44
1000	21.90	21.00	20.33	19.82	19.42	19.11	18.87
2000	43.80	42.00	40.66	39.64	38.84	38.23	37.74
5000	109.49	105.01	101.65	99.09	97.11	95.57	94.36
6000	131.39	126.01	121.98	118.91	116.53	114.68	113.23
7000	153.29	147.02	142.31	138.73	135.96	133.80	132.10
8000	175.18	168.02	162.64	158.54	155.38	152.91	150.98
9000	197.08	189.02	182.97	178.36	174.80	172.03	169.85
10000	218.98	210.02	203.30	198.18	194.22	191.14	188.72
15000	328.47	315.03	304.96	297.27	291.34	286.71	283.08
20000	437.96	420.05	406.61	396.36	388.45	382.28	377.44
25000	547.45	525.06	508.26	495.45	485.56	477.85	471.80
30000	656.94	630.07	609.91	594.54	582.67	573.42	566.16
35000	766.43	735.08	711.56	693.63	679.78	668.99	660.52
36000	788.33	756.08	731.89	713.45	699.21	688.11	679.39
37000	810.23	777.09	752.22	733.26	718.63	707.22	698.26
38000	832.12	798.09	772.55	753.08	738.05	726.34	717.14
39000	854.02	819.09	792.88	772.90	757.47	745.45	736.01
40000	875.92	840.09	813.21	792.72	776.90	764.56	754.88
41000	897.82	861.10	833.54	812.54	796.32	783.68	773.75
42000	919.72	882.10	853.87	832.35	815.74	802.79	792.62
43000	941.62	903.10	874.20	852.17	835.16	821.91	811.50
44000	963.51	924.10	894.53	871.99	854.58	841.02	830.37
45000	985.41	945.10	914.87	891.81	874.01	860.13	849.24
46000	1007.31	966.11	935.20	911.63	893.43	879.25	868.11
47000	1029.21	987.11	955.53	931.44	912.85	898.36	886.98
48000	1051.11	1008.11	975.86	951.26	932.27	917.48	905.86
49000	1073.00	1029.11	996.19	971.08	951.70	936.59	924.73
50000	1094.90	1050.12	1016.52	990.90	971.12	955.70	943.60
51000	1116.80	1071.12	1036.85	1010.71	990.54	974.82	962.47
52000	1138.70	1092.12	1057.18	1030.53	1009.96	993.93	981.35
53000	1160.60	1113.12	1077.51	1050.35	1029.39	1013.05	1000.22
54000	1182.49	1134.13	1097.84	1070.17	1048.81	1032.16	1019.09
55000	1204.39	1155.13	1118.17	1089.99	1068.23	1051.27	1037.96
56000	1226.29	1176.13	1138.50	1109.80	1087.65	1070.39	1056.83
57000	1248.19	1197.13	1158.83	1129.62	1107.08	1089.50	1075.71
58000	1270.09	1218.13	1179.16	1149.44	1126.50	1108.62	1094.58
59000	1291.98	1239.14	1199.49	1169.26	1145.92	1127.73	1113.45
60000	1313.88	1260.14	1219.82	1189.08	1165.34	1146.85	1132.32
65000	1423.37	1365.15	1321.47	1288.17	1262.45	1242.42	1226.68
70000	1532.86	1470.16	1423.12	1387.26	1359.57	1337.99	1321.04
75000	1642.35	1575.17	1524.78	1486.35	1456.68	1433.56	1415.40
80000	1751.84	1680.19	1626.43	1585.44	1553.79	1529.13	1509.76
85000	1861.33	1785.20	1728.08	1684.52	1650.90	1624.70	1604.12
90000	1970.82	1890.21	1829.73	1783.61	1748.01	1720.27	1698.48
95000	2080.31	1995.22	1931.38	1882.70	1845.13	1815.84	1792.84
100000	2189.80	2100.23	2033.03	1981.79	1942.24	1911.41	1887.20
105000	2299.29	2205.24	2134.69	2080.88	2039.35	2006.98	1981.56
110000	2408.78	2310.26	2236.34	2179.97	2136.46	2102.55	2075.92
120000	2627.76	2520.28	2439.64	2378.15	2330.69	2293.69	2264.64
130000	2846.74	2730.30	2642.94	2576.33	2524.91	2484.83	2453.36
140000	3065.72	2940.32	2846.25	2774.51	2719.13	2675.97	2642.08
150000	3284.70	3150.35	3049.55	2972.69	2913.36	2867.11	2830.80
175000	3832.15	3675.41	3557.81	3468.14	3398.92	3344.97	3302.60
200000	4379.61	4200.46	4066.07	3963.59	3884.48	3822.82	3774.40
225000	4927.06	4725.52	4574.33	4459.04	4370.04	4300.67	4246.20
250000	5474.51	5250.58	5082.58	4954.49	4855.59	4778.52	4718.01

21½%

Monthly Payments

necessary to amortize a loan

AMOUNT	15 YEARS	16 YEARS	17 YEARS	18 YEARS	19 YEARS	20 YEARS	21 YEARS
100	1.87	1.85	1.84	1.83	1.82	1.82	1.81
200	3.74	3.71	3.68	3.66	3.65	3.63	3.62
500	9.34	9.26	9.20	9.16	9.12	9.09	9.06
1000	18.68	18.53	18.41	18.31	18.23	18.17	18.12
2000	37.36	37.06	36.82	36.62	36.47	36.35	36.25
5000	93.40	92.65	92.04	91.56	91.17	90.86	90.62
6000	112.09	111.18	110.45	109.87	109.41	109.04	108.74
7000	130.77	129.70	128.86	128.18	127.64	127.21	126.86
8000	149.45	148.23	147.27	146.50	145.88	145.38	144.98
9000	168.13	166.76	165.68	164.81	164.11	163.56	163.11
10000	186.81	185.29	184.08	183.12	182.35	181.73	181.23
15000	280.21	277.94	276.13	274.68	273.52	272.59	271.85
20000	373.62	370.58	368.17	366.24	364.69	363.46	362.46
25000	467.02	463.23	460.21	457.80	455.87	454.32	453.08
30000	560.43	555.88	552.25	549.36	547.04	545.18	543.69
35000	653.83	648.52	644.29	640.92	638.22	636.05	634.31
36000	672.51	667.05	662.70	659.23	656.45	654.22	652.43
37000	691.19	685.58	681.11	677.54	674.68	672.39	670.55
38000	709.87	704.11	699.52	695.85	692.92	690.57	688.68
39000	728.55	722.64	717.93	714.17	711.15	708.74	706.80
40000	747.23	741.17	736.34	732.48	729.39	726.91	724.92
41000	765.91	759.70	754.74	750.79	747.62	745.09	743.05
42000	784.60	778.23	773.15	769.10	765.86	763.26	761.17
43000	803.28	796.75	791.56	787.41	784.09	781.43	779.29
44000	821.96	815.28	809.97	805.73	802.33	799.60	797.42
45000	840.64	833.81	828.38	824.04	820.56	817.78	815.54
46000	859.32	852.34	846.79	842.35	838.80	835.95	833.66
47000	878.00	870.87	865.19	860.66	857.03	854.12	851.79
48000	896.68	889.40	883.60	878.97	875.27	872.30	869.91
49000	915.36	907.93	902.01	897.28	893.50	890.47	888.03
50000	934.04	926.46	920.42	915.60	911.74	908.64	906.15
51000	952.72	944.99	938.83	933.91	929.97	926.81	924.28
52000	971.40	963.52	957.24	952.22	948.21	944.99	942.40
53000	990.08	982.05	975.64	970.53	966.44	963.16	960.52
54000	1008.77	1000.58	994.05	988.84	984.68	981.33	978.65
55000	1027.45	1019.10	1012.46	1007.16	1002.91	999.50	996.77
56000	1046.13	1037.63	1030.87	1025.47	1021.14	1017.68	1014.89
57000	1064.81	1056.16	1049.28	1043.78	1039.38	1035.85	1033.02
58000	1083.49	1074.69	1067.69	1062.09	1057.61	1054.02	1051.14
59000	1102.17	1093.22	1086.10	1080.40	1075.85	1072.20	1069.26
60000	1120.85	1111.75	1104.50	1098.72	1094.08	1090.37	1087.39
65000	1214.26	1204.40	1196.55	1190.28	1185.26	1181.23	1178.00
70000	1307.66	1297.04	1288.59	1281.84	1276.43	1272.10	1268.62
75000	1401.06	1389.69	1380.63	1373.40	1367.60	1362.96	1359.23
80000	1494.47	1482.33	1472.67	1464.95	1458.78	1453.83	1449.85
85000	1587.87	1574.98	1564.71	1556.51	1549.95	1544.69	1540.46
90000	1681.28	1667.63	1656.76	1648.07	1641.13	1635.55	1631.08
95000	1774.68	1760.27	1748.80	1739.63	1732.30	1726.42	1721.69
100000	1868.08	1852.92	1840.84	1831.19	1823.47	1817.28	1812.31
105000	1961.49	1945.56	1932.88	1922.75	1914.65	1908.15	1902.92
110000	2054.89	2038.21	2024.92	2014.31	2005.82	1999.01	1993.54
120000	2241.70	2223.50	2209.01	2197.43	2188.17	2180.74	2174.77
130000	2428.51	2408.79	2393.09	2380.55	2370.51	2362.47	2356.00
140000	2615.32	2594.08	2577.17	2563.67	2552.86	2544.19	2537.23
150000	2802.13	2779.38	2761.26	2746.79	2735.21	2725.92	2718.46
175000	3269.15	3242.60	3221.47	3204.59	3191.08	3180.24	3171.54
200000	3736.17	3705.83	3681.68	3662.39	3646.95	3634.56	3624.62
225000	4203.19	4169.06	4141.89	4120.19	4102.81	4088.88	4077.69
250000	4670.21	4632.29	4602.10	4577.98	4558.68	4543.20	4530.77

Monthly Payments 21½%

necessary to amortize a loan

AMOUNT	22 YEARS	23 YEARS	24 YEARS	25 YEARS	30 YEARS	35 YEARS	40 YEARS
100	1.81	1.81	1.80	1.80	1.79	1.79	1.79
200	3.62	3.61	3.60	3.60	3.59	3.59	3.58
500	9.04	9.03	9.01	9.00	8.97	8.96	8.96
1000	18.08	18.05	18.02	18.00	17.95	17.93	17.92
2000	36.17	36.10	36.05	36.01	35.89	35.85	35.84
5000	90.42	90.25	90.12	90.02	89.73	89.64	89.60
6000	108.50	108.31	108.15	108.02	107.68	107.56	107.52
7000	126.58	126.36	126.17	126.03	125.63	125.49	125.44
8000	144.66	144.41	144.20	144.03	143.57	143.42	143.36
9000	162.75	162.46	162.22	162.04	161.52	161.34	161.28
10000	180.83	180.51	180.25	180.04	179.47	179.27	179.20
15000	271.25	270.76	270.37	270.06	269.20	268.91	268.80
20000	361.66	361.02	360.50	360.08	358.93	358.54	358.40
25000	452.08	451.27	450.62	450.10	448.67	448.18	448.01
30000	542.49	541.53	540.75	540.12	538.40	537.81	537.61
35000	632.91	631.78	630.87	630.14	628.13	627.45	627.21
36000	650.99	649.83	648.90	648.15	646.08	645.37	645.13
37000	669.07	667.88	666.92	666.15	664.03	663.30	663.05
38000	687.16	685.93	684.95	684.16	681.97	681.23	680.97
39000	705.24	703.99	702.97	702.16	699.92	699.15	698.89
40000	723.32	722.04	721.00	720.16	717.87	717.08	716.81
41000	741.41	740.09	739.02	738.17	735.81	735.01	734.73
42000	759.49	758.14	757.05	756.17	753.76	752.93	752.65
43000	777.57	776.19	775.07	774.18	771.71	770.86	770.57
44000	795.66	794.24	793.10	792.18	789.65	788.79	788.49
45000	813.74	812.29	811.12	810.18	807.60	806.72	806.41
46000	831.82	830.34	829.15	828.19	825.55	824.64	824.33
47000	849.91	848.39	847.17	846.19	843.49	842.57	842.25
48000	867.99	866.44	865.20	864.20	861.44	860.50	860.17
49000	886.07	884.50	883.22	882.20	879.39	878.42	878.09
50000	904.16	902.55	901.25	900.21	897.33	896.35	896.01
51000	922.24	920.60	919.27	918.21	915.28	914.28	913.93
52000	940.32	938.65	937.30	936.21	933.23	932.20	931.85
53000	958.40	956.70	955.32	954.22	951.18	950.13	949.77
54000	976.49	974.75	973.35	972.22	969.12	968.06	967.69
55000	994.57	992.80	991.37	990.23	987.07	985.99	985.61
56000	1012.65	1010.85	1009.40	1008.23	1005.02	1003.91	1003.53
57000	1030.74	1028.90	1027.42	1026.23	1022.96	1021.84	1021.45
58000	1048.82	1046.95	1045.45	1044.24	1040.91	1039.77	1039.37
59000	1066.90	1065.00	1063.47	1062.24	1058.86	1057.69	1057.29
60000	1084.99	1083.06	1081.50	1080.26	1076.80	1075.62	1075.21
65000	1175.40	1173.31	1171.62	1170.27	1166.54	1165.26	1164.81
70000	1265.82	1263.56	1261.75	1260.29	1256.27	1254.89	1254.42
75000	1356.23	1353.82	1351.87	1350.31	1346.00	1344.53	1344.02
80000	1446.65	1444.07	1442.00	1440.33	1435.74	1434.16	1433.62
85000	1537.06	1534.33	1532.12	1530.35	1525.47	1523.80	1523.22
90000	1627.48	1624.58	1622.25	1620.37	1615.20	1613.43	1612.82
95000	1717.89	1714.84	1712.37	1710.39	1704.94	1703.07	1702.42
100000	1808.31	1805.09	1802.50	1800.41	1794.67	1792.70	1792.02
105000	1898.73	1895.35	1892.62	1890.43	1884.40	1882.34	1881.62
110000	1989.14	1985.60	1982.75	1980.45	1974.14	1971.97	1971.22
120000	2169.97	2166.11	2163.00	2160.49	2153.60	2151.24	2150.43
130000	2350.80	2346.62	2343.25	2340.53	2333.07	2330.51	2329.63
140000	2531.63	2527.13	2523.50	2520.57	2512.54	2509.78	2508.83
150000	2712.47	2707.64	2703.75	2700.62	2692.00	2689.05	2688.03
175000	3164.54	3158.91	3154.37	3150.72	3140.67	3137.23	3136.04
200000	3616.62	3610.18	3605.00	3600.82	3589.34	3585.40	3584.05
225000	4068.70	4061.46	4055.62	4050.92	4038.01	4033.58	4032.05
250000	4520.78	4512.73	4506.25	4501.03	4486.67	4481.75	4480.06

21¾% Monthly Payments

necessary to amortize a loan

AMOUNT	1 YEAR	2 YEARS	3 YEARS	4 YEARS	5 YEARS	6 YEARS	7 YEARS
100	9.35	5.18	3.81	3.14	2.75	2.50	2.33
200	18.69	10.35	7.61	6.27	5.50	5.00	4.65
500	46.74	25.88	19.03	15.69	13.74	12.49	11.64
1000	93.47	51.75	38.06	31.37	27.48	24.98	23.27
2000	186.95	103.51	76.12	62.74	54.95	49.96	46.54
5000	467.37	258.77	190.31	156.85	137.38	124.89	116.36
6000	560.84	310.53	228.37	188.22	164.86	149.87	139.63
7000	654.32	362.28	266.43	219.59	192.34	174.85	162.90
8000	747.79	414.04	304.49	250.96	219.82	199.82	186.17
9000	841.27	465.79	342.55	282.33	247.29	224.80	209.45
10000	934.74	517.55	380.61	313.71	274.77	249.78	232.72
15000	1402.11	776.32	570.92	470.56	412.15	374.67	349.08
20000	1869.48	1035.10	761.22	627.41	549.54	499.56	465.44
25000	2336.85	1293.87	951.53	784.26	686.92	624.45	581.80
30000	2804.22	1552.64	1141.84	941.12	824.31	749.34	698.15
35000	3271.59	1811.42	1332.14	1097.97	961.69	874.23	814.51
36000	3365.07	1863.17	1370.20	1129.34	989.17	899.21	837.78
37000	3458.54	1914.93	1408.27	1160.71	1016.65	924.18	861.06
38000	3552.02	1966.68	1446.33	1192.08	1044.12	949.16	884.33
39000	3645.49	2018.44	1484.39	1223.45	1071.60	974.14	907.60
40000	3738.96	2070.19	1522.45	1254.82	1099.08	999.12	930.87
41000	3832.44	2121.95	1560.51	1286.19	1126.56	1024.10	954.14
42000	3925.91	2173.70	1598.57	1317.56	1154.03	1049.07	977.42
43000	4019.39	2225.46	1636.63	1348.93	1181.51	1074.05	1000.69
44000	4112.86	2277.21	1674.69	1380.30	1208.99	1099.03	1023.96
45000	4206.33	2328.97	1712.76	1411.67	1236.46	1124.01	1047.23
46000	4299.81	2380.72	1750.82	1443.04	1263.94	1148.99	1070.50
47000	4393.28	2432.47	1788.88	1474.41	1291.42	1173.96	1093.77
48000	4486.76	2484.23	1826.94	1505.78	1318.89	1198.94	1117.05
49000	4580.23	2535.98	1865.00	1537.16	1346.37	1223.92	1140.32
50000	4673.71	2587.74	1903.06	1568.53	1373.85	1248.90	1163.59
51000	4767.18	2639.49	1941.12	1599.90	1401.32	1273.88	1186.86
52000	4860.65	2691.25	1979.18	1631.27	1428.80	1298.85	1210.13
53000	4954.13	2743.00	2017.25	1662.64	1456.28	1323.83	1233.41
54000	5047.60	2794.76	2055.31	1694.01	1483.76	1348.81	1256.68
55000	5141.08	2846.51	2093.37	1725.38	1511.23	1373.79	1279.95
56000	5234.55	2898.27	2131.43	1756.75	1538.71	1398.77	1303.22
57000	5328.02	2950.02	2169.49	1788.12	1566.19	1423.74	1326.49
58000	5421.50	3001.78	2207.55	1819.49	1593.66	1448.72	1349.76
59000	5514.97	3053.53	2245.61	1850.86	1621.14	1473.70	1373.04
60000	5608.45	3105.29	2283.67	1882.23	1648.62	1498.68	1396.31
65000	6075.82	3364.06	2473.98	2039.08	1786.00	1623.57	1512.67
70000	6543.19	3622.83	2664.29	2195.94	1923.39	1748.46	1629.03
75000	7010.56	3881.61	2854.59	2352.79	2060.77	1873.35	1745.39
80000	7477.93	4140.38	3044.90	2509.64	2198.16	1998.24	1861.74
85000	7945.30	4399.16	3235.21	2666.49	2335.54	2123.13	1978.10
90000	8412.67	4657.93	3425.51	2823.35	2472.93	2248.02	2094.46
95000	8880.04	4916.70	3615.82	2980.20	2610.31	2372.91	2210.82
100000	9347.41	5175.48	3806.12	3137.05	2747.70	2497.79	2327.18
105000	9814.78	5434.25	3996.43	3293.90	2885.08	2622.68	2443.54
110000	10282.15	5693.03	4186.74	3450.76	3022.47	2747.57	2559.90
120000	11216.89	6210.57	4567.35	3764.46	3297.23	2997.35	2792.62
130000	12151.63	6728.12	4947.96	4078.17	3572.00	3247.13	3025.33
140000	13086.37	7245.67	5328.57	4391.87	3846.77	3496.91	3258.05
150000	14021.12	7763.22	5709.19	4705.58	4121.54	3746.69	3490.77
175000	16357.97	9057.09	6660.72	5489.84	4808.47	4371.14	4072.57
200000	18694.82	10350.96	7612.25	6274.10	5495.39	4995.59	4654.36
225000	21031.67	11644.83	8563.78	7058.36	6182.32	5620.04	5236.16
250000	23368.53	12938.70	9515.31	7842.63	6869.24	6244.49	5817.95

Monthly Payments 21¾%

necessary to amortize a loan

AMOUNT	8 YEARS	9 YEARS	10 YEARS	11 YEARS	12 YEARS	13 YEARS	14 YEARS
100	2.21	2.12	2.05	2.00	1.96	1.93	1.91
200	4.41	4.23	4.10	4.00	3.92	3.86	3.81
500	11.03	10.58	10.25	10.00	9.80	9.65	9.53
1000	22.06	21.17	20.50	19.99	19.60	19.30	19.06
2000	44.11	42.33	41.00	39.98	39.20	38.59	38.11
5000	110.29	105.83	102.50	99.96	98.00	96.48	95.29
6000	132.34	127.00	123.00	119.95	117.60	115.77	114.34
7000	154.40	148.17	143.50	139.94	137.20	135.07	133.40
8000	176.46	169.33	164.00	159.93	156.80	154.37	152.46
9000	198.52	190.50	184.50	179.93	176.40	173.66	171.51
10000	220.57	211.67	205.00	199.92	196.00	192.96	190.57
15000	330.86	317.50	307.50	299.88	294.01	289.44	285.86
20000	441.15	423.34	409.99	399.84	392.01	385.92	381.14
25000	551.43	529.17	512.49	499.80	490.01	482.40	476.43
30000	661.72	635.01	614.99	599.76	588.01	578.87	571.71
35000	772.01	740.84	717.49	699.71	686.01	675.35	667.00
36000	794.06	762.01	737.99	719.71	705.61	694.65	686.06
37000	816.12	783.17	758.49	739.70	725.21	713.95	705.11
38000	838.18	804.34	778.99	759.69	744.81	733.24	724.17
39000	860.23	825.51	799.49	779.68	764.42	752.54	743.23
40000	882.29	846.67	819.99	799.67	784.02	771.83	762.28
41000	904.35	867.84	840.49	819.67	803.62	791.13	781.34
42000	926.41	889.01	860.99	839.66	823.22	810.42	800.40
43000	948.46	910.17	881.49	859.65	842.82	829.72	819.46
44000	970.52	931.34	901.99	879.64	862.42	849.02	838.51
45000	992.58	952.51	922.49	899.63	882.02	868.31	857.57
46000	1014.64	973.67	942.99	919.62	901.62	887.61	876.63
47000	1036.69	994.84	963.49	939.62	921.22	906.90	895.68
48000	1058.75	1016.01	983.99	959.61	940.82	926.20	914.74
49000	1080.81	1037.18	1004.49	979.60	960.42	945.50	933.80
50000	1102.86	1058.34	1024.99	999.59	980.02	964.79	952.86
51000	1124.92	1079.51	1045.49	1019.58	999.62	984.09	971.91
52000	1146.98	1100.68	1065.99	1039.58	1019.22	1003.38	990.97
53000	1169.04	1121.84	1086.49	1059.57	1038.82	1022.68	1010.03
54000	1191.09	1143.01	1106.99	1079.56	1058.42	1041.97	1029.08
55000	1213.15	1164.18	1127.49	1099.55	1078.02	1061.27	1048.14
56000	1235.21	1185.34	1147.99	1119.54	1097.62	1080.57	1067.20
57000	1257.27	1206.51	1168.49	1139.53	1117.22	1099.86	1086.26
58000	1279.32	1227.68	1188.98	1159.53	1136.82	1119.16	1105.31
59000	1301.38	1248.84	1209.48	1179.52	1156.42	1138.45	1124.37
60000	1323.44	1270.01	1229.98	1199.51	1176.02	1157.75	1143.43
65000	1433.72	1375.84	1332.48	1299.47	1274.03	1254.23	1238.71
70000	1544.01	1481.68	1434.98	1399.43	1372.03	1350.71	1334.00
75000	1654.30	1587.51	1537.48	1499.39	1470.03	1447.19	1429.28
80000	1764.58	1693.35	1639.98	1599.35	1568.03	1543.67	1524.57
85000	1874.87	1799.18	1742.48	1699.31	1666.03	1640.15	1619.86
90000	1985.16	1905.02	1844.98	1799.27	1764.03	1736.62	1715.14
95000	2095.44	2010.85	1947.48	1899.22	1862.04	1833.10	1810.43
100000	2205.73	2116.68	2049.97	1999.18	1960.04	1929.58	1905.71
105000	2316.02	2222.52	2152.47	2099.14	2058.04	2026.06	2001.00
110000	2426.30	2328.35	2254.97	2199.10	2156.04	2122.54	2096.28
120000	2646.88	2540.02	2459.97	2399.02	2352.05	2315.50	2286.85
130000	2867.45	2751.69	2664.97	2598.94	2548.05	2508.46	2477.43
140000	3088.02	2963.36	2869.96	2798.86	2744.05	2701.42	2668.00
150000	3308.59	3175.03	3074.96	2998.78	2940.06	2894.37	2858.57
175000	3860.03	3704.20	3587.45	3498.57	3430.07	3376.77	3335.00
200000	4411.46	4233.37	4099.95	3998.37	3920.08	3859.16	3811.42
225000	4962.89	4762.54	4612.44	4498.16	4410.09	4341.56	4287.85
250000	5514.32	5291.71	5124.94	4997.96	4900.10	4823.96	4764.28

21¾%

Monthly Payments
necessary to amortize a loan

AMOUNT	15 YEARS	16 YEARS	17 YEARS	18 YEARS	19 YEARS	20 YEARS	21 YEARS
100	1.89	1.87	1.86	1.85	1.84	1.84	1.83
200	3.77	3.74	3.72	3.70	3.69	3.67	3.66
500	9.43	9.36	9.30	9.25	9.22	9.19	9.16
1000	18.87	18.72	18.60	18.51	18.43	18.37	18.32
2000	37.74	37.44	37.20	37.01	36.86	36.74	36.65
5000	94.34	93.60	93.01	92.54	92.16	91.86	91.62
6000	113.21	112.32	111.61	111.04	110.59	110.23	109.94
7000	132.08	131.04	130.21	129.55	129.02	128.60	128.26
8000	150.95	149.76	148.81	148.06	147.45	146.97	146.59
9000	169.82	168.48	167.41	166.56	165.89	165.34	164.91
10000	188.69	187.20	186.02	185.07	184.32	183.72	183.23
15000	283.03	280.80	279.02	277.61	276.48	275.57	274.85
20000	377.38	374.40	372.03	370.14	368.64	367.43	366.46
25000	471.72	468.00	465.04	462.68	460.80	459.29	458.08
30000	566.07	561.60	558.05	555.22	552.96	551.15	549.70
35000	660.41	655.20	651.05	647.75	645.11	643.00	641.31
36000	679.28	673.92	669.66	666.26	663.55	661.38	659.64
37000	698.15	692.64	688.26	684.77	681.98	679.75	677.96
38000	717.02	711.36	706.86	703.27	700.41	698.12	696.28
39000	735.89	730.08	725.46	721.78	718.84	716.49	714.61
40000	754.76	748.80	744.06	740.29	737.27	734.86	732.93
41000	773.63	767.52	762.66	758.80	755.71	753.23	751.25
42000	792.50	786.24	781.27	777.30	774.14	771.60	769.57
43000	811.37	804.96	799.87	795.81	792.57	789.98	787.90
44000	830.23	823.68	818.47	814.32	811.00	808.35	806.22
45000	849.10	842.40	837.07	832.82	829.43	826.72	824.54
46000	867.97	861.12	855.67	851.33	847.86	845.09	842.87
47000	886.84	879.84	874.27	869.84	866.30	863.46	861.19
48000	905.71	898.56	892.88	888.35	884.73	881.83	879.51
49000	924.58	917.28	911.48	906.85	903.16	900.21	897.84
50000	943.45	936.00	930.08	925.36	921.59	918.58	916.16
51000	962.32	954.72	948.68	943.87	940.02	936.95	934.48
52000	981.19	973.44	967.28	962.37	958.46	955.32	952.81
53000	1000.05	992.16	985.88	980.88	976.89	973.69	971.13
54000	1018.92	1010.88	1004.48	999.39	995.32	992.06	989.45
55000	1037.79	1029.60	1023.09	1017.90	1013.75	1010.43	1007.78
56000	1056.66	1048.32	1041.69	1036.40	1032.18	1028.81	1026.10
57000	1075.53	1067.04	1060.29	1054.91	1050.62	1047.18	1044.42
58000	1094.40	1085.76	1078.89	1073.42	1069.05	1065.55	1062.75
59000	1113.27	1104.48	1097.49	1091.93	1087.48	1083.92	1081.07
60000	1132.14	1123.20	1116.09	1110.43	1105.91	1102.29	1099.39
65000	1226.48	1216.80	1209.10	1202.97	1198.07	1194.15	1191.01
70000	1320.83	1310.40	1302.11	1295.50	1290.23	1286.01	1282.62
75000	1415.17	1404.00	1395.12	1388.04	1382.39	1377.87	1374.24
80000	1509.52	1497.60	1488.13	1480.58	1474.55	1469.72	1465.86
85000	1603.86	1591.20	1581.13	1573.11	1566.71	1561.58	1557.47
90000	1698.21	1684.80	1674.14	1665.65	1658.87	1653.44	1649.09
95000	1792.55	1778.40	1767.15	1758.19	1751.03	1745.30	1740.70
100000	1886.90	1872.00	1860.16	1850.72	1843.18	1837.15	1832.32
105000	1981.24	1965.60	1953.16	1943.26	1935.34	1929.01	1923.94
110000	2075.59	2059.20	2046.17	2035.79	2027.50	2020.87	2015.55
120000	2264.28	2246.40	2232.19	2220.87	2211.82	2204.58	2198.79
130000	2452.96	2433.60	2418.20	2405.94	2396.14	2388.30	2382.02
140000	2641.65	2620.80	2604.22	2591.01	2580.46	2572.02	2565.25
150000	2830.34	2808.00	2790.24	2776.08	2764.78	2755.73	2748.48
175000	3302.07	3275.99	3255.27	3238.76	3225.57	3215.02	3206.56
200000	3773.79	3743.99	3720.31	3701.44	3686.37	3674.31	3664.64
225000	4245.52	4211.99	4185.35	4164.12	4147.16	4133.60	4122.72
250000	4717.24	4679.99	4650.39	4626.80	4607.96	4592.88	4580.80

Monthly Payments **21¾%**

necessary to amortize a loan

AMOUNT	22 YEARS	23 YEARS	24 YEARS	25 YEARS	30 YEARS	35 YEARS	40 YEARS
100	1.83	1.83	1.82	1.82	1.82	1.81	1.81
200	3.66	3.65	3.65	3.64	3.63	3.63	3.63
500	9.14	9.13	9.11	9.10	9.08	9.07	9.06
1000	18.28	18.25	18.23	18.21	18.15	18.13	18.13
2000	36.57	36.51	36.46	36.42	36.31	36.27	36.26
5000	91.42	91.27	91.14	91.04	90.77	90.67	90.64
6000	109.71	109.52	109.37	109.25	108.92	108.81	108.77
7000	127.99	127.77	127.60	127.46	127.07	126.94	126.90
8000	146.28	146.03	145.83	145.67	145.23	145.08	145.03
9000	164.56	164.28	164.05	163.87	163.38	163.21	163.15
10000	182.84	182.53	182.28	182.08	181.53	181.35	181.28
15000	274.27	273.80	273.42	273.12	272.30	272.02	271.92
20000	365.69	365.07	364.57	364.16	363.06	362.69	362.57
25000	457.11	456.33	455.71	455.20	453.83	453.36	453.21
30000	548.53	547.60	546.85	546.24	544.60	544.04	543.85
35000	639.96	638.87	637.99	637.29	635.36	634.71	634.49
36000	658.24	657.12	656.22	655.49	653.52	652.85	652.62
37000	676.52	675.37	674.45	673.70	671.67	670.98	670.75
38000	694.81	693.63	692.67	691.91	689.82	689.11	688.87
39000	713.09	711.88	710.90	710.12	707.98	707.25	707.00
40000	731.38	730.13	729.13	728.33	726.13	725.38	725.13
41000	749.66	748.39	747.36	746.53	744.28	743.52	743.26
42000	767.95	766.64	765.59	764.74	762.44	761.65	761.39
43000	786.23	784.89	783.82	782.95	780.59	779.79	779.52
44000	804.52	803.15	802.04	801.16	798.74	797.92	797.64
45000	822.80	821.40	820.27	819.37	816.89	816.06	815.77
46000	841.08	839.65	838.50	837.58	835.05	834.19	833.90
47000	859.37	857.91	856.73	855.78	853.20	852.33	852.03
48000	877.65	876.16	874.96	873.99	871.35	870.46	870.16
49000	895.94	894.41	893.19	892.20	889.51	888.60	888.28
50000	914.22	912.67	911.41	910.41	907.66	906.73	906.41
51000	932.51	930.92	929.64	928.62	925.81	924.86	924.54
52000	950.79	949.17	947.87	946.82	943.97	943.00	942.67
53000	969.08	967.43	966.10	965.03	962.12	961.13	960.80
54000	987.36	985.68	984.33	983.24	980.27	979.27	978.93
55000	1005.64	1003.93	1002.56	1001.45	998.43	997.40	997.05
56000	1023.93	1022.18	1020.78	1019.66	1016.58	1015.54	1015.18
57000	1042.21	1040.44	1039.01	1037.87	1034.73	1033.67	1033.31
58000	1060.50	1058.69	1057.24	1056.07	1052.89	1051.81	1051.44
59000	1078.78	1076.94	1075.47	1074.28	1071.04	1069.94	1069.57
60000	1097.07	1095.20	1093.70	1092.49	1000.10	1000.08	1087.70
65000	1188.49	1186.46	1184.84	1183.53	1179.96	1178.75	1178.34
70000	1279.91	1277.73	1275.98	1274.57	1270.73	1269.42	1268.98
75000	1371.33	1369.00	1367.12	1365.61	1361.49	1360.09	1359.62
80000	1462.76	1460.26	1458.26	1456.65	1452.26	1450.77	1450.26
85000	1554.18	1551.53	1549.40	1547.69	1543.02	1541.44	1540.90
90000	1645.60	1642.80	1640.55	1638.73	1633.79	1632.11	1631.54
95000	1737.02	1734.06	1731.69	1729.78	1724.56	1722.79	1722.19
100000	1828.44	1825.33	1822.83	1820.82	1815.32	1813.48	1012.83
105000	1919.87	1916.60	1913.97	1911.86	1906.09	1904.13	1903.47
110000	2011.29	2007.86	2005.11	2002.90	1996.85	1994.81	1994.11
120000	2194.13	2190.40	2187.39	2184.98	2178.39	2176.15	2175.39
130000	2376.98	2372.93	2369.68	2367.06	2359.92	2357.50	2356.67
140000	2559.82	2555.46	2551.96	2549.14	2541.45	2538.84	2537.96
150000	2742.67	2738.00	2734.24	2731.22	2722.98	2720.19	2719.24
175000	3199.78	3194.33	3189.95	3186.43	3176.81	3173.55	3172.45
200000	3656.89	3650.66	3645.66	3641.63	3630.64	3626.92	3625.65
225000	4114.00	4106.99	4101.36	4096.84	4084.47	4080.28	4078.86
250000	4571.11	4563.33	4557.07	4552.04	4538.31	4533.65	4532.07

Valuation of Assumable Mortgages

Many real estate mortgages on residential property are assumable, which means that a party other than the mortgagor may take over the monthly payments for the remaining term of the mortgage. This may be advantageous if the interest rate of the assumable mortgage is lower than the interest rate of a new mortgage.

One way to evaluate the relative merit of assuming a mortgage is to compare the monthly payment of the assumable mortgage with the monthly payment of a new mortgage that is based on (1) the principal and term remaining on the assumable mortgage and (2) the current interest rate. The following table shows the percentage increase, if any, from the monthly payment at the original interest rate to the monthly payment at the current interest rate. It covers current interest rates of 5% to 21% and original, or old, interest rates of 4% to 20%. The terms range from 5 years to 30 years. Here are some illustrative situations to help explain the use of the table:

Situation 1

Mr. Lane has an assumable mortgage with 20 years of monthly payments remaining. This mortgage was originally issued at an annual interest rate of 4%. Mr. Robertson wishes to purchase Mr. Lane's property and would like to assume the original mortgage (the remaining principal) and pay the monthly payments for the next 20 years. A new mortgage would have an interest rate of 8%, so it would be advantageous to assume Mr. Lane's mortgage. To find out how much more the monthly payment would be on a new mortgage, Mr. Robertson must (1) locate the 8% "current interest" page of this table, (2) look for the 4% interest line, and (3) scan across to the 20-year column, where he will find 38.03. This number is the percent that the current monthly payment would increase by, if he were to select a new mortgage with the current interest rate of 8%. Therefore, if the monthly payment of the assumable mortgage is $100.00, the monthly payment of a new mortgage would be $138.03. Mr. Robertson would save $38.03 on his monthly payments by assuming Mr. Lane's mortgage rather than refinancing at the current interest rate.

Situation 2

Mrs. Penny would like to buy a house from Mrs. Fine, who has an existing mortgage with 10 years to go and an interest rate of 8%. If the current interest rate is 12%, what would be the advantage of Mrs. Penny assuming Mrs. Fine's mortgage, with respect to the monthly mortgage payment?

To answer this, Mrs. Penny must (1) locate the 12% "current rate" page, (2) look down the left side until she finds 8%, and (3) search across the page to the number in the 10-year column (18.25). Mrs. Fine would spend 18.25% more per month if she were to finance the house purchase with a new mortgage at the current interest rate of 12% rather than assume the existing mortgage.

Valuation of Assumable Mortgages

CURRENT RATE: 5%

OLD RATE	5 YEARS	10 YEARS	15 YEARS	20 YEARS	21 YEARS	22 YEARS	23 YEARS
4.00	2.47	4.76	6.91	8.91	9.29	9.66	10.03
4.25	1.84	3.54	5.12	6.58	6.85	7.12	7.39
4.50	1.22	2.34	3.37	4.32	4.49	4.67	4.84
4.75	0.61	1.16	1.67	2.12	2.21	2.30	2.38
5.00	0.00	0.00	0.00	0.00	0.00	0.00	0.00

OLD RATE	24 YEARS	25 YEARS	26 YEARS	27 YEARS	28 YEARS	29 YEARS	30 YEARS
4.00	10.40	10.75	11.10	11.45	11.79	12.12	12.44
4.25	7.65	7.91	8.16	8.41	8.65	8.89	9.12
4.50	5.01	5.17	5.34	5.49	5.65	5.80	5.95
4.75	2.46	2.54	2.62	2.69	2.77	2.84	2.91
5.00	0.00	0.00	0.00	0.00	0.00	0.00	0.00

Valuation of Assumable Mortgages

CURRENT RATE: 5½%

OLD RATE	5 YEARS	10 YEARS	15 YEARS	20 YEARS	21 YEARS	22 YEARS	23 YEARS
4.00	3.72	7.19	10.46	13.52	14.10	14.67	15.24
4.25	3.08	5.94	8.61	11.09	11.56	12.02	12.47
4.50	2.46	4.72	6.81	8.73	9.09	9.45	9.80
4.75	1.84	3.51	5.05	6.45	6.71	6.97	7.22
5.00	1.22	2.32	3.32	4.23	4.40	4.57	4.73
5.25	0.61	1.15	1.64	2.08	2.17	2.25	2.33
5.50	0.00	0.00	0.00	0.00	0.00	0.00	0.00

OLD RATE	24 YEARS	25 YEARS	26 YEARS	27 YEARS	28 YEARS	29 YEARS	30 YEARS
4.00	15.79	16.34	16.88	17.40	17.92	18.43	18.93
4.25	12.92	13.36	13.78	14.20	14.62	15.02	15.42
4.50	10.14	10.48	10.81	11.13	11.45	11.76	12.06
4.75	7.47	7.71	7.95	8.18	8.41	8.63	8.85
5.00	4.89	5.05	5.20	5.35	5.49	5.63	5.77
5.25	2.40	2.48	2.55	2.62	2.69	2.76	2.82
5.50	0.00	0.00	0.00	0.00	0.00	0.00	0.00

Valuation of Assumable Mortgages

CURRENT RATE: 6%

OLD RATE	5 YEARS	10 YEARS	15 YEARS	20 YEARS	21 YEARS	22 YEARS	23 YEARS
4.00	4.98	9.66	14.08	18.23	19.02	19.80	20.57
4.25	4.33	8.38	12.17	15.70	16.37	17.03	17.67
4.50	3.70	7.12	10.31	13.24	13.80	14.34	14.88
4.75	3.07	5.89	8.49	10.86	11.31	11.75	12.18
5.00	2.45	4.67	6.71	8.56	8.90	9.24	9.57
5.25	1.83	3.48	4.97	6.32	6.57	6.82	7.06
5.50	1.21	2.30	3.28	4.15	4.31	4.47	4.62
5.75	0.60	1.14	1.62	2.04	2.12	2.20	2.27
6.00	0.00	0.00	0.00	0.00	0.00	0.00	0.00

OLD RATE	24 YEARS	25 YEARS	26 YEARS	27 YEARS	28 YEARS	29 YEARS	30 YEARS
4.00	21.32	22.06	22.79	23.51	24.21	24.90	25.58
4.25	18.31	18.93	19.54	20.14	20.73	21.31	21.87
4.50	15.40	15.92	16.42	16.91	17.39	17.87	18.33
4.75	12.60	13.01	13.41	13.81	14.19	14.57	14.93
5.00	9.90	10.21	10.52	10.82	11.12	11.41	11.69
5.25	7.29	7.52	7.74	7.96	8.17	8.37	8.57
5.50	4.77	4.92	5.06	5.20	5.34	5.47	5.59
5.75	2.35	2.42	2.48	2.55	2.61	2.68	2.74
6.00	0.00	0.00	0.00	0.00	0.00	0.00	0.00

Valuation of Assumable Mortgages

CURRENT RATE: 6½%

OLD RATE	5 YEARS	10 YEARS	15 YEARS	20 YEARS	21 YEARS	22 YEARS	23 YEARS
4.00	6.24	12.15	17.77	23.04	24.04	25.04	26.01
4.25	5.59	10.85	15.80	20.40	21.28	22.14	22.99
4.50	4.95	9.56	13.87	17.85	18.60	19.34	20.07
4.75	4.31	8.30	11.99	15.37	16.01	16.64	17.25
5.00	3.68	7.05	10.16	12.97	13.50	14.02	14.52
5.25	3.06	5.83	8.36	10.64	11.07	11.49	11.89
5.50	2.43	4.63	6.61	8.39	8.72	9.04	9.35
5.75	1.82	3.44	4.90	6.19	6.43	6.67	6.89
6.00	1.21	2.28	3.23	4.07	4.22	4.37	4.52
6.25	0.60	1.13	1.60	2.00	2.08	2.15	2.22
6.50	0.00	0.00	0.00	0.00	0.00	0.00	0.00

OLD RATE	24 YEARS	25 YEARS	26 YEARS	27 YEARS	28 YEARS	29 YEARS	30 YEARS
4.00	26.98	27.92	28.85	29.76	30.65	31.53	32.39
4.25	23.82	24.64	25.44	26.22	26.99	27.75	28.48
4.50	20.78	21.48	22.16	22.83	23.48	24.12	24.75
4.75	17.85	18.43	19.01	19.57	20.11	20.65	21.17
5.00	15.02	15.50	15.97	16.43	16.88	17.32	17.74
5.25	12.29	12.68	13.05	13.42	13.78	14.12	14.46
5.50	9.66	9.95	10.24	10.52	10.80	11.06	11.32
5.75	7.11	7.33	7.54	7.74	7.93	8.13	8.31
6.00	4.66	4.80	4.93	5.06	5.18	5.31	5.42
6.25	2.29	2.36	2.42	2.48	2.54	2.60	2.66
6.50	0.00	0.00	0.00	0.00	0.00	0.00	0.00

Valuation of Assumable Mortgages

CURRENT RATE: 7%

OLD RATE	5 YEARS	10 YEARS	15 YEARS	20 YEARS	21 YEARS	22 YEARS	23 YEARS
4.00	7.52	14.68	21.51	27.94	29.17	30.38	31.58
4.25	6.86	13.35	19.48	25.20	26.29	27.36	28.42
4.50	6.21	12.03	17.49	22.55	23.51	24.45	25.37
4.75	5.57	10.74	15.56	19.97	20.81	21.62	22.42
5.00	4.93	9.47	13.66	17.48	18.19	18.89	19.58
5.25	4.29	8.22	11.81	15.06	15.66	16.25	16.83
5.50	3.66	6.99	10.00	12.71	13.21	13.70	14.18
5.75	3.04	5.78	8.24	10.43	10.83	11.23	11.61
6.00	2.42	4.58	6.51	8.22	8.53	8.84	9.13
6.25	1.81	3.41	4.83	6.07	6.30	6.52	6.73
6.50	1.20	2.25	3.18	3.99	4.13	4.28	4.41
6.75	0.60	1.12	1.57	1.96	2.04	2.10	2.17
7.00	0.00	0.00	0.00	0.00	0.00	0.00	0.00

OLD RATE	24 YEARS	25 YEARS	26 YEARS	27 YEARS	28 YEARS	29 YEARS	30 YEARS
4.00	32.75	33.90	35.03	36.14	37.24	38.31	39.36
4.25	29.45	30.47	31.46	32.43	33.39	34.33	35.24
4.50	26.27	27.16	28.02	28.87	29.70	30.51	31.30
4.75	23.21	23.97	24.72	25.45	26.16	26.86	27.54
5.00	20.25	20.90	21.54	22.16	22.77	23.36	23.93
5.25	17.40	17.94	18.48	19.00	19.51	20.00	20.48
5.50	14.64	15.09	15.53	15.96	16.38	16.78	17.17
5.75	11.98	12.35	12.70	13.04	13.37	13.69	14.01
6.00	9.42	9.70	9.97	10.23	10.48	10.73	10.97
6.25	6.94	7.14	7.34	7.52	7.71	7.88	8.05
6.50	4.55	4.68	4.80	4.92	5.04	5.15	5.26
6.75	2.23	2.30	2.36	2.41	2.47	2.52	2.58
7.00	0.00	0.00	0.00	0.00	0.00	0.00	0.00

Valuation of Assumable Mortgages

CURRENT RATE: 7½%

OLD RATE	5 YEARS	10 YEARS	15 YEARS	20 YEARS	21 YEARS	22 YEARS	23 YEARS
4.00	8.80	17.24	25.32	32.94	34.40	35.84	37.25
4.25	8.14	15.88	23.23	30.10	31.40	32.69	33.95
4.50	7.48	14.53	21.18	27.34	28.50	29.65	30.77
4.75	6.83	13.21	19.18	24.66	25.70	26.71	27.70
5.00	6.18	11.91	17.23	22.07	22.98	23.87	24.73
5.25	5.54	10.63	15.32	19.55	20.34	21.12	21.87
5.50	4.90	9.38	13.45	17.11	17.79	18.45	19.10
5.75	4.27	8.14	11.63	14.74	15.32	15.88	16.42
6.00	3.65	6.92	9.85	12.45	12.92	13.39	13.84
6.25	3.03	5.72	8.12	10.22	10.60	10.97	11.33
6.50	2.41	4.54	6.42	8.05	8.35	8.64	8.92
6.75	1.80	3.38	4.76	5.95	6.16	6.37	6.58
7.00	1.20	2.23	3.14	3.91	4.05	4.18	4.31
7.25	0.60	1.11	1.55	1.93	1.99	2.06	2.12
7.50	0.00	0.00	0.00	0.00	0.00	0.00	0.00

OLD RATE	24 YEARS	25 YEARS	26 YEARS	27 YEARS	28 YEARS	29 YEARS	30 YEARS
4.00	38.64	40.00	41.34	42.66	43.95	45.22	46.46
4.25	35.19	36.41	37.60	38.77	39.92	41.04	42.13
4.50	31.87	32.95	34.01	35.04	36.05	37.03	38.00
4.75	28.67	29.62	30.55	31.45	32.34	33.20	34.04
5.00	25.58	26.41	27.22	28.01	28.78	29.52	30.25
5.25	22.60	23.32	24.02	24.70	25.36	26.00	26.62
5.50	19.73	20.34	20.93	21.51	22.07	22.62	23.15
5.75	16.95	17.47	17.97	18.45	18.92	19.38	19.82
6.00	14.27	14.70	15.11	15.50	15.89	16.26	16.62
6.25	11.69	12.02	12.35	12.67	12.98	13.27	13.56
6.50	9.19	9.45	9.70	9.94	10.18	10.40	10.62
6.75	6.77	6.96	7.14	7.32	7.48	7.65	7.80
7.00	4.44	4.56	4.67	4.79	4.89	5.00	5.10
7.25	2.18	2.24	2.30	2.35	2.40	2.45	2.50
7.50	0.00	0.00	0.00	0.00	0.00	0.00	0.00

Valuation of Assumable Mortgages

CURRENT RATE: 8%

OLD RATE	5 YEARS	10 YEARS	15 YEARS	20 YEARS	21 YEARS	22 YEARS	23 YEARS
4.00	10.10	19.84	29.20	38.03	39.72	41.39	43.03
4.25	9.43	18.44	27.03	35.08	36.61	38.12	39.60
4.50	8.76	17.07	24.92	32.21	33.59	34.95	36.28
4.75	8.10	15.72	22.86	29.44	30.68	31.89	33.08
5.00	7.45	14.39	20.85	26.74	27.85	28.93	29.99
5.25	6.80	13.08	18.88	24.13	25.11	26.07	27.00
5.50	6.15	11.80	16.96	21.60	22.46	23.30	24.12
5.75	5.51	10.53	15.08	19.14	19.89	20.62	21.33
6.00	4.88	9.28	13.25	16.75	17.40	18.02	18.63
6.25	4.25	8.06	11.46	14.44	14.98	15.51	16.02
6.50	3.63	6.85	9.71	12.19	12.64	13.08	13.50
6.75	3.01	5.66	7.99	10.01	10.37	10.72	11.06
7.00	2.40	4.50	6.32	7.89	8.17	8.44	8.70
7.25	1.79	3.34	4.69	5.83	6.03	6.23	6.42
7.50	1.19	2.21	3.09	3.83	3.96	4.09	4.21
7.75	0.59	1.10	1.53	1.89	1.95	2.01	2.07
8.00	0.00	0.00	0.00	0.00	0.00	0.00	0.00

OLD RATE	24 YEARS	25 YEARS	26 YEARS	27 YEARS	28 YEARS	29 YEARS	30 YEARS
4.00	44.64	46.22	47.78	49.30	50.80	52.26	53.70
4.25	41.05	42.47	43.87	45.23	46.57	47.88	49.16
4.50	37.58	38.86	40.11	41.32	42.52	43.68	44.82
4.75	34.24	35.38	36.49	37.57	38.63	39.66	40.66
5.00	31.02	32.03	33.01	33.97	34.90	35.80	36.69
5.25	27.91	28.80	29.66	30.50	31.32	32.11	32.88
5.50	24.91	25.69	26.44	27.17	27.88	28.57	29.23
5.75	22.02	22.68	23.33	23.96	24.57	25.16	25.74
6.00	19.22	19.79	20.34	20.88	21.40	21.90	22.39
6.25	16.52	17.00	17.47	17.91	18.35	18.77	19.17
6.50	13.91	14.31	14.69	15.06	15.42	15.76	16.09
6.75	11.39	11.71	12.02	12.31	12.59	12.87	13.13
7.00	8.96	9.20	9.44	9.66	9.88	10.09	10.29
7.25	6.60	6.78	6.95	7.11	7.27	7.42	7.56
7.50	4.33	4.44	4.55	4.65	4.75	4.85	4.94
7.75	2.13	2.18	2.23	2.28	2.33	2.38	2.42
8.00	0.00	0.00	0.00	0.00	0.00	0.00	0.00

Valuation of Assumable Mortgages

CURRENT RATE: 8½%

OLD RATE	5 YEARS	10 YEARS	15 YEARS	20 YEARS	21 YEARS	22 YEARS	23 YEARS
4.00	11.40	22.46	33.13	43.21	45.14	47.04	48.91
4.25	10.72	21.04	30.90	40.14	41.91	43.64	45.34
4.50	10.05	19.63	28.73	37.17	38.77	40.35	41.89
4.75	9.38	18.25	26.60	34.29	35.74	37.16	38.55
5.00	8.72	16.90	24.53	31.50	32.81	34.08	35.33
5.25	8.06	15.56	22.50	28.79	29.96	31.11	32.22
5.50	7.41	14.24	20.52	26.16	27.21	28.23	29.22
5.75	6.76	12.95	18.58	23.61	24.54	25.44	26.32
6.00	6.12	11.68	16.70	21.13	21.95	22.74	23.51
6.25	5.49	10.43	14.85	18.73	19.44	20.13	20.79
6.50	4.86	9.19	13.04	16.40	17.01	17.60	18.17
6.75	4.23	7.98	11.28	14.13	14.65	15.15	15.63
7.00	3.61	6.78	9.56	11.93	12.36	12.78	13.18
7.25	3.00	5.61	7.87	9.80	10.14	10.48	10.80
7.50	2.39	4.45	6.23	7.72	7.99	8.25	8.50
7.75	1.78	3.31	4.62	5.71	5.90	6.09	6.27
8.00	1.18	2.19	3.04	3.75	3.88	4.00	4.11
8.25	0.59	1.09	1.50	1.85	1.91	1.97	2.02
8.50	0.00	0.00	0.00	0.00	0.00	0.00	0.00

OLD RATE	24 YEARS	25 YEARS	26 YEARS	27 YEARS	28 YEARS	29 YEARS	30 YEARS
4.00	50.75	52.55	54.32	56.06	57.76	59.43	61.06
4.25	47.00	48.64	50.24	51.81	53.34	54.84	56.30
4.50	43.39	44.87	46.31	47.72	49.10	50.44	51.75
4.75	39.91	41.24	42.53	43.80	45.03	46.23	47.40
5.00	36.55	37.74	38.90	40.03	41.13	42.20	43.23
5.25	33.31	34.37	35.40	36.41	37.38	38.33	39.24
5.50	30.19	31.13	32.04	32.92	33.78	34.62	35.42
5.75	27.17	28.00	28.80	29.57	30.33	31.06	31.76
6.00	24.25	24.98	25.68	26.35	27.01	27.64	28.25
6.25	21.44	22.07	22.67	23.25	23.81	24.36	24.88
6.50	18.72	19.26	19.77	20.27	20.75	21.21	21.65
6.75	16.10	16.55	16.98	17.39	17.79	18.18	18.55
7.00	13.56	13.93	14.28	14.63	14.96	15.27	15.57
7.25	11.11	11.40	11.69	11.96	12.22	12.47	12.71
7.50	8.73	8.96	9.18	9.39	9.59	9.78	9.97
7.75	6.44	6.61	6.76	6.91	7.06	7.20	7.33
8.00	4.22	4.33	4.43	4.53	4.62	4.71	4.79
8.25	2.08	2.13	2.18	2.22	2.27	2.31	2.35
8.50	0.00	0.00	0.00	0.00	0.00	0.00	0.00

Valuation of Assumable Mortgages

CURRENT RATE: 9%

OLD RATE	5 YEARS	10 YEARS	15 YEARS	20 YEARS	21 YEARS	22 YEARS	23 YEARS
4.00	12.72	25.12	37.12	48.47	50.65	52.79	54.89
4.25	12.03	23.66	34.83	45.30	47.29	49.25	51.17
4.50	11.35	22.23	32.59	42.22	44.04	45.83	47.58
4.75	10.67	20.82	30.40	39.23	40.89	42.52	44.12
5.00	10.00	19.43	28.26	36.33	37.85	39.33	40.77
5.25	9.34	18.07	26.17	33.52	34.89	36.23	37.54
5.50	8.68	10.72	24.13	30.80	32.03	33.24	34.41
5.75	8.02	15.40	22.14	28.15	29.26	30.34	31.39
6.00	7.37	14.10	20.19	25.58	26.58	27.54	28.47
6.25	6.73	12.82	18.29	23.09	23.97	24.82	25.65
6.50	6.09	11.56	16.43	20.68	21.45	22.19	22.92
6.75	5.46	10.32	14.62	18.33	19.00	19.65	20.28
7.00	4.83	9.10	12.84	16.05	16.63	17.18	17.72
7.25	4.21	7.90	11.11	13.84	14.32	14.80	15.25
7.50	3.60	6.72	9.41	11.68	12.09	12.48	12.86
7.75	2.98	5.55	7.75	9.60	9.92	10.24	10.54
8.00	2.38	4.41	6.13	7.57	7.82	8.06	8.29
8.25	1.78	3.28	4.55	5.59	5.78	5.95	6.12
8.50	1.18	2.17	3.00	3.68	3.79	3.91	4.02
8.75	0.59	1.08	1.48	1.81	1.87	1.92	1.98
9.00	0.00	0.00	0.00	0.00	0.00	0.00	0.00

OLD RATE	24 YEARS	25 YEARS	26 YEARS	27 YEARS	28 YEARS	29 YEARS	30 YEARS
4.00	56.96	58.99	60.98	62.93	64.84	66.71	68.54
4.25	53.06	54.91	56.72	58.49	60.22	61.91	63.56
4.50	49.30	50.98	52.62	54.22	55.79	57.31	58.80
4.75	45.68	47.20	48.68	50.13	51.54	52.91	54.25
5.00	42.18	43.55	44.89	46.19	47.46	48.69	49.89
5.25	38.81	40.04	41.24	42.41	43.54	44.64	45.71
5.50	35.55	36.66	37.73	38.77	39.79	40.76	41.71
5.75	32.41	33.39	34.35	35.28	36.17	37.04	37.88
6.00	29.37	30.25	31.10	31.91	32.70	33.47	34.20
6.25	26.44	27.21	27.96	28.68	29.37	30.04	30.68
6.50	23.61	24.29	24.94	25.56	26.16	26.74	27.30
6.75	20.88	21.46	22.02	22.56	23.08	23.58	24.06
7.00	18.24	18.74	19.21	19.67	20.11	20.54	20.94
7.25	15.68	16.10	16.50	16.89	17.26	17.61	17.95
7.50	13.21	13.56	13.89	14.21	14.51	14.80	15.08
7.75	10.83	11.10	11.37	11.62	11.86	12.09	12.31
8.00	8.52	8.73	8.93	9.13	9.31	9.49	9.66
8.25	6.28	6.44	6.58	6.72	6.86	6.98	7.10
8.50	4.12	4.22	4.31	4.40	4.49	4.57	4.64
8.75	2.03	2.07	2.12	2.16	2.20	2.24	2.28
9.00	0.00	0.00	0.00	0.00	0.00	0.00	0.00

Valuation of Assumable Mortgages

CURRENT RATE: 9½%

OLD RATE	5 YEARS	10 YEARS	15 YEARS	20 YEARS	21 YEARS	22 YEARS	23 YEARS
4.00	14.04	27.81	41.17	53.82	56.24	58.63	60.97
4.25	13.34	26.32	38.81	50.53	52.76	54.95	57.10
4.50	12.65	24.85	36.50	47.34	49.39	51.40	53.37
4.75	11.97	23.41	34.25	44.24	46.13	47.97	49.77
5.00	11.29	22.00	32.05	41.24	42.97	44.65	46.29
5.25	10.62	20.60	29.90	38.33	39.90	41.44	42.93
5.50	9.95	19.23	27.80	35.51	36.94	38.33	39.68
5.75	9.29	17.88	25.75	32.77	34.06	35.32	36.54
6.00	8.63	16.55	23.74	30.11	31.28	32.41	33.51
6.25	7.98	15.25	21.79	27.53	28.58	29.59	30.58
6.50	7.34	13.96	19.87	25.02	25.96	26.86	27.74
6.75	6.70	12.69	18.00	22.59	23.42	24.22	24.99
7.00	6.06	11.45	16.18	20.23	20.96	21.66	22.34
7.25	5.43	10.22	14.39	17.94	18.57	19.18	19.77
7.50	4.81	9.01	12.64	15.71	16.25	16.78	17.28
7.75	4.19	7.82	10.94	13.54	14.01	14.45	14.87
8.00	3.58	6.65	9.27	11.44	11.82	12.19	12.54
8.25	2.97	5.50	7.64	9.40	9.71	10.00	10.28
8.50	2.37	4.36	6.04	7.41	7.65	7.88	8.10
8.75	1.77	3.25	4.48	5.48	5.65	5.82	5.98
9.00	1.17	2.15	2.95	3.60	3.71	3.82	3.92
9.25	0.58	1.07	1.46	1.78	1.83	1.88	1.93
9.50	0.00	0.00	0.00	0.00	0.00	0.00	0.00

OLD RATE	24 YEARS	25 YEARS	26 YEARS	27 YEARS	28 YEARS	29 YEARS	30 YEARS
4.00	63.27	65.52	67.74	69.90	72.02	74.10	76.13
4.25	59.21	61.28	63.30	65.27	67.20	69.09	70.93
4.50	55.30	57.19	59.03	60.83	62.58	64.29	65.95
4.75	51.53	53.25	54.92	56.56	58.14	59.69	61.19
5.00	47.89	49.45	50.97	52.45	53.89	55.28	56.64
5.25	44.38	45.80	47.17	48.51	49.80	51.06	52.27
5.50	41.00	42.28	43.51	44.72	45.88	47.00	48.09
5.75	37.73	38.88	39.99	41.07	42.11	43.12	44.09
6.00	34.57	35.60	36.60	37.56	38.49	39.38	40.25
6.25	31.53	32.44	33.33	34.19	35.01	35.80	36.57
6.50	28.58	29.40	30.18	30.94	31.66	32.36	33.03
6.75	25.74	26.46	27.15	27.81	28.44	29.06	29.64
7.00	22.99	23.62	24.22	24.80	25.35	25.88	26.39
7.25	20.33	20.88	21.40	21.89	22.37	22.82	23.26
7.50	17.77	18.23	18.67	19.10	19.50	19.89	20.26
7.75	15.28	15.67	16.04	16.40	16.74	17.06	17.37
8.00	12.88	13.20	13.51	13.80	14.08	14.34	14.59
8.25	10.55	10.81	11.06	11.29	11.51	11.72	11.92
8.50	8.30	8.50	8.69	8.87	9.04	9.20	9.36
8.75	6.13	6.27	6.41	6.54	6.66	6.77	6.88
9.00	4.02	4.11	4.20	4.28	4.36	4.43	4.50
9.25	1.98	2.02	2.06	2.10	2.14	2.18	2.21
9.50	0.00	0.00	0.00	0.00	0.00	0.00	0.00

Valuation of Assumable Mortgages

CURRENT RATE: 10%

OLD RATE	5 YEARS	10 YEARS	15 YEARS	20 YEARS	21 YEARS	22 YEARS	23 YEARS
4.00	15.37	30.53	45.28	59.25	61.92	64.55	67.13
4.25	14.67	29.01	42.85	55.84	58.31	60.74	63.12
4.50	13.97	27.51	40.47	52.54	54.82	57.06	59.25
4.75	13.28	26.04	38.15	49.33	51.44	53.50	55.51
5.00	12.59	24.59	35.89	46.23	48.16	50.05	51.90
5.25	11.91	23.17	33.68	43.21	44.99	46.72	48.41
5.50	11.23	21.77	31.52	40.29	41.91	43.50	45.03
5.75	10.57	20.39	29.41	37.45	38.93	40.38	41.77
6.00	9.90	19.03	27.34	34.70	36.05	37.36	38.62
6.25	9.24	17.70	25.33	32.03	33.25	34.43	35.58
6.50	8.59	16.38	23.36	29.43	30.54	31.60	32.63
6.75	7.94	15.09	21.44	26.92	27.91	28.86	29.78
7.00	7.30	13.82	19.56	24.47	25.35	26.21	27.03
7.25	6.67	12.56	17.72	22.10	22.88	23.63	24.36
7.50	6.03	11.33	15.92	19.79	20.48	21.14	21.77
7.75	5.41	10.12	14.16	17.55	18.15	18.72	19.27
8.00	4.79	8.92	12.45	15.37	15.89	16.38	16.85
8.25	4.17	7.74	10.77	13.26	13.69	14.11	14.51
8.50	3.56	6.59	9.13	11.20	11.56	11.91	12.24
8.75	2.95	5.44	7.52	9.20	9.49	9.77	10.04
9.00	2.35	4.32	5.95	7.26	7.48	7.70	7.90
9.25	1.76	3.22	4.41	5.37	5.53	5.69	5.84
9.50	1.17	2.13	2.91	3.53	3.63	3.74	3.83
9.75	0.58	1.06	1.44	1.74	1.79	1.84	1.89
10.00	0.00	0.00	0.00	0.00	0.00	0.00	0.00

OLD RATE	24 YEARS	25 YEARS	26 YEARS	27 YEARS	28 YEARS	29 YEARS	30 YEARS
4.00	69.67	72.16	74.59	76.98	79.31	81.59	83.82
4.25	65.45	67.74	69.97	72.15	74.28	76.36	78.39
4.50	61.39	63.48	65.53	67.52	69.46	71.36	73.20
4.75	57.47	59.39	61.26	63.07	64.84	66.56	68.23
5.00	53.69	55.44	57.14	58.80	60.41	61.96	63.48
5.25	50.05	51.64	53.19	54.69	56.15	57.56	58.92
5.50	46.53	47.98	49.38	50.74	52.06	53.33	54.56
5.75	43.13	44.44	45.71	46.94	48.13	49.27	50.38
6.00	40.00	41.04	42.18	43.29	44.35	45.38	46.37
6.25	36.68	37.75	38.78	39.77	40.73	41.65	42.53
6.50	33.62	34.58	35.50	36.39	37.24	38.06	38.84
6.75	30.67	31.52	32.34	33.13	33.88	34.61	35.30
7.00	27.81	28.57	29.30	29.99	30.66	31.30	31.91
7.25	25.05	25.72	26.36	26.97	27.55	28.11	28.64
7.50	22.38	22.97	23.52	24.05	24.56	25.05	25.51
7.75	19.80	20.31	20.79	21.25	21.68	22.10	22.50
8.00	17.31	17.74	18.15	18.54	18.91	19.26	19.60
8.25	14.89	15.25	15.60	15.92	16.24	16.53	16.81
8.50	12.55	12.85	13.13	13.40	13.66	13.90	14.13
8.75	10.29	10.53	10.76	10.97	11.17	11.37	11.55
9.00	8.10	8.28	8.46	8.62	8.78	8.93	9.07
9.25	5.98	6.11	6.24	6.35	6.47	6.57	6.67
9.50	3.92	4.01	4.09	4.16	4.24	4.30	4.37
9.75	1.93	1.97	2.01	2.05	2.08	2.11	2.14
10.00	0.00	0.00	0.00	0.00	0.00	0.00	0.00

Valuation of Assumable Mortgages

CURRENT RATE: 10½%

OLD RATE	5 YEARS	10 YEARS	15 YEARS	20 YEARS	21 YEARS	22 YEARS	23 YEARS
4.00	16.71	33.28	49.44	64.75	67.68	70.56	73.39
4.25	16.00	31.72	46.94	61.23	63.95	66.61	69.23
4.50	15.29	30.20	44.50	57.81	60.33	62.79	65.21
4.75	14.59	28.70	42.11	54.49	56.82	59.10	61.33
5.00	13.90	27.22	39.78	51.28	53.43	55.53	57.58
5.25	13.21	25.76	37.51	48.16	50.15	52.08	53.96
5.50	12.53	24.33	35.29	45.14	46.96	48.74	50.46
5.75	11.85	22.93	33.11	42.20	43.88	45.50	47.08
6.00	11.18	21.54	30.99	39.35	40.89	42.37	43.81
6.25	10.51	20.18	28.92	36.59	37.99	39.34	40.65
6.50	9.85	18.84	26.90	33.91	35.18	36.41	37.59
6.75	9.20	17.51	24.92	31.30	32.46	33.57	34.64
7.00	8.55	16.21	22.98	28.77	29.81	30.81	31.78
7.25	7.90	14.94	21.09	26.32	27.25	28.15	29.01
7.50	7.27	13.68	19.24	23.93	24.76	25.56	26.33
7.75	6.63	12.44	17.44	21.61	22.35	23.06	23.74
8.00	6.00	11.22	15.67	19.36	20.01	20.63	21.23
8.25	5.38	10.01	13.94	17.17	17.74	18.28	18.79
8.50	4.76	8.83	12.25	15.04	15.53	15.99	16.44
8.75	4.15	7.67	10.60	12.98	13.39	13.78	14.15
9.00	3.54	6.52	8.99	10.96	11.31	11.63	11.94
9.25	2.94	5.39	7.40	9.01	9.29	9.55	9.80
9.50	2.34	4.28	5.86	7.11	7.32	7.52	7.72
9.75	1.75	3.18	4.35	5.26	5.41	5.56	5.70
10.00	1.16	2.11	2.87	3.46	3.56	3.65	3.74
10.25	0.58	1.05	1.42	1.70	1.75	1.80	1.84
10.50	0.00	0.00	0.00	0.00	0.00	0.00	0.00

Valuation of Assumable Mortgages

CURRENT RATE: 10½%

OLD RATE	24 YEARS	25 YEARS	26 YEARS	27 YEARS	28 YEARS	29 YEARS	30 YEARS
4.00	76.16	78.88	81.54	84.14	86.69	89.18	91.60
4.25	71.78	74.29	76.73	79.12	81.46	83.73	85.95
4.50	67.56	69.87	72.12	74.31	76.44	78.52	80.53
4.75	63.50	65.61	67.67	69.68	71.63	73.52	75.36
5.00	59.57	61.51	63.40	65.23	67.01	68.73	70.40
5.25	55.79	57.56	59.28	60.95	62.57	64.14	65.65
5.50	52.13	53.75	55.32	56.84	58.31	59.73	61.11
5.75	48.61	50.08	51.51	52.89	54.23	55.51	56.75
6.00	45.20	46.54	47.84	49.09	50.30	51.46	52.57
6.25	41.91	43.13	44.30	45.43	46.52	47.56	48.56
6.50	38.74	39.84	40.89	41.91	42.89	43.82	44.72
6.75	35.67	36.66	37.61	38.52	39.39	40.23	41.03
7.00	32.70	33.59	34.44	35.25	36.03	36.78	37.49
7.25	29.84	30.63	31.38	32.11	32.80	33.46	34.09
7.50	27.06	27.77	28.44	29.08	29.69	30.27	30.82
7.75	24.38	25.00	25.59	26.15	26.69	27.20	27.68
8.00	21.79	22.33	22.85	23.34	23.80	24.24	24.66
8.25	19.28	19.75	20.20	20.62	21.02	21.40	21.76
8.50	16.86	17.26	17.64	18.00	18.34	18.66	18.97
8.75	14.51	14.84	15.16	15.46	15.75	16.02	16.28
9.00	12.23	12.51	12.77	13.02	13.26	13.48	13.69
9.25	10.03	10.25	10.46	10.66	10.85	11.02	11.19
9.50	7.90	8.07	8.23	8.38	8.52	8.66	8.79
9.75	5.83	5.95	6.07	6.18	6.28	6.38	6.47
10.00	3.83	3.90	3.98	4.05	4.12	4.18	4.24
10.25	1.88	1.92	1.96	1.99	2.02	2.05	2.08
10.50	0.00	0.00	0.00	0.00	0.00	0.00	0.00

Valuation of Assumable Mortgages

CURRENT RATE:11%

OLD RATE	5 YEARS	10 YEARS	15 YEARS	20 YEARS	21 YEARS	22 YEARS	23 YEARS
4.00	18.06	36.06	53.66	70.33	73.52	76.65	79.72
4.25	17.34	34.47	51.09	66.69	69.65	72.56	75.41
4.50	16.63	32.91	48.58	63.15	65.91	68.61	71.24
4.75	15.92	31.38	46.12	59.73	62.28	64.78	67.22
5.00	15.21	29.87	43.73	56.40	58.77	61.08	63.34
5.25	14.52	28.39	41.39	53.18	55.37	57.51	59.58
5.50	13.83	26.93	39.10	50.05	52.08	54.05	55.96
5.75	13.14	25.49	36.87	47.02	48.88	50.70	52.45
6.00	12.46	24.08	34.69	44.07	45.79	47.45	49.06
6.25	11.79	22.68	32.56	41.22	42.79	44.32	45.79
6.50	11.12	21.31	30.48	38.44	39.89	41.28	42.62
6.75	10.46	19.97	28.44	35.75	37.07	38.33	39.56
7.00	9.80	18.64	26.45	33.13	34.33	35.48	36.59
7.25	9.15	17.33	24.51	30.59	31.68	32.72	33.72
7.50	8.51	16.05	22.61	28.13	29.11	30.05	30.95
7.75	7.87	14.78	20.75	25.73	26.61	27.45	28.26
8.00	7.23	13.54	18.93	23.40	24.19	24.94	25.65
8.25	6.60	12.31	17.16	21.14	21.84	22.50	23.13
8.50	5.98	11.10	15.42	18.94	19.55	20.14	20.69
8.75	5.36	9.91	13.72	16.80	17.33	17.84	18.32
9.00	4.74	8.74	12.06	14.72	15.18	15.62	16.03
9.25	4.13	7.59	10.44	12.70	13.09	13.46	13.81
9.50	3.53	6.45	8.85	10.73	11.06	11.36	11.65
9.75	2.93	5.34	7.29	8.82	9.08	9.33	9.56
10.00	2.33	4.24	5.77	6.96	7.16	7.35	7.53
10.25	1.74	3.15	4.28	5.15	5.30	5.43	5.56
10.50	1.16	2.09	2.82	3.39	3.48	3.57	3.65
10.75	0.58	1.04	1.40	1.67	1.72	1.76	1.80
11.00	0.00	0.00	0.00	0.00	0.00	0.00	0.00

Valuation of Assumable Mortgages

CURRENT RATE: 11%

OLD RATE	24 YEARS	25 YEARS	26 YEARS	27 YEARS	28 YEARS	29 YEARS	30 YEARS
4.00	82.73	85.68	88.57	91.40	94.16	96.85	99.47
4.25	78.19	80.92	83.58	86.18	88.71	91.18	93.59
4.50	73.82	76.33	78.78	81.17	83.50	85.76	87.95
4.75	69.60	71.91	74.17	76.36	78.49	80.56	82.56
5.00	65.53	67.66	69.73	71.74	73.69	75.57	77.40
5.25	61.60	63.56	65.46	67.29	69.07	70.80	72.46
5.50	57.81	59.60	61.34	63.02	64.65	66.21	67.72
5.75	54.15	55.79	57.38	58.92	60.39	61.82	63.19
6.00	50.62	52.12	53.57	54.96	56.31	57.60	58.84
6.25	47.21	48.58	49.89	51.16	52.38	53.55	54.67
6.50	43.91	45.16	46.35	47.50	48.60	49.66	50.67
6.75	40.73	41.86	42.94	43.98	44.97	45.92	46.83
7.00	37.65	38.67	39.65	40.58	41.48	42.33	43.14
7.25	34.68	35.60	36.48	37.31	38.11	38.87	39.60
7.50	31.81	32.63	33.41	34.16	34.87	35.55	36.20
7.75	29.03	29.76	30.46	31.12	31.76	32.36	32.93
8.00	26.34	26.99	27.61	28.20	28.75	29.28	29.79
8.25	23.74	24.31	24.85	25.37	25.86	26.32	26.76
8.50	21.22	21.72	22.19	22.64	23.07	23.47	23.85
8.75	18.78	19.21	19.62	20.01	20.38	20.73	21.05
00	16.42	16.79	17.14	17.47	17.79	18.08	18.36
9.25	14.14	14.45	14.74	15.02	15.28	15.53	15.76
9.50	11.92	12.18	12.42	12.65	12.87	13.07	13.26
9.75	9.78	9.98	10.18	10.36	10.53	10.69	10.84
10.00	7.70	7.86	8.01	8.15	8.28	8.40	8.52
10.25	5.69	5.80	5.91	6.01	6.10	6.19	6.27
10.50	3.73	3.81	3.87	3.94	4.00	4.06	4.11
10.75	1.84	1.87	1.91	1.94	1.97	1.99	2.02
11.00	0.00	0.00	0.00	0.00	0.00	0.00	0.00

Valuation of Assumable Mortgages

CURRENT RATE: 11½%

OLD RATE	5 YEARS	10 YEARS	15 YEARS	20 YEARS	21 YEARS	22 YEARS	23 YEARS
4.00	19.42	38.87	57.93	75.98	79.43	82.81	86.13
4.25	18.69	37.25	55.29	72.22	75.43	78.58	81.67
4.50	17.97	35.66	52.71	68.57	71.56	74.49	77.35
4.75	17.25	34.09	50.19	65.02	67.81	70.53	73.19
5.00	16.54	32.56	47.72	61.59	64.18	66.70	69.16
5.25	15.84	31.04	45.32	58.26	60.66	63.00	65.28
5.50	15.14	29.55	42.97	55.03	57.26	59.42	61.52
5.75	14.44	28.08	40.68	51.89	53.96	55.96	57.89
6.00	13.76	26.64	38.43	48.85	50.76	52.60	54.38
6.25	13.08	25.22	36.24	45.90	47.66	49.35	50.99
6.50	12.40	23.82	34.10	43.03	44.65	46.21	47.71
6.75	11.73	22.44	32.01	40.25	41.74	43.16	44.54
7.00	11.07	21.09	29.97	37.55	38.91	40.21	41.47
7.25	10.41	19.76	27.97	34.93	36.17	37.35	38.49
7.50	9.75	18.44	26.02	32.38	33.51	34.58	35.62
7.75	9.11	17.15	24.11	29.90	30.92	31.90	32.83
8.00	8.46	15.88	22.24	27.50	28.42	29.30	30.14
8.25	7.83	14.63	20.41	25.16	25.99	26.78	27.53
8.50	7.19	13.40	18.63	22.89	23.62	24.33	25.00
8.75	6.57	12.18	16.88	20.68	21.33	21.95	22.55
9.00	5.95	10.99	15.18	18.53	19.10	19.65	20.17
9.25	5.33	9.81	13.51	16.44	16.94	17.42	17.87
9.50	4.72	8.65	11.87	14.41	14.84	15.25	15.63
9.75	4.11	7.51	10.27	12.43	12.80	13.14	13.47
10.00	3.51	6.39	8.71	10.51	10.81	11.10	11.37
10.25	2.91	5.28	7.18	8.64	8.88	9.11	9.33
10.50	2.32	4.19	5.68	6.82	7.01	7.18	7.35
10.75	1.73	3.12	4.21	5.04	5.18	5.31	5.43
11.00	1.15	2.07	2.78	3.32	3.41	3.49	3.57
11.25	0.57	1.03	1.38	1.64	1.68	1.72	1.76
11.50	0.00	0.00	0.00	0.00	0.00	0.00	0.00

Valuation of Assumable Mortgages

CURRENT RATE: 11½%

OLD RATE	24 YEARS	25 YEARS	26 YEARS	27 YEARS	28 YEARS	29 YEARS	30 YEARS
4.00	89.39	92.57	95.69	98.73	101.70	104.60	107.43
4.25	84.68	87.63	90.51	93.32	96.05	98.71	101.30
4.50	80.15	82.87	85.53	88.11	90.63	93.07	95.45
4.75	75.77	78.29	80.74	83.12	85.43	87.67	89.84
5.00	71.55	73.88	76.13	78.32	80.44	82.49	84.47
5.25	67.48	69.62	71.70	73.71	75.65	77.52	79.33
5.50	63.56	65.53	67.43	69.27	71.05	72.76	74.41
5.75	59.76	61.57	63.32	65.01	66.63	68.19	69.69
6.00	56.10	57.76	59.36	60.90	62.38	63.81	65.17
6.25	52.57	54.09	55.55	56.95	58.30	59.60	60.84
6.50	49.15	50.54	51.87	53.15	54.38	55.55	56.67
6.75	45.85	47.12	48.33	49.49	50.61	51.67	52.68
7.00	42.67	43.82	44.92	45.97	46.98	47.93	48.85
7.25	39.58	40.63	41.62	42.58	43.48	44.35	45.17
7.50	36.61	37.55	38.45	39.30	40.12	40.89	41.63
7.75	33.72	34.57	35.38	36.15	36.88	37.57	38.23
8.00	30.94	31.70	32.42	33.11	33.76	34.38	34.96
8.25	28.24	28.92	29.56	30.17	30.75	31.30	31.82
8.50	25.63	26.23	26.80	27.34	27.85	28.34	28.79
8.75	23.11	23.64	24.14	24.61	25.06	25.48	25.88
9.00	20.66	21.12	21.56	21.98	22.36	22.73	23.08
9.25	18.29	18.69	19.07	19.43	19.76	20.08	20.37
9.50	16.00	16.34	16.66	16.97	17.25	17.52	17.77
9.75	13.78	14.06	14.34	14.59	14.83	15.05	15.26
10.00	11.62	11.86	12.08	12.29	12.49	12.67	12.84
10.25	9.53	9.72	9.90	10.07	10.23	10.37	10.51
10.50	7.51	7.66	7.79	7.92	8.04	8.15	8.26
10.75	5.55	5.65	5.75	5.84	5.93	6.01	6.09
11.00	3.64	3.71	3.77	3.83	3.89	3.94	3.99
11.25	1.79	1.83	1.86	1.89	1.91	1.94	1.96
11.50	0.00	0.00	0.00	0.00	0.00	0.00	0.00

Valuation of Assumable Mortgages

CURRENT RATE:12%

OLD RATE	5 YEARS	10 YEARS	15 YEARS	20 YEARS	21 YEARS	22 YEARS	23 YEARS
4.00	20.79	41.71	62.25	81.70	85.41	89.05	92.62
4.25	20.05	40.06	59.54	77.81	81.28	84.67	88.00
4.50	19.32	38.43	56.89	74.04	77.28	80.44	83.53
4.75	18.59	36.84	54.30	70.39	73.41	76.35	79.22
5.00	17.87	35.27	51.77	66.84	69.65	72.39	75.06
5.25	17.16	33.72	49.30	63.40	66.02	68.56	71.04
5.50	16.46	32.20	46.88	60.07	62.50	64.86	67.15
5.75	15.76	30.70	44.53	56.83	59.09	61.28	63.39
6.00	15.06	29.23	42.22	53.69	55.78	57.81	59.76
6.25	14.37	27.78	39.97	50.64	52.58	54.45	56.25
6.50	13.69	26.35	37.77	47.68	49.47	51.20	52.86
6.75	13.01	24.95	35.63	44.81	46.46	48.05	49.57
7.00	12.34	23.57	33.53	42.02	43.54	45.00	46.39
7.25	11.67	22.21	31.47	39.31	40.70	42.04	43.32
7.50	11.01	20.87	29.47	36.68	37.96	39.18	40.34
7.75	10.36	19.55	27.50	34.12	35.29	36.40	37.46
8.00	9.71	18.25	25.59	31.64	32.70	33.71	34.67
8.25	9.06	16.97	23.71	29.23	30.19	31.10	31.97
8.50	8.42	15.72	21.88	26.88	27.75	28.57	29.35
8.75	7.79	14.48	20.08	24.60	25.38	26.12	26.82
9.00	7.16	13.26	18.33	22.38	23.08	23.73	24.36
9.25	6.54	12.06	16.61	20.22	20.84	21.42	21.97
9.50	5.92	10.88	14.93	18.13	18.67	19.18	19.66
9.75	5.30	9.71	13.29	16.09	16.56	17.00	17.42
10.00	4.69	8.57	11.68	14.10	14.51	14.89	15.25
10.25	4.09	7.44	10.11	12.17	12.51	12.84	13.14
10.50	3.49	6.33	8.57	10.29	10.57	10.84	11.09
10.75	2.90	5.23	7.07	8.46	8.69	8.90	9.11
11.00	2.31	4.15	5.59	6.67	6.85	7.02	7.18
11.25	1.72	3.09	4.15	4.94	5.07	5.19	5.30
11.50	1.15	2.05	2.74	3.25	3.33	3.41	3.48
11.75	0.57	1.01	1.35	1.60	1.64	1.68	1.72
12.00	0.00	0.00	0.00	0.00	0.00	0.00	0.00

Valuation of Assumable Mortgages

CURRENT RATE: 12%

OLD RATE	24 YEARS	25 YEARS	26 YEARS	27 YEARS	28 YEARS	29 YEARS	30 YEARS
4.00	96.12	99.54	102.88	106.14	109.33	112.43	115.45
4.25	91.24	94.42	97.51	100.52	103.46	106.32	109.09
4.50	86.55	89.49	92.35	95.13	97.83	100.46	103.01
4.75	82.02	84.74	87.38	89.95	92.44	94.85	97.19
5.00	77.65	80.16	82.60	84.97	87.26	89.47	91.61
5.25	73.43	75.76	78.01	80.18	82.29	84.32	86.27
5.50	69.37	71.51	73.58	75.58	77.51	79.37	81.16
5.75	65.44	67.42	69.32	71.16	72.93	74.63	76.26
6.00	61.65	63.47	65.22	66.90	68.52	70.07	71.56
6.25	57.99	59.66	61.27	62.81	64.29	65.70	67.06
6.50	54.45	55.99	57.46	58.87	60.21	61.50	62.74
6.75	51.04	52.44	53.78	55.07	56.30	57.47	58.59
7.00	47.73	49.02	50.24	51.41	52.53	53.60	54.61
7.25	44.54	45.71	46.83	47.89	48.91	49.87	50.78
7.50	41.46	42.52	43.53	44.50	45.41	46.28	47.11
7.75	38.48	39.44	40.36	41.23	42.05	42.84	43.58
8.00	35.59	36.46	37.29	38.07	38.81	39.52	40.18
8.25	32.80	33.58	34.33	35.03	35.69	36.32	36.92
8.50	30.10	30.80	31.46	32.09	32.69	33.25	33.77
8.75	27.48	28.11	28.70	29.26	29.79	30.28	30.75
9.00	24.95	25.50	26.03	26.52	26.99	27.43	27.84
9.25	22.49	22.99	23.45	23.88	24.29	24.67	25.03
9.50	20.12	20.55	20.95	21.33	21.69	22.02	22.33
9.75	17.82	18.19	18.54	18.86	19.17	19.46	19.72
10.00	15.59	15.90	16.20	16.48	16.74	16.98	17.21
10.25	13.42	13.69	13.94	14.18	14.39	14.60	14.79
10.50	11.33	11.55	11.75	11.95	12.13	12.29	12.45
10.75	9.30	9.47	9.64	9.79	9.93	10.07	10.19
11.00	7.32	7.46	7.59	7.70	7.81	7.92	8.01
11.25	5.41	5.51	5.60	5.68	5.76	5.84	5.90
11.50	3.55	3.62	3.67	3.73	3.78	3.83	3.87
11.75	1.75	1.78	1.81	1.84	1.86	1.88	1.90
12.00	0.00	0.00	0.00	0.00	0.00	0.00	0.00

Valuation of Assumable Mortgages

CURRENT RATE: 12½%

OLD RATE	5 YEARS	10 YEARS	15 YEARS	20 YEARS	21 YEARS	22 YEARS	23 YEARS
4.00	22.16	44.58	66.63	87.49	91.46	95.36	99.18
4.25	21.42	42.89	63.84	83.48	87.19	90.83	94.40
4.50	20.68	41.24	61.12	79.58	83.06	86.46	89.78
4.75	19.94	39.61	58.46	75.81	79.06	82.23	85.32
5.00	19.22	38.01	55.86	72.15	75.19	78.14	81.02
5.25	18.50	36.43	53.32	68.61	71.44	74.19	76.86
5.50	17.78	34.88	50.84	65.16	67.80	70.36	72.84
5.75	17.07	33.35	48.42	61.82	64.28	66.66	68.95
6.00	16.37	31.85	46.06	58.58	60.87	63.07	65.20
6.25	15.68	30.37	43.75	55.44	57.56	59.60	61.57
6.50	14.98	28.91	41.49	52.38	54.35	56.24	58.06
6.75	14.30	27.48	39.28	49.42	51.24	52.99	54.66
7.00	13.62	26.07	37.13	46.54	48.22	49.83	51.38
7.25	12.95	24.68	35.02	43.75	45.30	46.78	48.20
7.50	12.28	23.31	32.96	41.03	42.46	43.82	45.12
7.75	11.61	21.97	30.94	38.39	39.70	40.95	42.14
8.00	10.96	20.65	28.97	35.83	37.03	38.17	39.26
8.25	10.30	19.34	27.05	33.34	34.43	35.47	36.46
8.50	9.66	18.06	25.16	30.92	31.91	32.86	33.76
8.75	9.02	16.80	23.32	28.56	29.47	30.32	31.13
9.00	8.38	15.55	21.52	26.28	27.09	27.86	28.59
9.25	7.75	14.33	19.76	24.05	24.78	25.47	26.13
9.50	7.12	13.12	18.03	21.89	22.54	23.16	23.74
9.75	6.50	11.93	16.35	19.78	20.36	20.91	21.42
10.00	5.89	10.76	14.70	17.73	18.24	18.72	19.17
10.25	5.28	9.61	13.08	15.74	16.18	16.60	16.99
10.50	4.67	8.48	11.50	13.80	14.18	14.54	14.87
10.75	4.07	7.36	9.95	11.91	12.23	12.54	12.82
11.00	3.47	6.26	8.44	10.07	10.34	10.59	10.83
11.25	2.88	5.18	6.96	8.28	8.50	8.70	8.89
11.50	2.30	4.11	5.51	6.54	6.70	6.86	7.01
11.75	1.72	3.06	4.09	4.84	4.96	5.07	5.18
12.00	1.14	2.02	2.70	3.18	3.26	3.34	3.40
12.25	0.57	1.00	1.33	1.57	1.61	1.64	1.68
12.50	0.00	0.00	0.00	0.00	0.00	0.00	0.00

Valuation of Assumable Mortgages

CURRENT RATE: 12½%

OLD RATE	24 YEARS	25 YEARS	26 YEARS	27 YEARS	28 YEARS	29 YEARS	30 YEARS
4.00	102.92	106.57	110.14	113.62	117.02	120.33	123.55
4.25	97.87	101.27	104.58	107.80	110.94	113.99	116.95
4.50	93.01	96.17	99.23	102.21	105.11	107.91	110.64
4.75	88.33	91.25	94.09	96.84	99.51	102.09	104.59
5.00	83.81	86.52	89.14	91.68	94.14	96.52	98.81
5.25	79.45	81.95	84.38	86.72	88.99	91.17	93.27
5.50	75.24	77.56	79.80	81.96	84.04	86.04	87.97
5.75	71.18	73.32	75.38	77.37	79.28	81.12	82.88
6.00	67.25	69.23	71.13	72.96	74.71	76.40	78.01
6.25	63.47	65.29	67.04	68.72	70.32	71.86	73.34
6.50	59.81	61.48	63.09	64.63	66.10	67.51	68.85
6.75	56.27	57.81	59.29	60.70	62.04	63.33	64.55
7.00	52.86	54.27	55.62	56.91	58.14	59.31	60.42
7.25	49.56	50.85	52.08	53.26	54.38	55.44	56.45
7.50	46.36	47.55	48.67	49.74	50.76	51.72	52.64
7.75	43.28	44.35	45.38	46.35	47.27	48.15	48.97
8.00	40.29	41.27	42.20	43.08	43.92	44.71	45.45
8.25	37.40	38.29	39.13	39.93	40.68	41.39	42.06
8.50	34.61	35.41	36.17	36.89	37.56	38.20	38.80
8.75	31.90	32.62	33.31	33.95	34.56	35.13	35.66
9.00	29.28	29.93	30.54	31.12	31.66	32.16	32.64
9.25	26.74	27.32	27.87	28.38	28.86	29.31	29.73
9.50	24.28	24.80	25.28	25.73	26.16	26.55	26.93
9.75	21.90	22.36	22.78	23.18	23.55	23.90	24.22
10.00	19.59	19.99	20.36	20.71	21.03	21.33	21.61
10.25	17.36	17.70	18.02	18.32	18.60	18.86	19.10
10.50	15.19	15.48	15.76	16.01	16.25	16.47	16.67
10.75	13.08	13.33	13.56	13.78	13.97	14.16	14.33
11.00	11.04	11.25	11.44	11.61	11.78	11.93	12.07
11.25	9.06	9.23	9.38	9.52	9.65	9.77	9.88
11.50	7.14	7.27	7.39	7.49	7.59	7.69	7.77
11.75	5.28	5.37	5.45	5.53	5.60	5.67	5.73
12.00	3.47	3.53	3.58	3.63	3.68	3.72	3.76
12.25	1.71	1.74	1.76	1.79	1.81	1.83	1.85
12.50	0.00	0.00	0.00	0.00	0.00	0.00	0.00

Valuation of Assumable Mortgages

CURRENT RATE: 13%

OLD RATE	5 YEARS	10 YEARS	15 YEARS	20 YEARS	21 YEARS	22 YEARS	23 YEARS
4.00	23.55	47.47	71.05	93.34	97.57	101.73	105.80
4.25	22.79	45.76	68.19	89.20	93.17	97.06	100.86
4.50	22.05	44.07	65.39	85.19	88.91	92.54	96.09
4.75	21.31	42.41	62.66	81.30	84.78	88.18	91.48
5.00	20.57	40.77	60.00	77.52	80.78	83.95	87.04
5.25	19.84	39.16	57.39	73.86	76.91	79.87	82.74
5.50	19.12	37.58	54.85	70.32	73.16	75.92	78.59
5.75	18.40	36.02	52.36	66.87	69.52	72.09	74.57
6.00	17.69	34.49	49.94	63.53	66.00	68.39	70.69
6.25	16.99	32.98	47.56	60.29	62.59	64.81	66.94
6.50	16.29	31.50	45.25	57.14	59.28	61.34	63.31
6.75	15.59	30.03	42.98	54.08	56.07	57.98	59.81
7.00	14.91	28.60	40.77	51.11	52.95	54.72	56.41
7.25	14.23	27.18	38.60	48.23	49.93	51.57	53.13
7.50	13.55	25.79	36.49	45.43	47.01	48.51	49.95
7.75	12.88	24.41	34.42	42.71	44.16	45.55	46.87
8.00	12.21	23.06	32.40	40.07	41.40	42.68	43.89
8.25	11.56	21.73	30.42	37.50	38.73	39.89	41.00
8.50	10.90	20.43	28.48	35.00	36.13	37.19	38.20
8.75	10.25	19.14	26.59	32.57	33.60	34.57	35.49
9.00	9.61	17.87	24.74	30.21	31.15	32.03	32.87
9.25	8.97	16.62	22.94	27.92	28.77	29.57	30.32
9.50	8.34	15.39	21.17	25.69	26.45	27.17	27.85
9.75	7.71	14.18	19.43	23.52	24.20	24.85	25.46
10.00	7.09	12.99	17.74	21.40	22.02	22.59	23.13
10.25	6.47	11.81	16.08	19.35	19.89	20.40	20.88
10.50	5.86	10.65	14.46	17.35	17.83	18.27	18.69
10.75	5.25	9.51	12.87	15.40	15.82	16.21	16.57
11.00	4.65	8.39	11.32	13.50	13.86	14.20	14.51
11.25	4.05	7.29	9.80	11.66	11.96	12.25	12.51
11.50	3.46	6.20	8.31	9.86	10.11	10.35	10.57
11.75	2.87	5.13	6.85	8.11	8.31	8.50	8.68
12.00	2.29	4.07	5.42	6.40	6.56	6.71	6.84
12.25	1.71	3.03	4.02	4.74	4.85	4.96	5.06
12.50	1.13	2.00	2.65	3.12	3.19	3.26	3.32
12.75	0.56	0.99	1.31	1.54	1.58	1.61	1.64
13.00	0.00	0.00	0.00	0.00	0.00	0.00	0.00

Valuation of Assumable Mortgages

CURRENT RATE: 13%

OLD RATE	24 YEARS	25 YEARS	26 YEARS	27 YEARS	28 YEARS	29 YEARS	30 YEARS
4.00	109.78	113.67	117.47	121.17	124.78	128.29	131.71
4.25	104.57	108.19	111.71	115.14	118.48	121.72	124.86
4.50	99.55	102.91	106.18	109.36	112.44	115.43	118.32
4.75	94.70	97.83	100.86	103.80	106.64	109.40	112.06
5.00	90.03	92.93	95.74	98.45	101.08	103.62	106.06
5.25	85.52	88.21	90.81	93.32	95.74	98.08	100.32
5.50	81.17	83.66	86.07	88.38	90.62	92.76	94.83
5.75	76.97	79.28	81.50	83.64	85.69	87.66	89.56
6.00	72.91	75.05	77.10	79.07	80.96	82.77	84.50
6.25	69.00	70.97	72.86	74.68	76.41	78.07	79.66
6.50	65.21	67.04	68.78	70.45	72.04	73.56	75.01
6.75	61.56	63.24	64.84	66.38	67.84	69.23	70.55
7.00	58.03	59.57	61.05	62.45	63.79	65.06	66.27
7.25	54.62	56.04	57.39	58.67	59.90	61.06	62.16
7.50	51.32	52.62	53.86	55.03	56.15	57.21	58.21
7.75	48.12	49.32	50.45	51.52	52.54	53.50	54.41
8.00	45.04	46.13	47.16	48.14	49.06	49.93	50.76
8.25	42.05	43.04	43.99	44.87	45.71	46.50	47.24
8.50	39.16	40.06	40.92	41.72	42.48	43.19	43.87
8.75	36.36	37.18	37.96	38.68	39.37	40.01	40.61
9.00	33.65	34.39	35.09	35.75	36.36	36.94	37.48
9.25	31.03	31.70	32.33	32.91	33.46	33.98	34.46
9.50	28.49	29.09	29.65	30.18	30.67	31.13	31.56
9.75	26.03	26.56	27.06	27.53	27.97	28.37	28.75
10.00	23.64	24.12	24.56	24.97	25.36	25.72	26.05
10.25	21.33	21.75	22.14	22.50	22.84	23.15	23.45
10.50	19.09	19.45	19.79	20.11	20.40	20.68	20.93
10.75	16.91	17.23	17.52	17.80	18.05	18.28	18.50
11.00	14.80	15.07	15.32	15.56	15.77	15.97	16.16
11.25	12.75	12.98	13.19	13.39	13.57	13.74	13.89
11.50	10.77	10.96	11.13	11.29	11.44	11.58	11.70
11.75	8.84	8.99	9.13	9.26	9.38	9.49	9.59
12.00	6.97	7.08	7.19	7.29	7.38	7.47	7.54
12.25	5.15	5.23	5.31	5.38	5.45	5.51	5.56
12.50	3.38	3.44	3.49	3.53	3.57	3.61	3.65
12.75	1.67	1.69	1.72	1.74	1.76	1.78	1.80
13.00	0.00	0.00	0.00	0.00	0.00	0.00	0.00

Valuation of Assumable Mortgages

CURRENT RATE: 13½%

OLD RATE	5 YEARS	10 YEARS	15 YEARS	20 YEARS	21 YEARS	22 YEARS	23 YEARS
4.00	24.94	50.40	75.52	99.24	103.75	108.16	112.48
4.25	24.18	48.65	72.58	94.98	99.21	103.34	107.38
4.50	23.42	46.93	69.72	90.84	94.81	98.68	102.46
4.75	22.67	45.23	66.92	86.84	90.55	94.18	97.70
5.00	21.93	43.57	64.18	82.95	86.43	89.82	93.11
5.25	21.19	41.93	61.51	79.18	82.44	85.61	88.67
5.50	20.46	40.31	58.90	75.52	78.57	81.53	84.39
5.75	19.74	38.72	56.35	71.97	74.82	77.58	80.24
6.00	19.02	37.16	53.86	68.53	71.19	73.76	76.24
6.25	18.31	35.62	51.42	65.18	67.67	70.06	72.37
6.50	17.60	34.11	49.04	61.94	64.25	66.48	68.62
6.75	16.90	32.62	46.72	58.79	60.94	63.01	65.00
7.00	16.20	31.15	44.45	55.73	57.73	59.65	61.49
7.25	15.51	29.70	42.22	52.76	54.62	56.40	58.10
7.50	14.83	28.28	40.05	49.87	51.60	53.25	54.82
7.75	14.15	26.88	37.93	47.07	48.67	50.19	51.64
8.00	13.48	25.51	35.86	44.35	45.82	47.23	48.56
8.25	12.81	24.15	33.83	41.70	43.06	44.35	45.58
8.50	12.15	22.82	31.84	39.13	40.38	41.57	42.69
8.75	11.50	21.50	29.90	36.63	37.78	38.86	39.89
9.00	10.85	20.21	28.01	34.19	35.25	36.24	37.18
9.25	10.20	18.93	26.15	31.83	32.79	33.70	34.55
9.50	9.56	17.68	24.33	29.53	30.40	31.23	32.00
9.75	8.93	16.44	22.56	27.29	28.08	28.83	29.53
10.00	8.30	15.23	20.82	25.11	25.83	26.50	27.13
10.25	7.67	14.03	19.12	23.00	23.64	24.24	24.81
10.50	7.05	12.85	17.45	20.93	21.51	22.05	22.55
10.75	6.44	11.69	15.82	18.93	19.44	19.91	20.36
11.00	5.83	10.54	14.23	16.97	17.42	17.84	18.23
11.25	5.22	9.42	12.67	15.07	15.46	15.82	16.16
11.50	4.63	8.31	11.14	13.22	13.55	13.87	14.16
11.75	4.03	7.21	9.64	11.41	11.70	11.96	12.21
12.00	3.44	6.14	8.18	9.65	9.89	10.11	10.31
12.25	2.86	5.07	6.74	7.94	8.13	8.31	8.47
12.50	2.28	4.03	5.34	6.27	6.42	6.55	6.68
12.75	1.70	3.00	3.96	4.64	4.75	4.85	4.94
13.00	1.13	1.98	2.61	3.06	3.13	3.19	3.25
13.25	0.56	0.99	1.29	1.51	1.54	1.57	1.60
13.50	0.00	0.00	0.00	0.00	0.00	0.00	0.00

Valuation of Assumable Mortgages

CURRENT RATE: 13½%

OLD RATE	24 YEARS	25 YEARS	26 YEARS	27 YEARS	28 YEARS	29 YEARS	30 YEARS
4.00	116.71	120.83	124.86	128.78	132.60	136.31	139.92
4.25	111.33	115.17	118.91	122.54	126.08	129.51	132.84
4.50	106.14	109.71	113.19	116.56	119.83	122.99	126.06
4.75	101.13	104.46	107.68	110.81	113.83	116.75	119.58
5.00	96.30	99.40	102.39	105.28	108.07	110.77	113.37
5.25	91.65	94.52	97.29	99.97	102.55	105.04	107.43
5.50	87.15	89.82	92.39	94.86	97.25	99.53	101.73
5.75	82.81	85.29	87.67	89.95	92.15	94.26	96.28
6.00	78.62	80.92	83.12	85.23	87.25	89.19	91.05
6.25	74.58	76.70	78.74	80.69	82.55	84.33	86.03
6.50	70.67	72.64	74.51	76.31	78.02	79.66	81.22
6.75	66.90	68.71	70.44	72.10	73.67	75.17	76.60
7.00	63.25	64.92	66.52	68.04	69.49	70.86	72.16
7.25	59.72	61.27	62.74	64.13	65.46	66.72	67.91
7.50	56.31	57.73	59.09	60.37	61.58	62.73	63.81
7.75	53.02	54.32	55.56	56.74	57.84	58.89	59.88
8.00	49.83	51.03	52.16	53.23	54.25	55.20	56.10
8.25	46.74	47.84	48.88	49.86	50.78	51.65	52.46
8.50	43.76	44.76	45.71	46.60	47.44	48.23	48.97
8.75	40.87	41.78	42.64	43.45	44.21	44.93	45.60
9.00	38.07	38.90	39.68	40.42	41.11	41.75	42.35
9.25	35.36	36.11	36.82	37.49	38.11	38.69	39.23
9.50	32.73	33.42	34.05	34.65	35.21	35.73	36.22
9.75	30.19	30.80	31.38	31.92	32.42	32.88	33.32
10.00	27.72	28.28	28.79	29.27	29.72	30.13	30.52
10.25	25.33	25.83	26.29	26.71	27.11	27.48	27.82
10.50	23.02	23.46	23.86	24.24	24.59	24.92	25.22
10.75	20.77	21.16	21.52	21.85	22.16	22.44	22.70
11.00	18.59	18.93	19.24	19.53	19.80	20.05	20.28
11.25	16.48	16.77	17.04	17.29	17.52	17.73	17.93
11.50	14.43	14.68	14.91	15.12	15.32	15.50	15.66
11.75	12.43	12.64	12.84	13.02	13.18	13.33	13.47
12.00	10.50	10.67	10.83	10.98	11.12	11.24	11.36
12.25	8.62	8.76	8.89	9.01	9.12	9.21	9.31
12.50	6.80	6.91	7.00	7.09	7.18	7.25	7.32
12.75	5.03	5.10	5.17	5.24	5.30	5.35	5.40
13.00	3.30	3.35	3.40	3.44	3.48	3.51	3.54
13.25	1.63	1.65	1.67	1.69	1.71	1.73	1.74
13.50	0.00	0.00	0.00	0.00	0.00	0.00	0.00

Valuation of Assumable Mortgages

CURRENT RATE: 14%

OLD RATE	5 YEARS	10 YEARS	15 YEARS	20 YEARS	21 YEARS	22 YEARS	23 YEARS
4.00	26.34	53.36	80.04	105.21	109.98	114.66	119.23
4.25	25.57	51.57	77.03	100.82	105.30	109.69	113.97
4.50	24.81	49.82	74.09	96.56	100.77	104.88	108.89
4.75	24.05	48.09	71.21	92.43	96.38	100.23	103.98
5.00	23.30	46.39	68.41	88.42	92.14	95.74	99.24
5.25	22.55	44.71	65.66	84.54	88.02	91.39	94.66
5.50	21.82	43.07	62.99	80.77	84.03	87.19	90.24
5.75	21.08	41.45	60.37	77.12	80.17	83.12	85.96
6.00	20.36	39.85	57.82	73.57	76.43	79.18	81.83
6.25	19.64	38.28	55.32	70.13	72.80	75.37	77.84
6.50	18.92	36.74	52.88	66.79	69.28	71.67	73.97
6.75	18.21	35.22	50.49	63.54	65.87	68.10	70.23
7.00	17.51	33.73	48.16	60.39	62.56	64.63	66.62
7.25	16.81	32.25	45.89	57.33	59.35	61.28	63.12
7.50	16.12	30.80	43.66	54.36	56.24	58.03	59.73
7.75	15.44	29.38	41.48	51.47	53.22	54.87	56.45
8.00	14.76	27.97	39.35	48.67	50.28	51.82	53.28
8.25	14.08	26.59	37.27	45.94	47.44	48.86	50.20
8.50	13.41	25.23	35.24	43.29	44.67	45.98	47.22
8.75	12.75	23.89	33.25	40.72	41.99	43.20	44.33
9.00	12.09	22.57	31.30	38.21	39.38	40.49	41.54
9.25	11.44	21.27	29.40	35.78	36.85	37.87	38.82
9.50	10.79	19.99	27.53	33.41	34.39	35.32	36.19
9.75	10.15	18.73	25.71	31.10	32.00	32.85	33.64
10.00	9.51	17.49	23.93	28.86	29.68	30.45	31.17
10.25	8.88	16.27	22.18	26.68	27.42	28.12	28.77
10.50	8.26	15.07	20.48	24.55	25.23	25.85	26.44
10.75	7.63	13.88	18.80	22.49	23.09	23.65	24.18
11.00	7.02	12.72	17.17	20.47	21.01	21.52	21.98
11.25	6.41	11.57	15.57	18.51	18.99	19.44	19.85
11.50	5.80	10.43	14.00	16.61	17.03	17.42	17.78
11.75	5.20	9.32	12.47	14.75	15.11	15.45	15.77
12.00	4.60	8.22	10.96	12.94	13.25	13.54	13.81
12.25	4.01	7.14	9.49	11.17	11.44	11.69	11.91
12.50	3.42	6.07	8.05	9.45	9.67	9.88	10.07
12.75	2.84	5.02	6.64	7.78	7.95	8.12	8.27
13.00	2.26	3.99	5.26	6.14	6.28	6.41	6.53
13.25	1.69	2.97	3.90	4.55	4.65	4.74	4.83
13.50	1.12	1.96	2.57	2.99	3.06	3.12	3.17
13.75	0.56	0.98	1.27	1.48	1.51	1.54	1.57
14.00	0.00	0.00	0.00	0.00	0.00	0.00	0.00

Valuation of Assumable Mortgages

CURRENT RATE: 14%

OLD RATE	24 YEARS	25 YEARS	26 YEARS	27 YEARS	28 YEARS	29 YEARS	30 YEARS
4.00	123.70	128.06	132.31	136.44	140.47	144.38	148.18
4.25	118.14	122.20	126.16	130.00	133.73	137.35	140.86
4.50	112.78	116.57	120.25	123.81	127.27	130.61	133.85
4.75	107.62	111.14	114.56	117.87	121.07	124.16	127.14
5.00	102.63	105.92	109.09	112.16	115.12	117.97	120.72
5.25	97.82	100.88	103.83	106.67	109.41	112.04	114.57
5.50	93.18	96.02	98.76	101.39	103.92	106.35	108.68
5.75	88.71	91.34	93.88	96.32	98.65	100.89	103.04
6.00	84.38	86.83	89.18	91.44	93.59	95.66	97.63
6.25	80.21	82.48	84.66	86.74	88.73	90.63	92.44
6.50	76.17	78.28	80.29	82.22	84.05	85.80	87.46
6.75	72.28	74.23	76.09	77.86	79.55	81.16	82.68
7.00	68.51	70.32	72.04	73.67	75.22	76.70	78.10
7.25	64.87	66.54	68.13	69.63	71.06	72.41	73.69
7.50	61.35	62.89	64.35	65.74	67.05	68.29	69.46
7.75	57.95	59.37	60.71	61.99	63.19	64.32	65.39
8.00	54.66	55.96	57.20	58.37	59.47	60.50	61.48
8.25	51.47	52.67	53.81	54.88	55.88	56.83	57.72
8.50	48.39	49.49	50.53	51.51	52.43	53.29	54.10
8.75	45.41	46.42	47.37	48.26	49.10	49.88	50.61
9.00	42.52	43.44	44.31	45.12	45.88	46.59	47.26
9.25	39.72	40.56	41.35	42.09	42.78	43.43	44.03
9.50	37.01	37.78	38.49	39.16	39.79	40.37	40.91
9.75	34.39	35.08	35.73	36.34	36.90	37.42	37.91
10.00	31.84	32.47	33.06	33.60	34.11	34.58	35.02
10.25	29.38	29.94	30.47	30.96	31.41	31.83	32.23
10.50	26.98	27.49	27.96	28.40	28.81	29.18	29.53
10.75	24.67	25.12	25.54	25.93	26.29	26.62	26.93
11.00	22.42	22.82	23.19	23.54	23.85	24.15	24.42
11.25	20.23	20.59	20.92	21.22	21.50	21.76	21.99
11.50	18.12	18.43	18.71	18.98	19.22	19.44	19.65
11.75	16.06	16.33	16.58	16.80	17.01	17.21	17.38
12.00	14.06	14.29	14.50	14.70	14.88	15.04	15.19
12.25	12.12	12.32	12.50	12.66	12.81	12.95	13.07
12.50	10.24	10.40	10.55	10.68	10.81	10.92	11.02
12.75	8.41	8.54	8.66	8.76	8.86	8.95	9.03
13.00	6.63	6.73	6.82	6.91	6.98	7.05	7.11
13.25	4.90	4.98	5.04	5.10	5.16	5.20	5.25
13.50	3.22	3.27	3.31	3.35	3.38	3.42	3.45
13.75	1.59	1.61	1.63	1.65	1.67	1.68	1.70
14.00	0.00	0.00	0.00	0.00	0.00	0.00	0.00

Valuation of Assumable Mortgages

CURRENT RATE: 14½%

OLD RATE	5 YEARS	10 YEARS	15 YEARS	20 YEARS	21 YEARS	22 YEARS	23 YEARS
4.00	27.76	56.34	84.60	111.23	116.27	121.20	126.03
4.25	26.98	54.52	81.52	106.71	111.45	116.08	120.60
4.50	26.20	52.73	78.50	102.32	106.78	111.13	115.36
4.75	25.44	50.97	75.55	98.07	102.26	106.34	110.31
5.00	24.68	49.23	72.67	93.95	97.89	101.71	105.42
5.25	23.92	47.53	69.86	89.95	93.65	97.23	100.70
5.50	23.18	45.85	67.12	86.08	89.54	92.90	96.14
5.75	22.44	44.20	64.44	82.31	85.57	88.70	91.73
6.00	21.70	42.57	61.82	78.66	81.71	84.65	87.47
6.25	20.97	40.97	59.26	75.12	77.97	80.72	83.35
6.50	20.25	39.40	56.75	71.68	74.35	76.91	79.37
6.75	19.53	37.85	54.31	68.34	70.83	73.23	75.51
7.00	18.82	36.33	51.92	65.10	67.43	69.66	71.79
7.25	18.12	34.83	49.58	61.95	64.12	66.20	68.18
7.50	17.42	33.35	47.30	58.89	60.92	62.85	64.68
7.75	16.73	31.89	45.07	55.92	57.80	59.60	61.30
8.00	16.04	30.46	42.89	53.03	54.78	56.45	58.03
8.25	15.36	29.05	40.75	50.22	51.85	53.40	54.86
8.50	14.68	27.67	38.67	47.50	49.01	50.44	51.79
8.75	14.01	26.30	36.63	44.84	46.24	47.56	48.81
9.00	13.34	24.95	34.63	42.27	43.56	44.78	45.93
9.25	12.68	23.63	32.68	39.76	40.95	42.07	43.13
9.50	12.03	22.33	30.77	37.32	38.42	39.45	40.42
9.75	11.38	21.04	28.90	34.95	35.96	36.90	37.79
10.00	10.74	19.78	27.07	32.64	33.56	34.43	35.24
10.25	10.10	18.53	25.28	30.39	31.24	32.03	32.76
10.50	9.46	17.31	23.53	28.21	28.98	29.69	30.36
10.75	8.84	16.10	21.82	26.08	26.78	27.42	28.03
11.00	8.21	14.91	20.14	24.01	24.64	25.22	25.77
11.25	7.60	13.74	18.50	21.99	22.56	23.08	23.57
11.50	6.98	12.58	16.89	20.03	20.53	21.00	21.43
11.75	6.37	11.45	15.32	18.11	18.56	18.98	19.36
12.00	5.77	10.33	13.78	16.25	16.64	17.01	17.34
12.25	5.17	9.22	12.27	14.43	14.78	15.09	15.38
12.50	4.58	8.14	10.79	12.66	12.96	13.23	13.48
12.75	3.99	7.07	9.34	10.94	11.19	11.42	11.63
13.00	3.41	6.01	7.92	9.25	9.46	9.65	9.83
13.25	2.83	4.97	6.54	7.61	7.78	7.94	8.08
13.50	2.25	3.95	5.17	6.01	6.15	6.26	6.37
13.75	1.68	2.94	3.84	4.46	4.55	4.64	4.72
14.00	1.12	1.95	2.53	2.93	2.99	3.05	3.10
14.25	0.56	0.97	1.25	1.45	1.48	1.51	1.53
14.50	0.00	0.00	0.00	0.00	0.00	0.00	0.00

Valuation of Assumable Mortgages

CURRENT RATE: 14½%

OLD RATE	24 YEARS	25 YEARS	26 YEARS	27 YEARS	28 YEARS	29 YEARS	30 YEARS
4.00	130.74	135.33	139.81	144.16	148.39	152.51	156.50
4.25	125.01	129.29	133.46	137.51	141.43	145.24	148.92
4.50	119.48	123.48	127.36	131.12	134.76	138.28	141.68
4.75	114.15	117.88	121.49	124.98	128.35	131.61	134.75
5.00	109.01	112.48	115.84	119.08	122.21	125.22	128.11
5.25	104.05	107.29	110.41	113.41	116.31	119.09	121.78
5.50	99.27	102.28	105.18	107.96	110.64	113.21	115.67
5.75	94.65	97.45	100.14	102.72	105.20	107.57	109.84
6.00	90.19	92.79	95.29	97.68	99.97	102.16	104.25
6.25	85.88	88.30	90.62	92.83	94.95	96.96	98.88
6.50	81.72	83.97	86.12	88.16	90.11	91.97	93.74
6.75	77.70	79.79	81.77	83.67	85.47	87.18	88.80
7.00	73.82	75.75	77.59	79.34	81.00	82.57	84.06
7.25	70.06	71.85	73.55	75.17	76.69	78.14	79.51
7.50	66.43	68.09	69.66	71.15	72.55	73.88	75.13
7.75	62.92	64.45	65.90	67.27	68.56	69.78	70.93
8.00	59.53	60.94	62.28	63.54	64.72	65.84	66.89
8.25	56.24	57.54	58.77	59.93	61.02	62.04	63.00
8.50	53.06	54.26	55.39	56.45	57.45	58.38	59.26
8.75	49.98	51.09	52.13	53.10	54.01	54.86	55.66
9.00	47.00	48.02	48.97	49.86	50.69	51.47	52.19
9.25	44.12	45.05	45.92	46.73	47.49	48.19	48.85
9.50	41.32	42.17	42.97	43.71	44.39	45.04	45.63
9.75	38.62	39.39	40.11	40.78	41.41	41.99	42.53
10.00	35.99	36.70	37.35	37.96	38.53	39.05	39.54
10.25	33.45	34.09	34.68	35.23	35.74	36.22	36.65
10.50	30.98	31.56	32.10	32.59	33.05	33.48	33.87
10.75	28.59	29.11	29.59	30.04	30.45	30.83	31.18
11.00	26.27	26.74	27.17	27.57	27.94	28.27	28.59
11.25	24.02	24.44	24.82	25.18	25.50	25.80	26.08
11.50	21.83	22.20	22.54	22.86	23.15	23.41	23.66
11.75	19.71	20.04	20.34	20.62	20.87	21.10	21.31
12.00	17.65	17.94	18.20	18.44	18.66	18.86	19.05
12.25	15.65	15.90	16.13	16.34	16.53	16.70	16.86
12.50	13.71	13.92	14.12	14.29	14.46	14.60	14.74
12.75	11.82	12.00	12.17	12.31	12.45	12.57	12.69
13.00	9.99	10.14	10.27	10.39	10.51	10.61	10.70
13.25	8.21	8.32	8.43	8.53	8.62	8.70	8.77
13.50	6.47	6.56	6.65	6.72	6.79	6.85	6.91
13.75	4.79	4.85	4.91	4.97	5.02	5.06	5.10
14.00	0.10	0.10	0.20	0.20	0.20	0.02	0.00
14.25	1.55	1.57	1.59	1.61	1.62	1.64	1.65
14.50	0.00	0.00	0.00	0.00	0.00	0.00	0.00

Valuation of Assumable Mortgages

CURRENT RATE: 15%

OLD RATE	5 YEARS	10 YEARS	15 YEARS	20 YEARS	21 YEARS	22 YEARS	23 YEARS
4.00	29.18	59.35	89.21	117.30	122.61	127.80	132.88
4.25	28.39	57.50	86.05	112.65	117.65	122.53	127.29
4.50	27.61	55.67	82.95	108.14	112.84	117.43	121.89
4.75	26.83	53.88	79.93	103.77	108.19	112.50	116.68
5.00	26.06	52.11	76.99	99.53	103.69	107.73	111.65
5.25	25.30	50.37	74.10	95.41	99.33	103.12	106.78
5.50	24.55	48.66	71.29	91.43	95.10	98.65	102.08
5.75	23.80	46.98	68.54	87.55	91.01	94.33	97.54
6.00	23.05	45.32	65.86	83.80	87.04	90.15	93.15
6.25	22.32	43.69	63.23	80.15	83.19	86.11	88.91
6.50	21.59	42.09	60.67	76.61	79.46	82.19	84.80
6.75	20.86	40.51	58.16	73.18	75.84	78.39	80.83
7.00	20.14	38.95	55.71	69.84	72.34	74.72	76.99
7.25	19.43	37.42	53.32	66.60	68.93	71.16	73.27
7.50	18.72	35.92	50.98	63.46	65.63	67.71	69.68
7.75	18.02	34.43	48.69	60.40	62.43	64.36	66.19
8.00	17.33	32.97	46.45	57.43	59.32	61.12	62.82
8.25	16.64	31.54	44.27	54.54	56.30	57.97	59.55
8.50	15.95	30.12	42.13	51.73	53.37	54.92	56.39
8.75	15.28	28.73	40.04	49.01	50.53	51.97	53.32
9.00	14.60	27.36	37.99	46.35	47.77	49.10	50.35
9.25	13.94	26.01	35.99	43.78	45.08	46.31	47.47
9.50	13.28	24.68	34.03	41.27	42.48	43.61	44.67
9.75	12.62	23.37	32.12	38.83	39.94	40.99	41.96
10.00	11.97	22.08	30.24	36.45	37.48	38.44	39.34
10.25	11.32	20.81	28.41	34.14	35.08	35.96	36.79
10.50	10.68	19.56	26.61	31.89	32.76	33.56	34.31
10.75	10.05	18.33	24.86	29.70	30.49	31.23	31.91
11.00	9.42	17.12	23.14	27.57	28.29	28.96	29.58
11.25	8.79	15.93	21.46	25.50	26.15	26.75	27.31
11.50	8.17	14.75	19.81	23.48	24.06	24.61	25.11
11.75	7.56	13.59	18.20	21.51	22.04	22.53	22.98
12.00	6.95	12.45	16.62	19.59	20.06	20.50	20.90
12.25	6.34	11.33	15.07	17.72	18.14	18.53	18.88
12.50	5.74	10.22	13.55	15.90	16.27	16.61	16.92
12.75	5.15	9.13	12.07	14.13	14.45	14.74	15.01
13.00	4.56	8.05	10.62	12.39	12.67	12.93	13.16
13.25	3.97	6.99	9.19	10.71	10.94	11.16	11.35
13.50	3.39	5.95	7.80	9.06	9.26	9.44	9.60
13.75	2.81	4.92	6.43	7.46	7.61	7.76	7.89
14.00	2.24	3.91	5.09	5.89	6.01	6.13	6.23
14.25	1.67	2.91	3.78	4.36	4.45	4.53	4.61
14.50	1.11	1.93	2.50	2.87	2.93	2.98	3.03
14.75	0.55	0.96	1.24	1.42	1.45	1.47	1.50
15.00	0.00	0.00	0.00	0.00	0.00	0.00	0.00

Valuation of Assumable Mortgages

CURRENT RATE: 15%

OLD RATE	24 YEARS	25 YEARS	26 YEARS	27 YEARS	28 YEARS	29 YEARS	30 YEARS
4.00	137.83	142.66	147.35	151.92	156.36	160.67	164.85
4.25	131.92	136.43	140.81	145.06	149.18	153.17	157.03
4.50	126.23	130.43	134.51	138.47	142.29	145.98	149.55
4.75	120.73	124.66	128.46	132.13	135.68	139.10	142.39
5.00	115.44	119.10	122.64	126.05	129.34	132.50	135.54
5.25	110.32	113.74	117.03	120.20	123.25	126.17	128.98
5.50	105.39	108.57	111.64	114.58	117.40	120.11	122.70
5.75	100.63	103.60	106.44	109.17	111.78	114.28	116.67
6.00	96.03	98.79	101.44	103.97	106.39	108.70	110.90
6.25	91.59	94.16	96.62	98.96	101.20	103.33	105.36
6.50	87.31	89.69	91.97	94.15	96.21	98.18	100.05
6.75	83.16	85.38	87.50	89.51	91.42	93.23	94.95
7.00	79.16	81.22	83.18	85.04	86.80	88.48	90.06
7.25	75.29	77.20	79.02	80.74	82.36	83.90	85.35
7.50	71.55	73.32	75.00	76.59	78.09	79.50	80.84
7.75	67.93	69.57	71.13	72.59	73.97	75.27	76.50
8.00	64.43	65.95	67.38	68.74	70.01	71.20	72.32
8.25	61.04	62.45	63.77	65.02	66.19	67.28	68.31
8.50	57.77	59.06	60.28	61.43	62.50	63.51	64.45
8.75	54.59	55.79	56.91	57.97	58.95	59.87	60.73
9.00	51.52	52.63	53.66	54.62	55.52	56.36	57.15
9.25	48.55	49.56	50.51	51.39	52.22	52.99	53.70
9.50	45.67	46.60	47.47	48.28	49.03	49.73	50.38
9.75	42.88	43.73	44.52	45.26	45.95	46.58	47.17
10.00	40.17	40.95	41.68	42.35	42.97	43.55	44.08
10.25	37.55	38.26	38.92	39.53	40.10	40.62	41.11
10.50	35.01	35.66	36.25	36.81	37.32	37.79	38.23
10.75	32.54	33.13	33.67	34.17	34.64	35.06	35.45
11.00	30.15	30.68	31.17	31.62	32.04	32.42	32.77
11.25	27.83	28.31	28.75	29.16	29.53	29.87	30.19
11.50	25.58	26.01	26.40	26.77	27.10	27.40	27.68
11.75	23.39	23.78	24.13	24.45	24.75	25.02	25.27
12.00	21.27	21.61	21.92	22.21	22.47	22.71	22.93
12.25	19.21	19.51	19.78	20.04	20.26	20.47	20.66
12.50	17.21	17.47	17.71	17.93	18.13	18.31	18.48
12.75	15.26	15.49	15.70	15.89	16.06	16.21	16.36
13.00	13.37	13.57	13.74	13.90	14.05	14.18	14.31
13.25	11.53	11.70	11.85	11.98	12.11	12.22	12.32
13.50	9.75	9.88	10.00	10.12	10.22	10.31	10.39
13.75	8.01	8.12	8.22	8.31	8.39	8.46	8.53
14.00	6.32	6.40	6.48	6.55	6.61	6.67	6.72
14.25	4.67	4.73	4.79	4.84	4.88	4.92	4.96
14.50	3.07	3.11	3.15	3.18	3.21	3.23	3.26
14.75	1.52	1.54	1.55	1.57	1.58	1.59	1.60
15.00	0.00	0.00	0.00	0.00	0.00	0.00	0.00

Valuation of Assumable Mortgages

CURRENT RATE: 15½%

OLD RATE	5 YEARS	10 YEARS	15 YEARS	20 YEARS	21 YEARS	22 YEARS	23 YEARS
4.00	30.61	62.39	93.86	123.42	129.00	134.45	139.78
4.25	29.81	60.50	90.62	118.64	123.90	129.03	134.02
4.50	29.02	58.64	87.45	114.00	118.95	123.78	128.47
4.75	28.24	56.81	84.36	109.51	114.17	118.70	123.10
5.00	27.46	55.01	81.34	105.15	109.54	113.79	117.92
5.25	26.69	53.24	78.38	100.92	105.05	109.05	112.91
5.50	25.93	51.49	75.50	96.82	100.70	104.45	108.07
5.75	25.17	49.78	72.68	92.84	96.49	100.01	103.40
6.00	24.42	48.09	69.93	88.98	92.41	95.71	98.88
6.25	23.67	46.43	67.24	85.23	88.45	91.54	94.51
6.50	22.93	44.79	64.62	81.59	84.61	87.51	90.28
6.75	22.20	43.18	62.05	78.06	80.89	83.60	86.19
7.00	21.47	41.60	59.54	74.63	77.28	79.82	82.24
7.25	20.75	40.04	57.09	71.30	73.78	76.15	78.41
7.50	20.04	38.51	54.69	68.06	70.39	72.60	74.70
7.75	19.33	37.00	52.35	64.92	67.09	69.16	71.12
8.00	18.63	35.51	50.05	61.86	63.89	65.82	67.64
8.25	17.93	34.05	47.81	58.89	60.79	62.58	64.28
8.50	17.24	32.60	45.62	56.01	57.78	59.45	61.02
8.75	16.55	31.19	43.48	53.20	54.85	56.40	57.86
9.00	15.87	29.79	41.38	50.48	52.01	53.45	54.80
9.25	15.20	28.41	39.33	47.83	49.25	50.58	51.84
9.50	14.53	27.06	37.33	45.25	46.56	47.80	48.96
9.75	13.87	25.72	35.36	42.74	43.96	45.10	46.17
10.00	13.21	24.41	33.44	40.30	41.42	42.48	43.46
10.25	12.55	23.12	31.56	37.92	38.96	39.93	40.84
10.50	11.91	21.84	29.73	35.61	36.57	37.46	38.29
10.75	11.26	20.59	27.93	33.36	34.24	35.06	35.82
11.00	10.63	19.35	26.17	31.17	31.97	32.72	33.42
11.25	10.00	18.14	24.44	29.03	29.77	30.45	31.09
11.50	9.37	16.94	22.75	26.95	27.63	28.25	28.82
11.75	8.75	15.76	21.10	24.93	25.54	26.10	26.62
12.00	8.13	14.60	19.48	22.96	23.51	24.02	24.48
12.25	7.52	13.45	17.90	21.04	21.53	21.99	22.40
12.50	6.91	12.32	16.35	19.16	19.61	20.01	20.38
12.75	6.31	11.21	14.83	17.34	17.73	18.09	18.42
13.00	5.71	10.11	13.34	15.56	15.91	16.22	16.51
13.25	5.12	9.03	11.88	13.83	14.13	14.40	14.65
13.50	4.53	7.97	10.45	12.13	12.39	12.63	12.85
13.75	3.95	6.92	9.05	10.48	10.70	10.90	11.09
14.00	3.37	5.89	7.68	8.87	9.06	9.22	9.37
14.25	2.80	4.87	6.33	7.30	7.45	7.59	7.71
14.50	2.23	3.87	5.02	5.77	5.89	5.99	6.08
14.75	1.67	2.88	3.72	4.28	4.36	4.43	4.50
15.00	1.11	1.91	2.46	2.82	2.87	2.92	2.96
15.25	0.55	0.95	1.22	1.39	1.42	1.44	1.46
15.50	0.00	0.00	0.00	0.00	0.00	0.00	0.00

Valuation of Assumable Mortgages

CURRENT RATE: 15½%

OLD RATE	24 YEARS	25 YEARS	26 YEARS	27 YEARS	28 YEARS	29 YEARS	30 YEARS
4.00	144.97	150.03	154.95	159.73	164.37	168.88	173.25
4.25	138.89	143.61	148.20	152.65	156.97	161.14	165.18
4.50	133.02	137.44	141.71	145.86	149.86	153.73	157.46
4.75	127.36	131.49	135.47	139.33	143.04	146.63	150.08
5.00	121.90	125.76	129.47	133.05	136.50	139.82	143.01
5.25	116.64	120.23	123.70	127.02	130.22	133.29	136.24
5.50	111.56	114.91	118.13	121.23	124.19	127.03	129.75
5.75	106.65	109.78	112.78	115.65	118.40	121.03	123.54
6.00	101.92	104.83	107.62	110.29	112.84	115.27	117.58
6.25	97.35	100.06	102.66	105.13	107.49	109.73	111.87
6.50	92.93	95.46	97.87	100.16	102.35	104.42	106.39
6.75	88.66	91.02	93.25	95.38	97.40	99.32	101.13
7.00	84.54	86.73	88.80	90.78	92.64	94.41	96.08
7.25	80.55	82.59	84.51	86.34	88.06	89.69	91.23
7.50	76.70	78.59	80.37	82.06	83.65	85.16	86.57
7.75	72.97	74.72	76.38	77.94	79.41	80.79	82.09
8.00	69.37	70.99	72.52	73.97	75.32	76.59	77.78
8.25	65.88	67.38	68.80	70.13	71.38	72.55	73.64
8.50	62.50	63.90	65.21	66.43	67.58	68.65	69.66
8.75	59.24	60.52	61.73	62.86	63.92	64.90	65.82
9.00	56.07	57.26	58.38	59.41	60.38	61.29	62.13
9.25	53.01	54.11	55.13	56.09	56.98	57.80	58.57
9.50	50.04	51.05	51.99	52.87	53.69	54.44	55.14
9.75	47.17	48.10	48.96	49.76	50.51	51.20	51.84
10.00	44.38	45.23	46.03	46.76	47.44	48.07	48.65
10.25	41.68	42.46	43.19	43.86	44.48	45.05	45.58
10.50	39.06	39.78	40.44	41.05	41.61	42.13	42.61
10.75	36.52	37.17	37.78	38.33	38.84	39.31	39.75
11.00	34.06	34.65	35.20	35.70	36.17	36.59	36.98
11.25	31.67	32.21	32.70	33.16	33.58	33.96	34.31
11.50	29.35	29.84	30.28	30.69	31.07	31.42	31.73
11.75	27.10	27.54	27.94	28.31	28.65	28.95	29.24
12.00	24.91	25.31	25.67	26.00	26.30	26.57	26.82
12.25	22.79	23.14	23.46	23.76	24.02	24.27	24.49
12.50	20.73	21.04	21.32	21.58	21.82	22.04	22.23
12.75	18.72	19.00	19.25	19.48	19.68	19.87	20.04
13.00	16.77	17.02	17.24	17.43	17.62	17.78	17.93
13.25	14.88	15.09	15.28	15.45	15.61	15.75	15.88
13.50	13.04	13.22	13.38	13.53	13.66	13.78	13.89
13.75	11.25	11.40	11.54	11.66	11.77	11.87	11.96
14.00	9.51	9.64	9.75	9.85	9.94	10.02	10.10
14.25	7.82	7.92	8.01	8.09	8.16	8.23	8.29
14.50	6.17	6.25	6.32	6.38	6.43	6.48	6.53
14.75	4.56	4.62	4.67	4.72	4.76	4.79	4.82
15.00	3.00	3.04	3.07	3.10	3.13	3.15	3.17
15.25	1.48	1.50	1.51	1.53	1.54	1.55	1.56
15.50	0.00	0.00	0.00	0.00	0.00	0.00	0.00

Valuation of Assumable Mortgages

CURRENT RATE: 16%

OLD RATE	5 YEARS	10 YEARS	15 YEARS	20 YEARS	21 YEARS	22 YEARS	23 YEARS
4.00	32.04	65.45	98.56	129.59	135.44	141.15	146.72
4.25	31.24	63.53	95.23	124.67	130.19	135.57	140.80
4.50	30.44	61.63	91.99	119.91	125.11	130.17	135.08
4.75	29.65	59.77	88.82	115.29	120.19	124.95	129.56
5.00	28.86	57.93	85.72	110.81	115.43	119.90	124.23
5.25	28.08	56.13	82.70	106.47	110.81	115.02	119.08
5.50	27.31	54.35	79.75	102.25	106.34	110.29	114.10
5.75	26.55	52.60	76.86	98.16	102.01	105.72	109.29
6.00	25.79	50.88	74.05	94.19	97.81	101.29	104.64
6.25	25.03	49.19	71.29	90.34	93.74	97.01	100.14
6.50	24.29	47.53	68.60	86.60	89.80	92.86	95.79
6.75	23.55	45.89	65.97	82.97	85.97	88.84	91.58
7.00	22.81	44.27	63.40	79.45	82.27	84.95	87.51
7.25	22.08	42.68	60.89	76.02	78.67	81.18	83.58
7.50	21.36	41.12	58.43	72.70	75.18	77.53	79.76
7.75	20.64	39.58	56.03	69.47	71.79	73.99	76.07
8.00	19.93	38.07	53.69	66.33	68.50	70.56	72.50
8.25	19.23	36.58	51.39	63.28	65.31	67.23	69.04
8.50	18.53	35.11	49.15	60.32	62.21	64.00	65.69
8.75	17.84	33.66	46.95	57.43	59.20	60.87	62.44
9.00	17.15	32.24	44.80	54.63	56.28	57.83	59.29
9.25	16.47	30.84	42.70	51.91	53.44	54.88	56.23
9.50	15.79	29.46	40.65	49.26	50.68	52.02	53.27
9.75	15.12	28.10	38.64	46.68	48.00	49.25	50.40
10.00	14.45	26.76	36.67	44.17	45.40	46.55	47.62
10.25	13.79	25.44	34.75	41.73	42.87	43.93	44.92
10.50	13.14	24.14	32.87	39.35	40.41	41.39	42.30
10.75	12.49	22.87	31.02	37.04	38.01	38.91	39.75
11.00	11.85	21.61	29.22	34.79	35.68	36.51	37.28
11.25	11.21	20.37	27.45	32.59	33.42	34.18	34.88
11.50	10.57	19.15	25.72	30.46	31.21	31.91	32.55
11.75	9.95	17.94	24.03	28.38	29.07	29.70	30.29
12.00	9.32	16.76	22.37	26.35	26.98	27.56	28.09
12.25	8.70	15.59	20.75	24.38	24.95	25.47	25.95
12.50	8.09	14.44	19.16	22.45	22.97	23.44	23.87
12.75	7.48	13.31	17.61	20.58	21.04	21.46	21.85
13.00	6.88	12.19	16.08	18.75	19.16	19.54	19.89
13.25	6.28	11.09	14.59	16.97	17.33	17.67	17.97
13.50	5.69	10.01	13.12	15.23	15.55	15.85	16.11
13.75	5.10	8.94	11.69	13.53	13.82	14.07	14.30
14.00	4.51	7.89	10.28	11.88	12.12	12.34	12.54
14.25	3.93	6.85	8.91	10.27	10.47	10.66	10.83
14.50	3.36	5.83	7.56	8.69	8.86	9.02	9.16
14.75	2.79	4.82	6.23	7.16	7.29	7.42	7.53
15.00	2.22	3.83	4.94	5.66	5.76	5.86	5.95
15.25	1.66	2.85	3.67	4.19	4.27	4.34	4.40
15.50	1.10	1.89	2.42	2.76	2.81	2.86	2.90
15.75	0.55	0.94	1.20	1.36	1.39	1.41	1.43
16.00	0.00	0.00	0.00	0.00	0.00	0.00	0.00

Valuation of Assumable Mortgages

CURRENT RATE: 16%

OLD RATE	24 YEARS	25 YEARS	26 YEARS	27 YEARS	28 YEARS	29 YEARS	30 YEARS
4.00	152.16	157.44	162.59	167.58	172.43	177.12	181.67
4.25	145.89	150.84	155.64	160.29	164.79	169.15	173.36
4.50	139.85	144.48	148.95	153.28	157.47	161.51	165.40
4.75	134.03	138.35	142.53	146.56	150.44	154.19	157.79
5.00	128.41	132.45	136.35	140.10	143.70	147.17	150.50
5.25	122.99	126.77	130.40	133.88	137.23	140.45	143.53
5.50	117.76	121.29	124.67	127.91	131.02	134.00	136.84
5.75	112.71	116.00	119.15	122.17	125.05	127.81	130.44
6.00	107.84	110.91	113.84	116.65	119.32	121.87	124.29
6.25	103.13	106.00	108.73	111.33	113.81	116.16	118.40
6.50	98.59	101.26	103.80	106.21	108.51	110.69	112.76
6.75	94.20	96.68	99.04	101.29	103.41	105.43	107.33
7.00	89.95	92.26	94.46	96.54	98.51	100.37	102.13
7.25	85.85	88.00	90.04	91.97	93.79	95.51	97.13
7.50	81.88	83.88	85.78	87.56	89.25	90.83	92.32
7.75	78.05	79.91	81.66	83.32	84.87	86.33	87.71
8.00	74.33	76.06	77.69	79.22	80.66	82.01	83.27
8.25	70.74	72.35	73.86	75.27	76.60	77.84	79.00
8.50	67.27	68.76	70.15	71.46	72.68	73.83	74.89
8.75	63.91	65.29	66.58	67.78	68.91	69.96	70.94
9.00	60.65	61.93	63.12	64.23	65.27	66.23	67.13
9.25	57.50	58.68	59.78	60.80	61.76	62.64	63.46
9.50	54.44	55.53	56.55	57.49	58.37	59.18	59.93
9.75	51.48	52.49	53.42	54.29	55.09	55.83	56.52
10.00	48.62	49.54	50.40	51.20	51.93	52.61	53.24
10.25	45.84	46.69	47.48	48.20	48.88	49.50	50.07
10.50	43.14	43.92	44.64	45.31	45.93	46.49	47.01
10.75	40.53	41.24	41.90	42.51	43.07	43.59	44.06
11.00	37.99	38.65	39.25	39.80	40.31	40.78	41.21
11.25	35.53	36.13	36.68	37.18	37.64	38.07	38.45
11.50	33.14	33.69	34.19	34.64	35.06	35.44	35.79
11.75	30.83	31.32	31.77	32.19	32.56	32.91	33.22
12.00	28.58	29.02	29.43	29.80	30.14	30.45	30.74
12.25	26.39	26.79	27.16	27.49	27.80	28.08	28.33
12.50	24.27	24.63	24.96	25.26	25.53	25.78	26.00
12.75	22.20	22.53	22.82	23.09	23.33	23.55	23.75
13.00	20.20	20.49	20.75	20.98	21.20	21.39	21.57
13.25	18.25	18.50	18.73	18.94	19.13	19.30	19.45
13.50	16.36	16.58	16.78	16.96	17.12	17.27	17.40
13.75	14.52	14.71	14.88	15.04	15.18	15.30	15.42
14.00	12.72	12.89	13.03	13.17	13.29	13.40	13.49
14.25	10.98	11.12	11.24	11.35	11.46	11.55	11.63
14.50	9.28	9.40	9.50	9.59	9.67	9.75	9.82
14.75	7.63	7.72	7.81	7.88	7.95	8.01	8.06
15.00	6.02	6.09	6.16	6.21	6.27	6.31	6.35
15.25	4.46	4.51	4.55	4.60	4.63	4.67	4.69
15.50	2.93	2.97	3.00	3.02	3.05	3.07	3.08
15.75	1.45	1.46	1.48	1.49	1.50	1.51	1.52
16.00	0.00	0.00	0.00	0.00	0.00	0.00	0.00

Valuation of Assumable Mortgages

CURRENT RATE: 16½%

OLD RATE	5 YEARS	10 YEARS	15 YEARS	20 YEARS	21 YEARS	22 YEARS	23 YEARS
4.00	33.49	68.54	103.29	135.80	141.92	147.89	153.71
4.25	32.68	66.58	99.89	130.75	136.52	142.15	147.62
4.50	31.87	64.65	96.56	125.86	131.31	136.60	141.74
4.75	31.07	62.75	93.32	121.12	126.25	131.23	136.06
5.00	30.28	60.88	90.15	116.51	121.36	126.05	130.58
5.25	29.49	59.05	87.06	112.05	116.62	121.03	125.28
5.50	28.71	57.24	84.03	107.72	112.02	116.17	120.16
5.75	27.93	55.46	81.08	103.52	107.57	111.47	115.22
6.00	27.16	53.70	78.19	99.45	103.26	106.92	110.43
6.25	26.40	51.98	75.38	95.49	99.08	102.52	105.81
6.50	25.65	50.28	72.62	91.65	95.02	98.25	101.34
6.75	24.90	48.61	69.93	87.92	91.09	94.12	97.01
7.00	24.16	46.97	67.30	84.30	87.28	90.12	92.83
7.25	23.42	45.35	64.72	80.79	83.59	86.25	88.78
7.50	22.69	43.76	62.21	77.37	80.00	82.49	84.86
7.75	21.97	42.19	59.75	74.05	76.52	78.85	81.06
8.00	21.25	40.65	57.35	70.83	73.14	75.32	77.39
8.25	20.53	39.13	55.00	67.70	69.86	71.90	73.83
8.50	19.83	37.63	52.70	64.65	66.68	68.58	70.38
8.75	19.13	36.16	50.45	61.69	63.59	65.37	67.04
9.00	18.43	34.71	48.26	58.82	60.58	62.24	63.80
9.25	17.74	33.28	46.11	56.02	57.67	59.21	60.66
9.50	17.06	31.87	44.00	53.29	54.83	56.27	57.62
9.75	16.38	30.49	41.94	50.65	52.08	53.42	54.66
10.00	15.71	29.13	39.93	48.07	49.40	50.64	51.80
10.25	15.04	27.78	37.96	45.56	46.80	47.95	49.02
10.50	14.38	26.46	36.03	43.12	44.27	45.34	46.33
10.75	13.72	25.16	34.15	40.75	41.81	42.80	43.71
11.00	13.07	23.88	32.30	38.43	39.42	40.33	41.17
11.25	12.43	22.62	30.49	36.18	37.09	37.93	38.70
11.50	11.79	21.37	28.72	33.99	34.82	35.60	36.31
11.75	11.15	20.15	26.99	31.85	32.62	33.33	33.98
12.00	10.52	18.94	25.29	29.77	30.48	31.12	31.72
12.25	9.89	17.75	23.63	27.74	28.39	28.98	29.52
12.50	9.27	16.58	22.00	25.77	26.35	26.89	27.38
12.75	8.66	15.42	20.41	23.84	24.37	24.86	25.30
13.00	8.05	14.29	18.85	21.96	22.44	22.88	23.28
13.25	7.44	13.17	17.32	20.13	20.56	20.96	21.32
13.50	6.84	12.06	15.82	18.35	18.73	19.08	19.40
13.75	6.25	10.97	14.35	16.61	16.95	17.26	17.54
14.00	5.66	9.90	12.91	14.91	15.21	15.48	15.73
14.25	5.07	8.85	11.50	13.25	13.51	13.75	13.97
14.50	4.49	7.81	10.12	11.63	11.86	12.06	12.25
14.75	3.91	6.78	8.77	10.05	10.25	10.42	10.58
15.00	0.04	5.77	7.44	0.01	0.07	0.02	0.05
15.25	2.77	4.77	6.14	7.01	7.14	7.25	7.36
15.50	2.21	3.79	4.86	5.54	5.64	5.73	5.81
15.75	1.65	2.82	3.61	4.11	4.18	4.24	4.30
16.00	1.10	1.87	2.38	2.71	2.75	2.79	2.83
16.25	0.55	0.93	1.18	1.34	1.36	1.38	1.40
16.50	0.00	0.00	0.00	0.00	0.00	0.00	0.00

Valuation of Assumable Mortgages

CURRENT RATE: 16½%

OLD RATE	24 YEARS	25 YEARS	26 YEARS	27 YEARS	28 YEARS	29 YEARS	30 YEARS
4.00	159.38	164.90	170.26	175.46	180.51	185.40	190.13
4.25	152.94	158.10	163.11	167.96	172.65	177.19	181.57
4.50	146.73	151.56	156.23	160.75	165.11	169.32	173.37
4.75	140.74	145.26	149.62	153.82	157.88	161.78	165.53
5.00	134.96	139.18	143.25	147.17	150.94	154.56	158.03
5.25	129.38	133.33	137.13	140.78	144.28	147.63	150.84
5.50	124.00	127.69	131.24	134.63	137.88	140.99	143.95
5.75	118.81	122.26	125.56	128.72	131.73	134.61	137.36
6.00	113.80	117.02	120.09	123.03	125.83	128.49	131.03
6.25	108.96	111.96	114.83	117.56	120.15	122.62	124.96
6.50	104.28	107.08	109.75	112.29	114.70	116.98	119.15
6.75	99.76	102.38	104.86	107.22	109.45	111.56	113.56
7.00	95.40	97.83	100.14	102.33	104.40	106.35	108.20
7.25	91.17	93.45	95.60	97.63	99.54	101.35	103.05
7.50	87.09	89.21	91.21	93.09	94.86	96.53	98.10
7.75	83.15	85.12	86.97	88.72	90.36	91.90	93.35
8.00	79.33	81.16	82.89	84.50	86.02	87.44	88.77
8.25	75.64	77.34	78.94	80.44	81.84	83.15	84.38
8.50	72.06	73.65	75.13	76.51	77.81	79.02	80.14
8.75	68.61	70.07	71.45	72.73	73.92	75.04	76.07
9.00	65.26	66.62	67.89	69.07	70.17	71.20	72.15
9.25	62.01	63.27	64.45	65.54	66.56	67.50	68.37
9.50	58.87	60.04	61.12	62.13	63.07	63.93	64.73
9.75	55.83	56.91	57.91	58.84	59.69	60.49	61.22
10.00	52.88	53.87	54.80	55.65	56.44	57.17	57.84
10.25	50.02	50.94	51.79	52.57	53.30	53.96	54.57
10.50	47.24	48.09	48.87	49.59	50.26	50.87	51.43
10.75	44.55	45.33	46.05	46.71	47.32	47.88	48.39
11.00	41.96	42.66	43.32	43.92	44.48	44.99	45.45
11.25	39.42	40.07	40.67	41.22	41.73	42.19	42.61
11.50	36.96	37.56	38.11	38.61	39.07	39.49	39.87
11.75	34.58	35.12	35.62	36.08	36.50	36.88	37.22
12.00	32.26	32.76	33.21	33.63	34.01	34.35	34.66
12.25	30.01	30.46	30.88	31.25	31.59	31.90	32.18
12.50	27.83	28.24	28.61	28.95	29.26	29.53	29.79
12.75	25.71	26.08	26.41	26.71	26.99	27.24	27.46
13.00	23.65	23.98	24.28	24.55	24.79	25.02	25.22
13.25	21.64	21.94	22.20	22.45	22.66	22.86	23.04
13.50	19.60	19.95	20.10	20.41	20.60	20.77	20.93
13.75	17.80	18.03	18.24	18.43	18.60	18.75	18.89
14.00	15.95	16.16	16.34	16.50	16.65	16.78	16.90
14.25	14.16	14.34	14.49	14.64	14.76	14.88	14.98
14.50	12.42	12.57	12.70	12.82	12.93	13.03	13.11
14.75	10.72	10.84	10.96	11.06	11.15	11.23	11.30
15.00	9.06	9.17	9.26	9.34	9.42	9.49	9.55
15.25	7.45	7.54	7.61	7.68	7.74	7.79	7.84
15.50	5.88	5.95	6.01	6.06	6.10	6.14	6.18
15.75	4.36	4.40	4.44	4.48	4.51	4.54	4.57
16.00	2.87	2.90	2.92	2.95	2.97	2.99	3.00
16.25	1.41	1.43	1.44	1.45	1.46	1.47	1.48
16.50	0.00	0.00	0.00	0.00	0.00	0.00	0.00

Valuation of Assumable Mortgages

CURRENT RATE: 17%

OLD RATE	5 YEARS	10 YEARS	15 YEARS	20 YEARS	21 YEARS	22 YEARS	23 YEARS
4.00	34.95	71.66	108.06	142.05	148.44	154.67	160.74
4.25	34.12	69.66	104.58	136.87	142.90	148.77	154.48
4.50	33.31	67.70	101.18	131.85	137.54	143.07	148.44
4.75	32.50	65.76	97.86	126.98	132.35	137.56	142.60
5.00	31.70	63.86	94.62	122.26	127.32	132.23	136.97
5.25	30.90	61.99	91.45	117.68	122.46	127.07	131.52
5.50	30.11	60.14	88.35	113.23	117.74	122.08	126.26
5.75	29.33	58.33	85.33	108.92	113.17	117.25	121.18
6.00	28.55	56.55	82.38	104.74	108.74	112.58	116.26
6.25	27.78	54.79	79.49	100.68	104.44	108.06	111.51
6.50	27.02	53.06	76.67	96.73	100.28	103.67	106.91
6.75	26.26	51.36	73.92	92.91	96.25	99.43	102.47
7.00	25.51	49.69	71.22	89.19	92.33	95.32	98.17
7.25	24.77	48.04	68.59	85.58	88.53	91.34	94.01
7.50	24.03	46.42	66.02	82.08	84.85	87.48	89.98
7.75	23.30	44.82	63.50	78.67	81.28	83.74	86.08
8.00	22.57	43.25	61.04	75.36	77.81	80.12	82.30
8.25	21.85	41.70	58.64	72.15	74.44	76.60	78.64
8.50	21.13	40.18	56.29	69.02	71.17	73.19	75.10
8.75	20.43	38.68	53.99	65.98	68.00	69.89	71.66
9.00	19.72	37.20	51.74	63.03	64.91	66.68	68.34
9.25	19.03	35.74	49.54	60.15	61.92	63.57	65.11
9.50	18.34	34.31	47.38	57.36	59.01	60.55	61.98
9.75	17.65	32.90	45.28	54.64	56.18	57.61	58.95
10.00	16.97	31.51	43.22	52.00	53.43	54.77	56.01
10.25	16.30	30.15	41.20	49.42	50.76	52.00	53.15
10.50	15.63	28.80	39.23	46.92	48.16	49.31	50.38
10.75	14.96	27.47	37.29	44.48	45.63	46.70	47.69
11.00	14.30	26.17	35.40	42.11	43.18	44.17	45.08
11.25	13.65	24.88	33.55	39.79	40.79	41.70	42.54
11.50	13.00	23.62	31.74	37.54	38.46	39.30	40.08
11.75	12.36	22.37	29.97	35.35	36.20	36.97	37.69
12.00	11.72	21.14	28.23	33.21	33.99	34.71	35.36
12.25	11.09	19.93	26.53	31.13	31.85	32.50	33.11
12.50	10.47	18.73	24.87	29.10	29.76	30.36	30.91
12.75	9.84	17.56	23.24	27.13	27.73	28.27	28.77
13.00	9.23	16.40	21.64	25.20	25.74	26.24	26.70
13.25	8.62	15.26	20.07	23.32	23.81	24.27	24.68
13.50	8.01	14.13	18.54	21.49	21.93	22.34	22.71
13.75	7.41	13.03	17.04	19.70	20.10	20.47	20.80
14.00	6.81	11.94	15.56	17.96	18.31	18.64	18.94
14.25	6.22	10.86	14.12	16.25	16.57	16.86	17.12
14.50	5.63	9.80	12.71	14.59	14.87	15.13	15.36
14.75	5.05	8.75	11.32	12.97	13.22	13.44	13.64
15.00	4.47	7.72	9.96	11.39	11.60	11.79	11.96
15.25	3.89	6.71	8.63	9.85	10.03	10.19	10.33
15.50	3.32	5.71	7.32	8.34	8.49	8.62	8.74
15.75	2.76	4.72	6.04	6.87	6.99	7.10	7.19
16.00	2.20	3.75	4.79	5.43	5.52	5.61	5.68
16.25	1.64	2.79	3.56	4.03	4.09	4.15	4.21
16.50	1.09	1.85	2.35	2.65	2.70	2.74	2.77
16.75	0.54	0.92	1.16	1.31	1.33	1.35	1.37
17.00	0.00	0.00	0.00	0.00	0.00	0.00	0.00

Valuation of Assumable Mortgages

CURRENT RATE: 17%

OLD RATE	24 YEARS	25 YEARS	26 YEARS	27 YEARS	28 YEARS	29 YEARS	30 YEARS
4.00	166.65	172.39	177.97	183.38	188.63	193.71	198.62
4.25	160.03	165.40	170.62	175.66	180.54	185.25	189.81
4.50	153.64	158.67	163.54	168.24	172.78	177.16	181.37
4.75	147.48	152.19	156.74	161.12	165.34	169.40	173.30
5.00	141.54	145.95	150.19	154.28	158.20	161.97	165.50
5.25	135.81	139.93	143.90	147.70	151.34	154.84	158.18
5.50	130.28	134.14	137.83	141.37	144.76	148.00	151.09
5.75	124.94	128.55	132.00	135.29	138.44	141.44	144.30
6.00	119.79	123.16	126.37	129.44	132.36	135.15	137.79
6.25	114.81	117.96	120.96	123.81	126.52	129.10	131.55
6.50	110.00	112.94	115.74	118.39	120.91	123.30	125.56
6.75	105.36	108.10	110.71	113.17	115.51	117.72	119.81
7.00	100.87	103.43	105.85	108.15	110.32	112.36	114.29
7.25	96.53	98.92	101.18	103.31	105.32	107.21	108.99
7.50	92.33	94.56	96.66	98.64	100.50	102.25	103.90
7.75	88.28	90.35	92.31	94.14	95.87	97.49	99.00
8.00	84.35	86.29	88.10	89.81	91.40	92.90	94.30
8.25	80.56	82.36	84.04	85.62	87.10	88.48	89.77
8.50	76.88	78.56	80.12	81.59	82.95	84.23	85.41
8.75	73.33	74.88	76.34	77.69	78.96	80.13	81.22
9.00	69.88	71.33	72.68	73.93	75.10	76.18	77.19
9.25	66.55	67.89	69.14	70.30	71.38	72.37	73.30
9.50	63.32	64.56	65.72	66.79	67.78	68.70	69.55
9.75	60.19	61.34	62.41	63.40	64.32	65.16	65.94
10.00	57.16	58.23	59.21	60.13	60.97	61.74	62.46
10.25	54.22	55.21	56.12	56.96	57.73	58.44	59.10
10.50	51.37	52.28	53.12	53.89	54.60	55.26	55.86
10.75	48.60	49.44	50.22	50.93	51.58	52.18	52.73
11.00	45.92	46.70	47.41	48.06	48.66	49.21	49.70
11.25	43.32	44.03	44.69	45.28	45.83	46.33	46.79
11.50	40.80	41.45	42.05	42.60	43.10	43.55	43.97
11.75	38.34	38.94	39.49	39.99	40.45	40.86	41.24
12.00	35.97	36.51	37.01	37.47	37.88	38.26	38.60
12.25	33.65	34.15	34.61	35.03	35.40	35.74	36.05
12.50	31.41	31.87	32.28	32.66	33.00	33.30	33.58
12.75	29.23	29.64	30.02	30.36	30.67	30.94	31.19
13.00	27.11	27.48	27.82	28.13	28.41	28.66	28.88
13.25	25.05	25.39	25.69	25.97	26.21	26.44	26.64
13.50	23.04	23.35	23.62	23.87	24.09	24.28	24.47
13.75	21.10	21.37	21.61	21.83	22.03	22.21	22.00
14.00	19.20	19.44	19.66	19.85	20.03	20.18	20.32
14.25	17.36	17.57	17.76	17.93	18.08	18.22	18.34
14.50	15.56	15.75	15.92	16.00	16.20	16.32	16.42
14.75	13.82	13.98	14.12	14.25	14.37	14.47	14.56
15.00	12.12	12.26	12.38	12.49	12.59	12.67	12.75
15.25	10.46	10.58	10.68	10.77	10.86	10.93	10.99
15.50	8.85	8.95	9.03	9.11	9.17	9.23	9.29
15.75	7.28	7.36	7.42	7.48	7.54	7.59	7.63
16.00	5.75	5.81	5.86	5.91	5.95	5.98	6.02
16.25	4.26	4.30	4.34	4.37	4.40	4.43	4.45
16.50	2.80	2.83	2.85	2.87	2.89	2.91	2.93
16.75	1.38	1.40	1.41	1.42	1.43	1.44	1.44
17.00	0.00	0.00	0.00	0.00	0.00	0.00	0.00

Valuation of Assumable Mortgages

CURRENT RATE: 17½%

OLD RATE	5 YEARS	10 YEARS	15 YEARS	20 YEARS	21 YEARS	22 YEARS	23 YEARS
4.00	36.41	74.80	112.87	148.35	155.00	161.49	167.81
4.25	35.58	72.77	109.31	143.03	149.32	155.43	161.38
4.50	34.75	70.77	105.83	137.88	143.82	149.58	155.17
4.75	33.94	68.80	102.43	132.88	138.49	143.92	149.18
5.00	33.12	66.86	99.11	128.04	133.33	138.45	143.39
5.25	32.32	64.95	95.87	123.34	128.33	133.15	137.80
5.50	31.52	63.07	92.71	118.78	123.49	128.03	132.39
5.75	30.73	61.23	89.61	114.35	118.80	123.07	127.17
6.00	29.95	59.41	86.59	110.06	114.25	118.27	122.12
6.25	29.17	57.62	83.64	105.89	109.84	113.63	117.24
6.50	28.40	55.86	80.76	101.85	105.57	109.13	112.52
6.75	27.63	54.13	77.94	97.92	101.43	104.77	107.95
7.00	26.87	52.43	75.18	94.11	97.41	100.55	103.54
7.25	26.12	50.75	72.49	90.41	93.51	96.46	99.26
7.50	25.37	49.10	69.86	86.81	89.73	92.50	95.12
7.75	24.63	47.47	67.28	83.32	86.06	88.66	91.12
8.00	23.90	45.87	64.76	79.92	82.50	84.94	87.24
8.25	23.17	44.29	62.30	76.62	79.05	81.33	83.48
8.50	22.45	42.74	59.90	73.42	75.69	77.83	79.84
8.75	21.73	41.21	57.54	70.30	72.43	74.44	76.32
9.00	21.02	39.71	55.24	67.27	69.27	71.14	72.90
9.25	20.32	38.23	52.99	64.32	66.19	67.95	69.58
9.50	19.62	36.77	50.79	61.45	63.21	64.84	66.37
9.75	18.93	35.34	48.63	58.66	60.30	61.83	63.26
10.00	18.24	33.92	46.53	55.95	57.48	58.91	60.23
10.25	17.56	32.53	44.46	53.31	54.74	56.07	57.30
10.50	16.88	31.16	42.44	50.74	52.07	53.31	54.46
10.75	16.21	29.81	40.47	48.24	49.48	50.63	51.69
11.00	15.54	28.48	38.53	45.80	46.96	48.03	49.01
11.25	14.88	27.17	36.64	43.43	44.50	45.50	46.41
11.50	14.23	25.88	34.79	41.12	42.12	43.03	43.88
11.75	13.58	24.61	32.97	38.87	39.79	40.64	41.42
12.00	12.94	23.36	31.20	36.68	37.53	38.32	39.03
12.25	12.30	22.12	29.46	34.54	35.33	36.05	36.71
12.50	11.66	20.91	27.75	32.46	33.19	33.85	34.46
12.75	11.04	19.71	26.08	30.43	31.10	31.71	32.26
13.00	10.41	18.53	24.45	28.45	29.07	29.62	30.13
13.25	9.79	17.37	22.85	26.53	27.08	27.59	28.05
13.50	9.18	16.22	21.28	24.65	25.15	25.62	26.04
13.75	8.57	15.10	19.74	22.81	23.27	23.69	24.07
14.00	7.97	13.98	18.23	21.02	21.44	21.82	22.16
14.25	7.37	12.89	16.76	19.28	19.65	19.99	20.30
14.50	6.77	11.81	15.31	17.57	17.91	18.21	18.48
14.75	6.19	10.75	13.89	15.91	16.21	16.48	16.72
15.00	5.60	9.70	12.50	14.29	14.55	14.79	15.00
15.25	5.02	8.66	11.14	12.70	12.93	13.14	13.32
15.50	4.44	7.64	9.80	11.16	11.35	11.53	11.69
15.75	3.87	6.64	8.49	9.65	9.81	9.96	10.10
16.00	3.31	5.65	7.21	8.17	8.31	8.43	8.54
16.25	2.74	4.68	5.95	6.73	6.84	6.94	7.03
16.50	2.19	3.71	4.71	5.32	5.41	5.49	5.55
16.75	1.63	2.77	3.50	3.95	4.01	4.06	4.11
17.00	1.08	1.83	2.31	2.60	2.64	2.68	2.71
17.25	0.54	0.91	1.14	1.29	1.31	1.32	1.34
17.50	0.00	0.00	0.00	0.00	0.00	0.00	0.00

Valuation of Assumable Mortgages

CURRENT RATE: 17½%

OLD RATE	24 YEARS	25 YEARS	26 YEARS	27 YEARS	28 YEARS	29 YEARS	30 YEARS
4.00	173.95	179.92	185.72	191.33	196.78	202.04	207.14
4.25	167.15	172.74	178.15	183.39	188.46	193.35	198.07
4.50	160.58	165.82	170.88	175.77	180.48	185.02	189.40
4.75	154.26	159.16	163.89	168.45	172.83	177.05	181.10
5.00	148.15	152.75	157.16	161.41	165.49	169.40	173.15
5.25	142.27	146.56	150.69	154.65	158.44	162.07	165.54
5.50	136.58	140.61	144.46	148.15	151.67	155.04	158.25
5.75	131.10	134.86	138.46	141.89	145.17	148.29	151.27
6.00	125.80	129.32	132.68	135.88	138.92	141.82	144.57
6.25	120.69	123.98	127.11	130.09	132.92	135.60	138.15
6.50	115.75	118.83	121.75	124.52	127.15	129.63	131.99
6.75	110.98	113.85	116.58	119.15	121.59	123.90	126.08
7.00	106.37	109.05	111.59	113.99	116.25	118.39	120.40
7.25	101.91	104.42	106.78	109.01	111.11	113.09	114.95
7.50	97.60	99.94	102.14	104.21	106.16	107.99	109.71
7.75	93.43	95.61	97.66	99.59	101.40	103.09	104.68
8.00	89.40	91.44	93.34	95.13	96.81	98.37	99.84
8.25	85.50	87.40	89.17	90.83	92.38	93.83	95.18
8.50	81.73	83.49	85.14	86.68	88.12	89.46	90.70
8.75	78.07	79.72	81.25	82.68	84.01	85.24	86.39
9.00	74.54	76.06	77.49	78.81	80.04	81.18	82.24
9.25	71.11	72.53	73.85	75.08	76.21	77.27	78.24
9.50	67.79	69.11	70.34	71.47	72.52	73.49	74.39
9.75	64.58	65.80	66.94	67.99	68.95	69.85	70.67
10.00	61.46	62.60	63.65	64.62	65.51	66.33	67.09
10.25	58.44	59.49	60.47	61.36	62.18	62.94	63.63
10.50	55.51	56.49	57.39	58.21	58.97	59.66	60.30
10.75	52.67	53.57	54.40	55.16	55.86	56.50	57.08
11.00	49.92	50.75	51.52	52.21	52.86	53.44	53.97
11.25	47.25	48.01	48.72	49.36	49.95	50.48	50.97
11.50	44.65	45.36	46.01	46.60	47.13	47.62	48.07
11.75	42.13	42.78	43.38	43.92	44.41	44.86	45.27
12.00	39.69	40.29	40.83	41.33	41.78	42.18	42.55
12.25	37.31	37.86	38.36	38.81	39.22	39.59	39.93
12.50	35.01	35.51	35.96	36.38	36.75	37.09	37.39
12.75	32.77	33.22	33.64	34.01	34.35	34.66	34.93
13.00	30.59	31.01	31.38	31.72	32.03	32.31	32.56
13.25	28.47	28.85	29.19	29.50	29.78	30.03	30.25
13.50	26.41	26.76	27.06	27.34	27.59	27.82	28.02
13.75	24.41	24.72	25.00	25.25	25.47	25.67	25.85
14.00	22.47	22.74	22.99	23.21	23.42	23.59	23.75
14.25	20.57	20.82	21.04	21.24	21.42	21.58	21.72
14.50	18.73	18.95	19.15	19.32	19.48	19.62	19.74
14.75	16.93	17.13	17.30	17.46	17.59	17.72	17.83
15.00	15.19	15.36	15.51	15.64	15.76	15.87	15.97
15.25	13.49	13.63	13.76	13.88	13.99	14.08	14.16
15.50	11.83	11.96	12.07	12.17	12.26	12.33	12.40
15.75	10.22	10.32	10.42	10.50	10.57	10.64	10.70
16.00	8.64	8.73	8.81	8.88	8.94	8.99	9.04
16.25	7.11	7.18	7.24	7.30	7.35	7.39	7.43
16.50	5.62	5.67	5.72	5.76	5.80	5.83	5.86
16.75	4.16	4.20	4.23	4.26	4.29	4.31	4.34
17.00	2.74	2.76	2.79	2.81	2.82	2.84	2.85
17.25	1.35	1.36	1.38	1.38	1.39	1.40	1.41
17.50	0.00	0.00	0.00	0.00	0.00	0.00	0.00

Valuation of Assumable Mortgages

CURRENT RATE: 18%

OLD RATE	5 YEARS	10 YEARS	15 YEARS	20 YEARS	21 YEARS	22 YEARS	23 YEARS
4.00	37.88	77.97	117.72	154.68	161.60	168.34	174.91
4.25	37.04	75.90	114.07	149.23	155.77	162.13	168.31
4.50	36.21	73.86	110.51	143.94	150.12	156.12	161.94
4.75	35.38	71.85	107.04	138.82	144.66	150.31	155.78
5.00	34.56	69.88	103.65	133.85	139.37	144.70	149.84
5.25	33.75	67.94	100.33	129.03	134.24	139.26	144.10
5.50	32.94	66.03	97.09	124.36	129.27	134.00	138.55
5.75	32.14	64.15	93.93	119.82	124.46	128.92	133.19
6.00	31.35	62.30	90.84	115.42	119.80	123.99	128.01
6.25	30.56	60.48	87.82	111.14	115.27	119.23	123.00
6.50	29.78	58.69	84.87	107.00	110.89	114.61	118.15
6.75	29.01	56.92	81.99	102.97	106.64	110.14	113.47
7.00	28.24	55.19	79.17	99.06	102.52	105.81	108.93
7.25	27.48	53.48	76.41	95.26	98.52	101.61	104.54
7.50	26.73	51.80	73.72	91.57	94.64	97.55	100.30
7.75	25.98	50.14	71.09	87.99	90.88	93.61	96.19
8.00	25.24	48.51	68.52	84.51	87.23	89.79	92.20
8.25	24.50	46.91	66.00	81.13	83.68	86.09	88.35
8.50	23.77	45.33	63.54	77.84	80.24	82.49	84.61
8.75	23.05	43.77	61.13	74.64	76.89	79.01	80.99
9.00	22.33	42.24	58.78	71.53	73.65	75.63	77.48
9.25	21.62	40.73	56.47	68.51	70.49	72.35	74.08
9.50	20.91	39.25	54.22	65.57	67.43	69.17	70.78
9.75	20.21	37.79	52.02	62.71	64.45	66.08	67.58
10.00	19.52	36.35	49.86	59.93	61.56	63.07	64.48
10.25	18.83	34.93	47.75	57.22	58.74	60.16	61.47
10.50	18.14	33.53	45.69	54.58	56.01	57.33	58.55
10.75	17.46	32.16	43.67	52.02	53.35	54.58	55.71
11.00	16.79	30.81	41.69	49.52	50.76	51.91	52.96
11.25	16.13	29.47	39.75	47.09	48.24	49.31	50.29
11.50	15.46	28.16	37.86	44.72	45.79	46.78	47.69
11.75	14.81	26.86	36.00	42.41	43.41	44.33	45.17
12.00	14.16	25.59	34.18	40.16	41.09	41.94	42.72
12.25	13.51	24.33	32.40	37.97	38.83	39.62	40.34
12.50	12.87	23.10	30.66	35.84	36.63	37.36	38.02
12.75	12.23	21.88	28.95	33.76	34.49	35.16	35.77
13.00	11.60	20.68	27.28	31.73	32.41	33.02	33.58
13.25	10.98	19.49	25.64	29.75	30.37	30.94	31.45
13.50	10.36	18.33	24.04	27.82	28.39	28.91	29.38
13.75	9.74	17.18	22.47	25.94	26.46	26.93	27.36
14.00	9.13	16.05	20.93	24.11	24.58	25.01	25.40
14.25	8.53	14.93	19.42	22.32	22.75	23.14	23.49
14.50	7.93	13.83	17.94	20.57	20.96	21.31	21.62
14.75	7.33	12.75	16.49	18.87	19.22	19.53	19.81
15.00	6.74	11.68	15.06	17.20	17.51	17.80	18.05
15.25	6.15	10.63	13.67	15.58	15.86	16.10	16.33
15.50	5.57	9.59	12.30	13.99	14.24	14.45	14.65
15.75	4.99	8.57	10.96	12.44	12.66	12.85	13.02
16.00	4.42	7.56	9.65	10.93	11.11	11.28	11.42
16.25	3.85	6.57	8.36	9.45	9.61	9.75	9.87
16.50	3.29	5.59	7.10	8.01	8.14	8.25	8.35
16.75	2.73	4.63	5.86	6.60	6.70	6.79	6.87
17.00	2.18	3.68	4.64	5.22	5.30	5.37	5.43
17.25	1.63	2.74	3.45	3.87	3.93	3.98	4.03
17.50	1.08	1.81	2.28	2.55	2.59	2.62	2.65
17.75	0.54	0.90	1.13	1.26	1.28	1.30	1.31
18.00	0.00	0.00	0.00	0.00	0.00	0.00	0.00

Valuation of Assumable Mortgages

CURRENT RATE: 18%

OLD RATE	24 YEARS	25 YEARS	26 YEARS	27 YEARS	28 YEARS	29 YEARS	30 YEARS
4.00	181.29	187.48	193.49	199.31	204.95	210.40	215.68
4.25	174.30	180.10	185.72	191.16	196.40	201.47	206.36
4.50	167.56	173.00	178.25	183.32	188.21	192.91	197.44
4.75	161.07	166.16	171.07	175.80	180.35	184.71	188.91
5.00	154.80	159.57	164.16	168.57	172.80	176.86	180.74
5.25	148.75	153.22	157.51	161.62	165.56	169.32	172.92
5.50	142.92	147.10	151.11	154.94	158.60	162.10	165.43
5.75	137.29	141.20	144.95	148.52	151.92	155.17	158.25
6.00	131.85	135.52	139.01	142.34	145.50	148.51	151.37
6.25	126.60	130.03	133.29	136.39	139.33	142.12	144.77
6.50	121.53	124.74	127.78	130.67	133.40	135.99	138.44
6.75	116.63	119.63	122.47	125.16	127.70	130.10	132.36
7.00	111.89	114.70	117.35	119.85	122.21	124.43	126.53
7.25	107.32	109.94	112.41	114.73	116.93	118.99	120.92
7.50	102.89	105.34	107.64	109.81	111.84	113.75	115.54
7.75	98.61	100.90	103.04	105.06	106.94	108.71	110.37
8.00	94.47	96.61	98.60	100.48	102.23	103.86	105.39
8.25	90.47	92.46	94.32	96.06	97.68	99.20	100.61
8.50	86.59	88.45	90.18	91.79	93.30	94.70	96.00
8.75	82.84	84.57	86.18	87.68	89.07	90.37	91.57
9.00	79.21	80.82	82.32	83.71	85.00	86.20	87.30
9.25	75.69	77.19	78.58	79.87	81.07	82.17	83.19
9.50	72.28	73.68	74.97	76.17	77.27	78.29	79.23
9.75	68.98	70.28	71.48	72.59	73.61	74.55	75.41
10.00	65.78	66.99	68.10	69.13	70.07	70.94	71.73
10.25	62.68	63.80	64.83	65.78	66.65	67.45	68.18
10.50	59.68	60.71	61.67	62.54	63.35	64.08	64.76
10.75	56.76	57.72	58.60	59.41	60.15	60.83	61.45
11.00	53.93	54.82	55.64	56.38	57.07	57.69	58.25
11.25	51.19	52.01	52.76	53.45	54.08	54.65	55.17
11.50	48.52	49.28	49.98	50.61	51.19	51.71	52.19
11.75	45.94	46.64	47.28	47.86	48.39	48.87	49.30
12.00	43.43	44.07	44.66	45.20	45.68	46.12	46.52
12.25	40.99	41.59	42.13	42.61	43.06	43.46	43.82
12.50	38.62	39.17	39.66	40.11	40.52	40.88	41.21
12.75	36.32	36.82	37.28	37.68	38.05	38.39	38.69
13.00	34.09	34.54	34.96	35.33	35.67	35.97	36.24
13.25	31.91	32.33	32.71	33.05	33.35	33.63	33.87
13.50	29.80	30.18	30.52	30.83	31.11	31.35	31.58
13.75	27.74	28.09	28.40	28.68	28.93	29.15	29.35
14.00	25.74	26.06	26.34	26.59	26.81	27.01	27.19
14.25	23.80	24.08	24.33	24.56	24.76	24.94	25.10
14.50	21.91	22.16	22.39	22.59	22.77	22.93	23.07
14.75	20.06	20.29	20.49	20.67	20.83	20.98	21.10
15.00	18.27	18.47	18.65	18.81	18.95	19.08	19.19
15.25	16.52	16.70	16.86	17.00	17.12	17.23	17.33
15.50	14.82	14.98	15.12	15.24	15.35	15.44	15.53
15.75	13.17	13.30	13.42	13.53	13.62	13.70	13.78
16.00	11.55	11.67	11.77	11.86	11.94	12.01	12.07
16.25	9.98	10.08	10.16	10.24	10.30	10.36	10.41
16.50	8.44	8.52	8.59	8.66	8.71	8.76	8.80
16.75	6.95	7.01	7.07	7.12	7.16	7.20	7.24
17.00	5.49	5.54	5.58	5.62	5.65	5.68	5.71
17.25	4.07	4.10	4.13	4.16	4.19	4.21	4.23
17.50	2.68	2.70	2.72	2.74	2.75	2.77	2.78
17.75	1.32	1.33	1.34	1.35	1.36	1.37	1.37
18.00	0.00	0.00	0.00	0.00	0.00	0.00	0.00

Valuation of Assumable Mortgages

CURRENT RATE: 18½%

OLD RATE	5 YEARS	10 YEARS	15 YEARS	20 YEARS	21 YEARS	22 YEARS	23 YEARS
4.00	39.37	81.16	122.60	161.05	168.23	175.23	182.04
4.25	38.51	79.05	118.87	155.46	162.25	168.86	175.27
4.50	37.67	76.98	115.23	150.04	156.47	162.70	168.73
4.75	36.84	74.94	111.68	144.79	150.86	156.74	162.42
5.00	36.01	72.93	108.21	139.70	145.44	150.98	156.32
5.25	35.19	70.95	104.82	134.76	140.18	145.40	150.43
5.50	34.37	69.01	101.51	129.96	135.09	140.01	144.74
5.75	33.56	67.09	98.28	125.31	130.15	134.79	139.24
6.00	32.76	65.21	95.12	120.80	125.37	129.74	133.93
6.25	31.96	63.36	92.03	116.42	120.73	124.85	128.79
6.50	31.18	61.53	89.01	112.17	116.24	120.12	123.81
6.75	30.39	59.74	86.07	108.04	111.88	115.53	119.01
7.00	29.62	57.97	83.19	104.04	107.65	111.09	114.35
7.25	28.85	56.23	80.37	100.14	103.56	106.79	109.85
7.50	28.09	54.52	77.62	96.36	99.58	102.62	105.49
7.75	27.33	52.83	74.92	92.69	95.72	98.58	101.27
8.00	26.58	51.17	72.29	89.12	91.97	94.66	97.19
8.25	25.84	49.54	69.72	85.65	88.34	90.86	93.23
8.50	25.10	47.93	67.20	82.28	84.81	87.18	89.40
8.75	24.37	46.35	64.74	79.01	81.38	83.60	85.69
9.00	23.64	44.79	62.34	75.82	78.05	80.14	82.09
9.25	22.92	43.26	59.98	72.72	74.82	76.77	78.60
9.50	22.21	41.75	57.68	69.71	71.67	73.51	75.21
9.75	21.50	40.26	55.43	66.78	68.62	70.34	71.93
10.00	20.80	38.79	53.22	63.92	65.65	67.26	68.75
10.25	20.10	37.35	51.06	61.15	62.77	64.27	65.66
10.50	19.41	35.93	48.95	58.45	59.96	61.37	62.66
10.75	18.73	34.53	46.89	55.82	57.24	58.55	59.75
11.00	18.05	33.15	44.86	53.26	54.58	55.81	56.93
11.25	17.37	31.79	42.88	50.76	52.00	53.14	54.19
11.50	16.70	30.46	40.95	48.34	49.49	50.55	51.52
11.75	16.04	29.14	39.05	45.97	47.05	48.03	48.94
12.00	15.38	27.84	37.19	43.67	44.67	45.58	46.42
12.25	14.73	26.56	35.37	41.42	42.35	43.20	43.98
12.50	14.08	25.30	33.59	39.23	40.10	40.88	41.60
12.75	13.44	24.06	31.84	37.10	37.90	38.63	39.29
13.00	12.80	22.84	30.14	35.02	35.76	36.44	37.04
13.25	12.17	21.64	28.46	33.00	33.68	34.30	34.86
13.50	11.54	20.45	26.82	31.02	31.65	32.22	32.73
13.75	10.92	19.28	25.21	29.09	29.67	30.19	30.66
14.00	10.31	18.13	23.64	27.21	27.74	28.22	28.65
14.25	9.69	16.99	22.09	25.38	25.86	26.30	26.69
14.50	9.09	15.88	20.58	23.59	24.03	24.42	24.78
14.75	8.48	14.77	19.10	21.84	22.24	22.60	22.92
15.00	7.89	13.69	17.64	20.13	20.49	20.82	21.11
15.25	7.29	12.62	16.22	18.47	18.79	19.08	19.34
15.50	6.71	11.56	14.82	16.84	17.13	17.39	17.62
15.75	6.12	10.52	13.45	15.25	15.51	15.74	15.95
16.00	5.54	9.49	12.11	13.70	13.93	14.13	14.31
16.25	4.97	8.48	10.79	12.19	12.39	12.56	12.72
16.50	4.40	7.49	9.50	10.71	10.88	11.03	11.16
16.75	3.83	6.50	8.23	9.26	9.41	9.53	9.65
17.00	3.27	5.53	6.99	7.85	7.97	8.07	8.17
17.25	2.72	4.58	5.77	6.46	6.56	6.65	6.72
17.50	2.17	3.64	4.57	5.11	5.19	5.26	5.31
17.75	1.62	2.71	3.39	3.79	3.85	3.90	3.94
18.00	1.07	1.79	2.24	2.50	2.54	2.57	2.59
18.25	0.54	0.89	1.11	1.24	1.25	1.27	1.28
18.50	0.00	0.00	0.00	0.00	0.00	0.00	0.00

Valuation of Assumable Mortgages

CURRENT RATE: 18½%

OLD RATE	24 YEARS	25 YEARS	26 YEARS	27 YEARS	28 YEARS	29 YEARS	30 YEARS
4.00	188.65	195.07	201.29	207.32	213.15	218.79	224.23
4.25	181.48	187.50	193.32	198.94	204.37	209.61	214.66
4.50	174.57	180.21	185.65	190.90	195.96	200.82	205.50
4.75	167.90	173.19	178.28	183.17	187.88	192.40	196.74
5.00	161.47	166.42	171.18	175.75	180.13	184.33	188.35
5.25	155.27	159.91	164.36	168.62	172.70	176.60	180.32
5.50	149.28	153.63	157.78	161.76	165.55	169.18	172.63
5.75	143.50	147.57	151.46	155.16	158.69	162.06	165.25
6.00	137.92	141.73	145.36	148.82	152.10	155.22	158.18
6.25	132.53	136.10	139.49	142.71	145.77	148.66	151.41
6.50	127.33	130.67	133.83	136.84	139.68	142.36	144.90
6.75	122.30	125.42	128.38	131.18	133.82	136.31	138.66
7.00	117.44	120.36	123.12	125.73	128.18	130.49	132.67
7.25	112.75	115.48	118.05	120.48	122.76	124.90	126.91
7.50	108.20	110.76	113.16	115.42	117.54	119.52	121.38
7.75	103.81	106.20	108.44	110.54	112.51	114.35	116.07
8.00	99.57	101.79	103.88	105.84	107.66	109.37	110.96
8.25	95.46	97.54	99.48	101.30	103.00	104.57	106.04
8.50	91.48	93.42	95.23	96.92	98.50	99.96	101.32
8.75	87.63	89.44	91.13	92.70	94.16	95.51	96.76
9.00	83.90	85.59	87.16	88.62	89.97	91.22	92.38
9.25	80.29	81.87	83.33	84.68	85.93	87.09	88.16
9.50	76.80	78.26	79.62	80.88	82.04	83.11	84.09
9.75	73.41	74.77	76.04	77.20	78.28	79.26	80.17
10.00	70.13	71.40	72.57	73.65	74.64	75.55	76.39
10.25	66.94	68.13	69.21	70.21	71.13	71.97	72.74
10.50	63.86	64.96	65.97	66.89	67.74	68.51	69.22
10.75	60.87	61.89	62.82	63.68	64.46	65.17	65.82
11.00	57.96	58.91	59.77	60.57	61.29	61.95	62.54
11.25	55.15	56.02	56.82	57.55	58.22	58.82	59.37
11.50	52.41	53.22	53.97	54.64	55.25	55.81	56.31
11.75	49.76	50.51	51.19	51.82	52.38	52.89	53.35
12.00	47.18	47.88	48.51	49.08	49.60	50.07	50.49
12.25	44.68	45.32	45.90	46.43	46.90	47.33	47.72
12.50	42.25	42.84	43.38	43.86	44.29	44.69	45.04
12.75	39.89	40.43	40.92	41.37	41.77	42.12	42.45
13.00	37.60	38.09	38.54	38.95	39.31	39.64	39.93
13.25	35.37	35.82	36.23	36.60	36.94	37.23	37.50
13.50	33.20	33.62	33.99	34.33	34.63	34.90	35.14
13.75	31.09	31.47	31.81	32.12	32.39	32.64	32.86
14.00	29.04	29.38	29.70	29.97	30.22	30.44	30.64
14.25	27.04	27.36	27.64	27.89	28.12	28.32	28.49
14.50	25.10	25.38	25.64	25.87	26.07	26.25	26.41
14.75	23.21	23.47	23.70	23.90	24.08	24.24	24.39
15.00	21.37	21.60	21.81	21.00	22.16	22.28	22.42
15.25	19.58	19.78	19.97	20.13	20.27	20.40	20.51
15.50	17.83	18.01	18.18	18.32	18.45	18.56	18.66
15.75	16.13	16.29	16.44	16.56	16.67	16.77	16.86
16.00	14.47	14.61	14.74	14.85	14.95	15.03	15.11
16.25	12.86	12.98	13.09	13.18	13.27	13.34	13.41
16.50	11.28	11.39	11.48	11.56	11.63	11.70	11.75
16.75	9.75	9.84	9.92	9.98	10.04	10.10	10.14
17.00	8.25	8.32	8.39	8.45	8.49	8.54	8.58
17.25	6.79	6.85	6.90	6.95	6.99	7.02	7.05
17.50	5.37	5.41	5.45	5.49	5.52	5.54	5.57
17.75	3.98	4.01	4.04	4.06	4.08	4.10	4.12
18.00	2.62	2.64	2.66	2.67	2.69	2.70	2.71
18.25	1.29	1.30	1.31	1.32	1.33	1.33	1.34
18.50	0.00	0.00	0.00	0.00	0.00	0.00	0.00

Valuation of Assumable Mortgages

CURRENT RATE: 19%

OLD RATE	5 YEARS	10 YEARS	15 YEARS	20 YEARS	21 YEARS	22 YEARS	23 YEARS
4.00	40.85	84.38	127.51	167.45	174.90	182.15	189.20
4.25	40.00	82.23	123.70	161.72	168.77	175.62	182.26
4.50	39.14	80.12	119.99	156.17	162.84	169.30	175.55
4.75	38.30	78.04	116.35	150.79	157.10	163.19	169.08
5.00	37.46	76.00	112.81	145.57	151.53	157.29	162.83
5.25	36.63	73.99	109.34	140.51	146.15	151.57	156.79
5.50	35.81	72.01	105.96	135.60	140.93	146.05	150.96
5.75	34.99	70.06	102.66	130.84	135.87	140.70	145.32
6.00	34.18	68.14	99.43	126.22	130.97	135.52	139.87
6.25	33.38	66.26	96.27	121.73	126.22	130.51	134.60
6.50	32.58	64.40	93.19	117.37	121.61	125.65	129.50
6.75	31.79	62.57	90.17	113.15	117.15	120.95	124.57
7.00	31.00	60.77	87.23	109.04	112.82	116.40	119.80
7.25	30.23	59.00	84.35	105.05	108.61	111.99	115.18
7.50	29.46	57.26	81.54	101.18	104.54	107.71	110.71
7.75	28.69	55.55	78.79	97.42	100.58	103.57	106.39
8.00	27.93	53.86	76.10	93.76	96.74	99.55	102.20
8.25	27.18	52.20	73.47	90.21	93.02	95.66	98.14
8.50	26.44	50.56	70.90	86.75	89.40	91.88	94.21
8.75	25.70	48.95	68.38	83.40	85.89	88.22	90.40
9.00	24.96	47.36	65.92	80.13	82.48	84.67	86.71
9.25	24.24	45.80	63.51	76.96	79.16	81.22	83.13
9.50	23.52	44.26	61.16	73.87	75.94	77.87	79.66
9.75	22.80	42.75	58.86	70.87	72.81	74.62	76.30
10.00	22.09	41.26	56.60	67.94	69.77	71.47	73.03
10.25	21.39	39.79	54.40	65.10	66.81	68.40	69.87
10.50	20.69	38.34	52.24	62.33	63.94	65.42	66.79
10.75	20.00	36.92	50.13	59.64	61.14	62.53	63.81
11.00	19.31	35.52	48.06	57.01	58.42	59.72	60.92
11.25	18.63	34.13	46.04	54.46	55.78	56.99	58.10
11.50	17.95	32.77	44.06	51.97	53.21	54.34	55.37
11.75	17.28	31.43	42.12	49.55	50.70	51.76	52.72
12.00	16.62	30.11	40.22	47.19	48.26	49.24	50.14
12.25	15.96	28.81	38.36	44.89	45.89	46.80	47.63
12.50	15.30	27.53	36.54	42.65	43.58	44.43	45.20
12.75	14.65	26.27	34.76	40.46	41.33	42.12	42.83
13.00	14.01	25.02	33.01	38.33	39.14	39.87	40.52
13.25	13.37	23.80	31.30	36.26	37.00	37.67	38.28
13.50	12.74	22.59	29.62	34.23	34.92	35.54	36.10
13.75	12.11	21.40	27.98	32.26	32.89	33.47	33.98
14.00	11.48	20.23	26.37	30.33	30.92	31.44	31.92
14.25	10.87	19.07	24.79	28.45	28.99	29.47	29.91
14.50	10.25	17.93	23.24	26.62	27.11	27.55	27.95
14.75	9.64	16.81	21.73	24.83	25.28	25.68	26.04
15.00	9.04	15.70	20.24	23.08	23.49	23.86	24.18
15.25	8.44	14.61	18.78	21.37	21.74	22.08	22.37
15.50	7.85	13.54	17.36	19.71	20.04	20.34	20.61
15.75	7.26	12.48	15.96	18.08	18.38	18.65	18.89
16.00	6.67	11.44	14.58	16.49	16.76	17.00	17.22
16.25	6.09	10.41	13.24	14.94	15.18	15.39	15.58
16.50	5.52	9.39	11.92	13.42	13.63	13.82	13.99
16.75	4.94	8.39	10.62	11.94	12.12	12.29	12.43
17.00	4.38	7.41	9.35	10.49	10.65	10.79	10.91
17.25	3.82	6.44	8.10	9.08	9.21	9.33	9.43
17.50	3.26	5.48	6.88	7.69	7.80	7.90	7.99
17.75	2.70	4.53	5.68	6.34	6.43	6.51	6.58
18.00	2.15	3.60	4.50	5.01	5.08	5.15	5.20
18.25	1.61	2.68	3.34	3.72	3.77	3.81	3.85
18.50	1.07	1.78	2.21	2.45	2.49	2.51	2.54
18.75	0.53	0.88	1.09	1.21	1.23	1.24	1.26
19.00	0.[illegible]	0.00	0.00	0.00	0.00	0.00	0.00

Valuation of Assumable Mortgages

CURRENT RATE: 19%

OLD RATE	24 YEARS	25 YEARS	26 YEARS	27 YEARS	28 YEARS	29 YEARS	30 YEARS
4.00	196.05	202.68	209.12	215.34	221.37	227.19	232.81
4.25	188.69	194.92	200.94	206.75	212.36	217.77	222.99
4.50	181.60	187.44	193.07	198.50	203.72	208.75	213.59
4.75	174.76	180.24	185.51	190.57	195.44	200.11	204.59
5.00	168.17	173.30	178.23	182.95	187.49	191.83	195.98
5.25	161.81	166.61	171.22	175.63	179.85	183.89	187.74
5.50	155.66	160.17	164.48	168.60	172.52	176.27	179.84
5.75	149.74	153.96	157.99	161.83	165.48	168.96	172.27
6.00	144.02	147.97	151.74	155.32	158.72	161.95	165.01
6.25	138.49	142.19	145.71	149.05	152.22	155.22	158.06
6.50	133.15	136.62	139.91	143.02	145.97	148.75	151.38
6.75	128.00	131.24	134.31	137.22	139.96	142.54	144.97
7.00	123.01	126.05	128.92	131.62	134.17	136.57	138.82
7.25	118.19	121.04	123.72	126.24	128.61	130.83	132.92
7.50	113.54	116.20	118.70	121.04	123.25	125.31	127.24
7.75	109.03	111.52	113.85	116.04	118.09	120.00	121.78
8.00	104.08	107.00	109.18	111.21	113.11	114.89	116.54
8.25	100.46	102.64	104.67	106.56	108.32	109.97	111.50
8.50	96.38	98.41	100.31	102.07	103.71	105.23	106.64
8.75	92.44	94.33	96.09	97.73	99.25	100.66	101.97
9.00	88.61	90.38	92.03	93.55	94.98	96.26	97.47
9.25	84.91	86.56	88.09	89.51	90.82	92.02	93.14
9.50	81.32	82.86	84.29	85.60	86.82	87.93	88.96
9.75	77.85	79.29	80.61	81.83	82.95	83.99	84.94
10.00	74.48	75.82	77.05	78.18	79.23	80.18	81.06
10.25	71.22	72.46	73.61	74.66	75.62	76.50	77.31
10.50	68.05	69.21	70.28	71.25	72.14	72.96	73.70
10.75	64.99	66.06	67.05	67.95	68.78	69.53	70.21
11.00	62.01	63.01	63.92	64.76	65.52	66.21	66.84
11.25	59.12	60.05	60.90	61.67	62.37	63.01	63.59
11.50	56.32	57.18	57.96	58.68	59.33	59.91	60.45
11.75	53.60	54.40	55.12	55.78	56.38	56.92	57.41
12.00	50.95	51.69	52.37	52.97	53.52	54.02	54.47
12.25	48.39	49.07	49.69	50.25	50.76	51.22	51.63
12.50	45.90	46.53	47.10	47.62	48.08	48.50	48.88
12.75	43.47	44.06	44.58	45.06	45.49	45.87	46.21
13.00	41.12	41.66	42.14	42.58	42.97	43.32	43.64
13.25	38.83	39.33	39.77	40.17	40.53	40.85	41.14
13.50	36.61	37.06	37.47	37.84	38.16	38.46	38.72
13.75	34.45	34.86	35.24	35.57	35.87	36.14	36.37
14.00	32.34	32.72	33.07	33.37	33.64	33.88	34.10
14.25	30.30	30.64	30.95	31.23	31.48	31.70	31.89
14.50	28.30	28.62	28.90	29.16	29.38	29.58	29.75
14.75	26.36	26.65	26.91	27.14	27.34	27.52	27.68
15.00	24.48	24.74	24.97	25.17	25.36	25.52	25.66
15.25	22.64	22.87	23.08	23.27	23.43	23.57	23.70
15.50	20.85	21.06	21.25	21.41	21.56	21.69	21.80
15.75	19.10	19.29	19.46	19.61	19.74	19.85	19.95
16.00	17.41	17.57	17.72	17.85	17.97	18.07	18.15
16.25	15.75	15.90	16.03	16.14	16.24	16.33	16.41
16.50	14.13	14.26	14.38	14.48	14.57	14.64	14.71
16.75	12.56	12.67	12.77	12.86	12.93	13.00	13.06
17.00	11.02	11.12	11.20	11.28	11.34	11.40	11.45
17.25	9.53	9.61	9.68	9.74	9.79	9.84	9.88
17.50	8.06	8.13	8.19	8.24	8.29	8.33	8.36
17.75	6.64	6.69	6.74	6.78	6.82	6.85	6.87
18.00	5.25	5.29	5.32	5.36	5.38	5.41	5.43
18.25	3.89	3.92	3.94	3.97	3.99	4.00	4.02
18.50	2.56	2.58	2.60	2.61	2.62	2.64	2.65
18.75	1.27	1.28	1.28	1.29	1.30	1.30	1.31
19.00	0.00	0.00	0.00	0.00	0.00	0.00	0.00

Valuation of Assumable Mortgages

CURRENT RATE: 19½%

OLD RATE	5 YEARS	10 YEARS	15 YEARS	20 YEARS	21 YEARS	22 YEARS	23 YEARS
4.00	42.35	87.62	132.46	173.88	181.59	189.10	196.39
4.25	41.48	85.43	128.57	168.02	175.32	182.40	189.27
4.50	40.62	83.28	124.77	162.34	169.24	175.93	182.41
4.75	39.77	81.17	121.06	156.83	163.36	169.67	175.77
5.00	38.92	79.09	117.44	151.48	157.66	163.62	169.37
5.25	38.08	77.04	113.90	146.30	152.14	157.77	163.18
5.50	37.25	75.03	110.44	141.27	146.80	152.10	157.20
5.75	36.42	73.05	107.06	136.39	141.62	146.62	151.42
6.00	35.61	71.10	103.76	131.66	136.60	141.32	145.83
6.25	34.79	69.18	100.54	127.06	131.73	136.18	140.43
6.50	33.99	67.29	97.39	122.60	127.01	131.21	135.20
6.75	33.19	65.43	94.31	118.27	122.44	126.39	130.15
7.00	32.40	63.60	91.30	114.07	118.00	121.73	125.26
7.25	31.61	61.80	88.36	109.98	113.70	117.21	120.53
7.50	30.83	60.02	85.49	106.02	109.52	112.83	115.95
7.75	30.06	58.28	82.67	102.16	105.47	108.58	111.52
8.00	29.30	56.56	79.93	98.42	101.54	104.47	107.22
8.25	28.54	54.87	77.24	94.78	97.72	100.48	103.07
8.50	27.78	53.20	74.61	91.24	94.01	96.61	99.04
8.75	27.03	51.57	72.04	87.81	90.42	92.86	95.13
9.00	26.29	49.95	69.53	84.46	86.92	89.21	91.35
9.25	25.56	48.36	67.07	81.21	83.53	85.68	87.68
9.50	24.83	46.80	64.66	78.05	80.23	82.25	84.13
9.75	24.11	45.26	62.31	74.97	77.02	78.92	80.68
10.00	23.39	43.74	60.01	71.98	73.91	75.69	77.34
10.25	22.68	42.24	57.76	69.07	70.88	72.55	74.09
10.50	21.97	40.77	55.55	66.24	67.93	69.50	70.94
10.75	21.27	39.32	53.39	63.48	65.07	66.54	67.88
11.00	20.58	37.90	51.28	60.79	62.28	63.66	64.92
11.25	19.89	36.49	49.21	58.18	59.57	60.86	62.03
11.50	19.21	35.11	47.19	55.63	56.94	58.14	59.23
11.75	18.53	33.74	45.21	53.15	54.37	55.49	56.51
12.00	17.86	32.40	43.27	50.73	51.87	52.92	53.87
12.25	17.19	31.07	41.37	48.37	49.44	50.42	51.30
12.50	16.53	29.77	39.51	46.08	47.08	47.98	48.81
12.75	15.87	28.49	37.69	43.84	44.77	45.61	46.38
13.00	15.22	27.22	35.90	41.66	42.53	43.31	44.02
13.25	14.58	25.97	34.15	39.53	40.34	41.07	41.72
13.50	13.94	24.74	32.44	37.46	38.21	38.88	39.49
13.75	13.30	23.53	30.76	35.44	36.13	36.75	37.31
14.00	12.67	22.34	29.11	33.46	34.10	34.68	35.20
14.25	12.05	21.16	27.50	31.54	32.13	32.66	33.14
14.50	11.43	20.01	25.92	29.66	30.21	30.69	31.13
14.75	10.81	18.86	24.37	27.83	28.33	28.78	29.18
15.00	10.20	17.74	22.86	26.04	26.50	26.91	27.27
15.25	9.59	16.63	21.37	24.29	24.71	25.08	25.42
15.50	8.99	15.54	19.91	22.59	22.97	23.31	23.61
15.75	8.40	14.46	18.48	20.92	21.27	21.57	21.85
16.00	7.81	13.40	17.07	19.29	19.61	19.88	20.13
16.25	7.22	12.35	15.70	17.70	17.98	18.23	18.45
16.50	6.64	11.32	14.35	16.15	16.40	16.62	16.82
16.75	6.06	10.30	13.02	14.63	14.86	15.05	15.23
17.00	5.49	9.30	11.73	13.15	13.35	13.52	13.67
17.25	4.92	8.31	10.45	11.70	11.87	12.02	12.15
17.50	4.36	7.33	9.20	10.28	10.43	10.56	10.67
17.75	3.80	6.37	7.98	8.89	9.02	9.13	9.23
18.00	3.24	5.42	6.77	7.54	7.64	7.73	7.81
18.25	2.69	4.49	5.59	6.21	6.30	6.37	6.44
18.50	2.14	3.56	4.43	4.92	4.98	5.04	5.09
18.75	1.60	2.65	3.29	3.65	3.69	3.74	3.77
19.00	1.06	1.76	2.17	2.41	2.44	2.46	2.49
19.25	0.53	0.87	1.08	1.19	1.20	1.22	1.23
19.50	0.00	0.00	0.00	0.00	0.00	0.00	0.00

Valuation of Assumable Mortgages

CURRENT RATE: 19½%

OLD RATE	24 YEARS	25 YEARS	26 YEARS	27 YEARS	28 YEARS	29 YEARS	30 YEARS
4.00	203.47	210.32	216.97	223.39	229.61	235.61	241.41
4.25	195.93	202.36	208.58	214.58	220.37	225.95	231.33
4.50	188.66	194.69	200.51	206.12	211.51	216.70	221.68
4.75	181.65	187.31	192.76	197.99	203.01	207.83	212.46
5.00	174.89	180.20	185.29	190.18	194.86	199.34	203.62
5.25	168.37	173.34	178.11	182.67	187.03	191.19	195.17
5.50	162.07	166.74	171.20	175.45	179.51	183.38	187.06
5.75	156.00	160.37	164.54	168.51	172.29	175.89	179.30
6.00	150.13	154.23	158.13	161.83	165.35	168.69	171.86
6.25	144.47	148.31	151.95	155.41	158.69	161.79	164.72
6.50	139.00	142.59	146.00	149.23	152.27	155.15	157.87
6.75	133.71	137.08	140.26	143.27	146.11	148.78	151.30
7.00	128.60	131.76	134.73	137.54	140.18	142.66	144.00
7.25	123.66	126.62	129.40	132.01	134.47	136.77	138.93
7.50	118.89	121.65	124.25	126.69	128.97	131.11	133.11
7.75	114.27	116.86	119.28	121.55	123.68	125.66	127.51
8.00	109.81	112.23	114.40	110.01	118.58	120.42	122.13
8.25	105.48	107.75	109.80	111.83	113.67	115.37	116.96
8.50	101.31	103.42	105.39	107.23	108.93	110.51	111.98
8.75	97.26	99.24	101.07	102.78	104.36	105.83	107.18
9.00	93.34	95.19	06.00	90.49	99.98	101.32	102.57
9.25	89.55	91.27	92.87	94.34	95.71	96.97	98.12
9.50	85.87	87.48	88.97	90.34	91.61	92.77	93.84
9.75	82.31	83.81	85.20	86.47	87.65	88.72	89.71
10.00	78.86	80.26	81.55	82.73	83.82	04.82	85.73
10.25	75.51	76.82	78.02	79.12	80.13	81.05	81.89
10.50	72.27	73.48	74.60	75.62	76.55	77.41	78.18
10.75	69.12	70.25	71.29	72.24	73.10	73.89	74.61
11.00	66.07	67.12	68.09	68.97	60.76	70.49	71.15
11.25	63.11	64.09	64.98	65.80	66.54	67.21	67.81
11.50	60.23	61.15	61.98	62.73	63.41	64.03	64.59
11.75	57.45	58.29	59.06	59.76	60.39	60.96	61.47
12.00	54.74	55.52	56.23	56.88	57.46	57.99	58.46
12.25	52.11	52.84	53.49	54.09	54.62	55.11	55.54
12.50	49.55	50.23	50.84	51.38	51.88	52.32	52.72
12.75	47.07	47.69	48.26	48.76	49.22	49.62	49.99
13.00	44.66	45.23	45.75	46.22	46.64	47.01	47.34
13.25	42.31	42.85	43.32	43.75	44.13	44.48	44.78
13.50	40.03	40.52	40.96	41.36	41.71	42.02	42.30
13.75	37.82	38.27	38.67	39.03	39.35	39.64	39.89
14.00	35.66	36.07	36.44	36.77	37.07	37.33	37.56
14.25	33.56	33.94	34.28	34.58	34.85	35.09	35.30
14.50	31.52	31.87	32.18	32.45	32.70	32.91	33.10
14.75	29.53	29.85	30.13	30.38	30.60	30.80	30.97
15.00	27.60	27.89	28.14	28.37	28.57	28.75	28.90
15.25	25.71	25.98	26.21	26.41	26.59	26.75	26.90
15.50	23.88	24.12	24.33	24.51	24.67	24.82	24.94
15.75	22.09	22.30	22.49	22.66	22.81	22.94	23.05
16.00	20.35	20.54	20.71	20.86	20.99	21.10	21.21
16.25	18.65	18.82	18.97	19.11	19.22	19.32	19.41
16.50	16.99	17.15	17.28	17.40	17.50	17.59	17.67
16.75	15.38	15.52	15.63	15.74	15.83	15.91	15.98
17.00	13.81	13.92	14.03	14.12	14.20	14.27	14.33
17.25	12.27	12.37	12.46	12.54	12.61	12.67	12.72
17.50	10.77	10.86	10.94	11.00	11.06	11.11	11.16
17.75	9.31	9.39	9.45	9.51	9.56	9.60	9.63
18.00	7.88	7.95	8.00	8.05	8.09	8.12	8.15
18.25	6.49	6.54	6.58	6.62	6.65	6.68	6.70
18.50	5.13	5.17	5.20	5.23	5.26	5.28	5.30
18.75	3.80	3.83	3.86	3.88	3.89	3.91	3.92
19.00	2.51	2.52	2.54	2.55	2.56	2.57	2.58
19.25	1.24	1.25	1.25	1.26	1.27	1.27	1.28
19.50	0.00	0.00	0.00	0.00	0.00	0.00	0.00

Valuation of Assumable Mortgages

CURRENT RATE:20%

OLD RATE	5 YEARS	10 YEARS	15 YEARS	20 YEARS	21 YEARS	22 YEARS	23 YEARS
4.00	43.86	90.88	137.44	180.34	188.32	196.07	203.61
4.25	42.98	88.66	133.46	174.34	181.89	189.22	196.32
4.50	42.11	86.47	129.58	168.53	175.67	182.59	189.28
4.75	41.25	84.32	125.79	162.88	169.65	176.18	182.49
5.00	40.39	82.20	122.09	157.41	163.81	169.98	175.92
5.25	39.54	80.12	118.48	152.11	158.16	163.99	169.58
5.50	38.70	78.07	114.95	146.96	152.69	158.19	163.46
5.75	37.87	76.06	111.50	141.97	147.39	152.57	157.54
6.00	37.04	74.07	108.13	137.12	142.25	147.14	151.81
6.25	36.22	72.12	104.83	132.42	137.26	141.88	146.28
6.50	35.41	70.20	101.62	127.85	132.43	136.79	140.93
6.75	34.60	68.31	98.47	123.42	127.76	131.86	135.75
7.00	33.80	66.44	95.40	119.12	123.21	127.08	130.74
7.25	33.01	64.61	92.39	114.94	118.80	122.45	125.90
7.50	32.22	62.81	89.46	110.88	114.52	117.96	121.21
7.75	31.44	61.03	86.59	106.93	110.38	113.62	116.67
8.00	30.66	59.28	83.78	103.10	106.35	109.40	112.27
8.25	29.90	57.56	81.04	99.38	102.44	105.32	108.01
8.50	29.13	55.87	78.35	95.76	98.65	101.35	103.88
8.75	28.38	54.20	75.73	92.24	94.96	97.51	99.88
9.00	27.63	52.56	73.16	88.82	91.38	93.78	96.01
9.25	26.89	50.94	70.65	85.49	87.91	90.16	92.25
9.50	26.15	49.35	68.19	82.25	84.53	86.65	88.61
9.75	25.42	47.78	65.79	79.10	81.25	83.24	85.08
10.00	24.69	46.24	63.44	76.04	78.06	79.93	81.65
10.25	23.98	44.72	61.14	73.06	74.96	76.71	78.33
10.50	23.26	43.22	58.88	70.16	71.94	73.59	75.10
10.75	22.56	41.75	56.68	67.33	69.01	70.55	71.97
11.00	21.85	40.29	54.52	64.58	66.16	67.61	68.93
11.25	21.16	38.86	52.41	61.91	63.38	64.74	65.08
11.50	20.47	37.46	50.34	59.30	60.69	61.95	63.11
11.75	19.78	36.07	48.32	56.76	58.06	59.24	60.32
12.00	19.10	34.70	46.34	54.29	55.50	56.61	57.62
12.25	18.43	33.35	44.40	51.88	53.01	54.05	54.99
12.50	17.76	32.03	42.50	49.53	50.59	51.55	52.43
12.75	17.10	30.72	40.63	47.24	48.23	49.13	49.94
13.00	16.44	29.43	38.81	45.00	45.93	46.77	47.52
13.25	15.79	28.16	37.02	42.83	43.69	44.47	45.17
13.50	15.14	26.91	35.27	40.70	41.51	42.23	42.88
13.75	14.50	25.68	33.56	38.63	39.38	40.05	40.66
14.00	13.86	24.47	31.88	36.61	37.31	37.93	38.49
14.25	13.23	23.27	30.23	34.64	35.29	35.86	36.38
14.50	12.60	22.09	28.62	32.72	33.31	33.85	34.32
14.75	11.98	20.93	27.04	30.84	31.39	31.88	32.32
15.00	11.37	19.79	25.49	29.01	29.52	29.97	30.37
15.25	10.75	18.66	23.97	27.22	27.69	28.10	28.47
15.50	10.15	17.54	22.48	25.48	25.90	26.28	26.62
15.75	9.54	16.45	21.01	23.77	24.16	24.51	24.81
16.00	8.95	15.37	19.58	22.11	22.46	22.78	23.05
16.25	8.35	14.30	18.18	20.48	20.80	21.09	21.34
16.50	7.77	13.25	16.80	18.89	19.18	19.44	19.66
16.75	7.18	12.22	15.45	17.34	17.60	17.83	18.03
17.00	6.60	11.20	14.12	15.82	16.05	16.26	16.44
17.25	6.03	10.19	12.82	14.33	14.54	14.72	14.88
17.50	5.46	9.20	11.54	12.88	13.07	13.23	13.37
17.75	4.89	8.22	10.29	11.46	11.62	11.76	11.89
18.00	4.33	7.25	9.06	10.08	10.21	10.33	10.44
18.25	3.78	6.30	7.85	8.72	8.84	8.94	9.03
18.50	3.22	5.36	6.67	7.39	7.49	7.57	7.65
18.75	2.68	4.44	5.50	6.09	6.17	6.24	6.30
19.00	2.13	3.53	4.36	4.82	4.88	4.94	4.98
19.25	1.59	2.63	3.24	3.58	3.62	3.66	3.69
19.50	1.06	1.74	2.14	2.36	2.39	2.41	2.43
19.75	0.53	0.86	1.06	1.17	1.18	1.19	1.20
20.00	0.00	0.00	0.00	0.00	0.00	0.00	0.00

Valuation of Assumable Mortgages

CURRENT RATE:20%

OLD RATE	24 YEARS	25 YEARS	26 YEARS	27 YEARS	28 YEARS	29 YEARS	30 YEARS
4.00	210.91	217.99	224.84	231.46	237.86	244.05	250.01
4.25	203.19	209.83	216.24	222.43	228.40	234.14	239.68
4.50	195.74	201.97	207.97	213.75	219.32	224.66	229.79
4.75	188.56	194.40	200.02	205.42	210.60	215.57	220.33
5.00	181.63	187.12	192.38	197.42	202.24	206.86	211.28
5.25	174.95	180.09	185.02	189.72	194.22	198.51	202.61
5.50	168.50	173.32	177.93	182.33	186.51	190.50	194.30
5.75	162.28	166.80	171.11	175.21	179.11	182.82	186.34
6.00	156.27	160.51	164.54	168.37	172.00	175.45	178.71
6.25	150.46	154.44	158.21	161.78	165.17	168.37	171.39
6.50	144.86	148.58	152.11	155.44	158.59	161.57	164.37
6.75	139.44	142.93	146.23	149.34	152.27	155.04	157.64
7.00	134.21	137.48	140.56	143.46	146.19	148.76	151.17
7.25	129.15	132.21	135.09	137.80	140.34	142.72	144.95
7.50	124.26	127.13	129.82	132.34	134.71	136.92	138.99
7.75	119.53	122.21	124.73	127.08	129.28	131.33	133.25
8.00	114.96	117.47	119.82	122.01	124.05	125.96	127.73
8.25	110.53	112.88	115.07	117.12	119.02	120.79	122.43
8.50	106.24	108.44	110.49	112.40	114.16	115.80	117.32
8.75	102.10	104.16	106.07	107.84	109.48	111.00	112.41
9.00	98.08	100.01	101.79	103.44	104.97	106.38	107.68
9.25	94.20	95.90	97.66	99.19	100.61	101.92	103.12
9.50	90.43	92.11	93.66	95.09	96.41	97.62	98.73
9.75	86.78	88.35	89.79	91.12	92.35	93.47	94.50
10.00	83.24	84.71	86.06	87.29	88.43	89.46	90.41
10.25	79.82	81.18	82.44	83.59	84.64	85.60	86.48
10.50	76.49	77.77	78.94	80.00	80.98	81.87	82.68
10.75	73.27	74.46	75.54	76.54	77.44	78.26	79.01
11.00	70.14	71.25	72.26	73.18	74.02	74.78	75.47
11.25	67.11	68.14	69.08	69.93	70.71	71.41	72.05
11.50	64.17	65.13	66.00	66.79	67.51	68.15	68.74
11.75	61.31	62.20	63.01	63.74	64.41	65.00	65.54
12.00	58.53	59.36	60.11	60.79	61.41	61.96	62.45
12.25	55.84	56.61	57.31	57.93	58.50	59.01	59.46
12.50	53.22	53.94	54.58	55.16	55.68	56.15	56.57
12.75	50.68	51.34	51.94	52.47	52.95	53.39	53.77
13.00	48.21	48.82	49.37	49.87	50.31	50.71	51.06
13.25	45.80	46.37	46.88	47.34	47.74	48.11	48.43
13.50	43.47	43.99	44.46	44.88	45.26	45.59	45.89
13.75	41.20	41.68	42.11	42.50	42.84	43.15	43.42
14.00	38.99	39.43	39.83	40.19	40.50	40.78	41.03
14.25	36.84	37.25	37.61	37.94	38.23	38.48	38.71
14.50	34.75	35.12	35.46	35.76	36.02	36.25	36.46
14.75	32.71	33.06	33.36	33.63	33.88	34.09	34.27
15.00	30.73	31.04	31.32	31.57	31.79	31.98	32.15
15.25	28.80	29.09	29.34	29.57	29.77	29.94	30.10
15.50	26.92	27.18	27.41	27.62	27.80	27.96	28.09
15.75	25.08	25.32	25.53	25.72	25.88	26.03	26.15
16.00	23.30	23.52	23.71	23.87	24.02	24.15	24.26
16.25	21.56	21.76	21.93	22.08	22.21	22.32	22.42
16.50	19.86	20.04	20.19	20.33	20.45	20.55	20.64
16.75	18.21	18.37	18.51	18.63	18.73	18.82	18.90
17.00	16.60	16.74	16.86	16.97	17.06	17.14	17.21
17.25	15.03	15.15	15.26	15.35	15.43	15.50	15.56
17.50	13.49	13.60	13.69	13.77	13.84	13.91	13.96
17.75	11.99	12.09	12.17	12.24	12.30	12.35	12.40
18.00	10.53	10.61	10.68	10.74	10.79	10.84	10.88
18.25	9.10	9.17	9.23	9.28	9.32	9.36	9.40
18.50	7.71	7.77	7.82	7.86	7.89	7.92	7.95
18.75	6.35	6.40	6.43	6.47	6.50	6.52	6.54
19.00	5.02	5.06	5.09	5.11	5.13	5.15	5.17
19.25	3.72	3.75	3.77	3.79	3.80	3.82	3.83
19.50	2.45	2.47	2.48	2.49	2.51	2.51	2.52
19.75	1.21	1.22	1.23	1.23	1.24	1.24	1.25
20.00	0.00	0.00	0.00	0.00	0.00	0.00	0.00

Valuation of Assumable Mortgages

CURRENT RATE:20½%

OLD RATE	5 YEARS	10 YEARS	15 YEARS	20 YEARS	21 YEARS	22 YEARS	23 YEARS
4.00	45.37	94.16	142.45	186.83	195.07	203.08	210.84
4.25	44.49	91.90	138.39	180.69	188.49	196.06	203.38
4.50	43.61	89.68	134.43	174.74	182.13	189.27	196.18
4.75	42.74	87.49	130.56	168.97	175.96	182.71	189.22
5.00	41.87	85.34	126.78	163.37	169.99	176.37	182.50
5.25	41.01	83.22	123.09	157.95	164.21	170.23	176.01
5.50	40.16	81.14	119.48	152.68	158.61	164.29	169.74
5.75	39.32	79.09	115.96	147.57	153.18	158.55	163.68
6.00	38.48	77.07	112.52	142.61	147.92	152.99	157.82
6.25	37.65	75.08	109.16	137.80	142.82	147.60	152.15
6.50	36.83	73.13	105.87	133.13	137.87	142.39	146.67
6.75	36.02	71.20	102.66	128.60	133.08	137.34	141.37
7.00	35.21	69.31	99.52	124.19	128.43	132.45	136.25
7.25	34.41	67.45	96.45	119.91	123.92	127.71	131.28
7.50	33.61	65.61	93.45	115.76	119.55	123.12	126.48
7.75	32.82	63.80	90.52	111.73	115.30	118.67	121.83
8.00	32.04	62.03	87.66	107.80	111.18	114.35	117.33
8.25	31.26	60.28	84.85	103.99	107.18	110.17	112.97
8.50	30.49	58.55	82.11	100.29	103.30	106.11	108.74
8.75	29.73	56.86	79.43	96.69	99.53	102.18	104.65
9.00	28.97	55.19	76.81	93.19	95.87	98.36	100.68
9.25	28.22	53.54	74.25	89.78	92.31	94.66	96.84
9.50	27.48	51.92	71.74	86.47	88.85	91.06	93.11
9.75	26.74	50.33	69.29	83.25	85.49	87.57	89.49
10.00	26.01	48.76	66.88	80.12	82.23	84.18	85.98
10.25	25.28	47.21	64.53	77.07	79.05	80.89	82.58
10.50	24.56	45.69	62.24	74.10	75.97	77.69	79.28
10.75	23.85	44.19	59.98	71.21	72.97	74.59	76.07
11.00	23.14	42.71	57.78	68.40	70.05	71.57	72.96
11.25	22.43	41.25	55.63	65.66	67.21	68.63	69.94
11.50	21.74	39.82	53.52	62.99	64.45	65.78	67.00
11.75	21.04	38.41	51.45	60.39	61.76	63.01	64.15
12.00	20.36	37.02	49.42	57.86	59.14	60.31	61.38
12.25	19.68	35.65	47.44	55.39	56.60	57.69	58.68
12.50	19.00	34.30	45.50	52.99	54.12	55.14	56.06
12.75	18.33	32.97	43.60	50.64	51.70	52.65	53.52
13.00	17.67	31.66	41.74	48.36	49.35	50.24	51.04
13.25	17.01	30.37	39.92	46.13	47.05	47.89	48.63
13.50	16.35	29.10	38.13	43.96	44.82	45.59	46.29
13.75	15.71	27.84	36.38	41.84	42.64	43.36	44.01
14.00	15.06	26.61	34.66	39.78	40.52	41.19	41.79
14.25	14.42	25.39	32.98	37.76	38.45	39.07	39.63
14.50	13.79	24.19	31.33	35.79	36.44	37.01	37.52
14.75	13.16	23.01	29.72	33.87	34.47	35.00	35.48
15.00	12.54	21.85	28.13	32.00	32.55	33.04	33.48
15.25	11.92	20.70	26.58	30.17	30.68	31.13	31.53
15.50	11.31	19.57	25.06	28.38	28.85	29.27	29.64
15.75	10.70	18.45	23.57	26.64	27.07	27.45	27.79
16.00	10.09	17.35	22.10	24.93	25.33	25.68	25.99
16.25	9.50	16.27	20.67	23.27	23.63	23.95	24.23
16.50	8.90	15.20	19.26	21.64	21.97	22.26	22.52
16.75	8.31	14.15	17.88	20.05	20.35	20.62	20.85
17.00	7.73	13.11	16.53	18.50	18.77	19.01	19.22
17.25	7.15	12.09	15.20	16.98	17.22	17.44	17.62
17.50	6.57	11.08	13.89	15.50	15.71	15.90	16.07
17.75	6.00	10.08	12.61	14.04	14.24	14.41	14.55
18.00	5.43	9.10	11.36	12.62	12.79	12.94	13.07
18.25	4.87	8.13	10.13	11.24	11.38	11.51	11.63
18.50	4.31	7.18	8.92	9.88	10.01	10.12	10.21
18.75	3.76	6.24	7.73	8.55	8.66	8.75	8.83
19.00	3.21	5.31	6.56	7.25	7.34	7.42	7.48
19.25	2.66	4.39	5.42	5.98	6.05	6.11	6.17
19.50	2.12	3.49	4.30	4.73	4.79	4.83	4.88
19.75	1.59	2.60	3.19	3.51	3.55	3.59	3.62
20.00	1.05	1.72	2.11	2.32	2.34	2.36	2.38

Valuation of Assumable Mortgages

CURRENT RATE:20½%

OLD RATE	24 YEARS	25 YEARS	26 YEARS	27 YEARS	28 YEARS	29 YEARS	30 YEARS
4.00	218.38	225.67	232.73	239.55	246.14	252.50	258.64
4.25	210.47	217.31	223.92	230.30	236.44	242.35	248.05
4.50	202.84	209.27	215.45	221.41	227.13	232.64	237.92
4.75	195.49	201.52	207.31	212.87	218.21	223.33	228.23
5.00	188.40	194.05	199.48	204.67	209.65	214.40	218.95
5.25	181.55	186.86	191.94	196.79	201.42	205.85	210.06
5.50	174.95	179.93	184.68	189.21	193.53	197.64	201.55
5.75	168.58	173.25	177.69	181.93	185.95	189.77	193.40
6.00	162.42	166.80	170.96	174.91	178.66	182.21	185.58
6.25	156.48	160.59	164.48	168.17	171.66	174.96	178.08
6.50	150.74	154.59	158.23	161.68	164.93	167.99	170.89
6.75	145.19	148.80	152.21	155.42	158.45	161.30	163.98
7.00	139.83	143.22	146.40	149.40	152.22	154.87	157.35
7.25	134.65	137.82	140.80	143.60	146.23	148.69	150.99
7.50	129.65	132.62	135.40	138.01	140.45	142.74	144.87
7.75	124.80	127.58	130.19	132.62	134.90	137.02	138.99
8.00	120.12	122.72	125.16	127.43	129.54	131.51	133.34
8.25	115.58	118.02	120.30	122.41	124.38	126.21	127.91
8.50	111.20	113.48	115.60	117.58	119.41	121.10	122.68
8.75	106.95	109.09	111.07	112.91	114.61	116.19	117.64
9.00	102.84	104.84	106.69	108.40	109.99	111.45	112.79
9.25	98.86	100.73	102.46	104.05	105.52	106.88	108.12
9.50	95.00	96.75	98.36	99.85	101.22	102.47	103.62
9.75	91.27	92.90	94.40	95.79	97.06	98.22	99.29
10.00	87.64	89.17	90.57	91.86	93.04	94.12	95.10
10.25	84.13	85.56	86.87	88.07	89.16	90.16	91.07
10.50	80.73	82.06	83.28	84.39	85.41	86.33	87.18
10.75	77.43	78.67	79.81	80.84	81.78	82.64	83.42
11.00	74.23	75.39	76.44	77.41	78.28	79.07	79.79
11.25	71.12	72.20	73.19	74.08	74.89	75.62	76.28
11.50	68.11	69.12	70.03	70.86	71.61	72.28	72.90
11.75	65.18	66.12	66.97	67.74	68.43	69.06	69.62
12.00	62.34	63.21	64.00	64.72	65.36	65.94	66.46
12.25	59.58	60.39	61.13	61.79	62.38	62.91	63.39
12.50	56.90	57.66	58.34	58.95	59.50	59.99	60.43
12.75	54.30	55.00	55.63	56.19	56.70	57.15	57.56
13.00	51.77	52.42	53.00	53.52	53.99	54.41	54.78
13.25	49.31	49.91	50.45	50.93	51.36	51.75	52.09
13.50	46.91	47.47	47.97	48.42	48.81	49.17	49.48
13.75	44.59	45.10	45.57	45.98	46.34	46.67	46.95
14.00	42.33	42.80	43.23	43.61	43.94	44.24	44.50
14.25	40.12	40.56	40.96	41.30	41.61	41.89	42.13
14.50	37.98	38.39	38.75	39.07	39.35	39.60	39.82
14.75	35.90	36.27	36.60	36.89	37.15	37.38	37.58
15.00	33.87	34.21	34.51	34.78	35.02	35.23	35.41
15.25	31.89	32.21	32.48	32.73	32.94	33.13	33.30
15.50	29.96	30.25	30.51	30.73	30.93	31.10	31.25
15.75	28.09	28.35	28.58	28.79	28.97	29.12	29.26
16.00	26.26	26.50	26.71	26.90	27.06	27.20	27.32
16.25	24.48	24.70	24.89	25.06	25.20	25.33	25.44
16.50	22.74	22.94	23.11	23.26	23.40	23.51	23.61
16.75	21.05	21.23	21.38	21.52	21.64	21.74	21.83
17.00	19.40	19.56	19.70	19.82	19.92	20.02	20.10
17.25	17.79	17.93	18.06	18.16	18.26	18.34	18.41
17.50	16.22	16.34	16.45	16.55	16.63	16.70	16.77
17.75	14.68	14.79	14.89	14.98	15.05	15.11	15.17
18.00	13.10	13.20	13.37	13.44	13.51	13.56	13.61
18.25	11.72	11.81	11.88	11.95	12.00	12.05	12.09
18.50	10.30	10.37	10.43	10.49	10.54	10.58	10.61
18.75	8.90	8.97	9.02	9.06	9.10	9.14	9.17
19.00	7.54	7.59	7.64	7.68	7.71	7.74	7.76
19.25	6.21	6.25	6.29	6.32	6.35	6.37	6.39
19.50	4.91	4.95	4.97	5.00	5.02	5.03	5.05
19.75	3.64	3.67	3.69	3.70	3.72	3.73	3.74
20.00	2.40	2.42	2.43	2.44	2.45	2.46	2.46

Valuation of Assumable Mortgages

CURRENT RATE:21%

OLD RATE	5 YEARS	10 YEARS	15 YEARS	20 YEARS	21 YEARS	22 YEARS	23 YEARS
4.00	46.90	97.47	147.48	193.35	201.85	210.10	218.11
4.25	46.00	95.17	143.34	187.07	195.12	202.92	210.47
4.50	45.11	92.91	139.30	180.98	188.61	195.98	203.10
4.75	44.23	90.69	135.35	175.08	182.30	189.27	195.98
5.00	43.36	88.50	131.49	169.36	176.19	182.77	189.10
5.25	42.49	86.34	127.72	163.81	170.28	176.49	182.46
5.50	41.63	84.22	124.04	158.42	164.55	170.42	176.04
5.75	40.78	82.14	120.45	153.20	158.99	164.54	169.84
6.00	39.94	80.09	116.93	148.12	153.61	158.85	163.84
6.25	39.10	78.07	113.50	143.20	148.39	153.34	158.04
6.50	38.27	76.08	110.15	138.43	143.34	148.01	152.44
6.75	37.44	74.12	106.87	133.79	138.43	142.84	147.01
7.00	36.62	72.19	103.67	129.28	133.68	137.84	141.77
7.25	35.81	70.30	100.54	124.91	129.06	132.99	136.69
7.50	35.01	68.43	97.47	120.66	124.59	128.29	131.77
7.75	34.21	66.59	94.48	116.54	120.25	123.74	127.01
8.00	33.42	64.79	91.56	112.52	116.03	119.32	122.41
8.25	32.64	63.01	88.70	108.63	111.94	115.04	117.94
8.50	31.86	61.25	85.90	104.84	107.97	110.89	113.62
8.75	31.09	59.53	83.16	101.16	104.11	106.87	109.43
9.00	30.33	57.83	80.49	97.58	100.36	102.96	105.37
9.25	29.57	56.16	77.87	94.09	96.72	99.17	101.44
9.50	28.81	54.51	75.31	90.71	93.19	95.49	97.62
9.75	28.07	52.89	72.80	87.41	89.75	91.92	93.92
10.00	27.33	51.29	70.35	84.21	86.41	88.45	90.33
10.25	26.59	49.72	67.95	81.09	83.17	85.08	86.85
10.50	25.87	48.17	65.61	78.05	80.01	81.81	83.47
10.75	25.14	46.64	63.31	75.10	76.94	78.63	80.18
11.00	24.43	45.14	61.06	72.22	73.96	75.55	77.00
11.25	23.72	43.66	58.86	69.42	71.06	72.54	73.91
11.50	23.01	42.20	56.71	66.69	68.23	69.63	70.90
11.75	22.31	40.77	54.60	64.03	65.47	66.79	67.98
12.00	21.62	39.35	52.53	61.44	62.80	64.03	65.15
12.25	20.93	37.96	50.51	58.92	60.19	61.35	62.39
12.50	20.25	36.59	48.53	56.46	57.65	58.73	59.71
12.75	19.57	35.24	46.59	54.07	55.18	56.19	57.10
13.00	18.90	33.90	44.68	51.73	52.78	53.72	54.57
13.25	18.23	32.59	42.82	49.45	50.43	51.31	52.11
13.50	17.57	31.30	41.00	47.23	48.15	48.97	49.71
13.75	16.92	30.02	39.21	45.07	45.92	46.69	47.37
14.00	16.27	28.77	37.46	42.95	43.75	44.46	45.10
14.25	15.62	27.53	35.74	40.89	41.63	42.30	42.89
14.50	14.98	26.31	34.06	38.88	39.57	40.19	40.74
14.75	14.35	25.11	32.41	36.91	37.56	38.13	38.64
15.00	13.72	23.92	30.80	35.00	35.59	36.13	36.60
15.25	13.09	22.76	29.21	33.13	33.68	34.17	34.61
15.50	12.47	21.61	27.66	31.30	31.81	32.26	32.67
15.75	11.86	20.47	26.14	29.52	29.99	30.41	30.78
16.00	11.25	19.35	24.64	27.77	28.21	28.59	28.93
16.25	10.64	18.25	23.18	26.07	26.47	26.82	27.13
16.50	10.04	17.16	21.74	24.41	24.77	25.10	25.38
16.75	9.45	16.09	20.33	22.78	23.12	23.41	23.67
17.00	8.86	15.04	18.95	21.19	21.50	21.77	22.00
17.25	8.27	14.00	17.59	19.64	19.92	20.16	20.37
17.50	7.69	12.97	16.26	18.12	18.37	18.59	18.78
17.75	7.11	11.96	14.95	16.64	16.86	17.06	17.23
18.00	6.54	10.96	13.67	15.18	15.39	15.56	15.71
18.25	5.97	9.97	12.42	13.76	13.94	14.10	14.23
18.50	5.40	9.00	11.18	12.37	12.53	12.67	12.79
18.75	4.85	8.05	9.97	11.01	11.15	11.27	11.38
19.00	4.29	7.10	8.78	9.68	9.80	9.91	10.00
19.25	3.74	6.17	7.61	8.38	8.48	8.57	8.65
19.50	3.19	5.25	6.46	7.11	7.19	7.26	7.33
19.75	2.65	4.35	5.34	5.86	5.93	5.99	6.04
20.00	2.11	3.45	4.23	4.64	4.69	4.74	4.78

Valuation of Assumable Mortgages

CURRENT RATE:21%

OLD RATE	24 YEARS	25 YEARS	26 YEARS	27 YEARS	28 YEARS	29 YEARS	30 YEARS
4.00	225.86	233.37	240.63	247.65	254.43	260.96	267.27
4.25	217.77	224.82	231.62	238.18	244.49	250.57	256.43
4.50	209.96	216.58	222.95	229.08	234.97	240.62	246.05
4.75	202.44	208.65	214.61	220.34	225.83	231.09	236.13
5.00	195.18	201.01	206.59	211.94	217.06	221.95	226.63
5.25	188.17	193.65	198.88	203.87	208.64	213.19	217.53
5.50	181.42	186.55	191.45	196.11	200.56	204.79	208.81
5.75	174.89	179.71	184.29	188.65	192.79	196.73	200.46
6.00	168.59	173.11	177.40	181.47	185.33	188.99	192.45
6.25	162.51	166.75	170.77	174.57	178.16	181.56	184.77
6.50	156.64	160.61	164.37	167.92	171.27	174.43	177.41
6.75	150.96	154.69	158.20	161.52	164.64	167.58	170.34
7.00	145.47	148.97	152.26	155.35	158.26	160.99	163.55
7.25	140.17	143.45	146.53	149.41	152.12	154.66	157.03
7.50	135.05	138.12	141.00	143.69	146.21	148.57	150.77
7.75	130.09	132.97	135.66	138.17	140.52	142.71	144.75
8.00	125.29	127.99	130.51	132.85	135.04	137.07	138.96
8.25	120.65	123.18	125.53	127.72	129.75	131.64	133.39
8.50	116.16	118.53	120.73	122.77	124.66	126.41	128.04
8.75	111.82	114.03	116.09	117.99	119.75	121.38	122.88
9.00	107.61	109.68	111.60	113.38	115.01	116.52	117.92
9.25	103.54	105.48	107.27	108.92	110.44	111.85	113.13
9.50	99.59	101.40	103.08	104.62	106.03	107.33	108.53
9.75	95.76	97.46	99.02	100.46	101.77	102.98	104.08
10.00	92.06	93.65	95.10	96.44	97.66	98.78	99.80
10.25	88.46	89.95	91.31	92.55	93.69	94.73	95.67
10.50	84.98	86.37	87.64	88.79	89.85	90.81	91.68
10.75	81.60	82.90	84.08	85.16	86.14	87.03	87.83
11.00	78.33	79.54	80.64	81.64	82.55	83.37	84.12
11.25	75.15	76.28	77.30	78.23	79.08	79.84	80.53
11.50	72.06	73.12	74.07	74.93	75.72	76.42	77.06
11.75	69.07	70.05	70.94	71.74	72.47	73.12	73.71
12.00	66.16	67.07	67.90	68.65	69.32	69.92	70.46
12.25	63.33	64.19	64.96	65.65	66.27	66.83	67.33
12.50	60.59	61.38	62.10	62.74	63.31	63.83	64.29
12.75	57.93	58.66	59.33	59.92	60.45	60.93	61.35
13.00	55.34	56.02	56.64	57.19	57.68	58.12	58.51
13.25	52.82	53.45	54.02	54.53	54.99	55.39	55.75
13.50	50.37	50.96	51.49	51.96	52.38	52.75	53.08
13.75	47.99	48.54	49.03	49.46	49.85	50.19	50.49
14.00	45.67	46.18	46.63	47.03	47.39	47.70	47.98
14.25	43.42	43.89	44.31	44.68	45.00	45.29	45.55
14.50	41.23	41.66	42.05	42.39	42.69	42.95	43.19
14.75	39.09	39.49	39.85	40.16	40.44	40.68	40.89
15.00	37.01	37.38	37.71	38.00	38.25	38.47	38.67
15.25	34.99	35.33	35.63	35.90	36.13	36.33	36.51
15.50	33.02	33.33	33.61	33.85	34.06	34.25	34.41
15.75	31.10	31.39	31.64	31.86	32.05	32.22	32.37
16.00	29.23	29.49	29.72	29.92	30.10	30.25	30.39
16.25	27.41	27.65	27.86	28.04	28.20	28.34	28.46
16.50	25.63	25.85	26.04	26.21	26.35	26.48	26.59
16.75	23.90	24.09	24.27	24.42	24.55	24.66	24.76
17.00	22.21	22.39	22.54	22.68	22.80	22.90	22.99
17.25	20.56	20.72	20.86	20.98	21.09	21.18	21.26
17.50	18.95	19.09	19.22	19.33	19.43	19.51	19.58
17.75	17.38	17.51	17.62	17.72	17.80	17.88	17.94
18.00	15.85	15.96	16.06	16.15	16.22	16.29	16.34
18.25	14.35	14.45	14.54	14.62	14.68	14.74	14.79
18.50	12.89	12.98	13.06	13.12	13.18	13.23	13.27
18.75	11.47	11.54	11.61	11.67	11.72	11.76	11.79
19.00	10.07	10.14	10.20	10.24	10.29	10.32	10.35
19.25	8.71	8.77	8.82	8.86	8.89	8.92	8.95
19.50	7.38	7.43	7.47	7.50	7.53	7.55	7.58
19.75	6.08	6.12	6.15	6.18	6.20	6.22	6.24
20.00	4.81	4.84	4.86	4.88	4.90	4.92	4.93

Valuation of Assumable Mortgages

CURRENT RATE: 21½%

OLD RATE	5 YEARS	10 YEARS	15 YEARS	20 YEARS	21 YEARS	22 YEARS	23 YEARS
4.00	48.43	100.80	152.55	199.89	208.65	217.15	225.39
4.25	47.52	98.47	148.32	193.47	201.77	209.80	217.58
4.50	46.63	96.17	144.20	187.25	195.11	202.70	210.04
4.75	45.73	93.90	140.17	181.22	188.66	195.84	202.75
5.00	44.85	91.68	136.23	175.36	182.41	189.20	195.72
5.25	43.98	89.49	132.38	169.69	176.37	182.78	188.93
5.50	43.11	87.33	128.63	164.18	170.51	176.56	182.36
5.75	42.25	85.21	124.96	158.84	164.83	170.55	176.01
6.00	41.39	83.12	121.37	153.66	159.32	164.73	169.88
6.25	40.55	81.07	117.87	148.63	153.99	159.10	163.95
6.50	39.71	79.05	114.45	143.74	148.82	153.64	158.22
6.75	30.07	77.06	111.10	139.00	143.81	148.36	152.67
7.00	38.05	75.10	107.84	134.40	138.94	143.24	147.30
7.25	37.23	73.17	104.64	129.93	134.23	138.28	142.11
7.50	36.42	71.27	101.52	125.58	129.65	133.48	137.08
7.75	35.61	69.40	98.46	121.36	125.21	128.82	132.21
8.00	34.81	67.57	95.48	117.26	120.90	124.31	127.50
8.25	34.02	65.76	92.56	113.28	116.71	119.93	122.93
8.50	33.24	63.97	89.70	109.41	112.65	115.68	118.51
8.75	32.46	62.22	86.91	105.64	108.71	111.57	114.23
9.00	31.68	60.49	84.18	101.96	104.88	107.57	110.07
9.25	30.92	58.79	81.51	98.42	101.16	103.69	106.05
9.50	30.16	57.12	78.90	94.96	97.54	99.93	102.14
9.75	29.40	55.47	76.34	91.59	94.03	96.28	98.36
10.00	28.65	53.84	73.84	88.32	90.61	92.73	94.69
10.25	27.91	52.24	71.39	85.13	87.29	89.29	91.12
10.50	27.18	50.67	69.00	82.02	84.07	85.94	87.67
10.75	26.45	49.12	66.65	79.00	80.93	82.69	84.31
11.00	25.72	47.59	64.36	76.06	77.87	79.53	81.05
11.25	25.01	46.08	62.11	73.20	74.90	76.46	77.89
11.50	24.29	44.60	59.91	70.41	72.01	73.48	74.81
11.75	23.59	43.14	57.76	67.69	69.20	70.58	71.83
12.00	22.89	41.70	55.65	65.04	66.47	67.76	68.93
12.25	22.19	40.29	53.59	62.47	63.80	65.01	66.11
12.50	21.50	38.89	51.57	59.95	61.21	62.34	63.37
12.75	20.82	37.52	49.59	57.50	58.68	59.74	60.70
13.00	20.14	36.16	47.65	55.11	56.22	57.21	58.11
13.25	19.47	34.83	45.75	52.79	53.82	54.75	55.59
13.50	18.80	33.51	43.88	50.52	51.48	52.35	53.13
13.75	18.14	32.22	42.06	48.30	49.21	50.02	50.75
14.00	17.48	30.94	40.27	46.14	46.99	47.75	48.42
14.25	16.83	29.68	38.52	44.03	44.82	45.53	46.16
14.50	16.18	28.44	36.81	41.98	42.71	43.37	43.96
14.75	15.54	27.22	35.12	39.97	40.66	41.27	41.81
15.00	14.90	26.01	33.47	38.01	38.65	39.22	39.72
15.25	14.27	24.83	31.86	36.10	36.69	37.22	37.69
15.50	13.65	23.66	30.27	34.23	34.78	35.27	35.70
15.75	13.02	22.50	28.72	32.40	32.92	33.37	33.77
16.00	12.41	21.37	27.19	30.62	31.10	31.51	31.88
16.25	11.80	20.24	25.70	28.88	29.32	29.70	30.04
16.50	11.19	19.14	24.23	27.18	27.58	27.94	28.25
16.75	10.59	18.05	22.79	25.52	25.89	26.22	26.50
17.00	9.99	16.98	21.38	23.89	24.23	24.53	24.79
17.25	9.40	15.92	20.00	22.31	22.62	22.89	23.13
17.50	8.81	14.87	18.64	20.75	21.04	21.29	21.50
17.75	8.23	13.85	17.31	19.24	19.49	19.72	19.91
18.00	7.65	12.83	16.00	17.75	17.98	18.19	18.36
18.25	7.07	11.83	14.72	16.30	16.51	16.69	16.85
18.50	6.50	10.84	13.46	14.88	15.07	15.23	15.37
18.75	5.94	9.87	12.22	13.49	13.66	13.80	13.93
19.00	5.38	8.91	11.01	12.13	12.28	12.40	12.51
19.25	4.82	7.96	9.81	10.80	10.93	11.04	11.13
19.50	4.27	7.03	8.64	9.50	9.61	9.70	9.78
19.75	3.72	6.11	7.49	8.22	8.31	8.40	8.46
20.00	3.18	5.20	6.36	6.97	7.05	7.12	7.17

Valuation of Assumable Mortgages

CURRENT RATE:21½%

OLD RATE	24 YEARS	25 YEARS	26 YEARS	27 YEARS	28 YEARS	29 YEARS	30 YEARS
4.00	233.37	241.09	248.56	255.77	262.73	269.44	275.91
4.25	225.09	232.34	239.33	246.07	252.56	258.81	264.81
4.50	217.10	223.91	230.46	236.76	242.81	248.62	254.20
4.75	209.40	215.80	221.93	227.82	233.46	238.87	244.04
5.00	201.98	207.98	213.73	219.23	224.49	229.51	234.31
5.25	194.81	200.45	205.83	210.97	215.87	220.55	225.00
5.50	187.90	193.18	198.23	203.03	207.60	211.95	216.08
5.75	181.22	186.19	190.91	195.39	199.65	203.70	207.53
6.00	174.78	179.44	183.86	188.05	192.02	195.78	199.34
6.25	168.56	172.93	177.06	180.98	184.68	188.18	191.48
6.50	162.55	166.65	170.52	174.17	177.62	180.87	183.94
6.75	156.74	160.58	164.21	167.62	170.84	173.86	176.70
7.00	151.13	154.73	158.13	161.32	164.31	167.12	169.75
7.25	146.70	149.09	152.28	155.24	158.03	160.64	163.08
7.50	140.46	143.63	146.60	149.38	151.98	154.40	156.67
7.75	135.39	138.36	141.14	143.73	146.15	148.41	150.51
8.00	130.48	133.27	135.87	138.29	140.54	142.64	144.58
8.25	125.74	128.35	130.78	133.04	136.14	137.08	139.09
8.50	121.14	123.59	125.86	127.97	129.92	131.73	133.40
8.75	116.70	118.99	121.11	123.08	124.90	126.58	128.13
9.00	112.00	114.54	116.53	118.36	120.05	121.61	123.04
9.25	108.22	110.23	112.09	113.80	115.37	116.82	118.15
9.50	104.10	106.07	107.80	109.40	110.86	112.20	113.43
9.75	100.27	102.04	103.65	105.14	106.50	107.75	108.89
10.00	96.48	98.13	99.64	101.03	102.29	103.45	104.50
10.25	92.81	94.35	95.76	97.05	98.23	99.30	100.28
10.50	89.24	90.68	92.00	93.20	94.30	95.29	96.19
10.75	85.79	87.13	88.36	89.48	90.50	91.42	92.26
11.00	82.43	83.69	84.84	85.88	86.82	87.68	88.45
11.25	79.18	80.36	81.43	82.39	83.27	84.06	84.78
11.50	76.03	77.12	78.12	79.02	79.83	80.57	81.23
11.75	72.96	73.99	74.91	75.75	76.50	77.18	77.79
12.00	69.99	70.94	71.81	72.58	73.28	73.91	74.47
12.25	67.10	67.99	68.79	69.51	70.16	70.74	71.26
12.50	64.29	65.12	65.87	66.54	67.14	67.68	68.16
12.75	61.56	62.34	63.03	63.65	64.21	64.71	65.15
13.00	58.91	59.63	60.28	60.86	61.37	61.83	62.24
13.25	56.34	57.01	57.61	58.14	58.62	59.04	59.42
13.50	53.83	54.46	55.01	55.51	55.95	56.34	56.68
13.75	51.40	51.98	52.49	52.95	53.36	53.72	54.03
14.00	49.03	49.57	50.04	50.47	50.84	51.17	51.47
14.25	46.72	47.22	47.66	48.05	48.40	48.71	48.97
14.50	44.48	44.94	45.35	45.71	46.03	46.31	46.56
14.75	42.30	42.72	43.10	43.43	43.73	43.98	44.21
15.00	40.17	40.57	40.91	41.22	41.49	41.73	41.93
15.25	38.10	38.47	38.79	39.07	39.32	39.53	39.72
15.50	36.09	36.42	36.72	36.98	37.20	37.40	37.57
15.75	34.12	34.43	34.70	34.94	35.15	35.33	35.49
16.00	32.21	32.49	32.74	32.96	33.15	33.31	33.46
16.25	30.34	30.60	30.83	31.03	31.20	31.35	31.48
16.50	28.52	28.76	28.97	29.15	29.31	29.45	29.57
16.75	26.75	26.97	27.16	27.32	27.47	27.59	27.70
17.00	25.02	25.22	25.39	25.54	25.67	25.78	25.88
17.25	23.33	23.52	23.67	23.81	23.93	24.03	24.11
17.50	21.69	21.85	21.99	22.12	22.22	22.31	22.39
17.75	20.08	20.23	20.36	20.47	20.56	20.65	20.72
18.00	18.52	18.65	18.76	18.86	18.95	19.02	19.08
18.25	16.99	17.10	17.21	17.29	17.37	17.43	17.49
18.50	15.49	15.60	15.69	15.77	15.83	15.89	15.94
18.75	14.03	14.13	14.21	14.27	14.33	14.38	14.43
19.00	12.61	12.69	12.76	12.82	12.87	12.91	12.95
19.25	11.22	11.29	11.35	11.40	11.44	11.48	11.51
19.50	9.85	9.91	9.97	10.01	10.05	10.08	10.11
19.75	8.52	8.58	8.62	8.66	8.69	8.71	8.74
20.00	7.22	7.27	7.30	7.33	7.36	7.38	7.40

Points Discount Table

When shopping for a mortgage a real estate investor or prospective home buyer may find that, in order to obtain a mortgage, he or she must pay points, which represent a one-time charge associated with the loan agreement. The term *points* refers to a percentage of the total mortgage loan amount. Each point equals one percent of that amount. A mortgage generally requires between 1 and 5 points, which translates into 1% to 5% of the total mortgage loan. If you must pay 3 points on a mortgage and your total mortgage amount is $100,000, you must pay an up-front fee of $3,000. Therefore, the net amount received is $97,000. Paying points is equivalent to receiving a smaller net amount from the lender but with the same monthly repayment commitment. The effective rate of interest is thereby increased.

The points discount table shows the effective interest rate on mortgage loans with interest rates from 5% to 21% and with 1 to 5 points. Here are some illustrative situations to help you understand and use the table:

Situation 1

Miss Lake wishes to purchase property and has looked to several banks to help finance her purchase. ABC Savings Bank is offering her a mortgage at an interest rate of 11½% but requires that she pay 3 points. XYZ Bank is offering her a 12% interest rate with no points at all. Miss Lake prefers the mortgage with the smallest effective interest rate. The question is, which bank should Miss Lake use if her mortgage is for a ten-year term.

To find the answer she must (1) locate the 11½% interest rate along the left side of the points discount table and (2) read under the 10-year column the number next to 97. The number 97 is used because if she pays 3 points she will get a net loan of 97% of the mortgage. The number next to 97 is 12.25, or 12¼%. That shows that Miss Lake will receive from ABC Savings Bank a mortgage with an equivalent interest rate of 12¼%. This is higher than the 12% offered by XYZ Bank and therefore Miss Lake will choose a mortgage from the XYZ Bank at the 12% interest rate for the 10-year term.

Situation 2

Mr. Apple wishes to know the effective interest rate of a 30-year mortgage with an interest rate of 13½% and required payment of 2 points. He must (1) look down the left side of the table and find 13½%, (2) locate the 98 value, and (3) scan across the table to the 30-year column. The number shown there is 13.80. Thus, Mr. Apple will be paying an equivalent interest rate of 13.80% if he pays 2 points on the mortgage with an interest rate of 13½%.

Points Discount Table

RATE	PRICE	5 YEARS	10 YEARS	15 YEARS	20 YEARS	25 YEARS	30 YEARS	40 YEARS
5%	99	5.41	5.22	5.15	5.12	5.10	5.09	5.07
	98	5.84	5.44	5.31	5.24	5.20	5.18	5.15
	97	6.26	5.66	5.47	5.37	5.31	5.27	5.22
	96	6.69	5.89	5.63	5.49	5.41	5.36	5.30
	95	7.13	6.12	5.79	5.62	5.52	5.46	5.38
5¼%	99	5.67	5.47	5.40	5.37	5.35	5.34	5.32
	98	6.09	5.69	5.56	5.49	5.46	5.43	5.40
	97	6.51	5.92	5.72	5.62	5.56	5.52	5.48
	96	6.95	6.15	5.88	5.75	5.67	5.62	5.56
	95	7.39	6.38	6.04	5.88	5.78	5.71	5.64
5½%	99	5.92	5.72	5.66	5.62	5.60	5.59	5.58
	98	6.34	5.94	5.81	5.75	5.71	5.68	5.65
	97	6.77	6.17	5.97	5.87	5.82	5.78	5.73
	96	7.20	6.40	6.13	6.00	5.92	5.87	5.81
	95	7.64	6.64	6.30	6.13	6.03	5.97	5.90
5¾%	99	6.17	5.97	5.91	5.87	5.85	5.84	5.83
	98	6.59	6.20	6.06	6.00	5.96	5.94	5.91
	97	7.02	6.42	6.23	6.13	6.07	6.03	5.99
	96	7.46	6.66	6.39	6.26	6.18	6.13	6.07
	95	7.90	6.89	6.55	6.39	6.29	6.23	6.15
6%	99	6.42	6.22	6.16	6.13	6.11	6.09	6.08
	98	6.84	6.45	6.32	6.25	6.21	6.19	6.16
	97	7.27	6.68	6.48	6.38	6.32	6.29	6.24
	96	7.71	6.91	6.64	6.51	6.43	6.39	6.33
	95	8.15	7.15	6.81	6.65	6.55	6.49	6.41
6¼%	99	6.67	6.47	6.41	6.38	6.36	6.35	6.33
	98	7.10	6.70	6.57	6.50	6.47	6.44	6.41
	97	7.53	6.93	6.73	6.63	6.58	6.54	6.50
	96	7.96	7.16	6.90	6.77	6.69	6.64	6.58
	95	8.41	7.40	7.07	6.90	6.80	6.74	6.67
6½%	99	6.92	6.72	6.66	6.63	6.61	6.60	6.58
	98	7.35	6.95	6.82	6.76	6.72	6.70	6.67
	97	7.78	7.18	6.99	6.89	6.83	6.80	6.75
	96	8.22	7.42	7.15	7.02	6.95	6.90	6.84
	95	8.66	7.66	7.32	7.16	7.06	7.00	6.93
6¾%	99	7.17	6.98	6.91	6.88	6.86	6.85	6.83
	98	7.60	7.20	7.07	7.01	6.97	6.95	6.92
	97	8.03	7.44	7.24	7.14	7.09	7.05	7.01
	96	8.47	7.67	7.41	7.28	7.20	7.15	7.10
	95	8.92	7.91	7.58	7.41	7.32	7.26	7.19
7%	99	7.42	7.23	7.16	7.13	7.11	7.10	7.09
	98	7.85	7.46	7.33	7.26	7.23	7.20	7.17
	97	8.29	7.69	7.49	7.40	7.34	7.30	7.26
	96	8.73	7.93	7.66	7.53	7.46	7.41	7.35
	95	9.17	8.17	7.83	7.67	7.58	7.52	7.45
7¼%	99	7.67	7.48	7.41	7.38	7.36	7.35	7.34
	98	8.10	7.71	7.58	7.51	7.48	7.45	7.43
	97	8.54	7.94	7.75	7.65	7.59	7.56	7.52
	96	8.98	8.18	7.92	7.79	7.71	7.67	7.61
	95	9.43	8.42	8.09	7.93	7.83	7.77	7.71
7½%	99	7.92	7.73	7.66	7.63	7.61	7.60	7.59
	98	8.36	7.96	7.83	7.77	7.73	7.71	7.68
	97	8.79	8.20	8.00	7.90	7.85	7.81	7.77
	96	9.24	8.44	8.17	8.04	7.97	7.92	7.87
	95	9.69	8.68	8.35	8.19	8.09	8.03	7.97
7¾%	99	8.18	7.98	7.92	7.88	7.87	7.85	7.84
	98	8.61	8.21	8.08	8.02	7.98	7.96	7.93
	97	9.05	8.45	8.25	8.16	8.10	8.07	8.03
	96	9.49	8.69	8.43	8.30	8.23	8.18	8.13
	95	9.94	8.94	8.60	8.44	8.35	8.29	8.22

Points Discount Table

RATE	PRICE	5 YEARS	10 YEARS	15 YEARS	20 YEARS	25 YEARS	30 YEARS	40 YEARS
8%	99	8.43	8.23	8.17	8.14	8.12	8.11	8.09
	98	8.86	8.47	8.34	8.27	8.24	8.21	8.19
	97	9.30	8.70	8.51	8.41	8.36	8.32	8.29
	96	9.74	8.95	8.68	8.55	8.48	8.44	8.38
	95	10.20	9.19	8.86	8.70	8.61	8.55	8.48
8¼%	99	8.68	8.48	8.42	8.30	8.37	8.30	8.35
	98	9.11	8.72	8.59	8.53	8.49	8.47	8.44
	97	9.55	8.96	8.76	8.67	8.61	8.58	8.54
	96	10.00	9.20	8.94	8.81	8.74	8.69	8.64
	95	10.45	9.45	9.12	8.96	8.86	8.81	8.74
8½%	99	8.93	8.73	8.67	8.64	8.62	8.61	8.60
	98	9.36	8.97	8.84	8.78	8.74	8.72	8.70
	97	9.80	9.21	9.02	8.92	8.87	8.83	8.80
	96	10.25	9.46	9.19	9.07	8.99	8.95	8.90
	95	10.71	9.70	9.37	9.21	9.12	9.07	9.00
8¾%	99	9.18	8.98	8.92	8.89	8.87	8.86	8.85
	98	9.62	9.22	9.09	9.03	9.00	8.97	8.95
	97	10.06	9.46	9.27	9.18	9.12	9.09	9.05
	96	10.51	9.71	9.45	9.32	9.25	9.21	9.16
	95	10.96	9.96	9.63	9.47	9.38	9.32	9.26
9%	99	9.43	9.24	9.17	9.14	9.12	9.11	9.10
	98	9.87	9.47	9.35	9.28	9.25	9.23	9.20
	97	10.31	9.72	9.52	9.43	9.38	9.34	9.31
	96	10.76	9.96	9.70	9.58	9.51	9.46	9.42
	95	11.22	10.21	9.89	9.73	9.64	9.58	9.52
9¼%	99	9.68	9.49	9.42	9.39	9.38	9.36	9.35
	98	10.12	9.73	9.60	9.54	9.50	9.48	9.46
	97	10.56	9.97	9.78	9.68	9.63	9.60	9.56
	96	11.01	10.22	9.96	9.83	9.76	9.72	9.67
	95	11.47	10.47	10.14	9.99	9.90	9.84	9.78
9½%	99	9.93	9.74	9.67	9.64	9.63	9.62	9.61
	98	10.37	9.98	9.85	9.79	9.76	9.73	9.71
	97	10.82	10.22	10.03	9.94	9.89	9.85	9.82
	96	11.27	10.47	10.21	10.09	10.02	9.98	9.93
	95	11.73	10.73	10.40	10.24	10.16	10.10	10.05
9¾%	99	10.18	9.99	9.93	9.90	9.88	9.87	9.86
	98	10.62	10.23	10.10	10.04	10.01	9.99	9.97
	97	11.07	10.48	10.29	10.19	10.14	10.11	10.08
	96	11.52	10.73	10.47	10.35	10.28	10.23	10.19
	95	11.98	10.98	10.66	10.50	10.41	10.36	10.31
10%	99	10.43	10.24	10.18	10.15	10.13	10.12	10.11
	98	10.88	10.48	10.36	10.30	10.26	10.24	10.22
	97	11.32	10.73	10.54	10.45	10.40	10.37	10.33
	96	11.78	10.98	10.72	10.60	10.53	10.49	10.45
	95	12.24	11.24	10.91	10.76	10.67	10.62	10.57
10¼%	99	10.69	10.49	10.43	10.40	10.38	10.37	10.36
	98	11.13	10.74	10.61	10.55	10.52	10.50	10.47
	97	11.58	10.99	10.79	10.70	10.65	10.62	10.59
	96	12.03	11.24	10.98	10.86	10.79	10.75	10.71
	95	12.49	11.50	11.17	11.02	10.93	10.88	10.83
10½%	99	10.94	10.74	10.68	10.65	10.63	10.62	10.61
	98	11.38	10.99	10.86	10.80	10.77	10.75	10.73
	97	11.83	11.24	11.05	10.96	10.91	10.88	10.85
	96	12.29	11.49	11.24	11.11	11.05	11.01	10.97
	95	12.75	11.75	11.43	11.27	11.19	11.14	11.09
10¾%	99	11.19	10.99	10.93	10.90	10.88	10.88	10.87
	98	11.63	11.24	11.11	11.06	11.02	11.00	10.98
	97	12.08	11.49	11.30	11.21	11.16	11.13	11.10
	96	12.54	11.75	11.49	11.37	11.30	11.26	11.22
	95	13.01	12.01	11.68	11.53	11.45	11.40	11.35

Points Discount Table

RATE	PRICE	5 YEARS	10 YEARS	15 YEARS	20 YEARS	25 YEARS	30 YEARS	40 YEARS
	99	11.44	11.25	11.18	11.15	11.14	11.13	11.12
	98	11.88	11.49	11.37	11.31	11.28	11.26	11.24
11%	97	12.34	11.75	11.56	11.47	11.42	11.39	11.36
	96	12.80	12.00	11.75	11.63	11.56	11.52	11.48
	95	13.26	12.26	11.94	11.79	11.71	11.66	11.61
	99	11.69	11.50	11.43	11.40	11.39	11.38	11.37
	98	12.14	11.75	11.62	11.56	11.53	11.51	11.49
11¼%	97	12.59	12.00	11.81	11.72	11.67	11.64	11.62
	96	13.05	12.26	12.00	11.88	11.82	11.78	11.74
	95	13.52	12.52	12.20	12.05	11.97	11.92	11.87
	99	11.94	11.75	11.69	11.66	11.64	11.63	11.62
	98	12.39	12.00	11.87	11.81	11.78	11.76	11.75
11½%	97	12.84	12.25	12.06	11.98	11.93	11.90	11.87
	96	13.30	12.51	12.26	12.14	12.08	12.04	12.00
	95	13.77	12.78	12.46	12.31	12.23	12.18	12.13
	99	12.19	12.00	11.94	11.91	11.89	11.88	11.87
	98	12.64	12.25	12.13	12.07	12.04	12.02	12.00
11¾%	97	13.10	12.51	12.32	12.23	12.18	12.16	12.13
	96	13.56	12.77	12.51	12.40	12.33	12.30	12.26
	95	14.03	13.03	12.71	12.57	12.49	12.44	12.39
	99	12.44	12.25	12.19	12.16	12.14	12.13	12.13
	98	12.89	12.50	12.38	12.32	12.29	12.27	12.25
12%	97	13.35	12.76	12.57	12.49	12.44	12.41	12.39
	96	13.81	13.02	12.77	12.65	12.59	12.55	12.52
	95	14.28	13.29	12.97	12.82	12.74	12.70	12.66
	99	12.69	12.50	12.44	12.41	12.40	12.39	12.38
	98	13.15	12.76	12.63	12.57	12.54	12.53	12.51
12¼%	97	13.60	13.02	12.83	12.74	12.69	12.67	12.64
	96	14.07	13.28	13.03	12.91	12.85	12.81	12.78
	95	14.54	13.55	13.23	13.08	13.00	12.96	12.92
	99	12.95	12.75	12.69	12.66	12.65	12.64	12.63
	98	13.40	13.01	12.88	12.83	12.80	12.78	12.76
12½%	97	13.86	13.27	13.08	13.00	12.95	12.92	12.90
	96	14.32	13.53	13.28	13.17	13.11	13.07	13.04
	95	14.79	13.80	13.49	13.34	13.26	13.22	13.18
	99	13.20	13.00	12.94	12.91	12.90	12.89	12.88
	98	13.65	13.26	13.14	13.08	13.05	13.03	13.02
12¾%	97	14.11	13.52	13.34	13.25	13.21	13.18	13.16
	96	14.58	13.79	13.54	13.42	13.36	13.33	13.30
	95	15.05	14.06	13.74	13.60	13.52	13.48	13.44
	99	13.45	13.26	13.19	13.17	13.15	13.14	13.14
	98	13.90	13.51	13.39	13.33	13.30	13.29	13.27
13%	97	14.36	13.78	13.59	13.51	13.46	13.44	13.41
	96	14.83	14.04	13.79	13.68	13.62	13.59	13.56
	95	15.31	14.32	14.00	13.86	13.78	13.74	13.70
	99	13.70	13.51	13.45	13.42	13.40	13.39	13.39
	98	14.15	13.77	13.64	13.59	13.56	13.54	13.53
13¼%	97	14.62	14.03	13.85	13.76	13.72	13.69	13.67
	96	15.09	14.30	14.05	13.94	13.88	13.85	13.82
	95	15.56	14.57	14.26	14.12	14.04	14.00	13.97
	99	13.95	13.76	13.70	13.67	13.65	13.65	13.64
	98	14.41	14.02	13.90	13.84	13.81	13.80	13.78
13½%	97	14.87	14.28	14.10	14.02	13.97	13.95	13.93
	96	15.34	14.55	14.31	14.19	14.14	14.10	14.08
	95	15.82	14.83	14.52	14.38	14.30	14.26	14.23
	99	14.20	14.01	13.95	13.92	13.91	13.90	13.89
	98	14.66	14.27	14.15	14.09	14.07	14.05	14.04
13¾%	97	15.12	14.54	14.35	14.27	14.23	14.21	14.18
	96	15.59	14.81	14.56	14.45	14.39	14.36	14.34
	95	16.07	15.09	14.77	14.63	14.56	14.52	14.49
	99	14.45	14.26	14.20	14.17	14.16	14.15	14.14
	98	14.91	14.52	14.40	14.35	14.32	14.30	14.29
14%	97	15.38	14.79	14.61	14.53	14.48	14.46	14.44
	96	15.85	15.07	14.82	14.71	14.65	14.62	14.60
	95	16.33	15.34	15.03	14.89	14.82	14.78	14.75

Points Discount Table

RATE	PRICE	5 YEARS	10 YEARS	15 YEARS	20 YEARS	25 YEARS	30 YEARS	40 YEARS
14¼%	99	14.70	14.51	14.45	14.42	14.41	14.40	14.40
	98	15.16	14.78	14.66	14.60	14.57	14.56	14.55
	97	15.63	15.05	14.86	14.78	14.74	14.72	14.70
	96	16.10	15.32	15.08	14.97	14.91	14.88	14.85
	95	16.58	15.60	15.29	15.15	15.08	15.05	15.01
14½%	99	14.95	14.76	14.70	14.68	14.66	14.66	14.65
	98	15.42	15.03	14.91	14.86	14.83	14.81	14.80
	97	15.88	15.30	15.12	15.04	15.00	14.97	14.96
	96	16.36	15.58	15.33	15.22	15.17	15.14	15.11
	95	16.84	15.86	15.55	15.41	15.34	15.31	15.28
14¾%	99	15.21	15.01	14.95	14.93	14.91	14.91	14.90
	98	15.67	15.28	15.16	15.11	15.08	15.07	15.06
	97	16.14	15.55	15.37	15.29	15.25	15.23	15.21
	96	16.61	15.83	15.59	15.48	15.43	15.40	15.37
	95	17.10	16.11	15.81	15.67	15.60	15.57	15.54
15%	99	15.46	15.27	15.21	15.18	15.17	15.16	15.15
	98	15.92	15.54	15.42	15.36	15.34	15.32	15.31
	97	16.39	15.81	15.63	15.55	15.51	15.49	15.47
	96	16.87	16.09	15.84	15.74	15.68	15.66	15.63
	95	17.35	16.37	16.07	15.93	15.86	15.83	15.80
15¼%	99	15.71	15.52	15.46	15.43	15.42	15.41	15.41
	98	16.17	15.79	15.67	15.62	15.59	15.58	15.57
	97	16.64	16.06	15.88	15.80	15.77	15.74	15.73
	96	17.12	16.34	16.10	16.00	15.94	15.92	15.89
	95	17.61	16.63	16.32	16.19	16.12	16.09	16.06
15½%	99	15.96	15.77	15.71	15.68	15.67	15.66	15.66
	98	16.42	16.04	15.92	15.87	15.84	15.83	15.82
	97	16.90	16.32	16.14	16.06	16.02	16.00	15.99
	96	17.38	16.60	16.36	16.25	16.20	16.17	16.15
	95	17.86	16.88	16.58	16.45	16.39	16.35	16.33
15¾%	99	16.21	16.02	15.96	15.94	15.92	15.92	15.91
	98	16.68	16.29	16.18	16.12	16.10	16.09	16.08
	97	17.15	16.57	16.39	16.32	16.28	16.26	16.24
	96	17.63	16.85	16.61	16.51	16.46	16.43	16.41
	95	18.12	17.14	16.84	16.71	16.65	16.61	16.59
16%	99	16.46	16.27	16.21	16.19	16.17	16.17	16.16
	98	16.93	16.55	16.43	16.38	16.35	16.34	16.33
	97	17.40	16.83	16.65	16.57	16.53	16.51	16.50
	96	17.89	17.11	16.87	16.77	16.72	16.69	16.67
	95	18.38	17.40	17.10	16.97	16.91	16.88	16.85
16¼%	99	16.71	16.52	16.46	16.44	16.43	16.42	16.42
	98	17.18	16.80	16.68	16.63	16.61	16.59	16.58
	97	17.66	17.08	16.90	16.83	16.79	16.77	16.76
	96	18.14	17.37	17.13	17.03	16.98	16.95	16.93
	95	18.63	17.66	17.36	17.23	17.17	17.14	17.11
16½%	99	16.96	16.77	16.72	16.69	16.68	16.67	16.67
	98	17.43	17.05	16.93	16.89	16.86	16.85	16.84
	97	17.91	17.33	17.16	17.08	17.05	17.03	17.01
	96	18.40	17.62	17.38	17.28	17.24	17.21	17.19
	95	18.89	17.91	17.62	17.40	17.43	17.40	17.38
16¾%	99	17.21	17.03	16.97	16.94	16.93	16.93	16.92
	98	17.69	17.30	17.19	17.14	17.12	17.10	17.09
	97	18.16	17.59	17.41	17.34	17.30	17.29	17.27
	96	18.65	17.88	17.64	17.54	17.49	17.47	17.45
	95	19.14	18.17	17.87	17.75	17.69	17.66	17.64
17%	99	17.47	17.28	17.22	17.19	17.18	17.18	17.17
	98	17.94	17.56	17.44	17.39	17.37	17.36	17.35
	97	18.42	17.84	17.67	17.59	17.56	17.54	17.53
	96	18.90	18.13	17.90	17.80	17.75	17.73	17.71
	95	19.40	18.43	18.13	18.01	17.95	17.92	17.90
17¼%	99	17.72	17.53	17.47	17.45	17.44	17.43	17.43
	98	18.19	17.81	17.70	17.65	17.62	17.61	17.60
	97	18.67	18.10	17.92	17.85	17.82	17.80	17.79
	96	19.16	18.39	18.16	18.06	18.01	17.99	17.97
	95	19.65	18.68	18.39	18.27	18.21	18.18	18.16

Points Discount Table

RATE	PRICE	5 YEARS	10 YEARS	15 YEARS	20 YEARS	25 YEARS	30 YEARS	40 YEARS
	99	17.97	17.78	17.72	17.70	17.69	17.68	17.68
	98	18.44	18.06	17.95	17.90	17.88	17.87	17.86
17½%	97	18.92	18.35	18.18	18.11	18.07	18.06	18.04
	96	19.41	18.64	18.41	18.32	18.27	18.25	18.23
	95	19.91	18.94	18.65	18.53	18.47	18.45	18.43
	99	18.22	18.03	17.97	17.95	17.94	17.93	17.93
	98	18.70	18.32	18.20	18.15	18.13	18.12	18.11
17¾%	97	19.18	18.61	18.43	18.36	18.33	18.31	18.30
	96	19.67	18.90	18.67	18.57	18.53	18.51	18.49
	95	20.17	19.20	18.91	18.79	18.73	18.71	18.69
	99	18.47	18.28	18.23	18.20	18.19	18.19	18.18
	98	18.95	18.57	18.46	18.41	18.39	18.38	18.37
18%	97	19.43	18.86	18.69	18.62	18.59	18.57	18.56
	96	19.92	19.16	18.93	18.83	18.79	18.77	18.75
	95	20.42	19.46	19.17	19.05	19.00	18.97	18.95
	99	18.72	18.53	18.48	18.45	18.44	18.44	18.44
	98	19.20	18.82	18.71	18.66	18.64	18.63	18.62
18¼%	97	19.69	19.11	18.94	18.87	18.84	18.83	18.82
	96	20.18	19.41	19.18	19.09	19.05	19.03	19.01
	95	20.68	19.71	19.43	19.31	19.26	19.23	19.21
	99	18.97	18.78	18.73	18.71	18.70	18.69	18.69
	98	19.45	19.07	18.96	18.92	18.90	18.89	18.88
18½%	97	19.94	19.37	19.20	19.13	19.10	19.08	19.07
	96	20.43	19.67	19.44	19.35	19.31	19.29	19.27
	95	20.94	19.97	19.69	19.57	19.52	19.49	19.48
	99	19.22	19.04	18.98	18.96	18.95	18.94	18.94
	98	19.70	19.33	19.22	19.17	19.15	19.14	19.13
18¾%	97	20.19	19.62	19.45	19.39	19.36	19.34	19.33
	96	20.69	19.92	19.70	19.61	19.57	19.55	19.53
	95	21.19	20.23	19.95	19.83	19.78	19.76	19.74
	99	19.47	19.29	19.23	19.21	19.20	19.20	19.19
	98	19.96	19.58	19.47	19.42	19.40	19.40	19.39
19%	97	20.45	19.88	19.71	19.64	19.61	19.60	19.59
	96	20.94	20.18	19.96	19.86	19.82	19.81	19.79
	95	21.45	20.49	20.20	20.09	20.04	20.02	20.00
	99	19.73	19.54	19.48	19.46	19.45	19.45	19.45
	98	20.21	19.83	19.72	19.68	19.66	19.65	19.64
19¼%	97	20.70	20.13	19.97	19.90	19.87	19.86	19.85
	96	21.20	20.44	20.21	20.12	20.08	20.07	20.05
	95	21.70	20.74	20.46	20.35	20.30	20.28	20.27
	99	19.98	19.79	19.74	19.71	19.70	19.70	19.70
	98	20.46	20.09	19.98	19.93	19.91	19.90	19.90
19½%	97	20.95	20.39	20.22	20.15	20.13	20.11	20.10
	96	21.45	20.69	20.47	20.38	20.34	20.33	20.31
	95	21.96	21.00	20.72	20.61	20.56	20.54	20.53
	99	20.23	20.04	19.99	19.97	19.96	19.95	19.95
	98	20.71	20.34	20.23	20.19	20.17	20.16	20.15
19¾%	97	21.21	20.64	20.48	20.41	20.38	20.37	20.36
	96	21.71	20.95	20.73	20.64	20.60	20.59	20.58
	95	22.22	21.26	20.98	20.87	20.83	20.81	20.79
	99	20.48	20.29	20.24	20.22	20.21	20.21	20.20
	98	20.97	20.59	20.48	20.44	20.42	20.41	20.41
20%	97	21.46	20.90	20.73	20.67	20.64	20.63	20.62
	96	21.96	21.20	20.98	20.90	20.86	20.85	20.84
	95	22.47	21.52	21.24	21.13	21.09	21.07	21.06
	99	20.73	20.55	20.49	20.47	20.46	20.46	20.48
	98	21.22	20.86	20.74	20.70	20.68	20.67	20.66
20¼%	97	21.71	21.15	20.99	20.92	20.90	20.88	20.88
	96	22.22	21.46	21.24	21.16	21.12	21.11	21.10
	95	22.73	21.78	21.50	21.39	21.35	21.33	21.32
	99	20.98	20.80	20.74	20.72	20.71	20.71	20.71
	98	21.47	21.10	20.99	20.95	20.93	20.92	20.92
20½%	97	21.97	21.41	21.24	21.18	21.15	21.14	21.14
	96	22.47	21.72	21.50	21.42	21.38	21.36	21.36
	95	22.99	22.03	21.76	21.66	21.61	21.59	21.58

Points Discount Table

RATE	PRICE	5 YEARS	10 YEARS	15 YEARS	20 YEARS	25 YEARS	30 YEARS	40 YEARS
	99	21.23	21.05	21.00	20.97	20.97	20.96	20.96
	98	21.72	21.35	21.24	21.20	21.19	21.18	21.17
20¾%	97	22.22	21.66	21.50	21.44	21.41	21.40	21.39
	96	22.73	21.97	21.76	21.67	21.64	21.62	21.62
	95	23.24	22.29	22.02	21.92	21.87	21.85	21.84
	99	21.48	21.30	21.25	21.23	21.22	21.21	21.21
	98	21.98	21.60	21.50	21.46	21.44	21.43	21.43
21%	97	22.48	21.91	21.75	21.69	21.67	21.66	21.65
	96	22.98	22.23	22.01	21.93	21.90	21.88	21.88
	95	23.50	22.55	22.28	22.18	22.13	22.12	22.11
	99	21.74	21.55	21.50	21.48	21.47	21.47	21.47
	98	22.23	21.86	21.75	21.71	21.70	21.69	21.68
21¼%	97	22.73	22.17	22.01	21.95	21.92	21.91	21.91
	96	23.24	22.49	22.27	22.19	22.16	22.14	22.14
	95	23.75	22.81	22.54	22.44	22.40	22.38	22.37
	99	21.99	21.80	21.75	21.73	21.72	21.72	21.72
	98	22.48	22.11	22.01	21.97	21.95	21.94	21.94
21½%	97	22.98	22.42	22.27	22.21	22.18	22.17	22.17
	96	23.49	22.74	22.53	22.45	22.42	22.40	22.40
	95	24.01	23.07	22.80	22.70	22.66	22.64	22.63
	99	22.24	22.05	22.00	21.98	21.98	21.97	21.97
	98	22.73	22.36	22.26	22.22	22.20	22.20	22.19
21¾%	97	23.24	22.68	22.52	22.46	22.44	22.43	22.42
	96	23.75	23.00	22.79	22.71	22.68	22.66	22.66
	95	24.27	23.32	23.06	22.96	22.92	22.91	22.90

Glossary

acceleration clause A clause in a mortgage stipulating that, if certain defined conditions occur, any amount of money still outstanding is due and payable at once. Also called a *call-back clause.*

Adjustable Rate Mortgage (ARM) A mortgage, the interest rate of which varies during the term of the mortgage. Also called a *Variable Rate Mortgage.*

amortization The process of repaying a loan through a series of installment payments.

annual interest rate A percentage that, when multiplied by the principal, gives the amount of money that the principal will earn over the period of a year.

balloon note A note that usually calls for a final payment greater than the regular periodic payments.

blanket mortgage One mortgage that covers more than one parcel of real estate.

bridge loan A short-term loan in effect from the end of one loan to the beginning of another loan, or prior to permanent financing.

call-back clause *See* acceleration clause.

conventional mortgage A mortgage made by a bank or other private institution and not insured by a governmental agency.

discount points A charge, made by the lending institution to the borrower, that is based on the mortgage amount. A point is one percent of the principal mortgage amount.

Federal Housing Administration (FHA) mortgage A mortgage loan made by a lender and insured by the Federal Housing Administration.

first mortgage The primary mortgage on a property. If a foreclosure occurs, the first mortgage is repaid before any "junior" mortgages.

Flexible Payment Mortgage (FPM) A mortgage with payments that vary over the term of the mortgage. Usually the initial payments are lower than later payments.

Graduated Payment Mortgage (GPM) A mortgage with payments that increase in a specified manner over the term of the mortgage.

interest The amount of money earned by the principal during a specified period of time.

interest rate A percentage that, when multiplied by the principal, determines the amount of money that the principal earns over a period of time, usually one year.

junior mortgage A mortgage of lesser rank than the first mortgage. *See also* first mortgage.

mortgage A legal document that establishes real estate as the security for the loan which finances that real estate. Colloquially, the term *mortgage* is sometimes used to refer to the loan itself.

mortgage commitment A written offer of a mortgage loan by a lending institution. Often in the form of a letter, the commitment specifies the terms and conditions of the mortgage loan being offered to the prospective borrower.

mortgagee The institution or person who is the lender or creditor on a mortgage loan.

mortgagor The institution or person who is the borrower or debtor on a mortgage loan.

open-end mortgage A mortgage that provides for additional amounts to be loaned to the borrower without the need to create a new mortgage.

points *See* discount points.

prepayment clause A clause in a mortgage enabling the borrower to pay off the mortgage balance before the end of the mortgage term. This privilege sometimes involves a prepayment penalty.

Price Level Adjusted Mortgage (PLAM) A mortgage that provides for a periodic changing of the interest rate. A portion of the rate is determined by the contract rate, and an additional portion is determined by recalculating the mortgage balance based on a cost of living index.

principal Initial amount of money invested or borrowed.

Renegotiated Rate Mortgage (RRM) *See* Rollover Mortgage (ROM).

Reverse Annuity Mortgage (RAM) A type of mortgage that allows a borrower to draw on the current equity of the property.

Rollover Mortgage (ROM) A mortgage that provides for the renegotiation of the interest rate and the payment terms at specific intervals. Also called a *Renegotiated Rate Mortgage.*

Shared Appreciation Mortgage (SAM) A mortgage providing for the lender to receive a share in the appreciation of residential real estate. In return for this, the borrower is given an interest rate lower than the prevailing rate. Also called a *Shared Equity Mortgage.*

Shared Equity Mortgage (SEM) *See* Shared Appreciation Mortgage (SAM).

subject to mortgage A purchaser of mortgaged real estate having title but not being responsible for any of the mortgage debt beyond the value of his or her equity in the property.

Variable Rate Mortgage (VRM) *See* Adjustable Rate Mortgage.

Veterans Administration (VA) mortgage A mortgage made to veterans by a lender for residential real estate and insured by the Veterans Administration.

Telephone No.

Telephone No.